Southern Living®
2012 Annual Recipes

Oxmoor House®

Best Recipes of 2012

Members of our Food staff gather almost every day to taste-test recipes to ensure not only that they're reliable, but also that they taste as good as they possibly can. Here we share this year's favorites.

clockwise from top left:
- Roast Chicken (page 39)
- King Ranch Chicken Mac and Cheese (page 38)
- Fried Chicken Thighs & Biscuits (page 90)
- Tyler's Country-Fried Steak with Uncle Ellis' Cornmeal Gravy (page 31)

Down-South Banh Mi (page 48)

"Some Like It Hot" Grilled Pimiento
Cheese Sandwiches (page 55)

Strawberry Mousse Cake (page 83)

clockwise from top left:
• Blackberry-Peach Cobbler with Praline-Pecan Streusel (page 157)
• Mini Berry Cobblers (page 101)
• Peanut-Cola Cake (page 196)
• Swoon Pies (page 52)

clockwise from top left:
• Hush Puppies (page 195)
• The *Southern Living* Pulled
Pork Sandwich (page 144)
• Grilled Corn-and-
Butter Bean Salad
(page 196)
• Broccoli Slaw with
Candied Pecans (page 133)

Honeysuckle-Watermelon
Cocktails (page 203)

Peach Upside-Down Cake (page 127)

Praline Key Lime Pie (page 135)

Figgy Focaccia
(page 219)

clockwise from top left:

- Marinated Fig Salad
  (page 219)
- Fig-and-Bourbon Fizz
  (page 219)
- Pancetta-and-Fig Pasta
  (page 218)
- Rosemary Flank Steak
  with Fig Salsa (page 219)

clockwise from top left:

- Caramel Apple Coffee Cake (page 227)
- Caramel Apple Dip (page 226)
- Caramel Apple Muffins (page 227)
- Caramel Apple-Brownie Cheesecake (page 226)

Caramel Apple Ice-cream Tarts (page 228)

Mississippi Mud S'Mores-Fudge
Pie (page 256)

Our Year at
Southern Living®

Dear Food Friends,

Here at *Southern Living,* our passion is to inspire our dedicated readers to cook with success, experiment with flavors, and savor the bounty of the South. We research trends, study our Southern roots, and test and retest thousands of recipes until we know we have them just right. Every recipe we print is guaranteed spectacular for you to share with your friends and family.

We seek out local, fresh ingredients as well as our favorite convenience items to give you a delicious mix of menu ideas, easy weeknight fixes, and healthy indulgences. Our column "Quick-Fix Suppers" is targeted toward busy families to simplify weeknight cooking with fast prep, wholesome ingredients, and supermarket shortcuts. We also highlight the season's best produce in our "What to Cook Now" column, inspiring new ways to make the most of your farmers' market picks.

We research trends, study our Southern roots, and test and retest thousands of recipes...

And because Southerners are most known for their gracious hospitality, we offer a number of creative ideas for pulling off the perfect party in our "Hospitality" column, from fancy holiday spreads to laid-back gatherings. Don't forget to thank your guests with a thoughtful hostess gift—turn to our "Food Gift of the Month" column for simple homemade treats and clever packaging ideas. Whatever the occasion, you'll find something special on every page.

After more than 45 years, *Southern Living* remains dedicated to bringing you a balance of traditional flavors along with new classics that reflect trends happening in Southern kitchens across the region. We hope you enjoy this year's collection of recipes and continue to share some of your favorites with us. From the South's most trusted kitchen to yours, thank you for inviting us into your home.

Sincerely,

Shannon

Shannon Sliter Satterwhite
Food Director

ISBN-13: 978-0-8487-3655-2
ISBN-10: 0-8487-3655-9
ISSN: 0272-2003

Printed in the United States of America
First printing 2012

To order additional publications, call 1-800-765-6400.

For more books to enrich your life, visit **oxmoorhouse.com**

To search, savor, and share thousands of recipes, visit
myrecipes.com

Oxmoor House
Publisher: Jim Childs
Editorial Director: Leah McLaughlin
Creative Director: Felicity Keane
Brand Manager: Daniel Fagan
Senior Editor: Rebecca Brennan
Managing Editor: Rebecca Benton
Art Director: Claire Cormany

Southern Living® 2012 Annual Recipes
Editor: Susan Hernandez Ray
Project Editor: Emily Chappell
Photography Director: Jim Bathie
Photo Stylist: Mindi Shapiro Levine
Test Kitchen Director: Elizabeth Tyler Austin
Recipe Editor: Alyson Moreland Haynes
Food Stylist: Catherine Crowell Steele
Senior Production Manager: Greg A. Amason

Contributors
Designer: Nancy Johnson
Copy Editor: Donna Baldone
Proofreaders: Julie Bosché, Polly Linthicum, Barry Wise Smith
Indexer: Mary Ann Laurens
Editorial Interns: Emily Robinson, Katie Strasser

Southern Living®
Editor: M. Lindsay Bierman
Creative Director: Robert Perino
Managing Editor: Candace Higginbotham
Art Director: Chris Hoke
Executive Editors: Rachel Hardage Barrett,
    Hunter Lewis, Jessica S. Thuston
Food Director: Shannon Sliter Satterwhite
Test Kitchen Director: Rebecca Kracke Gordon
Senior Writer: Donna Florio
Senior Food Editor: Mary Allen Perry
Recipe Editor: JoAnn Weatherly
Assistant Recipe Editor: Ashley Arthur
Test Kitchen Specialist/Food Styling:
    Vanessa McNeil Rocchio
Test Kitchen Professionals: Norman King, Pam Lolley,
    Angela Sellers
Editorial Assistant: Pat York
Senior Photographer: Ralph Lee Anderson
Photographer: Laurey W. Glenn
Senior Photo Stylist: Buffy Hargett
Copy Chief: Susan Emack Alison
Assistant Copy Chief: Katie Bowlby
Copy Editor: Ashley Leath
Production Manager: Mary Elizabeth Davis
Assistant Production Manager: Christy Coleman
Production Coordinator: Paula Dennis
Photo Research Coordinator: Ginny P. Allen
Office Manager: Nellah Bailey McGough
Editor-at-Large: Kimberly Schlegel Whitman
Contributing Editors: Rick Bragg, Virginia Willis

Cover: Dreamy White Cake with Chocolate-Mint Cheesecake
Layers and Mint Buttercream Frosting, page 306
Page 1: Brown Sugar-Bourbon Bundt, page 275; Black Bottom
Pumpkin Pie, page 278

Contents

Favorite Columns

Each month, we focus on topics that are important to our readers—from delicious menus to healthy options to handy tips for almost anything.

QUICK-FIX SUPPERS

♥ Give boring chicken dinners a quick and delicious makeover. You'll have dinner in just half an hour when you try Pan-Grilled Chicken with Fresh Plum Salsa or Pecan-Crusted Chicken and Tortellini with Herbed Butter Sauce. (pages 58-59)

♥ Even the pickiest eaters can't complain with these scrumptious weeknight fixes. Baked Chicken Roulade and Chicken Risotto with Spring Vegetables come together in a snap with skinless, boneless chicken breasts. (pages 74-75)

♥ Eggs aren't meant just for breakfast dishes. We created four simple, flavorful meals that are ready to serve in 30 minutes or less. Try our twist on Fried Egg Sandwiches that use hollandaise, arugula, and pancetta to take this classic to a whole new level. (page 96)

♥ Fast homemade salsa revs up these weeknight dishes. Have 15 minutes? 30 minutes? 45 minutes? We make sure you have a delicious dinner in no time with these go-to recipes. Try the Greek Salsa, Garden Salsa, or even Blueberry Salsa in these recipes, or serve with chips as an appetizer at your next party. (pages 120-121)

♥ Fire up the grill, and pull out the skewers for these fast and easy recipes. Try our Grilled Scallop Kabobs or Peach and Pork Kabobs for a quick summer dinner with very easy cleanup. (page 138)

♥ Classic potato salad—move over—we're serving spuds for supper! We took away the gobs of mayo and added flavorful additions to make these spins on weeknight dinners. Go for Shrimp-Boil Potato Salad or Steak-and-Blue Cheese Potato Salad—recipes that are quick, easy, and out of this world. (pages 198-199)

♥ Turn to the garden for these fast flavor fixin's. We use heirloom tomatoes to brighten a robust pasta sauce. Make it ahead, freeze, and thaw for a quick pasta dish, or when you're craving a hearty meatball sub. Have even more veggies growing out back? Try Chicken with Ratatouille, which uses a variety of the best produce year-round. (page 222)

♥ We revisit our childhood with speedy spins on some of our all-time faves. "PB&J" Steak Stir-fry with Rice is our new take on the classic lunchbox sandwich. We use red pepper jelly and creamy peanut butter to spice up this dish for a weeknight meal that takes less than an hour to prepare. (page 233)

♥ Warm up to a hearty bowl of chili brimming with Mexican flair with these fall-inspired recipes. Chicken-and-Three-Bean Chili Verde is ready in under an hour. Spicy Slow-Cooker Beef Chili will be ready for you the second you walk in the door. (page 253)

HEALTHY INDULGENCE

♥ Mouthwatering mix-ins make these chicken salad variations healthier and tastier. We use simple ingredients, such as fresh fruit, chopped herbs, and red curry paste, to give this Southern staple a flavor-packed update. (page 117)

♥ No need to count calories with our version of Fried Green Tomatoes. We use olive oil in a nonstick skillet to give this fried favorite the crunch you love, without the unhealthy fat you don't. (page 137)

♥ Global inspiration led us to top hot dogs with everything from Thai-Style Dogs to Dixie Caviar Dogs. Now everyone can enjoy this ballpark favorite with more tang and less guilt. (page 193)

♥ This Southern spread is a delicacy in the South. And now, we can enjoy it with less fat and less calories! The Test Kitchen took our original recipe from 2001 and transformed it into creamy, flavorful healthy goodness. Don't believe us? Try the new and improved Classic Pimiento Cheese and more flavor-packed variations. (page 221)

♥ Say so long to triple-stuffed, overloaded baked potatoes. And say hello to healthy, scrumptious spuds. We replaced heaping mounds of butter and sour cream with caramelized roasted veggies. We cut the saturated fat and added more taste to make this a *hot* potato! (page 228)

SOUTHERN HOSPITALITY

♥ Impress your guests with this yummy take on a Louisiana staple. Adding crawfish and Creole seasoning to this creamy dip makes for the perfect Super Bowl starter. (page 61)

♥ There's no need to stress when you follow our simple guide to hosting "Our Easiest, Prettiest Brunch." Suitable for showers, garden club meetings, or any ladies lunch, menu standouts Peach-Basil Iced Tea and Creamy Egg Strata will delight your guests, and our easy presentation ideas and serving suggestions are sure to impress. (pages 62 and 65)

♥ Host an adult-savvy, kid-friendly Easter party with Sunday supper and egg hunt included. Decadent dishes for grown-ups and kid-approved plates for younger ones share the menu. Everyone will end the meal with cupcakes smothered in Buttermilk-Cream Cheese Frosting. (pages 92-94)

♥ Reintroduce your friends to communal cocktails. Our party punches are full of flavor and easy to put together. Serve these beverages by the bowlful at your next gathering. Warning: These have more kick than what Grandma used to make. (page 104)

♥ Silver platters, julep cups, and wide-brimmed show-stopping hats are a must for this Kentucky Derby party. Although it's one of the quickest sporting events of the year, there's plenty of time to enjoy Southern hors d'oeuvres on your finest presentation pieces. (page 106)

♥ Celebrate the best of summer's bounty with this backyard party menu. Make our version of Southern salsa using fresh lady peas, cool down with a Sweet Tea Spritzer, and then try one of our variations for Grilled Corn. You'll almost forget how hot it is with this scrumptious, refreshing meal. (pages 131-132)

♥ Fancify your next fish fry. Batter up fillets with our simple beer-batter recipe, and serve alongside Peach-Ginger Slaw and Grilled Corn-and-Butter Bean Salad for a winning menu. Be sure to save room for to-die-for Peanut-Cola Cake to round out the backyard fest. (pages 194-196)

♥ Olé! Pink Cadillac Margaritas and Chipotle Shrimp Cocktail are sure to spice up your next fiesta. And after a swing at the piñata or a turn at the tango, enjoy dessert. Our Mexican Chocolate Ice-cream Pie comes with a graham cracker crust spiked with ground cinnamon and red pepper for a real punch. (pages 216-218)

♥ Chef James Petrakis shares his secrets for the perfect riverside cookout. He keeps things casual and simple. It's all about good food and spending time together around the table. This tasty outdoor menu highlights the best of the season with a rich Butternut Squash Soup, a tangy kale salad, and a luscious Pineapple Upside-Down Cake his wife is known for. (pages 230-232)

♥ Host a backyard beer bash and serve our Bavarian-inspired menu. We've put a twist on Southern classics like Dry-Brined Beer-Can Chicken and Black Forest Pound Cake, and paired them with craft brews made right here in the South. (page 246 and 249)

CHEF'S TABLE

♥ Some of the country's greatest chefs competed in this comfort food face-off. Judge for yourself who made the best meatloaf, chicken-fried steak, mac-and-cheese, and shrimp and grits. How do these all-star recipes compare to Grandma's classics? We have to say, "Pretty darn well!" (pages 28-35)

♥ Winner of the James Beard Foundation Award's 2011 Best Chef: Southeast, Chef Andrea Reusing is using simple Southern techniques with fresh, local ingredients to create astonishing dishes. She shares her recipe for Spring Onion Pie, a dish that wows not only dining critics, but also her children. (page 118)

♥ Soup or Salad? No need to decide. Virginia-based chef Aaron Deal, a tried-and-true Southern chef who swears by Duke's mayo and sweet tea, shares his recipe for Salad in a Soup, the dish he loves to make on his day off. (page 129)

♥ He started as a busboy and is now one of Birmingham's finest Italian-trained chefs. James Lewis stopped by our Test Kitchen to show us how he whips up simple, savory summer pasta when he's off the clock. (page 200)

♥ His Southern roots inspire Chef Danny Trace of Brennan's of Houston. He shares his recipe for Sautéed Redfish, the sweet, buttery fish that pairs beautifully with his make-ahead black-eyed pea salad. Serve them with Grapefruit-Tequila Fizz, and you've got a dinner party. (page 242)

♥ A Georgia native, Kevin Gillespie knows how to make amazing Southern comfort food. He shares his *Top Chef* recipe for Gussied Up Mac 'n' Cheese. You'll never guess his secret ingredient that makes this oh-so creamy. (page 258)

Cook's Chat

Our readers chat online about what they think of our recipes and how they use them. Here, they brag about some of their favorites.

APPETIZERS

Pimiento Cheese Cookies, page 56—The perfect blend of savory and sweet. Each bite yields butter, pimiento cheese, strawberry preserves, and chopped pecans. Taking these to my weekend Super Bowl party, where I am sure they will be devoured in an instant.

Hot Crawfish Dip, page 61—My neighbor made this for Super Bowl Sunday, and it was delicious. In lieu of the green pepper, he added roasted poblano and served with toasted crusty bread. The flavor is very rich and satisfying. I had to be sure that I found and saved the recipe!

Shrimp in Cucumber Cups, page 115—Beautiful and so cool for a nice summer appetizer!

Sparkling Cherry Limeade, page 197—Very refreshing on a hot summer afternoon!

Honeysuckle-Watermelon Cocktails, page 203—This cocktail is spot on and so refreshing for the summertime! It makes a world of difference using CATHEAD HONEY-SUCKLE VODKA. Do not skimp on the proper ingredients—light rum or plain vodka does not lend any honeysuckle flavor and aroma. I made this up in a big batch and served it for about 50 guests. Should have made it up for 500 guests the way everyone enjoyed this cocktail!

Pink Cadillac Margaritas, page 216—I had this at a party last night, and it was very refreshing. Not the usual aftertaste I experience when I drink margaritas. This recipe is a keeper, and I'm making them tonight!

Apple Pie-Infused Bourbon, page 229—Awesome! Great tasting and very easy to make! This may become our new Fall Favorite!!

BREAKFAST

Creamy Egg Strata, page 65—Excellent recipe to serve for brunch. Our company raved, and it was convenient, as the prep happens a day ahead.

Fried Egg Sandwiches, page 96—Tastes as fabulous as the picture looks. My kids initially turned up their noses, but then they tasted it, and they loved it. Will definitely make again!

BREADS

Cornbread Madeleines, page 76—These are wonderful treats with soups or any meal you want to dress up your cornbread. They popped right out of the pan with no sticking with a good knock of the pan on its side on a countertop. I halve the recipe, which provides a generous portion for a family of six.

Fluffy Cream Cheese Biscuits, page 108—We had this for dinner tonight, and both of us thought it was very good. I baked the biscuits this afternoon for 10 minutes and froze the ones I wasn't going to use for another day. At dinner-time I finished baking the biscuits. That worked well. I bought honey ham at the deli. The Figgy Port Chutney and Blue Cheese Butter (page 110) were delicious. Great combination of flavors.

Lemon-Poppy Seed Zucchini Bread, page 224—The taste is rich and buttery, the texture more like a cake than a bread. The lemon adds just the right amount of zest to perk up the flavors.

SALADS

Easy Potato Salad, page 48—Fresh take on potato salad. Terrific taste with simple ingredients. A winner!

Waldorf Spinach Salad, page 60—This is an absolutely delicious salad. I did have trouble finding honey-roasted cashews, but as necessity is the mother of invention, I created my own. Drizzled with honey, stirred with brown sugar, and toasted. That made them sticky, so I tossed with granulated sugar, and they were great. Also soaked the apples in OJ to keep them fresh. I served this at a luncheon, and it was a huge hit! Many requests for the recipe!

Strawberry Chicken Salad, page 85—Great summer salad. I didn't have any basil, so I used a little chopped up rosemary, and it was a great substitute. Will definitely make this again and again.

Mixed Fruit Chicken Salad, page 117—I substituted fresh clementines for the canned mandarin oranges. The salad dressing is excellent. Very fresh and delicious—will make again!

Heirloom Tomato Salad, page 130—This was delicious! We love a salad that has no oil and yet is so flavorful. The recommended Lady Pea Salsa (page 131) was amazing. I followed the recipe exactly, and you can't go wrong. Took the dish to a Memorial Day cookout, and everyone raved about it. The presentation is beautiful!

Steak-and-Blue Cheese Potato Salad, page 199—This salad was easy to prepare and very tasty. It was even better the next day as a cold salad tossed over greens.

SIDES

Farmers' Market Roasted Vegetables (Farmers' Market Pizza), page 91—The eggplant is especially delicious and flavorful in this recipe. I replaced the fennel with a sliced onion (fennel is hard to find where I live). This made enough vegetables to cover two pizzas, so I froze one and used it a few weeks later. It was still just as delicious as the day I made it!

Hoppin' John Parfaits, page 103—Loved it even more the next day after it chilled in fridge. Next time I made it as a salad and served it over artisan baby greens and used an Italian dressing in lieu of the vinegar and olive oil...got rave reviews from my bridge club.

Sweet, Salty, and Spicy Watermelon Refresher, page 147—What a refreshing alternative to a fruit salad! I couldn't wait to bring this as a side dish to our neighbor's party.

ENTRÉES

Michelle's Lowcountry Shrimp and Grits, page 34—I made this for my Southern husband, who is a true foodie. It completely changed his opinion of my cooking skills! He and I both now list it as our favorite dish and enjoy it often. I have made it for entertaining as well, and it is a sure hit.

King Ranch Chicken Mac and Cheese, page 38—Terrific taste and sure to please everyone. I haven't used pasteurized cheese product in a long time, but when I saw this combination with cellentani pasta, I couldn't resist. This kicked-up version of King Ranch was a hit with all the boys at our table. Fun to make and a crowd-pleasing hearty meal.

Ratatouille, page 40—Great side dish. I served it with rice. The ingredients can be flexible. I didn't have yellow pepper so used only the red and green. It was a hit with everyone, even those who weren't so fond of vegetables. I'm making it again today!

Slow-cooked Barbecued Chicken, page 46—Quick and easy, and my kids loved it. Requires minimal ingredients, which most home cooks have on hand. Perfect for a crowd as well as a good meal after running around to kids' sporting events. I served this dish with couscous to soak up the plentiful gravy! Yum!

Pan-Grilled Chicken with Fresh Plum Salsa, page 58—We thought it had tons of flavor—plums, jalapeños, cumin, lime juice, red onion, basil—that's a whole lotta stuff in there! It was easy to make and very quick. We've added it to our list of "keepers."

Baked Chicken Roulade, page 74—Excellent and easy! This will be a keeper for dinner parties.

Chicken Risotto with Spring Vegetables, page 75—It was my first time making risotto. The recipe was easy to follow and put together. I will be making this again for sure. I will probably try other vegetables as well, depending on what's in season. Awesome dish!

Shrimp Destin Linguine, page 80—My (picky eater) son has already requested this again. All the family liked it. I liked that it uses ingredients that we typically have on hand. Very quick and easy.

Vietnamese Barbecue Tacos, page 90—Will be making these again and again; easy and full of flavor. Husband was very pleased.

Country Ham Carbonara, page 97—Great weeknight meal that the whole family enjoyed.

ENTRÉES (continued)

Grilled Chicken and Garden Salsa, page 121—Have made this several times now. The chicken was very flavorful and outstanding—like something from a quality restaurant. The vegetables were better on the grill than cooking them on the stove-top. Don't skip the lemon zest—it adds a lot of flavor. My guests loved it.

Brown Sugar Pork Chops with Peach Barbecue Sauce, page 125—I made this last night, and it was absolutely delicious! I brined the chops for several hours, and they were so juicy, and the sauce adds the perfect sweetness. This is definitely a keeper.

Chipotle-Bacon Mac and Cheese, page 146—Best macaroni and cheese I have ever had! I halved the recipe and used just regular chili powder, and will for sure make it again. Perfect for guests!

DESSERTS

Caramelized Banana Pudding, page 50—This was FANTASTIC...very rich. My husband's favorite dessert is banana pudding, and he loved the twist on this one. I don't even like eating bananas, but I ate my whole serving, bananas and all! It was not difficult to make and will be a go-to recipe when I'm entertaining. My husband said they looked like a dessert we would get in a restaurant. I'll certainly make this one again!

Hummingbird Bundt Cake, page 52—This is my first time making a hummingbird cake. I had seen recipes and vowed I would try but I'm always a bit intimidated by layer cakes. So, when I saw this version I immediately had to try it. It was outstanding!!! My husband has eaten two slices already, and I can't stop licking my food processor...it has the icing in it. :) I can't wait to share this with my co-workers tomorrow—there's NO WAY I'm keeping this in my house!

Banana Pudding Cheesecake, page 72—Excellent! This was very easy, and I do not have a lot of experience making cheesecakes. The taste was a perfect blend of banana pudding and cheesecake. I am definitely making this again!!

Lemon Icebox Pie Ice Cream, page 113—Excellent! Easy and a hit with guests!

Peanut Butter-Banana Icebox Pie, page 134—All I can say is WOW! What a sensational dessert. Absolutely sure to be a hit with any crowd!

Red Velvet-Berry Cobbler, page 158-159—This was delicious. The Cream Cheese Ice Cream is the perfect complement to the cobbler. The whole pan was gone in minutes, and my kids asked me to make it again tomorrow.

EXTRAS

Sweet Basil Vinaigrette (Spring Garden Strawberry Salad), page 86—This is my new favorite dressing. I love the flavors, and it can be used on many different salads. This is so good I could almost drink it. LOL.

Bourbon Vinaigrette (Kentucky Bibb Lettuce Salad), page 89—This is a great dressing. It's not too sweet, and the bourbon gives it a nice kick.

January

The Greatest, Gooeyest Comfort Food Cook-Off

We asked 10 of the South's most celebrated chefs to share their inspired takes on down-home classics from meatloaf to mac and cheese. Who really brought home the bacon? Who showed the most grit? Decide for yourself by making the recipes at home, or head to their restaurants to sample them for yourself!

THE CHALLENGE
MEATLOAF

Edward Lee

Open-Faced Meatloaf Sandwiches

610 MAGNOLIA
LOUISVILLE, KY

"I love steak and eggs. There's something about adding a runny egg over beef, so I thought, 'Why not apply that idea to meatloaf?' It almost has a breakfast-for-supper feel." *610magnolia.com*

Edward's Open-Faced Meatloaf Sandwiches

party perfect

MAKES: 8 servings
HANDS-ON TIME: 1 hr., 5 min.
TOTAL TIME: 4 hr.
(Pictured on page 162)

MEATLOAF

- 7 **bacon slices, diced**
- 2 **cups finely chopped onion (1 large)**
- ½ **cup finely chopped celery**
- 2 **garlic cloves, minced**
- 2 **cups chopped fresh mushrooms**
- 2 **lb. ground chuck**
- 1½ **cups soft, fresh breadcrumbs**
- 3 **large eggs**
- ¼ **cup cola soft drink**
- 2 **Tbsp. bourbon***
- 2 **tsp. Worcestershire sauce**
- 1 **cup ketchup**
- 1½ **tsp. salt**
- ½ **tsp. freshly ground pepper**
- 2 **Tbsp. light brown sugar**
- 1 **Tbsp. soy sauce**

GRAVY

- 1½ **Tbsp. butter**
- 1 **Tbsp. all-purpose flour**
- ½ **cup chicken broth**
- ¼ **tsp. salt**
- 1 **tsp. freshly ground pepper**
- ¼ **tsp. fresh lemon juice**

REMAINING INGREDIENTS

- 8 **Texas toast slices**
- 1 **Tbsp. butter**
- 8 **large eggs**
- 8 **thick tomato slices**
- 4 **Tbsp. mayonnaise**
  Chopped fresh parsley

1. Prepare Meatloaf: Preheat oven to 350°. Cook bacon in a large skillet over medium heat, stirring often, 8 to 10 minutes or until crisp. Remove bacon, and drain on paper towels, reserving drippings in skillet. Add onions and next 2 ingredients to hot drippings, and sauté 3 minutes. Add mushrooms; sauté 4 minutes. Transfer mixture to a large bowl, and let cool to room temperature (about 30 minutes).
2. Add ground chuck, next 5 ingredients, ½ cup ketchup, 1½ tsp. salt, ½ tsp. pepper, and cooked bacon to onion mixture in bowl, and combine mixture, using hands. Stir together brown sugar, soy sauce, and remaining ½ cup ketchup in a separate bowl.
3. Transfer meat mixture to a lightly greased 9- x 5-inch loafpan. Brush top with ketchup mixture.
4. Bake at 350° for 1 hour and 20 minutes to 1 hour and 30 minutes or until a meat thermometer inserted in center registers 155°. Let cool in pan on a wire rack 1 hour, reserving 1 cup drippings.
5. Prepare Gravy: Melt butter in a saucepan over medium heat. Whisk in flour until smooth. Slowly whisk in broth and meatloaf drippings. Reduce heat to medium-low, and simmer, whisking constantly, 2 minutes or until slightly thickened. Stir in ¼ tsp. salt, 1 tsp. pepper, and ¼ tsp. lemon juice. Remove from heat.

6. Preheat oven to 350°. Arrange Texas toast slices on a baking sheet, and bake 8 minutes on each side or until golden. Remove from oven.

7. Melt I Tbsp. butter in a large nonstick skillet over medium heat. Gently break 4 eggs into a hot skillet. Cook 2 to 3 minutes on each side or to desired degree of doneness. Remove from skillet, and cover with aluminum foil. Repeat procedure with remaining 4 eggs.

8. Cut meatloaf into 8 slices. Sprinkle tomato slices with desired amount of salt. Spread I side of each toast slice with I½ tsp. mayonnaise. Top each toast slice, mayonnaise sides up, with I tomato slice and I meatloaf slice. Gently place I cooked egg on each meatloaf slice. Serve with gravy; sprinkle with chopped fresh parsley and freshly ground pepper.

*2 Tbsp. cola soft drink may be substituted.

Ashley's Meatloaf-and-Mashed Potato Sandwiches

party perfect

MAKES: 12 servings
HANDS-ON TIME: I hr., 20 min.
TOTAL TIME: 3 hr., 30 min.

Have your butcher grind the pork shoulder roast. The meatloaf and gravy are equally as good served as a traditional plated dinner with the potatoes on the side. (Pictured on page 161)

MEATLOAF

½ (16-oz.) package hickory-smoked bacon slices, coarsely chopped
2½ lb. pork shoulder roast (Boston butt), ground
4 large eggs
2 cups panko (Japanese bread-crumbs)
¼ cup grated red onion
I Tbsp. finely ground pepper
I Tbsp. Asian sriracha hot chili sauce
I Tbsp. Dijon mustard
I Tbsp. Worcestershire sauce
2 tsp. sea salt

TOMATO-BACON GRAVY

5 hickory-smoked bacon slices, cut into I-inch pieces
1½ lb. tomatoes, halved
½ large yellow onion, sliced
2 Tbsp. apple cider vinegar
I Tbsp. Dijon mustard
I tsp. sea salt

MASHED POTATOES

2 lb. Yukon gold potatoes, cut into I-inch-thick pieces
I Tbsp. sea salt
I cup panko (Japanese bread-crumbs)
2 cups freshly grated sharp Cheddar cheese
½ cup chopped green onions
½ cup sour cream
2 Tbsp. butter
I tsp. sea salt

REMAINING INGREDIENTS

24 hearty bread slices, grilled
Garnish: green onions

1. Prepare Meatloaf: Preheat oven to 325°. Pulse chopped bacon 4 to 5 times in a food processor until finely chopped. Combine bacon, pork, and next 8 ingredients, using hands. Transfer pork mixture to a lightly greased 8½- x 4½-inch loaf pan.

2. Bake at 325° for I hour and 45 minutes to 2 hours or until a meat thermometer inserted in center registers 160°.

3. Prepare Gravy: Cook bacon slices in a large cast-iron skillet 8 to 10 minutes or until crisp; remove bacon, and drain on paper towels, reserving drippings in skillet. Increase heat to medium-high. Add tomatoes, cut sides down, and onion slices. Cook 6 to 7 minutes on each side or until charred. Remove from heat. Pulse tomatoes, onions, vinegar, and next 2 ingredients in a food processor just until coarsely chopped and combined. Stir in bacon.

4. Prepare Potatoes: Preheat broiler with oven rack placed in middle position. Bring Yukon gold potatoes, I Tbsp. sea salt, and water to cover to a boil in a large saucepan over medium-high heat; reduce heat to medium, and cook 15 minutes or until tender; drain. Combine potatoes, panko, and next 5 ingredients in a large bowl; mash with a potato masher to desired consistency.

5. Place 12 meatloaf slices on a lightly greased rack in a broiler pan. Spoon potato mixture generously over meatloaf. Broil 4 to 5 minutes or until potatoes are golden and crisp. Serve between bread slices with gravy. Garnish if desired.

Ashley Christensen

Meatloaf-and-Mashed Potato Sandwiches

POOLE'S DINER
RALEIGH, NC

"This dish is packed with familiar notes that give you that warm-in-your-belly feeling. The loaded mashed potatoes are definitely a harbinger of comfort, and the tangy tomato gravy balances out the recipe."
poolesdowntowndiner.com

David Bull

Chicken-Fried Steak with
Redeye Gravy*

SECOND BAR + KITCHEN
AUSTIN, TX

"I wanted to punch up the flavor
with a touch of cayenne, hot sauce,
and buttermilk, yet still make it taste
familiar." *congressaustin.com/second*

David's Chicken-Fried Steak with Redeye Gravy

party perfect

MAKES: 4 servings
HANDS-ON TIME: 45 min.
TOTAL TIME: 2 hr., 30 min.

To serve with Chef Bull's Grilled Escarole and Browned Butter Parsnips, visit southernliving. com/comfort. (Pictured on page 162)

- 4 (4-oz.) rib-eye steaks
- 3 cups all-purpose flour
- 1 tsp. baking powder
- ½ tsp. baking soda
- ¼ tsp. ground red pepper
- 2 large eggs
- 2 cups buttermilk
- ½ tsp. hot sauce
- 1 tsp. salt
- ¼ tsp. freshly ground black pepper
- 3 cups vegetable oil
  Redeye Gravy

1. Place steaks between 2 sheets of heavy-duty plastic wrap, and flatten to ¼-inch thickness, using flat side of a meat mallet. Lightly pound steak, using textured side of meat mallet. Wrap tightly with plastic wrap, and chill 1 hour.
2. Combine flour and next 3 ingredients in a bowl. Whisk together eggs and next 2 ingredients in a separate bowl. Sprinkle both sides of steaks with salt and black pepper.
3. Dip steaks in egg mixture, and dredge in flour mixture, shaking off excess. Repeat procedure two more times.
4. Fry steaks, 1 at a time, in hot oil in a nonstick skillet over medium-high heat 4 to 6 minutes on each side or until golden. Drain on a wire rack in a jelly-roll pan. Serve with gravy.

Redeye Gravy

quick prep • party perfect

MAKES: about 4 cups
HANDS-ON TIME: 45 min.
TOTAL TIME: 45 min.

- ¼ cup butter
- 1½ thick smoked bacon slices, diced
- ½ cup chopped smoked ham
- 1 small onion, diced
- 2 garlic cloves, minced
- 2 tsp. finely chopped fresh sage
- 2 Tbsp. all-purpose flour
- 1 cup milk
- 1 cup beef broth
- ¾ cup brewed coffee
- 1 Tbsp. chopped fresh chives
- 2 tsp. cracked pepper

1. Melt butter in a large saucepan over medium heat; add bacon, and cook, stirring occasionally, 5 to 7 minutes or until done. Add ham and next 3 ingredients; sauté 3 to 4 minutes or until onion is translucent. Reduce heat to medium-low. Add flour. Cook, stirring constantly, 3 to 5 minutes or until golden brown.
2. Slowly whisk in milk and next 2 ingredients; bring to a boil over high heat, stirring occasionally. Reduce heat to low. Simmer, stirring often, 14 to 18 minutes or until thickened. Remove from heat. Stir in chives and pepper.

Tyler's Country-Fried Steak with
Uncle Ellis' Cornmeal Gravy

1. Sprinkle cubed steaks with salt and pepper. Combine flour, crackers, and marjoram in a shallow dish. Whisk eggs and buttermilk in a bowl.

2. Dip steaks in egg mixture; dredge in cracker mixture. Repeat procedure.

3. Pour oil to depth of 1½ inches in a large heavy skillet. Heat to 325°. Fry steaks, in batches, 5 to 7 minutes on each side or until golden. Drain on a wire rack in a jelly-roll pan. Serve with gravy.

Uncle Ellis' Cornmeal Gravy

quick prep • party perfect

MAKES: about 1⅔ cups
HANDS-ON TIME: 20 min.
TOTAL TIME: 20 min.

- ½ cup plain red or white cornmeal
- ½ tsp. salt
- ½ tsp. pepper
- 1 tsp. bacon drippings
- 1 cup buttermilk
- 1 cup hot water

1. Cook cornmeal in a heavy skillet over medium-high heat, stirring constantly, 4 to 5 minutes or until golden brown. Stir in salt, pepper, and drippings. Stir together buttermilk and hot water; gradually whisk into cornmeal mixture. Bring to a boil, whisking constantly. Reduce heat, and cook, whisking constantly, until thickened. Whisk in additional buttermilk for desired consistency.

Tyler Brown

Country-Fried Steak with Uncle Ellis' Cornmeal Gravy

CAPITOL GRILLE
NASHVILLE, TN

"This recipe is a compilation of my journey through the South. Most recently, I've been really interested in the culture of the Delta. My chef de cuisine grew up in Cleveland, Mississippi, and the cornmeal gravy is inspired by something he enjoyed as a child." *capitolgrillenashville.com*

Tyler's Country-Fried Steak with Uncle Ellis' Cornmeal Gravy

party perfect

MAKES: 6 servings
HANDS-ON TIME: 15 min.
TOTAL TIME: 1 hr., 5 min.

Serve Chef Brown's Country-Fried Steak with Butternut Squash Hash (recipe available at southernliving.com/comfort). (Also pictured on page 3)

- 6 (6-oz.) top sirloin steaks, cubed
- 1 tsp. kosher salt
- ¼ tsp. ground pepper
- 3 cups all-purpose flour
- 1½ cups finely crushed round buttery crackers
- 6 Tbsp. chopped fresh marjoram
- 3 large eggs
- 2 cups buttermilk
  Vegetable oil
  Uncle Ellis' Cornmeal Gravy

Hugh Acheson

Southern Mac and Cheese

EMPIRE STATE SOUTH
ATLANTA, GA

"This recipe's roots are classically Southern with the hearty addition of leeks and bacon. I also like to use Canadian Cheddar, which reminds me of my childhood growing up outside of Ottawa. That's a key element to comfort food—it has that resonating chord in your history. The dish, like me, is a lot of Canada happily enmeshed in the South."

empirestatesouth.com

Hugh's Southern Mac and Cheese

party perfect

MAKES: 4 to 6 servings
HANDS-ON TIME: 45 min.
TOTAL TIME: 1 hr., 35 min.

Microwave milk in a microwave-safe bowl at HIGH 1 minute to warm.

- ¼ **lb. thick bacon slices, diced (about 4 slices)**
- 2 **medium leeks, cut into ½-inch rounds (about 1 cup)**
- ⅓ **(16-oz.) package uncooked cavatappi pasta**
- 1½ **Tbsp. unsalted butter**
- 1½ **Tbsp. all-purpose flour**
- 1 **cup milk, warmed**
- ½ **tsp. dry mustard**
- ¼ **tsp. salt**
- ¼ **tsp. ground black pepper**
  Pinch of ground red pepper
- 1 **cup (4 oz.) freshly grated 2-year-old aged Cheddar cheese, divided**
- 1 **egg yolk**
- ½ **cup freshly grated Gruyère cheese**
- 2 **Tbsp. heavy cream**
- ¼ **cup toasted soft, fresh breadcrumbs**

1. Preheat oven to 375°. Cook bacon in a skillet over medium heat, stirring occasionally, 6 to 8 minutes or until crisp; remove bacon, and drain on paper towels. Discard drippings.
2. Cook leeks in 4 qt. boiling water in a large Dutch oven 5 minutes. Remove leeks with a slotted spoon, reserving boiling water in Dutch oven. Plunge leeks into ice water to stop the cooking process; drain.
3. Add pasta to boiling water, and cook 10 minutes or until al dente. Drain.
4. Melt butter in a large skillet over medium heat. Reduce heat to medium-low, and whisk in flour until smooth; cook, whisking constantly, 2 minutes or until golden brown. Slowly whisk in milk, and cook, whisking constantly, 3 minutes or until thickened. Whisk in dry mustard, next

3 ingredients, and ½ cup Cheddar cheese, stirring until cheese is melted. Remove from heat. Season with salt to taste.
5. Gently stir together pasta, cheese sauce, half each of cooked bacon and leeks, and egg yolk. Stir in Gruyère cheese and remaining ½ cup Cheddar cheese. Spoon pasta mixture into a buttered 8-inch cast-iron skillet, and sprinkle with remaining bacon and leeks. Drizzle with cream; sprinkle with breadcrumbs.
6. Bake at 375° for 35 minutes or until golden and bubbly. Let stand 15 minutes before serving.

Chris' Tex-Mex Mac and Cheese

party perfect

MAKES: 6 servings
HANDS-ON TIME: 40 min.
TOTAL TIME: 1 hr., 30 min.

Save time by substituting chopped green chiles for roasted poblanos. (Pictured on page 163)

- 2 **poblano peppers**
- 2 **ears fresh corn, husks removed**
- 8 **oz. uncooked rotini or fusilli pasta**
- ½ **cup chopped cooked Mexican-style chorizo**
- 3 **Tbsp. butter**
- 3 **Tbsp. all-purpose flour**
- 3 **cups milk**
- 3 **cups (12 oz.) shredded pepper Jack cheese**
- 1 **tsp. salt**
- ¼ **tsp. freshly ground pepper**
- ¾ **cup crushed tortilla chips**
- ¼ **cup panko (Japanese breadcrumbs)**
- 3 **Tbsp. melted butter**

1. Preheat broiler with oven rack 5½ inches from heat. Broil peppers and corn at the same time on an aluminum foil-lined jelly-roll pan. Broil peppers 10 minutes or until blistered, turning after 5 minutes. Broil corn 20 minutes or until charred, turning every 5 minutes. Place peppers in a zip-top plastic freezer bag; seal and let

Chris Shepherd
Tex-Mex Mac and Cheese

UNDERBELLY
HOUSTON, TX

"Having that little bit of heat from the poblano peppers is a very Tex-Mex addition to comfort food. When you hear Tex-Mex mac and cheese, you know it's gonna be satisfying and delicious." *underbellyhouston.com*

Wesley's Gulf Coast Shrimp and Grits
party perfect

MAKES: 6 servings
HANDS-ON TIME: 50 min.
TOTAL TIME: 1 hr., 40 min.
(Pictured on page 162)

GRITS

- 1½ cups milk
- ¼ cup unsalted butter
- 1½ cups uncooked quick-cooking grits
- 1 Tbsp. unsalted butter
- 4 garlic cloves, minced
- 3 shallots, minced
- ¾ cup dry white wine
- ½ cup freshly grated Parmesan cheese
- 2 Tbsp. minced fresh chives
- 1½ tsp. salt
- ¼ tsp. black pepper

SHRIMP SAUCE

- 30 unpeeled, jumbo raw shrimp (21/25 count)
- ⅛ tsp. salt
- ⅛ tsp. ground black pepper
- ¼ cup extra virgin olive oil, divided
- 3 garlic cloves, chopped
- 1 Tbsp. minced shallots
- 1 pt. cherry tomatoes, halved
- 1 Tbsp. fresh lemon juice
- 1½ tsp. drained capers
- ¼ tsp. ground red pepper
    Dash of hot sauce
- 3 Tbsp. unsalted butter, cubed
- 1 Tbsp. chopped fresh chives

1. Prepare Grits: Preheat oven to 350°. Bring milk, ¼ cup butter, and 4 cups water to a boil in an ovenproof Dutch oven over medium-high heat. Whisk in grits; bring mixture to a boil, whisking occasionally. Cover and bake 45 minutes or until grits are creamy, whisking every 15 minutes.
2. Meanwhile, melt 1 Tbsp. butter in a large skillet over medium heat; add 4 garlic cloves and 3 shallots, and sauté 3½ minutes

---

Wesley True
Gulf Coast Shrimp and Grits

TRUE MIDTOWN KITCHEN
MOBILE, AL

"I worked with a cook who had this great recipe for Italian red sauce, so I translated that into shrimp and grits. For me, this is the perfect comfort food because you have buttery Parmesan grits combined with a rich, tomato-based sauce that's both familiar and just a little bit different." *kitchen.truedine.com*

---

stand 10 minutes to loosen skins. Peel peppers; remove and discard seeds. Chop peppers. Cut corn kernels from cobs. Reduce oven temperature to 400°.
2. Cook pasta in boiling salted water to cover 8 to 10 minutes or until al dente. Drain.
3. Cook chorizo in a medium skillet over medium heat, stirring often, 2 to 3 minutes or until crisp; remove chorizo, and drain on paper towels. Discard drippings.
4. Melt 3 Tbsp. butter in a large heavy saucepan over medium heat; whisk in flour until smooth, and cook, whisking constantly, 2 minutes or until golden brown. Slowly whisk in milk, and cook, whisking often, 10 to 12 minutes or until thickened. Remove from heat, and gradually add cheese, stirring until smooth. Stir in chopped peppers, corn kernels, chorizo, salt, and pepper. Gently stir together cheese mixture and pasta in a large bowl. Spoon into 6 (8-oz.) ramekins.
5. Combine tortilla chips, panko, and 3 Tbsp. melted butter; sprinkle over pasta.
6. Bake at 400° for 12 to 15 minutes or until golden and bubbly. Let stand 5 minutes before serving.

or until shallots are translucent. Add wine, stirring to loosen particles from bottom of skillet. Cook, stirring often, 4 minutes or until liquid is reduced by two-thirds; fold into hot cooked grits. Stir in cheese and next 3 ingredients.
3. Prepare Shrimp Sauce: Peel shrimp; devein, if desired. Sprinkle shrimp with ⅛ tsp. each salt and pepper.
4. Cook shrimp, in 2 batches, in 2 Tbsp. hot oil in a large skillet over medium-high heat 2 minutes on each side or just until shrimp turn pink. Remove shrimp from skillet.
5. Sauté 3 garlic cloves and 1 Tbsp. minced shallots in remaining 2 Tbsp. hot oil in skillet over medium-high heat 1 minute. Add tomatoes and next 4 ingredients. Cook, stirring often, 5 to 7 minutes or until tomatoes begin to break apart. Remove from heat. Stir in shrimp and 3 Tbsp. butter. Serve over grits with chives.

Michelle's Lowcountry Shrimp and Grits

party perfect

MAKES: 6 servings
HANDS-ON TIME: 30 min.
TOTAL TIME: 1 hr., 35 min.

Chef Weaver suggests using Anson Mills grits.

GRITS

2 cups uncooked white coarse-ground grits
½ cup freshly grated Parmigiano-Reggiano cheese
¼ cup unsalted butter

Michelle Weaver

Lowcountry Shrimp and Grits

CHARLESTON GRILL
CHARLESTON, SC

"Our wonderful local products make this recipe—from the fresh shrimp to the Anson Mills grits. Add in herbs, butter, and a little love, and how can you not feel comforted?" *charlestongrill.com*

SHRIMP SAUCE

1 lb. unpeeled, medium-size raw shrimp (28/31 count)
4 thick hickory-smoked bacon slices, diced
6 Tbsp. unsalted butter
1 medium-size Vidalia onion, diced
½ poblano pepper, diced
3 garlic cloves, minced
½ tsp. kosher salt
¼ tsp. ground white pepper
¼ tsp. ground red pepper
1 Tbsp. all-purpose flour
½ cup chicken broth
¼ cup Madeira
2 Tbsp. fresh lemon juice
1 Tbsp. chopped fresh parsley
1 green onion, chopped

1. Prepare Grits: Bring 7 cups water to a boil in a 4-qt. saucepan over medium-high heat. Slowly whisk in grits; reduce heat to medium, and cook, whisking constantly, 5 minutes. Cover, reduce heat to low, and cook, stirring occasionally, 1 hour or until tender. Fold in cheese and ¼ cup butter.
2. Prepare Shrimp Sauce: Peel shrimp; devein, if desired.
3. Cook bacon in a large skillet over medium-high heat, stirring often, 4 to 5 minutes or until crisp; remove bacon, and drain on paper towels, reserving 2 Tbsp. drippings in skillet.
4. Melt 6 Tbsp. butter in hot drippings in skillet. Reduce heat. Add onion, poblano pepper, and garlic; sauté 2 minutes or until onion is translucent. Add shrimp; cook, stirring often, 1 to 2 minutes. Add salt and next 2 ingredients; toss to coat.
5. Sprinkle flour over shrimp mixture; toss. Add broth and next 2 ingredients. Cook just until shrimp turn pink, stirring to loosen particles from skillet. Stir in bacon and parsley. Serve over grits with green onion.

THE CHALLENGE
BEANS & RICE

José's Black Beans & Rice

party perfect

MAKES: 6 to 8 servings
HANDS-ON TIME: 1 hr., 15 min.
TOTAL TIME: 4 hr., 16 min.
(Pictured on page 162)

BLACK BEANS

1 (16-oz.) package dried black beans
6 thick bacon slices, diced
1 large yellow onion, chopped
3 garlic cloves, minced
1 red bell pepper, chopped
2 (32-oz.) containers chicken broth
2 bay leaves
1 tsp. salt
½ tsp. ground cumin

José Mendin

Black Beans & Rice

PUBBELLY
MIAMI BEACH, FL

"This is a very traditional Cuban recipe, where the beans are cooked with pork. To punch up the flavor of the rice, I use a sofrito—a garlic-, tomato-, and pepper-based sauce popular in Latin cooking. The combination of rice and sweet plantains is one of my all-time favorite comfort foods." *pubbelly.com*

FRIED PLANTAIN AND MOJO

   Vegetable oil
1 plantain, cut into ½-inch cubes
2 garlic cloves, minced
1 Tbsp. chopped fresh cilantro
2 Tbsp. fresh lime juice
1 Tbsp. fresh orange juice
½ cup olive oil

SOFRITO

7 garlic cloves
2 shallots, coarsely chopped
1 green bell pepper, coarsely chopped
1 cup chopped fresh cilantro
1 Tbsp. olive oil
1 Tbsp. smoked paprika
2 Tbsp. tomato sauce
2 Tbsp. chopped roasted red bell peppers
1 Tbsp. tomato paste
   Hot cooked rice

1. Prepare Beans: Place beans in a large Dutch oven; add water to depth of 2 inches above beans. Bring to a boil. Boil 1 minute; cover, remove from heat, and let stand 1 hour. Drain.

2. Cook bacon in Dutch oven over medium heat, stirring often, 8 to 10 minutes or until crisp. Remove bacon, and drain on paper towels; reserve drippings in Dutch oven.

3. Add onion, 3 garlic cloves, and red bell pepper to hot drippings; cook, stirring often, 10 minutes or until tender.

4. Add broth, next 3 ingredients, and beans; bring to a boil over medium-high heat. Reduce heat to medium-low. Simmer, stirring occasionally, 2 hours or until beans are tender.

John Harris
Red Beans & Rice

LILETTE RESTAURANT
NEW ORLEANS, LA

"Red beans and rice is something everybody in Louisiana enjoys, especially at parties or festivals. The recipe's not complicated, but like a lot of classic comfort foods, it takes time to do it right. And that's what I love about it. I really like to invest the time to let the flavors develop. That's comfort." *liletterestaurant.com*

5. Meanwhile, prepare Plantain: Pour vegetable oil to depth of 1 inch in a 10-inch cast-iron skillet; heat to 340°. Fry plantain 2 to 3 minutes or until golden. Drain on paper towels.

6. Prepare Mojo: Stir together 2 garlic cloves and next 3 ingredients. Heat ½ cup olive oil in a small skillet over medium heat 2 to 3 minutes; whisk into juice mixture. Add salt and pepper to taste.

7. Prepare Sofrito: Pulse 7 garlic cloves and next 3 ingredients in a food processor until finely chopped. Sauté garlic mixture in 1 Tbsp. hot olive oil in a medium saucepan over medium-high heat 5 to 7 minutes. Add paprika and next 3 ingredients; sauté 1 minute.

8. Spoon desired amount hot cooked rice onto individual serving plates. Top each with 1 cup black bean mixture and 1 Tbsp. Sofrito. Drizzle each with 1 Tbsp. Mojo. Sprinkle with bacon and plantain cubes.

John's Red Beans & Rice
party perfect

MAKES: 10 to 12 servings
HANDS-ON TIME: 30 min.
TOTAL TIME: 3 hr., 55 min.

Serve over hot cooked rice.

1 (16-oz.) package dried red kidney beans
1 lb. mild smoked sausage, cut into ¼-inch-thick slices
1 (½-lb.) smoked ham hock, cut in half
¼ cup vegetable oil
3 celery ribs, diced
1 medium-size yellow onion, diced
1 green bell pepper, diced
3 bay leaves
3 garlic cloves, chopped
2 Tbsp. salt-free Cajun seasoning
1 tsp. kosher salt
1 tsp. dried thyme
1 tsp. ground pepper
3 (32-oz.) containers low-sodium chicken broth

1. Place beans in a large Dutch oven; add water 2 inches above beans. Boil 1 minute; cover, remove from heat, and let stand 1 hour. Drain.

2. Cook sausage and ham in hot oil in Dutch oven over medium-high heat 8 to 10 minutes or until browned. Drain sausage and ham on paper towels, reserving 2 Tbsp. drippings. Add celery and next 8 ingredients to drippings; cook over low heat, stirring occasionally, 15 minutes.

3. Add broth, beans, sausage, and ham to Dutch oven. Bring to a simmer. Cook, stirring occasionally, 2 hours or until beans are tender. Discard ham hock and bay leaves.

5 Shortcut Chicken Suppers

These recipes all start with a deli-roasted chicken, saving you time (hey, winter days are short!) while still pleasing your flock.

Skillet Chicken Pot Pie

Skillet Chicken Pot Pie
party perfect

MAKES: 6 to 8 servings
HANDS-ON TIME: 30 min.
TOTAL TIME: 1 hr., 30 min.

CHICKEN PIE FILLING
⅓ cup butter
⅓ cup all-purpose flour
1½ cups chicken broth
1½ cups milk
1½ tsp. Creole seasoning
2 Tbsp. butter
1 large sweet onion, diced
1 (8-oz.) package sliced fresh mushrooms
4 cups shredded cooked chicken
2 cups frozen cubed hash browns
1 cup matchstick carrots
1 cup frozen small sweet peas
⅓ cup chopped fresh parsley

PASTRY CRUST
1 (14.1-oz.) package refrigerated piecrusts
1 egg white

1. Prepare Filling: Preheat oven to 350°. Melt ⅓ cup butter in a large saucepan over medium heat; add all-purpose flour, and cook, whisking constantly, 1 minute. Gradually add chicken broth and milk, and cook, whisking constantly, 6 to 7 minutes or until thickened and bubbly. Remove from heat, and stir in Creole seasoning.
2. Melt 2 Tbsp. butter in a large Dutch oven over medium-high heat; add onion and mushrooms, and sauté 10 minutes or until tender. Stir in chicken, next 4 ingredients, and sauce.
3. Prepare Crust: Place 1 piecrust in a lightly greased 10-inch cast-iron skillet. Spoon chicken mixture over piecrust, and top with remaining piecrust.
4. Whisk egg white until foamy; brush top of piecrust with egg white. Cut 4 to 5 slits in top of pie for steam to escape.
5. Bake at 350° for 1 hour to 1 hour and 5 minutes or until golden brown and bubbly.

TRY THIS TWIST!

Chicken Pot Pie with Bacon-and-Cheddar Biscuits: Omit piecrusts and egg white. Preheat oven to 425°. Prepare Chicken Pie Filling as directed through Step 2. Spoon filling into a lightly greased 13- x 9-inch baking dish. Cut ½ cup cold butter into ½-inch cubes. Cut butter cubes into 2 cups self-rising flour with a pastry blender or fork until crumbly and mixture resembles small peas. Add ¾ cup (3 oz.) shredded sharp Cheddar cheese, ¼ cup finely chopped cooked bacon, 2 Tbsp. chopped fresh chives, and I cup whipping cream, stirring just until dry ingredients are moistened. Turn dough out onto a lightly floured surface, and knead lightly 3 or 4 times. Roll or pat dough to ¾-inch thickness; cut with a 2½-inch round cutter to form 15 biscuits. Bake Chicken Pie Filling at 425° for 15 minutes. Remove from oven, and arrange biscuits on top of hot chicken mixture. Bake 25 to 30 more minutes or until biscuits are golden brown and chicken mixture is bubbly. Remove from oven, and brush biscuits with 2 Tbsp. melted butter. Hands-on time: 50 min.; Total time: I hr., 30 min.

SOUTHERN KNOW-HOW
Seasoning a Cast-iron Skillet

For the love of cornbread! Return the sparkle to a Southern kitchen staple with these five easy steps.

Your trusty cast-iron skillet will eventually lose its sheen and, as a result, its super nonstick powers. Bringing back its luster and protecting it from rusting is as easy as a scrub, oil, and bake. Here's what to do.

{1}
Scrub skillet well in hot soapy water.

{2}
Dry thoroughly.

{3}
Spread a thin layer of melted shortening or vegetable oil over the skillet.

{4}
Place it upside down on a middle oven rack at 375°. (Place foil on a lower rack to catch drips.)

{5}
Bake I hour; let cool in the oven.

FAST FIX:
For day-to-day TLC, clean cast iron under hot water only (never use soap), and dry with towel before storing.

Chicken-and-Cornbread Dressing

quick prep • party perfect

MAKES: 8 to 10 servings
HANDS-ON TIME: 20 min.
TOTAL TIME: 45 min.

A favorite Southern side dish moves front and center as an all-in-one skillet supper.

- 1 cup chopped sweet onion
- 1 cup chopped celery
- 2 Tbsp. chopped fresh sage
- 1 tsp. freshly ground pepper
- 2 Tbsp. canola oil
- 2 cups self-rising white cornmeal mix
- 2 cups buttermilk
- ½ cup all-purpose flour
- 2 large eggs, lightly beaten
- ¼ cup butter, melted
- 2 Tbsp. sugar
- 2 cups chopped cooked chicken

1. Preheat oven to 425°. Sauté first 4 ingredients in hot oil in a 12-inch cast-iron skillet over medium heat 8 to 10 minutes or until tender. Remove from skillet; wipe skillet clean.
2. Stir together cornmeal mix, buttermilk, and next 4 ingredients just until moistened. Stir in onion mixture and chicken just until blended. Pour batter into hot 12-inch skillet.
3. Bake at 425° for 25 to 30 minutes or until golden brown.

> ### TAKE COMFORT IN THIS!
>
> White Lightning Chicken Chili takes only 30 minutes from start to finish.

White Lightning Chicken Chili

quick prep • party perfect

MAKES: 11½ cups
HANDS-ON TIME: 30 min.
TOTAL TIME: 30 min., not including salsa

Don't drain the chopped green chiles or navy beans. Serve chili with cornbread.

- 1 large sweet onion, diced
- 2 garlic cloves, minced
- 2 Tbsp. olive oil
- 4 cups shredded cooked chicken
- 2 (14½-oz.) cans chicken broth
- 2 (4.5-oz.) cans chopped green chiles
- 1 (1.25-oz.) package white chicken chili seasoning mix
- 3 (16-oz.) cans navy beans
  Toppings: Avocado-Mango Salsa, sour cream, shredded Monterey Jack cheese, fresh cilantro leaves

1. Sauté onion and garlic in hot oil in a large Dutch oven over medium-high heat 5 minutes or until onion is tender. Stir in chicken, next 3 ingredients, and 2 cans navy beans. Coarsely mash remaining can navy beans, and stir into chicken mixture. Bring to a boil, stirring often; cover, reduce heat to medium-low, and simmer, stirring occasionally, 10 minutes. Serve with desired toppings.
NOTE: We tested with McCormick White Chicken Chili Seasoning Mix.

Avocado-Mango Salsa

1. Stir together 1 large avocado, cubed; 1 cup diced fresh mango; ⅓ cup diced red onion; 2 Tbsp. chopped fresh cilantro; and 2 Tbsp. fresh lime juice. Makes: about 2 cups. Hands-on time: 10 min., Total time: 10 min.

King Ranch Chicken Mac and Cheese

quick prep • party perfect

MAKES: 6 servings
HANDS-ON TIME: 20 min.
TOTAL TIME: 45 min.
(Pictured on page 3)

- ½ (16-oz.) package cellentani pasta
- 2 Tbsp. butter
- 1 medium onion, diced
- 1 green bell pepper, diced
- 1 (10-oz.) can diced tomatoes and green chiles
- 1 (8-oz.) package pasteurized prepared cheese product, cubed
- 3 cups chopped cooked chicken
- 1 (10¾-oz.) can cream of chicken soup
- ½ cup sour cream
- 1 tsp. chili powder
- ½ tsp. ground cumin
- 1½ cups (6 oz.) shredded Cheddar cheese

1. Preheat oven to 350°. Prepare pasta according to package directions.
2. Meanwhile, melt butter in a large Dutch oven over medium-high heat. Add onion and bell pepper, and sauté 5 minutes or until tender. Stir in tomatoes and green chiles and prepared cheese product; cook, stirring constantly, 2 minutes or until cheese melts. Stir in chicken, next 4 ingredients, and hot cooked pasta until blended. Spoon mixture into a lightly greased 10-inch cast-iron skillet or 11- x 7-inch baking dish; sprinkle with shredded Cheddar cheese.
3. Bake at 350° for 25 to 30 minutes or until bubbly.

Every Recipe has a Story

Former *Southern Living* Food Editor Kate Nicholson shares her collection of Southern comforts, in memory of her mom.

Before the Barefoot Contessa, Emeril, and a slew of other celebrity chefs, my mom, Carolyn Flournoy, was a celebrity in her own right. As food editor for *The Times* in Shreveport, Louisiana, for three decades, she developed a loyal following, both in and beyond the state. At any given time, you could find her jetting off to Italy to teach and cook with culinary greats, such as James Beard, Jacques Pépin, and Simone Beck. Back home, of course, she was just Mom.

After she passed away eight years ago, I left *Southern Living*, where I was an editor in the Food department, and immersed myself in her work—reading newspaper articles, sorting through photographs, and thumbing through weathered, old recipe cards. I especially loved seeing her handwritten notes in the margins; it was like I could hear her voice again, playfully pronouncing ra-tuh-TOO-ee or talking to a blackberry as if it were king of the fruits. Someday, I plan to pay tribute to her in a cookbook of all her best recipes and the stories behind them. In the meantime, here are a few sentimental (and delicious) favorites. In my mind, all of these qualify as comfort foods. They bring her back to life. And what's more comforting than that?

THE ROAST CHICKEN TEST

"When it comes to a basic culinary skill, Mom always thought one must learn to roast a chicken. She agreed with Julia Child that you could judge the quality of a cook or restaurant by his, her, or its roast chicken."

Roast Chicken
good for you • party perfect

MAKES: 4 to 6 servings
HANDS-ON TIME: 20 min.
TOTAL TIME: I hr., 35 min.
(Pictured on page 3)

- 1 (4- to 5-lb.) whole chicken
- 1½ tsp. kosher salt, divided
- 1 lemon half
- 1 tsp. seasoned pepper
- 1 tsp. dried rosemary
- 1 Tbsp. olive oil
- 1 Tbsp. butter, melted

1. Preheat oven to 450°. If applicable, remove neck and giblets from chicken, and reserve for another use. Rinse chicken with cold water, and drain cavity well. Pat dry with paper towels. Sprinkle ½ tsp. salt inside cavity. Place lemon half inside cavity.
2. Stir together pepper, rosemary, and remaining 1 tsp. salt. Brush outside of chicken with oil. Rub 2½ tsp. pepper mixture into skin. Sprinkle remaining pepper mixture over both sides of breast. Place chicken, breast side up, on a lightly greased wire rack in a lightly greased shallow roasting pan. Add ¾ cup water to pan.
3. Bake at 450° for 20 minutes. Reduce heat to 375°, and bake 30 minutes. Baste chicken with pan juices; drizzle with melted butter. Bake 15 to 25 minutes or until a meat thermometer inserted in thigh registers 165°, shielding with aluminum foil to prevent excessive browning, if necessary. Remove chicken from oven, and baste with pan juices. Let stand 10 minutes before slicing.
NOTE: We tested with McCormick Gourmet Collection Crushed Rosemary.

ra-tuh-TOO-ee

"Mom loved to teach new dishes, and she often included one of my favorites, ratatouille, in her cooking demonstrations. She explained that it was worth all the chopping and dicing of the vegetables. I also recall her saying, 'As delicious as it is to eat, you've got to admit it's pretty fun to say.'"

Ratatouille

good for you • party perfect

MAKES: 4 to 6 servings
HANDS-ON TIME: 45 min.
TOTAL TIME: 45 min.

- 1 green bell pepper
- 1 red bell pepper
- 1 yellow bell pepper
- ½ lb. zucchini
- ½ lb. yellow squash
- 1 large onion, coarsely chopped
- 2 garlic cloves, minced
- 3 Tbsp. olive oil
- 2 (14.5-oz.) cans diced tomatoes
- 1 small eggplant (about 1 lb.), peeled and cut into 1-inch pieces
- ¼ tsp. salt
- 2 Tbsp. chopped fresh basil

1. Cut first 5 ingredients into 1-inch pieces.
2. Sauté onion and garlic in hot oil in a large skillet over medium heat 5 to 7 minutes or just until onion is tender. Stir in tomatoes and next 2 ingredients, and sauté 8 to 10 minutes or just until eggplant begins to soften. Stir in bell peppers, zucchini, and squash; cover and cook, stirring occasionally, 8 to 10 minutes or until vegetables are tender and liquid is slightly reduced. Stir in basil. Add salt and freshly ground pepper to taste, and sauté 3 minutes.

Ham Salad

quick prep • party perfect

MAKES: about 6 cups
HANDS-ON TIME: 20 min.
TOTAL TIME: 20 min.

- 2 lb. fully cooked boneless ham, cut into large chunks
- 1 cup sweet pickle relish
- 1 cup mayonnaise
- 1 Tbsp. celery seeds
- 1½ tsp. yellow mustard
- 1 tsp. refrigerated horseradish
- 1 tsp. fresh lemon juice
- ¼ tsp. seasoned pepper
- 3 to 5 hard-cooked eggs, peeled and chopped
   Toasted French bread slices (optional)
   Garnishes: fresh parsley leaves, small sweet pickle halves

1. Process ham, in batches, in a food processor until coarsely ground, stopping to scrape down sides as needed. Place ground ham in a bowl; stir in pickle relish and next 6 ingredients. Fold in chopped eggs. Serve on toasted bread slices, if desired. Garnish, if desired.

Mom's Lucky Black-eyed Peas

party perfect

MAKES: 4 to 6 servings
HANDS-ON TIME: 15 min.
TOTAL TIME: 8 hr.

For convenience, look for a 12-oz. package of sliced salt pork from Hormel. You'll need three slices.

- 1 (16-oz.) package dried black-eyed peas
- 2 oz. salt pork
- 1 large onion, chopped
- 1 tsp. bacon drippings
- ½ tsp. ground pepper
- 1 jalapeño pepper, seeded and diced (optional)
   Garnishes: chopped green onions, cooked and crumbled bacon

1. Rinse and sort peas according to package directions. Place peas in a large Dutch oven; cover with cold water 2 inches above peas, and let soak 6 to 8 hours (or see "Quick-Soak" method below). Drain peas, and rinse thoroughly.
2. Bring salt pork and 1 qt. water to a boil in Dutch oven over medium-high heat; reduce heat to medium-low, and simmer 30 minutes. Add peas, onion, next 2 ingredients, water to cover, and, if desired, jalapeño pepper. Bring to a boil over medium-high heat. Cover, reduce heat, and cook, stirring occasionally, 1 hour to 1 hour and 30 minutes or until peas are tender and liquid thickens slightly. (Uncover after 1 hour to allow liquid to evaporate, if necessary.) Season with salt and pepper to taste. Garnish, if desired.

QUICK-SOAK BLACK-EYED PEAS:

Place peas in a Dutch oven; cover with cold water 2 inches above peas. Bring to a boil; boil 1 minute. Cover, remove from heat, and let stand 1 hour. Drain peas, and rinse thoroughly. Proceed as directed in Step 2.

Roquefort Noodles

party perfect

MAKES: 6 to 8 servings
HANDS-ON TIME: 20 min.
TOTAL TIME: 20 min.

Don't skimp on the quality of the blue cheese in this recipe.

- 1 (12-oz.) package wide egg noodles
- 1 Tbsp. jarred chicken soup base
- ½ tsp. olive oil
- ½ cup butter
- 6 to 8 green onions, sliced
- 4 to 6 oz. Roquefort or other blue cheese, crumbled
- 1 (8-oz.) container sour cream

1. Prepare noodles according to package directions, adding chicken soup base and oil to water.

2. Meanwhile, melt butter in a large heavy skillet over medium heat. Add onions, and sauté 5 to 7 minutes or until tender. Reduce heat to medium-low, and stir in Roquefort cheese, stirring constantly, until cheese is melted. Remove from heat, and stir in sour cream until blended and smooth.

3. Toss together Roquefort cheese sauce and hot cooked egg noodles. Add seasoned pepper to taste.

NOTE: We tested with Superior Touch Better Than Bouillon Chicken Base.

THE BELOVED BLACKBERRY

"We all loved whatever fruit found its way into Mom's cobbler, but I know which was her favorite. While we were making a cobbler together one day, she held up a plump blackberry and announced, 'Oh ye of all the berries, you are indeed my most coveted of all.' And with that, she popped it into her mouth."

Winter Blackberry Cobbler

party perfect

MAKES: 8 to 10 servings
HANDS-ON TIME: 45 min.
TOTAL TIME: 2 hr., 20 min.

- 2½ cups all-purpose flour
- 1¾ tsp. baking powder
- ¾ tsp. salt
- ½ cup shortening
- ⅔ cup milk
- 2 cups sugar
- ⅓ cup all-purpose flour
- 1 tsp. fresh lemon juice
- 2 (16-oz.) packages frozen blackberries
- ¼ cup butter, cut into ¼-inch pieces and divided
- 1 Tbsp. sugar
  Vanilla ice cream

1. Preheat oven to 425°. Whisk together first 3 ingredients in a medium bowl. Cut shortening into flour mixture with a pastry blender or fork until mixture is slightly crumbly. Add milk, stirring with a fork until dry ingredients are moistened and mixture is soft enough to form a soft ball.

2. Turn dough out onto a lightly floured surface, and knead 6 to 8 times. Divide dough in half. Roll 1 dough half to ¼-inch thickness on a lightly floured surface, and cut into 1-inch-wide strips. Place on a lightly greased baking sheet.

3. Bake strips at 425° for 15 minutes or until lightly browned. Transfer strips to a wire rack, and let cool completely (about 30 minutes). Reduce oven temperature to 350°.

4. Meanwhile, roll remaining dough half to ¼-inch thickness; cut dough into 1-inch-wide strips.

5. Sprinkle 2 cups sugar, ⅓ cup flour, and lemon juice over frozen blackberries in a large bowl, and gently stir.

6. Spoon half of blackberry mixture into a lightly greased 13- x 9-inch baking dish. Break each baked dough strip into 2 or 3 pieces, and place on top of blackberry mixture in baking dish. Dot blackberry mixture with half of butter pieces. Spoon remaining blackberry mixture over baked dough strips.

7. Arrange unbaked dough strips in a lattice design over filling, and sprinkle with 1 Tbsp. sugar. Dot blackberry mixture with remaining butter pieces.

8. Bake at 350° for 50 to 60 minutes or until pastry is golden and mixture is bubbly. Serve with vanilla ice cream.

TRY THIS TWIST!
Summer Blackberry Cobbler: Substitute 8 cups fresh blackberries for frozen. Prepare recipe as directed, letting berries stand 10 minutes after stirring together mixture in Step 5. Hands-on time: 45 min.; Total time: 2 hr., 30 min.

Hostess Gift of the Month

This year, resolve to think beyond a ho-hum box of chocolates for a hostess gift. Instead, pass on this sweet treat, which marries two Southern specialties, coffee cake and pound cake, to create one buttery, best-of-both-worlds dessert.

Coffee Cake Pound Cake

make-ahead • party perfect

MAKES: 12 servings
HANDS-ON TIME: 30 min.
TOTAL TIME: 3 hr., 25 min.

Coffee Cake Pound Cake

PECAN STREUSEL

- ½ cup firmly packed brown sugar
- ½ cup all-purpose flour
- 1 tsp. ground cinnamon
- ¼ cup butter
- ¾ cup chopped pecans

POUND CAKE BATTER

- 1 cup finely chopped pecans
- 1 cup butter, softened
- 2½ cups granulated sugar
- 6 large eggs
- 3 cups all-purpose flour
- ¼ tsp. baking soda
- 1 (8-oz.) container sour cream
- 2 tsp. vanilla extract
- ¼ cup firmly packed brown sugar
- 1½ tsp. ground cinnamon

1. Prepare Pecan Streusel: Combine first 3 ingredients in a bowl. Cut in butter with a pastry blender or fork until mixture resembles small peas. Stir in ¾ cup pecans.
2. Prepare Pound Cake Batter: Preheat oven to 350°. Bake 1 cup pecans in a single layer in a shallow pan 5 to 7 minutes or until lightly toasted and fragrant, stirring halfway through. Cool 20 minutes. Reduce oven temperature to 325°.
3. Beat butter at medium speed with a heavy-duty electric stand mixer until creamy. Gradually add granulated sugar, beating until light and fluffy. Add eggs, 1 at a time, beating just until blended after each addition.

4. Stir together flour and baking soda; add to butter mixture alternately with sour cream, beginning and ending with flour mixture. Beat at low speed just until blended after each addition. Stir in vanilla.
5. Pour half of batter into a greased and floured 10-inch (12-cup) tube pan. Stir together toasted pecans, brown sugar, and cinnamon; sprinkle over batter. Spoon remaining batter over pecan mixture; sprinkle with Pecan Streusel.
6. Bake at 325° for 1 hour and 20 minutes to 1 hour and 30 minutes or until a long wooden pick inserted in center comes out clean. Cool in pan on a wire rack 10 to 15 minutes; remove from pan to wire rack, and cool completely (about 1 hour).

Coffee with Your Cake?

For the perfect warm-the-soul present, pair our Coffee Cake Pound Cake with a bag of java from one of our favorite Southern roasters.

COUNTER CULTURE COFFEE, Durham, NC

This community-focused company offers free cuppings at 10 a.m. every Friday.

BEST BEANS: Colombia La Golondrina. Smooth, with a chocolaty aroma and hints of butter and orange. $14/12 oz.; *counterculturecoffee.com*

CUP TO CUP, Savannah, GA

This one-man roaster specializes in ethically sourced coffees from around the globe.

BEST BEANS: Brazil Bob-O-Link. Bold with bright berry flavors. $10/12 oz.; *cuptocupcoffee.com*

FINERGRIND, Birmingham, AL

Woody Wiginton micro-roasts heirloom beans.

BEST BEANS: Panama Elida Estate. Caramel and blackberry notes. $16/12 oz.; *finergrind.com*

KALDI'S COFFEE, St. Louis, MO

Kaldi's serves certified kosher roasts at coffee-houses across the Show-Me State.

BEST BEANS: Organic Ethiopian Koke. Bright with a touch of toffee and lemon. $13/12 oz.; *kaldiscoffee.com*

SWEETWATER ORGANIC, Gainesville, FL

It's one of the South's largest wholesalers of fair trade organic coffee—100,000 pounds a year.

BEST BEANS: Moka Java. A low-acid coffee with a malty finish. $13/16 oz.; *sweetwaterorganiccoffee.com*

Wrap it Up!

Bundle cake and/or coffee in cheesecloth with bay sprigs.

Make-Ahead Muffins

When you have sweet and savory muffins at the ready, it's a whole lot easier to come out from under those covers. Here, our fix-and-freeze favorites.

Applesauce Muffins with Cinnamon Streusel Topping

quick prep • make-ahead • party perfect

MAKES: 1 dozen
HANDS-ON TIME: 15 min.
TOTAL TIME: 48 min., including topping

- 4 cups all-purpose baking mix
- ½ cup sugar
- 2 tsp. ground cinnamon
- ⅔ cup chunky applesauce
- ½ cup milk
- ¼ cup vegetable oil
- 2 large eggs
  Cinnamon Streusel Topping

1. Preheat oven to 400°. Whisk together baking mix, sugar, and cinnamon in a large bowl; make a well in center of mixture.
2. Whisk together applesauce and next 3 ingredients in a small bowl; add to sugar mixture, stirring just until dry ingredients are moistened. Spoon batter into a lightly greased 12-cup muffin pan, filling almost completely full. Sprinkle Cinnamon Streusel Topping over batter.
3. Bake at 400° for 18 to 20 minutes or until a wooden pick inserted in center comes out clean and tops are golden brown. Cool in pan on a wire rack 5 minutes. Remove from pan to a wire rack.
NOTE: We tested with Bisquick Original Pancake and Baking Mix.

Cinnamon Streusel Topping

quick prep

MAKES: about 1 cup
HANDS-ON TIME: 10 min.
TOTAL TIME: 10 min.

- ⅓ cup granulated sugar
- ¼ cup firmly packed light brown sugar
- 3 Tbsp. all-purpose baking mix
- ¼ tsp. ground cinnamon
- 2 Tbsp. butter, melted

1. Whisk together first 4 ingredients until blended. Stir melted butter into sugar mixture until well blended and crumbly.

Buttermilk-Poppy Seed Muffins

quick prep • make-ahead • party perfect

MAKES: 1 dozen
HANDS-ON TIME: 15 min.
TOTAL TIME: 45 min., including glaze

- 2 cups all-purpose flour
- 1 cup sugar
- 1 Tbsp. orange zest
- 1½ tsp. baking powder
- ½ tsp. baking soda
- ½ tsp. salt
- 1 cup buttermilk
- 3 large eggs
- 2 Tbsp. poppy seeds
- 1 tsp. vanilla extract
- ½ cup butter, melted
  Orange Glaze

1. Preheat oven to 375°. Combine first 6 ingredients in a large bowl; make a well in center of mixture.
2. Whisk together buttermilk and next 3 ingredients in a medium bowl. Add buttermilk mixture to flour mixture, stirring just until dry ingredients are moistened. Stir in melted butter. Spoon batter into a lightly greased 12-cup muffin pan, filling three-fourths full.
3. Bake at 375° for 20 to 25 minutes or until a wooden pick inserted in center comes out clean. Cool in pans on a wire rack 5 minutes. Remove from pans to a wire rack, and drizzle with Orange Glaze.

RECIPE FROM JEAN VOAN
SHEPHERD, TEXAS

Orange Glaze

quick prep

MAKES: about ½ cup
HANDS-ON TIME: 5 min.
TOTAL TIME: 5 min.

- 1 cup powdered sugar
- 1 tsp. vanilla extract
- 2 Tbsp. orange juice

1. Stir together powdered sugar, vanilla, and 1 Tbsp. orange juice. Stir in remaining 1 Tbsp. orange juice, 1 tsp. at a time, for desired consistency.

> *"These breakfast sandwich sliders will be the talk of your next brunch!"*
>
> **ASHLEY ARTHUR**
> ASSISTANT RECIPE EDITOR

Bacon-and-Cheddar Corn Muffins

quick prep • make-ahead • party perfect

MAKES: 1 dozen
HANDS-ON TIME: 22 min.
TOTAL TIME: 52 min.

Heating the pan beforehand results in a nice crispy bottom.

- 6 **bacon slices**
- 2 **cups self-rising white cornmeal mix**
- 1 **Tbsp. sugar**
- 1½ **cups buttermilk**
- 1 **large egg**
- 4 **Tbsp. butter, melted**
- 1 **cup (4 oz.) shredded sharp Cheddar cheese**
  Vegetable cooking spray

1. Preheat oven to 425°. Cook bacon in a large skillet over medium-high heat 12 to 14 minutes or until crisp; remove bacon, and drain on paper towels. Crumble bacon.
2. Heat a 12-cup muffin pan in oven 5 minutes.
3. Combine cornmeal mix and sugar in a medium bowl; make a well in center of mixture.
4. Stir together buttermilk and egg; add to cornmeal mixture, stirring just until dry ingredients are moistened. Stir in melted butter, cheese, and bacon. Remove pan from oven, and coat with cooking spray. Spoon batter into hot muffin pan, filling almost completely full.
5. Bake at 425° for 15 to 20 minutes or until golden. Remove from pan to a wire rack, and let cool 10 minutes.
NOTE: We tested with White Lily White Cornmeal Mix.

TRY THESE TWISTS!
Scrambled Egg Muffin Sliders: Prepare recipe as directed. Whisk together 8 large eggs, 1 Tbsp. water, and ½ tsp. Creole seasoning in a medium bowl. Melt 1 Tbsp. butter in a large nonstick skillet. Add egg mixture, and cook, without stirring, 2 to 3 minutes or until eggs begin to set on bottom. Gently draw cooked edges away from sides of pan to form large pieces. Cook, stirring occasionally, 4 to 5 minutes or until eggs are thickened and moist. (Do not overstir.) Cut muffins in half, and spoon eggs over bottom halves. Cover with top halves of muffins.

Ham-and-Swiss Corn Muffins: Substitute Swiss cheese for Cheddar cheese and 1 cup diced cooked ham for bacon. Reduce butter in batter to 3 Tbsp. Brown ham in remaining 1 Tbsp. melted butter in a nonstick skillet over medium-high heat 5 to 6 minutes. Proceed as directed, whisking in 2 Tbsp. Dijon mustard with buttermilk and egg.

Southwestern Chile-Cheese Corn Muffins: Omit bacon. Substitute pepper Jack cheese for Cheddar cheese. Proceed as directed, stirring in 1 (4.5-oz.) can chopped green chiles, drained, with cheese and butter.

Beer-Pimiento Cheese Muffins

quick prep • make-ahead • party perfect

MAKES: 1½ dozen
HANDS-ON TIME: 15 min.
TOTAL TIME: 38 min.

The cracker topping adds a crunchy surprise. Serve the mini version as party bites.

- 1 **(12-oz.) bottle beer, at room temperature**
- 1 **(4-oz.) jar diced pimiento, drained**
- 1 **large egg**
- 1 **tsp. finely grated onion**
- 4 **cups all-purpose baking mix**
- 2 **cups (8 oz.) shredded sharp Cheddar cheese**
- 1 **cup crushed bite-size Cheddar cheese crackers (about 1½ cups crackers)**

1. Preheat oven to 400°. Stir together first 4 ingredients; stir in baking mix just until ingredients are blended. (Batter may be lumpy.) Stir in cheese. Spoon batter into lightly greased 12-cup muffin pans, filling 18 cups three-fourths full. Sprinkle with crushed crackers.
2. Bake at 400° for 13 to 15 minutes or until lightly browned. Remove from pans to a wire rack, and let cool 10 minutes.
NOTE: We tested with Bisquick Original Pancake and Baking Mix.

INSPIRED BY PATSY BELL HOBSON
LIBERTY, MISSOURI

TRY THIS TWIST!
Miniature Beer-Pimiento Cheese Muffins: Omit Cheddar cheese crackers. Pour batter into 2 lightly greased 24-cup miniature muffin pans. Bake and cool as directed. Makes: 4 dozen.

Slow-cooker Winter Barbecue

Why wait 'til July to enjoy beef brisket and baked beans? These hearty dishes are made for wintry days. Just consider the slow cooker your very own pit master.

TRY THIS TWIST!

Slow-cooked Barbecued Chicken Sandwiches: Prepare recipe as directed through Step 3. Remove chicken from slow cooker, and let cool slightly (about 10 to 15 minutes). Discard lemons. Skin, bone, and shred chicken. Skim fat from pan juices, and pour over chicken. Serve chicken over sliced Sweet Potato Cornbread (recipe below). Top with Pickled Peppers & Onions and Simple Slaw (facing page). **NOTE:** To make ahead, cool shredded chicken completely. Freeze in an airtight container up to 3 months.

Slow-cooked
Barbecued Chicken

Sweet Potato Cornbread

quick prep • party perfect

MAKES: 6 servings
HANDS-ON TIME: 15 min.
TOTAL TIME: 50 min.

- 2 cups self-rising white cornmeal mix
- 3 Tbsp. sugar
- ¼ tsp. pumpkin pie spice
- 5 large eggs
- 2 cups cooked mashed sweet potatoes (about 1½ lb. sweet potatoes)
- 1 (8-oz.) container sour cream
- ½ cup butter, melted

1. Preheat oven to 425°. Stir together first 3 ingredients in a large bowl; make a well in center of mixture. Whisk together eggs and next 3 ingredients; add to cornmeal mixture, stirring just until moistened. Spoon batter into a lightly greased 9-inch square pan.

2. Bake at 425° for 35 minutes or until golden brown.

Slow-cooked Barbecued Chicken

make-ahead • party perfect

MAKES: 6 servings
HANDS-ON TIME: 20 min.
TOTAL TIME: 5 hr., 20 min.

- 2 tsp. salt
- 1½ tsp. paprika
- ½ tsp. garlic powder
- ½ tsp. pepper
- 1 (3- to 3½-lb.) cut-up whole chicken
- ½ cup cola soft drink
- ⅓ cup ketchup
- ¼ cup firmly packed light brown sugar
- 2 Tbsp. apple cider vinegar
- 2 Tbsp. bourbon
- 1 lemon, sliced

1. Stir together first 4 ingredients in a small bowl. Sprinkle over chicken. Place chicken in a single layer in a lightly greased 6-qt. slow cooker.

2. Whisk together cola soft drink and next 4 ingredients in a small bowl. Slowly pour mixture between chicken pieces (to avoid removing spices from chicken). Place lemon slices in a single layer on top of chicken.

3. Cover and cook on HIGH 5 hours (or on LOW 6½ to 7½ hours) or until done.

4. Transfer chicken pieces to a serving platter; discard lemon slices. Skim fat from pan juices in slow cooker. Pour pan juices over chicken; serve immediately.

Top Your Sandwich with Slaw

{1}

SIMPLE SLAW:

Whisk together ¼ cup apple cider vinegar, ¼ cup canola oil, 2 Tbsp. mayonnaise, 1 Tbsp. honey, ½ tsp. salt, ¼ tsp. pepper, and ¼ tsp. celery seeds in a large bowl. Stir in 1 (16-oz.) package shredded coleslaw mix. Serve immediately, or chill up to 24 hours.

{2}

LONE STAR SLAW:

Prepare Simple Slaw as directed, stirring in ½ tsp. grapefruit zest; 2 Tbsp. fresh grapefruit juice; 1 grapefruit, sectioned; ¾ cup toasted chopped pecans; and 1 Tbsp. chopped fresh cilantro.

{3}

LOWCOUNTRY SLAW:

Prepare Simple Slaw as directed, stirring in 1 cup sliced pickled okra and 2 Tbsp. pickled okra juice.

NOTE: We tested with Wickles Wicked Okra.

Pickled Peppers & Onions

make-ahead • party perfect

MAKES: 1 qt.
HANDS-ON TIME: 20 min.
TOTAL TIME: 1 hr., 35 min., plus 24 hr. for chilling

- ½ **small red onion, cut into ¼-inch-thick slices**
  Ice water
- ½ **red bell pepper, cut lengthwise into ¼-inch-wide strips**
- ½ **yellow bell pepper, cut lengthwise into ¼-inch-wide strips**
- ½ **green bell pepper, cut lengthwise into ¼-inch-wide strips**
- 1 **cup white vinegar**
- 6 **Tbsp. sugar**
- 2 **Tbsp. kosher salt**
- ½ **tsp. dried crushed red pepper**

1. Soak onion slices in ice water to cover in a small bowl 10 minutes; drain. Place onion slices and bell pepper strips in 1 (1-qt.) canning jar.
2. Bring vinegar, next 3 ingredients, and 1 cup water to a boil in a small nonaluminum saucepan over medium-high heat, stirring occasionally, until sugar is dissolved.
3. Pour hot vinegar mixture over vegetables in jar. Let stand, uncovered, 1 hour. Cover and chill 24 hours. Store in an airtight container in refrigerator up to 1 week.

Slow-cooker Mustard Barbecued Pork

make-ahead • party perfect

MAKES: 10 to 12 servings
HANDS-ON TIME: 20 min.
TOTAL TIME: 8 hr., 35 min.

This recipe was inspired by the popular mustard barbecue sauce found in parts of South Carolina.

- ⅓ **cup firmly packed light brown sugar**
- 2½ **tsp. salt**
- 1½ **tsp. garlic powder**
- 1½ **tsp. paprika**
- 1 **tsp. onion powder**
- ½ **tsp. ground red pepper**
- 1 **(4- to 5-lb.) bone-in pork shoulder roast (Boston butt)**
- 1 **cup yellow mustard**
- ⅓ **cup honey**
- ¼ **cup apple cider vinegar**
- 1½ **tsp. Worcestershire sauce**

1. Stir together first 6 ingredients. Rub brown sugar mixture over roast; place roast in a lightly greased 6-qt. slow cooker.
2. Whisk together mustard and next 3 ingredients. Pour mustard mixture over top of roast. Cover and cook on LOW 8 to 10 hours (or on HIGH 4 to 6 hours) or until meat shreds easily with a fork. Let stand 15 minutes. Shred pork with a fork; stir until sauce is incorporated.
NOTE: To make ahead, prepare recipe as directed, and let pork cool completely (about 1 hour), stirring occasionally. Freeze in an airtight container up to 3 months.

TRY THIS TWIST!
South Carolina Sliders: Prepare recipe as directed. Bake 1 (15-oz.) package slider miniature sandwich buns according to package directions. Split buns. Spoon ¼ cup barbecued pork and ¼ cup Lowcountry Slaw (recipe above) onto each bun bottom. Cover with tops of buns, and serve immediately. Makes: 4 to 6 servings. Hands-on time: 10 min.; Total time: 9 hr., 10 min., including barbecued pork and slaw.
NOTE: We tested with Pepperidge Farm Classic Sliders Mini Buns.

Down-South Banh Mi

party perfect

MAKES: 3 main-dish servings
HANDS-ON TIME: 25 min.
TOTAL TIME: 25 min., not including pork and peppers and onions

Here's a Southern spin on a classic Vietnamese-French sub. Keep the pickled pepper mixture and shredded pork on hand for a fast meal. (Pictured on page 4)

- 1 (18-inch) French bread baguette
- 3 Tbsp. mayonnaise
- 1 tsp. Asian sriracha hot chili sauce
- ¼ cup thinly sliced carrots
- 1 tsp. fish sauce
- 1 cup Slow-cooker Mustard Barbecued Pork (see page 47)
- ⅓ cup Pickled Peppers & Onions (see page 47)
- 1 small serrano pepper, thinly sliced*
- Fresh cilantro leaves

1. Preheat oven to 350°. Bake baguette on an ungreased baking sheet 10 minutes or until warm.

2. Meanwhile, stir together mayonnaise and sriracha in a small bowl. Stir together carrots and fish sauce in a separate bowl.

3. Split baguette horizontally. Cut each half into 3 (6-inch-long) pieces. Spread cut sides of bread with mayonnaise mixture. Layer bottom halves with Slow-cooker Mustard Barbecued Pork, Pickled Peppers & Onions, serrano pepper slices, carrot mixture, and cilantro to taste. Top with remaining bread slices. Serve immediately.

* ½ small jalapeño pepper may be substituted.

NOTE: To make appetizer servings, cut baguette into 6 (3-inch-long) pieces instead of 3 (6-inch-long) pieces.

TAKE COMFORT IN THIS!

Down-South Banh Mi doubles as an easy party pick up. Just cut the sandwiches into smaller portions.

Texas-Style Barbecued Beef Brisket

MAKES: 4 to 6 servings
HANDS-ON TIME: 20 min.
TOTAL TIME: 7 hr., 40 min.

Serve this with Lone Star Slaw (see page 47), and sop up the pan juices with Texas toast.

- 1 large sweet onion, sliced
- 3 garlic cloves, chopped
- 1 Tbsp. chili powder
- 1 Tbsp. jarred beef soup base
- 1 Tbsp. Worcestershire sauce
- 1 tsp. ground cumin
- ½ tsp. pepper
- 1½ tsp. hickory liquid smoke
- 1 (2- to 3-lb.) beef brisket flat, trimmed
- ¼ cup beer
- 3 Tbsp. bottled chili sauce

1. Lightly grease a 6-qt. slow cooker; add onion and garlic. Stir together chili powder and next 5 ingredients. Rub over brisket; place brisket over mixture in slow cooker.

2. Whisk together beer and chili sauce. Slowly pour mixture around brisket (to avoid removing spices from brisket).

3. Cover and cook on LOW 7 to 8 hours (or on HIGH 4 to 5 hours) or until fork-tender. Uncover and let stand in slow cooker 20 minutes.

4. Remove brisket from slow cooker; cut brisket across the grain into thin slices. Return brisket to slow cooker, and spoon pan juices over meat.

TAKE COMFORT IN THIS!

No browning required: Let your slow cooker do the work for a tender, juicy brisket every time.

Hearty BBQ Sides

Tangy "Baked" Beans

Let the beans cook (Step 1) while you sleep; continue with Step 2 the next day.

- 1 (16-oz.) package dried navy beans
- 1 cup ketchup
- ½ cup chopped onion
- ½ cup firmly packed light brown sugar
- 3 Tbsp. apple cider vinegar
- 3 Tbsp. cane syrup
- 2 Tbsp. yellow mustard
- 1 tsp. salt
- 1 tsp. Worcestershire sauce
- ½ tsp. garlic powder
- 2 bacon slices, diced

1. Combine beans and 6 cups water in a 6-qt. slow cooker. Cover and cook on LOW 8 hours.

2. Stir together ketchup and next 8 ingredients; stir into beans. Sprinkle bacon over top. Cover and cook on LOW 5 hours. Uncover and cook on LOW 30 minutes or until slightly thickened.

Easy Potato Salad

You can also use two packages refrigerated potato wedges.

- 2½ lb. small red potatoes, cut into wedges
- 2 Tbsp. olive oil
- 1 tsp. kosher salt
- ½ tsp. pepper
- 8 cooked bacon slices, crumbled
- 4 green onions, chopped
- ¾ cup bottled Ranch dressing

1. Preheat oven to 425°. Toss together first 4 ingredients; arrange in a 15- x 10-inch jelly-roll pan. Bake 45 minutes, stirring occasionally.

2. Toss together bacon, next 2 ingredients, and potatoes. Serve warm or cold.

February

New Classic Desserts

These inspired twists on iconic sweets—apple cobbler, banana pudding, and more—will have you scooping up seconds.

Caramelized Banana Pudding

make-ahead • party perfect

MAKES: 8 servings
HANDS-ON TIME: 30 min.
TOTAL TIME: 1 hr., 15 min.

For the best flavor, choose firm, ripe bananas with brown speckles. (Also pictured on page 168)

½ **cup firmly packed light brown sugar**
¼ **cup butter**
¼ **tsp. ground cinnamon**
4 **large ripe bananas, sliced**
1 **cup granulated sugar, divided**
⅓ **cup all-purpose flour**
2 **large eggs**
2 **cups milk**
4 **large eggs, separated**
2 **tsp. vanilla extract**
48 **vanilla wafers**

OUR TWIST ON
Banana Pudding

Forget everything you know about this creamy classic. Caramel-glazed bananas offer a whole new taste experience that's unforgettable.

Caramelized Banana Pudding

1. Preheat oven to 325°. Cook first 3 ingredients in a large skillet over medium heat, stirring constantly, 2 to 3 minutes or until bubbly. Add bananas; cook 2 to 3 minutes or until thoroughly heated. Remove from heat.

2. Whisk together ¾ cup granulated sugar, next 3 ingredients, and 4 egg yolks in a heavy saucepan. Cook over medium-low heat, whisking constantly, 8 to 10 minutes or until a pudding-like thickness. (Mixture will just begin to bubble and will hold soft peaks when whisk is lifted.) Remove from heat, and stir in vanilla.

3. Divide half of banana mixture, pudding, and wafers among 8 (1-cup) ramekins or ovenproof glass dishes. Layer with remaining banana mixture, pudding, and vanilla wafers.

4. Beat 4 egg whites at high speed with an electric mixer until foamy. Add remaining ¼ cup granulated sugar, 1 Tbsp. at a time, beating until stiff peaks form and sugar dissolves (2 to 4 minutes). Spread meringue over ramekins. Place ramekins on a baking sheet.

5. Bake at 325° for 15 to 20 minutes or until meringue is golden. Let cool on a wire rack 30 minutes.

Tangerine Chess Pie

party perfect

MAKES: 6 to 8 servings
HANDS-ON TIME: 15 min.
TOTAL TIME: 2 hr., 18 min.
(Pictured on page 168)

- 1 (14.1-oz.) package refrigerated piecrusts
- 1½ cups sugar
- 1 Tbsp. all-purpose flour
- 1 Tbsp. plain yellow cornmeal
- ¼ tsp. salt
- ¼ cup butter, melted
- 2 tsp. tangerine or orange zest
- ⅓ cup fresh tangerine or orange juice
- 1 Tbsp. lemon juice
- 4 large eggs, lightly beaten
  Garnishes: sweetened whipped cream, tangerine slices

1. Preheat oven to 450°. Unroll piecrusts; stack on a lightly floured surface. Roll into a 12-inch circle. Fit piecrust into a 9-inch pie plate; fold edges under, and crimp. Prick bottom and sides of crust with a fork. Bake 8 minutes; cool on a wire rack 15 minutes. Reduce oven temperature to 350°.
2. Whisk together sugar and next 8 ingredients until blended. Pour into prepared piecrust.
3. Bake at 350° for 40 to 45 minutes or until center is set, shielding edges with foil after 20 minutes to prevent excessive browning. Cool 1 hour.

Apple-Cherry Cobbler with Pinwheel Biscuits

party perfect

MAKES: 8 to 10 servings
HANDS-ON TIME: 1 hr.
TOTAL TIME: 1 hr., 15 min.
(Pictured on page 168)

APPLE-CHERRY FILLING

- 8 large Braeburn apples, peeled and cut into ½-inch-thick wedges (about 4½ lb.)
- 2 cups granulated sugar
- ¼ cup all-purpose flour
- ¼ cup butter
- 1 (12-oz.) package frozen cherries, thawed and well drained
- 1 tsp. lemon zest
- ⅓ cup fresh lemon juice
- 1 tsp. ground cinnamon

PINWHEEL BISCUITS

- 2¼ cups all-purpose flour
- ¼ cup granulated sugar
- 2¼ tsp. baking powder
- ¾ tsp. salt
- ¾ cup cold butter, cut into pieces
- ⅔ cup milk
- ⅔ cup firmly packed light brown sugar
- 2 Tbsp. butter, melted
- ¼ cup finely chopped roasted unsalted almonds

SERVE WITH

Sweetened whipped cream (optional)

1. Prepare Filling: Preheat oven to 425°. Toss together first 3 ingredients. Melt ¼ cup butter in a large skillet over medium-high heat; add apple mixture. Cook, stirring often, 20 to 25 minutes or until apples are tender and syrup thickens. Remove from heat; stir in cherries and next 3 ingredients. Spoon apple mixture into a lightly greased 3-qt. baking dish. Bake apple mixture 12 minutes, placing a baking sheet on oven rack directly below baking dish to catch any drips.
2. Prepare Biscuits: Stir together 2¼ cups flour and next 3 ingredients in a large bowl. Cut cold butter pieces into flour mixture with a pastry blender or fork until crumbly; stir in milk. Turn dough out onto a lightly floured surface; knead 4 to 5 times. Roll dough into a 12-inch square. Combine brown sugar and 2 Tbsp. melted butter; sprinkle over dough, patting gently. Sprinkle with almonds. Roll up, jelly-roll fashion; pinch seams and ends to seal. Cut roll into 12 (1-inch) slices. Place slices in a single layer on top of apple mixture.
3. Bake at 425° for 15 to 17 minutes or until biscuits are golden. Serve with whipped cream, if desired.

Hummingbird Bundt Cake

make-ahead • party perfect

MAKES: 10 to 12 servings
HANDS-ON TIME: 20 min.
TOTAL TIME: 3 hr., 45 min.
(Pictured on page 169)

CAKE BATTER

- 1½ cups chopped pecans
- 3 cups all-purpose flour
- 2 cups sugar
- 1 tsp. baking soda
- 1 tsp. ground cinnamon
- ½ tsp. salt
- 3 large eggs, lightly beaten
- 1¾ cups mashed ripe bananas (about 4 large)
- 1 (8-oz.) can crushed pineapple (do not drain)
- ¾ cup canola oil
- 1½ tsp. vanilla extract

GLAZE

- 4 oz. cream cheese, cubed and softened
- 2 cups sifted powdered sugar
- 1 tsp. vanilla extract
- 1 to 2 Tbsp. milk

1. Prepare Cake Batter: Preheat oven to 350°. Bake pecans in a single layer in a shallow pan 8 to 10 minutes or until toasted and fragrant, stirring halfway through.

2. Stir together flour and next 4 ingredients in a large bowl; stir in eggs and next 4 ingredients, stirring just until dry ingredients are moistened. Sprinkle 1 cup toasted pecans into a greased and floured 14-cup Bundt pan. Spoon batter over pecans.

3. Bake at 350° for 1 hour to 1 hour and 10 minutes or until a long wooden pick inserted in center comes out clean. Cool cake in pan on a wire rack 15 minutes; remove from pan to wire rack, and cool completely (about 2 hours).

4. Prepare Glaze: Process cream cheese, powdered sugar, vanilla, and 1 Tbsp. milk in a food processor until well blended. Add remaining 1 Tbsp. milk, 1 tsp. at a time, processing until smooth. Immediately pour glaze over cooled cake, and sprinkle with remaining ½ cup toasted pecans.

Swoon Pies

make-ahead • party perfect

MAKES: 1 dozen
HANDS-ON TIME: 45 min.
TOTAL TIME: 2 hr., 40 min., including filling
(Pictured on page 7)

- 1 cup all-purpose flour
- ½ tsp. baking powder
- ½ tsp. baking soda
- ½ tsp. salt
- 1 cup graham cracker crumbs
- ½ cup butter, softened
- ½ cup granulated sugar
- ½ cup firmly packed light brown sugar
- 1 large egg
- 1 tsp. vanilla extract
- 1 (8-oz.) container sour cream
  Parchment paper
  Marshmallow Filling
- 1 (12-oz.) package semisweet chocolate morsels
- 2 tsp. shortening
  Toppings: chopped roasted salted pecans, chopped crystallized ginger, sea salt

1. Preheat oven to 350°. Sift together flour and next 3 ingredients in a medium bowl; stir in graham cracker crumbs.

2. Beat butter and next 2 ingredients at medium speed with a heavy-duty electric stand mixer until fluffy. Add egg and vanilla, beating until blended.

3. Add flour mixture to butter mixture alternately with sour cream, beginning and ending with flour mixture. Beat at low speed until blended after each addition, stopping to scrape bowl as needed.

4. Drop batter by rounded tablespoonfuls 2 inches apart onto 2 parchment paper-lined baking sheets. Bake, in batches, at 350° for 13 to 15 minutes or until set and bottoms are golden brown. Remove cookies (on parchment paper) to wire racks, and cool completely (about 30 minutes).

5. Turn 12 cookies over, bottom sides up. Spread each with 1 heaping tablespoonful Marshmallow Filling. Top with remaining 12 cookies, bottom sides down, and press gently to spread filling to edges. Freeze on a parchment paper-lined baking sheet 30 minutes or until filling is set.

6. Pour water to depth of 1 inch in a medium saucepan over medium heat; bring to a boil. Reduce heat, and simmer; place chocolate and shortening in a medium-size heatproof bowl over simmering water. Cook, stirring occasionally, 5 to 6 minutes or until melted. Remove from heat, and let cool 10 minutes.

7. Meanwhile, remove cookies from freezer, and let stand 10 minutes.

8. Dip half of each cookie sandwich into melted chocolate mixture. Place on parchment paper-lined baking sheet. Sprinkle with desired toppings, and freeze l0 minutes or until chocolate is set. **NOTE:** Cookie sandwiches may be covered with plastic wrap and stored in refrigerator up to 24 hours.

TRY THIS TWIST!

Full Swoon Pies: Increase semisweet chocolate morsels to l (16-oz.) package and shortening to 3 tsp. Prepare recipe as directed, dipping cookie sandwiches completely in chocolate mixture. (Use a fork to easily remove sandwiches from chocolate.)

Marshmallow Filling

MAKES: about 1½ cups
HANDS-ON TIME: 5 min.
TOTAL TIME: 5 min.

- ½ **cup butter, softened**
- l **cup sifted powdered sugar**
- l **cup marshmallow crème**
- ½ **tsp. vanilla extract**

1. Beat butter at medium speed with an electric mixer until creamy; gradually add sugar, beating well. Add remaining ingredients, beating until well blended.

SOUTHERN SAMPLER
Artisanal Chocolate Makers

These cocoa connoisseurs are raising the bar with from-scratch chocolate roasted south of the Mason Dixon.

{1}
Askinosie Chocolate, **SPRINGFIELD, MO** Shawn Askinosie makes 42,000 pounds of chocolate annually sourced from farmers he personally meets on four continents. **TRY:** The White Chocolate Nibble Bar cocoa butter laced with nibs ($10.50). *askinosie.com*

{2}
French Broad Chocolates, **ASHEVILLE, NC** Truffle pros Jael and Dan Rattigan are now making from-scratch chocolate, some with a newly rediscovered Peruvian heirloom bean. **TRY:** 65% cacao La Red Cooperative ($7). *frenchbroadchocolates.com*

{3}
Escazú Artisan Chocolates, **RALEIGH, NC** Former chef Hallot Parson is committed to sourcing his beans only from Latin America, where cacao originated. **TRY:** The Roasted Cocoa Nibs 65% dark chocolate bar ($5), with a pleasant crunch from nibs (bits of roasted beans). *escazuchocolates.com*

{4}
Potomac Chocolate, **WOODBRIDGE, VA** Working from his home workshop, Ben Rasmussen produces about 500 artisan chocolate bars a week. **TRY:** The Upala 70% Chocolate Bar with flavor notes of raspberry and caramel ($7). *potomacchocolate.com*

{5}
Cacao Atlanta Chocolate Company, ATLANTA, GA Kristen Hard ditched law school to open Cacao in 2004, and four years later became the female pioneer of bean-to-bar chocolate. **TRY:** The beautifully packaged 'Love Bar,' Straight Up ($8), with 75% dark chocolate sourced from the Dominican Republic. *cacaoatlanta.com*

{6}
Olive & Sinclair Chocolate Company, NASHVILLE, TN Chef Scott Witherow uses brown sugar, molasses, and a stone-grinding process much like the one used to make grits. **TRY:** The creamy-tart Buttermilk White Chocolate ($6). *oliveandsinclair.com*

Pimiento Cheese

{The Pâté of the South}

It's the best thing to happen to the sandwich since, well, sliced bread. Here's everything you need to know about the South's most iconic spread.

Pick a Spread

Spelled pimiento or pimento (both correct), this cheese concoction is as essential to our Southern identity as sweet tea. Dress it up or down, but be sure to use freshly shredded cheese. Trust us. That preshredded stuff just doesn't cut it.

CREAMY

{1}

LOUIS OSTEEN'S PIMIENTO CHEESE: Beat 6 cups freshly grated sharp Cheddar cheese (1½ lb.); ½ (8-oz.) package cream cheese, softened; ¾ cup mayonnaise; 1 Tbsp. grated yellow onion; and 1 tsp. ground red pepper with a heavy-duty electric stand mixer at medium speed 1 to 2 minutes or until blended but not smooth. Add 1 (7-oz.) jar whole peeled pimiento, drained and cut into fourths; beat 1 to 2 minutes or until pimiento is shredded and mixture is blended and somewhat smooth. Garnish with freshly ground pepper, if desired. Makes: about 4 cups.

HERBY

{2}

FOOD SHARK'S PIMIENTO CHEESE: Stir together 1 (12-oz.) jar roasted red bell peppers, drained and finely chopped; 1 cup mayonnaise; ¼ cup finely chopped red onion; ¼ cup chopped fresh parsley; 1 Tbsp. chopped fresh dill; 2 Tbsp. Dijon mustard; 2 Tbsp. chopped jarred pepperoncini salad peppers; 1 Tbsp. liquid from pepperoncini salad peppers; and 1 tsp. grated fresh horseradish. Gently stir in 4 cups (16 oz.) shredded sharp Cheddar cheese and 3 cups (12 oz.) shredded Havarti cheese until well blended. Cover and chill until ready to serve. Garnish with pepperoncini salad peppers and fresh dill, if desired. Makes: 6 cups.

Hot Tubs
Tired of shredding? Try one of our favorite mail-order varieties

Callie's Pimento Cheese has a fantastic full-Cheddar flavor (two 15-oz. containers for $20 plus shipping). *calliesbiscuits.com*

Palmetto Cheese is great for dipping (one 12-oz. container for $5.50 plus shipping; other varieties available). *palmettocheese.com*

Blackberry Farm Aged Cheddar Pimento Cheese is rich and smoky (one 8-oz. container for $10 plus shipping). *blackberryfarm.com*

Belle Chevre Pimento Cheese Spread is made with goat cheese (one 6-oz. container for $7 plus shipping). *bellechevre.com*

Cast Iron Gourmet Spicy Pimento Cheese is made with bacon grease (one 8-oz. jar for $13 plus shipping). *castirongourmetla.com*

SWEET & SPICY

{3}

MISS MATTIE'S SOUTHERN PIMIENTO CHEESE: Bake ½ cup chopped pecans at 350° in a shallow pan 8 to 10 minutes or until toasted and fragrant, stirring halfway through. Cool 20 minutes. Stir together 1 cup mayonnaise; 1 (7-oz.) jar diced pimiento, drained; ½ cup chopped jarred sweet-hot pickled jalapeño pepper slices; 1 Tbsp. liquid from sweet-hot pickled jalapeño pepper slices; and toasted pecans. Stir in 4 cups freshly grated mild Cheddar cheese (1 lb.) until well blended. Garnish with sweet-hot pickled jalapeño pepper slices and toasted chopped pecans, if desired. **MAKES:** about 5 cups. **NOTE:** We tested with The Original Texas Sweet & Hot Jalapeños.

ZESTY

{4}

MARY ANN'S PIMIENTO CHEESE: Stir together ½ cup mayonnaise; 3 (4-oz.) jars diced pimiento, drained; ¼ cup sliced green onions; 1 Tbsp. dry mustard; 1½ Tbsp. Worcestershire sauce; 1½ tsp. hot sauce; ¾ tsp. celery seeds; ¾ tsp. apple cider vinegar; ¼ tsp. salt; and ¼ tsp. pepper. Stir in 5 cups freshly grated white Cheddar cheese (1¼ lb.) until well blended. Cover and chill 8 to 24 hours. Garnish with sliced green onions, if desired. Makes: about 5 cups.

TIPSY

{5}

HOMINY GRILL'S PIMIENTO CHEESE: Stir together ¾ cup mayonnaise; ½ cup jarred sliced pimiento, rinsed and finely chopped; 1½ Tbsp. bourbon; 1 tsp. ancho chile powder; ¼ tsp. ground cumin; and ¼ tsp. freshly ground pepper. Stir in 6 cups freshly grated sharp Cheddar cheese (1½ lb.) and ¾ cup freshly grated Parmesan cheese until well blended. Garnish with fresh cilantro, if desired. Makes: about 4 cups.

"Some Like It Hot" Grilled Pimiento Cheese Sandwiches

THE MOTHER OF ALL PIMIENTO CHEESE SANDWICHES

"Some Like It Hot" Grilled Pimiento Cheese Sandwiches

quick prep • party perfect

MAKES: 8 servings
HANDS-ON TIME: 20 min.
TOTAL TIME: 1 hr., including pimiento cheese
(Also pictured on page 5)

Miss Mattie's Southern Pimiento Cheese (recipe at left)
⅓ **cup butter, softened**
16 **sourdough bread slices**
16 **thick applewood-smoked bacon slices, cooked**
Strawberry preserves

1. Prepare Miss Mattie's Southern Pimiento Cheese as directed.
2. Butter 1 side of each bread slice. Place 8 bread slices, buttered sides down, on a hot griddle or in a large skillet over medium heat.
3. Spread ½ cup pimiento cheese over each bread slice on griddle. Top each with 2 cooked bacon slices.
4. Place remaining 8 bread slices, buttered sides up, on bacon. Turn sandwiches, and cook 5 to 7 minutes or until golden brown. (Pimiento cheese should be slightly melted.) Serve with strawberry preserves.

How Do YOU Take Your Pimiento Cheese?

Here are some delicious ideas showing up in kitchens across the South

READERS WEIGH IN

Stuff it into a large Spanish olive and place in a martini. **TAMAR F.**

Spoon onto a grilled hot dog in a bun. Top with chili and onions. Serve with plenty of cold beer. **BRENT G.**

Stir into hot cooked pasta until melted and top with crumbled, cooked bacon for a creamy mac and cheese. **NATALIE M.**

Use in place of Cheddar cheese in squash casserole, omitting any mayonnaise in the recipe. **SUSANNE D.**

Spread on white bread and grill in a waffle iron. Serve with strawberry jam. **PATTY C.**

Use as a quesadilla filling with pickled sliced jalapeño peppers on whole grain tortillas. **CYNTHIA B.**

Dollop on saltine crackers and top with a dash of Asian sriracha hot chili sauce and sweet-hot pickle chips. **TAD C.**

Stuff into a seeded jalapeño pepper, wrap with bacon, and smoke slowly on a grill over 300° to 350° (medium) heat. **TIGER R.**

Spoon onto hot fried green tomatoes. **LEE C.**

Spoon into celery pieces; sprinkle with chopped Spanish olives and pecans. **MELODY L.**

My favorite way to enjoy it is on a gingersnap or graham cracker— slightly sweet and savory, too. **DOROTHY B.**

Spread on cornbread and broil until melted. **HEATHER S.**

Smother sweet potato fries with chili, and then top with pimiento cheese. **INSPIRED BY BOTTLETREE CAFE AND BAR IN BIRMINGHAM**

Serve with sliced, tart Granny Smith apples. **DORI L.**

MORE WAYS TO GET YOUR FILL

Just when you thought pimiento cheese was a mere sandwich spread, think again!

Pimiento Cheese Cookies
make-ahead • party perfect

MAKES: 2 dozen
HANDS-ON TIME: 30 min.
TOTAL TIME: 3 hr., 35 min.

We used Palmetto Cheese (see page 54), a South Carolina favorite, in these treats.

- 1 cup all-purpose flour
- 1 cup refrigerated pimiento cheese
- ½ cup pecans, finely chopped
- ¼ cup butter, softened
  Parchment paper
- 4 Tbsp. strawberry preserves

1. Beat together flour and pimiento cheese at medium speed with a heavy-duty electric stand mixer 1 minute. Add pecans and butter; beat until blended. Wrap dough in plastic wrap; chill 2 hours.
2. Preheat oven to 400°. Place dough on a well-floured surface, and roll to ⅛-inch thickness. Cut into 48 rounds with a 2-inch round cutter, rerolling scraps once. Arrange half of rounds 2 inches apart on parchment paper-lined baking sheets; spoon ½ tsp. strawberry preserves onto center of each round, and top with remaining rounds, pressing edges to seal.
3. Bake at 400° for 12 to 15 minutes or until golden brown. Cool on baking sheets 10 minutes; transfer to wire racks, and cool completely (about 30 minutes).

RECIPE FROM PAWLEYS ISLAND SPECIALTY FOODS, PALMETTO CHEESE
PAWLEYS ISLAND, SOUTH CAROLINA

Pimiento Cheese Rolls

make-ahead • party perfect

MAKES: 1 dozen
HANDS-ON TIME: 15 min.
TOTAL TIME: 1 hr., 15 min.

- 1 **(25-oz.) package frozen Southern-style biscuits All-purpose flour**
- 2 **cups pimiento cheese**

1. Arrange biscuits, with sides touching, in 3 rows of 4 biscuits on a lightly floured surface. Let stand 30 to 45 minutes or until biscuits are thawed but cool to the touch.
2. Preheat oven to 375°. Sprinkle biscuits lightly with flour. Press edges together, and pat to form a 12- x 10-inch rectangle of dough; spread dough with pimiento cheese.
3. Roll up, starting at one long end; cut into 12 (1-inch-thick) slices. Place 1 slice into each muffin cup of a lightly greased 12-cup muffin pan.
4. Bake at 375° for 20 to 25 minutes or until golden. Let cool in pan on a wire rack 5 minutes; remove from pan, and serve immediately.
NOTE: We tested with Pillsbury Grands! Southern Style Biscuits.

Smoky Pimiento Cheese Deviled Eggs

quick prep • make-ahead • party perfect

MAKES: 2 dozen
HANDS-ON TIME: 20 min.
TOTAL TIME: 35 min.

This recipe comes from chef Jason Hill at Wisteria Restaurant in Atlanta.

- 12 **large eggs**
- ¼ **cup mayonnaise**
- ¾ **cup freshly grated smoked or sharp Cheddar cheese**
- ¼ **cup finely chopped jarred roasted red bell pepper**
- 1 **Tbsp. Dijon mustard Pinch of ground red pepper Toppings: sliced green onions, diced country ham, sliced pickled okra, spiced pecans**

1. Place eggs in a large stainless steel saucepan (not nonstick). Add water to depth of 3 inches. Bring to a rolling boil; cook 1 minute. Cover, remove from heat, and let stand 10 minutes. Drain.
2. Place eggs under cold running water until cool enough to handle. Peel under cold running water. Cut eggs in half lengthwise; remove yolks. Reserve 6 yolks for another use.
3. Mash remaining 6 yolks with mayonnaise using a fork. Stir in cheese and next 3 ingredients. Season with salt and pepper to taste. Spoon into egg whites. Serve with desired toppings.

On a Menu Near You

PIMENTO CHEESE PIZZA
Hutch & Harris Pub,
Winston-Salem, NC

BROWN SUGAR HAM & PIMENTO CHEESE PANINI
Wellington's at The Carnegie Hotel,
Johnson City, TN

CARPETBAGGER: FILET MIGNON WITH PIMENTO CHEESE
Blue Marlin, Columbia, SC

PIMENTO MAC-AND-CHEESE WITH JALAPEÑOS
The Bistro at the Bijou,
Knoxville, TN

4 Ways with Chicken Cutlets

Need to get dinner on the table in about a half hour? Consider fast-cooking chicken cutlets your saving grace.

Pan-Grilled Chicken with Fresh Plum Salsa

TIPS FROM OUR TEST KITCHEN

- Buy chicken cutlets on sale and keep them in the freezer. To thaw quickly, place chicken under warm running water.

- Make your own cutlets by cutting a boneless skinless chicken breast lengthwise into two thin pieces.

- Mix up your main-dish options by substituting turkey or pork cutlets in any of these recipes.

SWEET & SPICY

{1}

Pan-Grilled Chicken with Fresh Plum Salsa

quick prep • party perfect

MAKES: 4 servings
TOTAL TIME: 26 min.

- 1 cup chopped ripe plums (about 2 plums)
- 1 small jalapeño pepper, seeded and diced
- 2 Tbsp. chopped fresh basil
- 2 Tbsp. chopped red onion
- 2 tsp. fresh lime juice
- ¾ tsp. salt, divided
- 2 Tbsp. brown sugar
- ½ tsp. ground cumin
- 4 (4-oz.) chicken breast cutlets
- 2 tsp. olive oil

1. Stir together plums, next 4 ingredients, and ¼ tsp. salt in a medium bowl.
2. Stir together brown sugar, cumin, and remaining ½ tsp. salt in a small bowl. Rub chicken with brown sugar mixture.
3. Cook chicken in hot oil in a grill pan or nonstick skillet over medium heat 3 minutes on each side or until done. Serve with plum mixture.

NUTTY & BUTTERY

{2}

Pecan-Crusted Chicken and Tortellini with Herbed Butter Sauce

quick prep • party perfect

MAKES: 4 servings
TOTAL TIME: 30 min.

- 2 (9-oz.) packages refrigerated cheese-filled tortellini
- 4 (4-oz.) chicken breast cutlets
- ½ tsp. salt
- ¼ tsp. freshly ground pepper
- ¾ cup finely chopped pecans
- 1 large egg, lightly beaten
- 3 Tbsp. olive oil
- ½ cup butter
- 3 garlic cloves, thinly sliced
- 3 Tbsp. chopped fresh basil
- 3 Tbsp. chopped fresh parsley
- ¼ cup (1 oz.) shredded Parmesan cheese

1. Prepare tortellini according to package directions.
2. Meanwhile, sprinkle chicken with salt and pepper. Place pecans in a shallow bowl. Place egg in a second bowl. Dip chicken in egg mixture, allowing excess to drip off. Dredge chicken in pecans, pressing firmly to adhere.
3. Cook chicken in hot oil in a large nonstick skillet over medium-high heat 2 minutes on each side or until done. Remove from skillet; wipe skillet clean.
4. Melt butter in skillet over medium heat. Add garlic, and sauté 5 to 7 minutes or until garlic is caramel-colored and butter begins to turn golden brown. Immediately remove from heat, and stir in basil, parsley, and hot cooked tortellini. Sprinkle with cheese. Serve immediately with chicken.

SPICY & CRUNCHY

{3}

Hot Sauce Fried Chicken with Pickled Okra Slaw

quick prep • party perfect

MAKES: 6 servings
TOTAL TIME: 35 min.

- 6 (4-oz.) chicken breast cutlets
- 1½ tsp. salt, divided
- ¾ tsp. pepper, divided
- 1¼ cups all-purpose flour
- 30 saltine crackers, crushed
- ½ tsp. baking powder
- 2 large eggs, lightly beaten
- ⅓ cup hot sauce
  Peanut oil
- ½ cup sour cream
- ½ tsp. sugar
- 1 (16-oz.) package shredded coleslaw mix
- ½ cup sliced pickled okra
- 1 (4-oz.) jar diced pimiento, drained

1. Sprinkle chicken with ½ tsp. salt and ½ tsp. pepper. Place ½ cup flour in a shallow dish. Stir together cracker crumbs, baking powder, and remaining ¾ cup flour in a second shallow dish. Whisk together eggs and hot sauce in a third shallow dish. Dredge chicken in flour, dip in egg mixture, and dredge in cracker mixture, pressing to adhere.
2. Pour oil to depth of 1 inch into a 10-inch cast-iron skillet; heat to 360°. Fry half of chicken 3 to 4 minutes. Turn and fry 2 to 3 minutes or until golden brown and done. Repeat procedure with remaining half of chicken.
3. Stir together sour cream, sugar, and remaining 1 tsp. salt and ¼ tsp. pepper. Toss together coleslaw mix, pickled okra, diced pimiento, and sour cream mixture. Serve slaw and chicken with additional hot sauce.

SWEET & TANGY

{4}

Honey-Lime Chicken with Coconut-Black Bean Rice

quick prep • party perfect

MAKES: 6 servings
TOTAL TIME: 35 min.

- 1 (13.5-oz.) can coconut milk
- 1½ tsp. salt, divided
- 1 cup uncooked long-grain rice
- 6 (4-oz.) chicken breast cutlets
- ¼ tsp. freshly ground pepper
- ¾ cup finely crushed tortilla chips
- ¼ cup honey
- 1 tsp. lime zest
- ⅓ cup fresh lime juice
- ¼ cup extra virgin olive oil
- 1 (15.5-oz.) can seasoned black beans, drained and rinsed
- ½ cup chopped red bell pepper
- ⅓ cup sliced green onions
- ¼ cup chopped fresh cilantro

1. Bring coconut milk and 1 tsp. salt to a boil over medium-high heat; stir in rice. Cover, reduce heat to low, and simmer 20 minutes or until rice is tender.
2. Meanwhile, sprinkle chicken with pepper and remaining ½ tsp. salt. Place crushed tortilla chips in a shallow bowl. Whisk together honey and next 2 ingredients in a second shallow bowl. Reserve 2 Tbsp. honey mixture. Dip chicken in remaining honey mixture, allowing excess to drip off. Dredge in crushed chips.
3. Cook half of chicken in 2 Tbsp. hot oil in a large nonstick skillet over medium-high heat 2 minutes on each side or until done. Repeat procedure with remaining chicken and oil. Spoon reserved honey mixture over chicken.
4. Stir black beans and next 2 ingredients into rice; spoon onto serving plates. Top with chicken and cilantro.

Spinach Salads

Give that hot bacon dressing a breather and spiff up your greens with fruits, nuts, and creamy cheeses.

Blueberry Fields Salad

quick prep • good for you • party perfect

MAKES: 8 servings
HANDS-ON TIME: 20 min.
TOTAL TIME: 20 min.
(Pictured on page 167)

- 1 **cup chopped walnuts**
- ½ **cup balsamic vinegar**
- ⅓ **cup blueberry preserves**
- ⅓ **cup olive oil**
- 2 **(5.5-oz.) packages spring greens and baby spinach mix**
- 2 **cups fresh blueberries**
- 1 **small red onion, halved and sliced**
- 1 **cup crumbled blue cheese**

1. Heat walnuts in a small skillet over medium-high heat, stirring constantly, 5 minutes or until toasted and fragrant.
2. Whisk together balsamic vinegar, next 2 ingredients, and salt and freshly ground pepper to taste in a small bowl. Combine walnuts, spinach mix, and next 3 ingredients in a large bowl. Drizzle with desired amount of vinaigrette, and toss to combine. Serve immediately with remaining vinaigrette.

MARY HERSHISER
DAPHNE, ALABAMA

Spinach-Grape Chopped Salad

quick prep • good for you • party perfect

MAKES: 4 servings
HANDS-ON TIME: 15 min.
TOTAL TIME: 15 min.

- ¼ **cup chopped walnuts**
- 1 **(6-oz.) package fresh baby spinach**
- 1 **cup seedless red grapes**
- ¼ **cup crumbled reduced-fat feta cheese**
- ¼ **cup bottled light raspberry-walnut vinaigrette**

1. Heat chopped walnuts in a small skillet over medium-high heat, stirring constantly, 5 minutes or until toasted and fragrant.
2. Coarsely chop spinach and grapes; toss with feta cheese and vinaigrette. Sprinkle with walnuts. Serve immediately.

Waldorf Spinach Salad

quick prep • good for you • party perfect

MAKES: 6 servings
HANDS-ON TIME: 25 min.
TOTAL TIME: 25 min.

- ¼ **cup honey**
- 3 **Tbsp. vegetable oil**
- 2 **Tbsp. cider vinegar**
- ½ **tsp. dry mustard**
- ¼ **tsp. ground cinnamon**
- 1 **garlic clove, pressed**
- ⅛ **tsp. salt**
- 1 **(9-oz.) package fresh spinach, torn**
- 2 **large Gala apples, thinly sliced**
- 4 **oz. extra-sharp white Cheddar cheese, shaved**
- 1 **cup thinly sliced celery**
- 1 **cup honey-roasted cashews**
- ½ **cup golden raisins**

1. Whisk together first 7 ingredients in a large serving bowl until well blended. Add spinach and remaining ingredients, tossing gently to coat. Serve immediately.

Grilled Shrimp and Spinach Salad

good for you • party perfect

MAKES: 8 servings
HANDS-ON TIME: 35 min.
TOTAL TIME: 1 hr., 10 min., including vinaigrette
(Pictured on page 166)

- 8 **(12-inch) wooden skewers**
- 2 **lb. peeled, large raw shrimp (31/40 count)**
   Basil Vinaigrette, divided
- 2 **(6-oz.) packages fresh baby spinach**
- 2 **mangoes, peeled and sliced**
- 1 **small red onion, halved and sliced**
- 1 **(4-oz.) package goat cheese, crumbled**
- 1 **cup fresh raspberries**

1. Soak wooden skewers in water to cover 30 minutes.
2. Meanwhile, preheat grill to 350° to 400° (medium-high) heat. Devein shrimp, if desired. Combine shrimp and ¾ cup Basil Vinaigrette in a large zip-top plastic freezer bag; seal and chill 15 minutes, turning occasionally.
3. Remove shrimp from marinade, discarding marinade. Thread shrimp onto skewers.
4. Grill shrimp, covered with grill lid, 2 minutes on each side or just until shrimp turn pink. Remove shrimp from skewers.
5. Toss spinach, mangoes, and onion with ¼ cup Basil Vinaigrette in a large bowl; arrange on a serving platter. Top with grilled shrimp. Sprinkle with crumbled goat cheese and raspberries. Serve with remaining Basil Vinaigrette.

Basil Vinaigrette

MAKES: 1½ cups
HANDS-ON TIME: 5 min.
TOTAL TIME: 5 min.

1. Whisk together ½ cup chopped fresh basil; ½ cup raspberry vinegar; 2 garlic cloves, minced; 1 Tbsp. brown sugar; 2 tsp. Dijon mustard; and ½ tsp. each salt and dried crushed red pepper until blended. Add 1 cup olive oil in a slow, steady stream, whisking constantly until smooth.

TRY THIS TWIST!
Tropical Spinach Salad with Grilled Chicken: Omit skewers. Substitute 2 lb. skinned and boned chicken breasts for shrimp. Prepare recipe as directed, increasing grill time to 4 to 6 minutes on each side or until done. Let chicken stand 10 minutes; slice and serve as directed. Hands-on time: 38 min.; Total time: 1 hr., 8 min., including vinaigrette.

Hot Crawfish Dip

SOUTHERN HOSPITALITY

Crawfish Dip

In Louisiana, February means two things: Mardi Gras and crawfish. Two-thirds of all mudbugs are harvested this month. Most locals start with a boil (corn, sausage, and 'taters optional), but what's left goes into étouffée, crawfish pie, and luscious appetizer dips. This one works as well for a Super Bowl party as a formal Mardi Gras ball. You'll need 6 to 7 pounds of cooked whole crawfish for 1 pound of hard-earned meat. Or sub in frozen, peeled crawfish tails.

Hot Crawfish Dip

MAKES: 8 to 10 servings
HANDS-ON TIME: 30 min.
TOTAL TIME: 30 min.

- ½ cup butter
- 1 bunch green onions, sliced (about 1 cup)
- 1 small green bell pepper, diced
- 1 (1-lb.) package frozen cooked, peeled crawfish tails, thawed and undrained
- 2 garlic cloves, minced
- 1 (4-oz.) jar diced pimiento, drained
- 2 tsp. Creole seasoning
- 1 (8-oz.) package cream cheese, softened
- French bread baguette slices
- Garnishes: sliced green onion, chopped flat-leaf parsley

1. Melt butter in a Dutch oven over medium heat; add green onions and bell pepper. Cook, stirring occasionally, 8 minutes or until bell pepper is tender. Stir in crawfish and next 3 ingredients; cook, stirring occasionally, 10 minutes. Reduce heat to low. Stir in cream cheese until mixture is smooth and bubbly. Serve with toasted French bread slices.

TEST KITCHEN TIP

Crusty French bread pairs perfectly with Crawfish Dip.

Our Easiest, Prettiest Brunch

Hosting the garden club? Throwing a shower? Look to this colorful menu, inspired by the first signs of spring.

Spring Brunch

SERVES 8

Peach-Basil Iced Tea

Sunshine Citrus Platter

Herbed Dip with Baby Vegetables

Spring Greens with Strawberries

Chutney Chicken Salad

Creamy Egg Strata

Brown Sugar Bacon

Chilled Carrot Soup

Lemon-Rosemary Coffee Cake

Peach-Basil Iced Tea

quick prep • make-ahead • party perfect

MAKES: about 3 qt.
HANDS-ON TIME: 10 min.
TOTAL TIME: 20 min.

2 **family-size tea bags**
1 **cup loosely packed fresh basil leaves**
⅔ **cup sugar**
3 **cups peach nectar**
   Crushed ice
   Garnish: fresh basil sprigs

1. Bring 8 cups water to a boil in a large saucepan. Pour boiling water over tea bags and basil in a pitcher; cover and steep 6 minutes.
2. Remove and discard tea bags and basil. Add sugar, stirring until dissolved; stir in peach nectar. Serve over crushed ice.

Herbed Dip with Baby Vegetables

quick prep • good for you • party perfect

MAKES: 8 to 10 appetizer servings
HANDS-ON TIME: 15 min.
TOTAL TIME: 4 hr., 15 min.

- 1   cup mayonnaise
- ½   cup sour cream
- 2   Tbsp. chopped fresh parsley
- 1   Tbsp. finely chopped sweet onion
- 1   Tbsp. chopped fresh dill
- 1   tsp. Beau Monde seasoning
- 1   tsp. hot sauce
- ½   tsp. salt
- 1   lb. thin fresh asparagus
- ½   lb. haricots verts (tiny green beans), trimmed

1. Stir together first 8 ingredients in a small bowl until well blended. Cover and chill 4 to 24 hours.

2. Meanwhile, snap off and discard tough ends of asparagus. Cut asparagus into 6-inch pieces, reserving any remaining end portions for another use. Cook asparagus in boiling water to cover in a large saucepan 1 to 2 minutes or until crisp-tender; drain. Plunge into ice water to stop the cooking process; drain. Repeat procedure with haricots verts. Place vegetables in zip-top plastic bags; seal and chill until ready to serve. Serve mayonnaise mixture with chilled vegetables.

Spring Greens with Strawberries

quick prep • good for you
make-ahead • party perfect·

MAKES: 8 servings
HANDS-ON TIME: 25 min.
TOTAL TIME: 25 min.

This dish is a wonderful accompaniment to Chutney Chicken Salad (page 64) served in dainty pastry shells.

- ½   cup olive oil
- ¼   cup red wine vinegar
- 3   Tbsp. honey
- 1   small shallot, finely chopped
- 1   tsp. Dijon mustard
- ½   tsp. salt
- ¼   tsp. freshly ground pepper
- 1   (5-oz.) package arugula
- 1   (4-oz.) package watercress
- 1   pt. fresh strawberries, sliced
- ¼   cup chopped fresh dill
- 1   avocado, cut into 1-inch pieces

1. Whisk together first 7 ingredients in a small bowl until blended. Cover and chill until ready to serve.

2. Toss together arugula and next 3 ingredients in a large bowl. Top with avocado, and drizzle with half of vinaigrette just before serving; toss. Serve with remaining vinaigrette.

Sunshine Citrus Platter

quick prep • good for you • party perfect

MAKES: 8 servings
HANDS-ON TIME: 20 min.
TOTAL TIME: 1 hr., 20 min.
(Pictured on page 164)

- 4   navel oranges
- 2   Ruby Red or Rio Star grapefruit
- 2   Tbsp. powdered sugar
      Ground cinnamon
      Garnish: fresh mint leaves

1. Peel oranges and grapefruit; cut into ½-inch-thick rounds. Cover and chill 1 to 24 hours.

2. Arrange fruit on a large platter. Sift powdered sugar over fruit; sprinkle with cinnamon. Serve immediately.

Chutney Chicken Salad

make-ahead • party perfect

MAKES: 8 servings
HANDS-ON TIME: 40 min.
TOTAL TIME: 3 hr., 30 min.

If you love curry powder, feel free to add more. The exact size of your brioche molds may vary depending on the brand. (Also pictured on page 164)

⅓ cup slivered almonds
1 cup mayonnaise
½ cup Greek yogurt
⅓ cup mango chutney
1 Tbsp. curry powder
1 tsp. salt
¼ tsp. freshly ground pepper
5 cups diced cooked chicken
1 (8-oz.) can sliced water chestnuts, drained
4 green onions, chopped (about 1 cup)
½ (14.1-oz.) package refrigerated piecrusts
Garnish: thinly sliced green onions

1. Preheat oven to 350°. Bake almonds in a single layer in a shallow pan 5 to 7 minutes or until toasted and fragrant, stirring half-way through. Cool 20 minutes.

2. Whisk together mayonnaise and next 5 ingredients in a large bowl. Add chicken, next 2 ingredients, and toasted almonds, and toss until well blended. Cover and chill 2 to 24 hours.

3. Preheat oven to 450°. Cut piecrust into 8 (4½-inch) rounds. Press each dough round into a lightly greased 3½-inch brioche mold, pressing dough up sides. Fold dough over edge of molds, and pinch to secure. Arrange molds on a baking sheet.

4. Bake at 450° for 8 minutes or until lightly browned. Cool pastry shells in molds on a wire rack 1 minute. Loosen shells from molds using a small knife; remove shells from molds to wire racks, and cool completely (about 20 minutes).

5. Fill cooled pastry shells with chicken salad just before serving.

NOTE: Baked, unfilled pastry shells may be stored in an airtight container up to 3 days or frozen up to 6 months.

Serving Suggestion

These easy tart shells offer a pretty display for chicken salad. You can also serve it over fresh spring greens.

Creamy Egg Strata

make-ahead • party perfect

MAKES: 8 to 10 servings
HANDS-ON TIME: 35 min.
TOTAL TIME: 10 hr., 10 min.
(Pictured on page 164)

- ½ (16-oz.) French bread loaf, cubed (about 5 cups)
- 6 Tbsp. butter, divided
- 2 cups (8 oz.) shredded Swiss cheese
- ½ cup freshly grated Parmesan cheese
- ⅓ cup chopped onion
- 1 tsp. minced garlic
- 3 Tbsp. all-purpose flour
- 1½ cups chicken broth
- ¾ cup dry white wine
- ½ tsp. salt
- ½ tsp. freshly ground pepper
- ¼ tsp. ground nutmeg
- ½ cup sour cream
- 8 large eggs, lightly beaten
- Garnish: chopped fresh chives

1. Place bread cubes in a well-buttered 13- x 9-inch baking dish. Melt 3 Tbsp. butter, and drizzle over bread cubes. Sprinkle with cheeses.

2. Melt remaining 3 Tbsp. butter in a medium saucepan over medium heat; add onion and garlic. Sauté 2 to 3 minutes or until tender. Whisk in flour until smooth; cook, whisking constantly, 2 to 3 minutes or until lightly browned. Whisk in broth and next 4 ingredients until blended. Bring mixture to a boil; reduce heat to medium-low, and simmer, stirring occasionally, 15 minutes or until thickened. Remove from heat. Stir in sour cream. Add salt and pepper to taste.

3. Gradually whisk about one-fourth of hot sour cream mixture into eggs; add egg mixture to remaining sour cream mixture, whisking constantly. Pour mixture over cheese in baking dish. Cover with plastic wrap, and chill 8 to 24 hours.

4. Let strata stand at room temperature 1 hour. Preheat oven to 350°. Remove plastic wrap, and bake 30 minutes or until set. Serve immediately.

Chilled Carrot Soup and Brown Sugar Bacon

Brown Sugar Bacon

quick prep • make-ahead • party perfect

MAKES: 8 servings
HANDS-ON TIME: 10 min.
TOTAL TIME: 45 min.
(Also pictured on page 164)

- ½ cup firmly packed light brown sugar
- 1½ tsp. freshly ground pepper
- 16 thick bacon slices

1. Preheat oven to 350°. Line 2 (16- x 11-inch) jelly-roll pans with aluminum foil; place lightly greased wire racks on top of foil.

2. Stir together sugar and pepper. Arrange bacon in a single layer on wire racks; sprinkle with sugar mixture.

3. Bake at 350° for 30 to 35 minutes or until bacon is crisp and lightly browned. Cool on racks in pans 5 minutes.

Chilled Carrot Soup

make-ahead • party perfect

MAKES: 5 cups
HANDS-ON TIME: 30 min.
TOTAL TIME: 6 hr., 5 min.
(Also pictured on page 164)

- 3 cups peeled and diced baking potatoes
- 2 cups diced carrots
- 1½ cups chopped leeks
- 1 (32-oz.) container chicken broth
- 1 Tbsp. jarred chicken soup base
- 1 cup half-and-half
- ½ tsp. salt
- ¼ tsp. ground white pepper
- Garnish: finely shredded carrots

1. Combine first 5 ingredients in a Dutch oven; bring to a boil over medium-high heat. Cover, reduce heat to low, and simmer 10 minutes or until vegetables are tender. Cool 10 minutes.

2. Puree vegetable mixture, in batches, in a blender until smooth. Transfer puree to a large bowl; whisk in half-and-half, salt, and white pepper until blended. Let cool 1 hour; cover and chill 4 to 48 hours.

3. Add salt and white pepper to taste. Serve in chilled cups.

NOTE: We tested with Superior Touch Better Than Bouillon Chicken Base.

Lemon-Rosemary Coffee Cake

make-ahead • party perfect

MAKES: 8 to 10 servings
HANDS-ON TIME: 25 min.
TOTAL TIME: 2 hr., 20 min.
(Also pictured on page 165)

Parchment paper
3 large lemons
2 cups all-purpose flour
1¼ cups sugar
½ tsp. salt
½ cup very cold butter, cubed
1 tsp. baking powder
½ tsp. baking soda
¾ cup buttermilk*
1 large egg
1½ tsp. chopped fresh rosemary
1 (10-oz.) jar lemon curd
Powdered sugar
Garnishes: fresh rosemary sprigs, lemon slices

1. Preheat oven to 350°. Lightly grease bottom and sides of a 9-inch springform pan. Line bottom of pan with parchment paper.

2. Grate zest from lemons to equal 1 Tbsp. Cut lemons in half; squeeze juice from lemons into a bowl to equal 5 Tbsp. Reserve zest and 1 Tbsp. lemon juice.

3. Combine flour, sugar, and salt in bowl of a food processor; pulse 3 to 4 times or until blended. Add butter; pulse 6 to 7 times or until mixture resembles coarse crumbs. Reserve 1 cup flour mixture.

4. Transfer remaining flour mixture to bowl of a heavy-duty electric stand mixer. Add baking powder and baking soda; beat at low speed until well blended. Add buttermilk, egg, and ¼ cup lemon juice; beat at medium speed 1½ to 2 minutes or until batter is thoroughly blended, stopping to scrape bowl as needed. Stir in rosemary. Spoon half of batter into prepared pan.

5. Whisk lemon curd in a small bowl about 1 minute or until loosened and smooth; carefully spread over batter in pan. Top with remaining half of batter.

6. Stir together reserved lemon zest, 1 Tbsp. lemon juice, and 1 cup flour mixture; sprinkle lemon zest mixture over batter in pan.

7. Bake at 350° for 45 to 50 minutes or until a long wooden pick inserted in center comes out clean.

8. Let cool in pan on a wire rack 10 minutes. Gently run a sharp knife around edge of cake to loosen; remove sides of pan. Cool cake completely on wire rack (about 1 hour). Dust with powdered sugar just before serving.

*Greek yogurt may be substituted.

NOTE: A 9-inch round cake pan may be substituted for springform pan. Line bottom and sides of cake pan with aluminum foil, allowing 2 to 3 inches to extend over sides; grease foil well. Proceed with recipe as directed through Step 7. Let cool in pan on a wire rack 10 minutes. Lift cake from pan, using foil sides as handles. Carefully remove foil. Cool and dust with powdered sugar as directed.

Love It? Get It!

This turquoise charger is by Philippe Deshoulieres (Bromberg's; 205/871-3276). *(Also pictured on page 165)*

Lemon-Rosemary Coffee Cake

March

The New Ladies Lunch

Inspired by the South's most beloved department store restaurants, we developed a classic lunch-with-the-girls menu, complete with tea sandwiches, chicken salad, and—hold on to your napkin, honey—the dessert cart.

The Dainty & Delicious Menu

SERVES 6

Neiman Marcus Cheddar
Cheese Biscuits

Tomato-Basil Bisque

Tarragon Chicken Salad

Cranberry-Strawberry Salad

Mixed greens

Caramelized Onion Quiche

Crowd-Pleasing Tea Sandwiches

Assorted desserts

One of the greatest pleasures in life is dining out someplace where, for a time, you belong to a rarified world in which everything is a little bit brighter, richer, and more deluxe than in your real life. Nothing says soigné better than an old-fashioned department store dining room.

These places, usually open only for lunch, were wallpapered dens of polite and excited chatter. The guests were almost exclusively ladies in a time when a lady's job primarily entailed keeping up her house and keeping up herself. The attire: white gloves, felt hats trimmed with gossamer veils, swirling skirts, pumps. The food: daintily divided, toothpick-speared club sandwiches on thin bread with homemade mayonnaise.

Department store dining has always been popular in Europe, but we Southerners have our own way of doing things. Our department stores had refined tearooms for people-watching and gossiping over pink-tipped shrimp cocktails. There was the dining room of Dallas' flagship Neiman Marcus, built in the late 1940s for store founder Herbert Marcus when his eyesight began to wane. Herbert's private dining room evolved into the ultimate stage for ladies who lunch, thanks to the irresistible civility of the dining experience—and the rich, fluffy popovers, served gratis with every meal.

There was the Magnolia Room in the renowned Atlanta-based Rich's, the original local department store that came to define, for a time, the city's style. The gregarious cookbook author Nathalie Dupree ran Rich's cooking school for years. Eating at the Magnolia Room meant chicken salad amandine with frozen fruit salad (the frosty blush of ice on the grapes made your toes tingle) and the lightest triple-layer coconut cake.

That was a long time ago. Women went to work, locally owned department stores have all but disappeared, and suburban culture spread across the South. But you can revive the tradition in your own dining room. Invite your best gals over, break out the pearls, and make some fabulous chicken salad—garnished with greens...and a dash of gossip.

Neiman Marcus Cheddar Cheese Biscuits

make-ahead • party perfect

MAKES: about 2½ dozen
HANDS-ON TIME: 20 min.
TOTAL TIME: 1 hr., 40 min.

- 2½ **cups all-purpose flour**
- 1½ **Tbsp. baking powder**
- 1 **tsp. salt**
- 1 **cup vegetable shortening**
- 1 **cup (4 oz.) freshly shredded sharp Cheddar cheese**
- 1 **cup buttermilk**
  Parchment paper

1. Whisk together first 3 ingredients in a large bowl. Cut in shortening with a pastry blender until mixture resembles small peas and dough is crumbly; stir in cheese. Add buttermilk, stirring just until dry ingredients are moistened.
2. Turn dough out onto a lightly floured surface; knead 3 to 4 times. Place dough in a bowl; cover and chill 1 hour.

3. Preheat oven to 350°. Turn dough out onto a lightly floured surface. Pat or roll dough to a 1-inch thickness; cut with a 1½-inch round cutter, and place on parchment paper-lined baking sheets.

4. Bake at 350° for 20 to 22 minutes or until golden brown.

NOTE: Unbaked biscuits may be frozen up to 1 month. Bake frozen biscuits as directed for 26 to 28 minutes or until golden brown.

KEVIN GARVIN AND JOHN HARRISSON
NEIMAN MARCUS COOKBOOK

5 More Ideas for the Bread Plate

Stir in one of the following flavor combos with the Cheddar cheese, and prepare the biscuit recipe as directed.

{1}

½ cup finely chopped dried apricots and 2 Tbsp. finely chopped fresh ginger

{2}

½ cup freshly grated Asiago cheese and 2 tsp. minced fresh rosemary

{3}

⅓ cup each finely chopped sweetened dried cranberries and toasted pecans

{4}

½ cup finely chopped cooked bacon and ¼ cup minced green onion

{5}

½ cup finely chopped baked ham and ⅓ cup finely chopped pimiento-stuffed green olives

Fast Flourish!

Toss gourmet mixed salad greens with chopped fresh herbs and edible flowers or flower petals. Serve with **Fresh Lemon Vinaigrette:** Whisk together ¼ cup fresh lemon juice; 1 tsp. Dijon mustard; 1 large garlic clove, pressed; ¼ tsp. salt; and ¼ tsp. each sugar and freshly ground pepper. Add ⅓ cup olive oil in a slow, steady stream, whisking constantly until smooth. Store in refrigerator up to 1 week; let stand at room temperature 20 minutes, and whisk just before serving. Makes: about ⅔ cup.

Tomato-Basil Bisque

quick prep • party perfect

MAKES: about 7 cups
HANDS-ON TIME: 15 min.
TOTAL TIME: 15 min.
(Pictured on page 171)

- 2 (10¾-oz.) cans tomato soup
- 1 (14½-oz.) can fire-roasted diced tomatoes
- 2½ cups buttermilk
- 2 Tbsp. chopped fresh basil
- ¼ tsp. freshly ground pepper
  Toppings: fresh basil leaves, freshly ground pepper, Parmesan cheese

1. Cook first 5 ingredients in a 3-qt. saucepan over medium heat, stirring often, 6 to 8 minutes or until thoroughly heated. Serve immediately with desired toppings.

Tarragon Chicken Salad

make-ahead • party perfect

MAKES: about 6 cups
HANDS-ON TIME: 25 min.
TOTAL TIME: 2 hr., 25 min.
(Pictured on page 171)

- 1 Tbsp. butter
- ¾ cup chopped pecans
- 1 cup mayonnaise
- 3 Tbsp. chopped fresh tarragon
- 1 tsp. lemon zest
- 1 Tbsp. fresh lemon juice
- 4 cups chopped cooked chicken breasts
- 1½ cups diced Granny Smith apples
- 1 cup diced celery
- ¼ cup finely chopped red onion

1. Melt butter in a small skillet over medium-low heat. Add pecans, and cook, stirring constantly, 6 to 8 minutes or until toasted and fragrant.

2. Whisk together mayonnaise and next 3 ingredients in a large bowl; stir in chicken and next 3 ingredients just until blended. Add salt and freshly ground pepper to taste. Cover and chill 2 to 24 hours; stir in ½ cup toasted pecans just before serving. Sprinkle with remaining pecans.

Cranberry-Strawberry Salad

make-ahead • party perfect

MAKES: 12 servings
HANDS-ON TIME: 20 min.
TOTAL TIME: 8 hr., 50 min.

This congealed salad is a cool, delicious twist on a retro luncheon staple. (Pictured on page 171)

1½ cups fresh or frozen cranberries
2 cups diced fresh strawberries
½ cup sugar
2 cups boiling water
3 (3-oz.) packages strawberry-flavored gelatin
2 cups cranberry juice, chilled
1 (8-oz.) can crushed pineapple, undrained
1 cup diced celery

1. Process cranberries in a food processor 30 seconds or until coarsely chopped, stopping once to scrape down sides.
2. Stir together cranberries, strawberries, and sugar in a medium bowl.
3. Stir together 2 cups boiling water and gelatin in a large bowl, stirring 2 minutes or until gelatin dissolves. Stir in juice, and chill 30 minutes or until consistency of unbeaten egg whites. Stir in cranberry mixture, pineapple, and celery. Spoon mixture into 12 lightly greased (⅔-cup) molds; cover and chill molds 8 hours or until firm.

Caramelized Onion Quiche

party perfect

MAKES: 6 to 8 servings
HANDS-ON TIME: 45 min.
TOTAL TIME: 2 hr.

1 (14.1-oz.) package refrigerated piecrusts
3 large sweet onions, sliced (about 1½ lb.)
2 Tbsp. olive oil
½ cup chopped fresh flat-leaf parsley
6 cooked bacon slices, crumbled
2 cups (8 oz.) shredded Gruyère cheese
1½ cups half-and-half
4 large eggs
½ tsp. salt
¼ tsp. freshly ground pepper
¼ tsp. ground nutmeg

1. Preheat oven to 425°. Unroll piecrusts; stack on a lightly greased surface. Roll stacked piecrusts into a 12-inch circle. Fit piecrust into a 10-inch deep-dish tart pan with removable bottom; press into fluted edges. Trim off excess piecrust along edges. Line piecrust with aluminum foil or parchment paper, and fill with pie weights or dried beans. Place pan on a foil-lined baking sheet. Bake 12 minutes. Remove weights and foil, and bake 8 more minutes. Cool completely on baking sheet on a wire rack (about 15 minutes). Reduce oven temperature to 350°.
2. Meanwhile, cook onions in hot oil in a large skillet over medium-high heat, stirring often, 15 to 20 minutes or until onions are caramel colored. Remove from heat, and stir in parsley and bacon. Place half of onion mixture in tart shell, and top with half of cheese; repeat with remaining onion mixture and cheese.
3. Whisk together half-and-half and next 4 ingredients; pour over cheese.
4. Bake at 350° for 40 to 45 minutes or until set. Cool on baking sheet on a wire rack 15 minutes before serving.

Crowd-Pleasing Tea Sandwiches

make-ahead • party perfect
(Also pictured on page 170)

1. Choose your favorite fillings, and prepare up to a day ahead. Plan on ¼ cup filling for each whole sandwich. Freeze bread slices until firm. (This makes it easier to trim and cut the sandwiches.)
2. Trim crusts from bread with a long serrated knife after sandwiches are filled; cut each sandwich into 4 triangles.
3. Make sandwiches up to 4 hours ahead. Place in an airtight container, cover loosely with wax paper and a damp paper towel, cover, and refrigerate.

HAM SALAD

Process 1 lb. chopped baked ham, in batches, in a food processor until coarsely ground, stopping to scrape down sides as needed. Place ground ham in a bowl, and stir in 3 hard-cooked eggs, peeled and grated; ⅔ cup mayonnaise; and ½ cup finely chopped sweet-hot pickled okra. Add salt and pepper to taste. **SPREAD ON:** rye bread slices. Makes: about 3 cups.

CURRIED SHRIMP

Stir together 2½ cups finely chopped peeled and deveined, cooked shrimp (about 1 lb. of any size); ½ cup finely diced celery; ½ cup toasted sweetened flaked coconut; 1½ (8-oz.) packages cream cheese, softened; 3 Tbsp. minced green onions; 1 Tbsp. freshly grated ginger; 1½ tsp. curry powder; ¼ tsp. salt; and ¼ tsp. ground red pepper until well blended. **SPREAD ON:** white bread. Makes: about 3 cups.
Curried Chicken: Substitute 2½ cups finely chopped cooked chicken for shrimp. Prepare recipe as directed. **SPREAD ON:** raisin bread.

CUCUMBER AND STRAWBERRY

Stir together 1 (8-oz.) package cream cheese, softened; ½ cup peeled, seeded, and finely chopped cucumber; ⅓ cup mayonnaise; ¼ cup minced red onion; 3 Tbsp. finely chopped fresh basil; ½ tsp. freshly ground pepper; and ¼ tsp. salt. **SPREAD ON:** white bread; sandwich with diced fresh strawberries. Makes: about 2 cups.

GOAT CHEESE AND PECAN

Stir together 4 oz. each softened cream cheese and goat cheese, 1 cup (4 oz.) shredded white Cheddar cheese, ½ cup finely chopped toasted pecans, and 2 Tbsp. chopped fresh cilantro. **SPREAD ON:** whole wheat bread slices. Spread a thin layer of red pepper jelly on an equal number of whole wheat bread slices; sandwich cream cheese mixture slices with pepper jelly slices. Makes: about 2 cups.

ORANGE AND CRANBERRY

Stir together 1 (8-oz.) package cream cheese, softened; ⅔ cup sweetened dried cranberries; ⅓ cup orange marmalade; and ½ cup chopped toasted pecans. **SPREAD ON:** pumpernickel bread; sandwich with thinly sliced smoked turkey and fresh arugula. Makes: about 2 cups.

EGG SALAD

Stir together 8 hard-cooked eggs, peeled and grated; ⅔ cup mayonnaise; ½ cup finely diced celery; ¼ cup finely chopped chives; 2 Tbsp. minced red onion; 1 Tbsp. chopped fresh tarragon; 1 tsp. freshly ground pepper; and ½ tsp. seasoned salt. **SPREAD ON:** whole grain bread slices. Spread mayonnaise on an equal number of whole grain bread slices. Sandwich egg salad slices and mayonnaise slices with fresh watercress. Makes: about 3 cups.

The Dessert Cart

What is it about this rolling relic that delights us so much? Maybe it's the sound of the squeaky wheels that signifies sweets are a-comin', the colorful assortment of confections that makes us feel like a kid in a candy shop, or the irresistible invitation to linger just a little longer over a shared slice of—oh, forget it, your own slice of something sinful. Whatever it is, we'll have the cheesecake, please.

Banana Pudding Cheesecake

make-ahead • party perfect

MAKES: 10 to 12 servings
HANDS-ON TIME: 45 min.
TOTAL TIME: 11 hr., 10 min.

- 1½ cups finely crushed vanilla wafers
- ½ cup chopped pecans
- ¼ cup butter, melted
- 17 vanilla wafers
- 2 large ripe bananas, diced
- 1 Tbsp. lemon juice
- 2 Tbsp. light brown sugar
- 3 (8-oz.) packages cream cheese, softened
- 1 cup granulated sugar
- 3 large eggs
- 2 tsp. vanilla extract
- ½ cup coarsely crushed vanilla wafers
  Garnishes: sweetened whipped cream, vanilla wafers, sliced bananas tossed in lemon juice

1. Preheat oven to 350°. Stir together first 3 ingredients in a small bowl until well blended. Press mixture onto bottom of a greased and floured 9-inch springform pan. Stand 17 vanilla wafers around edge of pan (rounded sides against pan), pressing gently into crust to secure. Bake 10 minutes. Cool completely on a wire rack (about 30 minutes).

2. Combine bananas and lemon juice in a small saucepan. Stir in brown sugar. Cook over medium-high heat, stirring constantly, 1 minute or just until sugar has dissolved.

3. Beat cream cheese at medium speed with an electric mixer 3 minutes or until smooth. Gradually add granulated sugar, beating until blended. Add eggs, 1 at a time, beating just until yellow disappears after each addition. Beat in vanilla. Gently stir banana mixture into cream cheese mixture. Pour batter into prepared crust.

4. Bake at 350° for 45 to 55 minutes or until center is almost set. Remove cheesecake from oven; gently run a knife around edge of cheesecake to loosen. Sprinkle top of cheesecake with coarsely crushed wafers. Cool completely on a wire rack (about 1 hour). Cover and chill 8 hours.

Lemon-Orange Chiffon Cake

make-ahead • party perfect

MAKES: 12 servings
HANDS-ON TIME: 30 min.
TOTAL TIME: 2 hr., 10 min., including frosting

2½ cups sifted cake flour
1⅓ cups sugar
1 Tbsp. baking powder
1 tsp. salt
½ cup vegetable oil
5 large eggs, separated
¾ cup fresh orange juice
3 Tbsp. orange zest
½ tsp. cream of tartar
    Lemon-Orange Buttercream
    Frosting
    Garnishes: edible flowers,
    kumquat slices

1. Preheat oven to 350°. Combine first 4 ingredients in bowl of a heavy-duty electric stand mixer. Make a well in center of flour mixture; add oil, egg yolks, and orange juice. Beat at medium-high speed 3 to 4 minutes or until smooth. Stir in zest.
2. Beat egg whites and cream of tartar at medium-high speed until stiff peaks form. Gently fold into flour mixture. Spoon batter into 3 greased and floured 9-inch round cake pans.
3. Bake at 350° for 17 to 20 minutes or until a wooden pick inserted in center comes out clean. Cool in pans on wire racks 10 minutes; remove from pans to wire racks, and cool completely (about 1 hour).
4. Spread Lemon-Orange Buttercream Frosting between layers and on top and sides of cake.

Lemon-Orange Buttercream Frosting

quick prep • party perfect

1. Beat 1 cup softened butter, 3 Tbsp. orange zest, and 1 Tbsp. lemon zest at medium speed with an electric mixer 1 to 2 minutes or until creamy; gradually add 1 (32-oz.) package powdered sugar alternately with 3 Tbsp. fresh lemon juice and 5 Tbsp. fresh orange juice, beating at low speed until blended after each addition. Add up to 1 Tbsp. additional fresh orange juice, 1 tsp. at a time, until desired consistency is reached. Makes: about 6 cups. Hands-on time: 10 min., Total time: 10 min.

Vanilla-Buttermilk Tarts

make-ahead • party perfect

MAKES: 8 tarts
HANDS-ON TIME: 30 min.
TOTAL TIME: 4 hr., 30 min.

⅔ cup sugar
¼ cup all-purpose flour
1½ cups buttermilk
3 large eggs
2 tsp. vanilla bean paste
1 (8- or 10-oz.) package frozen
    tart shells
    Toppings: fresh fruit, fresh basil
    sprigs

1. Whisk together sugar and flour in a 3-qt. heavy saucepan; add buttermilk and eggs, and whisk until blended. Cook over medium heat, whisking constantly, 7 to 8 minutes or until a pudding-like thickness. Remove from heat, and stir in vanilla bean paste. Cover and chill 4 to 24 hours.
2. Meanwhile, bake frozen tart shells according to package directions, and cool completely (about 30 minutes). Spoon custard into tart shells, and top with desired toppings just before serving.

Chocolate-Espresso Pots de Crème

make-ahead • party perfect

MAKES: 3¾ cups
HANDS-ON TIME: 30 min.
TOTAL TIME: 12 hr., 45 min.

2 cups half-and-half
½ cup firmly packed brown sugar
¼ cup unsweetened cocoa
¼ cup coffee liqueur
2 large eggs, lightly beaten
1 Tbsp. instant espresso
8 oz. high-quality bittersweet
    chocolate, chopped
    Toppings: sweetened whipped
    cream, edible flowers, fresh
    mint sprigs

1. Pour water to depth of 1 inch into bottom of a double boiler over medium heat; bring to a boil. Reduce heat to low, and simmer. Whisk together first 6 ingredients in top of double boiler; whisk in chocolate. Cook, whisking constantly, 15 minutes or until mixture reaches 160°. (Mixture will continue to thicken as it cools.) Remove from heat, and cool 10 minutes. Spoon into demitasse, espresso, or tea cups. Cover and chill 12 hours. Serve with desired toppings.

Spring Chicken

Skinless, boneless breasts rule the roost when it comes to these fast week-night meals.

Baked Chicken Roulade

Baked Chicken Roulade

quick prep

MAKES: 4 servings
HANDS-ON TIME: 30 min.
TOTAL TIME: 45 min.

- 4 skinned and boned chicken breasts (about 1½ lb.)
- ½ tsp. pepper
- ¼ tsp. salt
- 1 (5-oz.) package baby spinach
- 4 garlic cloves, minced and divided
- 2 tsp. olive oil
- 12 fresh thin asparagus spears (about 1 lb.)
  Wooden picks
- 5 Tbsp. butter, divided
- 2 Tbsp. olive oil
- 1 Tbsp. all-purpose flour
- 2 Tbsp. dry white wine
- ¾ cup chicken broth
- 1 tsp. fresh lemon juice
- 2 Tbsp. chopped fresh flat-leaf parsley
- 2 Tbsp. drained capers

1. Preheat oven to 425°. Place chicken between 2 sheets of heavy-duty plastic wrap, and flatten to ¼-inch thickness using flat side of a meat mallet or rolling pin. Sprinkle chicken with pepper and salt.
2. Sauté spinach and 2 minced garlic cloves in 2 tsp. hot oil in a large ovenproof skillet over medium heat 1 minute or until spinach begins to wilt. Transfer spinach mixture to a plate. Wipe skillet clean.

3. Spoon spinach mixture over each breast, leaving a ½-inch border around edges. Top with asparagus, and roll up, starting at 1 short side. Tuck in ends of chicken, and secure with wooden picks.
4. Melt 3 Tbsp. butter with 2 Tbsp. olive oil in skillet over medium-high heat; add chicken. Cook 6 to 8 minutes, turning to brown on all sides. Transfer skillet to oven, and bake at 425° for 15 minutes. Transfer to a serving plate, and cover loosely with aluminum foil to keep warm.

5. Melt remaining 2 Tbsp. butter in skillet over medium-high heat; add remaining garlic. Sauté 1 to 2 minutes or until tender and fragrant. Whisk in flour; cook 1 minute. Add white wine; cook, stirring constantly, 1 minute. Whisk in chicken broth and lemon juice; cook 2 minutes or until thickened. Stir in parsley and capers; spoon sauce over chicken, and serve immediately.

Chicken (Not So) Little

Our Test Kitchen generally prefers smaller chicken breasts—4 to 6 ounces—that are increasingly harder to find. In fact, an informal survey of our local supermarkets found that most packages contain breasts weighing in at a whopping 8 to 12 ounces each. (Of the brands we sampled, only Springer Mountain Farms' individually packed breasts weighed in at around 4 ounces.) If you're stuck with huge portions, which can be hard to cook properly, we suggest pounding your unwieldy pieces, or cutting larger breasts in half lengthwise.

Our Test Kitchen weighs in! →

Smoky Chicken Panini with Basil Mayo
quick prep

MAKES: 4 servings
HANDS-ON TIME: 35 min.
TOTAL TIME: 45 min.

- 4 **skinned and boned chicken breasts (about 1 lb.)**
- ½ **tsp. salt**
- ⅛ **tsp. freshly ground pepper**
- ½ **cup mayonnaise**
- 2 **Tbsp. chopped fresh basil**
- ½ **tsp. lemon zest**
- 8 **sourdough bread slices**
- ½ **lb. smoked Gouda cheese, sliced**
- 1 **cup loosely packed baby spinach**
- ¼ **cup thinly sliced sun-dried tomatoes**
- 3 **Tbsp. butter, melted**

1. Preheat grill to 350° to 400° (medium-high) heat. Sprinkle chicken with salt and pepper. Grill chicken, covered with grill lid, 7 to 10 minutes on each side or until done. Let stand 10 minutes, and cut into slices.

2. Stir together mayonnaise and next 2 ingredients. Spread mixture on 1 side of each bread slice. Top 4 bread slices with chicken, Gouda, and next 2 ingredients. Top with remaining bread slices, mayonnaise mixture sides down. Brush sandwiches with melted butter.

3. Cook sandwiches, in batches, in a preheated panini press 2 to 3 minutes or until golden brown.

Chicken Risotto with Spring Vegetables
party perfect

MAKES: 6 to 8 servings
HANDS-ON TIME: 1 hr., 10 min.
TOTAL TIME: 1 hr., 15 min.

- 4 **cups chicken broth**
- ½ **lb. fresh asparagus spears**
- ¾ **lb. skinned and boned chicken breasts, cut into 1-inch strips**
- ½ **tsp. herbes de Provence**
- 1¼ **tsp. salt, divided**
- 3 **Tbsp. butter, divided**
- 2 **Tbsp. olive oil, divided**
- 2 **medium zucchini, thinly sliced into half moons**
- 1 **medium onion, finely chopped**
- 2½ **cups uncooked Arborio rice (short-grain)**
- 1 **cup dry white wine**
- 1 **cup freshly grated Parmesan cheese**
- ½ **cup freshly grated fontina cheese**
- ¼ **cup chopped fresh parsley**
- ½ **tsp. pepper**
  Garnish: Parmesan cheese

1. Bring chicken broth and 4 cups water to a simmer in a large saucepan over low heat. Snap off and discard tough ends of asparagus. Cut into 2-inch pieces.

2. Sprinkle chicken with herbes de Provence and ¾ tsp. salt.

3. Melt 2 Tbsp. butter with 1 Tbsp. olive oil in a Dutch oven over medium-high heat; add chicken, and sauté 5 to 6 minutes or until done. Remove chicken; cover and keep warm.

4. Melt remaining 1 Tbsp. butter in Dutch oven; add zucchini, onion, and asparagus, and sauté 3 minutes or until tender. Remove vegetables; cover and keep warm.

5. Sauté rice in remaining 1 Tbsp. hot oil in Dutch oven over medium-high heat 1 minute. Reduce heat to medium. Add wine and remaining ½ tsp. salt, and cook, stirring often, until liquid is absorbed. Add 1 cup hot broth mixture; cook, stirring often, until liquid is absorbed. Repeat procedure with remaining broth mixture, 1 cup at a time. (Total cooking time is about 30 minutes.)

6. Stir in grated cheeses, chicken, and vegetables until creamy. Stir in parsley and pepper. Serve immediately.

NOTE: Herbes de Provence can be found online (try mccormick.com) or at Whole Foods Market.

Chicken-and-Veggie Stir-fry

quick prep • good for you • make-ahead

MAKES: 4 servings
HANDS-ON TIME: 30 min.
TOTAL TIME: 30 min.

- 1 lb. skinned and boned chicken breasts, cut into thin strips
- ½ tsp. salt
- ¼ cup cornstarch
- 4 Tbsp. vegetable oil, divided
- ½ lb. Broccolini, cut into 1-inch pieces
- 1 cup chicken broth, divided
- 1 red bell pepper, cut into thin strips
- 1 small yellow squash, thinly sliced into half moons
- ¼ cup sliced green onions
- 2 tsp. cornstarch
- 1 Tbsp. fresh lime juice
- 1½ tsp. soy sauce
- 1 tsp. Asian chili-garlic sauce
  Hot cooked rice

1. Sprinkle chicken with salt; toss with ¼ cup cornstarch.

2. Stir-fry chicken in 3 Tbsp. hot oil in a large skillet or wok over medium-high heat 5 to 6 minutes or until golden brown and done. Transfer to a plate, using a slotted spoon; keep warm. Add Broccolini and ¼ cup broth; cover and cook 1 to 2 minutes or until crisp-tender. Transfer to plate with chicken, using slotted spoon.

3. Add remaining 1 Tbsp. oil to skillet. Sauté bell pepper and next 2 ingredients in hot oil 2 minutes or until crisp-tender.

4. Whisk together 2 tsp. cornstarch and remaining ¾ cup broth until cornstarch dissolves. Add broth mixture, chicken, and Broccolini (with any accumulated juices) to bell pepper mixture in skillet. Cook, stirring often, 1 minute or until liquid thickens. Stir in lime juice and next 2 ingredients. Serve over hot cooked rice.

FOOD GIFT OF THE MONTH
Cornbread Madeleines

This delicate Southern twist on the traditional French sponge cake is one of our favorite hostess gifts. Light and airy, and not too sweet, they'd have Proust swooning "Lawdamercy."

MAKES: 4 dozen
HANDS-ON TIME: 10 min.
TOTAL TIME: 1 hr., 14 min.
(for 4 batches)
(Also pictured on page 171)

1. Preheat oven to 400°. Whisk together 2 cups self-rising white cornmeal mix, ½ cup all-purpose flour, and ¼ cup sugar in a large bowl. Add 2 cups buttermilk; and 2 large eggs, lightly beaten. Whisk together just until blended.

2. Spoon batter into lightly greased shiny madeleine pans, filling three-fourths full. Bake, in batches, 16 to 18 minutes or until golden brown. Remove from pans immediately.

3. Serve hot, or cool completely on wire racks (about 20 minutes), and freeze in zip-top plastic bags up to 1 month.

4. To serve, arrange desired amount of madeleines on a baking sheet, and bake at 350° for 5 to 6 minutes or until thoroughly heated.

NOTE: The traditional shiny heavy-gauge, tinned steel madeleine pan, which makes one dozen 3- x 2-inch madeleines, yields the prettiest results. (Dark nonstick versions tend to over-brown.) Look for shiny pans in bake shops, or order online from *baeandcooco.com* ($17.95) or *amazon.com*. To prevent overbrowning if you do use a dark nonstick madeleine pan, wrap the bottom of the pan with a sheet of heavy-duty aluminum foil, shiny side out.

TRY THESE TWISTS!

Orange-Rosemary: Prepare recipe as directed, adding 2 Tbsp. orange zest and 1½ Tbsp. finely chopped fresh rosemary to dry ingredients.

Lemon-Thyme: Prepare recipe as directed, adding 1 Tbsp. lemon zest and 1 Tbsp. finely chopped fresh thyme to dry ingredients.

Spicy White Cheddar: Reduce sugar to 2 Tbsp. Prepare recipe as directed, adding ¾ cup finely shredded white Cheddar cheese and ¼ tsp. ground red pepper to dry ingredients.

Peas, Please!

Six easy ways to enjoy these bright green gems just in time for your next spring gathering.

{1}
Sweet Pea Crostini
quick prep • make-ahead • party perfect

Sauté 4 sliced green onions and I minced garlic clove in I Tbsp. hot olive oil 2 minutes. Add 1½ cups blanched fresh sweet peas and 2 tsp. fresh lemon juice; cook until heated. Remove from heat; stir in ¼ cup freshly grated Parmesan cheese and 3 Tbsp. chopped fresh basil. Add salt and pepper to taste. Pulse in a food processor until coarsely chopped. Spoon onto 24 toasted French baguette slices. Drizzle with balsamic vinegar. Top with shaved Parmesan cheese. Makes: 24 servings.

{2}
Pea Salad Deviled Eggs
quick prep • make-ahead • party perfect

Slice 12 hard-cooked eggs in half length-wise; carefully remove yolks, reserving egg whites. Mash together yolks; ½ cup blanched fresh sweet peas, coarsely chopped; 4 cooked bacon slices, finely chopped; ¼ cup mayonnaise; 2 Tbsp. minced red onion; 2 Tbsp. sour cream; I Tbsp. chopped fresh mint; ¼ tsp. salt; and ⅛ tsp. freshly ground pepper. Spoon into egg white halves. Serve immediately, or chill up to I hour. Makes: 2 dozen.

Test Kitchen Notebook

HOW TO BLANCH PEAS:
Cook desired amount of fresh sweet peas, snow peas, or sugar snap peas in boiling salted water to cover I to 3 minutes or until crisp-tender; drain. Plunge into ice-cold water to stop the cooking process; drain.

{3}
Roasted Garlic-Sweet Pea Spread
quick prep • make-ahead • party perfect

Preheat oven to 425°. Cut off pointed end of I garlic bulb; place garlic bulb on a piece of aluminum foil, and drizzle with I Tbsp. olive oil. Fold foil to seal. Bake 30 minutes; let cool 10 minutes. Process 2 cups blanched fresh sweet peas in a food processor until smooth. Squeeze pulp from roasted garlic bulb into food processor bowl with peas; add ½ cup ricotta cheese, ¼ cup chopped fresh basil, and 2 Tbsp. fresh lemon juice. Process until smooth. With processor running, pour ¼ cup olive oil through food chute in a slow, steady stream, processing until smooth. Stir in I tsp. kosher salt and ½ tsp. freshly ground pepper. Serve with crackers. Makes: about 2½ cups.

{4}
Shrimp-Snow Pea Stir-fry
quick prep • good for you

Peel I lb. medium-size raw shrimp; devein, if desired. Stir-fry shrimp in I Tbsp. hot peanut oil in a wok over high heat I minute. Add I large red bell pepper, cut into thin strips, and I garlic clove, chopped; stir-fry 2 minutes. Add I cup fresh snow peas, trimmed and cut into thin strips; stir-fry I minute. Add ⅓ cup bottled stir-fry sauce; stir-fry I minute. Serve over hot cooked rice. Makes: 4 servings.

{5}
Chilled Green Pea Soup
quick prep • make-ahead • party perfect

Process 4 cups blanched peas; 2 cups water; I cup chopped, peeled English cucumber; ¼ cup chopped sweet onion; ¼ cup chopped fresh mint; and ¼ cup sour cream in a blender until smooth. Stir in 1¼ tsp. salt and ¼ tsp. pepper. Cover and chill I to 8 hours. Makes: 8 cups.

{6}
Ginger-Snow Pea Slaw
quick prep • good for you • party perfect

Toss together 4 cups thinly sliced napa cabbage (I head); 2 cups fresh snow peas, trimmed and cut into thin strips; ⅓ cup bottled sesame-ginger dressing; ¼ cup chopped roasted almonds; 3 sliced green onions; I shredded carrot; and 3 Tbsp. chopped fresh cilantro. Makes: 8 servings.

Pretty, Quick-Toss Pastas

Take a breather from that jar of marinara and freshen up your dishes with seasonal vegetables and lightweight sauces.

Green Bean Pasta Salad with Lemon-Thyme Vinaigrette

Green Bean Pasta Salad with Lemon-Thyme Vinaigrette

quick prep • party perfect

MAKES: 4 to 6 servings
HANDS-ON TIME: 15 min.
TOTAL TIME: 30 min.

Casarecce [cah-sah-RECH-ee] pasta looks similar to a scroll with the long sides curled inward toward the center.

- 12 oz. uncooked casarecce pasta*
- ½ lb. haricots verts (tiny green beans), cut in half lengthwise
- 1 Tbsp. fresh thyme
- 5 tsp. lemon zest, divided
- ¼ cup finely chopped roasted, salted pistachios
- 2 Tbsp. Champagne vinegar
- 1 Tbsp. minced shallots
- 1 garlic clove, minced
- 1 tsp. salt
- ½ tsp. freshly ground pepper
- 5 Tbsp. olive oil
- 1½ cups loosely packed arugula
  Toppings: roasted, salted pistachios; Parmesan cheese

1. Cook pasta according to package directions, adding green beans to boiling water during last 2 minutes of cooking time; drain. Rinse pasta mixture with cold running water; drain well.

2. Place pasta mixture, thyme, and 3 tsp. lemon zest in a large bowl; toss gently to combine.

3. Whisk together pistachios, next 5 ingredients, and remaining 2 tsp. lemon zest in a small bowl. Add oil in a slow, steady stream, whisking constantly until blended. Drizzle over pasta mixture. Add arugula, and toss gently to coat. Serve with desired toppings.

*Penne pasta may be substituted.

NOTE: We tested with Whole Foods Market Organic Casarecce pasta.

Test Kitchen Tip

Only rinse pasta with water if you are making a cold pasta dish.

Roasted Vegetable Gnocchi with Spinach-Herb Pesto

quick prep • good for you

MAKES: 4 servings
HANDS-ON TIME: 10 min.
TOTAL TIME: 55 min., including pesto

Dumpling-like gnocchi [NYOH-kee] are sold near the dried pastas.

- **6 yellow squash (about 1¼ lb.)**
- **8 sweet mini bell peppers**
- **2 Tbsp. olive oil**
- **1 tsp. salt**
- **½ tsp. coarsely ground pepper**
- **1 (16-oz.) package gnocchi* Spinach-Herb Pesto**
- **½ (5-oz.) package baby spinach**
- **¼ to ⅓ cup (1 to 1½ oz.) freshly shredded Parmesan cheese**

1. Preheat oven to 425°. Cut squash into 1-inch pieces. Cut bell peppers in half lengthwise; remove seeds. Stir together squash, bell peppers, oil, salt, and ground pepper. Arrange vegetables in a single layer on a jelly-roll pan, and bake 15 minutes. Stir and bake 5 minutes or until tender and golden.
2. Cook gnocchi according to package directions in a Dutch oven; drain. Return to Dutch oven. Add Spinach-Herb Pesto to gnocchi, and toss to coat. Add squash mixture and spinach, and gently toss to combine. Sprinkle with Parmesan cheese. Serve immediately.
*Medium-size pasta shells may be substituted.
NOTE: We tested with Gia Russa Gnocchi With Potato.

Test Kitchen Tip

Test pasta for doneness by taking a bite. It should be slightly chewy with a tiny white speck in the center.

Spinach-Herb Pesto

quick prep • good for you • make-ahead

MAKES: ¾ cup
HANDS-ON TIME: 15 min.
TOTAL TIME: 15 min.

- **½ (5-oz.) package baby spinach**
- **1 Tbsp. chopped fresh cilantro**
- **1 Tbsp. chopped fresh basil**
- **1 tsp. lemon zest**
- **2 Tbsp. lemon juice**
- **1 tsp. chopped fresh mint**
- **1 garlic clove, minced**
- **¼ tsp. salt**
- **½ cup (2 oz.) freshly shredded Parmesan cheese**
- **¼ cup olive oil**

1. Pulse first 8 ingredients in a food processor 6 to 7 times or until finely chopped. Add Parmesan cheese and oil; process until smooth, stopping to scrape down sides as needed. Use immediately, or store in refrigerator up to 48 hours. If chilled, let stand at room temperature 30 minutes before using; stir until blended.

Fettuccine-and-Asparagus al Burro

quick prep

MAKES: 3 to 4 servings
HANDS-ON TIME: 30 min.
TOTAL TIME: 30 min.

Al burro means "buttered." This simple sauce is a more authentic version of today's popular Alfredo, which calls for whipping cream. Buy a high-quality cheese—it makes a difference. (Pictured on page 175)

- **1 lb. fresh thin asparagus**
- **4 to 6 oz. thick pancetta slices, diced**
- **1 (9-oz.) package refrigerated fettuccine**
- **2 Tbsp. butter, at room temperature**
- **3 Tbsp. extra virgin olive oil**
- **½ cup freshly shredded Parmigiano-Reggiano cheese**
- **2 Tbsp. chopped fresh flat-leaf parsley**
- **¼ tsp. salt**
- **¼ tsp. freshly ground pepper Toppings: shaved Parmesan cheese, freshly ground pepper**

1. Snap off and discard tough ends of asparagus. Cut diagonally into 1½-inch pieces.
2. Sauté pancetta in a large skillet over medium heat 5 minutes or until crisp; remove from skillet.
3. Cook fettuccine and asparagus in boiling salted water to cover 2 to 3 minutes. Drain, reserving ¼ cup pasta water.
4. Melt butter with oil in skillet over medium heat; add hot cooked pasta and asparagus, cheese, and next 3 ingredients. Toss to coat, adding enough reserved pasta water to make a glossy sauce. Remove from heat; sprinkle with pancetta. Serve immediately with desired toppings.
NOTE: We tested with Buitoni All Natural Fettuccine.

Shrimp Destin Linguine

Marinated Greek-Style Pasta

make-ahead • party perfect

MAKES: 14 to 16 servings
HANDS-ON TIME: 30 min.
TOTAL TIME: 2 hr., 40 min.

This big-batch salad is great for parties. Leftovers are perfect for next-day lunches straight from the fridge.

- 1 (16-oz.) package orecchiette*
- ½ lb. hard salami slices, cut into strips
- ¼ lb. assorted deli olives, pitted, drained, and cut in half
- 1 (7-oz.) jar roasted red bell peppers, drained and chopped
- 6 pepperoncini salad peppers, cut in half lengthwise
- ½ English cucumber, thinly sliced into half moons
- 1½ cups bottled Greek vinaigrette with feta, divided
- 1 pt. grape tomatoes, cut in half
- ¼ cup firmly packed fresh flat-leaf parsley leaves
- 4 oz. feta cheese, crumbled

1. Cook pasta according to package directions; drain. Rinse with cold running water.
2. Toss together pasta, salami, and next 4 ingredients. Add 1 cup vinaigrette, and toss to coat. Cover and chill 2 to 24 hours.
3. Toss in tomatoes, parsley, and remaining ½ cup vinaigrette just before serving. Sprinkle with feta cheese.
*Penne pasta may be substituted.
NOTE: We tested with De Cecco Orecchiette Pasta and Seeds of Change Certified Organic Greek Feta Vinaigrette.

Shrimp Destin Linguine

quick prep

MAKES: 2 to 3 servings
HANDS-ON TIME: 30 min.
TOTAL TIME: 30 min.

For a little kick, add a pinch of dried crushed red pepper just before serving. (Also pictured on page 174)

- 1½ lb. unpeeled, large raw shrimp (21/25 count)
- 1 (9-oz.) package refrigerated linguine
- ¼ cup butter
- ¼ cup olive oil
- ¼ cup chopped green onions
- 2 garlic cloves, minced
- 1 Tbsp. dry white wine
- 2 tsp. fresh lemon juice
- ½ tsp. salt
- ¼ tsp. coarsely ground pepper
- 1 Tbsp. chopped fresh dill
- 1 Tbsp. chopped fresh parsley

1. Peel shrimp, leaving tails on, if desired. Devein, if desired.
2. Prepare pasta according to package directions.
3. Meanwhile, melt butter with oil in a large skillet over medium-high heat; add green onions and garlic, and sauté 4 to 5 minutes or until onions are tender. Add shrimp, wine, and next 3 ingredients. Cook over medium heat, stirring occasionally, 3 to 5 minutes or just until shrimp turn pink. Stir in dill and parsley. Remove shrimp with a slotted spoon, reserving sauce in skillet.
4. Add hot cooked pasta to sauce in skillet, tossing to coat. Transfer pasta to a serving bowl, and top with shrimp.

April

Strawberry Delights

15 fresh and easy ways to celebrate the sweet taste of spring, from sugar-kissed salsa to featherlight muffins and layer cakes. U-pick your favorite!

Strawberry Cream Pie
quick prep • party perfect

MAKES: 8 servings
HANDS-ON TIME: 35 min.
TOTAL TIME: 5 hr., 45 min.

- 3 Tbsp. cornstarch
- 2 Tbsp. all-purpose flour
- ¼ tsp. salt
- 1 cup sugar, divided
- 3 cups half-and-half
- 6 egg yolks
- 2 tsp. vanilla extract
- 1 (9-oz.) package chocolate wafer cookies
- ½ (4-oz.) semisweet chocolate baking bar, chopped
- ½ cup butter, melted
- 1 qt. fresh strawberries
- ¼ cup red currant jelly
- 1 Tbsp. orange liqueur

1. Whisk together first 3 ingredients and ⅔ cup sugar in a medium-size heavy saucepan. Whisk together half-and-half and next 2 ingredients in a small bowl; gradually add to cornstarch mixture, whisking constantly.

2. Bring to a boil over medium heat, whisking constantly, and cook, whisking constantly, 1 minute. Remove from heat, and transfer to a bowl; cover and chill 4 to 24 hours.

3. Preheat oven to 350°. Pulse wafer cookies and chopped chocolate in a food processor 8 to 10 times or until finely crushed. Stir together cookie crumb mixture, melted butter, and remaining ⅓ cup sugar; firmly press mixture on bottom, up sides, and onto lip of a lightly greased 9-inch pie plate.

4. Bake at 350° for 10 minutes. Transfer to a wire rack, and cool completely (about 30 minutes).

5. Spoon chilled half-and-half mixture into prepared crust. Cut 8 to 10 strawberries in half, and arrange around outer edge of pie (leaving tops on, if desired); hull and slice remaining strawberries, and arrange in center of pie.

6. Cook jelly in a small saucepan over medium heat 2 to 3 minutes or until melted. Remove from heat, and stir in liqueur. Brush jelly mixture gently over strawberries. Chill, uncovered, 30 minutes.

Strawberry Cream Pie

Strawberry Showstopper

A dark-chocolate crust and jewel-bright berries brushed with jelly turn this down-home pie into company-worthy fare.

Strawberry Mousse Cake

make-ahead • party perfect

MAKES: 10 to 12 servings
HANDS-ON TIME: 45 min.
TOTAL TIME: 5 hr., 15 min.
(Pictured on page 6)

CAKE LAYERS

1¼ cups butter, softened
2¼ cups granulated sugar
7 egg whites, at room temperature
3½ cups cake flour
4 tsp. baking powder
2 tsp. vanilla extract
½ tsp. almond extract

STRAWBERRY MOUSSE

1 envelope unflavored gelatin
2 cups sliced fresh strawberries
¼ cup granulated sugar
1 cup whipping cream

REFRESHER COURSE

Strawberry-Amaretto Milk Shake

quick prep • party perfect

MAKES: 3 cups
HANDS-ON TIME: 10 min.
TOTAL TIME: 30 min.

2 cups sliced fresh strawberries
½ cup amaretto liqueur
2 Tbsp. sugar
2 cups vanilla ice cream
Garnishes: sweetened whipped cream, chopped fresh strawberries

1. Stir together sliced fresh strawberries, amaretto liqueur, and 2 Tbsp. sugar; let stand 20 minutes.
2. Process strawberry mixture and ice cream in a blender until smooth, stopping to scrape down sides as needed. Serve immediately.

STRAWBERRY FROSTING

¾ cup butter, softened
5 cups powdered sugar, sifted
¾ cup finely chopped fresh strawberries

GARNISHES

Halved fresh strawberries, edible flowers

1. Prepare Cake Layers: Preheat oven to 350°. Beat 1¼ cups softened butter and 2¼ cups granulated sugar at medium speed with a heavy-duty electric stand mixer until fluffy. Gradually add egg whites, one-third at a time, beating well after each addition.
2. Sift together cake flour and baking powder; gradually add to butter mixture alternately with 1 cup water, beginning and ending with flour mixture. Stir in vanilla and almond extracts. Pour batter into 4 greased and floured 8-inch round cake pans.
3. Bake at 350° for 22 to 25 minutes or until a wooden pick inserted in center comes out clean. Cool in pans on wire racks 10 minutes; remove from pans to wire racks, and cool completely (about 30 minutes).
4. Prepare Strawberry Mousse: Sprinkle gelatin over ¼ cup water in a small bowl; let stand 5 minutes. Process 2 cups sliced strawberries and ¼ cup granulated sugar in a blender or food processor until smooth, stopping to scrape down sides as needed. Transfer strawberry mixture to a small saucepan; bring to a boil over medium-high heat. Remove from heat. Add gelatin to strawberry mixture, stirring constantly until gelatin dissolves. Cover and chill until consistency of unbeaten egg whites, stirring occasionally (about 30 minutes).
5. Beat cream at low speed until foamy; increase speed to medium-high, and beat until soft peaks form. Fold whipped cream into strawberry mixture until well blended. Cover and chill 30 minutes or just until mixture is thick enough to hold its shape when mounded.

6. Spread about 1 cup Strawberry Mousse between each cake layer, leaving a ¼-inch border around edges; cover and chill 3 hours or until mousse is set.
7. Prepare Strawberry Frosting: Beat ¾ cup softened butter at medium speed 20 seconds or until fluffy. Gradually add powdered sugar and ¾ cup finely chopped strawberries, beating at low speed until creamy. Spread frosting on top and sides of cake.

Strawberry-Basil Frozen Yogurt

make-ahead • party perfect

MAKES: about 1 qt.
HANDS-ON TIME: 20 min.
TOTAL TIME: 1 hr., 50 min., not including freezing

Garnish this refreshing dessert with basil sprigs. (Pictured on page 173)

2 cups sliced fresh strawberries
1 cup sugar
2 Tbsp. chopped fresh basil
1 tsp. lime zest
1 cup plain Greek yogurt
1 cup whipping cream

1. Stir together strawberries and sugar in a medium bowl. Let stand 30 minutes, stirring occasionally. Pulse strawberry mixture, basil, and lime zest in a food processor 9 to 10 times or until berries are finely chopped (almost pureed), stopping to scrape down sides as needed.
2. Whisk together yogurt and cream in a medium bowl until smooth; stir strawberry mixture into yogurt mixture until well blended. Cover and chill 1 hour.
3. Pour strawberry mixture into freezer container of a 1½-qt. electric ice-cream maker, and freeze according to manufacturer's instructions. (Instructions and times may vary.)

Fresh Strawberry Meringue Cake

make-ahead • party perfect

MAKES: 10 to 12 servings
HANDS-ON TIME: 1 hr.
TOTAL TIME: 4 hr., 20 min.

Securing parchment paper with masking tape (it won't melt at the low temp) makes it easy to spread picture-perfect layers of meringue.

- 1 cup chopped pecans
- Parchment paper
- Masking tape
- 2 Tbsp. cornstarch
- ⅛ tsp. salt
- 2 cups sugar, divided
- 7 egg whites, at room temperature
- ½ tsp. cream of tartar
- 2 (8-oz.) containers mascarpone cheese
- 2 tsp. vanilla extract
- 3 cups whipping cream
- 4½ cups sliced fresh strawberries
- Halved fresh strawberries

1. Preheat oven to 350°. Bake pecans in a single layer in a shallow pan 10 to 12 minutes or until toasted and fragrant, stirring halfway through. Remove from oven, and cool completely (about 10 minutes). Reduce oven temperature to 250°.

2. Cover 2 large baking sheets with parchment paper. Draw 2 (8-inch) circles on each piece of paper. Turn paper over; secure with masking tape.

3. Process cornstarch, salt, toasted pecans, and ½ cup sugar in a food processor 40 to 45 seconds or until pecans are finely ground.

4. Beat egg whites and cream of tartar at high speed with an electric mixer until foamy. Gradually add 1 cup sugar, 1 Tbsp. at a time, beating at medium-high speed until mixture is glossy, stiff peaks form, and sugar dissolves (2 to 4 minutes; do not overbeat). Add half of pecan mixture to egg white mixture, gently folding just until blended. Repeat procedure with remaining pecan mixture.

5. Gently spoon egg white mixture onto circles drawn on parchment paper (about 1½ cups mixture per circle), spreading to cover each circle completely.

6. Bake at 250° for 1 hour, turning baking sheets after 30 minutes. Turn oven off; let meringues stand in closed oven with light on 2 to 2½ hours or until surface is dry and meringues can be lifted from paper without sticking to fingers.

7. Just before assembling cake, stir together mascarpone cheese and vanilla in a large bowl just until blended.

8. Beat whipping cream at low speed until foamy; increase speed to medium-high, and gradually add remaining ½ cup sugar, beating until stiff peaks form. (Do not overbeat or cream will be grainy.) Gently fold whipped cream into mascarpone mixture.

9. Carefully remove 1 meringue from parchment paper; place on a serving plate. Spread one-fourth mascarpone mixture (about 2 cups) over meringue; top with 1½ cups sliced strawberries. Repeat layers 2 times; top with remaining meringue, mascarpone mixture, and halved strawberries. Serve immediately, or chill up to 2 hours. Cut with a sharp, thin-bladed knife.

Fresh Strawberry Meringue Cake

Strawberry-Lemonade Muffins

quick prep • party perfect

MAKES: 15 muffins
HANDS-ON TIME: 15 min.
TOTAL TIME: 42 min.

We loved these fresh from the oven and topped with Strawberry Curd (at right). (Pictured on page 173)

2½   cups self-rising flour
1¼   cups sugar, divided
1   (8-oz.) container sour cream
½   cup butter, melted
1   Tbsp. lemon zest
¼   cup fresh lemon juice
2   large eggs, lightly beaten
1½   cups diced fresh strawberries

1. Preheat oven to 400°. Combine flour and 1 cup sugar in a large bowl; make a well in center of mixture.
2. Stir together sour cream and next 4 ingredients; add to flour mixture, stirring just until dry ingredients are moistened. Gently fold strawberries into batter. Spoon batter into lightly greased 12-cup muffin pans, filling three-fourths full. Sprinkle remaining ¼ cup sugar over batter.
3. Bake at 400° for 16 to 18 minutes or until golden brown and a wooden pick inserted in center comes out clean. Cool in pans on a wire rack 1 minute; remove from pans to wire rack, and cool 10 minutes.

Strawberry Chicken Salad

good for you • make-ahead • party perfect

MAKES: about 7 cups
HANDS-ON TIME: 20 min.
TOTAL TIME: 2 hr., 20 min.
(Pictured on page 172)

1. Stir together ½ cup bottled poppy-seed dressing, ¼ cup minced green onions, 3 Tbsp. chopped fresh basil, and ½ tsp. freshly ground pepper in a large bowl. Fold in 4 cups chopped cooked chicken and 2 cups diced fresh strawberries; add salt to taste. Cover and chill 2 hours. Stir in 1 cup chopped toasted pecans just before serving.

Chilled Strawberry Soup

good for you • make-ahead • party perfect

MAKES: about 4 cups
HANDS-ON TIME: 10 min.
TOTAL TIME: 2 hr., 10 min.
(Pictured on page 172)

1. Process 3 cups sliced fresh strawberries, 1 cup plain Greek yogurt, ½ cup Riesling, and ⅓ cup sugar in a blender or food processor until smooth, stopping to scrape down sides as needed. Cover and chill 2 hours. Garnish with a drizzle of olive oil, freshly ground pepper, and sliced fresh strawberries.

REFRESHER COURSE

Strawberry Limeade

make-ahead • party perfect

MAKES: 7 cups
HANDS-ON TIME: 10 min.
TOTAL TIME: 2 hr., 40 min.

3   cups sliced fresh strawberries
1   cup sugar
4   cups cold water
⅔   cup fresh lime juice
    (about 4 large limes)

1. Stir together strawberries and sugar in a large bowl; crush strawberries with a wooden spoon, and let stand at room temperature 30 minutes.
2. Process strawberry mixture in a blender or food processor until smooth, stopping to scrape down sides as needed. Press mixture through a wire-mesh strainer into a large pitcher, using back of spoon to squeeze out juice; discard solids. Add cold water and lime juice, stirring until blended. Cover and chill 2 to 24 hours.

SIP ON THIS
Strawberry-Limeade Iced Tea: Prepare Strawberry Limeade as directed, substituting 4 cups cold unsweetened tea for cold water.

Strawberry Curd

make-ahead • party perfect

MAKES: about 3⅓ cups
HANDS-ON TIME: 30 min.
TOTAL TIME: 8 hr., 30 min.

1. Process 4 cups sliced fresh strawberries in a blender or food processor until smooth, stopping to scrape down sides as needed. Press strawberries through a large wire-mesh strainer into a medium bowl, using back of a spoon to squeeze out juice; discard pulp and seeds. Combine ½ cup sugar and 2 Tbsp. cornstarch in a 3-qt. saucepan; gradually whisk in strawberry puree and ¼ cup fresh lime juice. Whisk in 3 large eggs and 2 egg yolks. Bring mixture to a boil over medium heat, whisking constantly, and cook, whisking constantly, 1 minute. Remove from heat, and whisk in 3 Tbsp. butter. Place plastic wrap directly on warm curd (to prevent a film from forming); chill 8 hours. Serve with hot biscuits, Strawberry-Lemonade Muffins, or use as a filling for tart shells.

Strawberry Salsa

good for you • make-ahead • party perfect

MAKES: about 2½ cups
HANDS-ON TIME: 15 min.
TOTAL TIME: 1 hr., 15 min.
(Pictured on page 173)

1. Whisk together ½ cup red pepper jelly; ⅓ cup each chopped fresh chives and cilantro; 1 Tbsp. lime zest; ¼ cup fresh lime juice; and ¼ tsp. dried crushed red pepper in a medium bowl. Stir in 2 cups chopped fresh strawberries and ⅓ cup sweetened dried cranberries; cover and chill 1 hour. Stir in 1 small avocado, diced, just before serving. Serve with grilled or pan-fried meats, poultry, or seafood.

Spring Garden Strawberry Salad

quick prep • good for you • party perfect

MAKES: 6 servings
HANDS-ON TIME: 30 min.
TOTAL TIME: 40 min.

- 1½ **cups trimmed fresh sugar snap peas (about 5 oz.)**
- 1 **(4-oz.) package baby arugula**
- 2 **cups sliced fresh strawberries**
- 1 **cup seeded and chopped English cucumber**
- ¾ **cup frozen baby English peas, thawed**
- 4 **oz. Gorgonzola cheese, crumbled**
- 6 **cooked bacon slices, coarsely chopped**
  Sweet Basil Vinaigrette

1. Arrange sugar snap peas in a steamer basket over boiling water. Cover and steam 1 to 2 minutes or until crisp-tender. Plunge peas into ice water to stop the cooking process; drain. Cut peas diagonally in half.

2. Toss together arugula, next 5 ingredients, and sugar snap peas on a large serving platter. Serve with Sweet Basil Vinaigrette.

Sweet Basil Vinaigrette

quick prep • make-ahead • party perfect

MAKES: 1½ cups
HANDS-ON TIME: 10 min.
TOTAL TIME: 10 min.

- ⅓ **cup red wine vinegar**
- 2 **shallots, chopped**
- 3 **Tbsp. sugar**
- 3 **Tbsp. chopped fresh basil**
- 1 **Tbsp. fresh lemon juice**
- 2 **tsp. Dijon mustard**
- ¾ **tsp. freshly ground pepper**
- ½ **tsp. salt**
- ¾ **cup canola oil**

1. Process first 8 ingredients in a blender until smooth. With blender running, add canola oil in a slow, steady stream, processing until smooth.

Strawberry Caprese Salad and Strawberry Bruschetta

Strawberry Caprese Salad

MAKES: 4 to 6 servings
HANDS-ON TIME: 20 min.
TOTAL TIME: 2 hr., 50 min.
(Also pictured on page 173)

1. Whisk together 3 Tbsp. white balsamic vinegar; 1 small garlic clove, minced; 1 Tbsp. light brown sugar; and ¼ tsp. each salt and freshly ground pepper in a large bowl until sugar is dissolved. Add 3 Tbsp. olive oil in a slow, steady stream, whisking constantly until smooth. Add ⅓ cup chopped fresh basil and 1 (8-oz.) tub fresh small mozzarella cheese balls; toss to coat. Cover and chill 2 hours. Stir in 4 cups halved fresh strawberries; let stand at room temperature 30 minutes, stirring occasionally. Serve over fresh arugula or as an appetizer with toasted French bread baguette slices. Garnish with thinly sliced fresh basil.

Strawberry Bruschetta

quick prep • good for you • party perfect

MAKES: 10 to 12 servings
HANDS-ON TIME: 20 min.
TOTAL TIME: 35 min.
(Also pictured on page 173)

1. Preheat oven to 375°. Stir together 1½ cups sliced fresh strawberries; 1 nectarine, diced; 1 cup quartered grape tomatoes; 3 Tbsp. thinly sliced fresh basil; 1 shallot, minced; 2 Tbsp. olive oil; 1 Tbsp. balsamic vinegar; 1 tsp. each sugar and freshly ground pepper; and ¼ tsp. salt.

2. Split 1 (12-oz.) French bread baguette in half; cut each half crosswise into 4 equal pieces. Spread cut sides of bread with 1 (10.5-oz.) goat cheese log, softened. Place bread pieces on a baking sheet, and bake 13 to 15 minutes or until thoroughly heated. Remove from oven, and top with strawberry mixture. Cut into 2-inch slices.

The Local Flavor Cookbook

Our recipes celebrate the iconic ingredients of the 10 winning cities.

E arlier in 2012, we asked our readers to vote for the best food destinations in the South. Now that a whopping 500,000 votes were cast, we share with you some of our favorite recipes from our 10 winners. Dig in!

LAFAYETTE, LA

Andouille-Stuffed Pork Chops

party perfect

MAKES: 6 servings
HANDS-ON TIME: 40 min.
TOTAL TIME: 1 hr., 15 min.

Spicy stuffed chops are a beloved staple in Cajun delis and meat markets.

- ½ lb. andouille sausage, casings removed
- ½ cup finely chopped onion
- ¼ cup finely chopped celery
- ¼ cup finely chopped green bell pepper
- 3 garlic cloves, minced
- 1 Tbsp. Cajun seasoning, divided
- 2 cups French bread cubes
- ½ cup chicken broth
- 6 (2-inch-thick) bone-in, center-cut pork loin chops
- 2 Tbsp. paprika
- 2 tsp. pepper
- 2 Tbsp. olive oil
  Garnish: fresh thyme

1. Preheat oven to 350°. Cook sausage in a large skillet over medium heat, stirring often, 5 to 6 minutes or until sausage crumbles and is no longer pink. Remove sausage; drain on paper towels, reserving drippings in skillet.
2. Sauté onion and next 3 ingredients in hot drippings 5 minutes or until tender. Remove from heat; stir in sausage and 1 tsp. Cajun seasoning.
3. Stir together sausage mixture, bread cubes, and chicken broth in a large bowl.
4. Cut a lengthwise slit in 1 side of each pork chop to form a pocket, cutting to but not through opposite side. Sprinkle both sides and pocket of each chop with desired amount of salt and pepper. Spoon sausage mixture into each pocket.
5. Stir together paprika, pepper, and remaining 2 tsp. Cajun seasoning; rub over chops.
6. Cook 3 pork chops in 1 Tbsp. hot olive oil in a large skillet over medium-high heat 1 to 2 minutes on each side or until golden. Place pork chops in a lightly greased roasting pan or large shallow baking dish. Repeat with remaining pork chops and olive oil.
7. Bake at 350° for 30 to 40 minutes or until done. Let stand 10 minutes before serving.

CHARLOTTESVILLE, VA

"Jefferson" Virginia Ham Pasta

quick prep • party perfect

MAKES: 6 to 8 servings
HANDS-ON TIME: 30 min.
TOTAL TIME: 30 min.

Our nod to the Virginia wine country and Thomas Jefferson's love of pasta.

- 2 (8.8-oz.) packages strozzapreti pasta
- ¼ lb. country ham, cut into ⅛-inch-thick strips (about ¾ cup)
- 2 Tbsp. olive oil
- 3 shallots, thinly sliced
- 8 oz. assorted wild mushrooms, sliced
- 1 garlic clove, thinly sliced
- 1 cup Viognier or dry white wine
- ½ cup frozen sweet peas
- ⅓ cup coarsely chopped fresh flat-leaf parsley
- ¼ cup heavy cream
- 3 Tbsp. butter
- ¼ tsp. pepper
- 1 cup freshly grated pecorino Romano cheese

1. Prepare pasta according to package directions.
2. Meanwhile, sauté ham in hot oil in a large skillet over medium heat 2 minutes or until lightly browned and crisp. Add shallots; sauté 1 minute. Add mushrooms and garlic, and cook, stirring often, 2 minutes or until mushrooms are tender. Stir in wine, and cook 5 minutes or until reduced by half.
3. Add peas, next 4 ingredients, and ½ cup cheese, stirring until cheese begins to melt and cream begins to thicken. Stir in hot cooked pasta, and toss until coated. Serve immediately with remaining ½ cup cheese.
NOTE: We tested with Jefferson Vineyards Viognier.

INSPIRED BY, AMONG OTHERS, DEAN MAUPIN
EXECUTIVE CHEF, KESWICK HALL AT MONTICELLO

CHARLESTON, SC

Hoppin' John Hush Puppies

quick prep • party perfect

MAKES: about 2 dozen
HANDS-ON TIME: 40 min.
TOTAL TIME: 55 min., including relish

A Lowcountry classic is transformed into a crispy, satisfying fritter.

Peanut oil
1 (15-oz.) can seasoned field peas
and snaps, drained and rinsed
(about 1 cup)*
1 cup yellow self-rising cornmeal
mix
¾ cup buttermilk
½ cup all-purpose flour
½ cup chopped country ham
½ cup cooked long-grain rice
½ cup sliced green onions, light
green parts only
1 jalapeño pepper, seeded and diced
2 garlic cloves, pressed
1 tsp. baking powder
1 tsp. freshly ground pepper
2 large eggs, lightly beaten
Tomato-Corn Relish

1. Pour oil to depth of 3 inches into a large, heavy skillet or Dutch oven; heat over medium-high heat to 350°.
2. Meanwhile, stir together field peas and next 11 ingredients in a large bowl.
3. Scoop pea mixture by rounded tablespoonfuls, in batches, and drop into hot oil. Fry 3 to 4 minutes or until hush puppies are golden brown. Drain on paper towels; keep warm. Serve with relish.
*1 (15.5-oz.) can seasoned black-eyed peas may be substituted.

Tomato-Corn Relish

quick prep • make-ahead • party perfect

1 thick bacon slice
1 cup fresh corn kernels (about 1 ear)
1 garlic clove, pressed
1 (8-oz.) jar green tomato relish
2 tsp. hot sauce
¼ tsp. salt

1. Cook bacon in a medium skillet over medium-high heat 3 minutes or until crisp; remove bacon, and drain on paper towels, reserving 1 Tbsp. drippings in skillet. Crumble bacon.
2. Sauté corn and garlic in hot drippings 3 minutes or until tender. Stir in tomato relish, next 2 ingredients, and bacon. Serve immediately.

BIRMINGHAM, AL

Highlands Baked Grits

party perfect

MAKES: 4 servings
HANDS-ON TIME: 40 min.
TOTAL TIME: 1 hr., 55 min.

Look no further for the most decadent grits around.

GRITS

1 tsp. kosher salt
1 cup uncooked yellow stone-ground
grits
2 Tbsp. unsalted butter,
at room temperature
¼ cup finely grated
Parmigiano-Reggiano cheese
1 large egg, beaten

SAUCE

½ cup dry white wine
¼ cup sherry vinegar
1 oz. country ham, diced
2 shallots, minced
1 bay leaf
1 tsp. dried crushed red pepper
1 Tbsp. heavy cream
½ cup unsalted butter, cut into cubes
2 Tbsp. finely grated
Parmigiano-Reggiano cheese
1 Tbsp. fresh lemon juice
Hot sauce

MUSHROOM TOPPING

½ cup assorted fresh mushrooms,
cut into 1- to 2-inch pieces
2 oz. country ham, cut into thin
strips
1 shallot, minced
1 Tbsp. olive oil

1. Prepare Grits: Bring salt and 4 cups water to a boil in a large heavy saucepan over medium heat. Gradually stir in grits. Bring to a boil; reduce heat to medium-low, and cook, stirring often, 45 minutes to 1 hour or until grits are thick. Remove from heat, and stir in 2 Tbsp. butter, ¼ cup cheese, and freshly ground white pepper to taste. Stir in egg until blended.
2. Preheat oven to 375°. Divide grits among 4 (4- to 6-oz.) buttered ramekins; place ramekins in a 13- x 9-inch pan, and add hot water to pan halfway up sides of ramekins. Cover pan with aluminum foil.
3. Bake at 375° for 15 minutes. Uncover and bake 20 minutes or until tops begin to brown.
4. Meanwhile, prepare Sauce: Combine wine and next 5 ingredients in a medium saucepan, and bring to a boil over medium heat. Cook, stirring often, 5 to 7 minutes or until liquid is reduced to 1 Tbsp. Reduce heat to low; stir in cream. Gradually whisk in cubed butter, 1 cube at a time, whisking until blended after each addition. Remove from heat.
5. Pour mixture through a wire-mesh strainer into a small saucepan. Stir in cheese and lemon juice. Season with kosher salt, white pepper, and hot sauce to taste. Keep warm.
6. Prepare Mushroom Topping: Sauté mushrooms and next 2 ingredients in hot oil 3 to 4 minutes or until mushrooms are just tender.
7. Unmold grits onto serving plates, and serve with sauce and mushroom topping.

FRANK STITT,
FRANK STITT'S SOUTHERN TABLE
BIRMINGHAM, ALABAMA

BALTIMORE, MD

Fried Soft-Shell Crabs Benedict

quick prep • party perfect

MAKES: 6 servings
HANDS-ON TIME: 30 min.
TOTAL TIME: 40 min.

Pass the Bloody Marys: This Chesapeake staple now stars for brunch.

Vegetable oil
1 (12-oz.) can evaporated milk
7 large eggs
6 soft-shell crabs
1½ tsp. seasoned salt
1½ cups self-rising flour
6 (¾-inch-thick) French bread loaf slices
2 Tbsp. butter, melted
1 (0.9-oz.) envelope hollandaise sauce mix
1 cup milk
1 Tbsp. lemon juice
½ tsp. white vinegar
2 cups loosely packed baby arugula
2 Tbsp. chopped fresh chives

1. Pour oil to depth of 3 inches into a Dutch oven; heat to 360°. Whisk together evaporated milk, 1 egg, and ¼ cup water in a large bowl.

2. Rinse crabs, pat dry, and sprinkle with seasoned salt. Dredge crabs in flour; dip in evaporated milk mixture, and dredge in flour again. Fry crabs, in 2 batches, in hot oil 2 minutes on each side or until golden brown. Drain on a wire rack over paper towels. Keep warm.

3. Preheat oven to 375°. Brush 1 side of each bread slice with butter. Bake bread slices, buttered sides up, 5 minutes or until toasted.

4. Prepare hollandaise sauce mix according to package directions, omitting butter and using 1 cup milk and 1 Tbsp. lemon juice.

5. Pour water to depth of 2 inches into a large saucepan. Bring to a boil; reduce heat, and maintain at a light simmer. Add vinegar. Break remaining 6 eggs, and slip into water, 1 at a time, as close as possible to surface. Simmer 3 to 5 minutes or to desired degree of doneness. Remove with a slotted spoon. Trim edges, if desired.

6. Top bread slices with arugula, fried crabs, poached eggs, and hollandaise sauce. Sprinkle with chives and salt and pepper to taste.

LOUISVILLE, KY

Kentucky Bibb Lettuce Salad with Bourbon Vinaigrette

party perfect

MAKES: 8 servings
HANDS-ON TIME: 30 min.
TOTAL TIME: 1 hr., 20 min., including vinaigrette and cakes

Tender Bibb lettuce comes from Kentucky. Dress it up with bourbon-infused vinaigrette, and serve with Country Ham Corn Cakes.

1½ cups pecan halves and pieces
2 Tbsp. butter, melted
3 Tbsp. light brown sugar
⅛ tsp. ground red pepper
6 bacon slices, cooked and crumbled
8 cups torn Bibb lettuce (2 to 3 medium heads)
4 cups trimmed watercress
4 large peaches, peeled and sliced
1 small red onion, halved and thinly sliced
4 oz. Gorgonzola cheese, crumbled
   Bourbon Vinaigrette
   Country Ham Corn Cakes

1. Preheat oven to 350°. Toss pecans in butter. Stir together brown sugar and red pepper in a bowl; add pecans, tossing to coat. Spread pecans in a single layer in a lightly greased aluminum foil-lined shallow pan. Bake 10 to 12 minutes or until lightly browned, toasted, and fragrant. Remove from oven, and toss pecans with crumbled bacon. Cool in pan on a wire rack 20 minutes; separate pecans with a fork.

2. Combine Bibb lettuce, next 3 ingredients, and pecan mixture in a large bowl. Top with crumbled cheese. Serve with Bourbon Vinaigrette and Country Ham Corn Cakes.

Bourbon Vinaigrette

quick prep • make-ahead • party perfect

1. Whisk together ⅓ cup apple cider vinegar, 1 Tbsp. light brown sugar, 3 Tbsp. bourbon, 2 tsp. Dijon mustard, ¾ tsp. salt, and ½ tsp. freshly ground pepper in a medium bowl. Add ⅔ cup canola oil in a slow, steady stream, whisking constantly until smooth.

Country Ham Corn Cakes

quick prep • party perfect

1. Stir together 1 (6-oz.) package buttermilk cornbread mix and ⅔ cup water in a small bowl until smooth. Stir in ¾ cup fresh corn kernels and ⅓ cup finely chopped country ham. Pour about ¼ cup batter for each corn cake onto a hot, lightly greased griddle or large nonstick skillet. Cook cakes over medium heat 3 to 4 minutes or until tops are covered with bubbles and edges look dry and cooked; turn and cook other side.

HOUSTON, TX

Vietnamese Barbecue Tacos

good for you • party perfect

MAKES: 8 servings
HANDS-ON TIME: 30 min.
TOTAL TIME: 8 hr., 50 min., including sauce

Houston's vibrant Vietnamese flavors are served Tex-Mex style.

- 3 beef strip steaks (about 2½ lb.)
- ¼ cup fish sauce
- ¼ cup rice wine vinegar
- 2 Tbsp. grated fresh ginger
- 3 garlic cloves, minced
- 2 Tbsp. sugar
- 2 Tbsp. honey
- 1 Tbsp. sesame oil
- 1 tsp. freshly ground pepper
- ½ medium-size red onion, sliced
- 8 (8-inch) soft taco-size flour tortillas, warmed
  Vietnamese Dipping Sauce
  Toppings: thinly sliced red cabbage, matchstick carrots, thinly sliced red onion, chopped fresh cilantro, chopped fresh mint, cucumber slices

1. Place steaks in a large zip-top plastic freezer bag. Whisk together fish sauce and next 7 ingredients. Stir in red onion, and pour mixture over steaks in freezer bag. Seal and chill 8 to 24 hours, turning once.
2. Preheat grill to 350° to 400° (medium-high) heat. Remove steaks from marinade, discarding marinade.
3. Grill steaks 7 to 8 minutes on each side or to desired degree of doneness, turning every 3 to 5 minutes. Cover loosely with aluminum foil, and let stand 10 minutes.
4. Cut steaks diagonally across the grain into thin strips, and serve in warm flour tortillas with Vietnamese Dipping Sauce and desired toppings.

Vietnamese Dipping Sauce

quick prep • make-ahead • party perfect

1. Stir together ½ cup water; ¼ cup fish sauce; ¼ cup white vinegar; 3 Tbsp. sugar; 2 Tbsp. fresh lime juice; 2 garlic cloves, minced; and 1 sliced and seeded serrano pepper or Thai chile pepper in a medium bowl. Store in an airtight container in refrigerator up to 1 week.

RALEIGH, NC

Fried Chicken Thighs & Biscuits

party perfect

MAKES: 8 servings
HANDS-ON TIME: 40 min.
TOTAL TIME: 1 hr., 5 min.

Two Southern icons make the ultimate sandwich, generously topped with pickled green tomatoes and local Raleigh honey. (Pictured on page 3)

FRIED CHICKEN THIGHS

- 8 skinned and boned chicken thighs (about 2¼ lb.)
- 1 tsp. salt
- ½ tsp. pepper
- ⅛ tsp. onion powder
- 1 cup buttermilk
- 1 large egg
  Vegetable oil
- 2 cups all-purpose flour

BISCUITS

- 2 cups bread flour
- 2 cups all-purpose flour
- 2 Tbsp. baking powder
- 2 Tbsp. sugar
- 1 tsp. salt
- 1 cup butter, cut into small cubes
- 1½ cups buttermilk
- 1 large egg
  Parchment paper

TOPPINGS

  Chopped pickled green tomatoes, local honey

1. Prepare Chicken: Sprinkle chicken thighs with salt and next 2 ingredients. Whisk together 1 cup buttermilk and 1 egg in a large bowl; add chicken, tossing to coat.
2. Pour oil to depth of 1 inch into a large cast-iron skillet; heat to 325°. Place flour in a shallow dish; dredge chicken in flour, shaking off excess. Fry chicken, in 2 batches, 5 to 6 minutes on each side or until golden brown and done. Drain on a wire rack over paper towels, and keep warm.
3. Prepare Biscuits: Combine bread flour and next 4 ingredients in a large bowl. Place cubed butter in a zip-top plastic freezer bag. Freeze flour mixture and butter separately 10 minutes or until well chilled. Whisk together 1½ cups buttermilk and 1 egg in a small bowl.
4. Cut chilled butter into flour mixture with a pastry blender or fork until crumbly. Add buttermilk mixture, stirring just until dry ingredients are moistened.
5. Preheat oven to 450°. Turn dough out onto a lightly floured surface, and knead lightly 3 to 4 times. Pat or roll dough to 1-inch thickness; cut into 8 squares, and place on a parchment paper-lined baking sheet.
6. Bake at 450° for 15 to 16 minutes or until golden brown. Split biscuits; fill each with 1 cooked chicken thigh and desired toppings.

**INSPIRED BY ASHLEY CHRISTENSEN
BEASLEY'S CHICKEN + HONEY**
RALEIGH, NORTH CAROLINA

DECATUR, GA

Farmers' Market Pizza

good for you • party perfect

MAKES: 6 servings
HANDS-ON TIME: 20 min.
TOTAL TIME: 1 hr., 50 min., including sauce and vegetables

Dekalb Farmers Market, in the Decatur area, inspired the vegetable medley that tops this homemade pizza.

- **Plain white cornmeal**
- 1 **lb. bakery pizza dough**
- ½ to ¾ cup **Quick Tomato Sauce**
- 1 **(8-oz.) package sliced fresh mozzarella cheese**
- ¼ **lb. mild Italian sausage, cooked and crumbled**
- 1½ cups **Farmers' Market Roasted Vegetables**

1. Preheat oven to 500°. Heat a pizza stone or baking sheet in oven 30 minutes.
2. Meanwhile, lightly dust a second baking sheet with cornmeal. Stretch pizza dough into a 12- to 14-inch circle on baking sheet.
3. Spread Quick Tomato Sauce over dough. Top with mozzarella slices and Italian sausage. Arrange Farmers' Market Roasted Vegetables over pizza; season with kosher salt and freshly ground pepper to taste.
4. Slide pizza from baking sheet onto hot pizza stone or baking sheet in oven.
5. Bake at 500° for 15 minutes or until crust is thoroughly cooked, edges are golden, and cheese is melted.

Quick Tomato Sauce

quick prep • good for you
make-ahead • party perfect

1. Stir together 1 (28-oz.) can whole peeled tomatoes with basil, 1½ Tbsp. extra virgin olive oil, and 1 tsp. kosher salt. Process with a handheld blender until smooth. Makes: 3 cups.

Farmers' Market Roasted Vegetables

good for you • make-ahead • party perfect

MAKES: 3 cups
HANDS-ON TIME: 15 min.
TOTAL TIME: 1 hr., 10 min.

These vegetables are delicious on their own. Or, toss with hot cooked pappardelle pasta, cooked Italian sausage, and our Quick Tomato Sauce.

- 1 **medium eggplant, cut into 1-inch pieces**
- 2 **large red bell peppers, cut into 1-inch pieces**
- 1 **fennel bulb, cut into ¼-inch slices**
- 3 **garlic cloves, thinly sliced**
- 3 **Tbsp. extra virgin olive oil**
- 1 **tsp. kosher salt**
- ½ **tsp. freshly ground pepper**
- 2 **Tbsp. chopped fresh basil**
- 1 **Tbsp. white balsamic vinegar**

1. Preheat oven to 450°. Toss together first 7 ingredients in a bowl until coated. Spread eggplant mixture in a single layer in a 15- x 10-inch jelly-roll pan. Bake 45 to 50 minutes or until vegetables are tender and slightly charred, stirring halfway through. Let cool slightly (about 10 minutes). Toss with basil and vinegar. Serve immediately. Store in an airtight container in refrigerator up to 2 days.

NEW ORLEANS, LA

Café Brûlot Bread Pudding

party perfect

MAKES: 10 servings
HANDS-ON TIME: 20 min.
TOTAL TIME: 1 hr., 30 min., including sauce

Two NOLA favorites, coffee and bread pudding, merge into one divine dessert.

- 3 **large eggs**
- 2 **cups milk**
- 1 **cup sugar**
- 1 **cup strong brewed chicory coffee**
- ¼ **cup butter, melted**
- 1 **Tbsp. orange zest**
- ¼ **cup fresh orange juice**
- ¾ **tsp. ground cinnamon**
- ¼ **tsp. salt**
- ⅛ **tsp. ground cloves**
- 1 **(8-oz.) French bread loaf, cut into 1-inch cubes**
  Café Brûlot Sauce

1. Preheat oven to 325°. Whisk together first 10 ingredients in a large bowl. Add bread cubes; cover and chill 10 minutes. Spoon bread into a lightly greased 11- x 7-inch baking dish.
2. Bake at 325° for 1 hour or until set. Serve immediately with Café Brûlot Sauce.

Café Brûlot Sauce

quick prep • party perfect

1. Cook ½ cup butter and ⅓ cup sugar in a heavy saucepan over low heat, stirring constantly, 3 minutes or until smooth. Stir in ¼ cup heavy cream and 1 Tbsp. strong brewed chicory coffee. Cook, stirring constantly, 5 minutes or until thickened. Remove from heat; stir in 1 Tbsp. brandy and 1 tsp. orange zest.

HOSPITALITY

Thrill of the Hunt

Hosting a full-on holiday feast can turn you into a basket case. Instead, opt for this easy-yet-elegant gathering where adults can graze and relax as kids enjoy the fun.

"My son is an only child—an only cousin, even—so I couldn't let him hunt alone!" says editor-at-large Kimberly Schlegel Whitman, who started hosting an annual Easter egg hunt at her family's Texas ranch, about 45 minutes north of Dallas, in 2009. These days, 4-year-old J.R. is far from flying solo. In fact, 150 friends and family members now make their way to the ranch every Easter afternoon after carving the requisite ham with their immediate families. "We don't want to interrupt the traditional post-church meal, so we always schedule the hunt for midafternoon," Kimberly says. That way, family rituals remain intact and the menu (think sandwiches and handheld sweets) remains manageable. Here, a few recipes and kid-friendly ideas (a petting zoo!) so that you can also rise to the occasion.

Easter Egg Hunt

SERVES 6

GROWN-UPS:
- Beef-and-Arugula Ciabatta Sandwiches
- Ham-and-Fontina Sourdough Sandwiches
- Roasted Vegetable Salad

YOUNG ONES:
- Hazelnut-Strawberry Sandwiches
- "Rabbit Food" Cups
- Two-Ingredient Chicken Strips

EVERYONE:
- Pineapple-Coconut or Pineapple-Carrot Cake Cupcakes with Buttermilk-Cream Cheese Frosting

---

SANDWICHES & SIDES

Beef-and-Arugula Ciabatta Sandwiches

quick prep • good for you
make-ahead • party perfect

MAKES: 8 servings
HANDS-ON TIME: 10 min.
TOTAL TIME: 25 min.

½ cup mayonnaise
3 Tbsp. red pepper jelly
1 (12-oz.) package frozen individual ciabatta rolls
8 rare deli roast beef slices (about ½ lb.)
8 Havarti cheese slices (about ½ lb.)
2 cups loosely packed arugula

1. Preheat oven to 400°. Whisk together first 2 ingredients.
2. Place rolls on a baking sheet. Bake at 400° for 5 minutes or until lightly toasted but still soft. Let cool 10 minutes; split rolls.
3. Spread cut sides of rolls with mayonnaise mixture. Layer bottom roll halves with beef, folding slices as needed to fit rolls. Top each with cheese, arugula, and remaining roll halves, mayonnaise mixture sides down.

Wrap Beef-and-Arugula Ciabatta Sandwiches with scrapbook paper.

Ham-and-Fontina Sourdough Sandwiches pair nicely with Roasted Vegetable Salad.

Ham-and-Fontina Sourdough Sandwiches

quick prep • good for you • party perfect

MAKES: 4 servings
HANDS-ON TIME: 10 min.
TOTAL TIME: 10 min.

½ cup mayonnaise
3 Tbsp. jarred refrigerated pesto sauce
1 tsp. fresh lemon juice
8 sourdough bakery bread slices
16 Fontina cheese slices (about ½ lb.)
1 large red bell pepper, cut into thin strips
16 thin deli ham slices (about ½ lb.)
12 fresh basil leaves
8 Bibb lettuce leaves

1. Stir together first 3 ingredients.
2. Spread 1 side of each bread slice generously with mayonnaise mixture. Layer cheese, bell pepper strips, ham, basil, and lettuce on half of bread slices. Top with remaining bread slices, mayonnaise mixture sides down. Cut sandwiches in half.

Roasted Vegetable Salad

quick prep • good for you
make-ahead • party perfect

MAKES: 6 servings
HANDS-ON TIME: 20 min.
TOTAL TIME: 1 hr., 23 min.

1 (8-oz.) package assorted sweet mini bell peppers, quartered
2 small zucchini, cut into ½-inch cubes
2 garlic cloves, chopped
2 Tbsp. olive oil
½ tsp. salt
4 cups coarsely chopped napa cabbage
½ cup chopped fresh basil
⅓ cup sesame-ginger dressing
¼ cup chopped fresh flat-leaf parsley

1. Preheat oven to 450°. Stir together first 5 ingredients. Spread in a single layer on a 15- x 10-inch jelly-roll pan.
2. Bake at 450° for 13 to 15 minutes or until just tender and lightly browned. Cool 20 minutes.
3. Combine roasted vegetables, cabbage, and next 3 ingredients. Chill 30 minutes to 4 hours. Stir just before serving.

Three Kid-Friendly Snacks

{1}
HAZELNUT-STRAWBERRY SANDWICHES: Smear hazelnut spread and strawberry jam on white bread. Wrap sandwiches in wax paper to keep them soft. Secure with stickers. Mix in a few creamy peanut butter-and-honey sandwiches, too.

{2}
"RABBIT FOOD" CUPS: Spoon hummus or green goddess dip into small plastic cups. Add thin strips of carrots, celery, and zucchini.

{3}
TWO-INGREDIENT CHICKEN STRIPS: Pump up the flavor of chicken tenders by marinating a few hours in Ranch dressing and grilling. They're so flavorful you don't need to serve a dipping sauce, which could mar those Easter outfits.

Pineapple-Coconut Cupcakes with Buttermilk-Cream Cheese Frosting

make-ahead • party perfect

MAKES: 2 dozen
HANDS-ON TIME: 30 min.
TOTAL TIME: 4 hr., 5 min., including filling and frosting

- 24 **paper baking cups**
  Vegetable cooking spray
- 3 **large eggs**
- 1 **(8-oz.) container sour cream**
- ⅓ **cup buttermilk**
- ⅓ **cup cream of coconut**
- ½ **tsp. vanilla extract**
- 1 **(18.25-oz.) package white cake mix**
  Pineapple Filling
  Buttermilk-Cream Cheese Frosting
  Birds' nests: egg-shaped chocolate-coated malted milk balls; bright green edible paper, cut into strips

1. Preheat oven to 325°. Place baking cups in 2 (12-cup) muffin pans, and lightly coat with cooking spray.

2. Beat eggs at medium speed with an electric mixer 2 minutes. Add sour cream and next 3 ingredients, beating well after each addition. Add cake mix, and beat at low speed just until blended. Spoon batter into prepared cups, filling three-fourths full.

3. Bake at 325° for 25 to 27 minutes or until a wooden pick inserted in center comes out clean. Remove from pans to wire racks, and cool completely (about 45 minutes).

4. Scoop out centers of cupcakes, using a 1-inch melon baller and leaving a ½-inch border around edges. Discard or reserve centers for another use. Spoon a heaping tablespoonful Pineapple Filling into center of each cupcake.

5. Pipe cupcakes with Buttermilk-Cream Cheese Frosting.

NOTE: We tested with Wilton Sugar Sheets Edible Decorating Paper.

Make birds' nests with malted milk balls and edible paper *(wilton.com)*.

Pineapple Filling

make-ahead • party perfect

MAKES: about 2 cups
HANDS-ON TIME: 15 min.
TOTAL TIME: 2 hr., 15 min.

- 2 **(8-oz.) cans crushed pineapple in juice, undrained**
- ¼ **cup sugar**
- 2 **Tbsp. cornstarch**
- 2 **Tbsp. butter**
- ½ **tsp. vanilla extract**

1. Stir together first 3 ingredients in a small saucepan. Cook over medium heat, stirring occasionally, 5 minutes or until a pudding-like thickness.

2. Remove from heat, and stir in butter and vanilla; pour mixture into a bowl. Place heavy-duty plastic wrap directly on warm filling (to prevent a film from forming); chill 2 to 24 hours.

Buttermilk-Cream Cheese Frosting

quick prep • make-ahead • party perfect

MAKES: about 3¼ cups
HANDS-ON TIME: 10 min.
TOTAL TIME: 10 min.

- 1 **(8-oz.) package cream cheese, softened**
- ½ **cup butter, softened**
- 1 **(16-oz.) package powdered sugar, sifted**
- ⅓ **cup buttermilk**
- 1 **tsp. vanilla extract**

1. Beat cream cheese and butter at medium speed with an electric mixer until creamy. Add powdered sugar alternately with buttermilk, beating at low speed until blended after each addition. Add vanilla, beating until blended.

Try This Twist!

PINEAPPLE-CARROT CAKE CUPCAKES WITH BUTTERMILK-CREAM CHEESE FROSTING: Omit buttermilk and cream of coconut. Prepare recipe as directed through Step 2, adding 1 cup finely grated carrots; 1 (8-oz.) can crushed pineapple in juice, well drained; ½ cup finely chopped toasted pecans; ¼ cup vegetable oil; 1 tsp. ground cinnamon; and ½ tsp. ground ginger before adding cake mix, beating well after each addition. Proceed with recipe as directed.

The Fun

{1}

COOL DOWN Let kids and adults help themselves to festive sodas and homemade lemonade (in Mason jars) over ice in a unique "cooler," such as an old horse trough. Try our Coconut Lemonade: Stir together 2 (12-oz.) cans frozen lemonade concentrate, thawed; ½ cup cream of coconut; and 2 lemons, thinly sliced, in a 3-qt. container. Stir in 6 cups water. Cover and chill 1 hour before serving.

{2}

CREATE A COLORING STATION Cover kid-size activity tables with butcher paper and display assorted crayons in colored sand (available at crayola.com). Kimberly even uses the colored sand, which is miraculously stain proof, in sandboxes.

{3}

INVITE FURRY FRIENDS When it comes to kids, a live petting zoo is always a hit. Kimberly's uncle, who lives at the ranch, provides supervised access to chicks and bunnies, but you can search "mobile petting zoo" online to find local hares-for-hire.

{4}

LET THE GAMES BEGIN After a friend reads the Easter story from an illustrated children's book (and signs and dates the book as a keepsake), it's time for the big event. To ensure that the little ones don't get out-hunted, designate, say, green and yellow eggs for those 3 and under. Kimberly, who is clearly all too familiar with Texas weather, advises against filling those eggs with melt-prone candy.

Dinner Over Easy

Break out the eggs for a fast meal anytime.

Fried Egg Sandwiches

Fried Egg Sandwiches

quick prep • good for you

MAKES: 4 servings
HANDS-ON TIME: 25 min.
TOTAL TIME: 27 min.

- 4 (½-inch-thick) challah bread slices
- 2 Tbsp. butter, melted
- 1 (0.9-oz.) envelope hollandaise sauce mix
- ¼ tsp. lemon zest
- 1½ tsp. fresh lemon juice, divided
- 2 cups loosely packed arugula
- ½ cup loosely packed fresh flat-leaf parsley leaves
- ¼ cup thinly sliced red onion
- 3 tsp. extra virgin olive oil, divided
- 4 large eggs
- ¼ tsp. kosher salt
- ¼ tsp. freshly ground pepper
- 12 thin pancetta slices, cooked
- 2 Tbsp. chopped sun-dried tomatoes

1. Preheat broiler with oven rack 5 to 6 inches from heat. Brush both sides of bread with butter; place on an aluminum foil-lined broiler pan. Broil 1 to 2 minutes on each side or until lightly toasted.
2. Prepare hollandaise sauce according to package directions; stir in zest and ½ tsp. lemon juice. Keep warm.
3. Toss together arugula, next 2 ingredients, 2 tsp. olive oil, and remaining 1 tsp. lemon juice.
4. Heat remaining 1 tsp. olive oil in a large nonstick skillet over medium heat. Gently break eggs into hot skillet; sprinkle with salt and pepper. Cook 2 to 3 minutes on each side or to desired degree of doneness.
5. Top bread slices with arugula mixture, pancetta slices, and fried eggs. Spoon hollandaise sauce over each egg, and sprinkle with tomatoes. Serve immediately.

BETTER THAN TAKEOUT

Chicken Fried Rice

quick prep • good for you

MAKES: 6 servings
HANDS-ON TIME: 25 min.
TOTAL TIME: 25 min.

- 3 Tbsp. vegetable oil, divided
- 4 large eggs, lightly beaten
- ¾ cup diced onion
- ¾ cup diced red bell pepper
- 1 lb. haricots verts (tiny green beans), trimmed and cut into 1½-inch pieces (about 2 cups)
- 2 cups chopped cooked chicken
- 4 cups cooked basmati rice
- ⅓ cup soy sauce
- 2 to 3 tsp. Asian chili-garlic sauce Toppings: sliced green onions, chopped toasted almonds

1. Heat 1 Tbsp. oil in a large skillet over medium-high heat 1 minute; add eggs, and cook, gently stirring, 1 to 2 minutes or until softly scrambled. Remove eggs from skillet; chop.

2. Heat remaining 2 Tbsp. oil in skillet; add onion, bell pepper, and green beans, and stir-fry 3 to 4 minutes or until vegetables are crisp-tender. Add chicken, and stir-fry 2 minutes. Add rice, soy sauce, and chili-garlic sauce; stir-fry 3 to 4 minutes or until thoroughly heated. Stir in scrambled eggs; sprinkle with desired toppings.

FRESH & FLAVORFUL

Asparagus Frittata

quick prep • good for you • party perfect

MAKES: 6 servings
HANDS-ON TIME: 30 min.
TOTAL TIME: 30 min.

- 1 lb. fresh thin asparagus
- 2 Tbsp. butter
- 1 small onion, coarsely chopped
- 1 garlic clove, minced
- 12 large eggs
- ½ cup sour cream
- ¾ tsp. freshly ground pepper
- ½ tsp. kosher salt
- 1 cup (4 oz.) shredded Gouda cheese
- ¼ cup freshly grated Parmesan cheese

1. Preheat oven to 350° with oven rack 6 inches from top of heat source. Snap off and discard tough ends of asparagus. Cut asparagus diagonally into 1-inch pieces. Melt butter in a 10-inch ovenproof skillet over medium-high heat; add onion, and sauté 3 to 4 minutes or until onion is tender. Add asparagus; sauté 3 to 4 minutes or until tender. Add garlic, and sauté 1 minute.

2. Whisk together eggs and next 3 ingredients until well blended. Stir in ¾ cup Gouda cheese. Fold egg mixture into vegetable mixture in skillet. Cook, stirring occasionally, 2 to 3 minutes or until almost set. Sprinkle with Parmesan cheese and remaining ¼ cup Gouda cheese.

3. Bake at 350° for 5 minutes or until set. Increase oven temperature to broil, and broil 3 to 4 minutes or until golden brown.

HEARTY, NOT HEAVY

Country Ham Carbonara

quick prep • good for you • party perfect

MAKES: 4 servings
HANDS-ON TIME: 30 min.
TOTAL TIME: 30 min.

- 1 (9-oz.) package refrigerated fettuccine
- ¾ cup chopped country ham
- 2 Tbsp. olive oil
- 2 shallots, thinly sliced
- 2 garlic cloves, pressed
- 2 pasteurized egg yolks
- ½ cup (2 oz.) freshly shredded Parmesan cheese
- 3 Tbsp. chopped fresh chives
- 3 Tbsp. chopped fresh parsley
- ½ tsp. freshly cracked pepper

1. Cook pasta according to package directions; drain, reserving 1½ cups hot pasta water.

2. Cook ham in hot oil in a large skillet over medium-high heat 4 to 5 minutes or until crisp. Remove ham, reserving drippings in skillet. Drain on paper towels.

3. Sauté shallots in hot drippings 3 to 4 minutes or until tender. Stir in garlic; sauté 1 minute. Add reserved pasta water to shallots and garlic; bring to a boil. Stir in hot cooked pasta, and remove from heat. Stir in egg yolks, 1 at a time.

4. Reduce heat to medium, and cook, stirring constantly, 2 to 3 minutes or until creamy. Remove from heat; add cooked ham, Parmesan cheese, and remaining ingredients. Sprinkle with additional Parmesan cheese, if desired. Serve immediately.

Bite-size Southern Favorites

We turned 14 classic dishes into adorable finger foods fit for company.

Cracker Spoons with Creamy Pimiento Cheese

make-ahead • party perfect

MAKES: about 5 dozen
HANDS-ON TIME: 25 min.
TOTAL TIME: 1 hr., 20 min., including pimiento cheese

For less than $2, a super-cute teaspoon-shaped cookie cutter makes down-home pimiento cheese party ready. (Also pictured on page 176)

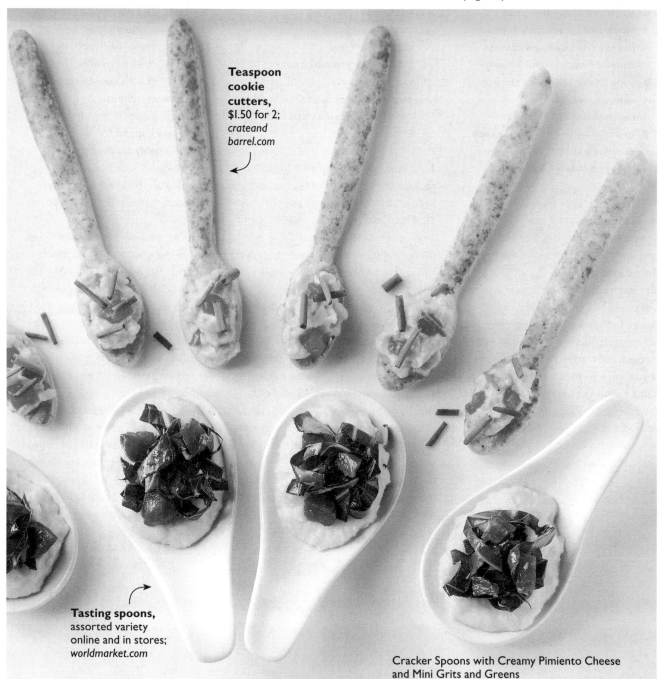

Teaspoon cookie cutters, $1.50 for 2; *crateand barrel.com*

Tasting spoons, assorted variety online and in stores; *worldmarket.com*

Cracker Spoons with Creamy Pimiento Cheese and Mini Grits and Greens

1½ **(14.1-oz.) package refrigerated piecrusts**
1 **egg white, beaten**
¾ **tsp. seasoned salt**
Parchment paper
Creamy Pimiento Cheese
Garnishes: diced pimiento, chopped fresh chives

1. Preheat oven to 400°. Unroll piecrusts; brush with egg white, and sprinkle with seasoned salt (about ¼ tsp. per crust). Cut dough into shapes using a 4½- or 5-inch teaspoon-shaped cutter. Place cutouts 1 inch apart on parchment paper-lined baking sheets.
2. Bake, in batches, at 400° for 9 to 11 minutes or until lightly browned and crisp. Remove from baking sheets to a wire rack, and cool completely (about 20 minutes). Store in an airtight container 1 day, or freeze up to 2 weeks.
3. Spoon Creamy Pimiento Cheese into a zip-top plastic freezer bag. (Do not seal.) Snip 1 corner of bag to make a small hole. Pipe pimiento cheese onto end of each spoon.

Creamy Pimiento Cheese
quick prep • make-ahead • party perfect
1. Beat 1 (10-oz.) block sharp Cheddar cheese, shredded; ½ cup mayonnaise; 1 (4-oz.) jar diced pimiento, drained; 1 tsp. grated onion; 1 tsp. Dijon mustard; ¼ tsp. ground red pepper; and a dash of Worcestershire sauce at medium speed with a heavy-duty electric stand mixer 1 minute or until creamy. Season with salt and pepper to taste. Makes: 1¾ cups. Hands-on time: 10 min., Total time: 10 min.

Mini Grits and Greens
quick prep • party perfect
MAKES: 3 dozen
HANDS-ON TIME: 25 min.
TOTAL TIME: 45 min.

Warm ceramic soup spoons in a 200° oven for 10 minutes before assembling. (Also pictured on page 176)

1 **cup chicken broth**
⅓ **cup half-and-half**
¼ **tsp. salt**
½ **cup uncooked regular grits**
½ **cup (2 oz.) freshly shredded Cheddar cheese**
¼ **cup freshly grated Parmesan cheese**
1 **Tbsp. butter**
½ **tsp. hot sauce**
¼ **tsp. freshly ground pepper**
8 **large fresh collard green leaves**
2 **small dry Spanish chorizo sausage links (about 2¾ oz.)**
1 **Tbsp. olive oil**
2 **tsp. apple cider vinegar**
½ **tsp. sugar**
36 **porcelain tasting spoons, warmed**

1. Bring first 3 ingredients and 1 cup water to a boil in a medium saucepan over high heat; gradually whisk in grits. Cover, reduce heat to medium-low, and simmer, stirring occasionally, 15 minutes or until thickened. Whisk in Cheddar cheese and next 4 ingredients, whisking constantly until cheese melts. Keep warm.
2. Rinse collard greens. Trim and discard thick stems from bottom of collard green leaves (about 2 inches). Stack collard greens on a cutting board. Tightly roll up leaves, and thinly slice into ⅛-inch strips. Quarter chorizo lengthwise, and cut into small pieces.
3. Sauté chorizo in hot oil in a large skillet over medium-high heat 2 minutes. Add collard greens, vinegar, and sugar. Cook, stirring constantly, 2 minutes or until greens are bright green and just tender. Season with salt and pepper to taste.

4. Place about 1 Tbsp. grits onto each warm spoon, and top with collard mixture. Serve immediately.
NOTE: We tested with Quijote Chorizos Caseros Home-Style Dry Sausage.

Fried Green Tomato Sliders
quick prep • make-ahead • party perfect
MAKES: 12 servings
HANDS-ON TIME: 20 min.
TOTAL TIME: 30 min.

Start with fried green tomatoes from your favorite meat 'n' three restaurant. Bake them on a baking sheet at 350° for 5 minutes or until warm and crispy. Add sweet-hot pickle chips to the bun with wooden picks for a fun garnish. (Pictured on page 176)

1½ **cups shredded red cabbage**
1½ **cups shredded napa cabbage**
1 **cup matchstick carrots**
⅓ **cup thinly sliced red onion**
3 **Tbsp. olive oil**
2 **Tbsp. fresh lime juice**
½ **cup chopped fresh cilantro, divided**
½ **cup mayonnaise**
2 **to 3 tsp. Asian sriracha hot chili sauce**
12 **slider buns or dinner rolls, warmed and split**
12 **cooked bacon slices**
12 **fried green tomatoes**

1. Stir together first 6 ingredients and ¼ cup cilantro in a medium bowl. Season with salt and pepper to taste. Let stand 10 minutes.
2. Stir together mayonnaise, sriracha, and remaining ¼ cup cilantro. Spread buns with mayonnaise mixture. Top bottom halves of buns with bacon, tomatoes, and cabbage mixture. Cover with top halves of buns, mayonnaise mixture sides down.

Cornbread Tartlets with Tomato-Lima Bean Relish

quick prep • party perfect

MAKES: 2 dozen
HANDS-ON TIME: 35 min.
TOTAL TIME: 2 hr., 20 min., including relish

Inspired by summery succotash, these petite tarts are buttery and fresh all in one bite.

- ½ **cup butter, softened**
- 4 **oz. cream cheese, softened**
- 1¼ **cups all-purpose flour**
- ½ **cup plain white cornmeal**
- ¼ **tsp. salt**
  Tomato-Lima Bean Relish
  Garnish: crumbled goat cheese

1. Beat butter and cream cheese at medium speed with a heavy-duty electric stand mixer until creamy. Combine flour and next 2 ingredients in a small bowl. Gradually add flour mixture to butter mixture, beating at low speed just until blended. Shape dough into 24 balls, and place dough balls on a baking sheet; cover and chill 1 hour.

Test Kitchen Tip

Baked pastry shells may be made up to 1 month ahead and frozen in an airtight container. Thaw at room temperature before filling.

2. Preheat oven to 400°. Place 1 dough ball into each of 24 greased assorted-shape tartlet tins; press dough into tins and all the way up sides, forming shells.
3. Bake at 400° for 15 to 17 minutes or until edges are golden. Carefully remove pastry shells from tins to wire racks, and cool completely (about 15 minutes). Let stand at room temperature up to 4 hours before filling, if desired.
4. Spoon 1 rounded tablespoonful Tomato-Lima Bean Relish into each pastry shell.

Tomato-Lima Bean Relish

quick prep • good for you
make-ahead • party perfect

1. Stir together 1 cup cooked baby lima beans, ¾ cup sliced grape tomatoes, 3 Tbsp. finely chopped red onion, 2 Tbsp. finely chopped fresh dill, 2 Tbsp. olive oil, 2 tsp. red wine vinegar, and 1 tsp. minced fresh garlic. Season with salt and pepper to taste. Makes: about 2 cups. Hands-on time: 15 min., Total time: 15 min.

Norpro Fancy Tartlet Pans,
$12 for 36; *amazon.com*

Cornbread Tartlets with
Tomato-Lima Bean Relish

Shrimp Boil Skewers

quick prep • good for you
make-ahead • party perfect

MAKES: 24 skewers
HANDS-ON TIME: 30 min.
TOTAL TIME: 1 hr.

*Serve this colorful appetizer in small
cups if you want to skip the skewers.
(Pictured on page 176)*

- 2 **Tbsp. butter**
- ¾ **cup finely chopped red bell**
  pepper
- ½ **cup finely chopped sweet onion**
- 1 **garlic clove, minced**
- 2 **cups fresh corn kernels**
  (about 4 medium ears)
- ½ to ¾ **tsp. Creole seasoning**
- ¼ **cup chopped fresh flat-leaf**
  parsley
- 1 **Tbsp. red wine vinegar**
- ¼ **cup Old Bay seasoning**
- 24 **baby red potatoes (about 1 lb.)**
- ½ **lb. smoked sausage, cut into**
  24 slices
- 24 **peeled and deveined,**
  extra-large raw shrimp
  (16/20 count, about 1¼ lb.)
- 24 **(6-inch) wooden skewers**

1. Melt butter in a medium skillet over
medium heat; add bell pepper and next
2 ingredients, and sauté 4 minutes. Stir
in corn and Creole seasoning, and sauté
3 minutes. Remove from heat, and stir in
parsley and vinegar.
2. Bring Old Bay seasoning and 5 qt.
water to a boil, covered, in a large stockpot. Add potatoes, and cook, uncovered,
10 minutes. Add sausage, and cook 3 minutes. Add shrimp; cook 3 minutes or just
until shrimp turn pink and potatoes are
tender. Drain.
3. Thread 1 potato, 1 shrimp, and 1 sausage
piece onto each skewer. Arrange on serving plates or a long shallow platter. Spoon
corn mixture over skewers.

Mini Berry Cobblers

Mini Berry Cobblers

quick prep • make-ahead • party perfect

MAKES: 12 servings
HANDS-ON TIME: 25 min.
TOTAL TIME: 1 hr.

*Use a mixture of blueberries, raspberries,
blackberries, and strawberries in these
charming individual desserts. (Also pictured
on page 7)*

- 18 **oz. mixed fresh berries (4 cups)**
- ¼ **cup sugar**
- 2 **Tbsp. butter, melted**
- 1 **Tbsp. cornstarch**
- 1½ **cups all-purpose flour**
- ⅓ **cup sugar**
- 3 **Tbsp. minced crystallized ginger**
- 2 **tsp. baking powder**
- ½ **tsp. salt**
- ⅔ **cup cold butter, cubed**
- ½ **cup buttermilk**
  Garnish: fresh mint sprigs

1. Preheat oven to 400°. Toss together
first 4 ingredients in a medium bowl.
2. Whisk together flour and next 4 ingredients in a large bowl. Cut cold butter
into flour mixture with a pastry blender
or fork until crumbly. Add buttermilk,
stirring just until dry ingredients are
moistened. Turn dough out onto a lightly
floured surface, and knead 3 to 4 times.
Pat into a 6- x 4-inch (1-inch-thick) rectangle. Cut into 6 squares; cut squares
diagonally into 12 triangles.
3. Arrange 12 (3½-inch) lightly greased
miniature cast-iron skillets on an aluminum
foil-lined baking sheet. Divide berry
mixture among skillets. Place 1 dough
triangle over berry mixture in each skillet.
4. Bake at 400° for 20 to 24 minutes or
until fruit bubbles and crust is golden
brown. Cool 15 minutes before serving.
Serve warm or at room temperature.

Mini More Options!

Six more bite-size versions of our favorite Southern foods and flavors, including the classiest gelatin shot known to man.

{1}

ANDOUILLE MINI DOGS
quick prep • make-ahead • party perfect

We tested with Aidells Cajun-Style Andouille Minis and Hillshire Farm Lit'l Smokies.

Sauté 1 (12-oz.) package Cajun-style andouille miniature sausages or cocktail-size smoked sausages in 1 Tbsp. hot olive oil over medium heat 5 minutes or until lightly browned and thoroughly heated. Cut slits in tops of 1 (9.25-oz.) package dinner rolls, warmed. Fill each roll with 1 sausage, and top with Creole mustard and sweet pepper relish. Makes: about 25

{2}

CHICKEN SALAD TARTS
quick prep • make-ahead • party perfect

Crisp 1 (1.9-oz.) package frozen mini phyllo pastry shells according to package directions; cool. Spoon ¾ cup store-bought chicken salad into cooled shells. Gently place 1 fresh mango sliver onto chicken salad in each shell, shaping mango sliver to resemble a flower. Place 1 small piece of blackberry and 1 small basil sprig next to each mango slice. Makes: 15 tarts

{3}

MINT JULEP GELÉES
quick prep • make-ahead • party perfect

To make these less strong, increase cold water to 2¼ cups and reduce bourbon to ¾ cup. Sprinkle 2 envelopes unflavored gelatin over 2 cups cold water in a medium saucepan. Let stand 5 minutes. Add ½ cup firmly packed fresh mint leaves and ½ cup sugar. Cook over medium-high heat, stirring often, 3 to 5 minutes or until steaming. Let stand 15 minutes. Remove and discard mint leaves. Stir in 1 cup bourbon. Pour mixture into a lightly greased 9- x 5-inch loaf pan. Chill 4 hours to 1 week. Cut into squares. Garnish with fresh mint sprigs and coarse sparkling sugar. Makes: 18 pieces

{4}

CRAB CAKE HUSH PUPPIES
quick prep • party perfect

Stir together 1 cup self-rising white cornmeal mix, ½ cup self-rising flour, 3 thinly sliced green onions, ½ cup finely chopped red bell pepper, 1 Tbsp. sugar, and ¼ tsp. salt in a large bowl. Stir in 8 oz. fresh lump crabmeat, picked; 1 large egg; and ¾ cup beer until just moistened. Let stand 10 minutes. Pour oil to depth of 2 inches into a Dutch oven; heat to 360°. Drop batter by tablespoonfuls into hot oil, and fry, in batches, 2 to 3 minutes or until golden brown, turning once. Serve with your favorite rémoulade or cocktail sauce. Makes: about 32

{5}

BOILED PEANUT HUMMUS
quick prep • good for you
make-ahead • party perfect

Process 1 cup shelled spicy boiled peanuts, ¼ cup water, 2 Tbsp. chopped fresh cilantro, 2 Tbsp. fresh lime juice, 2 Tbsp. olive oil, 2 Tbsp. creamy peanut butter, 1½ tsp. hot sauce, 1 tsp. minced fresh garlic, and ¼ tsp. ground cumin in a food processor 1 minute or until smooth. Spoon into shot glasses or small bowls, and drizzle with olive oil. Sprinkle with pepper. Serve with carrot or celery sticks. Garnish with fresh cilantro sprigs. Makes: 1½ cups

{6}

STRAWBERRY PRETZEL CROSTINI
quick prep • make-ahead • party perfect

We tested with Keebler Town House Flipsides Original Pretzel Crackers.

Stir together 2 cups finely chopped strawberries, ¼ cup chopped fresh basil, 2 Tbsp. dark brown sugar, 4 tsp. minced shallot, and a pinch of pepper. Spread 1 (3-oz.) package softened cream cheese onto 36 pretzel crackers. Top with strawberry mixture. Makes: 3 dozen

Buttermilk Chicken and Waffles

Buttermilk Chicken and Waffles

make-ahead • party perfect

MAKES: 14 to 16 appetizer servings
HANDS-ON TIME: 50 min.
TOTAL TIME: 1 hr., 5 min., including syrup

Keep waffles warm in a 200° oven up to 30 minutes before assembling. (Also pictured on page 177)

1½ cups all-purpose flour
 1 Tbsp. sugar
1½ tsp. baking powder
 ¾ tsp. baking soda
 ¾ tsp. salt
1¾ cups buttermilk
 ⅓ cup butter, melted
 2 large eggs
12 to 16 fried chicken breast tenders, cut into bite-size pieces
    Peach-Horseradish Maple Syrup
    Garnish: thinly sliced green onions

1. Stir together first 5 ingredients in a large bowl. Whisk together buttermilk and next 2 ingredients in a small bowl; stir buttermilk mixture into flour mixture just until combined.
2. Cook batter in a preheated, oiled mini-style waffle iron 3½ to 4 minutes or until golden (about ½ Tbsp. batter per waffle). Top waffles with chicken, and drizzle with Peach-Horseradish Maple Syrup.
NOTE: We tested with a Sunbeam Mini Waffle Maker. If you don't have a mini waffle iron, use ½ cup batter per waffle in a traditional (10- x 8½-inch) waffle iron, and cook 4 to 5 minutes or until golden; cut each waffle into fourths.

Peach-Horseradish Maple Syrup

quick prep • party perfect

1. Stir together 1 cup maple syrup, ¼ cup peach preserves, 2 tsp. prepared horseradish, ½ tsp. coarsely ground pepper, and ¼ tsp. salt in a small microwave-safe bowl. Microwave at HIGH 30 seconds or until warm. Makes: 1¼ cups. Hands-on time: 5 min., Total time: 5 min.

Hoppin' John Parfaits

quick prep • good for you • party perfect

MAKES: 12 servings
HANDS-ON TIME: 30 min.
TOTAL TIME: 30 min.
(Pictured on page 176)

 1 cup uncooked basmati rice
 3 bacon slices
 1 cup chopped sweet onion
 1 jalapeño pepper, seeded and minced
 2 (15.8-oz.) cans black-eyed peas, drained and rinsed
 1 large tomato, finely chopped
 2 green onions, thinly sliced
 1 celery rib, finely chopped
 ¼ cup chopped fresh parsley
 ¼ cup olive oil
 2 Tbsp. apple cider vinegar
 1 cup (4 oz.) shredded pepper Jack cheese

1. Prepare rice according to package directions.
2. Meanwhile, cook bacon in a medium skillet over medium-high heat 10 to 12 minutes or until crisp. Remove bacon, and drain on paper towels, reserving 1 Tbsp. drippings in skillet. Crumble bacon.
3. Sauté onion and jalapeño pepper in hot drippings 3 to 5 minutes or until lightly browned; stir in black-eyed peas and 1 cup water. Reduce heat to medium, and simmer, stirring occasionally, 5 to 7 minutes or until liquid has almost completely evaporated.
4. Stir together tomato and next 5 ingredients in a small bowl. Layer black-eyed pea mixture, hot cooked rice, and tomato mixture in 12 (7-oz.) glasses. Top with cheese and crumbled bacon.

Party Punches

The communal cocktail is again making a splash at spots like Atlanta's H. Harper Station and Houston's Anvil. But to be clear: We're not talking your grandmother's sherbet-laden concoctions.

The new beverages-by-the-bowlful are fresh and inspired, with just an occasional nod (or wink) to tradition. Try this trio of recipes from LeNell Camacho Santa Ana, the brains behind the booze at Birmingham's Little Donkey restaurant.

TANGY

MEXICAN SANGRÍA
quick prep • party perfect

If you order sangría below the border, you may be surprised to find it's not laden with chunks of fruit and lacks the extra liqueur kick usually expected from Spanish sangría. Mexican Sangría is light and refreshing, like a grown-up wine cooler.

Stir together 3 cups sugar and 2½ cups fresh lime juice in a large punch bowl until sugar is dissolved. Stir in 12 cups water, 1 (1-liter) bottle sparkling water, and 1 (750-milliliter) bottle dry red wine. Serve over ice. Garnish with lime and kumquat slices. Makes: about 1½ gal.
NOTE: We tested with Ménage à Trois California Red Wine.

CREAMY

PINEAPPLE-PEACH PUNCH
make-ahead • party perfect

This makes a great virgin punch, too; simply substitute an additional liter of club soda for the vodka.

Whisk together 1 (46-oz.) can pineapple juice, 2 (15-oz.) cans cream of coconut, 1½ cups peach nectar, and 1½ cups apricot nectar in a large pitcher. Divide pineapple mixture among 3 (2-gal.) zip-top plastic freezer bags, placing one-third mixture in each bag. Seal bags, and freeze 2 to 3 hours or until slushy. Remove bags from freezer, and let stand 5 minutes. Pour pineapple mixture into a large punch bowl; stir in 1 (1-liter) bottle chilled vodka, and top with 1 (1-liter) bottle chilled club soda. Makes: 5 qt.

BUBBLY

BERRY BUBBLY PUNCH
make-ahead • party perfect

This recipe is adapted from a Champagne punch found in the first-ever cocktail book published in the United States in 1862, The Bartender's Guide by Jerry Thomas.

Combine ¾ cup raspberry syrup, ¾ cup fresh orange juice, ¾ cup pineapple juice, and ¼ cup fresh lemon juice in a medium bowl, stirring until blended. Cover and chill 2 to 3 hours. Pour mixture into a punch bowl, and top with 2 (750-milliliter) chilled bottles Moscato d'Asti sparkling wine. Garnish with fresh, halved strawberries and blueberries. Makes: 2½ qt.
NOTE: We tested with Ricossa Moscato d'Asti.

May

Toast to the Derby

The most exciting two minutes in sports leaves plenty of time for ham biscuits, bourbon truffles, and flavorful juleps. Hats off to this Millionaires Row-worthy menu.

The Menu

SERVES 12

Roasted Brown-
Butter Pecans with Rosemary

Spring-on-a-Plate Salads

Assorted vegetables
with Whipped
Lemon Aïoli

Fluffy Cream Cheese Biscuits
filled with Ginger Ale-Brown
Sugar Smoked Ham
served with
Figgy Port Chutney and
Blue Cheese Butter

Ginger Ale-Brown Sugar
Smoked Ham

Watercress Canapés

Derby Truffles

Mint Julep Bar

Roasted Brown-Butter Pecans with Rosemary

MAKES: 4 cups
HANDS-ON TIME: 15 min.
TOTAL TIME: 1 hr.

Make two batches of these salty but slightly sweet pecans if you have a large crowd. (Also pictured on page 179)

¼ cup butter
4 cups pecan halves
2 tsp. kosher salt
2 tsp. sugar
1 Tbsp. chopped fresh rosemary
   Garnish: fresh rosemary leaves

1. Preheat oven to 350°. Cook butter in a medium saucepan over medium heat, stirring constantly, 3 to 5 minutes or just until butter begins to turn golden brown. Immediately remove pan from heat, and stir in pecans. Arrange pecans in a single layer on a baking sheet. Sprinkle with salt and sugar.

2. Bake pecans at 350° for 10 to 12 minutes or until toasted and fragrant, stirring halfway through. Sprinkle with rosemary. Bake 2 more minutes. Cool completely on baking sheet (about 30 minutes). Store in an airtight container.

MAKE AHEAD

Store these pecans in an airtight container up to 3 days, or freeze up to 1 month.

Roasted Brown-Butter
Pecans with Rosemary

Spring-on-a-Plate Salads

MAKES: 12 servings
HANDS-ON TIME: 30 min.
TOTAL TIME: 1 hr., 5 min., including vinaigrette

Look for tender, fresh baby greens and micro-greens at your local farmers' market; they should be abundant this time of year. Soaking vegetables in ice water crisps them up. (Pictured on page 179)

- **2 large carrots**
- **1 small fennel bulb**
- **¼ small red onion**
- **1¼ cups shelled edamame (green soybeans), cooked and chilled**
- **1 cup blanched fresh green peas, chilled**
- **Lemon-Dill Vinaigrette, divided**
- **1 lb. fresh lump crabmeat**
- **¼ cup minced red bell pepper**
- **2 tsp. lemon zest**
- **5 cups loosely packed assorted baby salad greens or microgreens**

1. Shave carrots into thin strips using a vegetable peeler. Cut fennel and onion into very thin slices using a mandoline. Place carrots, fennel, and onion in a large bowl; add ice water to cover. Let stand 30 minutes.
2. Combine edamame, peas, 2 Tbsp. Lemon-Dill Vinaigrette, and salt and pepper to taste.
3. Pick crabmeat, removing any bits of shell. Gently toss crab with red bell pepper and lemon zest; season with salt and pepper to taste.
4. Drain carrot mixture well. Divide pea mixture among 12 small plates; top with carrot mixture, salad greens, and crabmeat mixture. Drizzle with remaining Lemon-Dill Vinaigrette just before serving.

Lemon-Dill Vinaigrette

quick prep • make-ahead • party perfect

1. Whisk together ½ cup olive oil, 1½ Tbsp. chopped fresh dill, 2 tsp. lemon zest, ¼ cup fresh lemon juice, 1 tsp. Dijon mustard, and ¼ tsp. sugar. Season with salt and pepper to taste. Serve immediately, or store in an airtight container in refrigerator up to 3 days. Makes: ¾ cup.

Whipped Lemon Aïoli

Whipped Lemon Aïoli

quick prep • make-ahead • party perfect

MAKES: about 2½ cups
HANDS-ON TIME: 10 min.
TOTAL TIME: 10 min.

Indulgent and lightly flavored, this dip is the perfect partner to colorful spring veggies such as green and purple endive; assorted radishes; and blanched, chilled asparagus and haricots verts (tiny green beans). (Also pictured on page 179)

- **1 garlic clove**
- **1 cup mayonnaise**
- **2 tsp. lemon zest**
- **1 Tbsp. lemon juice**
- **¾ cup heavy cream**
- **Assorted vegetables**

1. Finely grate garlic into mayonnaise using a fine grater or zester. Stir in lemon zest and juice.
2. Beat cream at high speed with an electric mixer until medium peaks form. Add mayonnaise mixture, and beat until smooth. Season with salt to taste. Serve immediately with assorted vegetables, or cover and chill up to 1 day.

Fluffy Cream Cheese Biscuits

Ginger Ale-Brown Sugar Smoked Ham

make-ahead • party perfect

MAKES: 16 to 18 appetizer servings
HANDS-ON TIME: 15 min.
TOTAL TIME: 4 hr., 50 min.

Grab a bottle of your favorite spicy (or "hot") ginger ale (such as Blenheim from South Carolina, Buffalo Rock from Alabama, or a spicy Jamaican-style ginger beer) to use in this recipe. (Pictured on page 179)

- 1 (8- to 9-lb.) smoked, ready-to-cook, bone-in ham
- 2 (12-oz.) bottles or cans spicy ginger ale
- ½ cup bourbon
- ¼ cup firmly packed dark brown sugar
- 2 tsp. coarsely ground black pepper
- ½ tsp. kosher salt
- ½ tsp. dry mustard
- ¼ tsp. ground red pepper

1. Preheat oven to 325°. Remove skin from ham, and trim fat to ¼-inch thickness. Make shallow cuts in fat 1 inch apart in a diamond pattern. Place ham, fat side up, in a roasting pan; add ginger ale and bourbon to pan. Cover loosely with foil.

2. Bake, covered, at 325° for 4 to 4½ hours or until a meat thermometer inserted into ham registers 140°, basting with pan juices every 30 minutes.

3. Stir together brown sugar and next 4 ingredients. Remove ham from oven; uncover and sprinkle sugar mixture over ham, lightly pressing mixture into fat.

4. Bake, uncovered, at 325° for 20 to 25 minutes or until crust is browned and a meat thermometer registers 145°. Transfer ham to a cutting board, and let stand 15 minutes before carving.

Fluffy Cream Cheese Biscuits

quick prep • party perfect

MAKES: about 18 biscuits
HANDS-ON TIME: 15 min.
TOTAL TIME: 45 min.

Three leavening ingredients—yeast, baking powder, and baking soda—ensure light biscuits every time. (Also pictured on page 179)

- 1 (¼-oz.) envelope active dry yeast
- ¼ cup warm water (105° to 115°)
- 5 cups all-purpose flour
- 2 Tbsp. sugar
- 1 Tbsp. baking powder
- 1 tsp. baking soda
- 1 tsp. salt
- 1 (8-oz.) package cold cream cheese, cut into pieces
- ½ cup cold butter, cut into pieces
- 1¼ cups buttermilk
  Parchment paper
- 2 Tbsp. butter, melted

1. Preheat oven to 400°. Combine yeast and warm water in a small bowl; let stand 5 minutes.

2. Meanwhile, whisk together flour and next 4 ingredients in a large bowl; cut cream cheese and cold butter into flour mixture with a pastry blender or fork until crumbly.

3. Combine yeast mixture and buttermilk, and add to flour mixture, stirring just until dry ingredients are moistened. Turn dough out onto a lightly floured surface, and knead lightly 6 to 8 times (about 30 seconds to 1 minute), sprinkling with up to ¼ cup additional flour as needed to prevent sticking.

4. Roll dough to ¾-inch thickness. Cut with a 2½-inch round cutter, rerolling scraps once. Arrange biscuits on 2 parchment paper-lined baking sheets.

5. Bake at 400° for 13 to 15 minutes or until golden brown. Brush with melted butter.

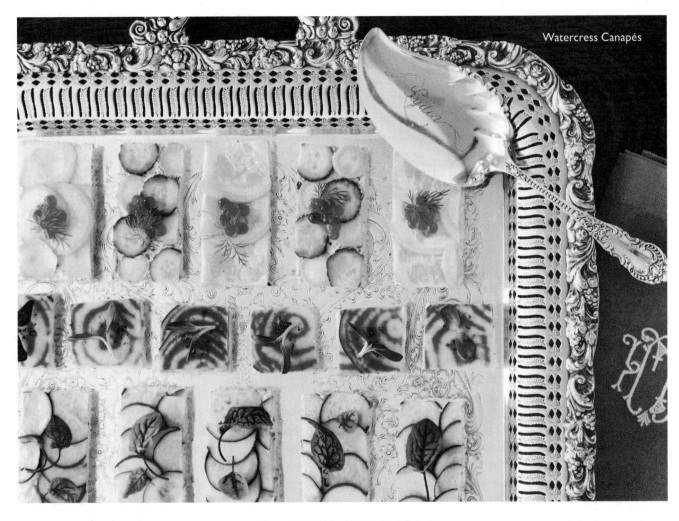

Watercress Canapés

Watercress Canapés

quick prep • make-ahead • party perfect

MAKES: 3 to 6 dozen
HANDS-ON TIME: 40 min.
TOTAL TIME: 40 min.

You can make the cream cheese mixture up to 2 days ahead. (Also pictured on page 178)

1 (8-oz.) package cream cheese, softened
2 Tbsp. sour cream
2 Tbsp. mayonnaise
1 cup lightly packed watercress
¼ cup firmly packed fresh parsley leaves
¼ tsp. salt
¼ tsp. pepper
18 white sandwich bread slices
Assorted vegetable slices and herbs

COLORFUL CANAPÉS

Top with cucumbers, yellow squash, candy-cane beets, salmon caviar, zucchini, herbs, radishes, sprouts, and other fresh finds.

1. Pulse first 3 ingredients in a food processor until smooth. Add watercress and next 3 ingredients; process until finely chopped.

2. Spread 1 Tbsp. cream cheese mixture onto each bread slice. Top with assorted vegetable slices and herbs in a single layer, pressing lightly. Trim crusts from bread. Cut each bread slice into 4 squares or 2 rectangles.

TRY THESE TWISTS:

Goat Cheese Canapés: Omit watercress and parsley. Reduce cream cheese to 4 oz. Add 1 (4-oz.) goat cheese log, softened, with cream cheese and 2 tsp. chopped fresh thyme with salt in Step 1. Top with: candy-cane beets and chives, or sliced squash and salmon caviar.

Bacon-and-Olive Canapés: Omit salt. Substitute ½ cup green olives, chopped, and 6 cooked and crumbled bacon slices for watercress and parsley. Add salt to taste. Top with: sliced grape tomatoes and hard-cooked eggs, or basil leaves, celery, and radishes.

Figgy Port Chutney

make-ahead • party perfect

MAKES: about 1¼ cups
HANDS-ON TIME: 30 min.
TOTAL TIME: 1 hr., 5 min.

Spread leftovers on a grilled cheese sandwich, or spoon over grilled or roasted pork tenderloin.

- 1 **Tbsp. butter**
- 1 **large shallot, finely chopped**
- 1 **cup chopped dried Mission figs**
- ½ **cup port**
- ¼ **cup honey**
- 2 **Tbsp. apple cider vinegar**
- ¼ **tsp. freshly ground pepper**
- ⅛ **tsp. salt**
- ½ **cup fig preserves**
- 2 **tsp. chopped fresh thyme**

1. Melt butter in a saucepan over medium heat; add shallot, and sauté 3 to 5 minutes or until tender. Stir in figs and next 5 ingredients. Bring to a boil; reduce heat to low, and simmer, stirring occasionally, 15 minutes or until liquid is almost completely absorbed. Remove from heat, and stir in preserves and thyme. Cool 30 minutes. Serve immediately, or store in an airtight container in refrigerator up to 1 week. (If chilled, let stand 30 minutes before serving.)

Blue Cheese Butter

quick prep • make-ahead • party perfect

MAKES: 1 cup
HANDS-ON TIME: 10 min.
TOTAL TIME: 10 min.

- 1 **(5-oz.) wedge soft ripened blue cheese, rind removed**
- ½ **cup butter**
- 1 **green onion, minced**
- 2 **Tbsp. chopped fresh parsley**
- 1 **tsp. Dijon mustard**
- ¼ **tsp. freshly ground pepper**

1. Let cheese and butter come to room temperature. Stir together cheese, butter, and remaining ingredients with a fork until thoroughly blended. Serve immediately. Store in refrigerator up to 1 week.

> Get ideas for Derby party games, hats, decorations, and more: *southernliving.com/derby*

What a Kentucky Bourbon Aficionado Drinks on Race Day

Julian Van Winkle, president of the legendary Old Rip Van Winkle Distillery in Frankfort, shares his go-to cocktail.

JULIAN'S OLD FASHIONED: Place 1 to 2 brown sugar cubes on a cocktail napkin. Sprinkle 2 to 3 drops orange bitters and 2 to 3 drops Angostura bitters over sugar cubes. (Napkin will soak up excess bitters.) Transfer cubes to a 10-oz. old-fashioned glass. Add 1 fresh orange slice and a few drops bourbon to glass. Mash sugar cubes and orange slice, using a muddler, until sugar is almost dissolved. (Avoid mashing the rind; doing so will release a bitter flavor.) Add 1½ to 2 oz. bourbon, and fill glass with ice cubes. Stir until well chilled. Add more bourbon, if desired.

Julian's Old Fashioned

SERVING IDEA

Display Derby Truffles with bakery macaroons and/or sugar cookies on tiered stands.

Derby Truffles

make-ahead • party perfect

MAKES: about 3 dozen
HANDS-ON TIME: 35 min.
TOTAL TIME: 4 hr., 35 min.

These make-ahead gems are easy enough for casual get-togethers and fancy enough for special occasions.

- **3 (4-oz.) bittersweet chocolate baking bars, chopped**
- **1½ Tbsp. cold butter, cubed**
- **2 tsp. vanilla extract**
- **9 Tbsp. heavy cream**
- **¼ cup bourbon**
- **1 (5.3-oz.) package pure butter shortbread cookies, crushed**
- **2 cups finely chopped roasted, salted pecans**
  Wax paper

1. Combine first 3 ingredients in a large glass bowl. Cook cream and bourbon in a small saucepan over medium heat 3 to 4 minutes or until mixture is hot but not boiling. (Mixture will steam, and bubbles will form around edge of pan.) Pour cream mixture over chocolate. Let stand 1 minute.
2. Stir chocolate mixture until melted and smooth. (If mixture doesn't melt completely, microwave at HIGH 30 seconds.) Stir in crushed cookies. Cover and chill 3 hours or until firm. (Mixture can be prepared and chilled up to 2 days ahead.)
3. Shape mixture into 1-inch balls (about 2 tsp. per ball). Roll in chopped pecans. Place on wax paper-lined baking sheets. Chill 1 hour. Store in an airtight container in refrigerator up to 5 days.
NOTE: We tested with Walkers Pure Butter Shortbread.

Derby Truffles

The Ultimate Julep Bar

An assortment of flavored syrups, worthy of your finest pewter.

Derby Julep

party perfect

MAKES: I serving
HANDS-ON TIME: 5 min.
TOTAL TIME: 5 min.
(not including syrup)

- 3 to 5 fresh mint leaves
- 2 Tbsp. desired julep syrup (see right)
  Crushed ice
- ¼ cup bourbon
- I fresh mint sprig

1. Place mint leaves and syrup in a chilled julep cup, and muddle. Pack cup tightly with crushed ice; add bourbon and mint sprig.

TO MUDDLE: Use the back of a spoon to press mint leaves against sides of cups, twisting slightly to release flavors.

I. MINT SYRUP: Boil 1½ cups sugar and 1½ cups water, stirring often, 2 to 3 minutes or until sugar dissolves. Remove from heat; add 15 fresh mint sprigs, and cool completely. Cover and chill 24 hours. Strain syrup; discard solids.

2. GRAPEFRUIT-HONEY SYRUP: Prepare Mint Syrup as directed, reducing sugar to ½ cup and stirring ¾ cup fresh grapefruit juice, ½ cup honey, 3 (2- x 4-inch) grapefruit rind strips, and rind from I lime, cut into strips, into sugar mixture with mint. For julep, muddle with I small grapefruit rind strip.

3. PEACH-BASIL SYRUP: Prepare Mint Syrup as directed, substituting basil for mint and stirring 2 (5.5-oz.) cans peach nectar and I split vanilla bean into sugar mixture with basil. For julep, muddle with I peach slice.

4. BLACKBERRY SYRUP: Prepare Mint Syrup as directed, adding 6 oz. fresh blackberries, halved, with mint. For julep, muddle with 2 fresh blackberries.

5. PINEAPPLE-LEMONGRASS SYRUP: Prepare Mint Syrup as directed, reducing granulated sugar to I cup, adding ½ cup light brown sugar to granulated sugar and water, and stirring I cup pineapple juice, 2 Tbsp. fresh lime juice, and 3 (3-inch) pieces fresh lemongrass into sugar mixture with mint after removing from heat. For julep, muddle with I small fresh pineapple chunk.

Sip the New Coke-tail

The American classic cola is embraced throughout the nation as the unofficial summer thirst quencher. But in Atlanta, where it's produced, bartender **Greg Best** of **Holeman & Finch Public House** (*holeman-finch.com*) is leading the charge to give the mixer an upgrade. We give you: Coke-tails. These are cocktails that creatively use cola as the star ingredient. Greg cooks the soda down into a gastrique (a syrupy reduction) for his Pause that Refreshes, a sparkly summer beverage that's balanced with sorghum—and delivers on its name (see below). At **Hector Santiago**'s tapas bar **Pura Vida** (*puravidatapas.com*), bar chef Paul Calvert showcases cola with Fernet-Branca and house lime shrub (a sweet, tart syrup) in his Cordoba Heights Coke-tail. And hot spot **Victory Sandwich Bar** (*vicsandwich.com*) serves up icy rum-and-cola slushies in Mason jars.

Pause that Refreshes

1. Add 1 Tbsp. Cola Gastrique* and 2 dashes of orange bitters to a Champagne flute or coupe glass. Top with 5 to 6 oz. sparkling wine. Garnish with a lemon rind curl.

*Cola Gastrique

1. Combine 3 cups cola soft drink, 3 cups apple cider vinegar, and 1 cup sorghum in a 4-qt. saucepan, and bring to a light boil over medium heat. Cook, stirring occasionally, 1 hour to 1 hour and 10 minutes or until mixture coats a metal spoon and runs off in a fluid stream. (Mixture should be reduced by two-thirds.) Remove from heat, and cool completely (about 1 hour). Store in an airtight container in refrigerator up to 2 weeks.

Try a Scoop of Pie

Homemade ice cream with four simple ingredients and a tangy citrus twist reinvents the classic Southern icebox pie.

Lemon Icebox Pie Ice Cream
make-ahead • party perfect

MAKES: about 1 qt.
HANDS-ON TIME: 20 min.
TOTAL TIME: 20 min.
(not including freezing)

- 3 **to 4 lemons**
- 2 **cups half-and-half**
- 1 **(14-oz.) can sweetened condensed milk**
- ¾ **cup coarsely crushed graham crackers**

1. Grate zest from lemons to equal 1 Tbsp. Cut lemons in half; squeeze juice from lemons into a measuring cup to equal ½ cup.

2. Whisk together half-and-half, sweetened condensed milk, and lemon juice. Pour mixture into freezer container of a 1½-qt. electric ice-cream maker, and freeze according to manufacturer's instructions. (Instructions and times may vary.) Stir in graham cracker crumbs and lemon zest; transfer to an airtight container. Freeze 2 hours before serving.

Lemon Icebox Pie Ice Cream

ICE CREAM-CONE COOKIES!
Jules Destrooper Butter Waffles; *amazon.com*

Gulf Shrimp, 10 Ways

The next best thing to being at the beach is getting a taste of it.

Why We Love Gulf Shrimp

AMAZING FLAVOR

Whether you choose white, brown, or pink varieties, wild-caught shrimp beat out farm raised every time. Gulf shrimp are sweet and succulent with a briny tang from the sea. Their all-natural diet has no added antibiotics.

GUILT-FREE EATING

All that swimming and plankton-eating builds strong muscles, so shrimp are protein powerhouses with hardly any fat. Six large boiled shrimp (about 3 ounces) contain a mere 100 calories!

HARVESTED BY SOUTHERN HANDS

Buying "local" shrimp is a win-win deal: We enjoy top-flight shellfish while helping shrimpers maintain their livelihood and seafaring lifestyle. It's great for the coastal economy and culture.

Perfect Poached Shrimp

quick prep • good for you
make-ahead • party perfect

Poach (don't boil) for moist, tender-crisp shrimp with loads of flavor.

1. Fill a large bowl halfway with ice and water. Pour 4 qt. water into a Dutch oven; squeeze juice from I lemon, halved, into Dutch oven. Stir in lemon halves, I Tbsp. black peppercorns, 2 bay leaves, and 2 tsp. salt; bring to a boil over medium-high heat. Remove from heat; add 2 lb. unpeeled, large raw shrimp (26/30 count). Cover and let stand 5 minutes or just until shrimp turn pink. Stir shrimp into ice water; let stand 10 minutes. Peel and devein shrimp. Makes: 3 to 4 servings.
TEST KITCHEN TIP: For more ways to use this recipe, see box on next page.

Marinated Shrimp Salad with Avocado

good for you • make-ahead • party perfect
MAKES: 6 servings
HANDS-ON TIME: 30 min.
TOTAL TIME: 5 hr., 10 min., including shrimp and vinaigrette

- I lb. Perfect Poached Shrimp (see recipe, above)
- 4 oranges, sectioned
- I large red bell pepper, thinly sliced
- ½ small red onion, sliced
- ½ cup chopped fresh cilantro
- ¼ cup chopped fresh mint
  Citrus Vinaigrette
- 2 cups chopped romaine lettuce
- 2 medium avocados, cubed

1. Combine first 6 ingredients in a large bowl; pour Citrus Vinaigrette over shrimp mixture, and gently toss to combine. Cover and chill 4 to 24 hours.
2. Place lettuce on a platter. Spoon shrimp mixture over lettuce, reserving vinaigrette. Drizzle with reserved vinaigrette. Top with avocado.

Citrus Vinaigrette

1. Whisk together ¼ cup fresh orange juice, ¼ cup olive oil, I Tbsp. country-style Dijon mustard, I Tbsp. fresh lemon juice, ¼ tsp. salt, and ⅛ tsp. freshly ground pepper. Makes: about ½ cup. Hands-on time: 5 min., Total time: 5 min.

Spicy Coconut Shrimp Soup

quick prep • party perfect
MAKES: 4 to 6 servings
HANDS-ON TIME: 55 min.
TOTAL TIME: 55 min.

- I lb. unpeeled, medium-size raw Gulf shrimp (36/40 count)
- I Tbsp. grated fresh ginger
- 4 garlic cloves, minced
- 2 tsp. olive oil
- 4 cups vegetable broth
- I (13.5-oz.) can unsweetened coconut milk
- 2½ Tbsp. fish sauce
- I Tbsp. light brown sugar
- I Tbsp. fresh lime juice
- 2 tsp. red curry paste
- I (8-oz.) package sliced fresh mushrooms
- I medium-size red bell pepper, chopped
- ¼ cup chopped fresh basil
- ¼ cup chopped fresh cilantro
- ¼ cup sliced green onions
- I Thai chile pepper, seeded and minced (optional)

1. Peel shrimp; devein, if desired.
2. Sauté ginger and garlic in hot oil in a large Dutch oven over medium-high heat I to 2 minutes or until fragrant. Add broth and next 5 ingredients. Bring broth mixture to a boil, and reduce heat to medium. Add mushrooms and bell pepper, and cook, stirring often, 3 to 5 minutes or until crisp-tender. Add shrimp, and cook I to 2 minutes or just until shrimp turn pink. Remove from heat. Add basil, next 2 ingredients, and, if desired, chile pepper.

5 Quick Ways to Use Poached Shrimp

These sure-to-please recipes use our Perfect Poached Shrimp (see recipe, page 114.)

Shrimp in Cucumber Cups

{1}

TEX-MEX MINI SHRIMP COCKTAIL

Place desired amount of guacamole and salsa in 1 small glass. Serve with peeled, skewered Perfect Poached Shrimp and tortilla chips. Makes: 1 serving.

{2}

SHRIMP PIZZA

Preheat oven to 450°. Spread 1 (16-oz.) prebaked Italian pizza crust with ⅓ cup refrigerated light pesto or Alfredo sauce. Top with 10 to 12 peeled Perfect Poached Shrimp, ½ cup coarsely chopped jarred roasted red bell peppers, and ⅓ cup freshly grated Parmesan cheese. Bake 20 minutes or until thoroughly heated. Top with 1 cup loosely packed arugula, shaved Parmesan cheese, and freshly ground pepper. Makes: 4 servings.

{3}

PEACHY SHRIMP CROSTINI

Spread 30 toasted French bread slices with softened goat cheese. Top each with 1 tsp. Ginger-Peach Chutney and 1 peeled Perfect Poached Shrimp. Makes: 30 appetizer servings.

Ginger-Peach Chutney: Peel and halve 3 medium peaches. Toss together peach halves; 1 shallot, halved; and 1 tsp. olive oil. Grill peach halves and shallots over 400° to 500° (high) heat, covered with grill lid, 4 minutes on each side. Remove from grill; cool 10 minutes. Coarsely chop peaches and shallot. Combine with 1 Tbsp. sugar, 2 Tbsp. white wine vinegar, 1 tsp. finely chopped fresh ginger, ⅛ tsp. salt, and ⅛ tsp. dried crushed red pepper. Makes: about 2 cups.

{4}

SHRIMP IN CUCUMBER CUPS

Stir together 1 (8-oz.) package cream cheese, softened; ¼ cup sour cream; 1 Tbsp. fresh dill; 1 Tbsp. chopped fresh chives; 1 Tbsp. fresh lemon juice; and ¼ tsp. salt. Cut 2 English cucumbers into 30 (¾-inch-thick) rounds. Scoop seeds from centers of cucumber rounds, using a melon baller or small spoon and leaving a ¼-inch-thick shell. Fill cucumber cups with cream cheese mixture; top each with 1 peeled Perfect Poached Shrimp. Garnish with fresh dill sprigs. Makes: 30 appetizer servings.

{5}

CREAMY SHRIMP-AND-MACARONI SALAD

Prepare 1 (8-oz.) package elbow macaroni according to package directions; rinse with cold running water. Stir together ½ cup chopped celery, ½ cup chopped green onions, ½ cup plus 3 Tbsp. mayonnaise, ¼ cup chopped fresh parsley, 1 Tbsp. country-style Dijon mustard, 1 Tbsp. chopped fresh tarragon, 2 tsp. white wine vinegar, 1 tsp. sugar, ½ tsp. salt, and ¼ tsp. pepper. Coarsely chop 1 lb. peeled Perfect Poached Shrimp; stir shrimp and mayonnaise mixture into pasta. Cover and chill 1 hour. Makes: 4 servings.

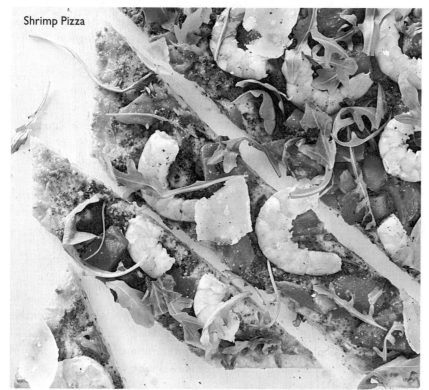

Shrimp Pizza

Grilled Blackened
Shrimp Skewers

Fritto Misto Po'boys
quick prep • party perfect

MAKES: 8 servings
HANDS-ON TIME: 35 min.
TOTAL TIME: 45 min., including coleslaw

Pepperoncini and sliced green tomatoes brighten our take on the Italian "mixed fried" seafood combo. If you have any leftover batter, simply discard it.

- 1½ **lb. unpeeled, large raw Gulf shrimp (26/30 count)**
- 3 **tsp. Creole seasoning, divided**
- 1 **cup jarred pepperoncini salad peppers, stemmed**
- 1 **(8-oz.) package tempura batter mix**
- 1 **cup cold light beer**
- 1 **Tbsp. lemon zest**
- 1 **Tbsp. hot sauce**
  Vegetable oil
  Cajun Coleslaw
- 8 **hoagie rolls, split and toasted**
- 2 **green tomatoes, sliced**

1. Peel shrimp; devein, if desired. Sprinkle with 1 tsp. Creole seasoning.
2. Pat peppers dry with paper towels.
3. Whisk together tempura batter mix, next 3 ingredients, and remaining 2 tsp. Creole seasoning in a large bowl; let stand 5 minutes.
4. Meanwhile, pour oil to depth of 3 inches into a Dutch oven; heat over medium-high heat to 350°.
5. Dip shrimp and peppers into batter. Shake off excess. Fry, in batches, 2 to 3 minutes or until golden. Drain on a wire rack over paper towels.
6. Spoon Cajun Coleslaw onto rolls. Layer with tomato slices, shrimp, and peppers.

Cajun Coleslaw
quick prep • party perfect

1. Stir together 1 cup mayonnaise, ½ cup red pepper jelly, 6 Tbsp. Creole mustard, and ½ tsp. salt in a large bowl. Reserve half of mixture. Add 1 (16-oz.) package coleslaw mix to remaining mayonnaise mixture, stirring until well coated. Serve reserved mayo mixture with po'boys. Makes: 8 servings. Hands-on time: 5 min., Total time: 5 min.

Grilled Blackened Shrimp Skewers
quick prep • good for you • party perfect

MAKES: 4 to 6 servings
HANDS-ON TIME: 25 min.
TOTAL TIME: 30 min., including drizzle

- 36 **unpeeled, large raw Gulf shrimp (about 1 lb., 26/30 count)**
- 1 **tsp. olive oil**
- 2 **tsp. Cajun blackened seasoning**
- 18 **(6-inch) wooden skewers**
- 36 **fresh blackberries**
- 18 **fresh mango slices**
  Mint-Lime Drizzle

1. Preheat grill to 350° to 400° (medium-high) heat. Peel shrimp, leaving tails on; devein, if desired.
2. Place shrimp in a large bowl, and drizzle with olive oil. Sprinkle with seasoning, and toss to coat.
3. Grill shrimp, covered with grill lid, 2 to 3 minutes on each side or just until shrimp turn pink.
4. Thread each skewer with 2 grilled shrimp, 2 blackberries, and 1 mango slice. Brush with Mint-Lime Drizzle, if desired.

Mint-Lime Drizzle:
quick prep • party perfect

1. Stir together 1 Tbsp. chopped fresh mint, 1 Tbsp. fresh lime juice, 1 Tbsp. olive oil, 1 tsp. sugar, and ⅛ tsp. salt. Makes: about ¼ cup.

Lighten Up Your Chicken Salad

The Southern staple gets four colorful makeovers.

Mixed Fruit Chicken Salad

quick prep • good for you • party perfect

MAKES: 7½ cups
HANDS-ON TIME: 30 min.
TOTAL TIME: 45 min., including vinaigrette

- ¼ **cup chopped pecans**
- 4 **cups chopped cooked chicken breasts**
- 2 **cups seedless red and green grapes, halved**
- 2 **celery ribs, chopped**
- 1 **(11-oz.) can mandarin oranges, drained**
- 1 **cup chopped fresh pineapple***
- ¼ **tsp. salt**
  Orange-Raspberry Vinaigrette

1. Preheat oven to 350°. Bake pecans in a single layer in a shallow pan 6 to 7 minutes or until toasted and fragrant, stirring halfway through.

2. Toss together chicken and next 5 ingredients in a large bowl. Add vinaigrette; toss to coat. Sprinkle with pecans, and serve immediately.

*1 (8-oz.) can pineapple tidbits, drained, may be substituted.

PER CUP: CALORIES 231; **FAT** 8.9G (**SAT** 1.5G, **MONO** 5.2G, **POLY** 1.7G); **PROTEIN** 22.5G; **CARB** 15.5G; **FIBER** 1.7G; **CHOL** 58.5MG; **IRON** 1.2MG; **SODIUM** 141MG; **CALC** 30MG

Orange-Raspberry Vinaigrette

quick prep • good for you make-ahead • party perfect

MAKES: 1 cup
HANDS-ON TIME: 10 min.
TOTAL TIME: 10 min.

- ½ **cup orange marmalade**
- ¼ **cup white balsamic-raspberry blush vinegar**
- 1 **medium-size jalapeño pepper, seeded and minced**
- 2 **Tbsp. chopped fresh cilantro**
- 2 **Tbsp. olive oil**

1. Stir together all ingredients.

NOTE: We tested with Alessi White Balsamic Raspberry Blush Vinegar.

PER TBSP.: CALORIES 17; **FAT** 1.8G (**SAT** 0.3G, **MONO** 1.4G, **POLY** 0.2G); **PROTEIN** 0G; **CARB** 0.3G; **FIBER** 0G; **CHOL** 0MG; **IRON** 0MG; **SODIUM** 0MG; **CALC** 0MG

Three More Favorites

SERVE ON:
toasted pita
bread wedges

SERVE ON:
whole grain
flatbread

SERVE ON:
baked
egg roll
wrappers

GREEK CHICKEN SALAD

Combine ½ cup bottled Greek vinaigrette, 1 Tbsp. chopped fresh oregano, and 1 tsp. lemon zest. Add 1 cucumber, halved and thinly sliced; 4 cups chopped cooked chicken breasts; 1 cup grape tomatoes, halved; 1 (16-oz.) can chickpeas, drained and rinsed; 1 (2¼-oz.) can sliced black olives, drained; and ⅓ cup diced red onion. Chill 1 hour. Add ¼ cup crumbled feta cheese.

LEMON-BASIL CHICKEN SALAD

Whisk together 1 Tbsp. chopped fresh basil; 3 Tbsp. olive oil; 2 tsp. Dijon mustard; 1 garlic clove, pressed; ½ tsp. sugar; ½ tsp. lemon zest; ¼ cup lemon juice; and ¼ tsp. salt. Combine 4 cups chopped cooked chicken breasts, 2 cups fresh baby spinach, and ⅓ cup diced sun-dried tomatoes in a large bowl. Drizzle with basil mixture, tossing to coat. Serve immediately.

CURRIED CHICKEN SALAD

Stir together ¾ cup light mayonnaise, 3 Tbsp. chopped fresh cilantro, 2 tsp. cider vinegar, 1 tsp. red curry paste, and ⅛ tsp. salt in a large bowl. Add 4 cups chopped cooked chicken breasts, 2 small grated carrots, and ½ cup golden raisins; toss to coat. Cover and chill 1 to 24 hours. Sprinkle with 2 Tbsp. chopped roasted, salted almonds before serving.

My Spring Onion Pie

Andrea Reusing, chef of Chapel Hill's Lantern restaurant, woos her pint-size dining critics with this elegantly simple dish.

ON THE FARM: Andrea and her children gather fresh eggs at Fickle Creek Farm.

Spring Onion Pie

quick prep • party perfect

MAKES: 6 servings
HANDS-ON TIME: 20 min.
TOTAL TIME: 45 min.

"What my kids eat on any given day is often a mystery, but they will always like anything with eggs and cheese."

10	thin spring onions
4	large eggs, lightly beaten
1	cup milk
¾	cup all-purpose flour
1	tsp. kosher salt
½	tsp. baking powder
¼	tsp. freshly ground pepper
2	Tbsp. butter
5	oz. Gruyère cheese, cubed

1. Preheat oven to 400°. Heat a 10-inch cast-iron skillet in oven. Trim roots from onions; discard roots. Chop half of onions.
2. Whisk together eggs and milk. Sift together flour and next 3 ingredients. Gradually add flour mixture to egg mixture, whisking rapidly 20 to 30 seconds or just until blended and smooth. (There should be no lumps.) Stir in chopped onions. Let stand 5 minutes.
3. Carefully remove hot skillet from oven. Add butter, and let stand until butter is melted. Place skillet over medium-high heat, and pour batter into skillet. Arrange cheese and remaining whole onions over top of batter, and cook 30 seconds to 1 minute or until edges begin to set.
4. Transfer skillet to top oven rack, and bake at 400° for 22 to 25 minutes or until golden brown and puffy. (Outside edges should be crispy, and inside texture should resemble a custard popover. Pie will deflate quickly.) Serve immediately.

PULL UP A CHAIR WITH...

Chef Andrea Reusing

LIVES IN: Chapel Hill, NC

RESTAURANT: Lantern

LATEST ACHIEVEMENT: James Beard Foundation Award's 2011 Best Chef: Southeast

FAVORITE KITCHEN GADGET: Well-seasoned cast-iron pans

FAVORITE SUMMER INGREDIENT: Very ripe tomatoes

FAVORITE SOUTHERN INDULGENCE: Fresh, cold buttermilk

FIRST FOOD JOB: Volunteer candy-striper waitress in a hospital coffee shop when I was 12

FAVORITE PANTRY STAPLE: Really good anchovies

Vidalia Onion & Peach Relish

MAKES: about 10 (8-oz.) jars
HANDS-ON TIME: 1 hr., 10 min.
TOTAL TIME: 1 hr., 40 min.;
plus 24 hours for standing

You will need a canner, jar lifter, and canning rack. Look for a 9- or 12-piece canning kit, which will include all of these pieces and more.

1. Bring canner half-full with water to a boil; simmer. Meanwhile, place 10 (8-oz.) jars in a large stockpot with water to cover; bring to a boil, and simmer. Place bands and lids in a large saucepan with water to cover; bring to a boil, and simmer. Remove hot jars 1 at a time using jar lifter.
2. Bring 2 cups water; 2 cups sugar; 2 cups apple cider vinegar; ¼ cup gin; 2 Tbsp. salt; 1 Tbsp. mustard seeds; 1 tsp. celery salt; ½ tsp. dried crushed red pepper; and 4 bay leaves, crushed, to a boil in a Dutch oven over medium-high heat. Add 3 lb. Vidalia onions, finely chopped; 3 lb. fresh peaches, peeled and chopped; and 4 garlic cloves, thinly sliced; boil, stirring occasionally, 15 minutes.
3. Pour hot mixture into hot jars, filling to ½ inch from top. Remove air bubbles, and wipe jar rims. Cover at once with metal lids, and screw on bands (snug but not too tight). Place jars in canning rack, and place in simmering water in canner. Add additional boiling water as needed to cover by 1 to 2 inches. Bring water to a rolling boil; boil 10 minutes. Turn off heat, and let stand 5 minutes. Remove jars from canner, and let stand at room temperature 24 hours. Test seals of jars by pressing center of each lid. If lids do not pop, jars are properly sealed. Store in a cool, dark place at room temperature up to 1 year.

TRY THIS TWIST!
Vidalia Onion & Peach Refrigerator Relish: Omit Steps 1 and 3. Prepare recipe as directed in Step 2. Let mixture cool completely (about 2 hours). Store in airtight containers in refrigerator up to 2 weeks. Hands-on time: 1 hr., 10 min.; Total time: 1 hr., 35 min.

GET THE LOOK
Decorative craft paper and homemade gift tags add a touch of charm to canned gifts—slip a serving spoon into the twine for extra thoughtfulness.

Just Add Salsa

Brighten up your favorite main dishes with fresh and colorful chopped ingredients.

Greek Salsa Salad with Grouper

IF YOU HAVE
15 MINUTES

Greek Salsa Salad with Grouper: Pick up steamed fish from your grocery seafood counter.

IF YOU HAVE
30 MINUTES

Grilled Chicken and Garden Salsa: Save time by buying pre-chopped veggies. Wrap them in foil, and grill as directed.

IF YOU HAVE
45 MINUTES

Jerk Pork Tenderloin with Blueberry Salsa: Take an extra 5 minutes to blanch fresh green beans for a fast side dish.

MAKE-AHEAD

Suadero Tacos with Serrano-Cilantro Salsa: This delicious flank steak dish is featured in *The Truck Food Cookbook* by John T. Edge.

15 MINUTES
Greek Salsa Salad with Grouper
quick prep • good for you • party perfect

MAKES: 4 servings
HANDS-ON TIME: 15 min.
TOTAL TIME: 15 min.

- 1 (8-oz.) round artisan bread loaf
- 2 Tbsp. butter, melted
- 1 tsp. minced garlic
- 1 (5-oz.) container mixed salad greens with herbs
- 1½ lb. steamed grouper fillets, broken into bite-size pieces
- 2 large tomatoes, quartered
- 1 cucumber, seeded and thinly sliced into half moons
- 1 (8-oz.) container refrigerated chopped assorted bell peppers
- 1 (3-oz.) container refrigerated sliced green onions
- 1 cup refrigerated Greek vinaigrette with feta cheese and garlic

1. Preheat oven to 425°. Cut bread into 1-inch cubes (about 2 cups), and place in a single layer on a jelly-roll pan. Combine butter and garlic; drizzle over bread cubes, and toss to coat. Bake 5 to 7 minutes or until lightly toasted, stirring twice. Transfer bread to a wire rack, and cool completely (about 5 minutes).
2. Arrange salad greens and next 5 ingredients on individual serving plates. Top with bread cubes, and serve with vinaigrette.
NOTE: We tested with Marie's Greek Vinaigrette with Feta Cheese & Garlic.

30 MINUTES
Grilled Chicken and Garden Salsa

quick prep • good for you • party perfect

MAKES: 4 servings
HANDS-ON TIME: 30 min.
TOTAL TIME: 30 min.

- 4 skinned and boned chicken breasts
- ½ tsp. salt
- ½ tsp. freshly ground pepper
- 3 Tbsp. freshly grated Parmesan cheese
- 3 Tbsp. mayonnaise
- 2 tsp. lemon zest
- 1 tsp. fresh lemon juice
- 2 medium zucchini, cut lengthwise into ½-inch-wide strips
- 1 small sweet onion, sliced
- 1 medium-size red bell pepper, quartered
- 2 Tbsp. olive oil
- ½ cup chopped fresh basil

1. Preheat grill to 300° to 350° (medium) heat. Sprinkle chicken with salt and pepper. Combine cheese and next 3 ingredients. Brush chicken with cheese mixture.

2. Toss zucchini, onion, and bell pepper in olive oil.

3. Grill chicken and vegetable mixture at the same time, covered with grill lid. Grill chicken 7 to 10 minutes on each side or until done. Grill vegetable mixture 2 to 3 minutes or until crisp-tender. Chop vegetable mixture, and toss with basil. Add salt and pepper to taste. Serve vegetable mixture with grilled chicken.

45 MINUTES
Jerk Pork Tenderloin with Blueberry Salsa

quick prep • good for you • party perfect

MAKES: 4 servings
HANDS-ON TIME: 20 min.
TOTAL TIME: 45 min.

easy side: *Cook 2 Tbsp. olive oil; 2 Tbsp. balsamic vinegar; 1 garlic clove, pressed; and salt and pepper to taste in a small saucepan over medium-low heat 2 minutes or until bubbly. Toss mixture with 1 lb. haricots verts (tiny green beans), trimmed and blanched.*

- 1 (2-lb.) package pork tenderloins
- 2 Tbsp. olive oil
- 2 Tbsp. Caribbean jerk seasoning
- 2 cups fresh blueberries
- 1 (8-oz.) can pineapple tidbits in juice, drained
- ¼ cup chopped green onions
- ¼ cup chopped fresh basil
- ¼ cup mango chutney
- 2 Tbsp. fresh lime juice
- ½ tsp. salt
- ½ tsp. dried crushed red pepper

1. Preheat grill to 350° to 400° (medium-high) heat. Remove silver skin from tenderloins, leaving a thin layer of fat. Brush pork with olive oil, and sprinkle with jerk seasoning.

2. Grill pork, covered with grill lid, 10 to 12 minutes on each side or until a meat thermometer inserted in thickest portion registers 145°. Remove from grill, and let stand 5 minutes.

3. Meanwhile, coarsely chop 1 cup blueberries. Toss together remaining whole blueberries, chopped berries, and next 7 ingredients. Slice pork, and serve with blueberry salsa.

Grilled Chicken and Garden Salsa

Suadero Tacos with Serrano-Cilantro Salsa

make-ahead • party perfect

MAKES: 6 servings
HANDS-ON TIME: 25 min.
TOTAL TIME: 2 hr., including salsa

- ½ cup fresh lemon juice
- 1 tsp. salt
- 1 tsp. dried Mexican oregano
- 1 tsp. fresh minced garlic
- 1 tsp. freshly ground pepper
- 6 Tbsp. vegetable oil, divided
- 1 (2-lb.) flank steak, diagonally cut into ¼-inch slices
- 12 (6-inch) fajita-size corn tortillas, warmed
- ½ cup chopped white onion
- ½ cup chopped fresh cilantro
  Serrano-Cilantro Salsa
  Lime wedges

1. Whisk together first 5 ingredients and 4 Tbsp. oil; drizzle lemon juice mixture over steak in a large shallow dish or zip-top plastic freezer bag. Cover or seal, and chill 1 to 12 hours. Remove steak from marinade, discarding marinade. Pat steak dry.

2. Heat remaining 2 Tbsp. oil in a 12-inch cast-iron skillet over medium-high heat. Add steak, and cook, stirring occasionally, 5 to 8 minutes or to desired degree of doneness. Transfer steak to a cutting board, and let stand 10 minutes. Chop steak.

3. Spoon steak into warm tortillas; top with chopped onion and cilantro. Serve with Serrano-Cilantro Salsa and lime wedges.

Serrano-Cilantro Salsa

quick prep • party perfect

MAKES: about 1 cup
HANDS-ON TIME: 25 min.
TOTAL TIME: 30 min.

- 10 serrano peppers, stemmed and seeded
- ½ cup diced onion
- 3 garlic cloves, minced
- 1 Tbsp. vegetable oil
- ½ cup chopped fresh cilantro
- 1 tsp. white vinegar
- ½ tsp. salt
- ¼ tsp. ground cumin

1. Cook first 3 ingredients in hot oil in a medium skillet over medium-high heat, stirring occasionally, 10 minutes or until peppers begin to brown and look blistered. Remove from heat, and cool slightly (about 5 minutes).

2. Process pepper mixture, cilantro, next 3 ingredients, and ¾ cup water in a blender until smooth.

Suadero Tacos with Serrano-Cilantro Salsa

The Secret to Deviled Eggs

"Years ago when we were making deviled eggs, she told me, 'If you turn those eggs upside down overnight, those yolks will center. Then when you boil them, they'll be right in the middle.' She was right. It worked."

TRISHA YEARWOOD
GRAMMY WINNER; *NEW YORK TIMES* BEST-SELLING COOKBOOK AUTHOR; AND STAR OF *TRISHA'S SOUTHERN KITCHEN,* HER NEW FOOD NETWORK SHOW; OWASSO, OK

Mama Yearwood's Deviled Eggs

quick prep • make-ahead • party perfect

- 12 large eggs
- ¼ cup mayonnaise
- 1½ Tbsp. sweet pickle relish
- 1 tsp. yellow mustard
  Paprika

1. Place eggs in a single layer in a stainless-steel saucepan. (Do not use nonstick.) Add water to depth of 3 inches. Bring to a rolling boil; cover, remove from heat, and let stand 20 minutes. Drain.

2. Place eggs under cold running water until just cool enough to handle. Tap eggs on the counter until cracks form; peel.

3. Slice eggs in half lengthwise, and carefully remove yolks, keeping egg whites intact. Mash together yolks, mayonnaise, next 2 ingredients, and salt and pepper to taste. Spoon yolk mixture into egg white halves. Serve immediately, or cover and chill 1 hour before serving. Sprinkle with paprika just before serving.

June

Peaches {Summer's First Blush}

We asked cookbook author and Georgia peach Virginia Willis to share her most inspired recipes for the iconic summer fruit. Turns out she was dripping with ideas.

Sweet Peach Pancakes

Sweet Peach Pancakes
party perfect

MAKES: 10 pancakes
HANDS-ON TIME: 1 hr., 5 min.
TOTAL TIME: 1 hr., 5 min.

The sweetness of the peaches combined with the natural sweetness of the cornmeal makes for a delicious morning. A well-seasoned griddle or skillet won't need much butter and oil; use only as much as you need to keep the pancakes from sticking.

¾ cup all-purpose soft-wheat flour
¾ cup plain yellow cornmeal
2 Tbsp. sugar
½ tsp. baking powder
½ tsp. baking soda
½ tsp. salt
1¼ cups buttermilk
2 large eggs
2 Tbsp. unsalted butter, melted
   Butter
   Canola oil
3 medium peaches (about 1¼ lb.), unpeeled and cut into 10 thin wedges each*
   Garnishes: sweetened whipped cream, syrup, fresh mint

1. Sift together first 6 ingredients in a large bowl. Whisk together buttermilk, eggs, and melted butter in a medium bowl. Add buttermilk mixture to flour mixture, and whisk just until combined.
2. Melt a small amount of butter with oil on a griddle or large nonstick skillet over medium heat. Place 3 peach wedges for

VIRGINIA'S TIP

SWEET PEACH PANCAKES
Hosting brunch? For a pretty presentation, place your peach slices in the skillet, then ladle your batter over them as opposed to dicing peaches right into the batter.

each pancake on griddle; starting at outside edge of peach slices, carefully pour ¼ cup batter over each group of slices to form a circle.

3. Cook pancakes 3 to 4 minutes or until tops are covered with bubbles and edges look dry and cooked. Turn and cook other sides 2 to 3 minutes or until golden. Transfer to a baking sheet; keep warm in a 300° oven. Repeat procedure with remaining peach slices and batter, adding more butter and oil to griddle as needed.

NOTE: We tested with White Lily All-Purpose Soft Wheat Flour.

*2 medium peaches, unpeeled and diced, may be substituted. Stir into batter at end of Step I. Cook pancakes as directed, using ¼ cup batter per pancake.

Peach Mojitos

quick prep • party perfect

MAKES: about 8½ cups
HANDS-ON TIME: I5 min.
TOTAL TIME: I5 min.

Enjoy this sparkling cooler all summer long. Use the back of a wooden spoon to muddle the mint.

- 2 **large peaches (about I lb.), unpeeled and chopped**
- ½ **cup superfine sugar**
- ¼ **cup fresh lemon juice (about I lemon)**
- ½ **cup firmly packed fresh mint leaves**
- 4 **cups club soda, chilled**
- 2 **cups white rum**
    Garnishes: fresh mint sprigs, peach wedges

1. Process first 3 ingredients in a blender or food processor until smooth. (Yield should be about 2 cups.)
2. Muddle mint leaves against bottom and sides of a glass pitcher to release flavors. (Leaves will be bruised and torn.) Add club soda, rum, and peach mixture; stir to combine. Serve immediately over ice.

Brown Sugar Pork Chops with Peach Barbecue Sauce

party perfect

MAKES: 4 servings
HANDS-ON TIME: 35 min.
TOTAL TIME: I hr., I0 min.

- ¾ **cup firmly packed dark brown sugar**
- ¼ **cup kosher salt**
- 2 **cups boiling water**
- 3 **cups ice cubes**
- 4 **bone-in pork loin chops (about 2 lb.)**
- I **medium-size sweet onion, finely chopped**
- I **Tbsp. canola oil**
- I **garlic clove, minced**
- I **(I-inch) piece fresh ginger, peeled and grated**
- I½ **cups ketchup**
- ½ **cup peach preserves or jam**
- 2 **large peaches (about I lb.), peeled and cut into ¾-inch chunks**
- 2 **Tbsp. apple cider vinegar**
    Kosher salt and freshly ground pepper to taste
    Garnish: fresh oregano sprigs

1. Combine sugar and salt in a large bowl; add boiling water, stirring until sugar and salt dissolve. Stir in ice cubes to cool mixture. Add pork chops; cover and chill 30 minutes.
2. Meanwhile, sauté onion in hot oil in a medium saucepan over medium heat 2 minutes or until tender. Add garlic and ginger; cook, stirring constantly, 45 to 60 seconds or until fragrant. Add ketchup, peach preserves, and peaches. Reduce heat to low, and simmer, stirring occasionally, 30 minutes or until sauce thickens. Add vinegar; season with kosher salt and freshly ground pepper to taste. Remove from heat.
3. Remove pork from brine, discarding brine. Rinse pork well, and pat dry with paper towels.
4. Preheat grill to 350° to 400° (medium-high) heat. Pour half of peach mixture into a bowl; reserve remaining mixture. Season both sides of pork with desired amount of kosher salt and freshly ground pepper.
5. Grill pork, covered with grill lid, 5 to 6 minutes on each side or until a meat thermometer inserted into thickest portion of each chop registers I45°, basting pork occasionally with peach mixture in bowl. Remove pork from grill; let stand 5 minutes before serving. Serve with reserved peach mixture.

"My peach mojito has a fragrant combination of sun-ripe peaches and crisp, refreshing mint that is certain to stir up summer fun."

VIRGINIA WILLIS

Peach-and-Tomato Gazpacho with Cucumber Yogurt

good for you • make-ahead • party perfect

MAKES: about 5 cups
HANDS-ON TIME: 20 min.
TOTAL TIME: 1 hr., 20 min.

This soup captures summer in a bowl. It's light and refreshing—the perfect balance of sweet peaches and ripe tomatoes.

- 5 large peaches, peeled and divided
- 3 large tomatoes, cored and divided
- ½ medium-size sweet onion, coarsely chopped (about ½ cup)
- 3 Tbsp. apple cider vinegar
  Kosher salt and freshly ground white pepper to taste
- ¾ cup finely diced English cucumber
- ⅓ cup plain Greek yogurt
- 2 Tbsp. chopped fresh chives
- 1 garlic clove, minced
  Extra virgin olive oil
  Garnishes: fresh chive pieces

1. Quarter 4 peaches and 2 tomatoes. Process quartered peaches and tomatoes and next 2 ingredients in a food processor until smooth.
2. Chop remaining peach and tomato. Stir into pureed mixture. Season with kosher salt and freshly ground white pepper to taste. Cover and chill 1 hour.
3. Meanwhile, combine cucumber and next 3 ingredients in a medium bowl. Season with kosher salt and freshly ground white pepper to taste. Cover and chill 1 to 24 hours. (Chilling can dull the seasoning, so you may need to add more salt and pepper before serving.)
4. Ladle gazpacho into bowls. Spoon cucumber mixture over gazpacho. Drizzle each serving with about 1 tsp. extra virgin olive oil. Serve immediately.

VIRGINIA'S TIP

PEACH-AND-TOMATO GAZPACHO: To up the refreshment factor, chill your serving bowls for 30 minutes in the fridge (or 15 in the freezer) before serving.

Crab Salad with Peaches and Avocados

quick prep • good for you • party perfect

MAKES: 6 servings
HANDS-ON TIME: 30 min.
TOTAL TIME: 30 min.

The crab salad can be made ahead, but the avocado and peach layers are best prepared just before serving.

- 1 lb. fresh jumbo lump crabmeat
- 2 Tbsp. lemon zest
- 1 Tbsp. mayonnaise
- ½ tsp. dry mustard
- 5 Tbsp. fresh lemon juice, divided
- ½ jalapeño pepper, seeded and finely diced
- ¼ cup finely diced celery
- 2 green onions, finely chopped
  Kosher salt and freshly ground white pepper to taste
- 5 to 6 medium peaches (about 1¾ lb.), unpeeled and coarsely chopped
- 1 Tbsp. honey
- 3 medium avocados, diced
  Arugula

1. Pick crabmeat, removing any bits of shell. Whisk together lemon zest, next 2 ingredients, and 1 Tbsp. lemon juice. Fold in jalapeño pepper, next 2 ingredients, and crabmeat, using a rubber spatula. Season with kosher salt and freshly ground white pepper to taste.

2. Stir together peaches and remaining 4 Tbsp. lemon juice. Reserve 3 cups peach mixture. Pulse honey and remaining peach mixture in a food processor 8 to 10 times or until smooth. Season pureed peach mixture with kosher salt and freshly ground white pepper to taste.
3. Spoon ¼ cup pureed peach mixture onto a chilled plate. Place a 3½-inch round cutter in center of peach mixture on plate. (A clean, empty tuna can with both ends removed may be used instead.) Spoon one-sixth of diced avocados and ½ cup reserved chopped peach mixture into cutter, packing each layer firmly and sprinkling with kosher salt and freshly ground white pepper to taste. Top with about ½ cup crab mixture. Carefully remove cutter from plate. Repeat procedure with remaining pureed peach mixture, avocado, chopped peach mixture, and crab mixture. Arrange desired amount of arugula around each layered salad; serve immediately.

VIRGINIA'S TIP

CRAB SALAD WITH PEACHES AND AVOCADOS: To get delicate cubes of avocado, cut in half lengthwise (around the pit), and twist to separate. After removing the pit, cut the flesh in a crosshatch fashion and gently scoop out the cubes using a large spoon.

Peach Upside-Down Cake

party perfect

MAKES: 8 to 12 servings
HANDS-ON TIME: 40 min.
TOTAL TIME: 1 hr., 40 min.

Be sure to use cake flour—not self-rising—for this recipe. (Also pictured on page 10)

> Parchment paper
> 4 medium peaches (about 1½ lb.), unpeeled and cut into ⅓-inch-thick wedges
> 2 Tbsp. fresh lemon juice (about 1 large lemon)
> 1 cup cake flour
> ¾ tsp. baking powder
> ¼ tsp. baking soda
> 1¼ cups granulated sugar, divided
> ¾ cup unsalted butter, at room temperature and divided
> ½ cup firmly packed light brown sugar
> 1 vanilla bean
> 2 large eggs
> ½ cup sour cream
> Sweetened whipped cream (optional)

1. Preheat oven to 350°. Line a baking sheet with parchment paper. (This helps with cleanup.) Toss peaches with lemon juice. Sift together flour, baking powder, and baking soda.

2. Cook ½ cup granulated sugar in a 10-inch cast-iron skillet over medium heat, stirring occasionally with a wooden spoon, 10 minutes or until sugar melts and turns a deep amber color. Remove from heat. Immediately add ¼ cup butter, stirring vigorously. Spread caramelized sugar to coat bottom of skillet evenly, and sprinkle with brown sugar. Arrange peach wedges in concentric circles over sugar mixture, overlapping as needed.

3. Split vanilla bean lengthwise, and scrape out seeds into bowl of a heavy-duty electric stand mixer. Beat vanilla seeds and remaining ¾ cup granulated sugar and ½ cup butter at medium speed until smooth. Add eggs, 1 at a time, beating until blended after each addition.

Peach Upside-Down Cake

"Peach Upside-Down Cake will turn your world right side up. Nothing's better than peaches married with tender, moist cake."

VIRGINIA WILLIS

Add sour cream, beating until blended. Gradually add sifted flour mixture, beating at low speed just until blended and stopping to scrape bowl as needed. Spoon batter over peaches in skillet, and spread to cover. Place skillet on prepared baking sheet.

4. Bake at 350° for 40 to 45 minutes or until golden brown and a wooden pick inserted in center comes out clean. Cool in skillet on a wire rack 10 minutes. Run a knife around edge to loosen.

5. Carefully pour out any excess liquid from skillet into a measuring cup, and reserve. (It's okay if you don't have any excess liquid—it all depends on how juicy your fruit is.) Carefully invert cake onto a serving plate, and drizzle with any reserved liquid. Cool slightly (about 10 minutes). Cut cake into wedges using a serrated knife. Top with sweetened whipped cream, if desired, and serve immediately.

Basil-Peach Chicken Breasts

quick prep • good for you • party perfect

MAKES: 4 servings
HANDS-ON TIME: 30 min.
TOTAL TIME: 45 min.

Starting the chicken on the stovetop and finishing in the oven helps prevent dry, overcooked chicken. The flavorful juices make a fresh and clean sauce—much lighter than a flour-thickened gravy. Serve with steamed rice, couscous, or quinoa for a simple summer meal.

4   **skinned and boned chicken breasts (about 2 lb.)**
1¼ **tsp. kosher salt**
½   **tsp. freshly ground pepper**
2   **Tbsp. canola oil**
1   **shallot, thinly sliced**
1   **tsp. freshly grated ginger**
2   **garlic cloves, minced**
12 **fresh basil leaves, finely chopped**
1   **cup reduced-sodium fat-free chicken broth**
4   **large peaches, peeled and cut into ¼-inch-thick slices (about 2 cups)**
    Garnish: fresh basil leaves

1. Preheat oven to 350°. Season chicken on both sides with salt and pepper. Cook chicken in hot oil in a large ovenproof skillet over medium-high heat 2 minutes on each side or until browned. Remove chicken from skillet, reserving drippings in skillet.

2. Reduce heat to medium. Add shallot to hot drippings in skillet, and sauté 3 minutes or until tender. Add ginger and garlic; sauté 45 to 60 seconds or until fragrant. Add basil, chicken broth, and peaches. Return chicken to skillet, and turn to coat.

3. Bake at 350° for 15 minutes or until chicken is done.

Country Ham-and-Peach Panini

Country Ham-and-Peach Panini

quick prep

MAKES: 4 servings
HANDS-ON TIME: 20 min.
TOTAL TIME: 20 min.

It's best to use very thinly sliced ham, not thick ham steaks. Ask your deli to slice it, or look for a packet of center- and end-cut slices, which tend to be smaller.

8   **ciabatta bread slices***
4   **tsp. coarse-grained Dijon mustard**
    Freshly ground pepper
4   **(1-oz.) fontina cheese slices**
4   **oz. thinly sliced country ham, prosciutto, or Serrano ham**
2   **medium peaches (about ¾ lb.), unpeeled and sliced**
4   **tsp. honey (optional)**
1   **Tbsp. extra virgin olive oil**

1. Spread each of 4 bread slices with 1 tsp. mustard, and sprinkle with desired amount of freshly ground pepper. Layer with cheese, ham, peaches, and, if desired, honey. Top with remaining bread slices, and press together gently. Brush sandwiches with olive oil.

2. Cook sandwiches, in batches, in a preheated panini press 3 to 4 minutes or until golden brown and cheese is melted. (Or use a preheated nonstick grill pan, and cook sandwiches over medium heat 3 to 4 minutes on each side.) Serve immediately.

*Any firm white bread may be substituted.

Try a Refreshing Summer Soup

Virginia-based chef Aaron Deal shares the light "salad in a soup" he whips up when he's off the clock.

Salad in a Soup

MAKES: 4 servings
HANDS-ON TIME: 30 min.
TOTAL TIME: 2 hr., 30 min., plus 24 hr. for chilling

- 8 to l0 large heirloom tomatoes (about 4½ lb.), cut into 8 wedges each
  Cheesecloth
- 2 medium tomatoes
- 2 Tbsp. extra virgin olive oil, divided
- ¾ tsp. sea salt, divided
- ¼ tsp. sugar
- 2 small yellow squash, thinly sliced
- ½ English cucumber, diced
- ½ cantaloupe, cut into ½-inch pieces
- l pt. assorted small tomatoes, halved
- l cup halved blueberries
- l tsp. fresh thyme leaves

1. Process heirloom tomatoes in a food processor 30 to 60 seconds or until pureed. Line a colander with 2 layers of cheesecloth; place colander over a large bowl. Pour tomato puree into cheesecloth. Tie ends of cheesecloth together. Chill 24 hours to allow puree to drain.

2. Remove bowl from refrigerator, and gently press cheesecloth using back of a spoon to extract remaining liquid. (Yield should be about 4 cups.) Cover and chill.
3. Preheat oven to 250°. Core medium tomatoes, removing stem ends. Cut tomatoes in half; place, cut sides up, on a lightly greased aluminum foil-lined baking sheet; sprinkle with l Tbsp. olive oil, ¼ tsp. sea salt, and ¼ tsp. sugar. Bake 2 hours.
4. Place l roasted tomato half in each of 4 serving bowls. Top with squash and next 4 ingredients; sprinkle with thyme and ¼ tsp. salt. Add remaining ¼ tsp. salt to tomato water, and divide tomato water among bowls. Drizzle with remaining l Tbsp. olive oil, and serve immediately.

PULL UP A CHAIR WITH...
Chef Aaron Deal

LIVES IN: Roanoke, VA

RESTAURANT: The River and Rail

FAVORITE SOUTHERN INDULGENCE: A secret passion of mine—Duke's mayo on everything

SWEET OR UNSWEET TEA: Sweet tea in a Styrofoam cup with lots of ice and lemon

FAVORITE SOUTHERN INGREDIENT: Smoked ham hocks

SOUTHERN CHEF WHO INSPIRES YOU: My friend Steven Satterfield

MOST MEMORABLE SOUTHERN MEAL: Butter beans, creamed corn, and fried chicken at my grandmother's house

Salad in a Soup

Meet Your New Summer Menu

Trust us: You'll swear by these no-fuss recipes all season long. Pick a meat, toss up a few sides, and let the backyard party begin.

Heirloom Tomato Salad

The Backyard Menu Planner

SERVES 6

PICK A MEAT

Buttermilk-Brined Grilled Chicken

Grilled Molasses Flank Steak with Watermelon Salsa

CHOOSE TWO SIDES

Heirloom Tomato Salad with Lady Pea Salsa

Fresh Herb Potato Salad

Broccoli Slaw with Candied Pecans

Grilled Corn with toppings

Shrimp Rémoulade Deviled Eggs

SIP WITH

Sweet Tea Spritzer (next page)

CAP IT OFF WITH

Icebox pie (page 134)

Heirloom Tomato Salad

good for you • party perfect

MAKES: 8 servings
HANDS-ON TIME: 15 min.
TOTAL TIME: 50 min., including pea salsa

    4 lb. assorted heirloom tomatoes
    2 small Kirby cucumbers, sliced
    I small red onion, halved and sliced
       Lady Pea Salsa
       Fresh basil leaves

1. Cut tomatoes into wedges or in half, depending on size. Gently toss tomatoes with cucumbers and onion. Top with Lady Pea Salsa and basil.

Lady Pea Salsa

quick prep • good for you
make-ahead • party perfect

MAKES: about 4 cups
HANDS-ON TIME: 20 min.
TOTAL TIME: 35 min.

This colorful salsa (and the twist made with watermelon) makes a delicious topping for sliced tomatoes, grilled chicken, or steak.

- 1 **cup diced unpeeled nectarine**
- 2 **jalapeño peppers,**
  seeded and minced
- 1 **Tbsp. sugar**
- 3 **Tbsp. fresh lime juice**
- 2 **tsp. orange zest**
- 2 **tsp. grated fresh ginger**
- 2 **cups cooked fresh lady peas**
- ½ **cup chopped fresh cilantro**
- ⅓ **cup diced red onion**

1. Stir together first 6 ingredients in a large bowl; let stand 15 minutes. Add peas and next 2 ingredients, and gently toss to coat. Serve immediately, or cover and chill up to 24 hours.

TRY THIS TWIST!

Watermelon Salsa: Prepare recipe as directed, substituting 2 cups seeded and diced watermelon for cooked fresh lady peas.

Grilled Molasses Flank Steak with Watermelon Salsa

make-ahead • party perfect

MAKES: 6 to 8 servings
HANDS-ON TIME: 30 min.
TOTAL TIME: 5 hr., 25 min., including salsa

- ¾ **cup molasses**
- ⅓ **cup soy sauce**
- ¼ **cup canola oil**
- ¼ **cup fresh lemon juice**
- 2 **Tbsp. Worcestershire sauce**
- 2 **Tbsp. grated fresh ginger**
- 3 **garlic cloves, minced**
- 1 **tsp. dried crushed red pepper**
- 1 **(2-lb.) flank steak**
  Watermelon Salsa

1. Place first 8 ingredients in a 2-gal. zip-top plastic freezer bag; squeeze bag to combine. Add steak; seal bag, and chill 4 to 12 hours. Remove steak from marinade, discarding marinade.

2. Preheat grill to 400° to 450° (high) heat. Grill steak, covered with grill lid, 9 minutes on each side or to desired degree of doneness. Remove from grill, and let stand 10 minutes. Cut diagonally across the grain into thin slices. Season with salt and pepper to taste. Top with Watermelon Salsa.

COCKTAIL OF THE MONTH
Sweet Tea Spritzer

If iced tea is the house wine of the South, consider this our summer sangría. Stir together 2 cups cranberry juice, 1 cup sweet tea-flavored vodka, and ½ cup fresh lemon juice in a large pitcher. Stir in 5 cups ice cubes, and top with 1 (12-oz.) can lemon-lime soft drink. Gently stir. Serve immediately. Makes: 4 to 6 servings.

Sweet Tea Spritzer

Buttermilk-Brined Grilled Chicken

make-ahead • party perfect

MAKES: 6 servings
HANDS-ON TIME: 20 min.
TOTAL TIME: I hr., 5 min., plus
I day for marinating

- 2 cups buttermilk
- 2 cups cold water
- ¼ cup firmly packed light brown sugar
- ¼ cup hot sauce
- 3 Tbsp. kosher salt
- I Tbsp. freshly cracked pepper
- I small sweet onion, thinly sliced
- I lemon, thinly sliced
- 3 garlic cloves, halved
- I (3½- to 4-lb.) cut-up whole chicken

1. Whisk together first 6 ingredients in a large bowl until sugar is dissolved; stir in onion and next 2 ingredients.

2. Place buttermilk mixture and chicken in a large zip-top plastic freezer bag; seal and chill 24 hours. Remove chicken from marinade, discarding marinade; pat chicken dry with paper towels.

3. Light I side of grill, heating to 300° to 350° (medium) heat. Place chicken, skin side up, over unlit side, and grill, covered with grill lid, 40 to 50 minutes or until a meat thermometer inserted in thickest portion registers 165°. Transfer chicken, skin side down, to lit side of grill, and grill 2 to 3 minutes or until skin is crispy. Let stand 5 minutes before serving.

3 Ways with Grilled Corn

Preheat grill to 350° to 400° (medium-high) heat. Pull back husks from 6 ears fresh corn; remove and discard silks. Tie husks together with kitchen string to form a handle. Soak corn in cold salted water to cover 10 minutes; drain. Grill corn, covered with grill lid, 15 minutes or until golden brown, turning occasionally. Serve with desired toppings. Makes: 6 servings.

{1}

HERBED COTIJA CHEESE: Toss together I cup crumbled Cotija cheese, 2 Tbsp. each chopped fresh cilantro and chives, and I tsp. each chili powder and lime zest. Brush corn with melted butter; sprinkle with Herbed Cotija Cheese. Serve with fresh lime wedges. Makes: 1¼ cups.

{2}

PARMESAN-PESTO BUTTER: Stir together ½ cup butter, softened; ½ cup freshly grated Parmesan cheese; 2 Tbsp. jarred refrigerated pesto sauce; 2 Tbsp. each finely chopped fresh flat-leaf parsley and chives; I garlic clove, pressed; and I tsp. freshly ground pepper in a bowl. Makes: ¾ cup.

{3}

CHIPOTLE BUTTER: Stir together ½ cup butter, softened; 2 Tbsp. each finely chopped fresh cilantro and chives; I Tbsp. finely chopped canned chipotle pepper in adobo sauce; I tsp. lime zest; and I tsp. freshly ground pepper. Makes: ¾ cup.

Broccoli Slaw with
Candied Pecans

Fresh Herb Potato Salad

make-ahead • party perfect

MAKES: 10 to 12 servings
HANDS-ON TIME: 30 min.
TOTAL TIME: 1 hr., 15 min.

- 4 lb. Yukon gold potatoes
- ½ cup diced celery
- ½ cup chopped fresh flat-leaf parsley
- ⅓ cup finely chopped green onions
- 3 hard-cooked eggs, peeled and grated
- 1 cup mayonnaise
- ½ cup sour cream
- 3 Tbsp. chopped fresh tarragon
- 2 garlic cloves, pressed
- 1 Tbsp. Dijon mustard
- 1 tsp. salt
- ¾ tsp. freshly ground pepper

1. Cook potatoes in boiling water to cover 30 to 40 minutes or until tender; drain and cool 15 minutes. Peel potatoes, and cut into 1-inch cubes.
2. Stir together potatoes, celery, and next 3 ingredients in a large bowl.
3. Stir together mayonnaise and next 6 ingredients; gently stir into potato mixture. Serve immediately, or cover and chill up to 12 hours.

Broccoli Slaw with Candied Pecans

MAKES: 6 servings
HANDS-ON TIME: 25 min.
TOTAL TIME: 1 hr., 25 min.
(Also pictured on page 8)

- 1 lb. fresh broccoli
- 1 cup mayonnaise
- ½ cup thinly sliced green onions
- ⅓ cup sugar
- ⅓ cup red wine vinegar
- 1 tsp. salt
- 1 tsp. lemon zest
- ¼ tsp. ground red pepper
- ½ small head napa cabbage (about 1 lb.), thinly sliced*
- ½ cup golden raisins
- 1 (3.5-oz.) package roasted glazed pecan pieces

1. Cut broccoli florets from stems; separate florets into small pieces using a paring knife. Peel away tough outer layer of stems; finely chop stems.
2. Whisk together mayonnaise and next 6 ingredients in a large bowl; add cabbage, raisins, and broccoli, and stir to coat. Cover and chill 1 hour. Stir in pecans just before serving.
*1 (16-oz.) package coleslaw mix may be substituted.

Shrimp Rémoulade Deviled Eggs

quick prep • make-ahead • party perfect

MAKES: 2 dozen
HANDS-ON TIME: 30 min.
TOTAL TIME: 1 hr.

- ¾ cup mayonnaise
- 3 Tbsp. minced green onions
- 1 Tbsp. minced fresh parsley
- 1½ Tbsp. Creole mustard
- 2 tsp. lemon zest
- 2 garlic cloves, pressed
- ¼ tsp. salt
- ¼ tsp. ground red pepper
- 12 large eggs
- 1 cup finely chopped cooked shrimp (about ¾ lb. peeled and deveined cooked shrimp)

1. Whisk together first 8 ingredients in a small bowl; cover and chill.
2. Place eggs in a single layer in a stainless-steel Dutch oven. (Do not use nonstick.) Add water to depth of 3 inches. Bring to a rolling boil; cover, remove from heat; let stand 15 minutes.
3. Drain immediately, and return eggs to Dutch oven. Fill Dutch oven with cold water and ice. Tap each egg firmly on the counter until cracks form all over the shell. Peel under cold water.
4. Slice eggs in half lengthwise, and carefully remove yolks, keeping egg white halves intact. Mash yolks with mayonnaise mixture until smooth using a fork; stir in shrimp. Spoon yolk mixture into egg whites. Serve immediately, or cover and chill up to 24 hours.

Cool Off with Icebox Desserts

These chilled, creamy pies are the dessert equivalent of a swimming hole—so refreshing that you can't help but dive in.

Peanut Butter-Banana Icebox Pie

make-ahead • party perfect

MAKES: 8 servings
HANDS-ON TIME: 30 min.
TOTAL TIME: 9 hr., 10 min.

- 2 cups cinnamon graham cracker crumbs (about 15 sheets)
- ½ cup finely chopped honey-roasted peanuts
- ½ cup butter, melted
- 1 (4-oz.) semisweet chocolate baking bar, chopped
- 2 cups whipping cream, divided
- 1 (8-oz.) package cream cheese, softened
- 1 cup creamy peanut butter
- ½ cup firmly packed light brown sugar
- 2 tsp. vanilla extract
- 2 large bananas, sliced
  Toppings: sweetened whipped cream, chocolate syrup, chopped honey-roasted peanuts

1. Preheat oven to 350°. Stir together first 3 ingredients; firmly press on bottom, up sides, and onto lip of a lightly greased 9-inch pie plate. Bake 10 to 12 minutes or until lightly browned. Remove from oven to a wire rack, and cool completely (about 30 minutes).
2. Microwave chocolate and ½ cup whipping cream in a small microwave-safe bowl at MEDIUM (50% power) 1½ minutes or until chocolate is almost melted, stirring at

Peanut Butter-Banana Icebox Pie

30-second intervals. Whisk until chocolate melts and mixture is smooth. (Do not overheat.) Spoon chocolate mixture into prepared crust.
3. Beat cream cheese, next 2 ingredients, and ¼ cup whipping cream at medium speed with an electric mixer until mixture is light and fluffy.
4. Beat vanilla and remaining 1¼ cups whipping cream at high speed until stiff peaks form. Fold one-third whipped cream mixture into peanut butter mixture to loosen; fold in remaining whipped cream mixture.
5. Arrange banana slices over chocolate mixture in crust. Spread peanut butter mixture over bananas. Cover and chill 8 hours. Serve pie with desired toppings.

Lemon-Mascarpone Icebox Tarts

make-ahead • party perfect

MAKES: 6 servings
HANDS-ON TIME: 30 min.
TOTAL TIME: 6 hr., 20 min.

- 2⅔ cups butter cookie crumbs (about 1½ [7.5-oz.] packages butter cookies)
- ⅓ cup butter, melted
- ¼ cup powdered sugar
- ½ tsp. almond extract
- 1 (14-oz.) can sweetened condensed milk
- 2 tsp. lemon zest
- ½ cup fresh lemon juice
- 6 egg yolks
- 1 (8-oz.) container mascarpone cheese
  Toppings: fresh berries, sliced peaches or plums, fresh mint or thyme sprigs

1. Preheat oven to 350°. Stir together first 4 ingredients; firmly press crumb mixture on bottom and up sides of 6 (3¾-inch) round tart pans with removable bottoms (about 6 Tbsp. per pan). Place tart pans on a baking sheet, and bake 10 to 12 minutes or until lightly browned. Cool completely on baking sheet on a wire rack (about 30 minutes).
2. Whisk together sweetened condensed milk and next 3 ingredients until well blended; whisk in mascarpone cheese just until blended. Spoon mixture into prepared tart shells.
3. Bake at 350° for 12 to 15 minutes or until almost set. (The centers will not be firm but will set up as they chill.) Cool completely on wire rack (about 1 hour). Cover and chill 4 hours. Arrange berries and fruit decoratively over tarts just before serving.
NOTE: We tested with Pepperidge Farm Chessmen Cookies.

Praline Key Lime Pie

Strawberry-Pretzel Icebox Pie

quick prep • party perfect

MAKES: 8 servings
HANDS-ON TIME: 30 min.
TOTAL TIME: 10 hr., 20 min.

Serve with lightly sweetened, sliced strawberries.

2 cups finely crushed pretzel sticks
¾ cup butter, melted
¼ cup firmly packed light brown sugar
2 cups sliced fresh strawberries
1 (14-oz.) can sweetened condensed milk
½ (8-oz.) package cream cheese, softened
4 Tbsp. plus 1 tsp. strawberry gelatin (½ [3-oz.] package)
2 cups whipping cream, divided
⅓ cup granulated sugar

1. Preheat oven to 350°. Stir together first 3 ingredients; firmly press on bottom, up sides, and onto lip of a lightly greased 10-inch pie plate. Bake 10 to 12 minutes or until lightly browned. Remove from oven to a wire rack, and cool completely (about 30 minutes).
2. Process strawberries in a food processor until finely chopped, stopping to scrape down sides as needed.
3. Beat condensed milk and next 2 ingredients at medium speed with an electric mixer until smooth. (Use the whisk attachment if using a stand mixer.) Add strawberries; beat at low speed just until blended. Transfer to a large bowl.
4. Beat ¾ cup whipping cream at high speed until soft peaks form; gently fold whipped cream into strawberry mixture. Spoon into prepared crust. Cover and freeze 8 to 12 hours or until firm.
5. Beat remaining 1¼ cups whipping cream at high speed until foamy; gradually add granulated sugar, beating until soft peaks form. Spread over pie. Freeze 1 hour or until whipped cream is firm.

Praline Key Lime Pie

make-ahead • party perfect

MAKES: 8 servings
HANDS-ON TIME: 30 min.
TOTAL TIME: 7 hr., 10 min.
(Also pictured on page 11)

1¼ cups chopped pecans
2 cups graham cracker crumbs
½ cup butter, melted
¼ cup firmly packed light brown sugar
½ cup plus 2 Tbsp. jarred caramel topping
2 (14-oz.) cans sweetened condensed milk
6 egg yolks
2 tsp. Key lime or lime zest
1 cup fresh Key lime or lime juice
1½ cups whipping cream
¼ cup plus 2 Tbsp. powdered sugar

1. Preheat oven to 350°. Bake pecans in a single layer in a shallow pan 8 to 10 minutes or until toasted and fragrant, stirring halfway through.
2. Stir together graham cracker crumbs, next 2 ingredients, and ½ cup toasted pecans until blended. Press crumb mixture on bottom, up sides, and onto lip of a lightly greased 10-inch deep-dish pie plate.
3. Bake at 350° for 10 to 12 minutes or until lightly browned. Remove from oven to a wire rack, and cool completely (about 45 minutes).
4. Sprinkle remaining ¾ cup toasted pecans over bottom of crust; drizzle caramel topping over pecans.
5. Whisk together sweetened condensed milk and next 3 ingredients. Gently pour into prepared crust.
6. Bake at 350° for 20 to 25 minutes or until almost set. (The center will not be firm but will set up as it chills.) Cool completely on a wire rack (about 1 hour). Cover and chill 4 hours.
7. Beat whipping cream at high speed with an electric mixer until foamy; gradually add powdered sugar, beating until soft peaks form. Spread over pie.

IT GETS EVEN BETTER!!

You'll find an irresistible layer of caramel and pecans between the crust and lime filling.

Pineapple-Coconut Icebox Pie

make-ahead • party perfect

MAKES: 8 servings
HANDS-ON TIME: 25 min.
TOTAL TIME: 6 hr., 25 min.

2   **cups pecan shortbread cookie crumbs (about 16 cookies)**
1   **cup sweetened flaked coconut**
¼   **cup butter, melted**
⅓   **cup sugar**
2   **Tbsp. cornstarch**
1   **(8-oz.) can crushed pineapple in juice**
1   **(8-oz.) package cream cheese, softened**
1½   **cups cream of coconut, divided**
2   **large eggs**
1   **cup whipping cream**
    Garnish: toasted coconut

1. Preheat oven to 350°. Stir together first 3 ingredients; firmly press on bottom and up sides of a lightly greased 9-inch pie plate. Bake 10 to 12 minutes or until lightly browned. Remove to a wire rack, and cool completely (about 30 minutes).

2. Meanwhile, stir together sugar and cornstarch in a small heavy saucepan; stir in pineapple. Bring to a boil over medium-high heat, stirring constantly, and cook, stirring constantly, 1 minute or until thickened. Remove from heat, and cool completely (about 20 minutes).

3. Beat cream cheese at medium speed with a heavy-duty electric stand mixer, using whisk attachment, until smooth. Gradually add 1 cup cream of coconut, beating at low speed just until blended. (Chill remaining ½ cup cream of coconut until ready to use.) Add eggs, 1 at a time, beating just until blended after each addition.

4. Spread cooled pineapple mixture over bottom of piecrust; spoon cream cheese mixture over pineapple mixture.

5. Bake at 350° for 38 to 42 minutes or until set. Cool completely on a wire rack (about 1 hour). Cover and chill 4 hours.

6. Beat whipping cream at high speed with an electric mixer until foamy; gradually add remaining ½ cup cream of coconut, beating until soft peaks form; spread over chilled pie.

NOTE: We tested with Keebler Sandies Pecan Shortbread and Coco Lopez Cream of Coconut.

Grasshopper Icebox Mini Pies

make-ahead • party perfect

MAKES: 12 servings
HANDS-ON TIME: 20 min.
TOTAL TIME: 5 hr.

The Grasshopper drink originated at Tujaque's in New Orleans.

12   **jumbo-size aluminum foil baking cups**
    Vegetable cooking spray
1   **(9-oz.) package chocolate wafer cookies**
½   **cup butter, melted**
3   **(8-oz.) packages cream cheese, softened**
1   **cup sugar**
⅓   **cup green crème de menthe**
3   **large eggs**
    Toppings: sweetened whipped cream, chocolate curls

1. Preheat oven to 350°. Place jumbo-size baking cups in 1 (12-cup) muffin pan, and coat with cooking spray.

2. Pulse chocolate wafer cookies in a food processor 8 or 10 times or until finely crushed. Stir together cookie crumbs and butter; firmly press on bottom and two-thirds up sides of each baking cup (about 3 Tbsp. crumbs per cup).

3. Beat cream cheese and sugar at medium speed with an electric mixer until blended. Add crème de menthe, beating at low speed until well blended. Add eggs, 1 at a time, beating just until yellow disappears after each addition. Spoon cream cheese mixture into prepared cups, filling completely full (it doesn't rise during baking!).

4. Bake at 350° for 20 minutes or until set. Cool in pans on wire racks 15 minutes. Gently remove from pans to wire racks, and cool completely (about 15 minutes). Cover and chill 4 hours. Top with sweetened whipped cream and chocolate shavings.

NOTE: We tested with Nabisco Famous Chocolate Wafers.

TRY THIS TWIST!

Mocha Icebox Mini Pies: Omit green crème de menthe. Microwave 1 cup (6 oz.) semisweet chocolate morsels and ¼ cup whipping cream in a small microwave-safe bowl at MEDIUM (50% power) 1½ minutes or until chocolate is almost melted, stirring at 30-second intervals. Whisk until chocolate melts and mixture is smooth (do not overheat.) Stir in 2 Tbsp. instant espresso. Prepare recipe as directed, adding chocolate mixture to cream cheese mixture after adding eggs in Step 3; beat just until blended. Top with sweetened whipped cream, caramel topping, sea salt, and chocolate shavings.

Lighten Up Fried Green Tomatoes

Get that familiar golden crunch with heart-healthy oil and a nonstick pan.

No saturated fat and only 65 calories!

Fried Green Tomatoes

quick prep • good for you • party perfect

MAKES: about 20 slices
HANDS-ON TIME: 30 min.
TOTAL TIME: 40 min.

- 4 **medium-size green tomatoes (about 1⅓ lb.)**
- ½ **tsp. salt**
- ½ **tsp. pepper**
- 1 **cup self-rising white cornmeal mix**
- ½ **cup panko (Japanese breadcrumbs)**
- ½ **cup all-purpose flour**
- 4 **egg whites**
- 3 **Tbsp. olive oil**

1. Cut tomatoes into ½-inch-thick slices; sprinkle with salt and pepper. Let stand 10 minutes.

2. Combine cornmeal mix and panko in a shallow dish or pie plate. Place flour in a second shallow dish or pie plate. Whisk egg whites in a medium bowl until foamy. Dredge tomato slices in flour, shaking off excess. Dip in egg whites, and dredge in cornmeal mixture.

3. Cook half of tomato slices in 1½ Tbsp. hot oil in a nonstick skillet over medium heat 4 to 5 minutes on each side or until golden brown. Season with salt to taste. Place on a wire rack in a jelly-roll pan, and keep warm in a 225° oven. Repeat procedure with remaining tomato slices and oil.

PER TOMATO SLICE: CALORIES 65; FAT 2.2G (SAT 0.3G, MONO 1.6G, POLY 0.2G); PROTEIN 2.1G; CARB 9.3G; FIBER 0.6G; CHOL 0MG; IRON 0.5MG; SODIUM 157MG; CALC 16MG

Skinny Dips

Each of these low-fat sauces can be stirred together in 10 minutes. Chill 1 hour, and store in an airtight container in the fridge up to 3 days.

{1}

PEPPER JELLY SAUCE: Stir together ⅔ cup red pepper jelly, 2 Tbsp. spicy brown mustard, 1 tsp. refrigerated horseradish, and 1 tsp. orange zest.

PER TBSP: CALORIES 29; FAT 0G

{2}

CITRUS-GINGER AÏOLI: Stir together 1 cup mayonnaise; 1 tsp. lime zest; 1 tsp. orange zest; 4 tsp. fresh lime juice; 1 Tbsp. fresh orange juice; 2 tsp. finely grated fresh ginger; 1 garlic clove, minced; ¼ tsp. salt, and ⅛ tsp. pepper.

PER TBSP: CALORIES 37; FAT 3.6G

{3}

BLUE CHEESE-DILL SAUCE: Stir together ½ cup sour cream, ½ cup 2% low-fat plain yogurt, 2 tsp. chopped fresh dill, 2 oz. crumbled blue cheese, 1 tsp. fresh lemon juice, and ¼ tsp. salt.

PER TBSP: CALORIES 23; FAT 1.8G

{4}

SRIRACHA RÉMOULADE: Stir together 1½ cups mayonnaise; 4 green onions, sliced; 2 Tbsp. chopped fresh parsley; 2 to 3 Tbsp. Asian Sriracha hot chili sauce; and 1 garlic clove, pressed.

PER TBSP: CALORIES 35; FAT 3.4G

Serve Dinner on a Stick

Grab the skewers, fire up the grill, and enjoy these easy and delicious kabobs, great for any night of the week.

15 MINUTES
Grilled Scallop Kabobs

quick prep • good for you • party perfect

MAKES: 4 to 6 servings

20	fresh thick asparagus spears
40	sea scallops (about 1½ lb.)
10	(6-inch) wooden skewers
¼	cup herb-flavored olive oil
	Lemon wedges

1. Preheat grill to 350° to 400° (medium-high) heat. Snap off and discard tough ends of asparagus. Cut asparagus into 2-inch pieces. Thread scallops alternately with asparagus pieces onto each skewer. Brush with olive oil.

2. Grill kabobs, covered with grill lid, 2½ minutes on each side or just until scallops are opaque. Sprinkle with salt to taste. Serve kabobs with lemon wedges.

NOTE: We tested with Benissimo Mediterranean Garlic Gourmet oil.

IF YOU HAVE 15 MINUTES

GRILLED SCALLOP KABOBS: Round out the meal with grilled pita wedges and deli tabbouleh salad.

---

30 MINUTES
Peach and Pork Kabobs

quick prep • party perfect

MAKES: 4 servings

½	cup bourbon
¼	cup fresh lemon juice
2	garlic cloves, minced
¼	cup olive oil, divided
2	tsp. chopped fresh rosemary, divided
1	lb. boneless pork loin, cut into 1½-inch cubes
¾	cup bottled barbecue sauce
8	(10-inch) metal skewers
1	tsp. salt
½	tsp. freshly ground pepper
2	large peaches, unpeeled and cut into 8 wedges each
1	large green bell pepper, cut into 1½-inch pieces

1. Preheat grill to 350° to 400° (medium-high) heat. Whisk together first 3 ingredients, 2 Tbsp. olive oil, and 1 tsp. rosemary; reserve ¼ cup. Pour remaining mixture into a large shallow dish or zip-top plastic freezer bag; add pork, turning to coat. Cover or seal, and let stand 10 minutes.

2. Meanwhile, cook barbecue sauce and reserved ¼ cup mixture in a medium saucepan over medium heat, stirring occasionally, 3 minutes or until bubbly. Remove from heat.

3. Remove pork from marinade, discarding marinade. Thread pork onto skewers, leaving a ⅛-inch space between pieces. Sprinkle pork with salt and pepper.

Peach and Pork Kabobs

4. Thread peaches and bell peppers alternately onto other skewers, leaving a ⅛-inch space between pieces. Drizzle with remaining 2 Tbsp. olive oil, and sprinkle with remaining 1 tsp. rosemary.

5. Grill pork and fruit-and-vegetable kabobs at the same time, covered with grill lid. Grill pork, turning occasionally, 7 to 8 minutes on each side or until done, brushing pork with barbecue sauce mixture during last 5 minutes of grilling. Grill fruit-and-vegetable kabobs 4 minutes on each side or until bell peppers are crisp-tender.

Grilled Shrimp and Smoky Grilled-Corn Grits

quick prep • party perfect

MAKES: 4 to 6 servings

- 2 ears fresh corn
- I tsp. salt
- I cup uncooked quick-cooking grits
- I cup (4 oz.) shredded Cheddar cheese
- 2 tsp. minced canned chipotle pepper in adobo sauce
- ½ cup olive oil
- ¼ cup fresh lemon juice
- I garlic clove, pressed
- ½ tsp. freshly ground pepper
- I lb. peeled, jumbo raw shrimp with tails (16/20 count), deveined
- 16 (6-inch) metal skewers
- I pt. grape tomatoes
- ½ (8-oz.) package fresh mushrooms, quartered
- I small green bell pepper, cut into I-inch pieces
- ⅓ cup chopped fresh cilantro

1. Preheat grill to 350° to 400° (medium-high) heat. Grill corn, covered with grill lid, 10 minutes or until done, turning once. Cut kernels from cobs. Discard cobs.

2. Bring salt and 4 cups water to a boil in a medium saucepan over medium-high heat. Gradually whisk in grits. Cook, stirring occasionally, 8 minutes or until thickened. Stir in corn kernels, cheese, and chipotle pepper. Cover and keep warm.

3. Stir together olive oil and next 3 ingredients in a large bowl. Toss shrimp with olive oil mixture; let stand at room temperature 3 minutes.

4. Remove shrimp from marinade, discarding marinade. Thread shrimp onto skewers alternately with tomatoes, mushrooms, and bell peppers.

5. Grill kabobs, covered with grill lid, 4 to 5 minutes on each side or just until shrimp turn pink. Serve kabobs with grits, and sprinkle with cilantro just before serving.

Great-Grandma Turano's Meatballs

We're always looking for a good meatball recipe, so we had to share this one from Jenny Rosenstrach's charming new cookbook, *Dinner: A Love Story* (out this month). And, of course, we gave it a Southern spin.

1. Combine 2 lb. ground beef; I cup Italian-seasoned breadcrumbs; I cup freshly grated Parmesan cheese; I cup chopped fresh flat-leaf parsley; 2 large eggs, lightly beaten; ½ tsp. salt; ¼ tsp. fennel seeds; and ¼ tsp. pepper. Shape into 37 (1½-inch) balls. Freeze up to I month. When ready to use, let stand at room temperature 10 minutes. Thread meatballs ⅛ inch apart onto 4 (10-inch) metal skewers. Grill, covered with grill lid, at 350° to 400° (medium-high) heat 3 to 4 minutes on each side or until centers are no longer pink, basting with bottled barbecue sauce during last 3 minutes. Serve on skewers or buns. Makes 37.

Grilled Chicken-Vegetable Kabobs

quick prep • good for you • party perfect

MAKES: 6 servings

- ½ cup red pepper jelly
- ¼ tsp. dried crushed red pepper
- ⅔ cup red wine vinegar, divided
- I tsp. salt, divided
- I tsp. freshly ground black pepper, divided
- 1½ lb. skinned and boned chicken breasts, cut into I-inch pieces
- I medium-size red onion, cut into 8 wedges
- 2 medium-size yellow squash, cut into I-inch pieces
- 24 small fresh okra (about ¾ lb.)
- 8 (12-inch) metal skewers, divided
- ¼ cup olive oil

1. Whisk together pepper jelly, red pepper, ⅓ cup red wine vinegar, and ½ tsp. each salt and pepper in a shallow dish or zip-top plastic freezer bag. Add chicken, turning to coat. Cover or seal, and chill 30 minutes, turning occasionally.

2. Preheat grill to 350° to 400° (medium-high) heat. Thread onion pieces and next 2 ingredients alternately onto 5 skewers, leaving a ⅛-inch space between pieces. Place skewers in a shallow pan. Whisk together olive oil and remaining ⅓ cup vinegar, ½ tsp. salt, and ½ tsp. pepper. Pour over vegetables.

3. Remove chicken from marinade, discarding marinade. Thread chicken onto remaining 3 skewers, leaving a ⅛-inch space between pieces.

4. Grill kabobs, covered with grill lid, 6 to 8 minutes on each side or until chicken is done and vegetables are crisp-tender.

Welcome to 'Cue Country. Down here,
barbecue is a ritual, a celebration,
a testament to all that's right. In our first-ever
'Cue Awards, we salute the people, places, and
recipes that keep our home fires burning.

Smokin' Hot List

The people behind the pits are often as compelling as the meat that emerges from them. We give you 10 of the South's best pitmasters, a diverse group united by a smoky passion.

Rodney Scott
SCOTT'S BAR-B-QUE
Hemingway, South Carolina

"Charcoal is good if you're lazy," says whole-hog maestro Rodney Scott, who started working his family's pits when he was 11. Rodney isn't lazy. He and his father cut trees weekly, salvaging the cords of hickory, oak, and pecan needed to power and perfume their concrete bunker pits. Those pits yield gorgeously crisp-skinned meat, mopped with a vinegar-pepper sauce that Rodney's never been tempted to tweak. His adherence to tradition has won him the respect of fellow Southern chefs, such as Husk's Sean Brock, who rates Scott's as his "most favorite place to eat in the entire world." Rodney says trading secrets with Sean and cooking with other pitmasters has solidified his passion for a hard, greasy job. "We have different styles, but we all have love for pork," he says. *thescottsbbq.com*

Francisca Andrin
OLD BRICK PIT BARBEQUE
Chamblee, Georgia

Francisca Andrin—who's in charge of the pit at this barn-shaped joint in north Atlanta—isn't the obvious choice to safeguard the city's dwindling vinegar tradition. She grew up in Indonesia, where the cuisine-defining meat dish is slathered with molasses and brown sugar. But she's shelved her sweet meat instincts and produces 'cue true to a local vinegar style that's lately been roughed up by ketchup. Acolytes proclaim her ribs to be Dekalb County's most tender. *oldbrickpitbbq.com*

Sam Jones
THE SKYLIGHT INN
Ayden, North Carolina

Sam Jones, 31, says he doesn't intend to change anything at the restaurant his grandfather Pete Jones opened in 1947. "My granddaddy would turn over in his casket two times," he says. In fact, Sam, heir to a 180-year-old family tradition of selling whole-hog barbecue, is working on a Skylight Inn T-shirt whose design features a meat cleaver and the phrase "Our idea of cutting edge." He became an apprentice after trying to shortcut his way through a college research paper by writing about barbecue. "That's when I put on a different set of spectacles as to how I look at it." He recalls long hours spent learning how to cook split hogs and hand chop meat and skin. "At 75, he would work me in the ground," Sam says of Skylight's patriarch. *252/746-4113*

Aaron Franklin
FRANKLIN BARBECUE
Austin, Texas

Hundreds of people line up every day to sample brisket from Aaron Franklin, a young Austinite who's nursed pitmaster dreams since age 12. But Aaron's popularity hasn't left him assuming there's nothing left to learn. "Anybody who thinks they've perfected barbecue should probably reassess," he says. His distinctive meat—heralded for its slinky marbling, flavorful bark, and whiff of white-oak smoke—keeps Aaron tied to the pit. He firmly believes the pitmaster adds to the flavor. "An old dude hands off the reins and it's never the same," he says. "It's safe to say I'm stuck." *franklinbarbecue.com*

Jack Easley
MARION PIT BAR-B-Q
Marion, Kentucky

Nearly 40 years ago, Jack Easley was paying too much rent on his sit-down restaurant, so he went looking for a more affordable avocation. There aren't any tables or chairs in the vinyl-sided hut known as Marion Pit Bar-B-Q, but out back there's a hickory-fired pit in which Jack smokes pork for 17 unhurried hours. When the shoulders are quivering on the cusp of fracture, he pulls them apart and soaks the meat with an exceptional tomato-based sauce, orange as a robin's breast. "The main thing for me is the sauce," says Jack, who refuses to disclose ingredients. "It's a little bit ketchup, a little bit everything else. So far everybody pretty well likes it." *270/965-3318*

Will Fleischman
LOCKHART SMOKEHOUSE

Dallas, Texas

Will Fleischman has studied literature and worked as a chef in China, but nothing daunts him like a brisket nearing the end of its run in a smoker. "The question of 'How do you know when it's done?' is where insecurity lives," he says. "You want the wood to speak to you, but the meat sits there in mute defiance." Will rejects the "cowboy wisdom" equating pounds and cook time: "That's like making a sweeping generalization about all redheads." Instead, he relies on instincts he's honed under the tutelage of a cattle rancher who sold beef to Leavenworth prison and a 350-pound man known as Pappy. "People need to humble themselves to the experience," he says. "Success depends on how many mistakes you're willing to make."
lockhartsmokehouse.com

Helen Turner
HELEN'S BBQ

Brownsville, Tennessee

Helen Turner's gotten used to customers poking around her modest barbecue shack looking for the man who runs the place. But she's been stacking hickory and hoisting pork shoulders since 1995. Customers who aren't diverted by the idea of a female-run barbecue joint are often equally struck by the thick smoke that clouds the interior of Helen's BBQ. She tried installing fans to clear the air, but the pit's heat melted them. "Some people say sauce makes it special, but the smoke is what makes the flavor," Helen says. *731/779-3255*

How They Do It *WAY* Down South

If you think Southerners are obsessed with cooking meat over fire, you should spend some time down south—South America, that is. That's just what 10 members of the **Fatback Collective**, a group of Southern "hambassadors" led by Nick Pihakis of Jim 'N Nick's Bar-B-Q (page 149), did in December 2011, traveling to Uruguay, a country where every house has an asado pit and even potato chips come in such flavors as beef tenderloin. At a ranch called **Estancia Belcampo**, *asadors* (imagine gaucho pitmasters) shared techniques with folks such as Rodney Scott (page 141) and chef Donald Link of New Orleans. On the surface, with both sides cooking for one another, it was as simple as I'll-try-yours, you-try-mine: Rodney's fiery, vinegar-based sauce versus the garlicky Uruguayan *chimichurri*. Appetizer bites of Donald's Cajun boudin versus fire-seared matambre (fatty flank steak) with beef-tallow crackers. But something deeper set in. You see, in Uruguay, organic, pastured meats aren't a trend—they're practically a birthright. As Nick points out, farms such as Belcampo are "taking good-quality food and bringing it to all the people, not just the elite." And it's that lesson the crew has brought back. Through the Fatback Pig Project they are working with local farmers to raise Mangalitsa stock for their restaurants. The end goal? Heritage hog—usually a fine-dining staple—on an $8 pulled pork sandwich. Now that's a delicious exchange. For a slide show of Fatback's asado adventure, go to *southernliving.com/BBQ*.

Chris Lilly
BIG BOB GIBSON BAR-B-Q

Decatur, Alabama

When Amy McLemore, great-granddaughter of Alabama barbecue legend Big Bob Gibson, looked at fellow University of North Alabama student Chris Lilly, she saw a husband. Her father saw a solution to a long-standing business problem. "My father-in-law hired me because he wanted to open a second location," says Chris, who'd never before minded a pit. He has since clinched the art of superlative 'cue— "It's just dry rub, patience, and sauce on the side," he says—and become a legend on the competition circuit. Unlike many professional pitmasters, Chris doesn't sneer at the prospect of smoking for prizes: He's won more than 10 World BBQ Championship titles, including three Memphis in May Grand Championships. Becoming a celebrity hasn't lured him out of Decatur: "My passion is in the pits," he says. "You'll still find me there, taking a turn." *bigbobgibson.com*

2012 'Cue Awards

Ed Mitchell
"THE PITMASTER"
Raleigh, North Carolina

The graybeard of whole-hog cooking, Ed Mitchell was a relatively late arrival to the barbecue business. After a lifetime of pig pickings at family gatherings, Ed inadvertently became a professional at 44 when his mother, a Wilson County grocer, asked him to smoke a pig for supper. She sold the leftovers at her corner store, which was soon after reinvented as Mitchell's Barbecue. These days, in a field that's made a mantra of low and slow, Ed cooks hot and fast, a technique he believes loosens the pig's juices. He's now plotting to open a chain of restaurants showcasing his signature whole-hog style. "I've tried ribs and butts, but you're missing about three-quarters of the flavors the animal can provide," he says. *thepitmasteredmitchell.com*

Avery Payne
COOK'S BARBECUE
Lexington, North Carolina

In 1984, when Avery Payne's parents purchased Cook's Barbecue from a childhood friend, millions of American boys were busy slipping quarters into Pac-Man machines. Avery, at 12, was working at Cook's. He recalls starting a few inadvertent fires that first week he learned to cook on the pit. Now more cautious, he is one of two Lexington-style pitmasters who mess with brisket. Cook's "went down to Texas and fell in love with it," he says. And the beef affair was no mere fling. "We thought we'd marry it and bring it back." What the Paynes didn't bring home was the Texan skepticism of sauce: "Sauce makes it good," says Avery, who builds his from ketchup, vinegar, and crushed red pepper. "Only way I can eat barbecue without sauce is off the chopping block or the pit." *cooksbbq.com*

Gettin' Saucy

Armed with loaves of white bread, pulled pork, and antacids, our Food staff sampled nearly 100 bottles of barbecue sauce to distill the pack down to this sweet, smoky, vinegary baker's dozen.

NIGHT OF THE LIVING BAR-B-Q SAUCE
Kansas City, KS
For chipotle fans: fiery yet sweet; $4.
oklahomajoesbbq.com

LAMBERT'S SWEET SAUCE O'MINE ORIGINAL
Olive Branch, MS
Honeyed tomato with a touch of apricot; $3.50. *ssomd.com*

KING'S FAMOUS NO. 2 BARBECUE SAUCE
Petersburg, VA
A tart, assertive blend of mustard, tomato, and vinegar; $4.
kingsfamousbarbecue.com

OKIE STEAK HOUSE BARBECUE SAUCE
Stroud, OK
Sweet and thick with a chili powder kick; $5. *okiesteakhouse.com*

BBQ FIGHT CLUB KICKIN' CHICKEN WHITE SAUCE
Nashville, TN
A peppery come-back sauce; $9.
615/329-1234

HILLSDALE BANK BAR B.Q. THE SAUCE (HOT)
Hillsdale, KS
Thick, sweet, and smoky; $4.
hillsdalebankbarbq.com

SAW'S SAUCE
Birmingham, AL
Just right: not too sweet, hot, or vinegary; $5.50. *sawsbbq.com*

WHOLE HOG CAFE SAUCE #2
Little Rock, AR
Lightly smoky tomato-vinegar with a warm finish; $7. *wholehogcafe.com*

HOG HEAVEN BARBECUE SAUCE EAST
Brewton, AL
Sweet and balanced; $4. *800/865-2262*

ABE'S BAR-B-Q SAUCE
Clarksdale, MS
Zippy with a punch of Worcestershire; $23 for 3 pt. *abesbbq.com*

HAROLD'S HOG WASH
Fayetteville, TN
A clove-tinged, authoritative mustard; $6. *haroldshogwash.com*

JIM'S OWN MILD BARBECUE SAUCE
Cary, NC
Sweet, peppery tomato with subtle floral notes; $6. *jimsownsauce.com*

WADMALAW ISLAND BARBEQUE SAUCE
Wadmalaw Island, SC
A bright and peppery twist on a classic mustard sauce; $5.
wadmalawislandbbq.com

The *Southern Living* Pulled Pork Sandwich

Our Test Kitchen took cues from the pros to bring pit-barbecue flavor to the backyard. Here's the breakdown. Definitely try it at home.

Smoked Pork Butt

1. Trim I (4- to 5-lb.) bone-in Boston butt pork roast. Rinse and pat dry. Sprinkle with ¼ cup Smoky-Sweet BBQ Rub (page 150); let stand at room temperature 30 minutes. Bring internal temperature of smoker to 225° to 250° according to manufacturer's directions, and maintain temperature 15 to 20 minutes. Place pork, fattier side up, on cooking grate directly over coals in center of smoker. Cover with lid, and adjust ventilation to maintain temperature between 225° and 250°.
2. Smoke, covered with lid and maintaining temperature, 5 hours; turn pork, fattier side down, and smoke 2 to 3 more hours or until a meat thermometer inserted into thickest portion registers 195°. Transfer to a cutting board; cool 15 minutes. Shred pork.
NOTE: For more details on this recipe, as well as a slow-cooker version, visit *southernliving.com/BBQ.*

THE SAUCE: (below) This tomato-based sauce perfectly balances heat, spice, and sweet, letting the meat shine. We love the dark molasses for that extra depth of flavor and the kick from the chili powder and black pepper.

THE MEAT: A juicy pork butt rubbed with salt, cumin, ginger, garlic, and sugar and scented with hickory smoke equals hog heaven. Pitmaster bonus: a crisp layer of bark.

THE BUN: Forget fancy. There's nothing we like better than a pillowy eight-pack of white-bread buns—soft and pliable and perfect for sopping up sauce. Sesame seeds are dealer's choice.

CHOWCHOW: (below) This tangy confetti of cabbage, green tomatoes, and peppers gives a fresh crunch—way better than plain ol' potato chips.

Fixin's for the Southern Living *Pulled Pork Sandwich*

CHOWCHOW: Stir together 3 cups chopped fresh cabbage, ¾ cup each chopped onion and green tomatoes, ½ cup each chopped green and red bell peppers, and I Tbsp. pickling salt. Cover and chill 2 to 8 hours. Transfer mixture to a Dutch oven. Stir in ¾ cup sugar, ½ cup white vinegar, ¼ cup water, ¾ tsp. mustard seeds, ¼ tsp. celery seeds, ¼ tsp. ground turmeric, and, if desired, ½ tsp. dried crushed red pepper. Bring to a boil over medium-high heat; reduce heat to medium, and simmer 3 minutes. Cool to room temperature (about 30 minutes). Stir in I jalapeño pepper, seeded and finely chopped, if desired. Cover and chill I to 8 hours before serving. Makes: about 3 cups. Hands-on time: 25 min.; Total time: 4 hr., 5 min.

SWEET-AND-TANGY TOMATO BARBECUE SAUCE:
Bring I cup ketchup, I cup water, ⅓ cup apple cider vinegar, ¼ cup firmly packed light brown sugar, I Tbsp. onion powder, I Tbsp. chili powder, 2 Tbsp. tomato paste, I½ Tbsp. dark molasses, and 2 tsp. freshly ground pepper to a boil in a large saucepan over medium heat, stirring occasionally. Reduce heat to low; cover and cook, stirring occasionally, 25 minutes or until slightly thickened. Cool 10 minutes. Cover and chill until ready to serve. Store in refrigerator up to I week. Makes: about 2 cups. Hands-on time: 10 min., Total time: 45 min.

(ALSO PICTURED ON PAGE 8)

A Little Something on the Side

For many, it's the delicious bounty of summer sides—not what's in the smoker—that makes a paper plate feel like fine china. So, in our first SIDE DISH SMACKDOWN, we set out to find the best reader recipes for slaw, baked beans, and more.

It's a good potato salad, but is it a $1,000 potato salad? That's what we asked as we tasted our way through stacks of mouthwatering side dish entries in our reader-recipe contest, which launched online in December 2011 and offered meaty cash prizes to winners in six categories (including an open-ended surprise option). Fortunately, when we stumbled across recipes such as Priscilla Yee's Spinach-Artichoke Dip Potato Salad, we knew we had an answer. And to those who didn't win: There's an entire summer ahead for experimenting—and we can't wait to dig in again next year.

Grandma Gwen's Beans

party perfect

MAKES: 10 servings
HANDS-ON TIME: 45 min.
TOTAL TIME: 2 hr., 5 min.

- 1 (1-lb.) package bacon slices
- 4 medium-size yellow onions, sliced
- ½ cup firmly packed light brown sugar
- ½ cup apple cider vinegar
- 1 tsp. salt
- 1 tsp. dry mustard
- ½ tsp. garlic powder
- 2 (16-oz.) cans butter beans, drained and rinsed
- 1 (15-oz.) can lima beans, drained and rinsed
- 1 (16-oz.) can kidney beans, drained and rinsed
- 1 (28-oz.) can baked beans

1. Preheat oven to 350°. Cook bacon, in batches, in a large skillet over medium-high heat 8 to 10 minutes or until crisp. Remove bacon, and drain on paper towels, reserving desired amount of drippings in skillet. (We reserved about 3 Tbsp.) Crumble bacon.
2. Sauté onions in hot drippings over medium heat 8 to 10 minutes or until onions are tender. Add brown sugar and next 4 ingredients. Cover and cook 20 minutes. Combine butter beans, next 3 ingredients, bacon, and onion mixture in a 13- x 9-inch baking dish.
3. Bake at 350° for 1 hour.

Chipotle-Cilantro Slaw

quick prep • make-ahead • party perfect

MAKES: 6 to 8 servings
HANDS-ON TIME: 15 min.
TOTAL TIME: 15 min.

- ¼ cup mayonnaise
- 1 Tbsp. sugar
- 2 Tbsp. sour cream
- 1 tsp. lime zest
- 2 Tbsp. fresh lime juice
- 2 tsp. red wine vinegar
- ½ tsp. salt
- ½ tsp. ground pepper
- 1 (16-oz.) package shredded coleslaw mix
- 1 carrot, shredded
- 2 canned chipotle chile peppers in adobo sauce, finely chopped
- ½ cup minced fresh cilantro

1. Whisk together first 8 ingredients in a large bowl. Add coleslaw mix and remaining ingredients, and stir until coated. Serve immediately, or cover and chill up to 1 hour.

WINNER:
BEST BAKED BEANS

GRANDMA GWEN'S BEANS

"My grandmother would make this dish for special family gatherings—it's a favorite. Sharing her recipe helps her legacy live on."

LIZ MATTHEWS
FULLERTON, CALIFORNIA

WINNER:
BEST COLESLAW

CHIPOTLE-CILANTRO SLAW:

"My family always enjoys a little heat with their meal, and this slaw delivers on that! It's great with grilled meats or on a sandwich."

NADINE MESCH
MOUNT HEALTHY, OHIO

Tangy Tzatziki Pasta Salad

good for you • make-ahead • party perfect

MAKES: 10 servings
HANDS-ON TIME: 35 min.
TOTAL TIME: 2 hr., 35 min.

- 1 (16-oz.) container low-fat plain Greek yogurt
- ¼ cup olive oil
- 1 Tbsp. chopped fresh dill
- 1 Tbsp. lemon juice
- 1 tsp. sea salt
- ½ tsp. freshly ground pepper
- 3 garlic cloves
- 1 (16-oz.) package penne pasta
- 1 cup pitted kalamata olives, sliced
- 2 cucumbers, peeled, seeded, and diced
- ¾ cup sun-dried tomatoes in oil, drained and chopped
- 1 (9.9-oz.) jar marinated artichoke hearts, drained and chopped
- 1½ cups crumbled feta cheese

1. Process first 7 ingredients in a food processor 30 seconds or until thoroughly blended. Transfer to a bowl, and cover and chill 1 to 24 hours.
2. Cook pasta according to package directions; drain and rinse with cold water.
3. Place cooled pasta in a large bowl. Stir in olives and next 3 ingredients until well blended. Add yogurt mixture, and stir just until well coated. Gently stir in feta cheese. Cover and chill 1 hour.

Chipotle-Bacon Mac and Cheese

party perfect

MAKES: 10 servings
HANDS-ON TIME: 40 min.
TOTAL TIME: 1 hr., 20 min.

- 3 tsp. sea salt, divided
- 1 (16-oz.) package cavatappi pasta
- 2 Tbsp. corn oil, divided
- ½ cup butter
- 1 small onion, diced
- 3 Tbsp. all-purpose flour
- 3 cups half-and-half
- 2 cups heavy cream
- 1 tsp. ground white pepper
- 3 cups freshly grated smoked Cheddar cheese
- 1 cup freshly grated Cheddar cheese
- 1 tsp. ground chipotle chile pepper
- 6 cooked bacon slices, chopped
- ¾ cup panko (Japanese breadcrumbs)

1. Preheat oven to 350°. Bring 1 gal. water and 1½ tsp. salt to a boil in a Dutch oven; add pasta. Cook 8 to 9 minutes or until al dente. Drain; rinse with cold water. Toss with 1 Tbsp. oil.
2. Melt butter in a large saucepan over medium-high heat. Add onion, and sauté 4 to 5 minutes or until tender. Add flour, and cook, whisking constantly, 1 to 2 minutes or until smooth. (Do not brown flour.) Add half-and-half, next 2 ingredients, and remaining 1½ tsp. sea salt, and bring to a simmer. Cook, whisking constantly, 5 to 6 minutes or until thickened. Gradually add cheeses, stirring until blended. Transfer mixture to a large bowl; stir in cooked pasta. Spoon into a lightly greased 13- x 9-inch baking dish.
3. Sauté chipotle pepper in remaining 1 Tbsp. hot corn oil in a small skillet over medium heat 30 seconds or until mixture begins to smoke. Remove from heat, and quickly stir in bacon and panko until coated. Sprinkle mixture over pasta.
4. Bake at 350° for 15 to 20 minutes or until golden and crisp on top. Serve immediately.

2012 'Cue Awards

Sweet, Salty, and Spicy Watermelon Refresher

quick prep • good for you
make-ahead • party perfect

MAKES: 10 to 12 servings
HANDS-ON TIME: 30 min.
TOTAL TIME: 50 min.

¼ cup fresh lime juice
1 Tbsp. turbinado sugar
2 Tbsp. fresh orange juice
1 jalapeño or 2 serrano peppers, seeded and minced
½ tsp. sea or kosher salt
¼ tsp. dried crushed red pepper
1 small red onion, diced
½ cup coarsely chopped fresh cilantro
2 Tbsp. coarsely chopped fresh mint
1 small seedless watermelon
1 small cantaloupe
2 English cucumbers
1 jicama
2 mangoes

1. Combine lime juice and next 5 ingredients.
2. Place red onion, cilantro, and mint in a large bowl. Dice watermelon and cantaloupe into 1-inch pieces; add to bowl. Peel and dice cucumbers, jicama, and mangoes; add to bowl. Stir in lime juice mixture. Cover and chill 20 minutes. Add salt and pepper to taste.

Spinach-Artichoke Dip Potato Salad

party perfect

MAKES: 10 to 12 servings
HANDS-ON TIME: 35 min.
TOTAL TIME: 1 hr., 10 min.

3 lb. small red potatoes
1 (9-oz.) package frozen chopped spinach
1 (8-oz.) package cream cheese, softened
¾ cup mayonnaise
½ cup buttermilk
¼ cup chopped fresh flat-leaf parsley
2 Tbsp. white wine vinegar
2 garlic cloves, minced
2 tsp. dried Italian seasoning
1 tsp. salt
½ tsp. freshly ground pepper
2 (6-oz.) jars marinated artichoke hearts, drained and chopped
¾ cup freshly grated Parmesan cheese
¾ cup chopped red onion
1½ cups coarsely crushed kettle-cooked potato chips

1. Cook potatoes in boiling water to cover 20 to 25 minutes or just until tender. Drain; cool 15 minutes. Cut into cubes.
2. Cook spinach according to package directions, and press between paper towels.
3. Whisk together cream cheese and next 8 ingredients in a large bowl. Stir in artichoke hearts, next 2 ingredients, and spinach; gently stir in potatoes. Sprinkle with potato chips; serve immediately.

The South's Best Butt

Chopped, pulled, shredded, or sliced, there's nothing like a pork sandwich from the pit. And everyone's got an opinion on which one is boss hog. One thing's for sure: These 20 barbecue joints do it right.

Readers' Picks

You voted on Facebook (and were pretty nice to each other). Here, your top pork sandwiches:

{1}

JIM 'N NICK'S BAR-B-Q, Birmingham, AL; *jimnnicks.com*

{2}

SOUTHERN SOUL BARBEQUE, St. Simons Island, GA; *southernsoulbbq.com*

{3}

MEMPHIS BARBECUE CO., Horn Lake, MS; *memphisbbqco.com*

{4}

FOX BROS. BAR-B-Q, Atlanta, GA; *foxbrosbbq.com*

{5}

MARTIN'S BAR-B-QUE JOINT, Nolensville, TN; *martinsbbqjoint.com*

{6}

THE SHED BARBEQUE & BLUES JOINT, Ocean Springs, MS; *theshedbbq.com*

{7}

THE SKYLIGHT INN, Ayden, NC; *252/746-4113*

{8}

HOME TEAM BBQ, Charleston, SC; *hometeambbq.com*

{9}

PAPA BUCK'S BBQ, Metter, GA; *papabucks.com*

{10}

MOE'S ORIGINAL BAR B QUE, Huntsville, AL; *moesoriginalbbq.com*

A&R Bar-B-Que

Memphis, Tennessee

A&R serves tamales, bologna, and barbecue spaghetti, but the star is the sloppy chopped-pork sandwich, twitching with tangy slaw and bathed in a sauce that doesn't obscure the robust smokiness of the meat. *aandrbbq.com*

Allen & Son BBQ

Chapel Hill, North Carolina

If a foreigner was studying for a barbecue exam, the Allen & Son flash card would surely get a workout. Keith Allen's restaurant straddles the dividing line between western and eastern Carolina 'cue, and idiosyncratically borrows from both traditions. They use a thin, vinegar-based sauce, the same as Eastern pitmasters, but cook only shoulders, considered the Piedmont's domain. *919/942-7576*

The Bar-B-Q Shop

Memphis, Tennessee

It's not hard to find an expertly smoked pork shoulder in Memphis, but this sandwich has won accolades for its accoutrements, including a mustard-tinged sauce, a fiery hot sauce, and sturdy Texas toast. *dancingpigs.com*

BBQ Barn

North Augusta, South Carolina

South Carolina is the only state with four distinct sauce regions, and BBQ Barn offers them all, including the thick mustard variety rarely found beyond Palmetto State borders. *803/278-7202*

2012 'Cue Awards

Bozo's Hot Pit Bar-B-Q

Mason, Tennessee

Bozo's had a bit part in *Walk the Line,* the 2005 Johnny Cash biopic, but the western Tennessee restaurant has long been famed for its treatment of pork shoulders, which emerge moist and tender from the pit, bearing the faintest trace of smoke. *901/294-3400*

The Brick Pit

Mobile, Alabama

On its website, The Brick Pit features testimonials from a car dealer, a banker, and a bonsai artist. But it doesn't take a professional palate to appreciate their succulent pulled pork, slathered with a thick tomato sauce. *brickpit.com*

Bunn's Barbecue

Windsor, North Carolina

Sandwiched between two flaps of crisp cornbread, Bunn's minced Boston butt is so good it may explain why the Russell family rebuilds every time the coastal restaurant suffers a hurricane-inflicted flood. *252/794-2274*

Georgia Pig Bar-B-Que

Fort Lauderdale, Florida

Wayne Anderson chops oak-smoked meat and crunchy bits of bark before saucing with his tangy original sauce. *954/587-4420*

Jim 'N Nick's Bar-B-Q

Multiple locations across the South

A multiunit chain might provoke skepticism from purists, but Jim 'N Nick's produces a phenomenal pork shoulder with traditional methods many have written off as too time-consuming. Committed to freshness and sustainability, the restaurant just launched its own heritage pork-raising program, and none of the 28 locations even has a freezer. *jimnnicks.com*

Jimmy's BBQ

Lexington, North Carolina

A prickly, red slaw tops the pork shoulder at Jimmy's, a Lexington mainstay that specializes in chewy, hickory-scented meat. *336/357-2311*

Leigh's Barbecue

Kevil, Kentucky

There aren't any pretensions at Leigh's, where the terrific hickory-kissed pork shoulder is chopped to order and sauced with vinegar. *270/488-3434*

Lexington Barbecue

Lexington, North Carolina

The defining Piedmont barbecue joint—known locally as The Monk's Place—chops its shoulders and slaw into an extraordinary mixture of sweetness and smoke. *336/249-9814*

Martin's Bar-B-Que Joint

Nolensville, Tennessee

Patrick Martin's open-faced sandwich, what he calls a Redneck Taco, piles hickory-smoked pork, slaw, and Piedmont-style tomato sauce atop a plate-size hoecake. *martinsbbqjoint.com*

Neely's

Marshall, Texas

Marooned in beef territory, Neely's is known by locals as The Brown Pig. The 85-year-old restaurant crowns ground smoked shoulder with mayonnaise, lettuce, and the signature sauce on a hamburger bun. *903/935-9040*

Papa Kayjoe's

Centerville, Tennessee

The flat disks of cornbread that bookend Papa Kayjoe's pork sandwich are fried to order in lard, in keeping with pitmaster Devin Pickard's philosophy that barbecue ought to be a celebration of swine fat. "I know when folks think of grease they think of unhealthy," he famously told a Southern Foodways Alliance oral historian in 2008. "But the key to good barbecue is grease." *931/729-2131*

Payne's Bar-B-Q

Memphis, Tennessee

Arguments rage over the best barbecue in Memphis, but the field narrows when you talk sandwiches. At Payne's, where lunch is so popular it's punctuated by the nonstop slap of a cleaver on the chopping block, the pork sandwich is graced with smoke-tinged bark, a robe of tomato-based sauce, and mustard slaw yellow as a buttercup. *901/272-1523*

2012 'Cue Awards

Pecan Lodge

Dallas, Texas

In a state known for barbecue, Dallas is rarely a player. But Pecan Lodge has reset 'cue expectations with killer pulled pork developed to satisfy the owners' Carolina nostalgia. *pecanlodge.com*

Red Bridges Barbecue Lodge

Shelby, North Carolina

Longtime customers know to request their sandwiches with "outside brown," the dark, chewy bark that lends textural zing and a woodsy demeanor to chopped meat. *bridgesbbq.com*

Saucy's Walk-up Bar.B.Q.

Petersburg, Virginia

The reclaimed shipping container that houses Saucy's may be the ultimate 21st-century symbol. But the meat served from within is smoked according to long-standing low-and-slow traditions, then swabbed with sauces such as mustard-jalapeño. *saucysbbq.com*

Sims Bar-B-Que

Little Rock, Arkansas

In 1937, Allen Sims and his wife, Amelia, opened a cafe, and quickly became known for great barbecue and their tangy, brown Sims Sauce, which they apply to every serving of chopped pork. *simsbarbeque-ar.com*

FOOD GIFT OF THE MONTH

Smoky-Sweet BBQ Rub

Prepare batches of this spicy gift and divvy it up by the cupful. It's the perfect base for our Smoked Pork Butt *(page 144)*.

MAKE IT!

MAKES: 1 cup
HANDS-ON TIME: 5 min.
TOTAL TIME: 5 min.

- ¼ cup kosher salt
- ¼ cup firmly packed dark brown sugar
- 2 Tbsp. plus 2 tsp. smoked paprika
- 2 Tbsp. granulated sugar
- 2 tsp. garlic powder
- 2 tsp. freshly ground pepper
- 1 tsp. dry mustard
- 1 tsp. ground cumin
- 1 tsp. ground ginger

1. Stir together all ingredients. Store in an airtight container up to 1 month.

TAKE IT!

These small jars, which come with a wooden spoon just right for dipping out spices, make charming gift wrap. Find them at Hobby Lobby ($2.67 each).

DOWNLOAD OUR GIFT TAGS:
southernliving.com/food-gift

SMOKY-SWEET BBQ RUB

Use 1 Tbsp. per pound of pork, beef, or chicken. Let stand 30 minutes before grilling or smoking.

July

Just Ripe for Summer

Cookbook author Virginia Willis shares some of her favorite fresh-off-the-vine tomato recipes in honor of the year's juiciest season.

Tomato Panzanella

Tomato Panzanella

quick prep • make-ahead • party perfect

MAKES: 4 to 6 servings
HANDS-ON TIME: 30 min.
TOTAL TIME: 1 hr.
(Also pictured on page 180)

1. Toss together 1 cup cooked fresh corn kernels; 2 lb. large heirloom tomatoes, coarsely chopped; 1 Tbsp. dry white wine; ½ (16-oz.) French bread loaf, cut into 1-inch cubes and toasted; 1 English cucumber, sliced; ½ cup extra virgin olive oil; ¼ red onion, thinly sliced; ⅓ cup torn fresh basil; and salt and pepper to taste. Let stand 30 minutes. Add 1 Tbsp. sherry vinegar, and toss to combine.

> ### VIRGINIA'S TIP
>
> **TOMATO PANZANELLA:**
> To layer the flavors further, substitute an unrefined corn oil, which tastes like fresh sweet corn, for some of the extra virgin olive oil. The wine seems like an unusual addition, but it will actually bring out the flavor of the tomatoes.

BLT Salad

quick prep • good for you • party perfect

MAKES: 4 servings
HANDS-ON TIME: 30 min.
TOTAL TIME: 40 min.
(Pictured on page 180)

- 6 artisan bread slices, halved
- 2 Tbsp. extra virgin olive oil
- 1 tsp. kosher salt, divided
- 1 tsp. freshly ground pepper, divided
- 6 thick applewood-smoked bacon slices, chopped
- 1 sweet onion, halved and sliced
- 1 garlic clove
- ½ cup mayonnaise
- 2 Tbsp. fresh lemon juice
- 1 lb. assorted heirloom tomatoes, cut into wedges
- 1 (5-oz.) package arugula

Tomato-and-Okra
Cornmeal Cakes

1. Preheat oven to 400°. Drizzle bread with oil; sprinkle with ½ tsp. each kosher salt and pepper. Bake bread in a single layer in a jelly-roll pan 12 minutes or until golden.

2. Cook bacon in a skillet over medium heat, stirring occasionally, 10 minutes or until crisp. Drain on paper towels; reserve 1 Tbsp. drippings in skillet.

3. Sauté onion in hot drippings over medium-low heat 3 to 5 minutes or until tender.

4. Smash garlic to make a paste. Whisk together mayonnaise, lemon juice, garlic paste, and remaining ½ tsp. each salt and pepper.

5. Toss together tomatoes, arugula, bacon, onion, and salt and pepper to taste in a large bowl. Pour mayonnaise mixture over tomato mixture, and toss to coat. Serve immediately with toasted bread.

VIRGINIA'S TIP

BLT SALAD: The garlicky, mayo-based dressing is a tangy addition to this reinvented BLT. Use the flat side of a knife to smash the garlic clove into a paste. If you want the dressing a tad thinner, add 1 to 2 Tbsp. water.

Tomato-and-Okra Cornmeal Cakes

quick prep • party perfect

MAKES: 16 appetizer servings
HANDS-ON TIME: 50 min.
TOTAL TIME: 50 min.

Other tasty additions to this recipe might include bacon pieces, microgreens, chopped avocado, or fresh broccoli sprouts.

  2 **cups plain yellow cornmeal**
  2 **tsp. baking powder**
  1 **tsp. fine sea salt**
  1 **large egg**
  1 **garlic clove**
  ½ **lb. fresh okra, thinly sliced**
  1 **jalapeño pepper, seeded and
      finely chopped**
  ¼ **cup canola oil**
      Kosher salt
      Freshly ground pepper
  ¾ **cup of your favorite pimiento
      cheese**
      Arugula
  1 **lb. small tomatoes, cut into
      ¼-inch-thick slices**
      Fresh basil leaves

1. Whisk together first 3 ingredients in a large bowl. Whisk together egg and 1½ cups water; add to cornmeal mixture, whisking until smooth.

VIRGINIA'S TIP

TOMATO-AND-OKRA CORNMEAL CAKES: If okra isn't quite in season, you can leave it out. Also, in place of pimiento cheese, you can try soft goat cheese, sheep's milk ricotta, or whipped cream cheese.

2. Smash garlic to make a paste. Stir okra, jalapeño, and garlic paste into cornmeal mixture. (Batter will be thick and will thicken even more as it sits, so add water, if needed.)

3. Heat 1 Tbsp. oil in a large cast-iron skillet over medium heat. Pour 1 Tbsp. batter for each cake into skillet, and gently flatten into a 2-inch cake. (Don't overcrowd the cakes in the skillet.) Cook 2 to 3 minutes or until tops are covered with bubbles. Turn and cook 2 to 3 more minutes. Transfer to a paper towel-lined plate. Season with kosher salt and pepper. Keep warm in a 200° oven. Repeat procedure with remaining batter and oil.

4. Spread each cake with about 1 tsp. pimiento cheese. Top with arugula, tomato, basil, and kosher salt and pepper.

Old-fashioned Tomato Pie

make-ahead • party perfect

MAKES: 6 to 8 servings
HANDS-ON TIME: 50 min.
TOTAL TIME: 3 hr., 25 min.
(Also pictured on page 181)

PIECRUST

- 1¼ **cups all-purpose flour**
- ¼ **cup cold vegetable shortening, cut into pieces**
- 4 **Tbsp. cold unsalted butter, cut into pieces**
- ½ **tsp. fine sea salt**
- 3 **to 4 Tbsp. ice-cold water**

FILLING

- 2¼ **lb. assorted heirloom tomatoes, thinly sliced**
- 1¼ **tsp. kosher salt, divided**
- 1 **sweet onion, chopped**
- 1¼ **tsp. freshly ground pepper, divided**
- 1 **Tbsp. canola oil**
- ½ **cup assorted chopped fresh herbs (such as chives, parsley, and basil)**
- ½ **cup freshly grated Gruyère cheese**
- ½ **cup freshly grated Parmigiano-Reggiano cheese**
- ¼ **cup mayonnaise**

Old-fashioned Tomato Pie

1. Prepare Piecrust: Process first 4 ingredients in a food processor until mixture resembles coarse meal. With processor running, gradually add 3 Tbsp. ice-cold water, 1 Tbsp. at a time, and process until dough forms a ball and leaves sides of bowl, adding up to 1 Tbsp. more water, if necessary. Shape dough into a disk, and wrap in plastic wrap. Chill 30 minutes.

2. Unwrap dough, and place on a lightly floured surface; sprinkle lightly with flour. Roll dough to ⅛-inch thickness.

3. Preheat oven to 425°. Press dough into a 9-inch pie plate. Trim dough 1 inch larger than diameter of pie plate; fold overhanging dough under itself along rim of pie plate. Chill 30 minutes or until firm.

4. Line piecrust with aluminum foil; fill with pie weights or dried beans. (This will keep the crust from bubbling up.) Place on an aluminum foil-lined baking sheet.

5. Bake at 425° for 20 minutes. Remove weights and foil. Bake 5 minutes or until browned. Cool completely on baking sheet on a wire rack (about 30 minutes). Reduce oven temperature to 350°.

6. Prepare Filling: Place tomatoes in a single layer on paper towels; sprinkle with 1 tsp. salt. Let stand 10 minutes.

7. Meanwhile, sauté onion and ¼ tsp. each salt and pepper in hot oil in a skillet over medium heat 3 minutes or until onion is tender.

8. Pat tomatoes dry with a paper towel. Layer tomatoes, onion, and herbs in prepared crust, seasoning each layer with pepper (1 tsp. total). Stir together cheeses and mayonnaise; spread over pie.

9. Bake at 350° for 30 minutes or until lightly browned, shielding edges with foil to prevent excessive browning. Serve hot, warm, or at room temperature.

VIRGINIA'S TIP

OLD-FASHIONED TOMATO PIE: This plate of goodness is always a home run. Don't skip salting the tomatoes. This step rids them of excess juice, so you'll have a nice firm pie, not a soggy mess.

Garden Cocktail

quick prep • party perfect

MAKES: 1 serving
HANDS-ON TIME: 10 min.
TOTAL TIME: 3 hr., 40 min., including tomato juice

You can make the Garden Tomato Juice up to 1 week ahead. It will yield 1 qt. homemade tomato juice, or enough for 8 cocktails. (Also pictured on page 180)

GARDEN TOMATO JUICE

- 3 lb. very ripe red or yellow tomatoes, coarsely chopped
- 1¼ cups chopped celery with leaves
- ⅓ cup chopped onion
- ½ tsp. kosher salt
- ½ tsp. freshly ground pepper

COCKTAIL

- 1 Tbsp. kosher salt
- 1 Tbsp. finely chopped fresh flat-leaf parsley
- 1 lime wedge
- ½ medium tomato, seeded and chopped
- 1 fresh basil sprig
- ¼ cup gin
  Garnishes: cucumber spears, celery ribs, fresh basil sprigs, lime wedges

1. Prepare Tomato Juice: Bring tomatoes and next 4 ingredients to a simmer in a large nonaluminum saucepan over medium heat; simmer 25 minutes or until mixture is soft. Cool 30 minutes. Process, in 2 batches, in a blender until smooth. Pour through a fine wire-mesh strainer into a container, discarding solids. Cover and chill 2 hours.

2. Prepare Cocktail: Combine kosher salt and parsley. Rub rim of a glass with lime wedge; dip rim in salt mixture to coat. Muddle tomato and basil sprig against sides of glass to release flavors. Fill glass with ice. Stir in gin and ½ cup Garden Tomato Juice. Sprinkle with ground pepper.

Garden Cocktail

VIRGINIA'S TIP

GARDEN COCKTAIL: You can substitute bottled juice for Garden Tomato Juice to save time. But if you make it fresh, don't use an aluminum saucepan—it will react with the tomato acid. Store in the fridge up to 1 week.

Mexican Tomato Soup

good for you • party perfect

MAKES: 4 to 6 servings
HANDS-ON TIME: 1 hr., 5 min.
TOTAL TIME: 1 hr., 40 min.
(Pictured on page 180)

- 6 (6-inch) corn tortillas
- 2 Tbsp. canola oil, divided
- 2 medium tomatoes, cored and halved
- 1 onion, chopped
- 2 garlic cloves
- 1 (32-oz.) container reduced-sodium fat-free chicken broth
- 2 cups low-sodium tomato juice
- 1 bay leaf
- ¼ tsp. ground cumin
- ¼ tsp. ground coriander
- ¼ tsp. ground red pepper
- 1½ lb. skinned and boned chicken breasts, cut into ½-inch-wide strips
- 4 green onions (white part only), thinly sliced
- ½ cup fresh lime juice
- ¼ cup chopped fresh cilantro
- ½ cup crumbled queso fresco (fresh Mexican cheese)
- 1 medium avocado, chopped

1. Preheat oven to 400°. Brush 1 side of tortillas with 1 Tbsp. oil; cut tortillas in half. Stack tortilla halves, and cut crosswise into ¼-inch-wide strips. Arrange strips in a single layer on a lightly greased baking sheet. Season with salt and pepper. Bake 15 minutes or until golden, stirring halfway through. Cool.

2. Meanwhile, heat a nonstick skillet over high heat 2 minutes. Add tomato halves, and cook, turning occasionally, 10 minutes or until charred on all sides. (Tomatoes may stick.) Transfer to a food processor.

3. Sauté onion in remaining 1 Tbsp. hot oil in skillet over medium heat 3 to 5 minutes or until tender. Add garlic, and sauté 2 minutes or until fragrant. Transfer onion mixture to food processor with tomatoes; process until smooth.

4. Cook tomato mixture in a Dutch oven over medium-high heat, stirring occasionally, 5 minutes or until thickened. Stir in broth and tomato juice. Add bay leaf and next 3 ingredients; bring to a boil. Reduce heat to medium-low, and simmer, partially covered and stirring occasionally, 20 minutes.

5. Add chicken; simmer, stirring occasionally, 5 to 7 minutes or until chicken is done.

6. Discard bay leaf. Stir in green onions and next 2 ingredients. Season with salt and pepper. Divide queso fresco among 4 to 6 soup bowls; top with tortilla strips. Ladle soup into bowls. Top with avocado.

Tomato Sandwiches

Go beyond the white bread-mayo combo with these twists. For smooth tomato slices, we like the Wüsthof 4109-7 Classic 5-inch Tomato Knife ($50; *amazon.com*).

TEXAS-STYLE BLT

Heat frozen five-cheese Texas toast bread slices according to package directions. Top with lettuce, cooked bacon slices, avocado slices, tomato slices, and hot banana peppers.

GRILLED TOMATO-AND-CHEESE

Layer provolone cheese slices and tomato slices between 2 Italian bread slices. Stir together equal parts mayonnaise and freshly grated Parmesan cheese; spread on outside of sandwich. Cook in a hot skillet over medium heat 3 minutes on each side or until golden.

CHERRY TOMATO CROSTINI

Spread toasted French bread slices with garlic-and-herb spreadable cheese. Top with assorted cherry tomatoes, thinly sliced, and fresh herbs.

CAPRESE SALAD SANDWICH

Layer fresh mozzarella cheese slices, tomato slices, fresh basil leaves, a drizzle of balsamic vinegar, and salt and pepper to taste between 2 ciabatta bread slices.

TOMATO-RICOTTA BRUSCHETTA

Toss together 1 pt. grape tomatoes, 1 Tbsp. honey, 1½ tsp. olive oil, and ¼ tsp. salt on a lightly greased baking sheet. Bake at 450° for 16 to 18 minutes. Top toasted baguette slices with ricotta cheese, roasted tomatoes, and thinly sliced fresh basil.

Lazy Day Summer Cobblers

Save the fussy layer cakes for *after* Labor Day. Summer calls for fast and easy scoopable desserts that celebrate the season's freshest ingredients. (And don't worry: We found the summer version of cream cheese frosting.)

Blackberry-Peach Cobbler with Praline-Pecan Streusel

COBBLE IT TOGETHER

Top scoops of our Blackberry-Peach Cobbler with Praline-Pecan Streusel with vanilla ice cream, Blackberry Syrup *(page 206)*, Mascarpone Cream *(page 159)*, and fresh raspberries.

Blackberry-Peach Cobbler with Praline-Pecan Streusel

make-ahead • party perfect

MAKES: 8 servings
HANDS-ON TIME: 35 min.
TOTAL TIME: 1 hr., 10 min.

Is there anything better than a fresh berry cobbler topped with ice cream? Best make that call after you taste this one with our Mascarpone Cream (page 159) (Also pictured on page 7).

STREUSEL

- ¾ cup firmly packed light brown sugar
- ½ cup butter, melted
- ⅛ tsp. salt
- 1½ cups all-purpose flour
- 1 cup coarsely chopped pecans

FILLING

- 4 cups peeled and sliced fresh peaches (about 4 large)
- ½ cup granulated sugar
- 3 Tbsp. all-purpose flour
- ¼ tsp. ground nutmeg
- 2 cups fresh blackberries

1. Prepare Streusel: Stir together first 3 ingredients in a large bowl; add flour and pecans, and stir until blended. Let stand 20 minutes or until mixture is firm enough to crumble into small pieces.

2. Meanwhile, prepare Filling: Preheat oven to 375°. Stir together peaches and next 3 ingredients in a large saucepan; bring to a boil over medium-high heat. Reduce heat to medium, and boil, stirring occasionally, 6 to 7 minutes or until juices have thickened. Remove from heat, and stir in blackberries. Spoon mixture into a lightly greased 9-inch square baking dish. Crumble streusel over hot peach mixture.

3. Bake at 375° for 30 to 35 minutes or until bubbly and golden brown.

Red Velvet-Berry Cobbler

Red Velvet-Berry Cobbler

make-ahead • party perfect

MAKES: 6 to 8 servings
HANDS-ON TIME: 20 min.
TOTAL TIME: 1 hr., 15 min.

Top with scoops of homemade Cream Cheese Ice Cream (facing page) for a cool summery twist on the classic Southern layer cake.

COBBLE IT TOGETHER

Layer scoops of Red Velvet-Berry Cobbler, Cream Cheese Ice Cream, and fresh berries in glasses. Top with sprigs of fresh mint.

1 Tbsp. cornstarch
1¼ cups sugar, divided
6 cups assorted fresh berries (We used 2 cups each blackberries, raspberries, and blueberries.)
½ cup butter, softened
2 large eggs
2 Tbsp. red liquid food coloring
1 tsp. vanilla extract
1¼ cups all-purpose flour
1½ Tbsp. unsweetened cocoa
¼ tsp. salt
½ cup buttermilk
1½ tsp. white vinegar
½ tsp. baking soda

1. Preheat oven to 350°. Stir together cornstarch and ½ cup sugar. Toss berries with cornstarch mixture, and spoon into a lightly greased 11- x 7-inch baking dish.

2. Beat butter at medium speed with an electric mixer until fluffy; gradually add remaining ¾ cup sugar, beating well. Add eggs, 1 at a time, beating just until blended after each addition. Stir in red food coloring and vanilla until blended.

3. Combine flour, cocoa, and salt. Stir together buttermilk, vinegar, and baking soda in a 2-cup liquid measuring cup. (Mixture will bubble.) Add flour mixture to butter mixture alternately with buttermilk mixture, beginning and ending with flour mixture. Beat at low speed until blended after each addition. Spoon batter over berry mixture.

4. Bake at 350° for 45 to 50 minutes or until a wooden pick inserted in center of cake topping comes out clean. Cool on a wire rack 10 minutes.

Top it Off

{1}
Hot Fudge Sauce

GREAT WITH: *Chocolate-Cherry Cobbler (see below)*

Microwave 1 (4-oz.) semisweet chocolate baking bar, chopped, and ¾ cup heavy cream in a small microwave-safe bowl at HIGH 1½ minutes or until chocolate melts and mixture is smooth, stirring at 30-second intervals. Makes: about 1 cup.

{2}
Butterscotch-Bourbon Sauce

GREAT WITH: *TennTucky Blackberry Cobbler and Summer Fruit Cobbler (page 160)*

Cook 1½ cups firmly packed light brown sugar and ½ cup butter in a large heavy saucepan over medium heat, stirring constantly, 3 to 4 minutes or until butter melts and mixture is smooth. Gradually stir in ¾ cup whipping cream. Bring mixture to a boil, stirring constantly; boil, stirring constantly, 3 minutes. Remove from heat, and stir in 3 Tbsp. bourbon. Cool 20 minutes. Makes: about 2 cups.

{3}
Mascarpone Cream

GREAT WITH: *Blackberry-Peach Cobbler with Praline-Pecan Streusel (page 157)*

Whisk together 1 (8-oz.) container mascarpone cheese, ⅓ cup heavy cream, 3 Tbsp. sugar, and 1 tsp. vanilla extract until blended. (Do not use an electric mixer.) Makes: about 1½ cups.

SWITCH IT UP
Chocolate-Cherry Cobbler: Omit red food coloring. Substitute 6 cups pitted fresh cherries (about 2½ to 3 lb.) for berries. Decrease flour to 1 cup, and increase unsweetened cocoa to ¼ cup. Proceed with recipe as directed.

For a **Chocolate-Cherry Cobbler sundae,** top scoops of Chocolate-Cherry Cobbler with vanilla ice cream, Hot Fudge Sauce (box above), sweetened whipped cream, and fresh cherries (with stems).

Cream Cheese Ice Cream
make-ahead • party perfect

MAKES: about 1 qt.
HANDS-ON TIME: 25 min.
TOTAL TIME: 9 hr., 25 min., not including freezing

- 3 **cups half-and-half**
- 1¼ **cups powdered sugar**
- 2 **egg yolks**
- 1 **(8-oz.) package cream cheese, cubed and softened**
- 2 **tsp. vanilla bean paste or vanilla extract**

1. Whisk together first 3 ingredients in a large heavy saucepan. Cook over medium heat, whisking constantly, 8 to 10 minutes or until mixture thickens slightly. Remove from heat, and whisk in cream cheese and vanilla bean paste until cheese is melted. Cool completely (about 1 hour), stirring occasionally. Place plastic wrap directly on mixture (to prevent a film from forming), and chill 8 to 24 hours.

2. Pour mixture into freezer container of a 1½-qt. electric ice-cream maker, and freeze according to manufacturer's instructions. (Instructions and times may vary.) Transfer ice cream to an airtight container. Freeze 4 hours before serving.

TennTucky Blackberry Cobbler

make-ahead • party perfect

MAKES: 6 to 8 servings
HANDS-ON TIME: 20 min.
TOTAL TIME: 1 hr., 25 min.

- 3 Tbsp. cornstarch
- 1½ cups sugar, divided
- 6 cups fresh blackberries
- ½ cup butter, softened
- 2 large eggs
- 1½ cups all-purpose flour
- 1½ tsp. baking powder
- 1 (8-oz.) container sour cream
- ½ tsp. baking soda

1. Preheat oven to 350°. Stir together cornstarch and ½ cup sugar. Toss berries with cornstarch mixture, and spoon into a lightly greased 11- x 7-inch baking dish.
2. Beat butter at medium speed with an electric mixer until fluffy; gradually add remaining 1 cup sugar, beating well. Add eggs, 1 at a time, beating just until blended after each addition.
3. Combine flour and baking powder. Stir together sour cream and baking soda. Add flour mixture to butter mixture alternately with sour cream mixture, beginning and ending with flour mixture. Beat at low speed just until blended after each addition. Spoon batter over berry mixture.
4. Bake at 350° for 45 minutes; shield loosely with aluminum foil to prevent excessive browning, and bake 20 to 25 minutes or until a wooden pick inserted in center of cake topping comes out clean.

SWITCH IT UP

Summer Fruit Cobbler: Substitute 3 cups coarsely chopped, peeled fresh nectarines; 2 cups fresh blueberries; and 1 cup fresh raspberries for blackberries.

COBBLE IT TOGETHER

Turn TennTucky Blackberry Cobbler into a cobbler sundae by layering it with vanilla ice cream, Butterscotch-Bourbon Sauce *(page 159)*, and lightly salted toasted pecans in tall soda fountain glasses.

TennTucky Blackberry Cobbler

Ashley's Meatloaf-and-Mashed Potato Sandwiches (page 29)

clockwise from top left:

• Edward's Open-Faced Meatloaf Sandwiches (page 28) • Wesley's Gulf Coast Shrimp and Grits (page 33) • José's Black Beans & Rice (page 34) • David's Chicken-Fried Steak with Redeye Gravy (page 30)

Chris' Tex-Mex Mac and
Cheese (page 32)

clockwise from top left:

- Chutney Chicken Salad (page 64) • Creamy Egg Strata (page 65) • Sunshine Citrus Platter (page 63) • Chilled Carrot Soup and Brown Sugar Bacon (page 65)

Lemon-Rosemary Coffee
Cake (page 66)

Grilled Shrimp and Spinach Salad (page 60)

Blueberry Fields Salad (page 60)

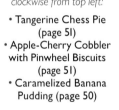

clockwise from top left:
- Tangerine Chess Pie (page 51)
- Apple-Cherry Cobbler with Pinwheel Biscuits (page 51)
- Caramelized Banana Pudding (page 50)

Hummingbird Bundt Cake (page 52)

Crowd-Pleasing
Tea Sandwiches (page 70)

Cornbread Madeleines (page 76) and
Tomato-Basil Bisque (page 69),
(below) Cranberry-Strawberry Salad,
(page 70) and Tarragon Chicken Salad (page 69)

Chilled Strawberry Soup and
Strawberry Chicken Salad (page 85)

clockwise from top left:
- Strawberry Salsa (page 85)
- Strawberry-Basil Frozen Yogurt (page 83)
- Strawberry Caprese Salad and Strawberry Bruschetta (page 86)
- Strawberry-Lemonade Muffins (page 85)

Shrimp Destin Linguine (page 80)

Fettuccine-and-Asparagus
al Burro (page 79)

clockwise from top left:

• Fried Green Tomato
Sliders (page 99)
• Shrimp Boil Skewers
(page 101) • Hoppin' John
Parfaits (page 103) • Cracker
Spoons with Creamy
Pimiento Cheese (page 98)
• Mini Grits and Greens
(page 99)

Buttermilk Chicken
and Waffles (page 103)

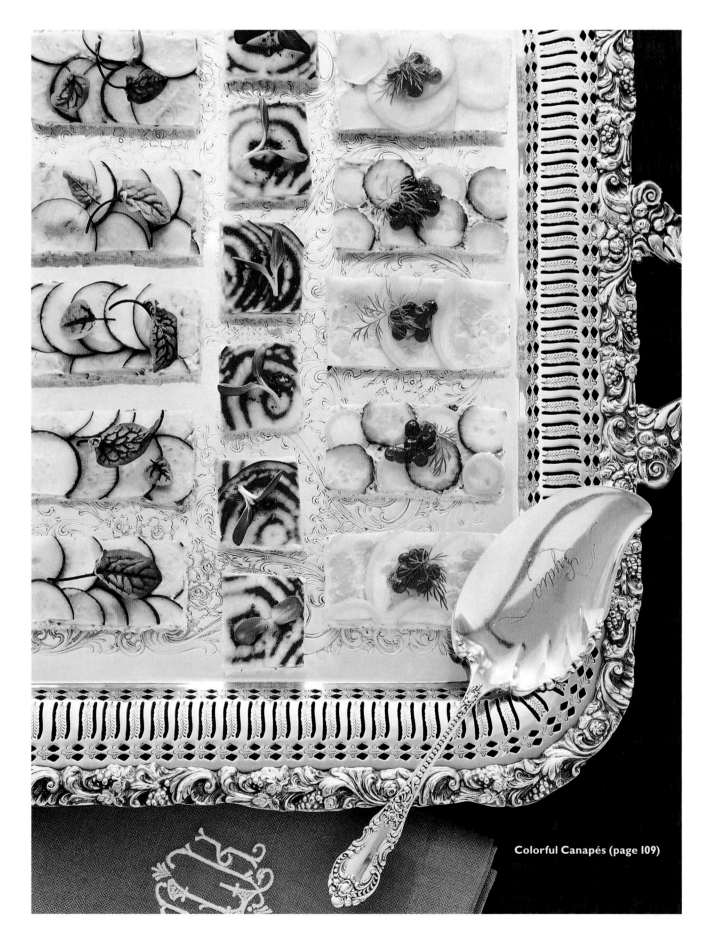

Colorful Canapés (page 109)

clockwise from top left:

• Roasted Brown-Butter Pecans with Rosemary (page 106)
• Spring-on-a-Plate Salads (page 107) • Assorted vegetables with Whipped Lemon Aïoli (page 107)
• Fluffy Cream Cheese Biscuits and Ginger Ale-Brown Sugar Smoked Ham (page 108)

clockwise from top left:
- Tomato Panzanella (page 152) • Garden Cocktail (page 155) • BLT Salad (page 152) • Mexican Tomato Soup (page 156)

Old-fashioned Tomato
Pie (page 154)

Grilled Watermelon with Blue
Cheese and Prosciutto (page 208)

182

clockwise from top left:
- Watermelon Bellini
  (page 209)
- Beef-and-Watermelon
  Stir-fry (page 208)
- Herbed Goat Cheese-
  Melon Party Bites
  (page 209)
- Tipsy Red-and-Yellow
  Watermelon Salad
  (page 209)

Mexican Chocolate Ice-cream Pie (page 218)

Chipotle Shrimp Cocktail
(page 2l7)

clockwise from top left:

- Butternut Squash Soup (page 231)
- Farmer Salad (page 230)
- Grilled Fingerling Potato Salad (page 232)

Pineapple Upside-Down
Cake (page 232)

Barbecue Bloody Mary, Apple Pie-Bourbon Sweet Tea, Brewmosa (page 235)

Mini Bourbon-and-Cola Bundt Cakes (page 240), Buttermilk Chess Tarts, Chocolate Chess Tarts, and Lemon-Coconut Tarts (page 241)

Peanut Butter-Banana Pudding (page 241)

Beef Ribs with Sorghum
Glaze (page 250)

Turkey, Brie, and Apple Panini with Bacon Marmalade (page 251)

Black Forest Pound Cake (page 249)

Build a Better Hot Dog

We dressed up a variety of store-bought favorites, and, frankly, they're delicious.

{1}

Thai-Style Dogs

good for you • party perfect

THE DOG: *Turkey hot dogs*
THE BUN: *Unsliced bakery buns*

Whisk together 2 Tbsp. seasoned rice wine vinegar, 1½ tsp. sesame oil, ½ tsp. honey, ¼ tsp. fish sauce, and ⅛ tsp. dried crushed red pepper. Stir in 2 cups chopped red cabbage, ½ cup sliced English cucumber, and ¼ cup grated carrot. Cover and chill 2 hours. Stir together ¼ cup light mayonnaise, ¾ tsp. fresh lime juice, and ½ tsp. Asian Sriracha hot chili sauce. Split tops of buns lengthwise. Grill 8 turkey dogs according to package directions; place in buns. Top with cabbage mixture, mayonnaise mixture, cilantro leaves, chopped cocktail peanuts, and sliced radishes. Makes: 8 servings

PER SERVING: **CALORIES** 210; **FAT** 5G (**SAT** 1G); **PROTEIN** 11G; **CARB** 31G; **FIBER** 2G; **CHOL** 20MG; **IRON** 2MG; **SODIUM** 968 MG (580MG FROM HOT DOG); **CALC** 71MG

{2}

Greek-Style Dogs

quick prep • good for you
make-ahead • party perfect

THE DOG: *Sun-dried tomato chicken sausages*
THE BUN: *Reduced-fat hot dog buns*

Stir together 1 (7-oz.) container 2% reduced-fat plain Greek yogurt, 2 Tbsp. light mayonnaise, 1 Tbsp. grated cucumber, 2 tsp. chopped fresh chives, 1 tsp. chopped fresh dill, ½ tsp. lemon zest, 2 tsp. fresh lemon juice; add salt and pepper. Cook 4 sausages according to package directions. Place sausages in buns. Top with yogurt mixture, shredded romaine lettuce, thinly sliced red onion, diced tomato and cucumber, and bottled Greek dressing. Makes: 4 servings

PER SERVING: **CALORIES** 304; **FAT** 13G (**SAT** 4G); **PROTEIN** 23G; **CARB** 27G; **FIBER** 3G; **CHOL** 76MG; **IRON** 3MG; **SODIUM** 789 MG (480MG FROM HOT DOG); **CALC** 66MG

{3}

Muffuletta Dogs

good for you • make-ahead • party perfect

THE DOG: *97% fat-free beef hot dogs*
THE BUN: *Hoagie rolls, split lengthwise and hollowed out*

Stir together 2 cups chopped fresh cauliflower; ½ cup grated carrot; 3 reduced-fat provolone cheese slices, chopped; ⅓ cup thinly sliced celery; ⅓ cup chopped jarred marinated roasted red bell peppers; ¼ cup chopped pimiento-stuffed Spanish olives; ¼ cup chopped kalamata olives; ¼ cup chopped fresh parsley; and ¼ cup bottled light olive oil vinaigrette. Cover and chill 2 hours. Grill 6 hot dogs according to package directions. Place hot dogs in rolls, and top with cauliflower mixture. Makes: 6 servings

PER SERVING: **CALORIES** 364; **FAT** 13G (**SAT** 4G); **PROTEIN** 17G; **CARB** 49G; **FIBER** 6G; **CHOL** 20MG; **IRON** 3MG; **SODIUM** 1,347 MG (520MG FROM HOT DOG); **CALC** 185MG

{4}

Dixie Caviar Dogs

good for you • make-ahead • party perfect

THE DOG: *Reduced-fat beef hot dogs*
THE BUN: *Reduced-fat wheat hot dog buns*

Stir together 1 (15-oz.) can no-salt-added black-eyed peas, drained and rinsed; ½ cup fresh corn kernels; ¼ cup diced red bell pepper; ¼ cup bottled olive oil-and-vinegar dressing; 2 Tbsp. chopped green onions; 2 Tbsp. chopped pickled jalapeño pepper slices; 2 Tbsp. chopped fresh cilantro; and 1 garlic clove, pressed, in a bowl. Cover and chill 2 hours. Cook 7 hot dogs according to package directions. Place hot dogs in buns; top with pea mixture and, if desired, light sour cream. Makes: 7 servings

PER SERVING: **CALORIES** 342; **FAT** 18G (**SAT** 6G); **PROTEIN** 14G; **CARB** 33G; **FIBER** 4G; **CHOL** 24MG; **IRON** 3MG; **SODIUM** 638MG (490MG FROM HOT DOG); **CALC** 73MG

The No-Fuss Fish Fry

You'll fall hook, line, and sinker for this classic menu of fried fish, perfectly crispy hush puppies, and peanut-topped cola cake.

Our Summer Fish Fry Menu

SERVES 8

FISH FRY

Beer-Battered Fried Fish

Malt Vinegar Mignonette

Buttermilk-Ranch-Herb Sauce

Peach-Ginger Slaw

Grilled Corn-and-Butter Bean Salad

Hush Puppies

SIP WITH

Sparkling Cherry Limeade

SAVE ROOM FOR

Peanut-Cola Cake

WE LOVE THIS!
Fancy up your fish fry with a summery mix of sturdy blue-and-white tableware.

Beer-Battered Fried Fish

quick prep • make-ahead • party perfect

MAKES: 8 servings
HANDS-ON TIME: 30 min.
TOTAL TIME: 30 min.

Any type of white, flaky fish may be substituted for grouper.

    Vegetable oil
2 lb. grouper fillets, cut into pieces
1 tsp. salt
½ tsp. freshly ground pepper
1½ cups all-purpose flour
1½ tsp. sugar
1 tsp. salt
1 (12-oz.) bottle beer
1 tsp. hot sauce

1. Pour oil to depth of 3 inches into a large Dutch oven; heat to 360°.
2. Meanwhile, sprinkle fish with salt and pepper.
3. Whisk together flour and next 2 ingredients in a large bowl. Whisk in beer and hot sauce. Dip fish in batter, allowing excess batter to drip off.
4. Gently lower fish into hot oil using tongs (to prevent fish from sticking to Dutch oven). Fry fish, in 4 batches, 2 to 3 minutes on each side or until golden brown. Place fried fish on a wire rack in a jelly-roll pan; keep warm in a 200° oven until ready to serve.

Hush Puppies

quick prep • make-ahead • party perfect

MAKES: 8 to 10 servings
(ABOUT 2 DOZEN HUSH PUPPIES)
HANDS-ON TIME: 25 min.
TOTAL TIME: 35 min.
(Pictured on page 8)

  Vegetable oil
1½ cups self-rising white cornmeal mix
¾ cup self-rising flour
¾ cup diced sweet onion (about ½ medium onion)
1½ Tbsp. sugar
1 large egg, lightly beaten
1¼ cups buttermilk

1. Pour oil to depth of 3 inches into a Dutch oven; heat to 375°. Combine cornmeal and next 3 ingredients. Add egg and buttermilk; stir just until moistened. Let stand 10 minutes.

2. Drop batter by rounded tablespoonfuls into hot oil, and fry, in 3 batches, 2 to 3 minutes on each side or until golden. Keep warm in a 200° oven.

TRY THESE TWISTS!

Bacon-and-Caramelized Onion Hush Puppies: Increase onion to 1½ cups. Cook 5 bacon slices in a medium skillet over medium heat 5 to 6 minutes or until crisp; drain bacon on paper towels, reserving 2 Tbsp. drippings in skillet. Crumble bacon. Sauté onion in hot drippings over medium-low heat 12 to 15 minutes or until golden brown. Proceed with recipe as directed, stirring in onion and bacon with cornmeal mix in Step 1.

Jalapeño-Pineapple Hush Puppies: Prepare recipe as directed, stirring in ½ cup canned pineapple tidbits and 2 to 3 Tbsp. seeded and diced jalapeño pepper with cornmeal mix in Step 1.

Shrimp-and-Corn Hush Puppies: Prepare recipe as directed, reducing buttermilk to ¾ cup and stirring 1½ cups chopped cooked shrimp (about ¾ lb. peeled) and 1 (8¼-oz.) can cream-style corn into batter in Step 1.

Peach-Ginger Slaw

quick prep • make-ahead • party perfect

MAKES: 8 servings
HANDS-ON TIME: 20 min.
TOTAL TIME: 30 min.

1 cup chopped pecans
3 Tbsp. pepper jelly
¼ cup rice wine vinegar
1 Tbsp. sesame oil
1 tsp. grated fresh ginger
⅓ cup canola oil
1 (16-oz.) package shredded coleslaw mix
2 large fresh peaches, unpeeled and coarsely chopped (about 2 cups)

1. Preheat oven to 350°. Bake pecans in a single layer in a shallow pan 10 to 12 minutes or until toasted and fragrant, stirring halfway through. Cool completely (about 10 minutes).

2. Meanwhile, microwave jelly in a large microwave-safe bowl at HIGH 15 seconds. Whisk in vinegar and next 2 ingredients until blended. Gradually add canola oil in a slow, steady stream, whisking constantly until well blended.

3. Add coleslaw mix, and toss to coat. Gently stir in peaches. Stir in pecans; add salt to taste. Serve immediately, or cover and chill up to 8 hours, stirring in pecans and salt to taste just before serving.

Grilled Corn-and-Butter Bean Salad

good for you • make-ahead • party perfect

MAKES: 8 to 10 servings
HANDS-ON TIME: 35 min.
TOTAL TIME: 3 hr., 20 min.
(Pictured on page 8)

- 1 (16-oz.) package frozen butter beans*
- 4 ears fresh corn, husks removed
- 1 large red onion, cut into thick slices
- 1 large red bell pepper, cut into thick rings
- ¾ cup mayonnaise
- 3 Tbsp. chopped fresh basil
- 1 garlic clove, pressed
- 1 tsp. salt
- 1 tsp. Worcestershire sauce
- ½ tsp. freshly ground pepper
- 1 cup halved grape tomatoes

1. Cook butter beans according to package directions; drain and cool completely (about 20 minutes).
2. Meanwhile, preheat grill to 350° to 400° (medium-high) heat. Grill corn, covered with grill lid, 15 minutes or until done, turning every 4 to 5 minutes. (Some kernels will begin to char and pop.) At the same time, grill onion and bell pepper, covered with grill lid, 5 minutes on each side or until tender. Cool all vegetables completely (about 20 minutes).
3. Cut kernels from cobs. Discard cobs. Chop onion and bell pepper into ½-inch pieces.
4. Stir together mayonnaise and next 5 ingredients. Stir in tomatoes, corn kernels, butter beans, and onion and pepper pieces. Add salt to taste. Cover and chill 2 to 8 hours before serving. Store in refrigerator up to 3 days.

*Fresh butter beans may be substituted.

Peanut-Cola Cake

quick prep • make-ahead • party perfect

MAKES: 12 servings
HANDS-ON TIME: 20 min.
TOTAL TIME: 1 hr., including frosting
(Also pictured on page 7)

- 1 cup cola soft drink
- ½ cup buttermilk
- 1 cup butter, softened
- 1¾ cups sugar
- 2 large eggs, lightly beaten
- 2 tsp. vanilla extract
- 2 cups all-purpose flour
- ¼ cup unsweetened cocoa
- 1 tsp. baking soda
  Peanut Butter Frosting
- 1 cup chopped honey-roasted peanuts

1. Preheat oven to 350°. Combine cola and buttermilk in a 2-cup measuring cup.
2. Beat butter at low speed with an electric mixer until creamy. Gradually add sugar, beating until blended. Add eggs and vanilla; beat at low speed just until blended.
3. Combine flour and next 2 ingredients in a medium bowl. Add to butter mixture alternately with cola mixture, beginning and ending with flour mixture. Beat at low speed just until blended after each addition. Pour batter into a lightly greased 13- x 9-inch pan.
4. Bake at 350° for 30 to 35 minutes or until a wooden pick inserted in center comes out clean. Cool in pan on a wire rack 10 minutes.
5. Meanwhile, prepare Peanut Butter Frosting. Pour over warm cake. Sprinkle with chopped peanuts.

Peanut Butter Frosting

MAKES: 3 cups
HANDS-ON TIME: 10 min.
TOTAL TIME: 10 min.

- ¼ cup butter
- ¾ cup milk
- 1 cup creamy peanut butter
- 1 (16-oz.) package powdered sugar
- 1 tsp. vanilla extract

1. Melt butter in a large saucepan over medium heat. Whisk in milk, and bring to a boil, whisking constantly. Reduce heat to low, and whisk in peanut butter until smooth. Gradually whisk in powdered sugar until smooth; remove from heat, and whisk in vanilla. Use immediately.

Peanut-Cola Cake

Sparkling Cherry Limeade

Sparkling Cherry Limeade

quick prep • make-ahead • party perfect

MAKES: about 8 cups
HANDS-ON TIME: 10 min.
TOTAL TIME: 10 min.

Add a little tequila and a splash of orange liqueur for a margarita-inspired sparkling cocktail.

1	lime, cut into wedges (optional)
	Margarita salt (optional)
1	(12-oz.) can frozen limeade concentrate, thawed
3½	cups cold water
½	cup liquid from jarred red maraschino cherries
2	cups sparkling water
	Garnishes: lime slices, maraschino cherries

1. Rub rims of 8 chilled glasses with lime wedges, and dip rims in salt to coat, if desired.
2. Stir together limeade concentrate and 3½ cups cold water; add liquid from maraschino cherries.
3. Fill prepared glasses with ice. Pour limeade mixture into glasses, filling each two-thirds full; add sparkling water to fill.
NOTE: We tested with San Pellegrino Sparkling Natural Mineral Water.

Try a Main-Dish Potato Salad

See how this summer staple goes from mayo-drenched side to satisfying meal.

IF YOU HAVE
30 MINUTES

Shrimp-Boil Potato Salad: You can substitute frozen peeled shrimp; toss in during the last 10 minutes of cooking.

IF YOU HAVE
45 MINUTES

Steak-and-Blue Cheese Potato Salad: Save more time by subbing store-bought vinaigrette for homemade.

IF YOU HAVE
1 HOUR

Tuna Potato Salad: Chill tuna in the fridge while you cook. Cutting the potatoes in half after cooking helps them cool quicker.

---

30 MINUTES
Shrimp-Boil Potato Salad

quick prep • good for you
make-ahead • party perfect

MAKES: 6 servings

- 1 (3-oz.) package boil-in-bag shrimp-and-crab boil
- 3 lb. baby red potatoes, halved
- 1 lb. smoked link sausage, cut into ½-inch pieces
- 4 ears fresh corn, husks removed
- 2 lb. peeled and deveined jumbo raw shrimp with tails (26/30 count)
- ½ cup fresh lemon juice
- ⅓ cup olive oil
- ¼ cup chopped fresh flat-leaf parsley
- 3 Tbsp. Creole mustard
- 4 green onions, sliced
- 1 garlic clove, pressed
- 1 tsp. paprika
- 1 tsp. refrigerated horseradish

1. Bring 10 cups water to a boil in a Dutch oven over high heat; add crab boil, potatoes, and sausage; return to a boil, and cook 10 minutes. Add corn, and return to a boil. Cook 3 minutes or until potatoes are tender. Add shrimp; cover, remove from heat, and let stand 5 minutes or just until shrimp turn pink.

2. Meanwhile, whisk together lemon juice and next 7 ingredients in a medium bowl.

3. Drain shrimp mixture. Cut kernels from cobs. Discard cobs. Stir together corn kernels, shrimp mixture, and lemon juice mixture in a large bowl. Serve immediately, or cover and chill up to 24 hours.

NOTE: We tested with Conecuh Original Smoked Sausage.

Potato Salad-Stuffed Spuds with Smoked Chicken

You can top your stuffed potatoes with any type of 'cue.

Preheat oven to 400°. Coat 4 large baking potatoes with vegetable cooking spray; pierce potatoes several times with a fork. Bake 1 hour or until tender. Remove from oven, and cool slightly (about 10 minutes). Cut off top one-third of each potato, and reserve for another use. Carefully scoop out pulp into a bowl, leaving ¼-inch-thick shells intact. Stir together 1 cup sour cream; ⅓ cup apple cider vinegar; 2 garlic cloves, minced; 1 Tbsp. coarsely ground pepper; 1 Tbsp. spicy brown mustard; 1 tsp. salt; 1 tsp. sugar; and 2 tsp. hot sauce. Stir 1 (4-oz.) jar diced pimiento, drained; ¾ cup sour cream mixture; ⅓ cup chopped sweet-hot pickles; and ¼ cup sliced green onions into potato pulp in bowl. Reserve remaining sour cream mixture. Spoon potato mixture into potato shells; cover and chill 1 to 24 hours. Divide ¾ lb. warm shredded smoked chicken; 6 bacon slices, cooked and crumbled; and 1 cup (4 oz.) shredded sharp Cheddar cheese among potatoes; top each with reserved sour cream mixture. Makes: 4 servings

Steak-and-Blue Cheese Potato Salad

quick prep • good for you • party perfect

MAKES: 6 servings

- 1 **lb. asparagus**
- 1½ **lb. baby yellow potatoes, halved**
- 2 **Tbsp. olive oil**
- 1 **(1½-lb.) flank steak**
- 1 **tsp. freshly ground pepper**
- ½ **tsp. salt**
- 1 **red bell pepper, cut into fourths**
- 1 **red onion, cut into 8 wedges**
- ½ **cup red wine vinegar**
- ⅓ **cup olive oil**
- 1 **Tbsp. coarse-grained mustard**
- 1 **tsp. lemon zest**
- 3 **Tbsp. lemon juice**
- 1 **garlic clove, pressed**
- 1 **tsp. salt**
- 1 **(4-oz.) wedge blue cheese, crumbled**

1. Preheat grill to 350° to 400° (medium-high) heat. Snap off and discard tough ends of asparagus. Place potatoes in a single layer in center of a large piece of heavy-duty aluminum foil, and drizzle with 2 Tbsp. olive oil. Bring up sides over potatoes; double fold top and side edges to seal, making a packet. Sprinkle steak with ground pepper and ½ tsp. salt.

2. Grill steak, potatoes (in foil packet), asparagus, bell pepper, and onion at same time, covered with grill lid. Grill potatoes and steak 7 to 8 minutes on each side or until steak reaches desired degree of doneness and potatoes are done, using tongs to shake foil packet just before turning. Grill asparagus, bell pepper, and onion 4 to 5 minutes or until tender. Let steak and vegetables stand 10 minutes.

3. Meanwhile, whisk together vinegar and next 6 ingredients in a small bowl. Place potatoes in a large bowl; toss with half of vinegar mixture, reserving remaining vinegar mixture.

4. Cut steak diagonally across the grain into thin strips. Toss together steak, potatoes, and grilled vegetables, and top with blue cheese. Drizzle with reserved vinegar mixture.

NOTE: We tested with Melissa's Dutch Yellow Baby Potatoes.

Toss Up a Summer Pasta

Even on James Lewis' days off, pasta is his go-to ingredient. The Italian-trained chef stopped by our Test Kitchen to whip up this fresh and healthy dish.

Summer Pasta

quick prep • good for you • party perfect

MAKES: 4 to 6 servings
HANDS-ON TIME: 30 min.
TOTAL TIME: 1 hr.

If you can't find pappardelle pasta, James suggests substituting fresh spaghetti or angel hair.

- 2 **medium-size yellow squash (about 1 lb.), divided**
- 2 **medium zucchini (about 1 lb.), divided**
- 2 **medium carrots, divided**
- 1 **small onion, chopped**
- 1 **garlic clove, minced**
- ¾ **cup vegetable broth, divided**
- 5 **Tbsp. olive oil, divided**
- 1 **tsp. salt, divided**
- ½ **cup chopped fresh basil, divided**
- 1 **(4-oz.) package prosciutto, torn into strips**
- 2 **(8.8-oz.) packages pappardelle pasta**
- 1 **Tbsp. butter**
- 3 **green onions, chopped**
- ½ **(8-oz.) container mascarpone cheese**
- ¾ **cup freshly grated Parmesan cheese**

1 HOUR

Tuna Potato Salad

quick prep • good for you

MAKES: 6 servings

- 2 **lb. assorted baby potatoes**
- 1 **(8-oz.) package fresh tiny green beans**
- 3 **large eggs**
- 1 **(7-oz.) package refrigerated fire-roasted red bell peppers in oil, drained and chopped**
- 3 **Tbsp. finely chopped red onion**
- 2 **Tbsp. chopped fresh dill**
- 2 **Tbsp. chopped fresh flat-leaf parsley**
- 2 **garlic cloves, pressed**
- ¼ **cup fresh lemon juice**
- 2 **Tbsp. olive oil**
- 1 **Tbsp. honey**
- 1 **tsp. Dijon mustard**
- ½ **tsp. salt**
- ¼ **tsp. ground pepper**
- 2 **(5-oz.) cans solid white tuna in spring water, drained**

1. Bring potatoes and water to cover to a boil; cook 15 minutes. Add beans and eggs; cook 5 minutes. Drain. Cut potatoes in half lengthwise, and cool 10 minutes.

2. Peel eggs under cold running water, and cut into wedges.

3. Gently stir together roasted red bell peppers, next 3 ingredients, potatoes, and beans. Whisk together garlic and next 6 ingredients; gently toss with potato mixture. Arrange on a serving plate with tuna and eggs.

Summer Pasta

1. Cut I squash, I zucchini, and I carrot into ¼-inch-thick slices. Place in a Dutch oven; add onion, garlic, ½ cup vegetable broth, 3 Tbsp. olive oil, and ½ tsp. salt. Cover and cook over medium-low heat, stirring occasionally, 20 to 30 minutes or until vegetables are very tender. Stir in ¼ cup basil; cool 10 minutes.

2. Meanwhile, sauté prosciutto in a lightly greased large nonstick skillet over medium heat 6 to 8 minutes or until browned and crisp; remove from skillet. Wipe skillet clean.

3. Process cooked squash mixture and remaining ¼ cup broth in a blender or food processor until smooth. Wipe Dutch oven clean.

4. Cook pasta in Dutch oven according to package directions; drain, reserving I cup hot pasta water. Return hot cooked pasta to Dutch oven.

5. Cut remaining squash, zucchini, and carrot lengthwise into very thin, ribbon-like strips using a mandoline or Y-shaped vegetable peeler. Stack ribbons, and cut in half lengthwise.

6. Melt butter with I Tbsp. olive oil in skillet over medium heat; add vegetable ribbons, green onions, and remaining ½ tsp. salt, and sauté 5 minutes or just until tender. Transfer to a plate, and cover.

7. Cook squash mixture, mascarpone cheese, and ¼ cup Parmesan cheese 3 to 4 minutes or just until sauce is hot and cheese is melted. Pour sauce over pasta; toss to coat, adding desired amount of reserved hot pasta water to thin sauce, if necessary. Top with vegetable ribbons, prosciutto, and remaining ½ cup Parmesan cheese and ¼ cup basil. Drizzle with remaining I Tbsp. olive oil.

NOTE: We tested with Bionaturae Organic Pappardelle Traditional Egg Pasta.

Chef James Lewis

LIVES IN: Birmingham, AL

RESTAURANT: Bettola

LATEST ACHIEVEMENT: My newly opened restaurant, Vittoria Macelleria (also located in Birmingham), which serves small plates and sells top-quality meats

FAVORITE SUMMER INGREDIENT: Zucchini with blossoms attached

FAVORITE SOUTHERN INDULGENCE: MoonPies

FIRST FOOD JOB: Busboy at an Original Pancake House in California

SOUTHERN CHEF WHO INSPIRES YOU: Frank Stitt

GO-TO COCKTAIL: Negroni or Aperol Sour

DISH YOU WOULD TAKE TO A POTLUCK: Brioche bread pudding

MOST MEMORABLE SOUTHERN MEAL: Fried chicken at a hunting plantation in Alabama

Thrill of the Scavenger Hunt

When we crashed Sela Ward's annual scavenger hunt in Meridian, Mississippi, we had no idea what to expect. We found a gorgeous setting, a delicious down-home menu, and a few intense (we're talkin' *cutthroat*) competitors.

S ela Ward's Southern roots run deep—six generations deep. Born and raised in Meridian, Mississippi, she attended the University of Alabama, where she cheered on "Bear" and the boys. Every July, she brings that same level of spirit-fingers enthusiasm to a 40-person scavenger hunt on Honeysuckle Farms, the 500-acre property in Meridian where she and her family spend summers. "Meridian offers a slice of life and culture that I want my children to have in their bones. And they do," says Sela.

Despite Sela's case-solving cred (she currently stars as investigator Jo Danville on *CSI: NY*), it's her husband, Howard Sherman, who masterminds the event that draws friends and family from as far as New York and California. "The hunt began as a simple way for our guests to explore and enjoy every corner of the property," he says. But, counters Sela, "After five years running, the bar has now been raised

Sela welcomes guests to the "It's All Good" Barn, designed by friend (and hunt attendee) Ann Runyon Carter of Ann Carter and Associates.

so high that Howard starts prepping in Los Angeles, and when we arrive at the farm, he sequesters himself in the library for days on end, piecing together extraordinarily complicated clues." Such clues might cover family history, be written in Italian or braille, or reference *The Amy Vanderbilt Complete Book of Etiquette.*

Friends bunk all over the property, but many stake out one of the 15 beds in the "It's All Good" Barn, a working horse stable with guest quarters created by decorator Ann Runyon Carter, architect Tim Taylor, and contractor Markey Joiner. The eclectic space,

initially renovated for Sela's surprise 50th birthday party, is filled with clever touches such as horse stirrups in lieu of bunk bed ladders and a working kitchen inside the barn's original grain storage silo. It's also where the hunt begins, and, thanks to a 20-seat farm table and working jukebox, the after-party takes place. "If guests don't know one another before the hunt, they certainly will afterward," says Sela, who, in addition to being a gracious hostess, sent thank-you notes to *SL* staffers after the photo shoot—which clued *us* in to this: Sela Ward will always be a Mississippi girl at heart.

The Honeysuckle-Watermelon Cocktails are named after Sela's farm.

Honeysuckle-Watermelon Cocktails

quick prep • party perfect

MAKES: 8 cups
HANDS-ON TIME: 20 min.
TOTAL TIME: 20 min.

As a nod to Honeysuckle Farms, we used Mississippi's Cathead Honeysuckle Flavored Vodka. (Also pictured on page 9)

- 8 **cups seeded and cubed watermelon (about 1 [6-lb.] watermelon)**
- 1 **cup honeysuckle vodka***
- ½ **cup fresh lime juice**
- ¼ **cup sugar**
- 4 **cups ice cubes**
- 2 **cups lemon-lime soft drink**
  Garnishes: lime slices, diced watermelon, fresh mint leaves

1. Process watermelon in a blender or food processor until smooth. Pour through a fine wire-mesh strainer into a large pitcher, using back of a spoon to squeeze out juice; discard solids.
2. Stir vodka and next 2 ingredients into watermelon juice. Add ice, and top with soft drink; gently stir. Serve immediately.
*Light rum or plain vodka may be substituted.

Stuffed Jalapeño Poppers

make-ahead • party perfect

MAKES: 24 poppers
HANDS-ON TIME: 1 hr.
TOTAL TIME: 1 hr., 45 min.

This recipe is inspired by Sela's friend Randy Chapman.

- 24 **jalapeño peppers**
- 1½ **(8-oz.) packages cream cheese, softened**
- 3 **Tbsp. chopped fresh cilantro**
- 2 **Tbsp. pepper jelly**
- 1 **Tbsp. fresh lime juice**
- ¼ **tsp. salt**
- 24 **bacon slices**

1. Cut stems off peppers. Cut each pepper lengthwise down 1 side, leaving other side intact; remove seeds and membranes using a small spoon. Rinse peppers under cold water to remove any remaining seeds.
2. Stir together cream cheese and next 4 ingredients. Spoon cream cheese mixture into a zip-top plastic freezer bag. (Do not seal.) Snip 1 corner of bag to make a small hole. Pipe a small amount of mixture into each pepper, and wrap each with 1 bacon slice. Secure with wooden picks.
3. Light 1 side of grill, heating to 400° to 500° (high) heat; leave other side unlit. Arrange peppers over unlit side, and grill, covered with grill lid, 22 to 25 minutes on each side.

Host Your Own Scavenger Hunt

Howard puts down his megaphone to share his tips for pulling off a (smaller scale) hunt.

- **ESTABLISH A LOCATION.** It can take place in your backyard or span an entire city. "Ideally, at least one person on each team should be familiar with the setting," he says.

- **SELECT TEAMS.** Nothing brings people together like a common enemy, so "feel free to form teams of semistrangers and assorted ages," he says. Order T-shirts at customink.com.

- **PINPOINT DESTINATIONS.** Choose 10 or so places (fewer if you're gallivanting around a city) that will be relatively easy to identify via clues. If you're looking beyond the backyard, assign each team a vehicle (bike, car, golf cart, you name it).

- **CREATE CLUES.** Pose simple questions or get creative. "Take a photo of a location, print it out, and cut it into small pieces," says Howard. "Place the pieces in an envelope so that each team has to complete the puzzle to know where to go." Or create a playlist of songs and ask participants to identify the common thread, which will lead them to the next location.

Smoked Chicken Summer Salad

make-ahead • party perfect

MAKES: 6 servings
HANDS-ON TIME: 20 min.
TOTAL TIME: 1 hr., 20 min., including vinaigrette and croutons

We turned the classic shredded sandwich into a salad.

Sweet Onion Vinaigrette
Toasted Bun Croutons
1 (4-oz.) package watercress
1 cup thinly sliced radishes (about 8 large radishes)
1 cup loosely packed fresh cilantro leaves
½ cup fresh corn kernels (about 1 ear)
½ English cucumber, thinly sliced into half moons
½ lb. shredded smoked chicken or barbecued pork without sauce
⅓ cup crumbled queso fresco (fresh Mexican cheese)
1 jalapeño pepper, halved, seeded, and thinly sliced

1. Prepare Sweet Onion Vinaigrette and Toasted Bun Croutons.
2. Toss together watercress, next 5 ingredients, and ¼ cup vinaigrette in a large bowl. Arrange mixture on a serving platter. Sprinkle with queso fresco, and top with jalapeño pepper slices and croutons. Serve salad with remaining vinaigrette.

Sweet Onion Vinaigrette

MAKES: 1¼ cups
HANDS-ON TIME: 10 min.
TOTAL TIME: 40 min.

½ cup finely chopped sweet onion
⅓ cup apple cider vinegar
3 Tbsp. sugar
2 Tbsp. coarse-grained mustard
1 tsp. kosher salt
¼ tsp. ground cumin
⅛ tsp. ground red pepper
½ cup canola oil

1. Whisk together first 7 ingredients. Gradually add oil in a slow, steady stream, whisking constantly until smooth. Cover and chill 30 minutes or until ready to serve.

Toasted Bun Croutons

MAKES: about 2½ cups
HANDS-ON TIME: 10 min.
TOTAL TIME: 50 min.

1 Tbsp. sugar
4 Tbsp. canola oil
1 tsp. chili powder
1 tsp. kosher salt
½ tsp. freshly ground pepper
4 hot dog or hamburger buns, cut into ½-inch cubes (about 4 cups)

1. Preheat oven to 375°. Whisk together first 5 ingredients. Add bun cubes, and toss. Spread in a single layer on a lightly greased 15- x 10-inch jelly-roll pan. Bake 10 to 12 minutes or until golden brown, stirring halfway through. Cool 30 minutes.

Serve a Cocktail on a Stick

These spiked treats are the sort of thing guests will rave about for years to come.

{1}

SWEET TEA JULEP POPS:
Bring 2 cups water to a boil in a 2-qt. saucepan. Remove from heat, add 2 family-size tea bags, and stir in I cup firmly packed fresh mint leaves. Cover and steep 10 minutes. Discard tea bags and mint. Stir in I cup cold water, ¾ cup bourbon, ½ cup sugar, and 3 Tbsp. fresh lemon juice, stirring until sugar dissolves. Pour mixture into 12 (3-oz.) paper cups; add a mint leaf and small lemon slice to each, if desired. Freeze as directed (see below). Makes: 12 pops

{2}

WHITE PEACH SANGRÍA POPS: Combine 1½ cups dry white wine, 1½ cups white grape juice, ⅓ cup sugar, and I Tbsp. fresh lemon juice in a 2-qt. measuring cup, stirring until sugar dissolves. Pour mixture into 12 (3-oz.) paper cups. Stir together ½ cup chopped, unpeeled white peaches; ½ cup raspberries; and ½ cup chopped, peeled kiwifruit; spoon fruit mixture into cups. Freeze as directed (see below). Makes: 12 pops

{3}

WATERMELON MARGARITA POPS:
Grate zest from I lime to equal I tsp. Squeeze juice from about 6 limes to equal ½ cup. Process lime juice and 4 cups chopped seedless watermelon in a blender until smooth. Pour through a fine wire-mesh strainer into a large measuring cup, discarding solids. Stir in ¾ cup tequila, ½ cup sugar, and I tsp. lime zest, stirring until sugar dissolves. Pour mixture into 12 (3-oz.) paper cups. Freeze as directed (see below). Makes: 12 pops

{4}

CHOCOLATE MILK PUNCH POPS: Combine 3 cups chocolate milk, ½ cup bourbon, ⅓ cup sugar, 2 tsp. vanilla extract, and ¼ tsp. grated nutmeg in a 2-qt. measuring cup, stirring until sugar dissolves. Pour half of mixture into 12 (3-oz.) paper cups; cover and chill remaining half. Freeze as directed (see below), reducing freeze time to 4 hours or until firm. Carefully remove foil from cups. Pour I Tbsp. chocolate syrup into each cup; freeze, uncovered, 2 hours. Pour remaining milk mixture into cups; freeze, uncovered, 8 hours or until firm. Makes: 12 pops

FREEZING INSTRUCTIONS
Cover each cup with aluminum foil; make a small slit in center, and insert I (3½-inch) food-safe wooden ice-cream spoon into each cup. Freeze 8 hours or until firm.

Blackberry Syrup

It's summer in a bottle! Bonus: In small jars, this signature sweet becomes a memorable party favor.

MAKE IT!

MAKES: about 2 cups
HANDS-ON TIME: 25 min.
TOTAL TIME: 55 min.

- **3 cups fresh blackberries***
- **1¼ cups sugar**
- **¼ cup light corn syrup**
- **1 tsp. cornstarch**

1. Process blackberries in a blender until smooth, stopping to scrape down sides as needed.

2. Press blackberry puree through a fine wire-mesh strainer into a medium saucepan, using back of a spoon to squeeze out juice (about 1½ cups). Discard pulp and seeds.

3. Add sugar and remaining ingredients to blackberry juice in pan, and bring mixture to a boil over medium heat, stirring occasionally. Boil, stirring occasionally, 1 to 2 minutes or until sugar is dissolved and mixture is smooth. Remove from heat, and cool slightly (about 30 minutes). Serve warm or at room temperature.

*1 (16-oz.) package frozen blackberries, thawed, may be substituted.

TAKE IT!

Pour this syrup into a glass swing-top bottle for a charming package. (We found ours at *specialtybottle.com*; $3.) Top it off with our downloadable gift tag and chunky, blackberry-adorned baker's twine. Adhere berries by inserting one end of a toothpick into the fruit. Thread what's still exposed of the toothpick through the twine.

SERVE IT!

We love this syrup on biscuits, fruit salad, and our Blackberry-Peach Cobbler sundae *(page 157)*.

DOWNLOAD OUR GIFT TAGS:
southernliving.com/food-gift

August

Livin' on the Wedge

Biting into a juicy slice of watermelon is a summer rite of passage. Here, cookbook author Virginia Willis shares a sticky handful of ways to enjoy the iconic fruit.

Beef-and-Watermelon Stir-fry

quick prep • good for you • party perfect

MAKES: 4 to 6 servings
HANDS-ON TIME: 25 min.
TOTAL TIME: 55 min.

This is inspired by a hot pepper beef recipe by Grace Young. (Pictured on page 183)

- 1 lb. sirloin strip steak, cut into thin strips
- 3 garlic cloves, minced
- 2 tsp. cornstarch
- 2 tsp. cold water
- 2 tsp. lite soy sauce
- 1½ tsp. sesame oil
- 2 Tbsp. dry white wine
- 2 Tbsp. hot water
- 2 Tbsp. hoisin sauce
- 1 tsp. kosher salt
- ½ tsp. ground black pepper
- 2 Tbsp. canola oil, divided
- 1 medium-size sweet onion, halved and sliced
- 12 oz. fresh sugar snap peas
- 1 tsp. grated fresh ginger
- ½ tsp. dried crushed red pepper
- 16 oz. watermelon, rind removed and cut into sticks (about 2 cups)
- 2 cups hot cooked rice

1. Toss together first 6 ingredients and 1 Tbsp. wine. Let stand 30 minutes. Meanwhile, stir together hot water, hoisin sauce, and remaining 1 Tbsp. wine.

2. Remove beef from marinade, discarding marinade. Sprinkle with salt and black pepper; cook half of beef in 1½ tsp. hot canola oil in a large skillet over high heat, without stirring, 45 seconds or until browned; turn beef, and cook 30 seconds or until browned. Transfer to a warm plate. Repeat with 1½ tsp. oil and remaining beef.

3. Stir-fry onion in remaining 1 Tbsp. hot canola oil in skillet over medium-high heat 2 minutes or until tender. Add sugar snap peas, ginger, and crushed red pepper; stir-fry 2 minutes. Add beef and hoisin mixture; stir-fry 1 minute or until slightly thickened. Remove from heat. Stir in watermelon. Add salt, black pepper, and red pepper to taste. Serve immediately with hot cooked rice.

VIRGINIA'S TIP

BEEF-AND-WATERMELON STIR-FRY: The sweet heat of this dish is surprisingly refreshing. Slice the watermelon into sticks about the same size as the sugar snap peas so you get a sweet crunch in every bite. Garnish with fresh cilantro leaves for extra flavor.

Grilled Watermelon with Blue Cheese and Prosciutto

quick prep • good for you • party perfect

MAKES: 4 servings
HANDS-ON TIME: 20 min.
TOTAL TIME: 20 min.
(Pictured on page 182)

- 3 (½-inch-thick) watermelon rounds, quartered
- 1 Tbsp. olive oil
  Kosher salt
  Freshly ground pepper
- 4 oz. thinly sliced prosciutto
- 4 oz. blue cheese, crumbled
  Fresh basil leaves
- 2 tsp. bottled balsamic glaze

1. Preheat grill to 350° to 400° (medium-high) heat. Brush both sides of each watermelon quarter with olive oil, and season with desired amount of salt and pepper. Cut prosciutto into thin strips.

2. Grill watermelon quarters, without grill lid, 1 minute on each side or until grill marks appear.

3. Transfer watermelon to a serving plate; top with blue cheese, prosciutto strips, and fresh basil. Drizzle watermelon with balsamic glaze. Serve immediately.

VIRGINIA'S TIP

GRILLED WATERMELON WITH BLUE CHEESE AND PROSCIUTTO: Pungent blue cheese and salty prosciutto are delicious with sweet melon. Grilling the watermelon enhances that sweetness and adds a touch of smoky flavor. Brushing the wedges with oil keeps them from sticking to the grill.

Herbed Goat Cheese-Melon Party Bites

quick prep • good for you •
make-ahead • party perfect
(Pictured on page 183)

1. Cut half of 1 small watermelon
into 1-inch-thick slices. Cut slices into
25 rounds, using a 2-inch round cutter.
Scoop just enough melon from tops to
form indentations, using a melon baller.
Stir together 1 (4-oz.) goat cheese log,
softened; 2 Tbsp. chopped fresh basil;
½ tsp. salt; and ¼ tsp. freshly ground
pepper. Spoon into indentations.
Chill 1 to 2 hours. Garnish with fresh
basil and freshly ground pepper.
Makes: 10 to 12 servings

VIRGINIA'S TIP

WATERMELON BELLINI:
Whirl up any summer melon in this
refreshing sipper. For a nonalcoholic
option, replace the sparkling wine
with sparkling white grape juice,
sparkling cider, or club soda.

Watermelon Bellini

quick prep • party perfect
(Pictured on page 183)

1. Cut 1 lime in half. Cut 1 half into wedges,
and rub on rims of 8 (6-oz.) cocktail glasses;
dip rims in 2 to 3 Tbsp. coarse sugar to
coat. Process 3 cups frozen, seedless
watermelon; 1 cup chilled sparkling wine;
2 Tbsp. sugar; a pinch of salt; and juice
from remaining lime half in a blender
until smooth. Pour mixture into prepared
glasses; top off with sparkling wine. Garnish
with watermelon wedges, if desired. Serve
immediately. Makes: 8 servings

Shrimp Salad over Zesty Watermelon

quick prep • good for you • party perfect

MAKES: 4 servings
HANDS-ON TIME: 30 min.
TOTAL TIME: 30 min.

*This salad uses just enough mayo to coat
the shrimp, which will keep them moist but
not drown them in a deluge of dressing.*

- 2 **lemons**
- 4 **(1-inch-thick) watermelon slices,
  rind removed**
- **Kosher salt**
- **Freshly ground pepper**
- 1 **Tbsp. finely chopped sweet onion**
- 3 **Tbsp. mayonnaise**
- 2 **Tbsp. finely chopped celery**
- 1 **lb. peeled and deveined, large
  cooked shrimp**
- 2 **Tbsp. chopped fresh tarragon**
- 1 **(5-oz.) package baby arugula**

1. Grate zest from lemons to equal
1 Tbsp. Cut lemons in half; squeeze juice
from lemons into a measuring cup to
equal 3 Tbsp.
2. Place each watermelon slice on a
chilled plate. Season with desired amount
of kosher salt and freshly ground pepper.
3. Microwave onion in a medium-size
microwave-safe bowl at HIGH 25 seconds
or just until onion is tender. Stir in mayonnaise, celery, 1 tsp. lemon zest, and 1 Tbsp.
lemon juice. Stir in shrimp and tarragon.
Season with salt and pepper to taste.
4. Place arugula in a medium bowl.
Sprinkle with remaining 2 tsp. lemon zest
and 2 Tbsp. lemon juice. Season with salt
and pepper to taste; toss to coat. Arrange
arugula mixture over watermelon; top
with shrimp mixture. Serve immediately.

Instant Watermelon Pops

Cut a 1-inch slit into the rind of a
just-cut watermelon wedge, and
insert a wooden stick. Serve pops
a variety of ways: Sprinkle with
flavored salts and freshly ground
pepper, drizzle with local honey
and fresh lime juice, dust with red
pepper, or add a splash of schnapps.

Tipsy Red-and-Yellow Watermelon Salad

make-ahead • party perfect

MAKES: 6 to 8 servings
HANDS-ON TIME: 20 min.
TOTAL TIME: 1 hr., 20 min.
(Pictured on page 183)

- ½ **(6-lb.) red watermelon**
- ½ **(6-lb.) yellow watermelon**
- 1 **cup fresh lemon juice
  (about 10 to 12 lemons)**
- ⅔ **cup sugar**
- ½ **cup vodka**
- ⅓ **cup black raspberry liqueur**
- **Pinch of fine sea salt**
- 1 **Tbsp. chopped fresh mint**
- **Garnish: fresh mint sprigs**

1. Scoop watermelons into balls using
various size melon ballers, and place
watermelon in a large bowl.
2. Whisk together lemon juice and next
4 ingredients in a medium bowl until sugar
dissolves. Pour lemon juice mixture over
watermelon balls; gently stir to coat.
Cover and chill 1 to 2 hours.
3. Gently toss watermelon balls. Sprinkle
with chopped fresh mint. Serve immediately with a slotted spoon.

Preserving Summer

What's more Southern than canning a whole mess of produce? Doing it with a whole mess of people—on an Oxford, Mississippi, farm, no less.

Elizabeth Heiskell will put up just about anything. Baby purple carrots, watermelon radishes, pattypan squash. You name it. "Just look at these tiny, baby, precious okra!" she squeals. "There's something special about putting those beautiful vegetables in jars. They become a treasure in the pantry for you to savor when the winter comes."

Elizabeth, the lead culinary instructor for Viking Cooking School in Greenwood, Mississippi, helps her husband, Luke, work 25 furrowed acres at Woodson Ridge Farm in Oxford, supplying produce to local Community Supported Agriculture members and 40 restaurants. And though she grew up packing Ball jars with her mama in the Delta—"the loveliest place on earth"—it wasn't until last year, the first harvest at Woodson Ridge, that she really found her mettle. "As a farmer and a chef,

there is nothing more terrifying than 2,000 pounds of squash staring you in the face," says Elizabeth. "Trying to use up all that squash is when I really got into canning."

Once she realized how easy it was, she started proselytizing from her kitchen pulpit, using the best tool any Delta girl knows—a party. She invited friends to the farm, plied them with her heirloom tomato Bloody Marys, and taught them this time-honored Southern skill. "People have this notion that canning is scary," Elizabeth says. "Our grandmothers wanted us to think they were martyrs and everything they did was hard—but it's not."

"Not only do we have a good ole time catching up over cocktails, but we become a vital step in continuing the tradition," she adds. "We're reclaiming it for our generation."

Elizabeth's Heirloom Bloody Mary Mix

good for you • make-ahead • party perfect

MAKES: 8 cups
HANDS-ON TIME: 35 min.

Because canning tomatoes requires extra care, try this refrigerator variety for your Bloody Marys (recipe above right). Trust us: You'll want to drink it immediately anyway. Learn how to safely can tomatoes—and prevent botulism—at the National Center for Home Food Preservation (nchfp.uga.edu).

8	ripe heirloom tomatoes, cored and quartered (about 6 lb.)
1	Tbsp. Worcestershire sauce
1	tsp. salt
1	tsp. celery salt
½	tsp. freshly ground pepper
½	tsp. hot sauce

1. Place tomatoes in a Dutch oven, and mash with a potato masher until chunky. Cook over medium heat, stirring often, 20 to 25 minutes or until peels are wilted and most of juices have been released.
2. Press tomatoes through a fine wire-mesh strainer into a medium bowl, pressing with a wooden spoon to squeeze out juices; discard solids. Return tomato juice to Dutch oven, and stir in Worcestershire sauce and remaining ingredients. Bring to a boil over medium heat, and cook, stirring often, 5 minutes. Remove from heat, and let cool to room temperature (about 30 minutes). Pour into 2 (1-qt.) jars; chill 2 to 4 hours. Store in refrigerator up to 5 days.

Her Garnish: Pickled Veggies

good for you • make-ahead • party perfect

Elizabeth uses this basic recipe for pickling okra, beets, baby purple carrots, radishes—whatever's coming in from the garden. She also throws in fresh dill or mustard green shoots. The recipe is very forgiving; you'd have to work to mess it up. If you've got very small okra, then use half-pint jars instead.

PICKLED OKRA: Brush 4½ lb. washed fresh okra lightly with a piece of nylon net or a brush to remove "fuzz." Trim stems from okra. Bring 8 cups apple cider vinegar, 1 cup water, and ½ cup salt to a boil in a 4-qt. saucepan over medium heat. Pack half of okra vertically in 2 layers in 5 (1-pt.) hot, sterilized jars, filling to ½ inch from top. (First layer should be packed with stems down and the next with stems up.) Add 1 garlic clove, 1 serrano pepper, 1 tsp. dill seeds, and 1 tsp. mustard seeds to each jar. Pour half of hot vinegar mixture over mixture in jars, filling to ½ inch from top. Seal and process as directed (see page 212). Repeat okra packing procedure with 5 more hot, sterilized jars. Seal and process as directed. Let stand at least 7 days before serving. Makes: 10 (1-pt.) jars. Hands-on time: 30 min.

PICKLED PURPLE CARROTS: Substitute 4½ lb. purple carrots, tops removed, for okra. Cut carrots lengthwise into quarters. Prepare Pickled Okra recipe as directed, packing carrots in 6 (1-pt.) hot, sterilized jars. Seal and process as directed (see page 212), increasing boiling time in Step 3 of canning instructions to 15 minutes. Makes: 6 (1-pt.) jars.

PICKLED RADISHES: Substitute 5 lb. radishes, tops removed, for okra. Trim radishes; cut into wedges. Prepare Pickled Okra recipe as directed, packing radishes in 6 (1-pt.) hot, sterilized jars. Seal and process as directed (see page 212), increasing boiling time in Step 3 of canning instructions to 15 minutes. Makes: 6 (1-pt.) jars.

STEP 2:
Now Get Canning!

We asked some of our favorite canning enthusiasts (including chefs, gardeners, and cookbook authors) to share their favorite recipes. Turn to page 212 for our easy canning how-to.

Cardamom-Plum Jam

make-ahead • party perfect

MAKES: 5 (8-oz.) jars
HANDS-ON TIME: 1 hr.

RECIPE FROM LIANA KRISSOFF,
AUTHOR OF *CANNING FOR A NEW GENERATION*

"Spices! In jam! This was the jam that made me realize how good homemade preserves could be—and I'm pretty sure it landed me my book deal. You can use any kind of plums. Tart, even under-ripe, plums too puckery to eat out of hand make especially good jams."

1. Bring 4 lb. diced black plums and 2 cups sugar to a light boil in a Dutch oven over medium-high heat, stirring often, and simmer, stirring often, 5 minutes. Pour through a fine wire-mesh strainer into a bowl, gently pressing with a wooden spoon to squeeze out juices. Reserve plum pieces. Return juice to Dutch oven; bring to a boil over medium-high heat, stirring occasionally. Boil, stirring occasionally, 10 to 15 minutes or until syrupy and a candy thermometer registers 220°. Add reserved plum pieces and any accumulated juices. Stir in 3 Tbsp. fresh lime juice and 1 to 2 tsp. freshly ground cardamom. Bring to a light boil over medium-high heat, stirring often; simmer, stirring often, 15 minutes. Skim off foam with a metal spoon, if necessary. Pour hot mixture into 5 (8-oz.) hot, sterilized jars, filling to ½ inch from top. Seal and process as directed (see page 212).

Muscadine Jelly

make-ahead • party perfect

MAKES: 8 (8-oz.) jars
HANDS-ON TIME: 20 min.

RECIPE FROM GWEN POWELL,
CO-OWNER OF PETALS FROM THE PAST

"I've always enjoyed the bouquet and flavor of muscadine grapes ripening in late summer. Our muscadine vineyard gives me the opportunity to make lots of jelly."

1. Bring 5 cups sugar, 5 cups muscadine juice, and ½ tsp. butter to a rolling boil in a Dutch oven over medium-high heat, stirring constantly. Add ½ (6-oz.) package (1 pouch) liquid pectin; boil, stirring constantly, 1 minute. Skim off foam with a metal spoon, if necessary. Pour hot mixture into 8 (8-oz.) hot, sterilized jars, filling to ½ inch from top. Seal and process in canner as directed (see page 212).
NOTE: We tested with Premium Bronze 100% Muscadine Grape Juice from Ward Farms of Whitsett (*wardfarmsofwhitsett.com*).

Test Kitchen Tip

Some jellies, such as Cardamom-Plum Jam and Muscadine Jelly, can take up to 2 weeks to jell. If yours doesn't set, learn how to reprocess it at *nchfp.uga.edu*.

A Three-Step Guide to Puttin' Up

Yes, it really is that easy. To get started, you'll need a basic canner, a jar lifter, and a canning rack. Look for a 9- or 12-piece canning kit, which will include all of these pieces and more.

{1}
STERILIZE

Bring a canner half full of water to a boil; simmer. Place jars in a large stockpot with water to cover; bring to a boil, and simmer 10 minutes. Place bands and lids in a large saucepan. (Always use new lids.) Using a ladle, cover bands and lids with hot water from canner to soften gaskets. Let stand 10 minutes.

{2}
PREPARE RECIPE

Meanwhile, prepare desired recipe. Remove hot jars from stockpot, 1 at a time, using jar lifter, and fill as directed in recipe.

{3}
SEAL & PROCESS

Wipe rims of filled jars. Cover at once with metal lids, and screw on bands (snug but not too tight). Place jars in canning rack, and place in simmering water in canner. Add more boiling water as needed to cover jars by 1 to 2 inches. Bring water to a rolling boil; boil 10 minutes, adjusting processing time for altitude.* Turn off heat, and let stand 5 minutes. Remove jars from canner, and let stand at room temperature 24 hours. Test seals of jars by pressing centers of lids. If lids do not pop, jars are properly sealed. Store in a cool, dark place at room temperature up to 1 year. Refrigerate after opening.

*Consult the USDA Complete Guide to Home Canning at *nchfp.uga.edu/publications/publications_usda.html* to adjust processing times for altitude.

Spicy Habanero-Mint Jelly

make-ahead • party perfect

MAKES: 9 (8-oz.) jars
HANDS-ON TIME: 45 min.

RECIPE FROM PAM LOLLEY,
SL TEST KITCHEN

"Most pepper jellies are too sweet and mild. But the mint and habaneros make this one special. I use it in vinaigrettes, to glaze meats, and even on grilled cheese. Add another pepper for extra spice."

1. Bring ½ cup firmly packed fresh mint leaves and ½ cup water to a boil in a sauce-pan. Remove from heat, cover, and let stand 30 minutes. Meanwhile, process 1½ lb. red bell peppers, seeded and coarsely chopped; 3 habanero peppers, seeded and coarsely chopped; 1 small onion, coarsely chopped; and ½ cup white vinegar in a food processor until finely chopped. Pour mint mixture through a wire-mesh strainer into a large Dutch oven, pressing mint with a wooden spoon to release flavors. Discard mint. Add pepper mixture, 7 cups sugar, 1 cup white vinegar, and 3 Tbsp. fresh lime juice to Dutch oven. Bring to a boil over medium-high heat, stirring often; boil, stirring constantly, 2 minutes. Remove from heat, and stir in 2 (3-oz.) packages liquid pectin. Return to heat, and bring to a boil, stirring often. Boil, stirring constantly, 1 minute; remove from heat. Let stand 5 minutes; skim off foam with a metal spoon, if necessary. Pour hot mixture into 9 (8-oz.) hot, sterilized jars, filling to ¼ inch from top. Seal and process as directed (see left), reducing boiling time in Step 3 of canning instructions to 5 minutes. Let stand at least 7 days before serving.

Test Kitchen Tip

If you do not have enough mixture to fill all of your jars completely, store it (after completely cooled) in your refrigerator, and use within 2 weeks. Do not process any partially filled jars.

Judy's Pickled Squash

good for you • make-ahead • party perfect

MAKES: 4 (1-pt.) jars
HANDS-ON TIME: 30 min.

RECIPE FROM SARA FOSTER, CHEF AND AUTHOR OF
SARA FOSTER'S SOUTHERN KITCHEN

"An overabundance of fast-growing yellow squash inspired my sister, Judy, to make these unusually gratifying sweet squash pickles. They can elevate anything from a simple dish of beans and rice to a fried egg sandwich. You can use any kind of summer squash, from sundrops to pattypans to zucchini."

1. Place 2 lb. squash, cut into ¼-inch-thick rounds; 2 medium-size red bell peppers, chopped; and 1 onion, thinly sliced; in a colander. Sprinkle with 2 Tbsp. kosher salt; cover and let stand at room tempera-ture 1 hour. (Do not rinse.) Tightly pack squash mixture in 4 (1-pt.) hot, sterilized jars, filling to ½ inch from top. Bring 3 cups sugar, 2½ cups apple cider vinegar, 2 tsp. mustard seeds, and 2 tsp. celery seeds to a boil in a Dutch oven over high heat; boil, stirring constantly, 1 minute or until sugar dissolves. Pour hot liquid over squash mixture in jars, filling to ½ inch from top. Remove air bubbles by gently stirring with a long wooden skewer. Seal and process as directed (see left), increasing boiling time in Step 3 of canning instructions to 15 minutes.

Uncle Hoyt's Bread-and-Butter Pickles

good for you • make-ahead • party perfect

MAKES: 14 (1-pt.) jars
HANDS-ON TIME: 2 hr., 10 min.

RECIPE FROM JAMES T. FARMER, III,
AUTHOR OF *A TIME TO PLANT*

"My family starts clamoring for my Uncle Hoyt Harwell's pickles—a perfect combination of sweet and savory—as soon as summer's heat gives us cucumbers. I put them on sandwiches and in deviled eggs or just eat them out of the jar."

1. Cut 25 to 30 medium cucumbers (about 9½ lb.) into ¼-inch-thick slices and 8 large onions into ⅛-inch-thick slices. Chop 2 large bell peppers. Place vegetables in a bowl; toss with ½ cup pickling salt. Let stand 3 hours; drain. Bring 5 cups white vinegar, 4 cups sugar, 2 Tbsp. mustard seeds, 1 tsp. ground turmeric, and ½ tsp. whole cloves to a boil in a large stockpot, boiling just until sugar dissolves. Add drained cucumber mixture, and cook, stirring often, 7 to 10 minutes or until mixture is thoroughly heated and cucum-ber peels turn dark green. Pack half of hot mixture in 7 (1-pt.) hot, sterilized jars, filling to ½ inch from top. Remove air bubbles by gently stirring with a long wooden skewer. Seal and process as directed (see left). Repeat procedure with remaining mixture and 7 more hot, sterilized jars.

Think Outside the Toast

Once you have your stash of canned goods, here's how you can spread the wealth beyond jam on bread.

{1}
JELLY-CHEDDAR THUMBPRINTS

Pulse 2¼ cups all-purpose flour; 2 cups (8 oz.) freshly shredded white Cheddar cheese; and I cup butter, softened and cut into I-inch pieces; in a food processor at 5-second intervals until dough forms a ball. Shape dough into ¾-inch balls; place 2 inches apart on lightly greased baking sheets. Press thumb in center of each to make an indentation. Cover and chill 30 minutes. Bake, in batches, at 350° for 15 to 18 minutes or until light golden brown. Transfer to wire racks; cool 30 minutes. Spoon ¼ tsp. desired jam or jelly into each indentation. Makes: 4½ dozen

{2}
PICKLED SUMMER SQUASH QUESADILLAS

Sprinkle ¼ cup freshly shredded pepper Jack cheese on I side of I soft taco-size flour tortilla; top with 2 Tbsp. chopped Judy's Pickled Squash *(page 213)*, I tsp. chopped fresh cilantro, and ½ tsp. finely chopped jalapeño pepper. Fold in half. Cook in a lightly greased nonstick skillet over medium-high heat I to 2 minutes on each side or until golden. Cut into wedges, and serve with sour cream. Makes: I serving

{3}
MINI CHEESE-AND-JAM PASTRIES

Divide ½ cup (2 oz.) desired shredded cheese (such as Gouda, Jarlsberg, or Dubliner) among I (1.9-oz.) package frozen mini-phyllo pastry shells. Spoon ½ tsp. desired jam or jelly into each shell. Bake on a lightly greased baking sheet at 350° for 10 minutes or until cheese is melted. Sprinkle with I Tbsp. finely chopped mixed nuts. Serve immediately. Makes: 15 tartlets

{4}
SPICY HABANERO-MINT JELLY ON CREAM CHEESE

Microwave I cup Spicy Habanero-Mint Jelly *(page 213)* in a large microwave-safe bowl at HIGH I minute or until smooth, stirring at 30-second intervals. Stir in 3 tsp. chopped fresh cilantro and 2 tsp. fresh lime juice. Spoon over I (8-oz.) block cream cheese. Serve immediately with crackers. Makes: 8 servings

{5}
BREAD-AND-BUTTER CHICKEN SALAD

Stir ¼ cup chopped Uncle Hoyt's Bread-and-Butter Pickles *(page 213)*, I Tbsp. chopped fresh parsley, and ¼ tsp. lemon zest into 2 cups of your favorite prepared chicken salad. Makes: 4 servings

{6}
GRILLED ANDOUILLE SAUSAGE WITH PICKLES

Serve Judy's Pickled Squash *(page 213)* or Uncle Hoyt's Bread-and-Butter Pickles *(page 213)* with grilled andouille sausages.

{7}
GOAT CHEESE LOG WITH MUSCADINE JELLY

Press or roll I (10.5-oz.) goat cheese log in ½ cup chopped roasted, salted pecans, thoroughly covering cheese. Arrange on a serving platter with any remaining pecans. Serve with Muscadine Jelly *(page 211)* and assorted crackers. Makes: 8 appetizer servings

{8}
BRIE WITH CARDAMOM-PLUM JAM GLAZE

Trim rind from top of I (7-oz.) Brie round. Place Brie on a lightly greased baking sheet. Bake at 400° for 7 minutes or until cheese is just melted. Meanwhile, microwave ½ cup Cardamom-Plum Jam *(page 211)*, 2 tsp. grated sweet onion, I tsp. Champagne vinegar, ⅛ tsp. salt, and ⅛ tsp. freshly ground pepper in a microwave-safe bowl at HIGH I minute or until smooth, stirring at 30-second intervals. Place Brie on a serving dish; immediately top with warm jam mixture. Serve with crackers and fresh fruit. Makes: 6 servings

Party Flavors

As both political sides huddle up for the ultimate scrimmage, do some campaign trail-gating with these recipes.

Left Wings

party perfect

MAKES: 12 servings

- 2 tsp. ground chipotle chile pepper
- 2 tsp. black pepper
- 2 tsp. salt, divided
- 4½ to 5 lb. chicken wings
- 1 Tbsp. olive oil
- 3 Tbsp. butter
- ½ cup chopped onion
- 2 garlic cloves, pressed
- 1 cup apple cider vinegar
- 1 (8-oz.) can tomato sauce
- 1 (6-oz.) can tomato paste
- 2 Tbsp. light brown sugar
- 2 Tbsp. Worcestershire sauce
- 2 tsp. hot sauce
  Blue Cheese Sauce

1. Light 1 side of grill, heating to 350° to 400° (medium-high) heat. Combine first 2 ingredients and 1 tsp. salt. Cut off chicken wing tips, and discard; cut wings in half at joint. Toss wings with oil. Sprinkle chicken with pepper mixture, and toss.

2. Arrange wings over unlit side of grill, and grill, covered with grill lid, 18 to 20 minutes on each side or until done.

3. Meanwhile, melt butter in a saucepan over medium-high heat; add onion and garlic, and sauté 5 minutes or until tender. Reduce heat to medium. Add vinegar, next 5 ingredients, and remaining 1 tsp. salt. Cook, stirring occasionally, 10 to 12 minutes or until bubbly.

4. Transfer wings to a clean bowl; add half of butter mixture, reserving remaining mixture. Toss wings gently to coat. Place wings on lit side of grill. Grill, covered with grill lid, 10 minutes or until browned, turning occasionally. Toss wings with reserved butter mixture. Serve with Blue Cheese Sauce.

Blue Cheese Sauce

1. Stir together 1 (8-oz.) container sour cream; ⅓ cup buttermilk; 1 (3-oz.) wedge blue cheese, crumbled; 2 Tbsp. chopped fresh chives; 1 tsp. lemon zest; 1 Tbsp. fresh lemon juice; 1 tsp. coarse-grained mustard; ½ tsp. salt; and ¼ tsp. pepper.

Right Wings

party perfect

MAKES: 12 servings

- 2½ cups all-purpose flour
- 2 tsp. salt
- 1 tsp. paprika
- ¼ tsp. ground red pepper
- 4½ to 5 lb. chicken wings
  Vegetable oil
  Rom-esco Sauce

1. Combine all-purpose flour and next 3 ingredients in a large bowl.

2. Cut off chicken wing tips, and discard; cut wings in half at joint. Add wings to flour mixture; toss to coat. Cover and chill in flour mixture 1½ hours.

3. Pour oil to depth of 2 inches into a Dutch oven; heat to 375°. Remove wings from flour mixture, shaking off excess. Fry wings, in batches, 10 to 12 minutes or until golden brown. Drain on a wire rack over paper towels. Transfer wings to a wire rack in a jelly-roll pan, and keep warm in a 225° oven. Place wings in a large bowl, and add ¾ to 1 cup Rom-esco Sauce; toss to coat. Serve hot wings with remaining sauce.

Rom-esco Sauce

quick prep • party perfect

1. Tear 1 (1-inch-thick) crusty French bread slice into 1-inch pieces. Heat ¼ cup olive oil in a medium skillet over medium heat. Cook bread and ⅓ cup slivered almonds in hot oil, stirring often, 1 to 2 minutes or until almonds are fragrant and bread is golden. Stir in 6 garlic cloves, chopped (about ¼ cup), and cook, stirring constantly, 1 minute. Process bread mixture; 1 (14.5-oz.) can diced tomatoes, undrained; 1 (8-oz.) jar roasted red bell peppers, drained; 1 Tbsp. smoked paprika*; 2 to 3 Tbsp. sherry vinegar; 1 tsp. salt; and 2 Tbsp. water in a food processor 30 seconds to 1 minute or until smooth. *Regular paprika may be substituted.

Toast Your Party!

Try these politicocktails inspired by Heaven Hill's special edition election-year bourbons.

BOURBON ON THE BARACKS: Place ½ cup halved blueberries and ¼ cup chopped crystallized ginger in an ice-cube tray. Top with a mix of 1¼ cups ginger ale and 3 to 4 dashes of Angostura bitters, and freeze. Place 3 to 4 cubes in an old-fashioned glass, and add a liberal pour of bourbon. Top with club soda.

GRAND OLD FASHIONED: Muddle 2 chopped strawberries, 1 (2-inch) orange zest strip, 2 tsp. Demerara sugar, and 2 dashes Peychaud's bitters against sides of an old-fashioned glass. Fill with ice, and add 3 Tbsp. bourbon; stir until blended. Top with a conservative splash of chilled seltzer water.

Spice Up Your Fiesta!

What's on the menu? A bright mix of sunny
Tex-Mex favorites inspired by summer's bounty.

Make-Ahead Tex-Mex Menu

SERVES 8

DRINKS

Pink Cadillac Margaritas

Iced Hibiscus Sweet Tea

STARTERS

Spicy Roasted Chile Peanuts
and Pepitas

Chipotle Shrimp Cocktail

THE MAIN DISH & SIDES

Chicken Enchiladas

Three Sisters Salad

Mango Tango

DESSERT

Mexican Chocolate
Ice-cream Pie

Pink Cadillac Margaritas

quick prep • party perfect

MAKES: 3¼ cups
HANDS-ON TIME: 10 min.
TOTAL TIME: 10 min.

*Fast Flourish: Rub rims of chilled glasses
with a lime wedge, dip in a saucer of coarse
salt and sparkling sugar, and twirl to coat.*

- 1 **cup tequila**
- 1 **cup fresh lime juice**
- ½ **cup powdered sugar**
- ½ **cup orange liqueur**
- ½ **cup cranberry juice**

1. Stir together all ingredients until sugar is
dissolved. Pour desired amount of mixture
into a cocktail shaker filled with ice cubes.
Cover with lid, and shake 30 seconds.
Strain into chilled cocktail glasses. Repeat
with remaining mixture. Serve immediately
(or make ahead; see tip below).
NOTE: We tested with Cointreau orange
liqueur.

Test Kitchen Tip

Mix up several batches of Pink
Cadillac Margaritas 3 to 4 hours
before the party starts, and chill
in decorative bottles or pitchers,
ready to shake or stir and serve
when guests arrive.

Iced Hibiscus Sweet Tea

make-ahead • party perfect

MAKES: 7 cups
HANDS-ON TIME: 5 min.
TOTAL TIME: 2 hr., 20 min.

- 8 **regular-size hibiscus tea bags**
- ¾ **cup sugar**
- 1 **navel orange, sliced**
- 1 **lime, sliced**
- 3 **cups ginger ale, chilled**

1. Bring 4 cups water to a boil in a 2-qt.
saucepan. Remove from heat, and add
tea bags. Cover and steep 10 minutes.
Discard tea bags. Stir in sugar until
dissolved; add orange and lime slices.
Cover and chill 2 to 6 hours. Stir in ginger
ale, and serve over ice.
NOTE: We tested with Celestial Seasonings
Red Zinger Herbal Tea.

Spicy Roasted Chile Peanuts and Pepitas

quick prep • good for you • party perfect

MAKES: about 3 cups
HANDS-ON TIME: 10 min.
TOTAL TIME: 40 min.

- 2 **cups unsalted,**
  dry-roasted peanuts
- 2 **Tbsp. butter, melted**
- 2 **Tbsp. light brown sugar**
- 2 **tsp. chili powder**
- ½ **tsp. ground cinnamon**
- ¼ **tsp. ground red pepper**
- 1 **cup roasted, salted shelled**
  pumpkin seeds (pepitas)

1. Preheat oven to 350°. Stir together peanuts and melted butter in a medium bowl.
2. Stir together brown sugar and next
3 ingredients. Add to peanut mixture,
tossing to coat. Place peanuts in a single
layer on a lightly greased baking sheet.
3. Bake at 350° for 10 to 15 minutes or
until golden brown, stirring once. Remove
from oven, and stir in pumpkin seeds.
Cool completely in pan on a wire rack
(about 20 minutes).

Chipotle Shrimp Cocktail

Chipotle Shrimp Cocktail

good for you • make-ahead • party perfect

MAKES: 8 servings
HANDS-ON TIME: 20 min.
TOTAL TIME: 12 hr., 20 min.
(Also pictured on page 185)

- 1 large red onion
- 1 medium-size red bell pepper
- 1 medium-size yellow bell pepper
- 2 lb. peeled and deveined, large cooked shrimp with tails
- 1 cup ketchup
- ½ cup chopped fresh cilantro
- ½ cup fresh lime juice
- 3 Tbsp. orange zest
- ½ cup fresh orange juice
- 2 to 3 canned chipotle peppers in adobo sauce, chopped

1. Cut onion and bell peppers into thin strips; layer with shrimp in a large zip-top plastic freezer bag.
2. Whisk together ketchup and next 5 ingredients; pour over shrimp mixture. Seal and chill 12 to 24 hours, turning bag occasionally. Serve using a slotted spoon.

Chicken Enchiladas

good for you • make-ahead • party perfect

MAKES: 6 to 8 servings
HANDS-ON TIME: 25 min.
TOTAL TIME: 2 hr., 45 min., including salsa

Fast Flourish: Char one side of the tortillas directly over gas flames for a few seconds using tongs.

- 1 cup diced sweet onion
- 3 garlic cloves, minced
- 1 Tbsp. canola oil
- 2 cups chopped fresh baby spinach
- 2 (4.5-oz.) cans chopped green chiles, drained
- 3 cups shredded cooked chicken
- 1 (8-oz.) package ⅓-less-fat cream cheese, cubed and softened
- 2 cups (8 oz.) shredded pepper Jack cheese
- ⅓ cup chopped fresh cilantro
- 8 (8-inch) soft taco-size flour tortillas
  Vegetable cooking spray
  Tomatillo Salsa

1. Preheat oven to 350°. Sauté onion and garlic in hot oil in a large skillet over medium heat 5 minutes or until tender. Add spinach and green chiles; sauté 1 to 2 minutes or until spinach is wilted. Stir in chicken and next 3 ingredients, and cook, stirring constantly, 5 minutes or until cheeses melt. Add salt and pepper to taste. Spoon about ¾ cup chicken mixture down center of each tortilla; roll up tortillas.
2. Place rolled tortillas, seam sides down, in a lightly greased 13- x 9-inch baking dish. Lightly coat tortillas with cooking spray.
3. Bake at 350° for 30 to 35 minutes or until golden brown. Top with Tomatillo Salsa.

TO MAKE AHEAD: Prepare recipe as directed through Step 2. Cover and chill overnight. Let stand at room temperature 30 minutes. Uncover and proceed as directed in Step 3.

Tomatillo Salsa

1. Stir together 2 cups diced tomatillo; ⅓ cup sliced green onions; ⅓ cup lightly packed fresh cilantro leaves; 1 jalapeño pepper, seeded and minced; 1 Tbsp. fresh lime juice; and ½ tsp. salt. Cover and chill 1 to 4 hours. Let stand at room temperature 30 minutes. Stir in 1 cup diced avocado just before serving. Makes: 3 cups

Three Sisters Salad

good for you • make-ahead • party perfect

MAKES: 8 to 10 servings
HANDS-ON TIME: 20 min.
TOTAL TIME: 3 hr., 10 min., including vinaigrette

- 2 lb. butternut squash
- 2 Tbsp. olive oil
- 1 (15.5-oz.) can cannellini beans, drained and rinsed
- 2 cups fresh corn kernels
- ½ small red onion, sliced
- ½ cup chopped fresh basil
  Balsamic Vinaigrette
- 3 cups loosely packed arugula

1. Preheat oven to 400°. Peel and seed butternut squash; cut into ¾-inch cubes. Toss squash with olive oil to coat; place in a single layer in a lightly greased aluminum foil-lined 15- x 10-inch jelly-roll pan. Bake 20 minutes or until squash is just tender and begins to brown (do not overcook), stirring once after 10 minutes. Cool completely (about 20 minutes).
2. Toss together cannellini beans, next 4 ingredients, and squash in a large bowl; cover and chill 2 to 4 hours. Toss with arugula just before serving.

Balsamic Vinaigrette

1. Whisk together 2 Tbsp. balsamic vinegar; 1 large shallot, minced; 1 tsp. minced garlic; ½ Tbsp. light brown sugar; ¼ tsp. salt; and ¼ tsp. seasoned pepper. Gradually add ¼ cup canola oil in a slow, steady stream, whisking until blended.

Mango Tango

good for you • make-ahead • party perfect

MAKES: 6 to 8 servings
HANDS-ON TIME: 20 min.
TOTAL TIME: 2 hr., 20 min.

- ¼ cup fresh lime juice
- 3 Tbsp. sugar
- 1 Tbsp. seeded and minced jalapeño pepper
- 2 mangoes, peeled and sliced
- 3 large peaches, peeled and sliced
- 3 cups sliced assorted plums
- 1 Tbsp. chopped fresh mint
- 1 Tbsp. chopped fresh cilantro

1. Stir together first 3 ingredients in a large bowl until sugar dissolves. Add mangoes and next 4 ingredients, tossing to coat. Cover and chill 2 to 6 hours.

Mexican Chocolate Ice-cream Pie

make-ahead • party perfect

MAKES: 8 servings
HANDS-ON TIME: 30 min.
TOTAL TIME: 10 hr., 50 min.
(Pictured on page 184)

- 3 cups cinnamon graham cracker crumbs (about 22 whole crackers), divided
- ½ cup butter, melted
- ¼ tsp. ground red pepper
- 1 (4-oz.) semisweet chocolate baking bar, finely chopped
- 1 (3.5-oz.) package roasted glazed pecan pieces
- 1 pt. chocolate ice cream, softened
- 1 pt. coffee ice cream, softened
- 1 cup whipping cream
- ¼ cup coffee liqueur

1. Preheat oven to 350°. Stir together 2½ cups cinnamon graham cracker crumbs and next 2 ingredients; firmly press mixture on bottom and up sides of a lightly greased 9-inch pie plate. Bake 10 to 12 minutes or until lightly browned. Cool completely on a wire rack (about 30 minutes).
2. Stir together semisweet chocolate, pecan pieces, and remaining ½ cup cinnamon graham cracker crumbs. Reserve ½ cup chocolate-pecan mixture to top pie.
3. Spread chocolate ice cream in bottom of prepared crust; top with remaining chocolate-pecan mixture. Freeze 30 minutes. Spread coffee ice cream over chocolate mixture. Cover and freeze 8 hours.
4. Beat whipping cream and coffee liqueur at medium speed with an electric mixer until stiff peaks form. Spread whipped cream mixture over pie; sprinkle with reserved ½ cup chocolate-pecan mixture. Cover and freeze 1 hour or until whipped cream is firm. Let stand 10 to 15 minutes before serving.

Test Kitchen Tip

A crisp, over-the-rim graham cracker crust spiked with ground cinnamon and red pepper adds a spicy cowboy kick to this showstopping pie. Make and freeze it up to one month ahead.

Celebrate Fig Season

Try these nine effortless recipes, each well worth a mad dash to the farmers' market.

Pancetta-and-Fig Pasta

quick prep • party perfect

MAKES: 6 servings
HANDS-ON TIME: 25 min.
TOTAL TIME: 35 min.

Bucatini is a hearty, hollow, spaghetti-like pasta. You can easily substitute linguine or fettuccine if you prefer. (Pictured on page 13)

- 1 (16-oz.) package bucatini pasta
- 5 oz. thinly sliced pancetta, chopped (about 1 cup)
- 2 shallots, minced
- 1 garlic clove, minced
- ¾ cup heavy cream
- ½ cup freshly grated Parmesan cheese
- 12 fresh figs, quartered
- ⅓ cup torn basil leaves

1. Cook pasta in boiling salted water according to package directions; drain, reserving 1 cup hot pasta water.
2. Sauté pancetta, shallots, and garlic in a large skillet over medium heat 6 to 7 minutes or until pancetta is golden and shallots are tender. Add cream, cheese, and hot cooked pasta; cook, stirring constantly, 2 to 3 minutes or until cheese is melted. Stir in ¾ to 1 cup reserved pasta water until creamy. Season with salt and pepper to taste. Transfer to a serving dish. Sprinkle with figs and basil. Serve immediately.

Figgy Focaccia

quick prep • party perfect

MAKES: 4 to 6 servings
HANDS-ON TIME: 20 min.
TOTAL TIME: 35 min.

Turn this into a pizza by adding grated fontina cheese and sliced dry salami. (Pictured on page 12)

- 1 medium-size red onion
- 3 Tbsp. olive oil, divided
  Coarse sea or kosher salt and freshly ground pepper to taste
  Plain cornmeal
- 1 lb. bakery pizza dough
- 8 fresh figs, halved
- 1 Tbsp. fresh rosemary leaves

1. Preheat grill to 350° to 400° (medium-high) heat. Cut onion into ¾- to 1-inch slices. Brush onion slices with 1 Tbsp. olive oil, and season with sea salt and freshly ground pepper to taste. Grill onion slices, without grill lid, 3 to 4 minutes on each side or until tender and lightly charred.

2. Preheat oven to 425°. Lightly dust work surface with cornmeal. Stretch dough into a 10- to 12-inch oval on work surface. Place dough, cornmeal side down, on a greased baking sheet; drizzle with remaining 2 Tbsp. olive oil. Rub oil into dough. Arrange fig halves and grilled onion over dough, pressing lightly. Sprinkle with rosemary and salt and pepper to taste.

3. Bake at 425° on lowest oven rack 15 to 20 minutes or until golden.

Fig-and-Bourbon Fizz

quick prep • party perfect

MAKES: 1 serving
HANDS-ON TIME: 5 min.
TOTAL TIME: 5 min.

We liked this recipe using a Black Mission fig or other purple-skinned variety because of the pretty tint it gives the drink. (Pictured on page 13)

1. Muddle 1 fresh whole, ripe fig; 6 fresh mint leaves; and 2 to 3 brown sugar cubes against sides of a cocktail shaker. (Fig needs to be fairly broken down.) Add ¼ cup bourbon and enough ice cubes to fill shaker (about 1 cup). Cover with lid, and shake vigorously until thoroughly chilled (about 30 seconds). Strain into a 10-oz. glass filled with ice cubes. Top with ½ cup chilled ginger ale. Stir gently, and garnish with a mint sprig, if desired. Serve immediately.

Marinated Fig Salad

quick prep • good for you • party perfect

MAKES: 4 servings
HANDS-ON TIME: 15 min.
TOTAL TIME: 45 min.
(Pictured on page 13)

- ¼ cup extra virgin olive oil
- 3 Tbsp. balsamic vinegar
- 1 Tbsp. honey
- 1 tsp. coarse-grained Dijon mustard
- 16 fresh figs, halved
- 1 (8-oz.) package fresh mozzarella cheese slices
- 4 oz. thinly sliced Serrano ham or prosciutto, torn into strips
- 2 cups loosely packed arugula

1. Whisk together first 4 ingredients and salt and pepper to taste in a medium bowl. Stir in figs; let stand 30 minutes.

2. Arrange mozzarella and ham on 4 salad plates or a large platter. Spoon fig mixture over cheese and ham. Sprinkle with arugula, and season with salt and pepper to taste.

Rosemary Flank Steak with Fig Salsa

good for you • make-ahead • party perfect

MAKES: 6 servings
HANDS-ON TIME: 30 min.
TOTAL TIME: 1 hr., 5 min.
(Pictured on page 13)

- 1 Tbsp. chopped fresh rosemary
- 2 garlic cloves, minced
- ¾ tsp. kosher salt
- ½ tsp. freshly ground pepper
- 3 Tbsp. olive oil, divided
- 1 (1¼-lb.) flank steak
- 3 cups chopped fresh figs
- 1 green onion, minced
- 2 Tbsp. chopped fresh parsley
- 2 Tbsp. seasoned rice wine vinegar
- 3 oz. Gorgonzola cheese, crumbled

1. Stir together first 4 ingredients and 1 Tbsp. olive oil. Rub onto steak; cover and chill 30 minutes to 4 hours.

2. Preheat grill to 400° to 450° (high) heat. Toss together figs, next 3 ingredients, and remaining 2 Tbsp. oil. Add salt and pepper to taste.

3. Grill steak, covered with grill lid, 5 minutes on each side or to desired degree of doneness. Let stand 5 minutes.

4. Cut steak diagonally across the grain into thin strips, and arrange on a serving platter. Spoon fig salsa over steak, and sprinkle with Gorgonzola.

4 More Reasons To Love Fig Season

FIGGY FROZEN YOGURT:
Blend 2 cups Greek yogurt, 1 cup heavy cream, ⅓ cup sugar, ¼ cup cane syrup, 2 tsp. vanilla extract, and a pinch of salt. Stir in 1 cup mashed fresh figs. Chill 2 hours. Freeze in a 1½-qt. ice-cream maker, swirling in ¼ cup chopped roasted, salted pecans and 3 Tbsp. caramel topping the last few minutes of freezing.

FIG-CHEESE TARTLETS:
Bake 1 (1.9-oz.) package mini-phyllo pastry shells on a baking sheet at 350° for 5 minutes. Cool 10 minutes. Fill each with 1 tsp. crumbled goat cheese; top each with 2 fresh fig quarters. Sprinkle with kosher salt and pepper to taste. Drizzle with bottled balsamic glaze.

FIG-BARBECUE PANINI:
Spread 4 bread slices with 4 Tbsp. fig preserves. Layer with 1 lb. shredded barbecued pork, ¼ cup thinly sliced red onion, 8 sliced fresh figs, 4 provolone cheese slices, and 1 cup loosely packed baby spinach. Top each with a bread slice. Brush with melted butter. Cook in a panini press 2 to 3 minutes.

FIG-CHERRY SHORTCAKES:
Stir together 1½ cups chopped figs; ¾ cup pitted, halved fresh cherries; 2 Tbsp. chopped fresh basil; 1 Tbsp. granulated sugar; and 2 Tbsp. orange liqueur. Let stand 30 minutes. Stir together 1 cup sour cream, 3 Tbsp. light brown sugar, and 2 Tbsp. heavy cream. Fill 6 warm biscuits with fig and cream mixtures.

SAVE ROOM

Bake It Easy

Put your own twist on our classic icebox cookies.

Icebox Butter Cookies
make-ahead • party perfect

MAKES: 8 to 10 dozen
HANDS-ON TIME: 20 min.
TOTAL TIME: 9 hr., 45 min.

Bake 8 minutes for a soft and chewy cookie or up to 12 minutes for a crisp cookie.

- 1 cup butter, softened
- 1½ cups granulated sugar
- ½ cup firmly packed light brown sugar
- 1 Tbsp. vanilla extract
- 2 large eggs
- 3½ cups all-purpose flour
- ½ tsp. baking soda
- ½ tsp. salt
- Parchment paper

1. Beat first 4 ingredients at medium speed with an electric mixer until fluffy. Add eggs, 1 at a time, beating just until blended after each addition.

2. Stir together flour and next 2 ingredients; gradually add to butter mixture, beating just until blended after each addition.

3. Shape dough into 4 logs (about 2 inches in diameter); wrap each log in plastic wrap. Chill 8 hours to 3 days.

4. Preheat oven to 350°. Cut each log into ¼-inch-thick slices; place on parchment paper-lined baking sheets. Bake 8 to 12 minutes or until lightly browned. Remove from baking sheets to wire racks, and cool completely (about 20 minutes).

Try These Stir-ins!

LIME-COCONUT: Stir in 1 cup sweetened flaked coconut, 1 cup finely chopped macadamia nuts, and 2 Tbsp. lime zest after adding flour mixture.

CHOCOLATE CONFETTI: Stir in 1 cup chopped honey-roasted peanuts and 1 (4-oz.) semisweet chocolate baking bar, finely chopped, after adding flour mixture.

ROSEMARY-BERRY: Stir in 1 cup finely chopped sweetened dried cranberries, 2 Tbsp. minced fresh rosemary, and 2 Tbsp. orange zest after adding flour mixture.

PRALINE PECAN: Stir in 1½ cups roasted glazed pecan pieces after adding flour mixture.

JAVA CHIP: Add 3 Tbsp. instant coffee granules with first 4 ingredients; stir in 4 (1.4-oz.) chocolate-covered toffee candy bars, finely chopped, after adding flour mixture.

LEMON-BASIL: Add ¼ cup finely chopped fresh basil, 2 Tbsp. lemon zest, and 2 Tbsp. poppy seeds with first 4 ingredients.

SPICED SWEET TEA: Add 3 Tbsp. unsweetened instant tea mix, 2 Tbsp. orange zest, 1 Tbsp. lemon zest, and 2 tsp. pumpkin pie spice with first 4 ingredients. Roll logs in Demerara sugar before chilling.

Lighten Up Pimiento Cheese

To all you pimiento cheese purists, we dare you not to love these healthier twists.

Potato Skin Party Bites

{1}

Classic Pimiento Cheese

quick prep • good for you • make-ahead • party perfect

Flashback: *We lightened up the original that ran in August 2001 and got 35% fewer calories and 45% fewer fat grams!*

1. Stir together ¾ cup light mayonnaise; I (4-oz.) jar diced pimiento, drained; I tsp. finely grated onion; I tsp. lemon juice; I tsp. Worcestershire sauce; and ¼ tsp. ground red pepper. Stir in I (8-oz.) block 2% reduced-fat extra-sharp Cheddar cheese, finely shredded, and I (8-oz.) block 2% reduced-fat sharp Cheddar cheese, shredded. Makes: about 3 cups

PER TBSP: CALORIES 43; FAT 3.3G (SAT 1.6G); PROTEIN 2.4G; CARB 0.7G; CHOL 8MG; SODIUM 113MG; CALC 68MG

{2}

Jalapeño-Pimiento Cheese

quick prep • good for you • make-ahead • party perfect

1. Stir together 1¼ cups low-fat or fat-free Greek yogurt; I (4-oz.) jar diced pimiento, drained; 2 Tbsp. finely chopped fresh cilantro; I Tbsp. chopped jarred pickled jalapeño peppers; and I Tbsp. liquid from pickled jalapeño peppers. Stir in I (8-oz.) block 2% reduced-fat extra-sharp Cheddar cheese, shredded, and ½ (8-oz.) block Monterey Jack cheese, shredded. Makes: about 3 cups

PER TBSP: CALORIES 28; FAT 1.8G (SAT 1.1G); PROTEIN 2.3G; CARB 0.6G; CHOL 5.9MG; SODIUM 61MG; CALC 55MG

{3}

Three-Cheese Pimiento Cheese

quick prep • good for you • make-ahead • party perfect

1. Process I (8-oz.) block fat-free cream cheese, softened, and ½ cup 1% low-fat cottage cheese in a food processor until smooth. Stir in I (4-oz.) jar diced pimiento, drained; 2 tsp. coarse-grained mustard; 2 tsp. finely grated onion; I tsp. lemon juice; and a dash of hot sauce. Stir in I (8-oz.) block 2% reduced-fat sharp white Cheddar cheese, shredded. Season with salt and freshly ground pepper to taste. Makes: about 2 ½ cups

PER TBSP: CALORIES 27; FAT 1.3G (SAT 0.8G); PROTEIN 2.6G; CARB 0.8G; CHOL 5.2MG; SODIUM 105MG; CALC 73MG

Cook Fast, Eat Fresh

Brighten up your plate with simple, colorful ingredients and flavors from the garden.

IF YOU HAVE
15 MINUTES

Garden Tomato Sauce over Pasta: Make an even faster meal by freezing the sauce in batches so that all you have to do is reheat.

IF YOU HAVE
30 MINUTES

Chicken with Ratatouille: Thin cutlets cook fast. Make your own cutlets by slicing chicken breasts in half lengthwise.

IF YOU HAVE
45 MINUTES

Shrimp Succotash: While the butter beans simmer, prep the other ingredients. Save more time by asking for peeled and deveined shrimp at the seafood counter.

---

15 MINUTES

Garden Tomato Sauce over Pasta

quick prep • good for you • party perfect

MAKES: about 3 cups

We love this sauce as a meatless meal over hearty pasta. Or try it in lasagna or a meatball sub.

1	onion, diced (about 1 cup)
1	Tbsp. olive oil
1	garlic clove, minced
4	medium-size heirloom tomatoes (about 2 lb.), cored and chopped
	Kosher salt
	Freshly ground pepper
¼	cup dry red wine
3	Tbsp. chopped fresh oregano or marjoram
	Hot cooked pasta
	Garnish: fresh oregano leaves

1. Sauté onion in hot oil in a Dutch oven over medium-high heat 3 minutes or until tender. Add garlic; sauté 1 minute. Add tomatoes, kosher salt, and freshly ground pepper to taste. Cook, stirring often, 2 to 3 minutes or until tomatoes start to release their juices. Add wine, and cook, stirring occasionally, 5 to 8 minutes or until almost all liquid has evaporated. Remove from heat, and stir in oregano. Serve sauce over hot cooked pasta. Store sauce in an airtight container in refrigerator up to 1 week, or freeze up to 1 month.

---

30 MINUTES

Chicken with Ratatouille

quick prep • good for you

MAKES: 6 servings

This is the perfect one-dish dinner when the garden is in full swing. Feel free to substitute whatever is overflowing in your garden or at the market for the vegetables in the ratatouille.

1	small red onion, chopped
½	(1-lb.) eggplant, peeled and chopped
2	Tbsp. olive oil
2	small summer squash, chopped
2	garlic cloves, minced
1	medium-size red bell pepper, chopped
1	medium tomato, diced
¼	cup chopped fresh basil
1¼	tsp. kosher salt, divided
¾	tsp. freshly ground pepper, divided
6	(4-oz.) chicken breast cutlets
⅓	cup all-purpose flour
1	cup canola oil
	Garnish: fresh basil leaves

1. Sauté onion and eggplant in hot olive oil in a large nonstick skillet over medium-high heat 5 minutes or until tender and light brown around edges. Add squash, garlic, and bell pepper; sauté 5 minutes or until tender. Add tomato, basil, and ¼ tsp. each kosher salt and freshly ground pepper. Cook, stirring constantly, 2 to 3 minutes or until mixture is thoroughly heated.

2. Remove vegetable mixture from skillet. Cover loosely with aluminum foil to keep warm. Wipe skillet clean.

3. Rinse chicken, and pat dry. Sprinkle with remaining 1 tsp. salt and ½ tsp. pepper. Dredge chicken in flour, shaking off excess.

4. Fry chicken, in 2 batches, in hot canola oil in skillet over medium-high heat 2 to 3 minutes on each side or until golden brown and done. Drain on a wire rack over paper towels; cover and keep warm. Transfer to a serving dish, and top with vegetable mixture.

45 MINUTES
Shrimp Succotash
quick prep • good for you

MAKES: 6 servings

This is a fantastic light summer meal. It's especially delicious with 'Silver Queen' corn and heirloom tomatoes, but you can use any of your favorite varieties.

- 2 **cups fresh butter beans (about ½ lb.)***
- 1¼ **tsp. kosher salt, divided**
- 1½ **lb. peeled and deveined, extra-large raw shrimp (16/20 count)**
- 2 **Tbsp. olive oil, divided**
- ¼ **tsp. freshly ground pepper**
- 1 **cup sliced fresh okra**
- 1 **small sweet onion, chopped**
- 1 **jalapeño pepper, seeded and minced**
- ½ **cup diced red bell pepper**
- 2 **garlic cloves, minced**
- 1 **medium-size heirloom tomato, seeded and diced**
- 1 **cup fresh corn kernels (2 ears)**
- ¼ **cup chopped fresh basil**
- 1 **Tbsp. butter**

1. Rinse, sort, and drain butter beans.

2. Bring butter beans, 1 tsp. salt, and 4 cups water to a boil in a saucepan over medium-high heat. Reduce heat to medium-low, and simmer, stirring occasionally, 35 minutes or until beans are tender; drain.

3. Meanwhile, combine shrimp, 1 Tbsp. oil, ¼ tsp. pepper, and remaining ¼ tsp. salt in a bowl, tossing to coat. Heat a grill pan over medium-high heat; cook shrimp 4 to 5 minutes or just until shrimp turn pink.

Transfer to a plate, and cover loosely with aluminum foil to keep warm.

4. Heat remaining 1 Tbsp. oil in a large skillet over medium heat. Add okra; cook 3 minutes or until lightly browned. Stir in onion and next 3 ingredients; cook 3 minutes or until vegetables are tender. Add tomato and corn; sauté 3 to 4 minutes or until corn is tender. Stir in basil, butter, shrimp, and butter beans. Cook 1 minute or until butter is melted and mixture is thoroughly heated. Season with salt and pepper to taste. Serve immediately.

*Frozen butter beans may be substituted. Omit Step 1.

MAKE-AHEAD
Pan-Seared Skirt Steaks

Halve, seed, and mince 1 jalapeño pepper. Combine ½ cup dry red wine; 3 Tbsp. Worcestershire sauce; ¼ cup chopped fresh cilantro; 1 Tbsp. olive oil; half of jalapeño pepper; and 1 garlic clove, minced, in a large zip-top plastic freezer bag. Add 2 lb. skirt steaks; seal and chill 30 minutes to 24 hours. (If marinating overnight, let steak stand in marinade at room temperature 30 minutes.) Remove from marinade, discarding marinade. Sprinkle steak with 1¼ tsp. kosher salt and 1 tsp. freshly ground pepper. Heat a grill pan over medium-high heat. Cook steaks, in batches, 2 minutes on each side (medium-rare) or to desired degree of doneness. Remove from grill pan, cover loosely with aluminum foil, and let stand 5 minutes. Stir together ¾ cup chopped fresh cilantro, 3 Tbsp. lime juice, 2 Tbsp. olive oil, 1 minced garlic clove, and remaining half of jalapeño pepper. Season with kosher salt and freshly ground pepper to taste. Cut steaks diagonally across the grain into thin slices. Serve with cilantro sauce and Sweet Potato Hash. Makes: 8 servings

Sweet Potato Hash: Melt 1 Tbsp. butter with 2 Tbsp. olive oil in a skillet over medium-high heat. Add 2 sweet potatoes, peeled and chopped; cook, stirring occasionally, 5 minutes. Add ½ red bell pepper, chopped; ½ red onion, chopped; 1 tsp. kosher salt; and ¼ tsp. freshly ground pepper. Reduce heat to medium; cover and cook, stirring occasionally, 8 to 10 minutes or until potatoes are tender.

Lemon-Poppy Seed Zucchini Bread

These little loaves freeze (and thaw) wonderfully, so keep them on hand by the bushelful for last-minute gifts.

MAKE IT!

MAKES: 3 (5- x 3-inch) loaves
HANDS-ON TIME: 20 min.
TOTAL TIME: I hr., 40 min.

The tender, fine-crumbed texture and bright citrus flavor offer a refreshing change from traditional spiced zucchini breads.

- ½ **cup butter, softened**
- 1⅓ **cups sugar**
- 3 **large eggs**
- 1½ **cups all-purpose flour**
- ½ **tsp. salt**
- ⅛ **tsp. baking soda**
- ½ **cup sour cream**
- I **cup shredded zucchini**
- I **Tbsp. lemon zest**
- 2 **tsp. poppy seeds**

1. Preheat oven to 325°. Beat butter at medium speed with a heavy-duty electric stand mixer until creamy. Gradually add sugar, beating until light and fluffy. Add eggs, I at a time, beating just until blended after each addition.

2. Stir together flour, salt, and baking soda. Add to butter mixture alternately with sour cream, beginning and ending with flour mixture. Beat at low speed just until blended after each addition. Stir in zucchini and next 2 ingredients. Spoon batter into 3 greased and floured 5- x 3-inch disposable aluminum foil loaf pans (about 1⅓ cups batter per pan).

3. Bake at 325° for 40 to 45 minutes or until a wooden pick inserted in center comes out clean. Cool in pans on wire racks I0 minutes; remove from pans to wire racks, and cool completely (about 30 minutes).

TAKE IT!

Package the bread in a pint-size wood berry box from *thinkgarnish.com* (75 cents each) for rustic charm. Add high style for low cost by wrapping the loaves with fabric scraps. (We used a Bed, Bath & Beyond curtain panel, torn and frayed at the edges.) Tie on our downloadable gift tag with embroidery thread for a pretty finish.

DOWNLOAD OUR GIFT TAGS:
southernliving.com/food-gift

September

Caramel Apples

The snap of a crisp fall apple wrapped in caramel is one of the sweetest temptations this side of paradise. But we'll go you one better with a slice of our Caramel Apple-Brownie Cheesecake. Of course, you wouldn't want to pass up the streusel-topped coffee cake or the Caramel Apple Muffins. Just take your pick!

Caramel Apple-Brownie Cheesecake

make-ahead • party perfect

MAKES: 12 servings
HANDS-ON TIME: 30 min.
TOTAL TIME: 4 hr., including topping and sauce
(Pictured on page 14)

- ¾ cup chopped pecans
- 2 (8-oz.) packages cream cheese, softened
- ½ cup granulated sugar
- 1 tsp. vanilla extract
- 4 large eggs, divided
- ½ cup firmly packed light brown sugar
- ½ cup butter, melted
- 1 cup all-purpose flour
- 1 tsp. ground cinnamon
- 1 tsp. baking powder
- ¼ tsp. salt
- 1½ cups peeled and diced Granny Smith apples
  Caramel Apple Topping
  Caramel Sauce (see recipe, next page)

1. Preheat oven to 350°. Bake pecans in a single layer in a shallow pan 8 to 10 minutes or until lightly toasted and fragrant, stirring halfway through. Reduce oven temperature to 325°. Sprinkle pecans over bottom of a greased and floured shiny 9-inch springform pan.
2. Beat cream cheese, granulated sugar, and vanilla at medium speed with a heavy-duty electric stand mixer until blended and smooth. Add 3 eggs, 1 at a time, beating just until blended after each addition.
3. Whisk together brown sugar, melted butter, and remaining egg in a large bowl until blended.
4. Stir together flour and next 3 ingredients; add to brown sugar mixture, and stir until blended. Stir in apples. Spoon batter into prepared pan. Carefully spoon cream cheese mixture over batter.
5. Bake at 325° for 1 hour and 10 minutes or until set. Remove from oven, and gently run a knife around outer edge of cheesecake to loosen from sides of pan. (Do not remove sides of pan.) Cool completely in pan on a wire rack (about 2 hours). Transfer to a serving plate.
6. Meanwhile, prepare Caramel Apple Topping and Caramel Sauce. Reserve 1 cup Caramel Sauce for another use. Spoon topping over cheesecake; drizzle with ½ cup Caramel Sauce.

Caramel Apple Topping

1. Melt ¼ cup butter in a large skillet over medium heat; add ½ cup sugar and 1 tsp. fresh lemon juice, and cook, stirring constantly with a long-handled wooden spoon, 5 to 6 minutes or until mixture turns a light golden brown. Add 5 large Granny Smith apples (about 2½ lb.), peeled and cut into ½-inch-thick wedges. Cook, stirring often, 15 to 18 more minutes or until apples are tender and caramelized. Remove from heat; cool 20 minutes.

Caramel Apple Dip

make-ahead • party perfect

MAKES: 4 servings
HANDS-ON TIME: 10 min.
TOTAL TIME: 2 hr., 20 min.

This dip offers a sugary spin on a cream cheese classic with a crisp bruléed topping. (Pictured on page 14)

- 1 (8-oz.) package cream cheese, softened
- ⅓ cup firmly packed dark brown sugar
- 1 tsp. vanilla bean paste or vanilla extract
- 1 Tbsp. granulated sugar
  Fresh apple slices

1. Stir together first 3 ingredients just until blended. Spoon mixture into a 10-oz. ramekin; level and smooth surface with a spatula. Cover and chill 2 to 8 hours.
2. Preheat broiler with oven rack 5 inches from heat. Sprinkle granulated sugar over mixture in ramekin. Fill an 8-inch cake pan with ice; place ramekin in pan.
3. Broil 3 to 5 minutes or until sugar is melted and caramelized. Let stand 5 minutes. Serve with apple slices.

Test Kitchen Secret

Test Kitchen Director Rebecca Gordon says... Use a shiny pan to prevent excessive browning when baking a coffee cake or cheesecake. Baking with dark pans? Try our trick on page 244.

Caramel Apple Muffins

party perfect

MAKES: I dozen
HANDS-ON TIME: 30 min.
TOTAL TIME: I hr., 30 min.

These are prettiest the day they are made. After standing overnight, the caramel melts into the muffins. (They're still delicious!) (Pictured on page 14)

    Cinnamon Topping
 I (8-oz.) container sour cream
 I cup sugar
 2 large eggs
 I Tbsp. vanilla extract
 2 cups all-purpose flour
 2 tsp. baking powder
 ½ tsp. baking soda
 ½ tsp. salt
 2 cups peeled and diced Granny
    Smith apples
 I (14-oz.) package caramels
 3 Tbsp. whipping cream
 I cup chopped lightly salted,
    roasted pecans
    Wax paper
    Food-safe twigs or craft sticks

1. Preheat oven to 375°. Prepare Cinnamon Topping as directed.
2. Beat sour cream and next 3 ingredients at low speed with an electric mixer 30 seconds or until blended.
3. Stir together flour and next 3 ingredients. Add to sour cream mixture, beating at low speed just until blended. (Do not overmix.) Stir in diced apples. Spoon into a lightly greased 12-cup muffin pan, filling three-fourths full; sprinkle with Cinnamon Topping.
4. Bake at 375° for 18 to 20 minutes or until golden brown and a wooden pick inserted in center comes out clean. Immediately remove from pans to wire racks; cool completely (about 30 minutes).
5. Microwave caramels and cream in a microwave-safe bowl at HIGH I to 2 minutes or until smooth, stirring at 30-second intervals. Let mixture stand, stirring occasionally, 5 minutes or until thick enough to coat muffins.

6. Quickly dip bottom three-fourths of each muffin into caramel mixture; roll bottom half of caramel-coated portion of muffin in chopped pecans, and place muffins, caramel sides up, on lightly greased wax paper. (If caramel mixture begins to harden before you've dipped all the muffins, microwave mixture a few seconds to soften.) Insert food-safe twigs or craft sticks into caramel-covered portions of muffins.

Cinnamon Topping

1. Stir together ⅓ cup firmly packed light brown sugar, I½ Tbsp. all-purpose flour, and ¼ tsp. ground cinnamon in a small bowl. Cut in I½ Tbsp. butter with a pastry blender or fork until mixture resembles coarse meal.

Caramel Apple Coffee Cake

MAKES: 8 to 10 servings
HANDS-ON TIME: 35 min.
TOTAL TIME: 4 hr., 50 min.
(Pictured on page 14)

 2 Tbsp. butter
 3 cups peeled and sliced Granny
    Smith apples (about 3 large)
    Streusel Topping
    Caramel Sauce (see recipe,
    at right)
 ½ cup butter, softened
 I cup sugar
 2 large eggs
 2 cups all-purpose flour
 2 tsp. baking powder
 ½ tsp. salt
 ⅔ cup milk
 2 tsp. vanilla extract

1. Preheat oven to 350°. Melt 2 Tbsp. butter in a large skillet over medium-high heat; add apples; sauté 5 minutes or until softened. Remove from heat; cool completely (about 30 minutes).
2. Meanwhile, prepare Streusel Topping and Caramel Sauce. Reserve ½ cup Caramel Sauce for another use.

3. Beat ½ cup butter at medium speed with an electric mixer until creamy; gradually add sugar, beating well. Add eggs, I at a time, beating until blended after each addition.
4. Combine flour, baking powder, and salt; add to butter mixture alternately with milk, beginning and ending with flour mixture. Beat at low speed until blended after each addition. Stir in vanilla. Pour batter into a greased and floured shiny 9-inch springform pan; top with apples. Drizzle with ½ cup Caramel Sauce; sprinkle with Streusel Topping.
5. Bake at 350° for 45 minutes. Cover loosely with aluminum foil to prevent excessive browning; bake 25 to 30 minutes or until center is set. (A wooden pick will not come out clean.) Cool in pan on a wire rack 30 minutes; remove sides of pan. Cool completely on wire rack (about I½ hours). Drizzle with ½ cup Caramel Sauce.

Streusel Topping

1. Stir together I½ cups all-purpose flour, I cup chopped pecans, ½ cup melted butter, ½ cup firmly packed light brown sugar, ¼ cup granulated sugar, I½ tsp. ground cinnamon, and ¼ tsp. salt until blended. Let stand 30 minutes or until firm enough to crumble into small pieces.

> ## Fast Flourish!
>
> **CARAMEL SAUCE:** Bring I cup firmly packed light brown sugar, ½ cup butter, ¼ cup whipping cream, and ¼ cup honey to a boil in a medium saucepan over medium-high heat, stirring constantly; boil, stirring constantly, 2 minutes. Remove from heat, and cool 15 minutes before serving. Store in an airtight container in refrigerator up to I week. To reheat, microwave at HIGH 10 to 15 seconds or just until warm; stir until smooth. Makes: about I½ cups.

Caramel Apple Ice-cream Tarts

make-ahead • party perfect

MAKES: 8 servings
HANDS-ON TIME: 30 min.
TOTAL TIME: 6 hr., 5 min.

This shortbread crust is the perfect foil for ice cream. (Pictured on page 15)

1⅔   cups all-purpose flour
¾   cup butter, cubed
⅔   cup powdered sugar
⅓   cup cornstarch
2   Tbsp. butter
2   cups peeled and diced Gala apples
⅓   cup firmly packed light brown sugar
2   Tbsp. bourbon
2   pt. vanilla ice cream
     Caramel Sauce (see recipe, page 227)
½   cup lightly salted, roasted pecans
     Garnish: Caramelized Apple Chips (see recipe below)

1. Preheat oven to 350°. Pulse first 4 ingredients in a food processor 10 to 12 times or until mixture resembles coarse meal. Firmly press on bottom and up sides of 8 (3¾-inch) round tart pans with removable bottoms (about 7 Tbsp. per pan). Place tart pans on a baking sheet. Bake 25 to 30 minutes or until lightly browned. Cool completely on baking sheet on a wire rack (about 30 minutes).
2. Melt 2 Tbsp. butter in a large skillet over medium-high heat; add apples and brown sugar. Cook, stirring constantly, 8 to 10 minutes or until tender and caramelized. Remove from heat, and stir in bourbon. Cool completely (about 30 minutes).
3. Let ice cream stand at room temperature 10 minutes or until softened; place ice cream in a large bowl, and stir in apple mixture. Cover and freeze 4 hours or until firm. Serve in tart shells with Caramel Sauce and pecans.

Fast Flourish!

CARAMELIZED APPLE CHIPS:
Preheat oven to 350°. Place a lightly greased wire rack in an aluminum foil-lined 15- x 10-inch jelly-roll pan. Cut 1 small apple into ¹⁄₁₆-inch-thick slices, cutting through stem and bottom end using a mandoline. Bring 1 cup sugar and 1 cup water to a boil in a 3-qt. saucepan over medium-high heat, stirring constantly. Add apple slices, and cook, stirring often, 10 to 12 minutes or until apples are slightly translucent and syrup begins to thicken. Remove from heat. Quickly remove apples from syrup, 1 at a time, using tongs, and place in a single layer on wire rack in pan. Discard remaining syrup, or save for another use. Bake apples at 350° for 10 to 15 minutes or until golden; remove from oven, and transfer apples to lightly greased wax paper, using tongs. Cool completely (about 10 minutes). Apples will crisp as they cool. Makes: about 2 dozen.

Caramel Apple Ice-cream Tarts

HEALTHY INDULGENCE

Lighten Up Your Spuds

Replace the restaurant-size scoops of butter and sour cream with these good-for-you toppings.

Test Kitchen Notebook

BASIC BAKED POTATOES:
Preheat oven to 400°. Drizzle 3 large baking potatoes with 2 tsp. vegetable oil, and rub with 2 tsp. kosher salt. Place on a 15- x 10-inch jelly-roll pan. Pierce potatoes several times with a fork. Bake 1 hour or until tender; cut in half.
PER SERVING: CALORIES 158; **FAT** 2g

Roasted Vegetable Loaded Potatoes

quick prep • good for you • party perfect

MAKES: 6 servings

3   cups chopped fresh cauliflower
2   cups sliced fresh Brussels sprouts
½   medium-size red onion, sliced
1   Tbsp. olive oil
½   tsp. kosher salt
½   tsp. freshly ground pepper
     Basic Baked Potatoes
¼   cup golden raisins
¼   cup chopped toasted walnuts
2   Tbsp. lite bottled Italian vinaigrette

1. Preheat oven to 400°. Toss together first 6 ingredients on a lightly greased 15- x 10-inch jelly-roll pan.

2. Prepare potatoes as directed. Bake cauliflower mixture, with potatoes, 25 minutes or until cauliflower is browned, stirring once. Toss with raisins, walnuts, and vinaigrette. Spoon over potatoes.

PER SERVING: CALORIES 264; FAT 7G (SAT 1G); PROTEIN 7G; CARB 45G; FIBER 7G; CHOL 0MG; IRON 3MG; SODIUM 891MG; CALC 61MG

TRY THESE TWISTS!

Country Ham & Cheese: Cook ½ cup chopped country ham in 1 tsp. hot vegetable oil in a small skillet over medium heat, stirring often, 5 to 7 minutes or until browned. (You can also use Canadian bacon.) Divide ham, ½ cup (2 oz.) shredded 2% reduced-fat Cheddar cheese, ¼ cup light sour cream, and 3 Tbsp. chopped fresh chives among Basic Baked Potatoes.

PER SERVING: CALORIES 231; FAT 6g

Spinach & Mushroom: Cook 1 (8-oz.) package sliced baby portobello mushrooms; 2 garlic cloves, minced; 1 (6-oz.) package fresh baby spinach; and ¼ tsp. each salt and pepper in 2 Tbsp. hot olive oil in a large skillet, stirring often, 5 minutes. Stir in ¼ cup toasted pine nuts, ½ cup crumbled reduced-fat feta cheese, and 2 Tbsp. bottled balsamic glaze. Serve over Basic Baked Potatoes.

PER SERVING: CALORIES 282; FAT 10g

Hawaiian Style: Cook 1 cup chopped cooked ham and ½ cup each chopped red bell pepper, fresh pineapple, and green onions in 1 tsp. hot vegetable oil in a large skillet, stirring constantly, 6 minutes or until tender. Stir in 2 Tbsp. each hoisin sauce and water. Serve over Basic Baked Potatoes. Sprinkle with 2 tsp. toasted sesame seeds.

PER SERVING: CALORIES 243; FAT 5g

FOOD GIFT OF THE MONTH

Upgrade Your Bourbon

Turn a plain bottle of hooch into a top-shelf indulgence, infused with sweet autumn flavor.

MAKE IT

Apple Pie-Infused Bourbon

make-ahead • party perfect

MAKES: 3¼ cups
HANDS-ON TIME: 10 min.
TOTAL TIME: 45 min., including simple syrup (plus 4 days for infusing)

- 1   **Golden Delicious apple, chopped**
- 2   **(3-inch) cinnamon sticks**
- ¼   **tsp. ground nutmeg**
- 1   **(750-milliliter) bottle bourbon**
- ¼   **cup Simple Syrup**

1. Place first 3 ingredients in a 1-qt. canning jar. Add bourbon; cover with metal lid, and screw on band. Let bourbon stand at room temperature 4 days.

2. Shake jar to distribute flavors. Pour bourbon mixture through a fine wire-mesh strainer into a pitcher, discarding solids. Stir in Simple Syrup, and pour into a clean 1-qt. canning jar or 3 to 4 small bottles. Cover and store in refrigerator up to 2 months.

Simple Syrup

1. Combine 1 cup sugar and ½ cup water in a small saucepan. Bring to a boil over medium heat, stirring occasionally. Boil 1 minute or until sugar is dissolved. Remove from heat, and cool 30 minutes. Store in an airtight container in refrigerator up to 2 weeks. Makes: ¾ cup

TRY THIS TWIST!

Orange-, Clove-, and Cranberry-Infused Bourbon: Omit apple, cinnamon, and nutmeg. Place 2 (2-inch) orange zest strips, 8 whole cloves, and 1 cup lightly crushed fresh or frozen cranberries in a 1-qt. canning jar. Add bourbon; cover with metal lid, and screw on band. Let bourbon stand at room temperature 4 days. Proceed with recipe as directed in Step 2.

TAKE IT

At 7 ounces, these cute corked bottles are the perfect size for gifts ($2.09 each; *specialtybottle.com*). You can also use mini Mason jars or any other food-safe glass container with a lid.

Cook Up A Rustic, Casual Feast

Chef James Petrakis' new cookbook, *The Ravenous Pig: Seasons of Florida,* is full of Old Florida charm, as is his riverside cookout.

The Menu

S ERVES 8

COCKTAIL

Umatilla Smash

STARTERS

Farmer Salad

Butternut Squash Soup

MAIN COURSE

Grilled Rib-Eye Steaks
with Béarnaise Butter
and Onion Relish

Grilled Fingerling
Potato Salad

Marinated Kale Salad
with Gouda and
Shaved Apples

DESSERT

Pineapple
Upside-Down Cake

KEEP IT LOW-KEY

"It's extremely important that we spend time around the table. Being out here is the perfect spot to relax and catch up," says James, chef/owner of *The Ravenous Pig* in Winter Park, Florida.

Umatilla Smash

quick prep • party perfect

MAKES: 1 serving
HANDS-ON TIME: 5 min.
TOTAL TIME: 50 min., including confit

1. Muddle 1 Tbsp. Kumquat Confit and 1 to 3 thin fresh jalapeño pepper slices against sides of an 8-oz. glass to release flavors. Stir in 3 Tbsp. whiskey and enough crushed ice to fill glass halfway; top with chilled club soda. Garnish with candied kumquat slices.
NOTE: We tested with Palm Ridge Reserve Handmade Micro Batch Florida Whiskey (*palmridgereserve.com*).

Kumquat Confit

quick prep • make-ahead • party perfect
1. Cut kumquats from 1 (8-oz.) container into thin slices, and place in a medium bowl. Combine 1 cup sugar and ½ cup water in a small saucepan; bring to a boil over medium-high heat, stirring often. Boil, stirring often, 1 minute. Pour mixture over kumquats; let stand at room temperature 30 minutes. Makes: about 1 cup.

Farmer Salad

quick prep • party perfect

MAKES: 8 servings
HANDS-ON TIME: 25 min.
TOTAL TIME: 45 min.
(Pictured on page 186)

- 8 **large eggs**
- 8 **thick bacon slices, coarsely chopped**
- 8 **cups loosely packed baby arugula**
- 4 **cups trimmed frisée**
- 2 **cups thinly sliced radicchio**
- 2 **cups brioche or challah bread cubes, toasted**
- ½ **cup shaved Parmesan cheese**
  Parmesan Vinaigrette
  Kosher salt and freshly ground pepper to taste

1. Bring 12 cups water to a boil in a large Dutch oven. Add eggs; boil 5 (soft cooked) to 7 (hard cooked) minutes or to desired degree of doneness. Remove from heat, and let eggs stand in hot water 1 minute; drain. Peel under cold running water. Cut eggs in half.
2. Cook bacon in a large skillet over medium-high heat 8 to 10 minutes or until crisp; remove bacon, and drain on paper towels.
3. Gently toss together bacon, arugula, next 4 ingredients, and desired amount of Parmesan Vinaigrette. Divide mixture among 8 salad bowls. Top each with 2 egg halves. Sprinkle with salt and pepper to taste. Serve with remaining Parmesan Vinaigrette.

Parmesan Vinaigrette

1. Process 1¼ cups freshly grated Parmesan cheese; ½ cup red wine vinegar; 4 anchovy fillets; 1 tsp. lemon zest; 1 Tbsp. fresh lemon juice; 1 garlic clove, pressed; 1 tsp. Dijon mustard; 1 tsp. Worcestershire sauce; ¼ tsp. kosher salt; and ¼ tsp. freshly ground pepper in a blender or food processor until smooth. With blender running, add ½ cup olive oil in a slow, steady stream, processing until smooth. Makes: 1½ cups.

Butternut Squash Soup

quick prep • party perfect

MAKES: 10½ cups
HANDS-ON TIME: 30 min.
TOTAL TIME: 1 hr., 10 min.
(Pictured on page 186)

- 2 carrots, cut into 1-inch pieces
- 1 sweet onion, chopped
- 3 Tbsp. olive oil
- 1 (3-lb.) butternut squash, peeled and cut into 1-inch pieces
- 6 cups chicken broth
- 1 tsp. orange zest
- 1 cup heavy cream
- 3 Tbsp. white wine vinegar
- 1 Tbsp. orange blossom honey
- ¾ tsp. kosher salt
- ½ tsp. freshly ground white pepper
- ½ tsp. hot sauce
   Garnish: smoked paprika, olive oil

1. Sauté carrots and onion in hot olive oil in a Dutch oven over medium-high heat 8 to 10 minutes or until lightly browned. Add squash, broth, and orange zest; bring to a boil. Cover, reduce heat to medium, and simmer 20 to 25 minutes or until squash is tender. Stir in cream and next 5 ingredients. Cool slightly (about 10 minutes).
2. Process mixture with a handheld blender until smooth. Serve warm.

Grilled Rib-eye Steaks with Béarnaise Butter and Onion Relish

party perfect

MAKES: 8 servings
HANDS-ON TIME: 20 min.
TOTAL TIME: 4 hr., 45 min.

- 8 Tbsp. roasted cacao nibs
- 8 (14-oz.) rib-eye steaks
- 3½ tsp. kosher salt
- 1½ tsp. freshly ground white pepper
   Béarnaise Butter, softened
   Onion Relish

1. Process roasted cacao nibs in a food processor until finely ground. Season steaks with kosher salt and pepper. Rub ground cacao nibs on both sides of steaks (about 1½ tsp. each). Let steaks stand at room temperature 30 minutes.
2. Preheat grill to 300° to 350° (medium) heat. Grill steaks, covered with grill lid, 5 to 7 minutes on each side or to desired degree of doneness. Let stand, loosely covered with aluminum foil, 10 minutes. Serve with Béarnaise Butter and Onion Relish.

NOTE: We tested with Taza Chocolate Organic Roasted Cacao Nibs.

Béarnaise Butter

1. Beat 1 cup butter, softened; 2 Tbsp. Pickled Shallots, minced (see recipe, next page); 1½ Tbsp. chopped fresh tarragon; and ¼ tsp. freshly ground pepper at medium speed with an electric mixer until combined. Spoon butter onto plastic wrap; roll tightly, forming a log. Serve immediately, or chill until ready to serve. Store in refrigerator up to 2 weeks. Makes: ½ cup.

Onion Relish

1. Bring 5 yellow onions, finely diced; 2 cups sugar; 2 cups white wine vinegar; 1 fresh bay leaf; 1 tsp. kosher salt; 1 tsp. yellow mustard seeds; 1 tsp. coriander seeds; and ½ tsp. freshly ground pepper to a boil in a heavy saucepan over high heat, stirring often. Reduce heat to medium-high, and simmer, stirring often, 30 minutes or until liquid is reduced by half and mixture reaches a syrup-like consistency. Discard bay leaf. Cool to room temperature (about 45 minutes) before serving. Makes: 3 cups.

Marinated Kale Salad with Gouda and Shaved Apples

good for you • make-ahead • party perfect

MAKES: 8 servings
HANDS-ON TIME: 15 min.
TOTAL TIME: 2 hr., 15 min.

Lacinato kale is also sold as dinosaur or Tuscan kale.

- 3 Pink Lady apples*
- ¼ cup fresh lemon juice
- ¼ cup extra virgin olive oil
- 1½ Tbsp. honey
- ¼ tsp. kosher salt
- ¼ tsp. freshly ground pepper
- 2 bunches Lacinato kale, stemmed and chopped (about 8 oz.)
- ¼ cup shaved aged Gouda cheese

1. Cut apples into ¼-inch-thick rings, cutting from 1 side through the other.
2. Whisk together lemon juice and next 4 ingredients in a large bowl. Add kale and apples; toss to coat. Cover and chill 2 to 24 hours. Add Gouda cheese, and toss just before serving.

*1 Granny Smith apple may be substituted.

Grilled Fingerling Potato Salad

good for you • party perfect

MAKES: 8 servings
HANDS-ON TIME: 20 min.
TOTAL TIME: 3 hr.
(Pictured on page 186)

- 6 cups fingerling potatoes (about 3 lb.), halved lengthwise
- 2 Tbsp. extra virgin olive oil
- 1 tsp. kosher salt
- ½ tsp. freshly ground pepper
- 3 Tbsp. Whole Grain Mustard Vinaigrette
- 3 Tbsp. Pickled Shallots
- 2 Tbsp. chopped fresh chives
- 2 Tbsp. chopped fresh flat-leaf parsley
- 1 tsp. chopped fresh thyme
- 3 Tbsp. cooked and crumbled bacon (optional)

1. Preheat grill to 350° to 400° (medium-high) heat. Toss potatoes with olive oil; sprinkle with salt and pepper. Place, cut sides down, on cooking grate; grill, covered with grill lid, 2 minutes or until grill marks appear.

2. Remove from grill. Place potatoes in a single layer in center of a large piece of heavy-duty aluminum foil. Bring up foil sides over potatoes; double fold top and side edges to seal, making a packet. Grill potatoes, in foil packet, covered with grill lid, 15 minutes on each side.

3. Remove packet from grill. Carefully open packet, using tongs. Cool 5 minutes. Toss together potatoes, vinaigrette, next 4 ingredients, and, if desired, bacon.

Whole Grain Mustard Vinaigrette

1. Whisk together ¼ cup white wine vinegar, 1 Tbsp. light brown sugar, 3 Tbsp. whole grain mustard, ½ tsp. freshly ground pepper, and ⅛ tsp. salt. Add ⅓ cup olive oil in a slow, steady stream, whisking constantly until smooth. Makes: ⅔ cup.

Pickled Shallots

1. Bring ¾ cup water, ¾ cup red wine vinegar, ⅓ cup sugar, 2 Tbsp. kosher salt, and ½ tsp. dried crushed red pepper to a boil, whisking until sugar and salt are dissolved. Pour over 1½ cups thinly sliced shallots in a sterilized canning jar. Cool to room temperature. Cover and chill 1 hour. Makes: 1½ cups.

Pineapple Upside-Down Cake

party perfect

MAKES: 12 servings
HANDS-ON TIME: 35 min.
TOTAL TIME: 1 hr., 25 min.

"My wife, Julie, is also a chef and creates our desserts," says James. "This is a terrific fall dessert—a real crowd-pleaser. The flavors of the caramel and pineapple are perfect together." (Pictured on page 187)

- 1 cup firmly packed light brown sugar
  Pinch of salt
- ½ cup butter, divided
- 1 medium-size peeled and cored pineapple
- 1¼ cups granulated sugar
- 2 large eggs
- 1 tsp. vanilla extract
- 1½ cups all-purpose flour
- 1 tsp. baking powder
- ¼ tsp. salt
- ½ cup sour cream
- 2 egg whites

1. Preheat oven to 325°. Combine brown sugar, pinch of salt, and ¼ cup butter in a heavy saucepan; cook over medium heat, stirring occasionally, 5 to 7 minutes or until mixture bubbles and sugar melts. Pour sugar mixture into a 10-inch cast-iron skillet.

2. Cut pineapple crosswise into 6 (¼-inch-thick) rings. Arrange pineapple rings in a single layer over brown sugar mixture.

3. Beat remaining ¼ cup butter and granulated sugar at medium speed with an electric mixer until creamy.

Add eggs, 1 at a time, beating until blended after each addition. Stir in vanilla.

4. Stir together flour, baking powder, and salt; add to butter mixture alternately with sour cream, beginning and ending with flour mixture. Beat batter at low speed until blended after each addition. Beat egg whites until stiff peaks form; fold into batter. Pour batter over pineapple slices.

5. Bake at 325° for 40 to 45 minutes or until a wooden pick inserted in center comes out clean. Cool in skillet on a wire rack 10 minutes. Carefully run a knife around edge of cake to loosen. Invert onto a serving plate; spoon any topping in skillet over cake.

QUICK-FIX SUPPERS

Revisit Your Childhood Favorites

In the spirit of back-to-school season, try one of these fast dinnertime twists on kid-approved classics for grown-up palates.

MAKE-AHEAD
Spaghetti Squash and Meatballs

1. Cut 2 (2¼-lb.) spaghetti squash in half lengthwise; discard seeds. Bake squash, cut sides down, on a lightly greased baking sheet at 400° for 1 hour. Cool 10 minutes. Combine 2 lb. ground chicken; 4 green onions, chopped; 2 Tbsp. chopped fresh flat-leaf parsley; 2 Tbsp. freshly grated Parmesan cheese; and 2 tsp. salt. Shape into 24 (2-inch) balls. Bake at 400° for 30 minutes. Scrape inside of squash to remove spaghetti-like strands (about 6 cups). Cover and chill squash and meatballs up to 24 hours. Cook 2 minced garlic cloves in 2 Tbsp. hot olive oil in a Dutch oven over medium-high heat, stirring occasionally, 1 minute. Add 1 (24-oz.) jar tomato-basil pasta sauce, 1 (14.5-oz.) can diced tomatoes, and meatballs; bring to a boil. Reduce heat to medium-low; simmer 10 minutes. Microwave squash, covered with plastic wrap, at HIGH 3 minutes. Stir ½ cup chopped fresh basil into sauce; serve over squash. Top with Parmesan cheese. Makes: 6 servings.

30 MINUTES

PANCAKES FOR SUPPER

Cornmeal Cakes with Smoked Chicken and Coleslaw

quick prep • good for you • party perfect

MAKES: 6 servings
TOTAL TIME: 30 min.

Pick up coleslaw, smoked chicken, and sauce from your favorite barbecue joint.

- 1 (6-oz.) package buttermilk cornbread mix
- ⅔ cup milk
- 2 Tbsp. butter, melted
- 1 cup fresh corn kernels (2 ears)
- 1 pt. prepared coleslaw
- 1 lb. chopped smoked chicken
- ½ cup barbecue sauce
- 2 avocados, sliced

1. Stir together first 3 ingredients in a small bowl until smooth. Stir in corn kernels. Drop mixture by ¼ cupfuls for each cornmeal cake onto a hot, lightly greased griddle or large nonstick skillet. Cook over medium heat 3 to 4 minutes on each side or until golden.
2. Divide coleslaw among cornmeal cakes; layer with chicken, barbecue sauce, and avocado slices.

45 MINUTES

PEANUT BUTTER & JELLY

"PB&J" Steak Stir-fry with Rice

make-ahead • party perfect

MAKES: 4 servings
TOTAL TIME: 45 min.

- ⅓ cup soy sauce
- ⅓ cup red pepper jelly
- 2 Tbsp. creamy peanut butter
- 2 tsp. cornstarch
- 1 lb. flank steak, thinly sliced
- 3 Tbsp. olive oil, divided
- 1 red, orange, or yellow bell pepper, thinly sliced
- 2 cups chopped broccoli florets
- ⅓ lb. sugar snap peas (1½ cups)
- 1 Tbsp. minced garlic
- 4 green onions, chopped
  Hot cooked rice

1. Combine first 3 ingredients in a small bowl; stir together cornstarch and ⅓ cup water, and add to soy sauce mixture.
2. Stir-fry half of steak in 1 Tbsp. hot olive oil in a large wok or skillet over high heat 3 to 4 minutes or to desired degree of doneness. Transfer steak to a plate; repeat procedure with 1 Tbsp. olive oil and remaining steak.
3. Stir-fry bell pepper, next 3 ingredients, and half of green onions in remaining 1 Tbsp. hot olive oil 2 to 3 minutes or until tender. Add soy sauce mixture and steak; bring to a boil, stirring constantly; cook, stirring occasionally, 1 minute or until sauce is slightly thickened. Remove from heat, and sprinkle with remaining green onions. Serve immediately over hot cooked rice.

60 MINUTES

TACO NIGHT

Grilled Pork Tacos

quick prep • good for you • party perfect

MAKES: 6 servings
TOTAL TIME: 1 hr.

Here's a delicious (and healthy) change of pace from the usual ground beef tacos.

- 6 (1-inch-thick) boneless pork chops
  Cilantro Slaw
- 2 Tbsp. olive oil
- 1 tsp. kosher salt
- ½ tsp. freshly ground pepper
- 12 (6-inch) fajita-size flour tortillas
  Lime wedges

1. Let pork stand at room temperature 30 to 40 minutes. Meanwhile, prepare Cilantro Slaw. Light 1 side of grill, heating to 350° to 400° (medium-high) heat; leave other side unlit. Brush pork with olive oil, and sprinkle with salt and pepper.
2. Grill pork over lit side of grill, covered with grill lid, 4 minutes on each side; transfer pork to unlit side, and grill, covered with grill lid, 10 minutes on each side or until a meat thermometer inserted into thickest portion registers 145°. Let stand 5 minutes. Thinly slice pork.
3. Place pork in warm tortillas; top with Cilantro Slaw. Serve with lime wedges.

Cilantro Slaw

quick prep • good for you • party perfect

MAKES: 6 servings

- ½ small head napa cabbage, thinly sliced (about 4 cups)
- 1 (8-oz.) can pineapple tidbits, drained
- ⅓ cup thinly sliced green onions
- ⅓ cup chopped radishes (about 2 large)
- ¼ cup thinly sliced sweet onion
- ¼ cup shredded carrot
- ¼ cup finely chopped fresh cilantro
- 2 Tbsp. Champagne vinegar
- 1 Tbsp. olive oil

1. Toss together all ingredients in a bowl. Season with salt and pepper to taste. Cover and chill 30 minutes.

SAVE ROOM

Raise the Bar

How do you improve the classic pecan pie bar? With buttery, cocoa-spiked shortbread and an over-the-top layer of chocolate, that's how.

OVERHEARD OUTSIDE OFFICE NUMBER 347*

"Gooey, chocolaty deliciousness!"

*Our Editor in Chief, Lindsay Bierman, sometimes misses tastings due to his meeting schedule, so we'll leave delicious remnants outside his office with Nellah McGough, our beloved Office Manager. Going forward, we'll include Nellah's colorful comments, in addition to more formal tasting notes, here.

German Chocolate-Pecan Pie Bars

make-ahead • party perfect

MAKES: about 2 dozen
HANDS-ON TIME: 20 min.
TOTAL TIME: 3 hr., 40 min.

- 3 cups pecan halves and pieces
- 1¾ cups all-purpose flour
- ¾ cup powdered sugar
- ¾ cup cold butter, cubed
- ¼ cup unsweetened cocoa
- 1½ cups semisweet chocolate morsels
- ¾ cup firmly packed brown sugar
- ¾ cup light corn syrup
- ¼ cup butter, melted
- 3 large eggs, lightly beaten
- 1 cup sweetened flaked coconut

1. Preheat oven to 350°. Bake pecans in a single layer in a shallow pan 8 to 10 minutes or until lightly toasted and fragrant, stirring halfway through.
2. Line bottom and sides of a 13- x 9-inch pan with heavy-duty aluminum foil, allowing 2 to 3 inches to extend over sides. Lightly grease foil.
3. Pulse flour and next 3 ingredients in a food processor 5 to 6 times or until mixture resembles coarse meal. Press mixture on bottom and ¾ inch up sides of prepared pan.
4. Bake crust at 350° for 15 minutes. Remove from oven, and sprinkle chocolate morsels over crust. Cool completely on a wire rack (about 30 minutes).
5. Whisk together brown sugar and next 3 ingredients until smooth. Stir in coconut and toasted pecans, and spoon into prepared crust.
6. Bake at 350° for 25 to 30 minutes or until golden and set. Cool completely on a wire rack (about 1 hour). Chill 1 hour. Lift baked bars from pan, using foil sides as handles. Transfer to a cutting board; cut into bars.

TRY THIS TWIST!
German Chocolate-Bourbon-Pecan Pie Bars: For a spirited kick, whisk ¼ cup of your favorite bourbon into brown sugar mixture in Step 5.

The South's Best Tailgate

We huddled to select the top 20 Southern schools with the greatest pregame celebrations. Turn the page for our preseason contenders. Plus: Get our top-ranked recipes for a winning game-day party at home or away.

"The Most Spirited"

Schools that turn "fan" into "fanatic," and spirited recipes to generate plenty of pregame buzz.

TOP-RANKED SPIRITS

Barbecue Bloody Mary

quick prep • party perfect
(Pictured on page 188)

Rub rim of an 8-oz. glass with a lime wedge; dip rim of glass in ¼ tsp. Barbecue Rub (see recipe, at right) to coat. Combine ½ cup vegetable juice, 1 Tbsp. lime juice, 1 tsp. Worcestershire sauce, 3 Tbsp. vodka, and ¼ tsp. Barbecue Rub in a cocktail shaker; fill with ice. Cover with lid; shake vigorously until chilled. Strain into prepared glass filled with ice. Garnish with fried pork rinds.

BARBECUE RUB: Stir together 2 Tbsp. kosher salt, 2 tsp. paprika, 1 tsp. celery salt, ½ tsp. garlic powder, ½ tsp. ground black pepper, and ¼ tsp. ground red pepper.

Brewmosa

quick prep • party perfect
(Pictured on page 188)

1. Combine ½ cup chilled orange juice, 1 Tbsp. orange liqueur, and 2 dashes Angostura bitters in a 12-oz. glass. Top with 1 (7-oz.) bottle chilled lager beer; gently stir. Garnish with an orange zest strip.

Apple Pie-Bourbon Sweet Tea

quick prep • party perfect
(Pictured on page 188)

1. Combine ¾ cup sweetened tea, 3 Tbsp. Apple Pie-Infused Bourbon (see recipe, page 229), and 1 Tbsp. fresh lemon juice in a cocktail shaker filled with ice. Cover with lid; shake vigorously until thoroughly chilled. Strain into a 10-oz. glass filled with ice. Top with club soda. Garnish with apple slice and cinnamon stick.

TOP CONTENDERS

UNIVERSITY OF FLORIDA The Gators and Georgia Bulldogs (see Powerhouses) meet up each year in Jacksonville, Florida, where the tailgate-turned-block party occupies 9 acres. Hot Dawgs, Gator Bites, and celebratory libations abound, earning it the moniker "World's Largest Outdoor Cocktail Party."

GRAMBLING STATE UNIVERSITY This Louisiana school turns its annual matchup against in-state rival Southern University, known as the Bayou Classic, into a weeklong extravaganza with an alumni mixer, gospel brunch, and battle of the bands, drawing more than 250,000 to host city New Orleans.

LOUISIANA STATE UNIVERSITY The Fighting Tigers enlist RVs and crawfish boils to cook up one heck of a tailgate. And that's just on the road. Their unofficial motto, "We don't travel. We take over," pretty much sums it up.

MCDANIEL COLLEGE With the nation's only drive-in stadium (really!), this Maryland school packs in four whole quarters of tailgating action.

MISSISSIPPI STATE UNIVERSITY Don't let the cowbells fool you. State has a rep as one of the friendliest fan bases. Ice cream made on campus (such as Muscadine Ripple) sweetens the deal.

Grilled Salsa

"The Traditionalists"

Schools renowned for game-day rituals, plus deviled eggs and dips to suit classic tastes.

Top Contenders

UNIVERSITY OF ARKANSAS

Have two stadiums, will tailgate. Since 1948, the Razorbacks have proudly claimed twice the tailgating with home fields in Fayetteville and Little Rock. Double Woo Pig Sooie!

AUBURN UNIVERSITY

Auburn fans are so proud of their traditions that there is an entire Wikipedia page devoted to rituals such as the pregame Tiger Walk, which weaves through thousands of revelers and lands them a spot on our list.

CLEMSON UNIVERSITY

Tailgating concludes with a dramatic player entrance known as the "Running Down the Hill," where players storm the grassy incline in the stadium's east endzone. (Veteran Clemson tailgaters may argue the best tradition is actually that your ticket gets you out and back in at halftime.)

UNIVERSITY OF SOUTH CAROLINA

Since 1990, South Carolina's Cockabooses, 22 train cabooses turned game-day suites, have offered fans a one-of-a-kind tailgating venue.

TEXAS A&M

The Aggie's Midnight Yell starts pregame revelry in the witching hour. For 80 years and counting, Yell Leaders have assembled with fans at Kyle Field to practice cheers and fight songs to warm up the Twelfth Man.

TOP-RANKED RECIPES
Grilled Salsa

quick prep • party perfect

MAKES: 4 cups
HANDS-ON TIME: 30 min.
TOTAL TIME: 45 min.

- 2 **ears fresh corn, husks removed**
- ½ **jalapeño pepper, seeded (optional)**
- 1 **small sweet onion, cut into ¼-inch-thick slices**
- 6 **medium tomatoes, halved (about 2 lb.)**
  Vegetable cooking spray
- 1 **small garlic clove, quartered**
- ¼ **cup loosely packed fresh cilantro leaves**
- 2 **Tbsp. fresh lime juice**
- 1½ **tsp. salt**
  Fried pork rinds

1. Preheat grill to 350° to 400° (medium-high) heat. Coat corn, jalapeño pepper, onion, and cut sides of tomatoes lightly with cooking spray. Grill corn and onion, covered with grill lid, 15 minutes or until golden brown, turning occasionally. At the same time, grill tomatoes and jalapeño pepper, covered with grill lid, 8 minutes or until grill marks appear, turning occasionally. Remove all from grill, and cool 15 minutes. Cut corn kernels from cobs; discard cobs. Coarsely chop onion.

2. Pulse garlic and next 2 ingredients in a food processor until finely chopped. Add grilled tomatoes, onion, and jalapeño pepper to food processor, in batches, and pulse each batch until well blended. Transfer to a large bowl. Stir in salt and corn. Serve with pork rinds.

Warm Gumbo Dip

Deviled Eggs

good for you • party perfect

MAKES: 2 dozen
HANDS-ON TIME: 30 min.
TOTAL TIME: I hr., 30 min.

- I **dozen hard-cooked eggs, peeled**
- ½ **cup light mayonnaise**
- I **Tbsp. chopped fresh flat-leaf parsley**
- 2 **Tbsp. sour cream**
- I **tsp. spicy brown mustard**
- ⅛ **tsp. salt**

1. Slice eggs in half lengthwise, and carefully remove yolks, keeping egg whites intact.
2. Mash together yolks, mayonnaise, and next 4 ingredients until smooth using a fork. Spoon yolk mixture into egg white halves. Cover and chill I hour before serving.

TRY THIS TWIST!
"The Pig Skin" Deviled Eggs:
1. Prepare recipe as directed, stirring in I Tbsp. finely chopped green onion, 3 Tbsp. sweet pickle relish, and I tsp. Asian Sriracha hot chili sauce with mayonnaise in Step 2. Top eggs with pickled okra slices and chopped pork crackling strips.

Warm Gumbo Dip

quick prep • party perfect

MAKES: 8 to 10 servings
HANDS-ON TIME: 35 min.
TOTAL TIME: I hr.

- ¼ **cup butter**
- 6 **green onions, sliced**
- 2 **celery ribs, diced**
- I **cup chopped assorted bell peppers**
- I½ **lb. peeled, large raw shrimp, chopped**
- I **garlic clove, pressed**
- I½ **tsp. Creole seasoning**
- I **(8-oz.) package cream cheese**
- ¾ **cup sliced pickled okra**
- ½ **cup plus 2 Tbsp. grated Parmesan cheese**
- 2 **Tbsp. chopped fresh flat-leaf parsley**
  Toasted French bread baguette slices

1. Preheat oven to 400°. Melt butter in a Dutch oven over medium heat; add green onions and next 2 ingredients. Cook, stirring occasionally, 6 to 8 minutes or until peppers are tender. Stir in shrimp and next 2 ingredients; cook, stirring occasionally, 2 minutes. Reduce heat to low; add cream cheese, stirring until cheese is melted. Remove from heat, and stir in okra and ½ cup Parmesan cheese. Spoon mixture into a 2-qt. baking dish, and sprinkle with remaining 2 Tbsp. cheese.
2. Bake at 400° for 25 to 30 minutes or until bubbly and lightly browned. Sprinkle with parsley. Serve with bread.

"The Powerhouses"

Southern schools with the most bowl victories, and hearty fare that satisfies the hunger to win.

Top Contenders

UNIVERSITY OF ALABAMA
Tents packed 1,000-deep on the Quad serve as the epicenter for this massive houndstooth-clad crowd. Families proudly proclaim their heritage by hanging signs that stake their claim, such as "Bessemer Bama Belles."

UNIVERSITY OF GEORGIA
Athens regularly welcomes more than 100,000 tailgaters. Large, active alumni groups gather for viewing parties in far-flung locales such as London and Shanghai, giving the Dawgs serious territory.

UNIVERSITY OF OKLAHOMA
When the grounds open on Fridays at noon, the Sooners live up to their property-rushing namesake with a frenzied staking of spots fondly known as "The Land Run." Plus, Oklahoma makes up half of an epic tailgate. (See Texas, below.)

UNIVERSITY OF TENNESSEE
With mammoth Neyland Stadium situated alongside the Tennessee River, UT's Vol Navy brings more than 150 houseboats and yachts together for Saturdays full of on-the-water "sailgating."

UNIVERSITY OF TEXAS
Each year the Longhorns and the Sooners face off on neutral territory during the Red River Rivalry in Dallas at the State Fair of Texas. Fans feast on fried Oreos and chicken-fried bacon.

TOP-RANKED RECIPES

Southern-Style Cuban Sandwiches

MAKES: 4 to 6 servings
HANDS-ON TIME: 15 min.
TOTAL TIME: 25 min.

Here's a smoky spin on a classic sub. Pick up sliced pork from your favorite barbecue restaurant.

1. Spread inside of bread shells (see "Test Kitchen Secret" at right) with Chipotle Rémoulade. Layer bottom shell with 1 lb. sliced barbecued pork without sauce, 4 (1-oz.) provolone cheese slices, and 1 cup sweet-hot pickles. Top with remaining bread shell. Cut into sandwiches.

Chipotle Rémoulade

1. Stir together ¾ cup mayonnaise; 2 Tbsp. Creole mustard; 2 Tbsp. sweet-hot pickle relish; 1 canned chipotle pepper in adobo sauce, chopped; 1 Tbsp. chopped fresh flat-leaf parsley; ½ tsp. lemon zest; 2 tsp. fresh lemon juice; and ⅛ tsp. each salt and pepper. Cover and chill up to 3 days before serving. Makes: 1 cup

Test Kitchen Secret

Start with 1 (12-oz.) French bread loaf cut in half horizontally; scoop out soft bread from center of each half, leaving a ½-inch-thick shell to make filling the sandwich easier. (Reserve soft bread for another use.)

SOUTHERN-
STYLE CUBAN

The South's **Best Tailgate**

Cobb Salad Sandwiches

MAKES: 4 to 6 servings
HANDS-ON TIME: 15 min.
TOTAL TIME: 25 min.

1. Spread inside of bread shells (see "Test Kitchen Secret" at left) with Avocado Mayonnaise. Layer bottom shell with 6 oz. smoked turkey slices; 6 oz. honey-maple ham slices; 6 (1-oz.) Swiss cheese slices; 8 cooked bacon slices; 2 hard-cooked eggs, sliced; 1 tomato, sliced; and 2 cups arugula. Season with salt and pepper. Top with remaining bread shell. Cut into sandwiches.

Avocado Mayonnaise

1. Process 1 avocado, coarsely chopped; ¾ cup mayonnaise; 1 jalapeño pepper, seeded and chopped; 2 Tbsp. fresh cilantro leaves; and 2 Tbsp. fresh lime juice in a food processor until smooth. Season with salt to taste. Makes: about 1 cup

Chicken & Honey Sandwiches

MAKES: 4 to 6 servings
HANDS-ON TIME: 15 min.
TOTAL TIME: 20 min.

1. Toss together 1 (10-oz.) package angel hair coleslaw and ¼ cup Honey-Mustard Dressing until coated. Layer bottom shell (see "Test Kitchen Secret" at left) with coleslaw and 15 to 20 fried chicken tenders. Top with remaining bread shell. Cut into sandwiches.

Honey-Mustard Dressing

1. Stir together 2 Tbsp. honey, ¼ cup mayonnaise, 2 Tbsp. country-style Dijon mustard, ⅛ tsp. paprika, and ⅛ tsp. pepper. Store in refrigerator up to 3 days. Makes: ½ cup

Eggs Benedict Sandwiches

MAKES: 4 to 6 servings
HANDS-ON TIME: 15 min.
TOTAL TIME: 25 min.

This brunch sub is ideal for a late-morning kickoff.

1. Spread inside of bread shells (see "Test Kitchen Secret" at left) with Hollandaise Dressing. Layer bottom shell with 10 Canadian bacon slices, cooked; 8 large eggs, fried; 4 (1-oz.) Colby cheese slices; and 2 cups loosely packed fresh baby spinach. Season with salt and pepper to taste. Top with remaining bread shell; cut into sandwiches.

Hollandaise Dressing

1. Stir together ½ cup mayonnaise, 3 Tbsp. olive oil, 1 Tbsp. chopped fresh chives, 1 Tbsp. Dijon mustard, 1 tsp. lemon zest, and 2 tsp. fresh lemon juice. Season with salt and pepper. Makes: ¾ cup

"The Style Setters"

Coeds in sundresses and desserts atop cake stands showcase true splendor in the grass.

Mini Bourbon-and-Cola Bundt Cakes

make-ahead • party perfect

MAKES: 3 dozen
HANDS-ON TIME: 20 min.
TOTAL TIME: 1 hr., 30 min., including glaze
(Also pictured on page 189)

- 1½ **cups butter, softened**
- 2½ **cups sugar**
- 3 **large eggs**
- 1½ **tsp. vanilla extract**
- 1 **cup cola soft drink**
- ¾ **cup buttermilk**
- ½ **cup bourbon**
- 3 **cups all-purpose flour**
- ½ **cup unsweetened cocoa**
- 1½ **tsp. baking soda**
- ½ **tsp. salt**
  Bourbon-and-Cola Glaze

1. Preheat oven to 350°. Beat butter at medium speed with an electric mixer until creamy. Gradually add sugar; beat until blended. Add eggs and vanilla; beat at low speed until blended.
2. Stir together cola, buttermilk, and bourbon in a small bowl. Combine flour and next 3 ingredients in another bowl. Add flour mixture to butter mixture alternately with cola mixture, beginning and ending with flour mixture. Beat at low speed just until blended after each addition, stopping to scrape bowl as needed. Pour batter into 3 lightly greased 12-cup Bundt brownie pans, filling each three-fourths full.

3. Bake at 350° for 12 to 15 minutes or until a wooden pick inserted in center comes out clean. Cool in pans on a wire rack 10 minutes. Remove from pans to wire racks, and cool 30 minutes. Drizzle warm Bourbon-and-Cola Glaze over cakes.

TRY THIS TWIST!
Go Big: Batter can be poured into 1 greased and floured 15-cup Bundt pan. Bake at 350° for 45 to 50 minutes or until a wooden pick inserted in center comes out clean.

Bourbon-and-Cola Glaze

MAKES: about 1 cup
HANDS-ON TIME: 15 min.
TOTAL TIME: 15 min.

- ¼ **cup butter**
- 3 **Tbsp. cola soft drink**
- 2½ **Tbsp. unsweetened cocoa**
- 1 **Tbsp. bourbon**
- 2 **cups plus 2 Tbsp. powdered sugar**

1. Cook first 3 ingredients in a 2-qt. saucepan over medium-low heat, stirring constantly, until butter melts. Remove from heat; stir in bourbon. Beat in powdered sugar at medium speed with an electric mixer until smooth.

The South's Best Tailgate

Mini Bourbon-and-Cola Bundt Cakes, Buttermilk Chess Tarts, Chocolate Chess Tarts, and Lemon-Coconut Tarts

Buttermilk Chess Tarts

quick prep • make-ahead • party perfect

MAKES: 4 dozen
HANDS-ON TIME: 30 min.
TOTAL TIME: 1 hr., 50 min.
(Also pictured on page 189)

- 1 (8-oz.) package cream cheese, softened
- 1 cup butter, softened
- 2½ cups all-purpose flour
- 4 large eggs
- 1 cup sugar
- ½ cup buttermilk
- ⅓ cup butter, melted
- 1 tsp. vanilla extract

1. Beat cream cheese and butter at medium speed with an electric mixer until creamy. Gradually add flour to butter mixture, beating at low speed until blended. Shape mixture into 48 balls, and place on a baking sheet; cover and chill 30 minutes.
2. Preheat oven to 350°. Place 1 dough ball into each cup of 2 lightly greased (24-cup) miniature muffin pans, and shape each into a pastry shell.

3. Whisk together eggs and next 4 ingredients. Pour into pastry shells.
4. Bake at 350° for 18 to 22 minutes or until filling is set. Cool in pans on wire racks 10 minutes. Remove from pans to wire racks; cool completely (about 20 minutes).

TRY THESE TWISTS!
Chocolate Chess Tarts: *(Also pictured on page 189)* Increase vanilla to 2 tsp. Microwave 2 (1-oz.) unsweetened chocolate baking squares, chopped, in a microwave-safe bowl at HIGH 1 to 1½ minutes or until melted and smooth, stirring at 30-second intervals. Prepare recipe as directed, stirring chocolate into egg mixture in Step 3. Garnish with shaved chocolate or chopped toasted pecans.

Lemon-Coconut Tarts: *(Also pictured on page 189)* Prepare Buttermilk Chess Tarts as directed, omitting buttermilk and vanilla and stirring ⅓ cup fresh lemon juice and 1 tsp. coconut extract into egg mixture in Step 3. Garnish with toasted coconut and lemon zest strips.

Peanut Butter-Banana Pudding

make-ahead • party perfect

MAKES: 10 servings
HANDS-ON TIME: 30 min.
TOTAL TIME: 2 hr., 30 min.

Layering pudding in half-pint jars gives you room to garnish and screw on the lids so you can place them in your cooler for easy transport. (Pictured on page 189)

- 3 cups milk
- 4 egg yolks
- 1 cup sugar
- ⅓ cup all-purpose flour
- ⅛ tsp. salt
- ½ cup creamy peanut butter
- 2 small ripe bananas, diced
- 2 tsp. vanilla extract
- 1 cup chopped salted, roasted peanuts
- 1 cup coarsely crushed vanilla wafers
  Garnishes: frozen whipped topping, thawed; cooked and crumbled bacon

1. Cook first 5 ingredients in a large saucepan over medium-low heat, whisking constantly, 15 to 20 minutes or until thickened. Remove from heat; whisk in peanut butter until blended. Stir in diced bananas and vanilla.
2. Combine peanuts and vanilla wafers. Divide 1 cup peanut mixture among 10 (8-oz.) jars. Top with pudding mixture and remaining peanut mixture. Cover and chill 2 to 24 hours.

"What's a great main dish for a late-summer dinner party?"

Chef Danny Trace of Brennan's of Houston serves up an answer.

PULL UP A CHAIR WITH...
Chef Danny Trace

HOMETOWN: New Orleans

LATEST ACHIEVEMENT: Hosting a James Beard Celebrity Chef Tour Dinner on Sept. 27 (*celebritycheftour.com*)

FAVORITE SOUTHERN INDULGENCE: Steen's molasses

PANTRY STAPLES: Stone-ground grits and Zatarain's rice

FIRST FOOD JOB: Dessert station at Commander's Palace

DREAM DINNER GUEST: Hank Williams III

SOUTHERN CHEF WHO INSPIRES YOU: Frank Stitt

LAST SUPPER REQUEST: Boudin and cracklins from The Best Stop Supermarket in Scott, LA

MOST MEMORABLE SOUTHERN MEAL: My grandpa's onion-braised wild rabbit and rice

Sautéed Redfish

good for you • make-ahead • party perfect

MAKES: 4 servings
HANDS-ON TIME: 50 min.
TOTAL TIME: 2 hr., 50 min.

Serve this flavorful sautéed fish over a black-eyed pea salad that you can make ahead.

- 2 **cups fresh black-eyed peas**
- 8 **cherry tomatoes, halved**
- ½ **cup diced assorted bell peppers**
- ¼ **small red onion, thinly sliced (about ¼ cup)**
- 3 **Tbsp. rice vinegar**
- 1 **Tbsp. Creole mustard**
- ¾ **cup canola oil, divided**
- ½ **tsp. kosher salt, divided**
- ½ **tsp. freshly ground pepper, divided**
- 4 **(6-oz.) skin-on redfish, grouper, or snapper fillets**
- 1 **tsp. chopped fresh thyme**
- 2 **Tbsp. thinly sliced fresh basil, divided**
- 2 **cups loosely packed baby arugula**
- 8 **pickled okra, halved**
- 2 **lemons, halved**

1. Cook peas, covered, in boiling salted water to cover 20 minutes or until tender. Remove peas from heat, and let stand, covered, 10 minutes. Drain and rinse with cold water. Combine cooked peas, tomatoes, bell peppers, and onion in a large bowl.

2. Whisk together vinegar, Creole mustard, ½ cup oil, ¼ tsp. salt, and ¼ tsp. pepper. Stir ½ cup vinaigrette into pea mixture, reserving remaining vinaigrette. Cover and chill pea mixture 1½ to 24 hours.

3. Rub both sides of fillets with 1 Tbsp. oil; sprinkle with remaining ¼ tsp. each salt and pepper. Press thyme and 1 Tbsp. basil leaves onto flesh side of fish.

4. Heat remaining 3 Tbsp. oil in a large nonstick skillet over medium heat. Place fish, flesh sides down, in hot oil; cook 3 minutes or until golden. (Do not allow herbs to burn.) Turn fish; cook 4 minutes or just until fish flakes with a fork.

5. Stir arugula and remaining 1 Tbsp. basil into pea salad; divide salad among 4 plates. Top each with a fish fillet. Serve with pickled okra, lemon halves, and remaining ¼ cup vinaigrette.

NOTE: Substitute mahi-mahi, triggerfish, or even salmon in a pinch.

COCKTAIL OF THE MONTH

Grapefruit-Tequila Fizz

MAKES: 1 serving

Kick back on the porch with this spritzer. Rub the rim of a 10-oz. glass with a **grapefruit wedge**; dip in **margarita salt** to coat. Fill glass with **ice cubes.** Fill a cocktail shaker half full with ice. Add **¼ cup fresh red grapefruit juice, 3 Tbsp. tequila,** and **1 jalapeño pepper slice.** Cover with lid, and shake vigorously until thoroughly chilled (about 30 seconds). Strain into prepared glass. Top with **citrus soft drink** (such as Squirt). Garnish with a **red grapefruit wedge** and a **jalapeño pepper slice.**

Community Cookbook

A taste of who and what recently got the highest raves in the *Southern Living* Test Kitchen.

FROM THE KITCHEN OF
LEAH STACEY
MONTGOMERY, AL

"I borrowed the recipe name from a former First Lady of Alabama who claimed her fried chicken had such powers."

"Man Catching" Fried Chicken with Honey-Pecan Glaze

make-ahead • party perfect

1. Place 4½ lb. chicken pieces (breast, drumsticks, and thighs) in a 13- x 9-inch baking dish. Whisk together 2 cups buttermilk and I large egg until blended; pour over chicken. Cover and chill I to 8 hours, turning chicken after 30 minutes. Pour vegetable oil to depth of 1½ inches into a cast-iron Dutch oven; heat over medium heat to 340°. Whisk together 2 cups self-rising flour, I Tbsp. salt, ½ tsp. ground red pepper, ¼ tsp. garlic powder, and ¼ tsp. ground black pepper in a shallow dish. Dredge chicken in flour mixture, shaking off excess. Fry chicken, in 2 batches, in hot oil 20 to 22 minutes or until done, turning occasionally. Drain on a wire rack over paper towels. Place on a wire rack in a jelly-roll pan, and keep warm in a 200° oven. Melt ½ cup butter in a small saucepan over medium heat; whisk in ¼ cup plus 2½ Tbsp. honey until blended. Stir in ½ cup pecans, coarsely chopped; bring mixture to a boil, whisking often. Reduce heat to low, and cook, stirring occasionally, 8 to 10 minutes or until slightly thickened. Drizzle over chicken, and serve immediately. Makes: 6 to 8 servings.

FROM THE KITCHEN OF
MELISSA SPERKA
GREENSBORO, NC

"My advice: Double the recipe, because these crispy bites will disappear fast!"

Potato-Skin Nests

quick prep • party perfect

1. Preheat oven to 450°. Stir together 3 cups frozen shredded hash browns, thawed; 2 egg whites, lightly beaten; ¾ cup (3 oz.) freshly shredded Parmesan cheese; I tsp. onion powder; ¾ tsp. salt; ½ tsp. garlic powder; and desired amount of freshly ground pepper. Press about ¼ cup potato mixture into each cup of a lightly greased 12-cup muffin pan; coat with vegetable cooking spray. Bake 20 to 25 minutes or until golden. (Bake in a 24-cup miniature muffin pan 20 minutes, if desired.) Remove from oven, and cool in pan on a wire rack 5 minutes. Gently run a knife around nests to loosen edges; remove from pan to a serving platter. Top nests with shredded colby-Jack cheese, sour cream, cooked and crumbled bacon, and chopped fresh chives. Makes: 12 servings.

FROM THE KITCHEN OF
ANDIE MITCHELL
BOSTON, MA

"These are just as indulgent baked as they are fried. Simply coat the rolls with cooking spray, and bake on a lightly greased baking sheet at 425° for 12 minutes. Turn and bake 8 to 10 more minutes."

Fried Buffalo Chicken Rolls

quick prep • party perfect

1. Stir together I cup shredded cooked chicken and ¼ cup hot sauce (such as Frank's RedHot Original Cayenne Pepper Sauce). Place 12 egg roll wrappers onto a work surface with I corner pointing toward you (like a diamond). Spoon I Tbsp. each shredded coleslaw mix (without dressing), chicken mixture, and crumbled blue cheese in centers of wrappers. Fold bottom corners of wrappers over filling. Fold in left and right corners. Moisten top corners with lightly beaten egg white; tightly roll up. Pour canola oil to depth of 3 inches into a heavy Dutch oven; heat to 350°. Fry rolls, in 2 batches, 3 minutes; drain. Serve with blue cheese dressing.

Test Kitchen Intervention

A little professional help from our resident foodies.

GRAB 'N' GO

Q Back-to-school season has arrived, and I'm still hopeful that I can pull off a healthy homemade breakfast before shuffling the kids out the door. Any fast suggestions?

MELISSA QUINONES
EUSTIS, FL

A The new school year breeds optimism, but don't set the breakfast bar too high. You can't whip up quinoa pancakes with the left hand while tying shoes with the right. The hardworking moms of our TK swear by these freezer-friendly rollups, which you can zap in the microwave on hectic mornings. Even better: They're portable, so Junior can eat one en route in the car—you know, when singing "Kumbaya" around the breakfast table just isn't going to happen.

Sausage-Egg Rollups

quick prep • make-ahead

Brown and drain ½ lb. ground pork sausage. Whisk together 5 large eggs, 1 Tbsp. milk, and a pinch of salt and pepper; scramble eggs in nonstick skillet over medium heat to desired consistency. Divide sausage, scrambled eggs, ¾ cup (3 oz.) shredded sharp Cheddar cheese, and salsa equally among 6 (6-inch) fajita-size flour tortillas, spooning ingredients down center of each tortilla. Roll up tortillas.

TO MAKE AHEAD: Chill in a zip-top plastic bag up to 3 days or freeze up to 1 month. (If frozen, thaw overnight in fridge before reheating.)
TO REHEAT: Microwave at HIGH 1 to 1½ minutes.

EASY GRILLING

Q Fall weather and football put me in a grilling mood. How can I avoid overcooked meat?

MELODY LEE
DOTHAN, AL

A Rebecca Gordon, our in-house tailgating enthusiast, was born with a pair of tongs in her hand. Her secret: an instant-read thermometer. "I remove meats about 5 degrees earlier than our guidelines state because the temp will rise as they rest," she says. Let meats rest, uncovered, 5 minutes before slicing.

TEMPERATURE GUIDELINES:
steak: 145° (medium-rare), 150° (medium), 165° (medium-well); pork: 150°; ground beef: 160°; chicken breasts: 165°; and chicken thighs: 175°

Editor's Tip
For easy handling, wrap rollups in parchment paper.

Your cake layers are too brown around the edges. Here's how to fix it.

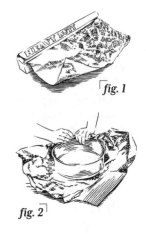

fig. 1

fig. 2

Not much dampens a Southerner's spirits like a dessert that doesn't merit cake-stand status. In this case, the culprit is probably the baking pan. We typically use dark pans when, say, the sugar mixture on an upside-down cake needs to caramelize, or we want the crust on pecan tassies to get good and golden. But because dark pans can sometimes cause the bottoms and sides of other baked goods to overbrown and dry out, we use shiny ones for more delicate recipes, such as cake layers and cheesecakes. Fortunately, you can brighten up your dark pans by wrapping the outside edges with heavy-duty aluminum foil (shiny side out) to reflect heat, like we did with the Caramel Apple Coffee Cake, page 227.

October

Host a Backyard Beer-Garden Bash

Feast on fall flavors with this Bavarian-inspired menu paired with our favorite Southern brews. Prost!

Backyard Bash

SERVES 8

APPETIZER

Plum-Glazed
Sausage Board

MAIN COURSE

Dry-Brined
Beer-Can Chicken

Tart Apple-and-
Cabbage Toss

Warm Lentil-and-
Potato Salad

DESSERT

Black Forest
Pound Cake

Test Kitchen Tip

PLUM-GLAZED SAUSAGE BOARD: Offer a hearty charcuterie board of Plum-Glazed Sausage, assorted pickled vegetables, various artisan cheeses, and fresh-from-the-oven soft pretzels with mustard. *(see recipe, facing page)*

Plum-Glazed Sausage

quick prep • party perfect

MAKES: 8 to 10 servings
HANDS-ON TIME: 20 min.
TOTAL TIME: 25 min.

Offer Bratwurst, Bockwurst, and weisswurst with fresh chicken or spicy pork sausage.

- ¾ cup plum preserves
- 2 Tbsp. balsamic vinegar
- 2 tsp. chopped fresh thyme
- ¼ tsp. freshly ground pepper
- 2 lb. assorted fresh sausages

1. Preheat grill to 300° to 350° (medium) heat. Cook first 4 ingredients in a small saucepan over low heat, stirring often, 5 minutes; reserve half of mixture.
2. Grill sausages, covered with grill lid, 10 to 12 minutes or until done, turning occasionally and brushing with remaining half of plum mixture during last 5 minutes of grilling. Remove from heat; let stand 5 minutes. Serve with reserved plum mixture.

Dry-Brined Beer-Can Chicken

good for you • make-ahead • party perfect

MAKES: 8 servings
HANDS-ON TIME: 20 min.
TOTAL TIME: 2 hr., plus 1 day for brining

- ¼ cup kosher salt
- 1 Tbsp. light brown sugar
- 2 tsp. pimentón (sweet smoked Spanish paprika)
- 1½ tsp. dried marjoram or oregano
- 1 tsp. dried thyme
- 1 tsp. freshly ground pepper
- 3 bay leaves, finely crumbled
- 2 (3½- to 4-lb.) whole chickens
- 1 large oven bag
- 2 (12-oz.) cans brown ale

1. Combine first 7 ingredients. Sprinkle skin and cavities of chickens with salt mixture. Place chickens in oven bag; twist end of bag, and close with tie. Chill 24 hours.
2. Light 1 side of grill, heating to 350° to 400° (medium-high) heat; leave other side unlit. Reserve ½ cup beer from each can for another use. Place each chicken upright onto a beer can, fitting into cavity. Pull legs forward to form a tripod, allowing chickens to stand upright.
3. Place chickens upright on unlit side of grill. Grill, covered with grill lid, 1 hour and 30 minutes to 1 hour and 40 minutes or until golden and a meat thermometer inserted in thickest portion registers 170°. Let stand 10 minutes. Carefully remove chickens from cans; cut into quarters.

Benne Seed Soft Pretzels

For a new twist on a hostess gift, try these buttery knots inspired by the Lowcountry.

MAKE IT!

MAKES: 8 pretzels
HANDS-ON TIME: 35 min.
TOTAL TIME: 2 hr., 10 min.

- 1 lb. fresh bakery pizza dough
  Parchment paper
- 3 Tbsp. baking soda
- ¼ cup butter, melted
- 2 Tbsp. benne (sesame) seeds
- 2 tsp. coarse sea salt

DOWNLOAD OUR LABELS: Get our gift tags: southernliving.com/food-gift

1. Turn dough out onto a lightly floured surface, and knead until smooth (about 2 to 3 minutes). Place in a lightly greased bowl, turning to grease top. Cover dough with plastic wrap, and let rise in a warm place (85°), free from drafts, 1 hour or until doubled in bulk.

2. Divide dough into 8 equal pieces. Roll each piece into a 16-inch-long rope on lightly floured surface, keeping unused dough covered with a damp towel. (If dough does not stretch easily, cover and allow to rest 5 minutes.) Form each rope into a U-shape on a parchment paper-lined baking sheet. Fold or twist each end down diagonally, and tuck under dough, forming pretzel shape. (See how on page 260.) Cover with a damp towel; let stand 15 minutes.

3. Preheat oven to 425°. Fill a 3½-qt. saucepan with water, and stir in baking soda; bring to a boil over medium-high heat. Reduce heat to medium-low,

and simmer. Gently lower 2 pretzels into simmering water mixture; cook 10 seconds on each side. Transfer to a lightly greased wire rack. Repeat procedure with remaining pretzels.

4. Transfer pretzels to parchment paper-lined baking sheet. Brush generously with melted butter, and sprinkle with benne seeds and sea salt. Bake at 425° for 12 to 15 minutes or until golden brown and thoroughly cooked.

TAKE IT!

Pack pretzels in a decorative box or basket that the hostess can reuse, and line it with fabric. Mini country Dijon mustard jars (at *worldmarket.com*) round out the gift. Secure our custom label to a small wooden spreader ($19 for 4; *table-matters.com*).

Noch Ein Bier, Bitte! *(Another Beer, Please!)*

Try one of these standout Southern brews with each course for a festive touch.

APPETIZER

Start with an Oktoberfest- or Märzen-style beer, each a delicious complement to the sausage board.

Bob's '47 Oktoberfest, Boulevard Brewing Co. (Missouri)
Clawhammer Oktoberfest, Highland Brewing Company (North Carolina)

MAIN COURSE

Feast with a pale ale or IPA. The robust flavor will hold its own with the smoky chicken and bold side dishes.

60 Minute IPA, Dogfish Head Craft Brewed Ales (Delaware)
IPA, Good People Brewing Company (Alabama)

DESSERT

Settle down with a stout or porter. Both styles will stand up to the rich chocolate cake and fruit.

Sue imperial porter, Yazoo Brewing Company (Tennessee)
Happy Ending imperial stout, SweetWater Brewing Company (Georgia)

Tart Apple-and-Cabbage Toss

good for you • make-ahead • party perfect

MAKES: 8 servings
HANDS-ON TIME: 20 min.
TOTAL TIME: I hr., 30 min.

Sauerkraut meets coleslaw in this vinegar-based salad.

- I to I½ tsp. caraway seeds
- ½ to I tsp. fennel seeds
- ½ tsp. freshly ground pepper
- ¼ cup apple cider vinegar
- ⅓ cup mayonnaise
- I tsp. sugar
- 8 cups finely shredded red cabbage (I medium head)
- I cup matchstick carrots
- 2 Granny Smith apples, thinly sliced
- ⅓ cup chopped fresh chives

1. Place caraway and fennel seeds in a mortar bowl or spice grinder; grind using a pestle or grinder until seeds become a medium powder. Combine pepper, vinegar, and crushed seeds in a small bowl; cover. Let stand I hour. Whisk in mayonnaise and sugar. Season with salt to taste.
2. Combine cabbage and next 3 ingredients in a large bowl. Add vinegar mixture, and toss until blended. Let stand 10 minutes to I hour before serving.

Warm Lentil-and-Potato Salad

quick prep • party perfect

MAKES: 8 servings
HANDS-ON TIME: 25 min.
TOTAL TIME: 50 min.

French green lentils add flavorful texture. They remain firm after cooking, while traditional brown lentils turn soft.

- ½ cup dried French green lentils
- I (28-oz.) package small red potatoes, halved
- 5 bacon slices
- 3 Tbsp. olive oil
- 2 large shallots, finely chopped
- I celery rib, sliced
- 2 garlic cloves
- 2 to 3 Tbsp. red wine vinegar
- 2 tsp. whole grain Dijon mustard
- I½ cups loosely packed fresh flat-leaf parsley leaves

1. Bring lentils and 4 cups salted water to a boil in a heavy 2-qt. saucepan over medium-high heat. Reduce heat to low; simmer 20 to 25 minutes or just until tender.
2. Meanwhile, cook potatoes in boiling salted water to cover 15 minutes or just until tender. Drain lentils and potatoes.
3. Cook bacon in a large, deep nonstick skillet over medium heat 6 to 7 minutes or until crisp; remove bacon, and drain on paper towels, reserving 2 Tbsp. drippings in skillet. Crumble bacon.
4. Add olive oil to hot drippings in skillet, and heat over medium heat. Sauté shallots, celery, and garlic in hot olive oil mixture 3 minutes. Remove from heat, and stir in vinegar and mustard. Season with salt and pepper to taste. Gently stir in lentils, potatoes, bacon, and parsley.

LESSON #350
SOUTHERN LIVING CHARM SCHOOL

Raise a Glass

Consuming beer straight from the can or bottle was fine when you were drinking the cheap college stuff, but suds enthusiasts know that pouring beer enhances unique flavor notes. (Seriously. Conduct your own at-home experiment to compare and contrast.) So be sure to offer partygoers a glass for their drinking enjoyment. But don't bother with a frosty mug—the ice-cold temp can kill flavor.

Ginger Beer

quick prep • party perfect

MAKES: 1¾ qt.
HANDS-ON TIME: 10 min.
TOTAL TIME: 10 min.

- 1 (4-inch) piece fresh ginger
- 2 (12-oz.) bottles amber beer, chilled
- 4 cups ginger ale, chilled
- ½ cup dark rum

1. Grate ginger, and squeeze to equal 2 tsp. juice; discard solids.
2. Stir together ginger juice, beer, ginger ale, and dark rum. Pour mixture into pilsner glasses, and garnish each with a fresh cherry, if desired. Serve immediately.

Black Forest Pound Cake

make-ahead • party perfect

MAKES: 10 servings
HANDS-ON TIME: 30 min.
TOTAL TIME: 3 hr., 15 min., including sauce

This decadent dessert is an easy, one-pan twist on the traditional layered cake. (Pictured on page 192)

- ⅔ cup butter, softened
- 1⅓ cups granulated sugar
- ⅔ cup firmly packed dark brown sugar
- 4 large eggs
- 1¼ tsp. vanilla extract, divided
- 1½ cups cake flour
- ½ cup unsweetened cocoa
- ½ tsp. salt
- ¼ tsp. baking soda
- ¾ cup sour cream
- 3 (1-oz.) bittersweet chocolate baking squares, finely chopped
  Cherry Sauce
- 1¼ cups heavy cream
- 1 Tbsp. granulated sugar
  Shaved bittersweet chocolate

1. Preheat oven to 325°. Beat butter at medium speed with a heavy-duty electric stand mixer until creamy. Gradually add 1⅓ cups granulated sugar and ⅔ cup brown sugar, beating until light and fluffy (about 5 minutes). Add eggs, 1 at a time, beating just until blended after each addition. Beat in 1 tsp. vanilla.
2. Whisk together flour and next 3 ingredients. Add to butter mixture alternately with sour cream, beginning and ending with flour mixture. Beat at low speed just until blended after each addition. Stir in chopped chocolate.
3. Pour batter into a greased and floured 10-inch round cake pan (with sides that are 3 inches high).
4. Bake at 325° for 1 hour and 10 minutes to 1 hour and 20 minutes or until a wooden pick inserted in center comes out clean. Cool in pan on a wire rack 15 minutes. Remove from pan to wire rack; cool completely (about 1 hour).

5. Meanwhile, prepare Cherry Sauce. Place cake on a serving plate or cake stand. Slowly pour Cherry Sauce over cake. Beat heavy cream, 1 Tbsp. granulated sugar, and remaining ¼ tsp. vanilla at medium-high speed until soft peaks form. Dollop whipped cream onto cake, and sprinkle with shaved chocolate.

Cherry Sauce

MAKES: 1⅓ cups
HANDS-ON TIME: 20 min.
TOTAL TIME: 1 hr., 20 min.

Kirsch is a fruit brandy made with sweet cherries, but the brandy in your liquor cabinet will work just fine. This sauce is also delicious over an ice-cream sundae. Try it on pancakes and waffles too.

1. Stir together 2 (12-oz.) packages frozen cherries, ⅓ cup sugar, ⅓ cup cold water, and 2 tsp. cornstarch in a medium saucepan. Cook over medium-low heat, stirring often, 12 to 15 minutes or until thickened. Remove from heat, and stir in 2 Tbsp. Kirsch or brandy, ½ tsp. vanilla extract, and a pinch of salt. Cool completely (about 1 hour).

Test Kitchen Tip

BLACK FOREST POUND CAKE: Prepare the cake layers and Cherry Sauce in advance. Make the whipped cream topping and shaved chocolate the day you serve the cake.

Sweet on Sorghum

The South's most deeply flavored drizzle connects us to our culinary past and offers untapped potential to make everything more delicious.

Restaurant Eugene, a sleek eatery in Atlanta with a pewter palette, has a stylish staff that orchestrates the evening with the precision of a Swiss clock. It's also where chef and Atlanta native Linton Hopkins serves the type of clever, passionately local fare that recently earned him a James Beard Foundation Award. Between bites, diners notice a subtle sweetness that connects the meticulously crafted plates. Sorghum, the richly flavored syrup made from the juice of sorghum cane, provides balance in a bourbon cocktail, adds a caramel chewiness to bacon caramel corn, glazes a crispy cube of pork belly, and tempers a vinaigrette.

Linton isn't the only chef sweet on sorghum. All over the South, the sticky elixir is being showcased as more than a condiment. (Its affinity for biscuits is well established.) Consider smoked sorghum milk tea at Hillbilly Tea in Louisville or sorghum-brined duck at Ashley's at The Capital Hotel in Little Rock.

To fully appreciate sorghum, it's important to see it in context, so Linton drives north into the windy hills of North Georgia to visit the Hughes family, one of his favorite producers. Olin Hughes has been producing syrup under his own label since 1954.

The future of sorghum is dangerously unclear. When Olin and Terry are asked who will take over their business, there are uneasy shrugs. Chefs like Linton are the first step in creating a broader audience, but it will take more devoted artisans and farmers to ensure this distinctive Southern flavor will survive. "I grew up putting it on biscuits, but have since started using it in everything possible," says Morgan Weber, owner of Revival Market in Houston and another sorghum evangelist. Morgan ages sorghum in whiskey barrels, swirls it into lattes, chili, and barbecue sauce, and uses it as a cure for "the best bacon ever."

That's the kind of enthusiasm needed to exploit sorghum's untapped culinary potential. To entice your interest, we're sharing the following recipes from Linton—as well as one from Olin that honors the memory of his wife. Enjoy their deep, bittersweet richness—a richness that connects our diverse tables across the South.

Southern Sorghums to Try

- **HUGHES SORGHUM** (706/400-8420) Linton's go-to variety (right), with a sunny citrus edge
- **KENTUCKY PURE CANE SWEET SORGHUM** (*bourbonbarrelfoods.com*) Earthy and sweet
- **MUDDY POND SORGHUM** (*muddypondsorghum.com*) Bright, appealingly tart flavor
- **TEXAS HEIRLOOM SORGHUM SYRUP** (*revivalmarket.com*) Just a tad bitter in a good way

Beef Ribs with Sorghum Glaze

make-ahead • party perfect

MAKES: 8 servings
HANDS-ON TIME: 45 min.
TOTAL TIME: 6 hr., 25 min., plus 12 hr. for chilling
(Pictured on page 190)

- 4 (2½-lb.) racks beef rib-back ribs (center-cut)
- ¼ cup sugar
- ¼ cup kosher salt
- 2 Tbsp. ground black pepper
- 1 tsp. garlic powder
- 1 tsp. onion powder
- 1 tsp. smoked paprika
- ½ tsp. ground red pepper
- 1 cup sorghum syrup
- 1 cup cider vinegar
- 1 Tbsp. coarsely ground black pepper

1. Rinse and pat ribs dry. Remove thin membrane from back of ribs by slicing into it and pulling it off.

2. Stir together sugar and next 6 ingredients. Massage sugar mixture into rib meat, covering all sides. Wrap ribs tightly with plastic wrap, and place in zip-top plastic freezer bags; seal and chill 12 hours.

3. Bring sorghum and next 2 ingredients to a boil in a 3-qt. saucepan over medium-high heat, stirring occasionally; reduce heat to medium, and cook, stirring occasionally, 6 to 7 minutes or until mixture is reduced by half. Cool completely (about 30 minutes).

4. Preheat oven to 275°. Place lightly greased wire racks in 2 aluminum foil-lined 15- x 10-inch jelly-roll pans. Remove plastic wrap from ribs, and place ribs on wire racks. Cover with aluminum foil to seal. Bake 2 hours. Remove foil, and bake 3 more hours or until meat begins to pull away from bones, basting with sorghum mixture every 30 minutes. Increase oven temperature to 400°, and bake 10 more minutes or until ribs are browned.

Turkey, Brie, and Apple Panini

party perfect

MAKES: 4 servings
HANDS-ON TIME: 20 min.
TOTAL TIME: 1 hr., 15 min., including marmalade
(Pictured on page 191)

1. Trim and discard rind from 1 (7-oz.) Brie round. Cut Brie into ¼-inch-thick slices. Cut 1 medium-size Gala apple into slices. Layer 4 Italian bread slices with Brie, apple slices, 1 cup loosely packed arugula, and 8 oz. thinly sliced smoked turkey. Top each with 1 bread slice spread with 1 Tbsp. Bacon Marmalade. Brush sandwiches with melted butter. Cook sandwiches, in batches, in a preheated panini press 3 to 4 minutes or until golden brown and cheese is melted. Serve immediately.

Bacon Marmalade

quick prep • make-ahead • party perfect

MAKES: 1¼ cups
HANDS-ON TIME: 25 min.
TOTAL TIME: 55 min.

Try this on toast with a triple-cream cheese, tossed with iceberg lettuce and blue cheese, or spooned over ice cream.
(Pictured on page 191)

   ½ **(16-oz.) package thick hickory-smoked bacon slices, diced**
   1 **cup sorghum syrup**
   1½ **cups cider vinegar**
   ½ **cup chicken broth**
   1 **bay leaf**
      Kosher salt and cracked pepper to taste

1. Cook bacon in a skillet over medium-high heat, stirring often, 4 minutes or until just dark golden brown; drain on paper towels. Wipe skillet clean; return bacon to skillet. Add sorghum; cook, stirring constantly, 1 minute. Add vinegar; cook, stirring often, 8 minutes or until liquid is reduced by half. Add broth and bay leaf; cook 5 minutes or until slightly thickened. Add seasonings. Cool 30 minutes. Discard bay leaf.

SIGNATURE COCKTAIL
The Slapping Incident

This cocktail is named after a famous incident involving General Patton in Italy during WWII. Like the controversial leader, the drink is crisp, strong, and gets the job done.

1. Stir together 2½ Tbsp. rye whiskey, 1½ Tbsp. lime juice, 1 Tbsp. Fernet-Branca, 1 Tbsp. sorghum syrup, and 1½ tsp. Faretti Biscotti Famosi in a 10-oz. glass. Add 4 ice cubes, and top with tonic water. Stir in a pinch of sea salt and cracked pepper.

The Slapping Incident Cocktail

Sorghum Caramel Corn

Sorghum Caramel Corn

make-ahead • party perfect

MAKES: about 14 cups
HANDS-ON TIME: 20 min.
TOTAL TIME: 2 hr., 5 min.

You'll love the salty-sweet taste.

   2 **(3.5-oz.) bags plain microwave popcorn, popped**
   1½ **cups cooked bacon, chopped**
   1 **cup unsalted roasted peanuts**
   1 **cup butter**
   2 **cups firmly packed light brown sugar**
   ½ **cup sorghum syrup**
   1½ **tsp. salt**
   1 **tsp. baking soda**
   1 **tsp. vanilla extract**

1. Preheat oven to 250°. Place popcorn, bacon, and peanuts in a lightly greased large bowl.
2. Melt butter in a large heavy saucepan over medium heat. Stir in brown sugar and next 2 ingredients; bring to a boil, stirring constantly. Boil, without stirring, 4 minutes or until a candy thermometer registers 240°. Remove from heat; stir in baking soda and vanilla.
3. Pour sorghum mixture over popcorn mixture, and stir until coated. Divide between 2 lightly greased 15- x 10-inch jelly-roll pans, and spread in a thin layer.
4. Bake at 250° for 1 hour, stirring every 15 minutes. Cool completely on wire racks (about 45 minutes). Break into pieces.
NOTE: For a less clumpy texture, stir popcorn constantly for 5 minutes after removing from oven.

Appalachian Primer

Many foods we consider emphatically Southern come from the heart of the mountains: cornbread, country ham, apple stack cake. But perhaps nothing is more prolific on area menus than beans. "Appalachians have a love affair with beans," says Rosann Kent of the Georgia Appalachian Studies Center. Here is one of our favorite bean recipes from the hills.

Appalachian Cider Baked Beans

Dishes like these cider-sorghum baked beans are at the heart of the Appalachian diet.

Place 3 cups dried pinto beans, rinsed and sorted, in a large bowl. Cover with cold water 3 inches above beans; cover and let soak 12 hours. Drain beans, and transfer to a Dutch oven. Add 3 cups fresh apple cider; bring to a boil over medium heat. Gently boil, uncovered and stirring occasionally, 30 minutes. Remove from heat; drain, reserving liquid. Layer 4 oz. thinly sliced salt pork in a 2-qt. Dutch oven. Spoon beans over salt pork; bury 2 small yellow onions, peeled, in beans. Cook 1 Tbsp. dry mustard, 6 Tbsp. sorghum syrup, and 1 tsp. salt over medium heat, stirring often, 3 minutes or until mustard and salt dissolve. Pour mixture over beans; top with 4 oz. thinly sliced salt pork. Add reserved bean liquid and, if necessary, hot water to cover. Bake, covered, at 300° for 3 hours, adding hot water as needed. Bake 2 more hours or until beans are tender.

ADAPTED FROM *CIDER BEANS, WILD GREENS, AND DANDELION JELLY: RECIPES FROM SOUTHERN APPALACHIA* BY JOAN ALLER

Lois' Dutch Sorghum Cake

make-ahead • party perfect

MAKES: 2 (9-inch) square cakes
HANDS-ON TIME: 25 min.
TOTAL TIME: 1 hr., 50 min., including glaze

Olin Hughes' wife, Lois, loved to cook with sorghum. Here, he shares one of her favorite recipes, to which we added a coffee glaze.

1 cup sugar
1 cup shortening
1 cup sorghum syrup
3 large eggs
3 cups all-purpose flour
1 tsp. baking soda
1 tsp. baking powder
1 tsp. ground ginger
1 tsp. ground cinnamon
1 cup buttermilk
1 cup raisins
1 cup chopped dates
1 cup chopped pecans, toasted
  Coffee Glaze

1. Preheat oven to 325°. Beat sugar and shortening at medium speed with a mixer until fluffy. Stop mixer, and add sorghum; beat just until blended. Add eggs, 1 at a time, beating until blended after each addition.
2. Combine flour and next 4 ingredients; gradually add to sugar mixture alternately with buttermilk. (Begin and end with flour mixture.) Beat at low speed just until blended after each addition. Stir in raisins, dates, and pecans. Spoon into 2 greased and floured 9-inch square pans.
3. Bake at 325° for 32 to 35 minutes or until a wooden pick inserted in center comes out clean. Cool completely on a wire rack (about 45 minutes). Drizzle each cake with Coffee Glaze.

Coffee Glaze

1. Whisk together 1 cup powdered sugar and 1½ Tbsp. strong brewed coffee in a small bowl until smooth. Makes: about ⅓ cup.

Spice Up Any Weeknight

Keep a slice of cornbread on hand to scoop up every drop of these hearty chilis.

30 MINUTES
Veggie Chili

quick prep • good for you • party perfect

MAKES: 6 cups
TOTAL TIME: 30 min.

2 large zucchini, chopped
1 large yellow squash, chopped
1 large onion, chopped
2 Tbsp. olive oil
½ tsp. salt
1 (12-oz.) package frozen meatless ground crumbles
1 (25-oz.) jar Texas chili starter with red bean and bock beer

1. Sauté zucchini, squash, and onion in hot oil in a large Dutch oven over medium-high heat 3 to 4 minutes or until tender.
2. Add salt and crumbles; cook 1 minute. Stir in chili starter. Bring to a boil over medium-high heat; reduce heat to medium-low, and simmer, stirring occasionally, 10 minutes.

NOTE: We tested with Frontera All Natural Texas Chili Starter with Red Bean and Bock Beer.

45 MINUTES

Chicken-and-Three-Bean Chili Verde

quick prep • good for you • party perfect

MAKES: 12 cups
TOTAL TIME: 45 min.

- 14 fresh tomatillos (about 3 lb.), husks removed
- 3 garlic cloves, minced
- 1 extra-large chicken bouillon cube
- 1 large onion, chopped
- 3 poblano peppers, seeded and chopped
- 2 Tbsp. olive oil
- 1 (16-oz.) package frozen whole kernel white corn
- 1 Tbsp. chili powder
- 1 tsp. ground cumin
- 3 cups chopped cooked chicken
- 1 (15-oz.) can black beans, drained and rinsed
- 1 (15-oz.) can navy beans, drained and rinsed
- 1 (15-oz.) can small kidney beans, drained and rinsed
- 2 cups crushed tortilla chips
- ½ cup fresh cilantro leaves, chopped
- 3 Tbsp. fresh lime juice
- 2 tsp. salt
- ½ tsp. pepper
  Toppings: avocado slices, shredded Jack cheese, fresh cilantro sprigs

1. Bring first 3 ingredients and 3 cups water to a boil in a 3-qt. saucepan; boil 10 minutes.

MAKE-AHEAD

Spicy Slow-Cooker Beef Chili

make-ahead • party perfect

1. Microwave 1 (10½-oz.) can condensed broth in a microwave-safe bowl at HIGH 2 to 3 minutes or until simmering. Place 4 dried ancho chile peppers, stemmed and seeded, in a blender. Pour hot broth over peppers; let stand 10 minutes. Holding lid down with a towel, process peppers and broth until smooth. Sprinkle 2 Tbsp. all-purpose flour, 1½ tsp. ground cumin, and 1 tsp. salt over 1 (2-lb.) London broil, cut into ½-inch cubes. Place beef in a 4-qt. slow cooker. Add 2 chopped onions, 4 minced garlic cloves, 1½ tsp. dried oregano, 1 (16-oz.) bottle dark beer, 1 cup water, and pepper mixture. Cover and cook on HIGH 3 to 4 hours (or on LOW 5 to 6 hours) or until beef is tender. Top with halved jalapeño peppers, sour cream, and refrigerated salsa. Serve with saltine crackers. Makes: about 8 cups.
NOTE: We tested with Los Chileros de Nuevo Mexico whole ancho chiles.

2. Meanwhile, sauté onion and peppers in hot oil in a large Dutch oven over medium-high heat 4 minutes or until tender. Add corn; sauté 2 minutes. Add chili powder and cumin; sauté 4 minutes.
3. Remove tomatillo mixture from heat, and cool 5 minutes. Process mixture in a blender until smooth.
4. Add chicken, beans, and tomatillo mixture to Dutch oven. Cook, stirring occasionally, 15 minutes. Stir in tortilla chips and next 4 ingredients; cook 5 minutes or until tortilla chips are soft. Serve with desired toppings.
NOTE: We tested with Knorr Extra Large Chicken Bouillon Cubes.

60 MINUTES

Beef-and-Black-eyed Pea Chili

quick prep • good for you • party perfect

MAKES: 10 cups
TOTAL TIME: 1 hr.

- 2 lb. ground chili meat
- 1 medium-size sweet onion, chopped
- 3 garlic cloves, minced
- 2 Tbsp. chili powder
- 2 tsp. ground cumin
- 1 Tbsp. olive oil
- 1 (6-oz.) can tomato paste
- 2 (14.5-oz.) cans diced tomatoes
- 1 (16-oz.) package frozen black-eyed peas
- 1 (12-oz.) bottle dark beer
- 1 cup beef broth
- 1 (4.5-oz.) can chopped green chiles
- 2 tsp. salt
- 1 tsp. smoked paprika
- ½ tsp. ground red pepper
  Toppings: pickled jalapeño pepper slices, shredded Cheddar cheese, pico de gallo

1. Cook first 3 ingredients in a Dutch oven over medium-high heat, stirring often, 8 to 10 minutes or until meat crumbles and is no longer pink; drain.
2. Cook chili powder and cumin in hot olive oil in Dutch oven over medium heat, stirring constantly, 2 to 3 minutes or until fragrant. Add tomato paste, and cook, stirring constantly, 2 minutes. Add diced tomatoes, next 7 ingredients, and beef mixture; bring to a boil over medium-high heat. Cover, reduce heat to medium-low, and simmer 30 minutes. Serve with desired toppings.

Sweet Potatoes

Hold the marshmallows. Here are five fresh ways to think outside the casserole—from a savory main-dish tart to a quick skillet fettuccine. And if you want another reason to root for this fall vegetable, know that these garnet gems are officially a super food: One medium-size sweet potato has 438% DV vitamin A, 37% DV vitamin C, and only 105 calories. Now that's sweet!

Roasted Sweet Potato Salad

good for you • make-ahead • party perfect

MAKES: 4 to 6 servings
HANDS-ON TIME: 20 min.
TOTAL TIME: 1 hr., 5 min.

- 1 (24-oz.) package fresh steam-in-bag petite sweet potatoes
- 1 Tbsp. Caribbean jerk seasoning
- 4 Tbsp. olive oil, divided
- 2 Tbsp. fresh lime juice
- ¼ tsp. salt
- 1 (5-oz.) package baby arugula
- 1 mango, peeled and diced
- 1 avocado, halved and thinly sliced
- ½ red bell pepper, sliced
- ½ small red onion, sliced
- ½ cup torn fresh basil

1. Preheat oven to 425°. Cut potatoes in half lengthwise; toss with jerk seasoning and 1 Tbsp. oil. Arrange, cut sides down, in a single layer on a lightly greased baking sheet. Bake 15 minutes; turn and bake 8 to 10 minutes or until tender. Cool on a wire rack 20 minutes.
2. Whisk together lime juice, salt, and remaining 3 Tbsp. oil in a large bowl. Add arugula and next 5 ingredients, and toss to coat. Arrange on a platter; top with potatoes.

Sweet Potato Crostini with Goat Cheese and Grape Salsa

quick prep • good for you • party perfect

MAKES: 10 appetizer servings
HANDS-ON TIME: 10 min.
TOTAL TIME: 30 min.

Spicy, sweet, and totally addictive, this easy appetizer starts with preseasoned fries.

- 20 large frozen waffle-cut sweet potato fries
- 2 Tbsp. red pepper jelly
- 1 Tbsp. fresh lime juice
- 1 cup quartered seedless red grapes
- ¼ cup finely diced yellow bell pepper
- 2 Tbsp. finely diced green onions
- 1 Tbsp. chopped fresh cilantro
- 1 (4-oz.) package crumbled goat cheese

1. Preheat oven to 425°. Bake potatoes in a single layer on a lightly greased baking sheet 12 minutes; turn potatoes, and bake 5 to 7 more minutes or until crisp and lightly browned. Remove from pan; cool on a wire rack 10 minutes.
2. Meanwhile, whisk together pepper jelly and lime juice in a small bowl; stir in grapes and next 3 ingredients.
3. Arrange potatoes on a serving platter; sprinkle with goat cheese. Top with grape mixture, using a slotted spoon. Serve immediately.

Sweet Potato Fettuccine

quick prep • good for you • party perfect

MAKES: 2 to 4 servings
HANDS-ON TIME: 20 min.
TOTAL TIME: 35 min., including gremolata

This clever technique for transforming sweet potatoes into "fettuccine" was inspired by a prize-winning recipe from the North Carolina Sweet Potato Commission.

- 1 large sweet potato (about 1 lb.)
- 3 Tbsp. butter
- ½ cup Pecan Gremolata
  Garnish: fresh parsley sprigs

1. Peel sweet potato, and cut lengthwise into ⅛-inch-thick slices using a mandoline. Stack 4 to 6 potato slices on a cutting board; cut lengthwise into ¼-inch-wide strips. Repeat procedure with remaining slices.
2. Melt butter in a large skillet over medium heat; add potato strips, and sauté 6 to 8 minutes or until al dente. (Don't overcook strips or they will fall apart.) Add ½ cup Pecan Gremolata, and toss gently to coat. Serve immediately.

Pecan Gremolata

quick prep • make-ahead • party perfect

1. Stir together ½ cup finely chopped fresh flat-leaf parsley; ⅓ cup finely chopped toasted pecans; 1 Tbsp. lemon zest; 2 garlic cloves, minced; and ¼ tsp. salt in a small bowl. Makes: about 1 cup.

> ### Test Kitchen Secret
>
> Start with a large, long sweet potato and a mandoline to create pasta-like strips. (See page 260 for more on mandolines.)

Creole Shrimp and Sweet Potato Grits

quick prep • party perfect

MAKES: 6 servings
HANDS-ON TIME: 40 min.
TOTAL TIME: 45 min.

- 2 **cups milk**
- 1 **cup uncooked regular grits**
- 1 **Tbsp. Creole seasoning**
- 2 **lb. large raw shrimp, peeled and deveined**
- 2 **garlic cloves, minced**
- 1 **Tbsp. canola oil**
- ¾ **cup chopped green onions**
- ¼ **cup chopped fresh cilantro**
- 1 **Tbsp. lemon zest**
- 2 **tsp. Asian Sriracha hot chili sauce**
- 1 **cup cooked, mashed sweet potatoes**
- 1 **cup (4 oz.) shredded smoked Gouda cheese**
- 2 **Tbsp. butter**
- 1 **tsp. salt**
- ½ **tsp. freshly ground pepper**
  Garnish: fresh cilantro sprigs

1. Bring milk and 1½ cups water to a boil in a large saucepan over medium-high heat; gradually whisk in grits. Reduce heat to medium-low, and simmer, stirring occasionally, 10 minutes or until thickened.
2. Meanwhile, sprinkle Creole seasoning over shrimp. Sauté garlic in hot oil in a large skillet over medium-high heat 30 seconds. Add shrimp, and sauté 3 minutes or until shrimp are almost pink. Add green onions and next 3 ingredients, and sauté 3 minutes.
3. Stir potatoes and next 4 ingredients into grits. Serve shrimp mixture over sweet potato grits.

Roasted Sweet Potato-
and-Onion Tart

Roasted Sweet Potato-and-Onion Tart

party perfect

MAKES: 6 to 8 servings
HANDS-ON TIME: 30 min.
TOTAL TIME: 2 hr., 40 min.

- 3 **cups ¾-inch-cubed sweet potatoes (about 1½ lb.)**
- 1 **cup chopped red onion**
- 2 **Tbsp. olive oil**
- 1 **tsp. seasoned pepper**
- 6 **cooked bacon slices, crumbled**
- ¼ **cup chopped fresh flat-leaf parsley**
- 1 **(14.1-oz.) package refrigerated piecrusts**
- 2 **cups (8 oz.) shredded Gruyère cheese**
- 1½ **cups half-and-half**
- 4 **large eggs**
- 1 **tsp. chopped fresh rosemary**
- ½ **tsp. salt**
  Garnish: fresh rosemary sprigs

1. Preheat oven to 425°. Toss together first 4 ingredients in a large bowl; arrange mixture in a single layer in a lightly greased 15- x 10-inch jelly-roll pan. Bake 20 minutes or just until potatoes are tender, stirring after 10 minutes. Cool completely in pan on a wire rack (about 30 minutes). Stir in bacon and parsley.
2. Unroll piecrusts; stack on a lightly greased surface. Roll stacked piecrusts into a 12-inch circle. Fit piecrust into a 10-inch deep-dish tart pan with removable bottom; press into fluted edges. Trim off excess piecrust along edges. Line piecrust with aluminum foil or parchment paper, and fill with pie weights or dried beans. Place pan on a foil-lined baking sheet.
3. Bake at 425° for 12 minutes. Remove weights and foil; bake 5 more minutes. Cool completely on baking sheet on a wire rack (about 15 minutes). Reduce oven temperature to 350°.
4. Layer half of sweet potato mixture and half of cheese in tart shell; repeat layers once.
5. Whisk together half-and-half and next 3 ingredients; pour over cheese.
6. Bake at 350° on lowest oven rack 35 to 40 minutes or until set. Cool tart on baking sheet on a wire rack 15 minutes.

Mississippi Madness

Five tricked-out twists on a wickedly delicious Southern treat.

Mississippi Mud S'Mores-Fudge Pie

party perfect

MAKES: 10 to 12 servings
HANDS-ON TIME: 20 min.
TOTAL TIME: 2 hr., including frosting
(Pictured on page 16)

 2 **cups graham cracker crumbs**
 ½ **cup butter, melted**
 2¼ **cups sugar, divided**
 1½ **cups coarsely chopped pecans, toasted and divided**
 1 **(4-oz.) semisweet chocolate baking bar, chopped**
 1 **cup butter**
 1½ **cups all-purpose flour**
 ½ **cup unsweetened cocoa**
 4 **large eggs**
 1 **tsp. vanilla extract**
 ¾ **tsp. salt**
 3 **cups regular marshmallows, cut in half horizontally**
 2 **cups miniature marshmallows Chocolate Frosting**

Test Kitchen Tip

Marshmallows cut easily if you coat scissors with cooking spray before you snip.

OVERHEARD OUTSIDE OFFICE NUMBER 347*

"Two thumbs up from this Mississippi gal!"

1. Stir together first 2 ingredients and ¼ cup sugar; press on bottom and 2 inches up sides of a shiny 9-inch springform pan. Sprinkle ¾ cup pecans over crust.
2. Microwave chopped chocolate and 1 cup butter in a large microwave-safe glass bowl at HIGH 1 minute or until melted and smooth, stirring at 30-second intervals.
3. Whisk flour, next 4 ingredients, and remaining 2 cups sugar into chocolate mixture, whisking until blended. Pour batter into prepared crust.
4. Bake at 350° for 1 hour to 1 hour and 15 minutes or until a wooden pick inserted in center comes out with a few moist crumbs. Remove from oven, and cool in pan on a wire rack 20 minutes.
5. Preheat broiler with oven rack on lowest level from heat. Place pie (in pan) on a jelly-roll pan. Toss together both marshmallows; mound on pie, leaving a ½-inch border around edge. Broil 30 seconds to 1 minute or until marshmallows are golden brown. Remove from oven, and immediately remove sides of pan. Cool on a wire rack 10 minutes.
6. Meanwhile, prepare Chocolate Frosting. Drizzle over marshmallows; sprinkle with remaining ¾ cup pecans.

Chocolate Frosting

1. Cook ¼ cup butter, 3 Tbsp. unsweetened cocoa, and 3 Tbsp. milk in a saucepan over medium heat, whisking constantly, 4 minutes or until slightly thickened; remove from heat. Whisk in 2 cups powdered sugar and ½ tsp. vanilla extract until smooth.

Test Kitchen Secret

For a dramatic and delicious effect, use a small kitchen torch to brown the marshmallows topping your Mississippi Mudslides.

Mississippi Mudslides

Mississippi Mudslides

MAKES: about 4 cups
HANDS-ON TIME: 10 min.
TOTAL TIME: 10 min.

 1 **pt. chocolate ice cream**
 1 **pt. coffee ice cream**
 1 **cup milk**
 ½ **cup bourbon**
  Toppings: whipped cream, chocolate syrup, marshmallows

1. Process first 4 ingredients in a blender until smooth. Serve with desired toppings.

*Our Editor in Chief, Lindsay Bierman, sometimes misses tastings due to his meeting schedule, so we'll leave delicious remnants outside his office with Nellah McGough, our beloved Office Manager. Every month, we're including Nellah's colorful comments in addition to our Test Kitchen's tasting notes.

Mississippi Mud Cupcakes

make-ahead • party perfect

MAKES: 1 dozen
HANDS-ON TIME: 20 min.
TOTAL TIME:: 1 hr., 20 min.

- ⅓ **cup butter, softened**
- ⅔ **cup sugar**
- 2 **large eggs**
- 1 **cup all-purpose flour**
- ⅓ **cup unsweetened cocoa**
- ¼ **tsp. salt**
- ½ **cup sour cream**
- ¾ **tsp. baking soda**
- 1 **(4-oz.) semisweet chocolate baking bar, finely chopped and divided**
- 12 **paper baking cups**
  Vegetable cooking spray
  Marshmallow Frosting
- ⅓ **cup roasted glazed pecan pieces**

1. Preheat oven to 350°. Beat butter at medium speed with an electric mixer until fluffy; gradually add sugar, beating well. Add eggs, 1 at a time, beating just until blended.
2. Combine flour, cocoa, and salt. Stir together sour cream and baking soda. Add flour mixture to butter mixture alternately with sour cream mixture, beginning and ending with flour mixture. Beat at low speed just until blended after each addition. Stir in half of chopped chocolate.
3. Place paper baking cups in a 12-cup muffin pan, and coat with cooking spray; spoon batter into cups, filling two-thirds full.
4. Bake at 350° for 18 to 20 minutes or until a wooden pick inserted in center comes out clean. Remove from pan to a wire rack, and cool completely (about 30 minutes).
5. Pipe Marshmallow Frosting onto cupcakes; sprinkle with pecans and remaining chopped chocolate.

Marshmallow Frosting

1. Beat ½ (8-oz.) package cream cheese, softened; ¼ cup butter, softened; 1 (7-oz.) jar marshmallow crème; and 2 tsp. vanilla extract at medium speed with an electric mixer until creamy. Gradually add 2½ cups powdered sugar, beating at low speed until blended and smooth.

Peanut Butter Mississippi Mud Brownies

Peanut Butter Mississippi Mud Brownies

make-ahead • party perfect

MAKES: about 2½ dozen
HANDS-ON TIME: 20 min.
TOTAL TIME: 2 hr., 15 min.

- 4 **(1-oz.) unsweetened chocolate baking squares**
- 1⅓ **cups butter, softened and divided**
- 2½ **cups granulated sugar, divided**
- 4 **large eggs**
- 2 **cups all-purpose flour, divided**
- 1 **tsp. vanilla extract**
- ½ **cup creamy peanut butter**
- ½ **cup firmly packed light brown sugar**
- 2 **large eggs**
- 1 **tsp. baking powder**
- 3 **cups miniature marshmallows**
- 1½ **cups lightly salted roasted peanuts**
  Chocolate Frosting (see recipe, facing page)

1. Preheat oven to 350°. Microwave chocolate in a microwave-safe bowl at MEDIUM (50% power) 1½ minutes or until melted and smooth, stirring at 30-second intervals.
2. Beat 1 cup butter and 2 cups granulated sugar at medium speed with an electric mixer until light and fluffy. Add 4 eggs, 1 at a time, beating just until blended after each addition. Add melted chocolate, beating just until blended. Add 1 cup flour, beating at low speed just until blended. Stir in vanilla. Spread half of batter in a greased and floured 13- x 9-inch pan.
3. Beat peanut butter, brown sugar, and remaining ⅓ cup butter and ½ cup granulated sugar at medium speed with an electric mixer until light and fluffy. Add 2 eggs, 1 at a time, beating just until blended after each addition. Stir together baking powder and remaining 1 cup flour, and add to peanut butter mixture, beating at low speed just until blended.
4. Spoon peanut butter mixture over brownie batter; top with remaining brownie batter, and swirl together.
5. Bake at 350° for 45 to 55 minutes or until a wooden pick inserted in center comes out with a few moist crumbs. Remove from oven to a wire rack; sprinkle with marshmallows and peanuts.
6. Prepare Chocolate Frosting, and drizzle over brownies. Cool completely.

"What's a twist on mac 'n' cheese that will wow my family?"

Former *Top Chef* contestant Kevin Gillespie of Atlanta's Woodfire Grill serves up an answer.

THE RECIPE
Gussied Up Mac 'n' Cheese
party perfect

MAKES: 10 to 12 servings
HANDS-ON TIME: 35 min.
TOTAL TIME: 1 hr., 5 min.

- 1 (16-oz.) package cavatappi pasta
- 1 Tbsp. salt
- ½ lb. andouille sausage, casings removed
- 4 cups heavy cream
- 1 (16-oz.) package pasteurized prepared cheese product, cut into 1-inch cubes
- 2 cups (8 oz.) freshly shredded smoked Cheddar cheese
- ½ cup freshly shredded aged Gouda cheese
- ½ cup freshly shredded Parmigiano-Reggiano cheese
- 1 (5-oz.) package unsalted kettle-cooked potato chips, crumbled*

1. Preheat oven to 375°. Prepare pasta according to package directions for al dente, adding salt to water.

2. Meanwhile, cut sausage lengthwise into quarters. Cut each quarter into ¼-inch-thick pieces.

3. Sauté sausage in a Dutch oven over medium-high heat 3 minutes or until browned around edges; drain on paper towels.

4. Bring cream to a simmer in Dutch oven over medium-high heat; reduce heat to low, and stir in cheese product. Cook, stirring constantly, until cheese is melted. Stir in sausage and remaining cheeses; cook, stirring constantly, until cheeses are melted. Remove from heat; stir in hot cooked pasta.

5. Pour mixture into a buttered 3-qt. baking dish or 12 (8-oz.) ramekins; top with potato chips. Bake at 375° for 20 minutes or until bubbly and browned. Remove from oven, and let stand 5 minutes.

NOTE: We tested with Velveeta.

*Lightly salted potato chips may be substituted.

RECIPE ADAPTED FROM *FIRE IN MY BELLY*

PULL UP A CHAIR WITH...
Kevin Gillespie

HOMETOWN: Locust Grove, GA

LATEST ACHIEVEMENT: My new cookbook, *Fire In My Belly*, out this month

FAVORITE SOUTHERN INDULGENCE: Whole hog 'cue

PANTRY STAPLE: Kosher salt

FIRST FOOD JOB: Frying hot wings at The Chicken Coupe

DREAM DINNER GUEST: Mark Richt and the entire Georgia Bulldogs football team. Go Dawgs!

SOUTHERN CHEF WHO INSPIRES YOU: Edna Lewis

LAST SUPPER REQUEST: Anything made by my Granny—she's my favorite cook.

MOST MEMORABLE SOUTHERN MEAL: My bachelor party at Charleston's Husk. We tried the whole menu. Epic.

KEVIN'S SECRET INGREDIENT

"I've searched high and low, but Velveeta makes the creamiest, cheesiest mac 'n' cheese you've ever tasted!"

Community Cookbook

A taste of who and what got the highest raves in the *Southern Living* Test Kitchen.

FROM THE KITCHEN OF
CARA LYONS
WORCESTER, MA

"I deconstructed the flavors of California Pizza Kitchen's Chicken Tequila Fettuccine (minus heavy cream) to make healthier burgers. Panko or oatmeal yields moist results; use whichever is on hand."
(See Cara's blog, carascravings.com.)

Grilled Chicken Tequila Burgers

quick prep • good for you • party perfect

1. Preheat grill to 350° to 400° (medium-high) heat. Pulse 1 lb. ground chicken breast, 3 Tbsp. chopped fresh cilantro, 2 chopped garlic cloves, and 1 seeded and chopped jalapeño pepper in a food processor 3 to 4 times or until combined. Add ½ cup panko (Japanese breadcrumbs) or ¼ cup uncooked regular or quick-cooking oats, 2 Tbsp. tequila, 1 tsp. lime zest, ¾ tsp. salt, ½ tsp. pepper, and ¼ tsp. soy sauce; pulse until combined. Shape into 5 patties. Grill, covered with grill lid, 4 to 5 minutes on each side or until a meat thermometer inserted in thickest portion registers 165°; remove from grill. Keep warm. Reduce grill temperature to 300° to 350° (medium) heat. Grill sliced bell peppers and onions 4 minutes on each side or until tender. Serve burgers, bell peppers, and onions on buns with Cilantro-Lime Mayonnaise. Makes: 5 servings.

Cilantro-Lime Mayonnaise

1. Stir together ¾ cup mayonnaise, 1 tsp. chopped fresh cilantro, 1 tsp. chopped fresh chives, 1 tsp. lime zest, and 1 tsp. fresh lime juice.

FROM THE KITCHEN OF
BARBARA MAYO
COLLIERVILLE, TN

"This sauce gets better with age. Store it in an airtight container in the fridge up to 3 days. For parties, I like to serve it on a platter with grilled shrimp, fish tacos, or fried chicken tenders with a sprinkle of jerk seasoning for garnish. It always goes fast!"

Caribbean Jerk Rémoulade Sauce

make-ahead • party perfect

1. Whisk together 1 cup light mayonnaise; ¼ cup finely chopped red bell pepper; ¼ cup finely chopped fresh cilantro; ¼ cup capers, drained; 2 garlic cloves, minced; 1 Tbsp. Caribbean jerk seasoning; 2 Tbsp. olive oil; 2 Tbsp. Creole mustard; 1 Tbsp. bottled chili sauce; and 1 Tbsp. Worcestershire sauce. Cover and chill 2 hours before serving. Makes: 1⅓ cups.

JOIN OUR RECIPE SWAP!

Share your favorite—if it wows the Test Kitchen, we'll feature it here and send you a *SL* cookbook: *southernliving.com/recipeswap.*
NOTE: All submitted recipes become the property of *Southern Living* and may be used for any purpose.

Hot Mulled Bourbon Apple Cider

quick prep • party perfect

MAKES: 8 cups
HANDS-ON TIME: 25 min.
TOTAL TIME: 25 min.

Bring 5 cups apple cider, 2 cups pulp-free orange juice, ¼ cup firmly packed light brown sugar, 2 Tbsp. red cinnamon candies, 2 (3-inch) cinnamon sticks, and 4 whole cloves to a boil in a saucepan over medium heat, stirring occasionally. Boil, stirring occasionally, 10 minutes. Pour mixture through a wire-mesh strainer into a heatproof pitcher, discarding solids. Stir in ¾ cup bourbon. Serve warm.

FROM THE KITCHEN OF
JESSICA DICKENSON
ABINGDON, VA

"These are surprisingly hearty for a meatless main dish, perfect for any night of the week or when you need a vegetarian option at your next backyard burger cookout."

Portobello Burgers with Spicy Mayo

quick prep • good for you • party perfect

1. Preheat grill to 300° to 350° (medium) heat. Stir together 3 Tbsp. mayonnaise, 1 tsp. cider vinegar, 1 tsp. bottled chili sauce, ½ tsp. dried crushed red pepper, and ¼ tsp. dried Italian seasoning. Coat 4 medium-size portobello mushrooms, stemmed, with 2 tsp. olive oil; sprinkle with ¼ tsp. each kosher salt, pepper, and Greek seasoning. Grill, covered with grill lid, 7 minutes on each side or until tender. Serve on toasted buns with desired toppings. Makes: 4 servings.

Test Kitchen Intervention

A little professional help from our resident foodies.

SUGAR RUSH

Q Halloween is creeping up, which means I'll soon have leftover candy by the bagful. What are some creative ways I can use up the excess sweets?

ELIZABETH MEELAN
CHARLESTON, SC

A NORMAN SAYS: Once the jack-o'-lanterns have lost their grins and the costumes have been put away, leftover candy is the last frontier. For a win-win, send it to troops stationed overseas: *operationshoebox.com*. Or try one of these homemade treats.

CANDY BROWNIES: Bake your favorite brownies; top immediately with chopped and mini candies, such as peanut butter cups, malted milk balls, and chocolate-covered caramels. Add some pretzel pieces—you'll love the salty-sweet touch. Bake 5 more minutes or just until candy melts a bit.

PRETZEL-PECAN BITES: Top mini-pretzel twists or snaps (such as Snyder's of Hanover) each with a bite-size chocolate-caramel nougat bar (such as Milky Way), a chocolate-coated caramel-peanut nougat bar (such as Snickers), or a chocolate-coated caramel (such as Rolo). Microwave on a microwave-safe plate at HIGH 20 seconds or just until chocolate begins to melt. Press toasted pecan halves into centers. Drizzle with caramel topping, and sprinkle with kosher salt, if desired. Serve immediately.

FRIED CANDY CORN: Yep, that's right. It's like a sweet, gooey fritter. Candy corn never had it so good. You can find my step-by-step video at *southernliving.com*.

GOTTA HAVE IT!

Q What's a so-called "nonessential" kitchen tool that's actually worth its salt?

ALYSSA SAVINO
CARY, NC

A VANESSA SAYS: Try a kitchen mandoline, a super-sharp device for making paper-thin slices. We love it for cutting radishes, apples, cukes, and other firm fruits and vegetables, including the sweet potatoes on page 254. After testing several models and going through a few bandages (**NOTE:** a protective finger guard is vital!), we like the top-notch OXO Steel Chef's Mandoline Slicer (below; $100 at Bed Bath & Beyond, *oxo.com*, and *amazon.com*).

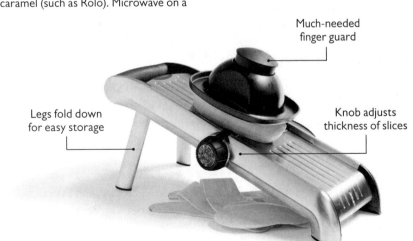

Much-needed finger guard

Legs fold down for easy storage

Knob adjusts thickness of slices

Bless Your Heart...

Homemade pretzels got you in knots? Relax. Follow our simple technique.

1. Let the dough come to room temp or it will be like rubber—hard to stretch. Roll each piece into a 16-inch-long rope.

2. Form each rope into a U-shape on a parchment paper-lined baking sheet. Paper keeps the dough from sticking to the pan.

3. Crisscross ends, folding or twisting each end diagonally. Tuck ends under dough to form a classic pretzel shape.

November

The Most Southern Thanksgiving Ever

Our Test Kitchen invites you to celebrate the season
with some of our favorite recipes.

Try a Meat 'n' Three Menu

Consider this our upscale version of the classic,
Southern-style blue-plate special

Deep South Meat 'n' Three

SERVES 8

THE MEAT

Herb-Roasted Turkey
with Easy Turkey Gravy

THE THREE

Cornbread Dressing with
Smoked Bacon and Pecans

Mashed Sweet Potatoes
with Autumn Spices

Fried Collards and Apples

THE TEA

Clementine Tea

Herb-Roasted Turkey

good for you • make-ahead • party perfect

MAKES: 8 servings
HANDS-ON TIME: 1 hr.
TOTAL TIME: 6 hr.

- 1 **(14-lb.) whole fresh turkey***
  Kitchen string
- 1 **tsp. dried thyme**
- 1 **tsp. ground sage**
- ½ **tsp. dried tarragon**
- 3 **tsp. salt**
- 1 **tsp. pepper**
- ¼ **cup butter, softened**
- 2 **medium onions, chopped**
- 2 **carrots, chopped**
- 2 **celery ribs, chopped**
- 1 **garlic bulb, halved**
- 1 **cup dry white wine**
  Garnish: fresh sage leaves

1. Remove giblets and neck from turkey,
and rinse turkey with cold water. Drain
cavity well; pat dry. Tie ends of legs
together with kitchen string; tuck wingtips
under. Place, breast side up, on a lightly
greased roasting rack in a large roasting
pan. Let stand at room temperature
1 hour.

2. Preheat oven to 400°. Stir together
thyme, next 2 ingredients, 1½ tsp. salt,
and ½ tsp. pepper; rub mixture into
cavity of turkey. Rub butter over turkey.
Sprinkle remaining salt and pepper over
outside of turkey; rub into skin. Arrange
onions and next 3 ingredients around
base of turkey in roasting pan; add wine
and 1 cup water to pan.

3. Place turkey in oven; reduce oven temperature to 325°. Bake at 325° for 3 hours
or until a meat thermometer inserted into
thickest portion of thigh registers 160°.

4. Remove turkey from oven; increase
heat to 425°. Baste turkey with pan
juices, and let stand 15 minutes; return
to oven. Bake at 425° for 10 to 15 minutes
or until golden brown and thermometer
registers 165°.

5. Let turkey stand in pan 30 minutes;
transfer to a serving platter. Reserve
pan drippings for Easy Turkey Gravy,
if desired.

*Frozen whole turkey, thawed, may be
substituted.

Southern Thanksgiving

Dress Up Your Turkey

We asked food stylist Marian Cooper Cairns to share her tricks of the trade when it comes to getting a centerpiece-worthy bird.

GET IT GOLDEN

Pat turkey dry with paper towels. Let sit at room temperature for 1 hour to encourage even cooking; then season it. Begin roasting at low heat (325°) to gently cook through; then increase heat (425°) to brown the skin to perfection.

WATCH THAT BIRD

Baste with pan juices or melted butter, and rotate the pan to avoid any hot spots in your oven. Shield areas that brown quickly with foil. "Wrap wingtips completely in foil for the best color," says Marian.

CARVE LIKE A PRO

Present the turkey Norman Rockwell-style at the table, but scoot back to the kitchen to carve. Set the turkey on a work surface, and remove the wings, legs, thighs, and breast with a sharp knife. Then carve into elegant slices and arrange on a platter. Take a bow.

GARNISH SIMPLY

Start with a base of green (Marian used late-season muscadine vines from *petalsfromthepast.com*), and add a pop of color. Fig leaves or collard greens paired with plums or citrus also work.

Easy Turkey Gravy

quick prep • party perfect

MAKES: about 6 cups
HANDS-ON TIME: 25 min.
TOTAL TIME: 25 min.

Reserved pan drippings from Herb-Roasted Turkey
Chicken broth (up to 2½ cups), divided
¼ cup butter
¼ cup all-purpose flour

1. Pour pan drippings through a wire-mesh strainer into a large measuring cup, discarding solids. Add broth to equal 3 cups.
2. Melt butter in a saucepan over medium heat; whisk in flour, and cook, whisking constantly, 10 to 12 minutes or until smooth and light brown. (Mixture should be the color of peanut butter.) Gradually whisk in drippings mixture. Bring to a boil, whisking constantly. Reduce heat to medium-low; simmer, stirring occasionally, 5 minutes or until thickened. Add up to ½ cup broth for desired consistency. Add salt and pepper to taste.

Cornbread Dressing with Smoked Bacon and Pecans

party perfect

MAKES: 8 servings
HANDS-ON TIME: 30 min.
TOTAL TIME: 1 hr., 50 min., including cornbread (*see recipe, page 264*)

½ cup pecan halves
4 oz. applewood-smoked bacon, cut into ¼-inch pieces
1 cup diced onions
1 cup diced carrots
1 cup diced celery
4 green onions, chopped
Classic Cornbread, crumbled (about 6½ cups)
¼ cup chopped fresh flat-leaf parsley
2 tsp. chopped fresh thyme
2 tsp. chopped fresh marjoram
6 Tbsp. butter, melted
¾ cup chicken broth
¾ tsp. salt
½ tsp. pepper

1. Preheat oven to 325°. Bake pecans in a single layer in a shallow pan 10 minutes or until toasted and fragrant, stirring halfway through. Remove from oven. Increase oven temperature to 375°.
2. Cook bacon in a Dutch oven over medium heat 5 to 6 minutes. (Do not crisp.) Remove bacon, and drain on paper towels, reserving drippings in Dutch oven. Sauté diced onion and next 2 ingredients in hot drippings 8 minutes or until tender. Stir in green onions; sauté 1 minute. Remove from heat.
3. Add bacon, cornbread, and next 3 ingredients. Stir together melted butter and broth, and stir into cornbread mixture. Add salt and pepper. Fold in pecans. Spoon dressing into a buttered, shallow 2-qt. baking dish; cover with aluminum foil.
4. Bake, covered, at 375° for 25 minutes. Remove from oven, and uncover. Transfer oven rack to highest position. Bake dressing, uncovered, 12 minutes or until top is crusty.

Southern Thanksgiving

Classic Cornbread
quick prep • make-ahead • party perfect

MAKES: 8 to 10 servings
HANDS-ON TIME: 10 min.
TOTAL TIME: 35 min.

- **4 Tbsp. butter, melted and divided**
- **3 Tbsp. warm bacon drippings, divided**
- **1½ cups stone-ground yellow cornmeal**
- **½ cup unbleached all-purpose flour**
- **1 tsp. salt**
- **1 tsp. coarsely ground pepper**
- **½ tsp. baking powder**
- **½ tsp. baking soda**
- **1 large egg, lightly beaten**
- **1¼ cups buttermilk**
- **½ cup milk**

1. Preheat oven to 450°. Place 1 Tbsp. melted butter and 1 Tbsp. bacon drippings in a 10-inch cast-iron skillet; heat in oven 5 minutes.
2. Meanwhile, sift together cornmeal and next 5 ingredients in a bowl. Whisk together egg and both milks; whisk into cornmeal mixture just until combined. Whisk in remaining 3 Tbsp. butter and 2 Tbsp. drippings. Pour into hot skillet.
3. Bake at 450° for 20 minutes or until golden brown and firm. Cool 5 minutes; remove from pan, and serve. Or cool completely in pan on a wire rack (about 1 hour).

TURKEY, GRAVY, AND DRESSING RECIPES BROUGHT TO THE TABLE BY CHEF FRANK STITT OF HIGHLANDS BAR AND GRILL IN BIRMINGHAM, ALABAMA.

Mashed Sweet Potatoes with Autumn Spices
make-ahead • party perfect

MAKES: 6 to 8 servings
HANDS-ON TIME: 30 min.
TOTAL TIME: 1 hr., 40 min.

- **3 lb. medium-size sweet potatoes (about 8 oz. each)**
- **⅓ cup peach preserves**
- **¼ cup butter, melted**
- **2 Tbsp. light brown sugar**
- **2 Tbsp. dry sherry**
- **2 tsp. lemon zest**
- **2 Tbsp. fresh lemon juice**
- **½ tsp. kosher salt**
- **½ tsp. freshly grated nutmeg**
- **½ tsp. ground ginger**
- **¼ tsp. ground cinnamon**
- **Garnish: crumbled gingersnaps**

1. Preheat oven to 350° with oven rack 8 inches from heat. Pierce potatoes several times with a fork; place potatoes on oven rack, and place a piece of aluminum foil on the rack below to catch drips. Bake potatoes 40 minutes or until tender. Cool slightly (about 10 minutes).
2. Peel potatoes, and press through a ricer or mash with a potato masher until smooth. (Do not use a mixer or food processor.) Stir in preserves and next 9 ingredients until well blended. Spoon sweet potato mixture into a lightly greased 2½-qt. baking dish.
3. Bake at 350° for 20 minutes or until hot.

BROUGHT TO THE TABLE BY SHERI CASTLE (ADAPTED FROM *THE NEW SOUTHERN GARDEN COOKBOOK*).

Fried Collards and Apples
quick prep • good for you • party perfect

MAKES: 8 servings
HANDS-ON TIME: 25 min.
TOTAL TIME: 25 min.

1. Separate 2 lb. fresh collard greens into leaves. Trim and discard tough stalk from center of leaves; stack leaves, and roll up, starting at 1 long side. Cut into ¼-inch-thick slices; rinse under cold running water. Drain well. Stir-fry collard greens in ¼ cup hot vegetable oil in a large Dutch oven over medium-high heat 2 minutes or until greens begin to wilt. Add ½ cup chicken broth, 1 tsp. salt, 4 tsp. apple cider vinegar, and ½ tsp. dried crushed red pepper; stir-fry 3 minutes or until greens are crisp-tender. Gently stir in 2 Fuji apples, cut into matchsticks; cook, stirring often, 2 minutes.

Clementine Tea
quick prep • party perfect

MAKES: 3 qt.
HANDS-ON TIME: 10 min.
TOTAL TIME: 30 min.

1. Bring 4 cups water to a boil in a 4-qt. saucepan over medium-high heat. Add 3 family-size or 8 regular-size black tea bags; boil 2 minutes. Remove pan from heat; add ½ cup fresh clementine juice and 2 clementines, sliced. Let steep 10 minutes. Discard tea bags and clementine slices. Stir in 1 cup sugar until dissolved. Pour into a 1-gal. container, and add 5½ cups cold water. Serve over ice.
NOTE: We tested with Lipton Iced Tea Family Size Tea Bags.

Southern Thanksgiving

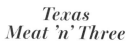

Texas Meat 'n' Three

SERVES 8

THE MEAT

Grilled Turkey Breast with Parsley-Mint Salsa Verde

THE THREE

Poblanos Stuffed with Goat Cheese Mashed Potatoes

Cauliflower Galettes with Chipotle Crème Fraîche

Roasted Carrot and Avocado Salad

THE TEA

Hibiscus-Mint Margaritas

Grilled Turkey Breast

good for you • make-ahead • party perfect

MAKES: 8 servings
HANDS-ON TIME: 20 min.
TOTAL TIME: 9 hr., 35 min., including salsa

⅓ cup kosher salt
⅓ cup sugar
3 bay leaves
2 jalapeño peppers, halved
2 Tbsp. cumin seeds
   Large, deep food-safe container
1 (5- to 6-lb.) boned, skin-on fresh turkey breast*
   Vegetable cooking spray
1 Tbsp. table salt
1 Tbsp. cumin seeds
1 Tbsp. paprika
2 tsp. freshly ground pepper
1 tsp. ground coriander
1 tsp. dried oregano
   Parsley-Mint Salsa Verde

1. Stir together kosher salt, next 4 ingredients, and 2 qt. water in a large, deep food-safe container or stockpot until sugar is dissolved. Add turkey. Chill 8 hours or overnight, turning once.
2. Coat cold cooking grate of grill with cooking spray, and place on grill. Light 1 side of grill, heating to 350° to 400° (medium-high) heat; leave other side unlit. Remove turkey from brine. Rinse turkey, drain well, and pat dry with paper towels.
3. Stir together table salt and next 5 ingredients. Rub skin of turkey with mixture.
4. Place turkey, skin side down, over lit side of grill, and grill, without grill lid, 4 to 5 minutes or until slightly charred. Transfer to unlit side, skin side up. Grill, covered with grill lid, 30 to 40 minutes or until a meat thermometer inserted into thickest portion registers 165°. Return turkey, skin side down, to lit side, and grill, covered with grill lid, 4 to 5 minutes or until skin is crisp.
5. Remove turkey from heat; cover loosely with aluminum foil. Let stand 10 minutes. Serve with salsa verde.

*Frozen turkey breast, thawed, may be substituted.

Parsley-Mint Salsa Verde

MAKES: 1¾ cups
HANDS-ON TIME: 15 min.
TOTAL TIME: 35 min.

⅔ cup extra virgin olive oil
⅓ cup sherry vinegar
¼ cup finely chopped shallots
2 garlic cloves, finely chopped
1 tsp. salt
½ tsp. pepper
1 cup chopped fresh flat-leaf parsley
¾ cup chopped fresh mint

1. Whisk together first 6 ingredients and 2 Tbsp. water until salt dissolves. Whisk in parsley and mint. Let stand 20 minutes.

BROUGHT TO THE TABLE BY ELIZABETH WINSLOW, COFOUNDER OF FARMHOUSE DELIVERY (FARMHOUSEDELIVERY.COM).

Poblanos Stuffed with Goat Cheese Mashed Potatoes

good for you • party perfect

MAKES: 8 servings
HANDS-ON TIME: 30 min.
TOTAL TIME: 1 hr., 15 min.

8 poblano peppers
6 medium-size Yukon gold potatoes, peeled (about 2 lb.)
2 tsp. salt
¼ cup buttermilk
2 Tbsp. butter
1 (4-oz.) can diced green chiles, drained
1 (4-oz.) package goat cheese, crumbled

1. Preheat grill to 350° to 400° (medium-high) heat. Grill peppers, without grill lid, 5 minutes on each side or until peppers look blistered.
2. Place peppers in a large zip-top plastic freezer bag; seal and let stand 10 minutes to loosen skins. Carefully peel peppers. Cut each pepper lengthwise down 1 side, being careful not to cut through other side. Remove and discard seeds and membranes.
3. Cut potatoes into 2-inch pieces. Bring potatoes, salt, and water to cover to a boil in a large Dutch oven over medium-high heat, and cook 20 minutes or until tender; drain. Return potatoes to Dutch oven, reduce heat to low, and cook, stirring occasionally, 3 to 5 minutes or until dry.
4. Mash potatoes with a potato masher. Stir in buttermilk, butter, chiles, and half of goat cheese until blended. Spoon mixture into a gallon-size zip-top plastic freezer bag. (Do not seal.) Snip 1 corner of bag, and pipe mixture into each pepper; top with remaining goat cheese.
5. Grill peppers, covered with grill lid, over 350° to 400° (medium-high) heat 10 to 12 minutes or until cheese is melted.

Southern Thanksgiving

Cauliflower Galettes with Chipotle Crème Fraîche

good for you • party perfect

MAKES: 8 servings
HANDS-ON TIME: 30 min.
TOTAL TIME: 1 hr., 10 min.

- 1 medium-size head cauliflower, cut into small florets
- 1 Tbsp. olive oil
- ¼ tsp. freshly ground black pepper
- 1¼ tsp. sea salt, divided
- 1 cup plain yellow or white cornmeal
- 2 tsp. baking powder
- ½ tsp. ground red pepper
- ½ tsp. ground cumin
- 2 large eggs
- 1 (6-oz.) container fat-free plain Greek yogurt
- 1 cup freshly grated Cheddar cheese
- 4 green onions, sliced and divided
- 4 Tbsp. vegetable oil
- 2 canned chipotle peppers in adobo sauce, finely chopped
- 1 cup crème fraîche or sour cream

1. Preheat broiler with oven rack 8 inches from heat. Place cauliflower in a 15- x 10-inch jelly-roll pan. Drizzle with olive oil, and sprinkle with black pepper and ¼ tsp. sea salt; toss to coat.

2. Broil cauliflower 10 minutes or until lightly browned, stirring halfway through. Remove from oven; cool in pan on a wire rack 30 minutes.

3. Whisk together cornmeal, next 3 ingredients, and remaining 1 tsp. sea salt in a medium bowl. Whisk together eggs, yogurt, and 1 cup water; whisk into dry ingredients. Fold in cheese and half of onions. Fold in cooled cauliflower.

4. Drop half of batter by spoonfuls (about 2 Tbsp.) into 2 Tbsp. hot vegetable oil in a nonstick skillet over medium-low heat (do not crowd pan), and fry 3 to 4 minutes on each side or until golden. Drain on paper towels. Repeat with remaining batter and oil. Sprinkle with remaining green onions.

5. Stir together chipotle peppers and crème fraîche; serve with galettes.

BROUGHT TO THE TABLE BY COOKBOOK AUTHOR ELLISE PIERCE (ADAPTED FROM *COWGIRL CHEF COOKBOOK*).

Roasted Carrot and Avocado Salad

good for you • make-ahead • party perfect

MAKES: 6 to 8 servings
HANDS-ON TIME: 20 min.
TOTAL TIME: 1 hr., 10 min.

- 3 (6-oz.) packages microwave-in-bag baby rainbow carrots with tops, cut in half lengthwise
- 2 lemons, halved
- 1 orange, halved
- 2 garlic cloves, minced
- 4 fresh thyme sprigs
- 1 tsp. ground cumin
- 1 tsp. paprika
- ½ cup olive oil, divided
- 1 tsp. kosher salt, divided
- 1 Tbsp. each sunflower seeds, sesame seeds, poppy seeds, and pumpkin seeds
- 1 medium avocado
- 1 tsp. fresh lemon juice
- 3 Tbsp. red wine vinegar
- 1 (5-oz.) package spring greens mix
- ½ small red onion, thinly sliced
- 2 Tbsp. Mexican crema

1. Preheat oven to 425°. Toss together first 7 ingredients in a 15- x 10-inch jelly-roll pan. Drizzle with 2 Tbsp. olive oil, and sprinkle with ½ tsp. salt; toss to coat. Bake 25 minutes or until lightly browned, stirring occasionally. Cool to room temperature (about 30 minutes).

2. Meanwhile, cook all seeds in a small skillet over medium-low heat, stirring constantly, 4 to 5 minutes or until toasted. Remove from heat; cool completely (about 15 minutes).

3. Cut avocado into slices, and toss with lemon juice.

4. Squeeze juice from roasted lemon and orange halves into a large bowl; stir in vinegar and remaining ½ tsp. salt. Slowly whisk in remaining 6 Tbsp. olive oil until blended; reserve half of dressing. Toss carrots, salad greens, and red onion with remaining dressing in bowl. Arrange greens on a serving platter or individual plates; top with avocado. Drizzle with crema; sprinkle with toasted seeds. Serve with reserved dressing.

BROUGHT TO THE TABLE BY ELIZABETH WINSLOW, CO-FOUNDER OF FARMHOUSE DELIVERY.

Hibiscus-Mint Margaritas

make-ahead • party perfect

MAKES: 8 servings
HANDS-ON TIME: 10 min.
TOTAL TIME: 1 hr., 30 min.

- 1½ cups boiling water
- 4 regular-size hibiscus tea bags
- 1 cup sugar
- 4 mint sprigs
- 2 cups silver or blanco tequila
- ½ cup orange liqueur
- ½ cup fresh lime juice
  Crushed ice
  Club soda

1. Pour boiling water over tea bags; stir in sugar and mint. Cover and steep 20 minutes. Discard tea bags and mint; cool completely (about 1 hour).

2. Stir together tequila, next 2 ingredients, and tea in a pitcher. Pour over crushed ice in 8 (10-oz.) glasses; top with a splash of club soda.

NOTE: We tested with Celestial Seasonings Red Zinger Herbal Tea.

Southern Thanksgiving

Lowcountry Meat 'n' Three

SERVES 8

THE MEAT

Turkey Tenderloins
with Madeira Gravy

THE THREE

Brussels Sprouts with
Applewood Bacon

Cornbread, Chestnut, and
Country Ham Dressing

Orange-Glazed Sweet Potatoes

THE TEA

Pineapple-Basil Tea

Turkey Tenderloins with Madeira Gravy

MAKES: 12 servings
HANDS-ON TIME: 40 min.
TOTAL TIME: 3 hr., 10 min.

- 3 cups dry **Madeira** or **fino sherry**
- ¾ cup **red wine vinegar**
- 12 **garlic cloves, crushed**
- 18 **fresh thyme sprigs**
- 3 tsp. **kosher salt, divided**
- 4 lb. **turkey tenderloins**
- 2 Tbsp. **vegetable oil, divided**
- 1 tsp. **freshly ground pepper**
- 3 Tbsp. **butter**
- 3 **large shallots, finely chopped**
- 2 tsp. **sifted all-purpose flour**
  Garnish: fresh thyme sprigs

1. Stir together first 4 ingredients and 2 tsp. salt in a 2-qt. measuring cup until salt dissolves. Reserve 1¼ cups. Pour remaining mixture into a zip-top plastic freezer bag. Add tenderloins; press out air, seal, and chill 2 to 4 hours, turning every 30 minutes.
2. Preheat oven to 450°. Remove tenderloins from marinade, discarding marinade. Pat tenderloins dry. Brush with 1 Tbsp. oil, and sprinkle with pepper and remaining 1 tsp. salt.
3. Cook tenderloins, in batches, in remaining 1 Tbsp. hot oil in a large cast-iron skillet over high heat 2 to 3 minutes on each side or until browned. Transfer to a plate; discard oil. Reduce heat to medium. Add butter and shallots to skillet, and cook, stirring constantly, until butter melts. Stir in flour. Cook, stirring often, 3 minutes or until shallots are tender. Whisk in reserved 1¼ cups sherry mixture, and bring to a simmer. Simmer 2 to 3 minutes or until slightly thickened. Remove from heat, and season with salt and pepper to taste. Place tenderloins in a 13- x 9-inch baking dish; pour sauce over tenderloins.

4. Bake at 450° for 10 to 12 minutes or until a meat thermometer inserted into thickest portion registers 165°. Transfer tenderloins to a cutting board, reserving gravy in baking dish. Cover loosely with foil, and let stand 10 minutes. Cut into ½-inch-thick medallions, and serve with gravy.

BROUGHT TO THE TABLE BY COOKBOOK AUTHORS MATT LEE AND TED LEE (ADAPTED FROM *THE LEE BROS. SIMPLE FRESH SOUTHERN COOKBOOK*).

Brussels Sprouts with Applewood Bacon

quick prep • party perfect

MAKES: 8 servings
HANDS-ON TIME: 35 min.
TOTAL TIME: 35 min.

- 2 lb. **fresh Brussels sprouts, halved**
- 5 **applewood-smoked bacon slices, diced**
- 2 Tbsp. **butter**
- ⅓ cup **firmly packed light brown sugar**
- ¼ tsp. **ground cinnamon**
- ⅛ tsp. **freshly grated nutmeg**

1. Cook Brussels sprouts in boiling salted water to cover 4 minutes; drain. Plunge sprouts into ice water to stop the cooking process; drain.
2. Cook bacon in a large skillet over medium heat, stirring often, 10 minutes or until crisp; remove bacon, and drain on paper towels, reserving 1 Tbsp. drippings in skillet.
3. Melt butter in hot drippings over medium-high heat; stir in brown sugar, cinnamon, and nutmeg. Cook, stirring constantly, 1 minute or until sugar is melted and sauce thickens slightly. Stir in Brussels sprouts; cook, stirring often, 10 to 12 minutes or until lightly browned. Add salt and pepper to taste.

BROUGHT TO THE TABLE BY CHEF BRETT MCKEE OF ELI'S TABLE IN CHARLESTON, SOUTH CAROLINA.

Southern Thanksgiving

Cornbread, Chestnut, and Country Ham Dressing

party perfect

MAKES: 10 servings
HANDS-ON TIME: 35 min.
TOTAL TIME: 2 hr., 50 min., including cornbread

- ½ cup chopped country ham
- 6 bacon slices, chopped
- 2 celery ribs, chopped
- 1 carrot, chopped
- ½ medium-size yellow onion, chopped
- Buttermilk Cornbread
- ⅓ cup whole roasted and peeled chestnuts, chopped*
- 1 cup chicken broth
- 2 Tbsp. butter, melted
- 1 Tbsp. chopped fresh thyme
- 1 Tbsp. chopped fresh sage
- ½ tsp. salt
- ¼ tsp. pepper

1. Preheat oven to 350°. Sauté ham and bacon in a large skillet over medium-high heat 8 to 10 minutes or until browned. Add celery and next 2 ingredients, and sauté 8 minutes or until vegetables are tender.

2. Crumble cornbread into a large bowl. Stir in chestnuts and ham mixture. Stir in broth and next 5 ingredients. Spoon into a lightly greased 13- x 9-inch baking dish.

3. Bake at 350° for 30 to 40 minutes or until lightly browned.

*Walnuts or pecans may be substituted.

NOTE: We tested with Lieber's Whole Roasted & Peeled Chestnuts.

BROUGHT TO THE TABLE BY JOHN ZUCKER OF CRU CAFÉ IN CHARLESTON, SOUTH CAROLINA.

Buttermilk Cornbread

make-ahead • party perfect

MAKES: 10 servings
HANDS-ON TIME: 10 min.
TOTAL TIME: 1 hr., 45 min.

You can make this a day ahead. If you're using it as a side (not in the dressing), then add ½ tsp. salt with the flour.

1. Preheat oven to 350°. Whisk together 1½ cups buttermilk, 3 large eggs, 4 Tbsp. sugar, and 1 tsp. baking soda in a large bowl; stir in ½ cup fresh corn kernels. Stir together 1½ cups fine yellow cornmeal and 1 cup all-purpose flour; gradually whisk flour mixture into buttermilk mixture. Whisk in ½ cup melted butter. Pour batter into a buttered 10-inch cast-iron skillet. Bake at 350° for 35 minutes or until a wooden pick inserted in center comes out clean. Remove from pan, and cool completely on a wire rack (about 1 hour).

Orange-Glazed Sweet Potatoes

good for you • make-ahead • party perfect

MAKES: 8 servings
HANDS-ON TIME: 15 min.
TOTAL TIME: 1 hr., 5 min.

- 6 medium-size sweet potatoes (about 4 lb.)
- ¼ cup firmly packed dark brown sugar
- ½ tsp. orange zest
- 1 cup fresh orange juice
- 2 Tbsp. butter, melted
- ¼ tsp. kosher salt
- ¼ tsp. ground cinnamon

1. Preheat oven to 325°. Peel potatoes, and cut into 1-inch-thick slices; arrange in a single layer in 2 lightly greased 13- x 9-inch baking dishes.

2. Stir together brown sugar and next 5 ingredients; pour over potatoes. Cover with aluminum foil.

3. Bake at 325° for 45 minutes or until fork-tender. Uncover and bake 5 more minutes or until glaze becomes syrupy.

MAKE AHEAD: Cover and chill cooked potatoes up to 1 day. To reheat, let stand at room temperature 1 hour. Bake, covered with foil, at 350° for 20 minutes.

BROUGHT TO THE TABLE BY COOKBOOK AUTHORS MATT LEE AND TED LEE (ADAPTED FROM *THE LEE BROS. SIMPLE FRESH SOUTHERN COOKBOOK*).

Pineapple-Basil Tea

quick prep • party perfect

MAKES: about 10 cups
HANDS-ON TIME: 30 min.
TOTAL TIME: 40 min.

1. Bring 2 cups chopped fresh pineapple, 1½ cups sugar, and 1 cup water to a boil in a saucepan over medium-high heat. Reduce heat to low; simmer, stirring often, 10 minutes. Cool slightly; process in a blender. Bring 3 cups water to a boil over medium-high heat in a saucepan. Add 8 regular-size black tea bags; boil 1 minute. Remove from heat; cover and steep 10 minutes. Discard tea bags. Pour pineapple mixture through a wire-mesh strainer into a 1-gal. container. Stir in tea, ¼ cup chopped fresh basil, and 6 cups cold water. Serve over ice.

Make, and Break, the Mold

Step away from the store-bought stuff and try these can-do ideas.

Cranberry-Apricot Sauce

good for you • make-ahead • party perfect

MAKES: about 3 cups
HANDS-ON TIME: 20 min.
TOTAL TIME: 9 hr.

- 1 cup sugar
- ½ cup fresh orange juice
- 1 Tbsp. red wine vinegar
- 2 (¼-inch-thick) fresh ginger slices
- 1 (3-inch) cinnamon stick
- 4 cups fresh or frozen cranberries
- ½ cup chopped dried apricots

1. Bring first 5 ingredients to a boil in a medium saucepan over medium-high heat, stirring until sugar is dissolved. Stir in cranberries and apricots, and return to a boil. Reduce heat to medium-low; simmer, stirring occasionally, 10 to 15 minutes or until berries begin to split and mixture begins to thicken.
2. Remove from heat; cool 30 minutes. Discard cinnamon and ginger. Pour into a 3-cup mold; cover and chill 8 hours or until set.

BREAKING THE MOLD

Not a fan of anything gelatinous? We won't revoke your Southern card. Just get (cranberry) sauced with a cocktail.

Cranberry Reduction

make-ahead • party perfect

MAKES: 1¼ cups
HANDS-ON TIME: 10 min.
TOTAL TIME: 2 hr., 5 min.

- 2 cups cranberry juice
- ½ cup canned jellied cranberry sauce
- ¼ cup sugar
- 4 dashes of Angostura bitters
- 1 (3-inch) rosemary sprig

1. Boil first 4 ingredients in a medium saucepan over medium heat, stirring often, 4 to 5 minutes or until smooth. Reduce heat to low, and simmer, stirring occasionally, 20 minutes or until liquid is reduced by half and slightly thickened.
2. Add rosemary; cover and let stand 5 minutes. Discard rosemary. Cool mixture 30 minutes. Cover and chill 1 hour. Store in an airtight container in refrigerator up to 1 week.

Make a Cocktail

make-ahead • party perfect

Each makes 1 serving and takes less than 5 minutes.

CRAN-BOURBON-AND-ORANGE: Stir together 3 Tbsp. bourbon, 1 Tbsp. Cranberry Reduction, and 1 Tbsp. fresh orange juice in a 10-oz. glass filled with ice cubes. Top with club soda. Garnish with fresh rosemary.

CRANBERRY-GIN FIZZ: Combine 3 Tbsp. gin, 1 Tbsp. Cranberry Reduction, and 1½ tsp. fresh lime juice in a cocktail shaker filled with ice cubes. Cover with lid; shake vigorously until thoroughly chilled (about 30 seconds). Strain into a 10-oz. glass filled with ice cubes. Top with lemon-lime soft drink.

CRANBERRY MOJITO: Muddle 3 mint leaves, 1 Tbsp. Cranberry Reduction, and 1½ tsp. fresh lime juice against sides of a cocktail shaker; add ice cubes and 3 Tbsp. rum. Cover with lid, and shake vigorously until thoroughly chilled (about 30 seconds). Strain into a 10-oz. glass filled with ice cubes. Top with lemon-lime soft drink. Garnish with a fresh mint sprig and lime slices.

HOLIDAY COSMOPOLITAN: Stir together 3 Tbsp. vodka, 1 Tbsp. orange liqueur (such as Triple Sec), 1 Tbsp. Cranberry Reduction, and 1½ tsp. fresh lemon juice in a cocktail shaker filled with ice cubes. Cover with lid, and shake vigorously until thoroughly chilled (about 30 seconds). Strain mixture into a chilled coupe or martini glass. Garnish with a lemon zest twist.

Cranberry Ice Cubes

make-ahead • party perfect

MAKES: 16 ice cubes
HANDS-ON TIME: 10 min.
TOTAL TIME: 4 hr., 10 min.

- ¼ cup sliced cranberries
- 16 thin lemon zest strips
- 5 to 6 fresh mint leaves, cut into thin strips
- 1 (8.4-oz.) can sparkling cranberry juice

1. Divide first 3 ingredients among each compartment of 1 ice-cube tray. Combine cranberry juice and ½ cup water. Pour into tray; freeze 4 hours or until firm.

MAKE AN ICE RING: Place ¼ cup sliced cranberries; ½ lemon, sliced; and 10 mint leaves, torn into pieces, in a 4-cup ring mold. Combine 2 (8.4-oz.) cans sparkling cranberry juice and 1½ cups water. Pour into mold; freeze 6 hours or until firm.

Set Up a Southern Sideboard

You can never have too many sides, so we dreamed up seven more dishes that are worthy of a spot in your holiday spread.

Fresh Corn Spoonbread

good for you • party perfect

MAKES: 12 servings
HANDS-ON TIME: 30 min.
TOTAL TIME: 1 hr., 5 min.

1   cup self-rising white cornmeal mix
½   cup all-purpose flour
2   Tbsp. sugar
1   tsp. salt
4   cups fresh corn kernels
     (about 8 ears)
2   cups plain yogurt
¼   cup butter, melted
¼   cup chopped fresh chives
2   Tbsp. chopped fresh parsley
1   tsp. minced fresh thyme
3   large eggs, lightly beaten
     Garnish: fresh thyme sprigs

1. Preheat oven to 350°. Stir together first 4 ingredients in a large bowl; make a well in center of mixture. Stir together corn and next 6 ingredients; add to cornmeal mixture, stirring just until dry ingredients are moistened. Divide mixture among 12 (6-oz.) buttered ramekins.
2. Bake at 350° for 35 to 40 minutes or until golden brown and set. Serve immediately.

Field Peas with Okra and Andouille Sausage

quick prep • party perfect

MAKES: 8 to 10 servings
HANDS-ON TIME: 10 min.
TOTAL TIME: 40 min.

½   lb. andouille sausage, cut into
     ¼-inch-thick slices
6   cups assorted fresh or frozen
     field peas
½   lb. small, fresh whole okra
12 fresh basil leaves, torn
     Salt and freshly ground pepper
     to taste

1. Sauté andouille in a Dutch oven over medium heat 5 minutes or until lightly browned.
2. Add field peas and water to cover 1 inch above peas; bring to a boil. Cover, reduce heat to medium-low, and simmer 20 minutes. Add okra; cover and simmer 5 minutes or until okra and peas are tender. Stir in basil and salt and pepper to taste. Transfer to a serving dish; serve with a slotted spoon.

BROUGHT TO THE TABLE BY COOKBOOK AUTHOR WHITNEY MILLER *(MODERN HOSPITALITY).*

Roasted Parsnips with Mint

quick prep • good for you • party perfect

MAKES: 8 servings
HANDS-ON TIME: 20 min.
TOTAL TIME: 55 min.

2   lb. parsnips
¼   tsp. freshly ground pepper
7   Tbsp. extra virgin olive oil, divided
1   tsp. kosher salt, divided
6   green onions, cut into 3-inch
     pieces
½   cup finely chopped fresh mint
2   Tbsp. finely chopped shallots
3   Tbsp. red wine vinegar
1   garlic clove, minced

1. Preheat oven to 400°. Peel parsnips, and cut into 2- to 3-inch-long pieces; cut each lengthwise into ⅓-inch-thick strips. Place in a lightly greased 15- x 10-inch jelly-roll pan; toss with pepper, 2 Tbsp. olive oil, and ½ tsp. kosher salt.
2. Bake at 400° for 25 minutes. Add green onions; toss. Bake 10 to 15 more minutes or until parsnips are tender and browned. Transfer to a serving platter.
3. Whisk together mint, next 3 ingredients, and remaining ½ tsp. salt until blended. Gradually add remaining 5 Tbsp. olive oil in a slow, steady stream, whisking until smooth. Spoon over vegetables. Serve immediately.

BROUGHT TO THE TABLE BY COOKBOOK AUTHORS MATT LEE AND TED LEE *(THE LEE BROS. SIMPLE FRESH SOUTHERN COOKBOOK).*

Southern Thanksgiving

Cranberry-Pecan Pilau

quick prep • good for you • party perfect

MAKES: 10 to 12 servings
HANDS-ON TIME: 35 min.
TOTAL TIME: 35 min.

- 1 cup coarsely chopped pecans
- 2 (7-oz.) packages wild pecan brown rice
- ¼ cup butter
- 1 lb. shallots, quartered lengthwise
- ⅔ cup sweetened dried cranberries
- ¼ cup dry sherry
- 1 tsp. orange zest
- ½ cup chopped fresh flat-leaf parsley

1. Heat pecans in small nonstick skillet over medium-low heat, stirring often, 5 to 7 minutes or until pecans are toasted and fragrant.
2. Prepare rice according to package directions.
3. Meanwhile, melt butter in a large skillet over medium-high heat; add shallots, and sauté 2 minutes. Reduce heat to medium-low, and sauté 10 minutes or until golden brown and tender. Add cranberries and next 2 ingredients, and sauté 3 minutes or until liquid is absorbed. Stir shallot mixture, toasted pecans, and parsley into hot cooked rice.
NOTE: Konriko Wild Pecan Brown Rice from Louisiana is one of our favorites. Find it in the supermarket or order directly from *konriko.com*.

Fresh Pear-and-Green Bean Salad with Sorghum Vinaigrette

good for you • party perfect

MAKES: 8 servings
HANDS-ON TIME: 15 min.
TOTAL TIME: 1 hr., 15 min., including pecans and vinaigrette

- 8 oz. haricots verts (tiny green beans), trimmed
- 1 (5-oz.) package gourmet mixed salad greens
- 2 red Bartlett pears, cut into thin strips
- ½ small red onion, sliced
- 4 oz. Gorgonzola cheese, crumbled
- 1 cup Sweet and Spicy Pecans
  Sorghum Vinaigrette

1. Cook beans in boiling salted water to cover 3 to 4 minutes or until crisp-tender; drain. Plunge beans into ice water to stop the cooking process; drain. Toss together salad greens, next 4 ingredients, and beans. Serve with Sorghum Vinaigrette.

Sweet and Spicy Pecans

quick prep • good for you • party perfect

MAKES: about 2 cups
HANDS-ON TIME: 10 min.
TOTAL TIME: 55 min.

- ¼ cup sorghum syrup
- 2 Tbsp. Demerara sugar
- ½ tsp. kosher salt
- ¼ tsp. ground red pepper
- 2 cups pecan halves
  Parchment paper

1. Preheat oven to 350°. Stir together first 4 ingredients. Add pecan halves; stir until coated. Line a jelly-roll pan with parchment paper, and lightly grease paper. Spread pecans in a single layer in pan.

2. Bake at 350° for 15 minutes or until glaze bubbles slowly and thickens, stirring once after 8 minutes. Transfer pan to a wire rack. Separate pecans into individual pieces; cool completely in pan. If cooled pecans are not crisp, bake 5 more minutes.

Sorghum Vinaigrette

quick prep • make-ahead • party perfect

MAKES: 2 cups
HANDS-ON TIME: 5 min.
TOTAL TIME: 5 min.

- ½ cup sorghum syrup
- ½ cup malt or apple cider vinegar
- 3 Tbsp. bourbon
- 2 tsp. grated onion
- 1 tsp. salt
- 1 tsp. freshly ground pepper
- ½ tsp. hot sauce
- 1 cup olive oil

1. Whisk together first 7 ingredients until blended. Add oil in a slow, steady stream, whisking until smooth.

BROUGHT TO THE TABLE BY CHEF OUITA MICHEL OF HOLLY HILL INN AND WOODFORD RESERVE DISTILLERY (*SWEET, SWEET SORGHUM COOKBOOK* BY RONA ROBERTS).

Four-Cheese Macaroni

party perfect

MAKES: 8 servings
HANDS-ON TIME: 40 min.
TOTAL TIME: 1 hr., 15 min.

- 12 oz. cavatappi pasta
- ½ cup butter
- ½ cup all-purpose flour
- ½ tsp. ground red pepper
- 3 cups milk
- 2 cups (8 oz.) freshly shredded white Cheddar cheese
- 1 cup (4 oz.) freshly shredded Monterey Jack cheese
- 1 cup (4 oz.) freshly shredded fontina cheese
- 1 cup (4 oz.) freshly shredded Asiago cheese
- 1½ cups soft, fresh breadcrumbs
- ½ cup chopped cooked bacon
- ½ cup chopped pecans
- 2 Tbsp. butter, melted

1. Preheat oven to 350°. Prepare pasta according to package directions.
2. Meanwhile, melt ½ cup butter in a Dutch oven over low heat; whisk in flour and ground red pepper until smooth. Cook, whisking constantly, 1 minute. Gradually whisk in milk; cook over medium heat, whisking constantly, 6 to 7 minutes or until milk mixture is thickened and bubbly. Remove from heat.
3. Toss together Cheddar cheese and next 3 ingredients in a medium bowl; reserve 1½ cups cheese mixture. Add remaining cheese mixture and hot cooked pasta to sauce, tossing to coat. Spoon into a lightly greased 13- x 9-inch baking dish. Top with reserved 1½ cups cheese mixture.
4. Toss together breadcrumbs and next 3 ingredients; sprinkle over cheese mixture.
5. Bake at 350° for 35 to 40 minutes or until bubbly and golden brown.

Butternut Squash Gratin

make-ahead • party perfect

MAKES: 8 servings
HANDS-ON TIME: 45 min.
TOTAL TIME: 3 hr., 30 min.

Slice the potatoes as you use them in each layer (rather than all at once) to help prevent oxidation.

- 1 (3-lb.) butternut squash
- 1 (3-lb.) spaghetti squash
- 2 Tbsp. butter, melted
- 1 cup firmly packed light brown sugar, divided
- ½ tsp. ground cinnamon
- ¼ tsp. ground nutmeg
- 3 cups whipping cream
- 5 large Yukon gold potatoes (about 2½ lb.)
- 1 tsp. salt
- 1 tsp. freshly ground pepper
- 4 cups (16 oz.) freshly shredded fontina cheese*
- Garnish: fresh rosemary sprigs

1. Preheat oven to 450°. Cut butternut and spaghetti squash in half lengthwise; remove and discard seeds. Place squash, cut sides up, in a lightly greased 17- x 12-inch jelly-roll pan. Drizzle with butter, and sprinkle with ½ cup brown sugar. Bake 40 minutes or until tender. Cool 20 minutes.
2. Using a fork, scrape inside of spaghetti squash to remove spaghetti-like strands, and place in a large bowl. Scoop pulp from butternut squash; coarsely chop pulp, and toss with spaghetti squash.
3. Stir together cinnamon, nutmeg, and remaining ½ cup brown sugar.
4. Cook cream in a heavy nonaluminum saucepan over medium heat, stirring often, 5 minutes or just until it begins to steam (do not boil); remove from heat.
5. Using a mandoline or sharp knife, cut potatoes into ⅛-inch-thick slices.

6. Arrange one-fourth of potato slices in a thin layer on bottom of a buttered 13- x 9-inch baking dish. Spoon one-third of squash mixture over potatoes (squash layer should be about ¼ inch thick); sprinkle with ¼ tsp. salt, ¼ tsp. pepper, 1 cup fontina cheese, and ¾ cup hot cream. Repeat layers twice, sprinkling one-third of sugar mixture over each of second and third squash layers. (Do not sprinkle sugar mixture over first squash layer.) Top with remaining potato slices, ¼ tsp. salt, and ¼ tsp. pepper. Gently press down layers with back of a spoon. Sprinkle top with remaining 1 cup cheese and ¾ cup hot cream; sprinkle with remaining brown sugar mixture. Place baking dish on an aluminum foil-lined baking sheet.
7. Bake, covered with foil, at 450° for 1 hour; uncover and bake 25 more minutes or until golden brown and potatoes are tender. Cool on a wire rack 20 minutes before serving.

*Gouda cheese may be substituted.

BROUGHT TO THE TABLE BY CHEF JOHN ZUCKER OF CRU CAFÉ IN CHARLESTON, SOUTH CAROLINA.

Serve a Mess of Greens

Green beans, that is. Here, three updates on the iconic casserole. Our only requirement? To retain crunch on top, 'cause we know y'all love those French fried onions.

Southern Thanksgiving

Balsamic Green Beans

good for you • party perfect

MAKES: 8 to 10 servings
HANDS-ON TIME: 30 min.
TOTAL TIME: 30 min.

Crunch Factor: Crispy fried shallots, crumbled bacon, and coarsely chopped roasted almonds top Balsamic Green Beans.

- 2 lb. fresh haricots verts (tiny green beans), trimmed
- 6 large shallots
  Vegetable oil
- ½ cup balsamic vinegar
- 1 Tbsp. light brown sugar
- 3 Tbsp. butter
  Salt and freshly ground pepper to taste
- ½ cup lightly salted roasted almonds, coarsely chopped
- ½ cup cooked and crumbled bacon (about 5 slices)

1. Cook beans in boiling salted water to cover 3 to 4 minutes or until crisp-tender; drain. Plunge beans into ice water to stop the cooking process; drain.
2. Cut shallots crosswise into thin slices; separate into rings. Pour oil to depth of 1 inch into a heavy saucepan; heat over medium-high heat to 350°. Fry shallots, in batches, 1 to 2 minutes or until crisp. Remove from skillet using a slotted spoon; drain on paper towels.
3. Cook vinegar and sugar in a large skillet over medium-high heat, stirring often, 5 to 6 minutes or until reduced to 3 Tbsp. Stir in butter until blended. Add beans, and sauté 5 minutes or until thoroughly heated; season with salt and pepper to taste. Arrange on a serving platter. Top with shallots, almonds, and bacon. Serve immediately.

Green Bean Lasagna

make-ahead • party perfect

MAKES: 8 servings
HANDS-ON TIME: 50 min.
TOTAL TIME: 2 hr., 25 min., including sauce

Crunch Factor: Crushed crackers and fried onions make for an over-the-top mix on Green Bean Lasagna.

- 2 (14.4-oz.) packages frozen French-cut green beans, thawed
- 12 uncooked lasagna noodles
- ¼ cup butter, divided
- 2 large sweet onions, halved and sliced
- 8 oz. assorted fresh mushrooms, trimmed and sliced
- ¼ cup white wine
- 1 (15-oz.) container ricotta cheese
- 5 cups (20 oz.) shredded Italian cheese blend, divided
  Parmesan Cream Sauce
- 1½ cups crushed round buttery crackers
- 1 (6-oz.) container French fried onions
- 3 Tbsp. butter, melted

1. Preheat oven to 350°. Drain green beans; pat dry with paper towels. Prepare noodles according to package directions.
2. Meanwhile, melt 2 Tbsp. butter in a large skillet over medium-high heat; add onions, and sauté 15 minutes or until golden brown. Transfer onions to a large bowl, and wipe skillet clean.
3. Melt remaining 2 Tbsp. butter in skillet; add mushrooms, and sauté 4 to 5 minutes or until tender. Add wine, and sauté 3 minutes or until liquid is absorbed. Add mushrooms and green beans to caramelized onions in bowl; toss.
4. Stir together ricotta cheese and 1 cup Italian cheese blend.

5. Layer 1 cup Parmesan Cream Sauce, 3 noodles, half of green bean mixture, and 1 cup cheese blend in a lightly greased 15- x 10-inch baking dish. Top with 1 cup Parmesan Cream Sauce, 3 noodles, and all of ricotta cheese mixture. Top with 3 noodles, remaining green bean mixture, 1 cup cheese blend, and 1 cup Parmesan Cream Sauce. Top sauce with remaining 3 noodles, 1 cup Parmesan Cream Sauce, and 2 cups cheese blend.
6. Bake at 350° for 50 minutes or until bubbly and golden brown. Toss together crackers and next 2 ingredients. Remove lasagna from oven; sprinkle cracker mixture over top. Bake 10 more minutes. Let stand on a wire rack 20 minutes before serving.

Parmesan Cream Sauce

MAKES: 4 cups
HANDS-ON TIME: 15 min.
TOTAL TIME: 15 min.

1. Melt ½ cup butter in a 3-qt. saucepan over medium-high heat. Whisk in ⅓ cup all-purpose flour; cook, whisking constantly, 1 minute. Gradually whisk in 4 cups milk. Bring to a boil, and cook, whisking constantly, 1 to 2 minutes or until thickened. Whisk in ½ cup grated Parmesan cheese, ¼ tsp. salt, and ¼ tsp. pepper.

Green Bean-Goat Cheese Gratin

good for you • party perfect

MAKES: 4 servings
HANDS-ON TIME: 20 min.
TOTAL TIME: 50 min.

Crunch Factor: Breadcrumbs and toasted pecans tossed with Parmesan and olive oil are sprinkled over Green Bean-Goat Cheese Gratin.

- 2 **white bread slices**
- 1 **Tbsp. olive oil**
- ¾ **cup (3 oz.) freshly shredded Parmesan cheese, divided**
- ⅓ **cup finely chopped pecans**
- 1 **lb. fresh haricots verts (tiny green beans), trimmed**
- 2 **oz. goat cheese, crumbled**
- ½ **cup whipping cream**
- ¼ **tsp. kosher salt**
- ¼ **tsp. pepper**

1. Preheat oven to 400°. Tear bread into large pieces; pulse in a food processor 2 or 3 times or until coarse crumbs form. Drizzle oil over crumbs; add ¼ cup Parmesan cheese. Pulse 5 or 6 times or until coated with oil. Stir in pecans.
2. Cut green beans crosswise into thirds. Cook in boiling water to cover 3 to 4 minutes or until crisp-tender; drain. Plunge into ice water to stop the cooking process; drain and pat dry with paper towels.
3. Toss together beans, next 4 ingredients, and remaining ½ cup Parmesan cheese. Firmly pack mixture into 4 (6-oz.) shallow ramekins. Cover each with aluminum foil, and place on a baking sheet.
4. Bake at 400° for 20 minutes. Uncover and sprinkle with crumb mixture. Bake 8 more minutes or until golden. Let stand 5 minutes.

BROUGHT TO THE TABLE BY COOKBOOK AUTHOR TASIA MALAKASIS, OWNER OF BELLE CHÈVRE CREAMERY IN ELKMONT, ALABAMA.

Pass the Rolls, Please!

We persuaded Pam Lolley, baker-in-chief of our Test Kitchen, to share her grandmother-in-law's coveted dinner roll recipe. Serve them with one of our favorite butter recipes.

Icebox Dinner Rolls

make-ahead • party perfect

MAKES: about 1½ dozen
HANDS-ON TIME: 30 min.
TOTAL TIME: 9 hr., 35 min.

- 1 **cup boiling water**
- 6 **Tbsp. shortening**
- ¼ **cup sugar**
- 1 **tsp. salt**
- 1 **(¼-oz.) envelope active dry yeast**
- ¼ **cup warm water (105° to 115°)**
- 1 **large egg, lightly beaten**
- 4 **cups all-purpose flour**
- ¼ **cup butter, melted and divided**

1. Pour boiling water over shortening and next 2 ingredients in bowl of a heavy-duty electric stand mixer, and stir until shortening melts and sugar and salt are completely dissolved. Let stand 10 minutes or until about 110°.
2. Meanwhile, combine yeast and warm water in a 1-cup liquid measuring cup; let stand 5 minutes.
3. Add yeast mixture and egg to shortening mixture; beat at low speed until combined. Gradually add flour, beating at low speed 2 to 3 minutes or until flour is blended and dough is soft and smooth.
4. Place dough in a lightly greased bowl, turning to grease top. Cover and chill 8 to 24 hours.
5. Turn dough out onto a lightly floured surface, and knead until smooth and elastic (about 1 minute). Gently shape dough into 60 (1-inch) balls; place 3 dough balls in each cup of 2 lightly greased 12-cup muffin pans. (You will fill only 20 cups.) Brush rolls with half of melted butter.
6. Cover pans with plastic wrap, and let rise in a warm place (85°), free from drafts, 45 minutes to 1 hour or until doubled in bulk.
7. Preheat oven to 400°. Bake rolls for 8 to 12 minutes or until golden brown. Brush with remaining melted butter. Serve immediately.

Pear Butter: Stir together ½ cup softened butter, 2 Tbsp. pureed pear preserves, and ½ tsp. finely chopped fresh rosemary.

Honey Butter: Stir together ½ cup softened butter, 1 Tbsp. honey, and ⅛ tsp. ground cinnamon.

Lemon-Herb Butter: Stir together ½ cup softened butter, 2 tsp. lemon zest, 2 tsp. finely chopped fresh flat-leaf parsley, and ½ tsp. finely chopped fresh thyme.

Goat Cheese-Garlic Butter: Stir together ½ cup softened butter; ½ (4-oz.) goat cheese log, softened; 4 roasted garlic cloves; and ¼ tsp. cracked pepper.

Mustard-Chive Butter: Stir together ½ cup softened butter, 4 tsp. spicy brown mustard, and 1 Tbsp. finely chopped fresh chives.

Pecan-Brown Sugar Butter: Stir together ½ cup softened butter, 2 Tbsp. finely chopped toasted pecans, and 1 Tbsp. light brown sugar.

THE DESSERTS

Save Room For Bundts and Pies

No, seriously. Leave ample space on your buffet for this deliciously indulgent assortment.

Rum-Glazed Sweet Potato Cakes

party perfect

MAKES: 3 dozen
HANDS-ON TIME: 40 min.
TOTAL TIME: 1 hr., 15 min.

- ¾ cup golden raisins
- ⅓ cup dark rum
- 4 large eggs, at room temperature
- 2 cups granulated sugar
- 1 cup vegetable oil
- 2 tsp. vanilla extract
- 2 cups pureed roasted sweet potatoes
- 3 cups all-purpose flour
- 1½ tsp. ground cinnamon
- 1 tsp. baking powder
- 1 tsp. baking soda
- ½ tsp. fine sea salt
- ½ tsp. ground nutmeg
- ¾ cup buttermilk
- ½ cup firmly packed dark brown sugar
- ¼ cup butter
- 3 Tbsp. whipping cream
- ½ cup finely chopped toasted pecans

1. Stir together first 2 ingredients. Let stand 30 minutes.
2. Meanwhile, beat eggs and granulated sugar at high speed with an electric mixer 2 to 4 minutes or until thick and pale. Add oil and vanilla, beating at low speed just until blended. Add sweet potato puree, beating just until blended and stopping to scrape down sides as needed.

3. Preheat oven to 350°. Sift together flour and next 5 ingredients; add to egg mixture alternately with buttermilk, beginning and ending with flour mixture. Beat at low speed just until blended after each addition. Drain raisins, reserving rum. Fold raisins into batter. Spoon batter into 3 lightly greased 12-cup Bundt brownie pans, filling each three-fourths full.
4. Bake at 350° for 14 to 16 minutes or until a wooden pick inserted in center comes out clean. Cool in pans on lightly greased wire racks 5 minutes. Remove from pans to wire racks.
5. While cakes are baking, bring brown sugar and next 2 ingredients to a boil in a heavy saucepan over medium-high heat. Boil, stirring constantly, 3 minutes or until mixture begins to thicken to a syrup-like consistency. Remove from heat; stir in reserved rum.
6. Pierce tops of cakes multiple times using a wooden pick. Dip top halves of cakes in glaze, and hold 1 to 2 seconds (to allow glaze to soak into cakes). Place, glazed sides up, on lightly greased racks. Sprinkle each cake with pecans.
NOTE: To puree roasted sweet potatoes, peel potatoes as soon as they are slightly cooled. Press pulp through a wire-mesh strainer with the back of a spoon. You'll need to roast about 1½ lb. potatoes for 2 cups puree.

BROUGHT TO THE TABLE BY SHERI CASTLE (ADAPTED FROM *THE NEW SOUTHERN GARDEN COOKBOOK*).

Brown Sugar-Bourbon Bundt

make-ahead • party perfect

MAKES: 12 servings
HANDS-ON TIME: 20 min.
TOTAL TIME: 2 hr., 35 min.
(Pictured on page 1)

- 1 cup butter, softened
- ½ cup shortening
- 1 (16-oz.) package light brown sugar
- 5 large eggs
- 1 (5-oz.) can evaporated milk
- ½ cup bourbon
- 3 cups all-purpose flour
- ½ tsp. baking powder
- ½ tsp. salt
- 1 Tbsp. vanilla bean paste
- 2 Tbsp. powdered sugar
  Garnishes: candied oranges, magnolia leaves

1. Preheat oven to 325°. Beat butter and shortening at medium speed with a heavy-duty electric stand mixer until creamy. Gradually add brown sugar, beating at medium speed until light and creamy. Add eggs, 1 at a time, beating just until blended after each addition.
2. Stir together evaporated milk and bourbon in a bowl. Stir together flour, baking powder, and salt in another bowl. Add flour mixture to butter mixture alternately with milk mixture, beginning and ending with flour mixture. Beat at low speed just until blended after each addition. Stir in vanilla bean paste. Pour batter into a greased and floured 10-inch (12-cup) Bundt pan.
3. Bake at 325° for 1 hour and 5 minutes to 1 hour and 10 minutes or until a long wooden pick inserted in center comes out clean. Cool in pan on a wire rack 10 to 15 minutes; remove from pan to wire rack. Cool completely (about 1 hour). Dust top lightly with powdered sugar.

Southern Thanksgiving

Robert E. Lee Bundt

make-ahead • party perfect

MAKES: 12 servings
HANDS-ON TIME: 20 min.
TOTAL TIME: 2 hr., 35 min.

1 cup butter, softened
½ cup shortening
3 cups granulated sugar
6 large eggs
3 cups all-purpose flour
½ tsp. baking powder
⅛ tsp. salt
1 cup milk
4 tsp. orange zest, divided
2 tsp. lemon zest, divided
¼ cup fresh lemon juice
2 cups powdered sugar
2 to 3 Tbsp. fresh orange juice
Garnishes: fresh raspberries, gold-gilded cranberries and gooseberries, fresh mint sprigs

1. Preheat oven to 325°. Beat butter and shortening at medium speed with a heavy-duty electric stand mixer until creamy. Gradually add granulated sugar, beating at medium speed until light and fluffy. Add eggs, 1 at a time, beating just until blended after each addition.

2. Stir together flour, baking powder, and salt. Add to butter mixture alternately with milk, beginning and ending with flour mixture. Beat at low speed just until blended after each addition. Stir in 2 tsp. orange zest, 1 tsp. lemon zest, and ¼ cup fresh lemon juice. Pour batter into a greased and floured 10-inch (12-cup) Bundt pan.

3. Bake at 325° for 1 hour and 5 minutes to 1 hour and 15 minutes or until a long wooden pick inserted in center comes out clean. Cool in pan on a wire rack 10 minutes; remove from pan to wire rack, and cool completely (about 1 hour).

4. Whisk together powdered sugar, orange juice, and remaining 2 tsp. orange zest and 1 tsp. lemon zest until smooth. Spoon mixture over cake.

Tennessee Jam Bundt

make-ahead • party perfect

MAKES: 12 servings
HANDS-ON TIME: 30 min.
TOTAL TIME: 4 hr., 30 min.

CAKE

1½ cups chopped pecans
1½ cups granulated sugar
1 cup butter, softened
4 large eggs
3 cups all-purpose flour
2 Tbsp. unsweetened cocoa
1 tsp. ground cinnamon
½ tsp. salt
½ tsp. ground allspice
¼ tsp. ground nutmeg
1 cup buttermilk
1 tsp. baking soda
1½ cups seedless blackberry jam
2 tsp. vanilla extract
Shortening

CARAMEL FROSTING

½ cup firmly packed dark brown sugar
¼ cup whipping cream
¼ cup butter
1 tsp. vanilla extract
1¼ cups powdered sugar

GARNISHES

Fresh mint, blackberries

1. Prepare Cake: Preheat oven to 350°. Bake pecans in a single layer in a shallow pan 8 to 10 minutes or until toasted and fragrant, stirring halfway through. Cool completely in pan on a wire rack (about 30 minutes). Reduce oven temperature to 325°.

2. Beat granulated sugar and 1 cup butter at medium speed with a heavy-duty electric stand mixer until light and fluffy. Add eggs, 1 at a time, beating just until blended after each addition.

3. Stir together flour and next 5 ingredients. Stir together buttermilk and baking soda. Add flour mixture to butter mixture alternately with buttermilk mixture, beginning and ending with flour mixture. Beat at low speed just until blended after each addition. Add jam and vanilla, and beat just until blended. Stir in toasted pecans. Grease (with shortening) and flour a 10-inch (12-cup) Bundt pan. Pour batter into prepared pan.

4. Bake at 325° for 1 hour to 1 hour and 15 minutes or until a long wooden pick inserted in center comes out clean. Cool cake in pan on a wire rack 20 minutes; remove from pan to wire rack, and cool completely (about 2 hours).

5. Prepare Frosting: Bring brown sugar and next 2 ingredients to a boil in a 2-qt. saucepan over medium heat, whisking constantly; boil, whisking constantly, 1 minute. Remove from heat; stir in vanilla. Gradually whisk in powdered sugar until smooth. Gently stir 3 to 5 minutes or until mixture begins to cool and thicken. Immediately pour frosting over cooled cake.

Southern Thanksgiving

Cranberry-Apple-Pumpkin Bundt

party perfect

MAKES: 12 servings
HANDS-ON TIME: 30 min.
TOTAL TIME: 4 hr., 30 min., including Sugared Pecans and Pepitas and glaze

- ¾ **cup finely chopped pecans**
- 1½ **cups peeled and diced Granny Smith apple**
- 2 **Tbsp. butter, melted**
- ½ **cup finely chopped sweetened dried cranberries**
- ½ **cup firmly packed light brown sugar**
- 3 **Tbsp. all-purpose flour**
- 2 **cups granulated sugar**
- 1 **cup butter, softened**
- 4 **large eggs**
- 1 **(15-oz.) can pumpkin**
- 1 **Tbsp. vanilla extract**
- 3 **cups all-purpose flour**
- 2 **tsp. baking powder**
- 2 **tsp. pumpkin pie spice**
- ½ **tsp. baking soda**
  Sugared Pecans and Pepitas
  Maple Glaze

1. Preheat oven to 350°. Bake pecans in a single layer in a shallow pan 6 to 8 minutes or until toasted, stirring halfway through. Cool 15 minutes. Reduce oven temperature to 325°.
2. Toss diced apples in 2 Tbsp. melted butter to coat in a medium bowl; add cranberries, next 2 ingredients, and toasted pecans, and toss until well blended.
3. Beat granulated sugar and 1 cup butter at medium speed with an electric mixer until light and fluffy. Add eggs, 1 at a time, beating just until blended after each addition. Add pumpkin and vanilla; beat just until blended.

4. Stir together 3 cups flour and next 3 ingredients. Gradually add flour mixture to butter mixture, beating at low speed just until blended after each addition. Spoon half of batter into a greased and floured 10-inch (12-cup) Bundt pan. Spoon apple mixture over batter, leaving a ½-inch border around outer edge. Spoon remaining batter over apple mixture.
5. Bake at 325° for 1 hour and 10 minutes to 1 hour and 20 minutes or until a long wooden pick inserted in center of cake comes out clean. Cool in pan on a wire rack 15 minutes. Remove from pan to wire rack; cool completely (about 2 hours).
6. Meanwhile, prepare Sugared Pecans and Pepitas.
7. Prepare Maple Glaze; immediately spoon onto cooled cake. Arrange pecans and pepitas on cake.

Sugared Pecans and Pepitas

1. Preheat oven to 350°. Stir together 1 cup pecan halves and pieces; ½ cup roasted, salted shelled pepitas (pumpkin seeds); and 2 Tbsp. butter, melted. Spread in a single layer in a 13- x 9-inch pan. Bake 12 to 15 minutes or until toasted and fragrant, stirring halfway through. Remove from oven; toss with 2 Tbsp. sugar. Cool completely in pan on a wire rack (about 30 minutes). Makes: 1½ cups.

Maple Glaze

1. Bring ½ cup pure maple syrup, 2 Tbsp. butter, and 1 Tbsp. milk to a boil in a small saucepan over medium-high heat, stirring constantly; boil, stirring constantly, 2 minutes. Remove from heat; whisk in 1 tsp. vanilla extract. Gradually whisk in 1 cup powdered sugar until smooth; stir gently 3 to 5 minutes or until mixture begins to thicken and cool slightly. Use immediately. Makes: about 1 cup.

Ambrosia Chess Tarts

MAKES: 14 tarts
HANDS-ON TIME: 30 min.
TOTAL TIME: 2 hr., 20 min.

- 2 **(14.1-oz.) packages refrigerated piecrusts***
- 1½ **cups sugar**
- 1 **Tbsp. all-purpose flour**
- 1 **Tbsp. plain white cornmeal**
- ½ **tsp. salt**
- 4 **large eggs**
- ½ **cup cream of coconut**
- ⅓ **cup butter, melted**
- ¼ **cup fresh lemon juice**
- 1 **cup sweetened flaked coconut**
- 1 **(8-oz.) can crushed pineapple**
- 2 **Tbsp. orange zest**
  Toppings: toasted coconut, sweetened whipped cream, orange sections, fresh rosemary sprigs

1. Preheat oven to 450°. Cut piecrusts into 14 (4½-inch) rounds. Press each dough round into a lightly greased 3½-inch brioche mold, pressing up sides. Fold dough over edge of molds, and pinch to secure. Arrange molds on a baking sheet. Bake 7 to 8 minutes or until lightly browned. Cool completely on baking sheet on a wire rack (about 30 minutes). Reduce oven temperature to 350°.
2. Meanwhile, whisk together sugar and next 3 ingredients in a large bowl; add eggs and next 3 ingredients, and whisk until blended. Stir in coconut and next 2 ingredients. Spoon coconut mixture into cooled pastry shells, filling almost full.
3. Bake at 350° for 22 to 25 minutes or until golden brown and center of tarts is almost set. (Filling will continue to cook as it cools.) Cool tarts completely on baking sheet on wire rack (about 1 hour). Loosen tarts from molds using a small knife; remove tarts from molds. Serve with desired toppings.
*2 (8- or 10-oz.) packages frozen tart shells may be substituted. Bake as directed in Step 1.

Southern Thanksgiving

Chocolate-Caramel Pecan Pie

make-ahead • party perfect

MAKES: 6 to 8 servings
HANDS-ON TIME: 20 min.
TOTAL TIME: 4 hr., 25 min.

- 1½ **cups pecan halves and pieces**
- 1 **(14.1-oz.) package refrigerated piecrusts**
- 1 **cup semisweet chocolate morsels**
- ½ **cup whipping cream, divided**
- 1 **(8-oz.) package cream cheese, softened**
- 1 **cup sugar, divided**
- 1 **large egg**
- 28 **caramels**
- ¼ **cup butter**
- 2 **large eggs**
- 1 **tsp. vanilla extract**
- ¼ **tsp. salt**

1. Preheat oven to 350°. Bake pecans in a single layer in a shallow pan 8 to 10 minutes or until toasted, stirring halfway through. Cool completely on a wire rack (about 30 minutes). Increase oven temperature to 425°.
2. Unroll piecrusts; stack on a lightly floured surface. Roll stacked piecrusts into a 12-inch circle. Fit piecrust into a 10-inch deep-dish tart pan with removable bottom; press into fluted edges. Trim off excess crust along edges. Line piecrust with aluminum foil or parchment paper, and fill with pie weights or dried beans. Place pan on a foil-lined baking sheet.
3. Bake at 425° for 12 minutes. Remove weights and foil, and bake 4 more minutes. Cool completely on baking sheet on a wire rack (about 15 minutes). Reduce oven temperature to 350°.
4. Microwave chocolate morsels and ¼ cup cream in a microwave-safe bowl at HIGH 1 minute or until melted and smooth, stirring at 30-second intervals.
5. Beat cream cheese and ¼ cup sugar at medium speed with an electric mixer

1 to 2 minutes or until smooth. Add 1 egg, beating at low speed just until blended. Add chocolate mixture, beating just until blended. Spoon batter into prepared crust.
6. Microwave caramels, butter, and remaining ¼ cup cream in a large microwave-safe bowl at HIGH 1 to 2 minutes or until smooth, stirring at 30-second intervals. Whisk together 2 eggs, vanilla, salt, and remaining ¾ cup sugar; whisk into caramel mixture until blended. Stir in pecans; spoon over chocolate mixture in prepared crust.
7. Bake at 350° for 55 minutes to 1 hour and 5 minutes or until center is almost set, shielding edges with aluminum foil after 45 minutes to prevent excessive browning. Cool completely on a wire rack (about 2 hours).

Black Bottom Pumpkin Pie

make-ahead • party perfect

MAKES: 6 to 8 servings
HANDS-ON TIME: 30 min.
TOTAL TIME: 10 hr., 20 min.
(Pictured on page 1)

- ½ **cup chopped pecans**
- 1 **cup cinnamon graham cracker crumbs**
- 1 **cup crushed gingersnaps**
- ½ **cup butter, melted**
- 1 **cup semisweet chocolate morsels**
- 2 **cups whipping cream, divided**
- 2 **(1.4-oz.) chocolate-covered toffee candy bars, finely chopped**
- ¾ **cup sugar**
- ⅓ **cup all-purpose flour**
- 2 **large eggs**
- 4 **egg yolks**
- 2 **cups milk**
- 1 **cup canned pumpkin**
- 1 **Tbsp. vanilla bean paste***
- ½ **cup maple syrup**
  Garnish: semisweet chocolate shavings

1. Preheat oven to 350°. Bake pecans in a single layer in a shallow pan 8 to 10 minutes or until toasted and fragrant, stirring halfway through. Cool 10 minutes.
2. Stir together graham cracker crumbs, next 2 ingredients, and toasted pecans until blended. Press crumb mixture on bottom, up sides, and onto lip of a lightly greased 10-inch pie plate.
3. Bake at 350° for 10 to 12 minutes or until lightly browned. Transfer to a wire rack, and cool completely (about 30 minutes).
4. Microwave 1 cup semisweet chocolate morsels and ½ cup whipping cream in a small microwave-safe bowl at HIGH 1 minute or until melted, stirring at 30-second intervals. Spoon chocolate mixture over bottom of pie crust; sprinkle candy bars over chocolate mixture. Cover and chill 1 hour or until chocolate mixture is set.
5. Meanwhile, whisk together sugar and flour in a heavy 3-qt. saucepan; add eggs, egg yolks, and milk, and whisk until blended. Cook over medium heat, whisking constantly, 8 to 10 minutes or until a pudding-like thickness. (Mixture will just begin to bubble and will hold soft peaks when whisk is lifted.) Remove from heat, and whisk in pumpkin and vanilla bean paste. Transfer to a bowl. Place heavy-duty plastic wrap directly on warm filling (to prevent a film from forming); chill 30 minutes. Spoon pumpkin mixture over chocolate; cover and chill 8 to 24 hours or until filling is firm.
6. Beat remaining 1½ cups cream at high speed with an electric mixer until foamy; gradually add syrup, beating until soft peaks form. Spread or pipe over pie.
*Vanilla extract may be substituted.

Southern Thanksgiving

Cranberry-Apple Pie with Pecan Shortbread Crust

MAKES: 12 servings
HANDS-ON TIME: 30 min.
TOTAL TIME: 3 hr., 55 min.

CRUST

1	cup finely chopped pecans
1½	cups butter, softened
¾	cup powdered sugar
3	cups all-purpose flour

FILLING

3	lb. Gala apples
1	cup firmly packed light brown sugar
¾	cup sweetened dried cranberries
¼	cup all-purpose flour
1	tsp. ground cinnamon
2	Tbsp. butter, melted

GARNISHES

Toasted pecan halves, powdered sugar

1. Prepare Crust: Preheat oven to 350°. Bake pecans in a single layer in a shallow pan 4 to 5 minutes or until lightly toasted and fragrant, stirring halfway through. Cool completely (about 20 minutes).
2. Meanwhile, beat butter at medium speed with an electric mixer 1 minute or until creamy; add powdered sugar, beating well. Gradually add flour, beating at low speed until mixture is no longer crumbly and starts to come together into a ball. Stir in pecans. Shape one-third of dough into an 8-inch log; wrap in plastic wrap, and chill until ready to use. Press remaining dough on bottom and up sides of a 9-inch springform pan. Cover and chill crust.
3. Prepare Filling: Peel apples. Cut into ¼-inch-thick wedges. Toss together apples and next 4 ingredients. Spoon mixture into prepared crust. Drizzle with melted butter.
4. Cut reserved dough log into 8 (1-inch) pieces. Gently shape each piece into a 6- to 8-inch rope. Lightly press each rope to flatten into strips. Arrange strips in a lattice design over filling.
5. Bake at 350° for 1 hour to 1 hour and 10 minutes or until juices are thick and bubbly, crust is golden brown, and apples are tender when pierced with a long wooden pick, shielding with foil during last 30 minutes to prevent excessive browning. Cool completely in pan on a wire rack. Remove sides of pan.

White Chocolate-Cranberry Cheesecake

MAKES: 6 to 8 servings
HANDS-ON TIME: 35 min.
TOTAL TIME: 12 hr., 40 min.

CRANBERRY TOPPING

1	(12-oz.) package fresh cranberries
1	cup sugar
½	cup seedless raspberry jam

PIECRUST

1	(9-oz.) package chocolate wafer cookies
½	(4-oz.) semisweet chocolate baking bar, chopped
½	cup butter, melted
⅓	cup sugar

CHEESECAKE FILLING

1	(6-oz.) package white chocolate baking squares, chopped
¼	cup whipping cream
2	(8-oz.) packages cream cheese, softened
2	Tbsp. all-purpose flour
⅓	cup sugar
4	large eggs
½	cup chopped sweetened dried cranberries
½	(4-oz.) semisweet chocolate baking bar, finely chopped
¼	cup amaretto liqueur

GARNISH

Fresh mint leaves

1. Prepare Topping: Bring first 2 ingredients and ¼ cup water to a boil in a 3-qt. saucepan over medium-high heat, stirring often. Boil, stirring often, 6 to 8 minutes or until mixture thickens to a syrup-like consistency. Remove from heat, and stir in jam. Cool completely (about 1 hour). Cover and chill 8 hours.
2. Meanwhile, prepare Piecrust: Preheat oven to 350°. Pulse wafer cookies and chopped semisweet chocolate in a food processor 8 to 10 times or until mixture resembles fine crumbs. Stir together crumb mixture, melted butter, and ⅓ cup sugar; firmly press on bottom, up sides, and onto lip of a lightly greased 10-inch pie plate. Bake 10 minutes. Transfer to a wire rack, and cool completely (about 30 minutes). Reduce oven temperature to 325°.
3. Prepare Filling: Microwave white chocolate and whipping cream at MEDIUM (50% power) 1 to 1½ minutes or until melted and smooth, stirring at 30-second intervals.
4. Beat cream cheese, flour, and ⅓ cup sugar at medium speed with an electric mixer 1 minute or until creamy and smooth. Add eggs, 1 at a time, beating just until blended after each addition. Add cranberries, next 2 ingredients, and white chocolate mixture. Beat at low speed just until blended. Spoon batter into prepared crust.
5. Bake at 325° for 30 to 35 minutes or until set. Cool completely on a wire rack (about 2 hours). Cover and chill 8 hours. Spoon topping over pie before serving.

Rethink Your Leftovers

Hold the mayo! We upgraded the iconic day-after sandwich with better spreads and breads.

IF YOU HAVE LEFTOVER SMOKED TURKEY...

Smoked Turkey-Blue Cheese Open-faced Sandwiches

quick prep • good for you • party perfect

1. Spread desired amount of fig paste on 12 (¼-inch-thick) toasted ciabatta or French bread slices; top with smoked turkey slices and soft-ripened blue-veined Brie. Place on a parchment paper-lined baking sheet. Bake at 425° for 8 minutes. Remove from oven. Top with arugula, and sprinkle with pepper just before serving.

IF YOU HAVE LEFTOVER GREEN-BEAN CASSEROLE...

Green-Bean-Casserole Sandwich

quick prep • party perfect

1. Spread butter on 1 side of 2 small pumpernickel party rye bread slices. Place 1 slice, buttered side down, on wax paper; top with 1 heaping tablespoonful green bean casserole and 1 shaved Parmesan cheese slice. Top with remaining bread slice, buttered side up. Cook in a nonstick skillet over medium heat 2 to 3 minutes on each side or until golden brown and cheese is melted.

IF YOU HAVE LEFTOVER SWEET POTATOES...

Open-faced Sweet Potato-Mushroom Sandwiches

quick prep • party perfect

1. Stir together 1 cup mashed sweet potatoes, 3 oz. crumbled goat cheese, and ½ tsp. ground chipotle chile pepper. Spread mixture on 12 (3-inch) square toasted rye bread slices. Cook 3 thick bacon slices in a skillet over medium heat 4 to 5 minutes or until crisp; remove bacon. Drain on paper towels, reserving 1 Tbsp. drippings in skillet. Crumble bacon. Sauté ½ cup sliced sweet onion in hot drippings until caramelized. Add 5 oz. sliced shiitake mushrooms and ½ tsp. chopped fresh thyme; sauté 2 minutes. Stir in bacon; spoon over sweet potato mixture. Place sandwiches on a baking sheet. Bake at 425° for 8 minutes. Top with fresh thyme sprigs.

IF YOU HAVE LEFTOVER ROASTED TURKEY...

Turkey-and-Spinach Wraps with Cranberry-Walnut-Cream Cheese Spread

quick prep • good for you • make-ahead • party perfect

1. Stir together 1 (8-oz.) package cream cheese, softened; 2 (4-oz.) packages goat cheese, softened; ¾ cup sweetened dried cranberries, coarsely chopped; ¼ cup chopped toasted walnuts; 2 tsp. honey; 1 garlic clove, minced; ½ tsp. chopped fresh rosemary; and ¼ tsp. pepper. Season with salt. Cover and chill up to 3 days. Spread 2 Tbsp. cream cheese mixture onto each of 8 (10-inch) flour tortillas, leaving a ½-inch border around edges. Divide 1 lb. thinly sliced turkey and 4 cups fresh baby spinach among tortillas. Roll up, and cut in half or into slices.

IF YOU HAVE LEFTOVER BAKED HAM...

Ham Waldorf Salad

quick prep • good for you • party perfect

1. Stir together 3 cups chopped cooked ham; 1 cup seedless red grapes, halved; 1 large Gala apple, diced; 1 cup diced celery; ½ cup chopped toasted walnuts; ½ cup mayonnaise; 2 Tbsp. chopped fresh flat-leaf parsley; 3 Tbsp. honey mustard; 2 green onions, chopped; and salt and pepper to taste in a large bowl. Serve in mini pita halves with fresh arugula. Makes: about 6 cups.

Slow It Down

We like to take our sweet time with things down here—we speak with a *drawwwl,* for goodness sake. So we developed slow-cooker suppers that you can leave simmering all day long.

Southern Thanksgiving

Spiced Beef Stew with Sweet Potatoes

make-ahead • party perfect

MAKES: 8 servings
HANDS-ON TIME: 50 min.
TOTAL TIME: 6 hr., 50 min.

- 1 (6-oz.) can tomato paste
- 1 (32-oz.) container beef broth
- 1 (3-lb.) boneless chuck roast, trimmed and cut into 1½-inch cubes
- 3 Tbsp. all-purpose flour
- 1½ tsp. salt
- 1 tsp. freshly ground pepper
- 2 Tbsp. olive oil
- 2 lb. small sweet potatoes, peeled and cubed
- 2 sweet onions, cut into eighths
- 2 cups cubed butternut squash (about 1 lb.)
- 2 cups frozen whole kernel corn, thawed
- 2 celery ribs, sliced
- 4 garlic cloves, minced
- 2 tsp. ancho chile powder
- 1 tsp. smoked paprika
- 1 tsp. dried thyme

1. Whisk together first 2 ingredients until smooth.
2. Sprinkle beef with flour, salt, and pepper; toss to coat.
3. Cook beef, in batches, in hot oil in a large skillet over medium-high heat, stirring occasionally, 10 to 12 minutes or until browned. Place in a 6-qt. slow cooker. Add sweet potatoes, next 8 ingredients, and broth mixture. Cover and cook on HIGH 6 to 7 hours or until tender.

SERVE WITH: HERBED BISCUITS
Preheat oven to 425°. Cut ½ cup cold butter, cubed, into 2 cups self-rising flour with a pastry blender or fork until mixture resembles small peas. Add 2 Tbsp. each chopped fresh chives and basil and 1 tsp. freshly ground pepper. Add 1 cup buttermilk, stirring just until dry ingredients are moistened. Turn dough out onto a lightly floured surface, and knead lightly 3 or 4 times. Pat or roll dough to ¾-inch thickness; cut into squares to form 15 biscuits. Place on a parchment paper-lined baking sheet. Bake 15 minutes or until golden. Makes: 15 biscuits.

Chicken and Cornbread Dumplings

make-ahead • party perfect

MAKES: 8 servings
HANDS-ON TIME: 30 min.
TOTAL TIME: 5 hr., 40 min.

CHICKEN
- 3 skinned, bone-in chicken breasts (about 1½ lb.)
- 6 skinned and boned chicken thighs (about 1 lb.)
- 1 tsp. salt
- ½ tsp. freshly ground pepper
- ½ tsp. poultry seasoning
- ½ lb. carrots, sliced
- ½ lb. parsnips, sliced
- 4 celery ribs, sliced
- 1 sweet onion, chopped
- 2 (10¾-oz.) cans cream of chicken soup
- 1 (32-oz.) container chicken broth

CORNBREAD DUMPLINGS
- 1½ cups all-purpose flour
- ½ cup self-rising yellow cornmeal
- 2 tsp. baking powder
- ½ tsp. salt
- 1 cup milk
- 3 Tbsp. butter, melted
- ¼ tsp. dried thyme
- 2 tsp. chopped fresh flat-leaf parsley

1. Prepare Chicken: Rub chicken pieces with salt, pepper, and poultry seasoning. Place breasts in a 6-qt. slow cooker; top with thighs. Add carrots and next 3 ingredients. Whisk together soup and broth until smooth. Pour soup mixture over vegetables. Cover and cook on HIGH 3½ hours or until chicken shreds easily with a fork. Remove chicken; cool 10 minutes. Bone and shred chicken. Stir chicken into soup-and-vegetable mixture. Cover and cook on HIGH 1 hour or until boiling.
2. Meanwhile, prepare Dumplings: Whisk together flour and next 3 ingredients. Make a well in center of mixture. Add milk, butter, thyme, and parsley to dry ingredients, gently stirring just until moistened.
3. Drop dough by ¼ cupfuls into simmering chicken mixture, leaving about ¼-inch space between dumplings. Cover and cook on HIGH 30 to 35 minutes or until dumplings have doubled in size.

SERVE WITH: STRAWBERRY SALAD
Toss together 1 (6-oz.) package fresh baby spinach; 2 cups quartered strawberries; 1¼ cups crumbled feta cheese; ¼ red onion, thinly sliced; ½ cup bottled vinaigrette; and ¼ cup sliced toasted almonds. Makes: 8 servings.

Southern Thanksgiving

Chicken-and-Squash Casserole

make-ahead • party perfect

MAKES: 6 servings
HANDS-ON TIME: 25 min.
TOTAL TIME: 5 hr., 5 min.

- 2 lb. yellow squash, sliced
- 1 lb. zucchini, sliced
- 1 large onion, chopped
- 1 tsp. salt
- ½ tsp. pepper
- 1 (14.5-oz.) can diced tomatoes
- 4 cups chopped cooked chicken
- 1 (10¾-oz.) can cream of chicken soup
- 1 (8-oz.) container sour cream
- ⅓ cup chopped fresh basil
- 2 garlic cloves, minced
- 2 cups soft, fresh breadcrumbs
- 3 cups (12 oz.) shredded sharp Cheddar cheese
- ⅓ cup (1½ oz.) shredded Parmesan cheese

1. Place first 3 ingredients in a large microwave-safe bowl. Cover tightly with plastic wrap, folding back a small edge to allow steam to escape. Microwave at HIGH 8 minutes or until squash is tender; drain. Sprinkle with salt and pepper.
2. Drain tomatoes well, pressing between paper towels. Stir together tomatoes, chicken, and next 4 ingredients. Layer one-third each soup mixture, squash mixture, breadcrumbs, and Cheddar cheese in a lightly greased 6-qt. slow cooker. Repeat layers twice. Top with Parmesan cheese.
3. Cover and cook on HIGH 4 hours or until bubbly and edges are golden. Uncover and cook on HIGH 30 minutes. Let stand 10 minutes before serving.

SERVE WITH: ARUGULA-APPLE SALAD
Whisk together ¼ cup each olive oil, fresh lime juice, and red pepper jelly; 1 tsp. each minced garlic and grated fresh ginger; and ½ tsp. salt. Combine 1 (5-oz.) package arugula and 1 cup each sliced apple and cucumber. Add ⅓ cup each sugared pecans and shaved Parmesan cheese. Drizzle with olive oil mixture before serving. Makes: 6 servings.

Good Luck Greens and Peas with Ham

good for you • make-ahead • party perfect

MAKES: 8 servings
HANDS-ON TIME: 15 min.
TOTAL TIME: 7 hr., 15 min.

- 1 (32-oz.) container vegetable broth
- 1 (16-oz.) package frozen black-eyed peas, thawed
- 1 sweet onion, cut into eighths
- ¼ cup apple cider vinegar
- ¼ tsp. dried crushed red pepper
- 2 Tbsp. dark brown sugar
- 2 Tbsp. country-style Dijon mustard
- 1 (5- to 6-lb.) smoked, fully cooked semiboneless ham
- 1 (1-lb.) package shredded fresh collard greens

1. Place first 5 ingredients in a 6-qt. slow cooker. Stir together brown sugar and mustard; rub mixture over ham. Place ham in slow cooker. Cover and cook on HIGH 6 to 7 hours or until ham is tender.
2. Uncover and add collard greens. Cover and cook on HIGH 1 hour or until tender. Slice ham, and serve with greens mixture.

SERVE WITH: CHEESY CORNBREAD
Preheat oven to 450°. Coat bottom and sides of an 8-inch cast-iron skillet with 3 tsp. vegetable oil; heat in oven 5 minutes. Whisk together 2 cups buttermilk, 1 large egg, 2 cups shredded sharp Cheddar cheese, and 1¾ cups self-rising yellow cornmeal. Pour into hot skillet. Bake 25 minutes. Makes: 8 servings.

Shrimp-and-Sausage Gumbo

make-ahead • party perfect

MAKES: 6 servings
HANDS-ON TIME: 35 min.
TOTAL TIME: 6 hr., 25 min.

- ½ cup all-purpose flour
- 1 lb. andouille sausage, sliced
- 1 (14.5-oz.) can diced tomatoes
- 1 large onion, chopped
- 1 large green bell pepper, chopped
- 2 celery ribs, chopped
- 4 garlic cloves, chopped
- 3 bay leaves
- 2 tsp. Creole seasoning
- ½ tsp. dried thyme
- 4 cups chicken broth
- 3 lb. unpeeled, large raw shrimp, peeled and deveined
- 1 bunch green onions, sliced
- ¼ cup chopped fresh flat-leaf parsley
  Garnish: sliced green onions

1. Preheat oven to 400°. Sprinkle flour in a 9-inch cast-iron skillet. Bake 10 to 15 minutes or until golden brown, stirring once. Cool 10 minutes.
2. Meanwhile, cook sausage in a Dutch oven over medium heat, stirring occasionally, 5 minutes or until browned. Drain on paper towels. Place sausage in a 6-qt. slow cooker; add tomatoes and next 7 ingredients.
3. Whisk together browned flour and broth until smooth. Pour into slow cooker. Cover and cook on HIGH 5 to 6 hours. Stir in shrimp, green onions, and parsley. Cover and cook on HIGH 30 minutes, stirring once. Discard bay leaves before serving.

SERVE WITH: HERBED RICE
Stir together 3 cups hot cooked rice and ¼ cup chopped fresh flat-leaf parsley. Makes: 6 servings.

Host a Grits Bar Brunch

Come Sunday morn, serve up any of our basic grits recipes (don't miss the grits waffles) with decadent toppings.

START WITH
Slow-Cooker Grits

MAKES: 8 servings
HANDS-ON TIME: 10 min.
TOTAL TIME: 10 hr., 10 min.

Simplify your morning: Soak the grits the night before.

- 2 **cups uncooked stone-ground grits**
- ¼ **cup heavy cream**
- 2 **Tbsp. butter**
- 1½ **tsp. salt**
- ½ **tsp. pepper**

1. Stir together grits and 6 cups water in a 5- or 6-qt. slow cooker. Let stand 1 to 2 minutes, allowing grits to settle to bottom. Tilt slow cooker slightly, and skim off solids using a fine wire-mesh strainer. Cover and soak 8 hours or overnight.
2. Cover and cook grits on HIGH 2 hours to 2 hours and 30 minutes, stirring halfway through. Stir in cream and remaining ingredients. Serve with desired toppings.

TRY THIS TWIST!
Slow-Cooker Cheese Grits: Prepare recipe as directed, stirring in 1 cup (4 oz.) shredded sharp Cheddar cheese and ½ cup freshly grated Parmesan cheese with cream until melted.

GREAT GRITS COMBOS

Boiled Shrimp + Easy Creole Sauce

Bourbon Mushrooms + Spinach + Swiss + Bacon

Chopped Ham + Shredded Cheddar

Caramelized Onions + Shredded Smoked Gruyère

Shredded Barbecued Pork + BBQ Sauce + Sautéed Spinach

CREATE A GRITS BAR

Offer these toppings with a few staples. (See our favorite flavor combos above.)

Bourbon Mushrooms

1. Melt ¼ cup butter with ¼ cup olive oil in a large skillet over medium heat; add 2 lb. sliced assorted fresh mushrooms, ¾ tsp. salt, and ¼ tsp. pepper. Cook, stirring occasionally, 12 to 15 minutes or until tender and almost all liquid has evaporated. Remove from heat. Stir in ½ cup bourbon or chicken broth; return to heat, and cook 2 to 3 minutes or until slightly thickened. Reduce heat to low; stir in 3 garlic cloves, minced; 2 Tbsp. chopped fresh parsley; and 1 Tbsp. chopped fresh thyme. Cook 1 more minute. Makes: 8 to 10 servings.

Easy Creole Sauce

Prepare up to 2 days ahead.
1. Sauté 2 celery ribs, chopped, in 2 Tbsp. olive oil in a saucepan over medium heat 3 to 4 minutes until tender. Stir in 2 (14.5-oz.) cans diced tomatoes with green peppers and onion; 3 garlic cloves, minced; 2 tsp. Creole seasoning; and 1 tsp. sugar. Reduce heat to low; simmer, stirring occasionally, 20 minutes. Stir in 2 Tbsp. chopped fresh flat-leaf parsley; 2 green onions, thinly sliced; and 1 tsp. hot sauce. Store in refrigerator up to 2 days. Makes: 3 cups.

WASH IT DOWN
Bloody Mary Punch
quick prep • party perfect

1. Combine 1 (46-oz.) container low-sodium vegetable juice, chilled; 1 Tbsp. freshly ground pepper; 3 Tbsp. fresh lime juice; 1 Tbsp. hot sauce; 1 Tbsp. Worcestershire sauce; ½ tsp. Old Bay seasoning; and, if desired, ½ cup vodka, chilled, in a punch bowl or pitcher. Rim glasses in salt and pepper, if desired. Serve punch over ice with any garnish such as celery, lemon wheels, and pickled okra. Makes: 1½ qt.

Georgia Grits Waffles
party perfect

MAKES: 8 servings
HANDS-ON TIME: 25 min.
TOTAL TIME: 50 min., not including toppings

Serve with Vanilla Crème Anglaise and Maple-Bacon Praline Syrup. (see recipes, page 284)

- ½ **cup uncooked regular grits**
- 6 **Tbsp. cold unsalted butter, cubed**
- ¾ **cup buttermilk**
- 2 **large eggs, lightly beaten**
- 1¼ **cups all-purpose flour**
- 1 **Tbsp. sugar**
- 2 **tsp. baking powder**
- ½ **tsp. baking soda**

1. Bring 2 cups water to a boil over medium-high heat in a medium saucepan. Whisk in grits; bring to a boil. Reduce heat to low; cook, stirring often, 15 minutes or until tender. Stir in butter until melted; cool to room temperature. Stir in buttermilk and eggs.
2. Whisk together flour and next 3 ingredients in a small bowl. Stir flour mixture into grits mixture until just combined.
3. Cook in a preheated, oiled waffle iron until golden (about ⅓ cup batter each).

BROUGHT TO THE TABLE BY COOKBOOK AUTHOR CONSTANCE SNOW (ADAPTED FROM *THE RUSTIC TABLE COOKBOOK*).

Vanilla Crème Anglaise

quick prep • party perfect

MAKES: 1 cup
HANDS-ON TIME: 20 min.
TOTAL TIME: 20 min.

½ cup 2% reduced-fat milk
½ cup heavy cream
3 egg yolks
¼ cup sugar
   Pinch of kosher salt
½ tsp. vanilla extract

1. Heat milk and cream in a heavy saucepan over medium-low heat just until bubbles and steam appear (do not boil).
2. Reduce heat to low. Whisk together egg yolks, sugar, and salt in a bowl; gradually whisk in one-fourth of hot milk mixture. Gradually add warm egg mixture to remaining hot milk mixture, whisking constantly; cook, whisking constantly, 7 minutes or until mixture thinly coats the back of a wooden spoon. Remove from heat. Whisk in vanilla.
3. Pour through a fine wire-mesh strainer into a bowl. Serve warm.

BROUGHT TO THE TABLE BY BLOGGER NEALEY DOZIER
(DIXIECAVIAR.COM).

Maple-Bacon Praline Syrup

1. Cook ½ cup butter, ½ cup chopped pecans, ½ cup pure maple syrup, and 2 thick hickory-smoked bacon slices, cooked and crumbled, in a saucepan over medium-low heat, stirring often, 5 minutes or until blended and sugar dissolves.

Reach for an Heirloom Recipe

We all have a cherished family recipe, each stain representing a story. For author Whitney Miller, that recipe was scribbled in the back of a church cookbook 100 years ago, and it's steeped in history.

Grandma's Tea Cakes

make-ahead • party perfect

MAKES: about 6 dozen
HANDS-ON TIME: 30 min.
TOTAL TIME: 1 hr., 35 min.

1 cup butter, softened
1¼ cups sugar
¾ cup cane syrup
1 Tbsp. vanilla extract
1½ tsp. fresh lemon juice
3 large eggs
4½ cups self-rising flour
   Parchment paper

1. Preheat oven to 350°. Beat butter and sugar at medium speed with an electric mixer until creamy. Add cane syrup and next 2 ingredients, beating just until blended. Add eggs, 1 at a time, beating just until blended after each addition. Gradually add flour, beating at low speed just until blended after each addition. Drop dough by rounded spoonfuls 2 inches apart onto parchment paper-lined baking sheets, using a small cookie scoop (about 1¼ inches).
2. Bake at 350° for 8 to 10 minutes or just until edges begin to turn golden brown. Cool on baking sheets on wire racks 1 minute; transfer to wire racks. Cool completely (about 15 minutes). Store in airtight containers 1 week.

WHITNEY MILLER IS THE FIRST WINNER (SEASON ONE)
OF *MASTERCHEF* AND AUTHOR OF THE COOKBOOK
MODERN HOSPITALITY: SIMPLE RECIPES WITH SOUTHERN CHARM.

Try These Twists!

PECAN TEA CAKES: Stir 1½ cups chopped toasted pecans into dough after adding flour in Step 1.

SNICKERDOODLE TEA CAKES: Stir 1½ tsp. ground cinnamon into flour before adding to butter mixture in Step 1. Stir together ⅔ cup sugar and 1 Tbsp. ground cinnamon in a shallow dish or pie plate; drop spoonfuls of dough into cinnamon-and-sugar mixture before placing on parchment paper-lined baking sheets. Bake as directed.

FOOD GIFT OF THE MONTH

Try a Sweet Send-off

Because a good Southerner doesn't let guests leave empty-handed.

Chocolate-Pecan Pie Granola

make-ahead • party perfect

MAKES: 6 cups
HANDS-ON TIME: 10 min.
TOTAL TIME: 1 hr., 5 min.

- ½ **cup butter, melted**
- ½ **cup dark corn syrup**
- ¼ **cup firmly packed light brown sugar**
- 1 **tsp. vanilla extract**
- ⅛ **tsp. salt**
- 3 **cups uncooked regular oats**
- 1½ **cups coarsely chopped pecans**
- ½ **cup toasted wheat germ**
- 1½ **(4-oz.) semisweet chocolate baking bars, chopped**

1. Preheat oven to 325°. Stir together first 5 ingredients in a large bowl. Add oats, pecans, and wheat germ, stirring to coat. Spread mixture in a lightly greased 15- x 10-inch jelly-roll pan. Bake 25 to 30 minutes or until toasted, stirring every 10 minutes. Cool completely in pan on a wire rack (about 30 minutes). Stir in chocolate. Store in an airtight container at room temperature up to 3 days, or freeze up to 6 months.

Chocolate-Dipped Praline Pretzels

make-ahead • party perfect

MAKES: 16 pretzels
HANDS-ON TIME: 20 min.
TOTAL TIME: 1 hr., 5 min.

1. Preheat oven to 350°. Stir together 1½ cups coarsely chopped pecans, ¼ cup firmly packed light brown sugar, and 2 Tbsp. heavy cream. Spread in a single layer in a lightly buttered 9-inch round cake pan. Bake 20 minutes or until sugar is slightly crystallized, stirring once. Cool in pan 10 minutes; finely chop. Spread mixture in a single layer on wax paper. Place 2 (4-oz.) semisweet chocolate baking bars, chopped, in a microwave-safe measuring cup. Microwave at HIGH 1 minute or until melted, stirring every 15 seconds. Immediately dip two-thirds of each of 16 pretzel rods into chocolate, twirling to coat all sides. Roll coated ends of pretzels in pecan mixture. Gently place on wax paper; let stand until chocolate is set. Store in airtight containers 4 days.

Pumpkin Biscotti

good for you • make-ahead • party perfect

MAKES: about 30 pieces
HANDS-ON TIME: 20 min.
TOTAL TIME: 3 hr., 25 min.

- 1 **cup shelled, raw pumpkin seeds**
- 1 **cup sugar**
- 6 **Tbsp. butter, softened**
- 1 **cup canned pumpkin**
- 2 **large eggs**
- 3½ **cups all-purpose baking mix**
- 1 **Tbsp. pumpkin pie spice**

1. Preheat oven to 325°. Bake pumpkin seeds in a single layer in a shallow pan 8 to 10 minutes or until toasted and fragrant, stirring halfway through. Cool 10 minutes.

2. Meanwhile, beat sugar and butter at medium speed with an electric mixer until creamy. Stir in canned pumpkin. Add eggs, 1 at a time, beating until blended after each addition. Add baking mix and pumpkin pie spice, beating until blended.

3. Gently fold pumpkin seeds into sugar mixture. Cover and freeze 1 hour or until firm.

4. Divide dough in half. Shape each portion into a 12- x 3-inch slightly flattened log on a lightly greased baking sheet, using lightly floured hands.

5. Bake at 325° for 35 minutes or until firm. Transfer to wire racks; cool completely (about 1 hour). Cut each log diagonally into ¾-inch-thick slices with a serrated knife, using a gentle sawing motion. Place on greased baking sheets.

6. Bake at 325° for 20 minutes; turn cookies over, and bake 20 more minutes. Transfer to wire racks; cool completely (about 30 minutes). Store in airtight containers up to 4 days.

Take It!

Recycled cardboard soft drink containers make perfect car carriers for the ride home—just stash a cellophane-wrapped snack in each slot. We gave our container a coat of white spray paint, glued on scrap fabric, and affixed a custom "Happy Trails!" label to the front.

AND FOR A LITTLE SOMETHING SAVORY...

Barbecue Roasted Nuts

good for you • make-ahead • party perfect

MAKES: 6 cups
HANDS-ON TIME: 30 min.
TOTAL TIME: 2 hr., 5 min.

Two kinds of sugar sweeten this happy hour munchie. Buy shelled nuts to save time.

- 2   egg whites
- 2   lb. assorted whole, raw nuts, shelled
- 1   Tbsp. kosher salt
- 1   Tbsp. light brown sugar
- 2   tsp. smoked paprika
- 1½ tsp. granulated sugar
- ½   tsp. garlic powder
- ½   tsp. dry mustard
- ¼   tsp. ground cumin
- ¼   tsp. ground ginger

1. Preheat oven to 350°. Whisk egg whites in a large bowl until foamy. Toss nuts with whites. Stir together salt and next 7 ingredients; sprinkle over nuts, and toss to coat. Bake nuts in a single layer in a 17- x 11-inch jelly-roll pan 25 to 30 minutes or until toasted and fragrant, stirring occasionally. Cool on a wire rack (about 1 hour). Store in airtight containers up to 1 week.

Mocktail of the Month

MULLED CRANBERRY SIPPER: Bring 32 oz. cranberry juice, 2 qt. water, 2 cups sugar, ¼ cup lemon juice, 4 (5-inch) cinnamon sticks, and 1 Tbsp. whole cloves to a boil over medium-high heat. Reduce heat to medium, and simmer, stirring occasionally, 10 minutes. Discard solids; stir in 1 cup orange juice. Serve warm or cold. Garnish with lemon zest twists. Makes: about 3½ quarts.

Community Cookbook

A taste of what got the highest raves in the *Southern Living* Test Kitchen. This Month: Fresh-from-the-Oven Muffins.

RECIPE SWAP WINNER!

PEGGY SHARPE ADDS A SWEET DRIZZLE OVER WARM LEMON MUFFINS:
Stir together 1 cup powdered sugar and 1½ Tbsp. lemon juice.

FROM THE KITCHEN OF
PEGGY SHARPE
COLLIERVILLE, TN

"My co-workers demand these any time we have an office breakfast."

Lemon Muffins

quick prep • make-ahead • party perfect

1. Whisk together 3 cups all-purpose flour, 1 cup sugar, 2½ tsp. baking powder, and ½ tsp. salt in a large bowl. Whisk together 2 large eggs, 1¼ cups milk, ½ cup melted butter, and 1 Tbsp. lemon zest; stir into dry ingredients just until moistened. Spoon into a lightly greased 12-cup muffin pan, filling two-thirds full. Bake at 350° for 25 to 30 minutes or until golden. Makes: 1 dozen.

FROM THE KITCHEN OF
NAOMI CORDILL
WINNSBORO, LA

"These are best served hot from the oven on Thanksgiving morning."

Banana-Blueberry Muffins

quick prep • make-ahead • party perfect

1. Toss 1 cup frozen blueberries with 2 Tbsp. all-purpose flour. Stir together 2¼ cups all-purpose flour, 2 tsp. baking powder, ½ tsp. ground cinnamon, and ¼ tsp. salt. Whisk together 1 cup mashed ripe banana, 2 large eggs, ¾ cup light brown sugar, ⅓ cup melted butter, and ½ tsp. vanilla extract; add to dry ingredients, stirring just until moistened. Fold in blueberries. Spoon into a lightly greased 12-cup muffin pan, filling two-thirds full. Bake at 375° for 20 minutes or until golden brown. Makes: 1 dozen.

FROM THE KITCHEN OF
DRAKEEL BURNS
GERMANTOWN, MD

"I usually include these in care packages for friends and family."

Garlic-and-Cheese Muffins

quick prep • party perfect

1. Whisk together 2 cups self-rising flour and 1 cup milk; stir in 1 cup grated Cheddar cheese, 2 to 4 minced garlic cloves, ¼ cup mayonnaise, and 2 Tbsp. sugar. Spoon into a lightly greased 12-cup muffin pan, filling two-thirds full. Bake at 375° for 18 minutes or until golden. Brush with melted butter. Makes: 1 dozen.

JOIN OUR RECIPE SWAP: Share your favorite—if it wows the Test Kitchen, we'll feature it here and send you a SL cookbook: *southernliving.com/recipeswap*.
NOTE: All submitted recipes become the property of *Southern Living* and may be used for any purpose.

December

A Month of Sunday Suppers

SUNDAY, DECEMBER 2

Super-Easy Soup & Salad

S E R V E S 8

Southern Italian
Chicken Soup

Shredded Kale Salad with Bacon
and Chopped Dates

Southern Italian Chicken Soup

MAKES: 8 servings
HANDS-ON TIME: 45 min.
TOTAL TIME: 50 min.

- l large onion, diced
- l celery rib, thinly sliced
- 2 carrots, chopped
- l garlic clove, minced
- 3 Tbsp. olive oil, divided
- 6 cups chicken broth
- l (14.5-oz.) can diced tomatoes
- l tsp. dried Italian seasoning
- ¼ tsp. dried crushed red pepper
- ½ tsp. salt
- ½ tsp. freshly ground black pepper
- 4 (6- to 8-oz.) skinned and boned chicken breasts
- 2 cups sliced fresh okra
- l (15.5-oz.) can black-eyed peas, drained and rinsed
- l (9-oz.) package refrigerated cheese-filled tortellini
  Freshly grated Parmesan cheese

1. Sauté first 4 ingredients in 2 Tbsp. hot oil in a large Dutch oven over medium-high heat 3 to 5 minutes or until tender.

Stir in broth and next 3 ingredients; bring to a boil, stirring occasionally. Reduce heat to medium, and simmer, stirring occasionally, l0 minutes.
2. Meanwhile, sprinkle salt and pepper over chicken. Cook chicken in remaining l Tbsp. hot oil in a large nonstick skillet over medium-high heat 5 minutes on each side or until lightly browned. Cool slightly (about 5 minutes), and cut into l-inch pieces.
3. Add okra, black-eyed peas, and chicken to mixture in Dutch oven. Simmer, stirring occasionally, l0 minutes or until okra is tender. Add pasta, and cook, stirring occasionally, 3 minutes or until pasta is done. Serve with Parmesan cheese.

Shredded Kale Salad with Bacon and Chopped Dates

MAKES: 8 servings
HANDS-ON TIME: 15 min.
TOTAL TIME: l hr., 15 min.

- 3 Tbsp. olive oil
- 2 Tbsp. red wine vinegar
- l tsp. Dijon mustard
- l tsp. lemon juice
- ¼ tsp. salt
- ¼ tsp. freshly ground black pepper
- l small shallot, minced
- 3 cups shredded fresh kale
- ll Medjool dates, pitted and cut into thin slices
- 3 cooked bacon slices, crumbled

1. Whisk together first 7 ingredients in a large serving bowl until smooth. Add kale, and toss to coat. Cover and chill l to 2 hours. Toss in dates and bacon just before serving.

SUNDAY, DECEMBER 9

*Hanukkah
Celebration*

S E R V E S 8

Red Wine-Braised Brisket with
Caramelized Onions

Sweet Potato Latkes served with
Thyme-Scented Applesauce

Red Wine-Braised Brisket with Caramelized Onions

MAKES: 8 servings
HANDS-ON TIME: l hr., 15 min.
TOTAL TIME: 5 hr., 45 min.

- l (4-lb.) beef brisket flat, cut into 3 pieces
- 1½ tsp. salt
- 1½ tsp. pepper
- 2 Tbsp. vegetable oil
- 3 large white onions, cut in half and thinly sliced (6 loosely packed cups, about 3 lb.)
- 4 shallots, sliced
- l tsp. sugar
- l (750-milliliter) dry red wine
- 1½ tsp. chopped fresh rosemary, divided
- l (10-oz.) package cipollini onions, peeled

1. Preheat oven to 350°. Sprinkle all sides of brisket pieces with salt and pepper. Cook brisket, in batches, in hot oil in an ovenproof Dutch oven over medium-high heat until browned on all sides (about l5 minutes). Transfer to a plate, reserving drippings in Dutch oven.
2. Add white onions and shallots to hot drippings in Dutch oven, and sprinkle with sugar. Cook over medium heat, stirring often, 25 minutes or until onions are soft and caramelized. Stir in wine, l tsp. rosemary, and brisket. Top with cipollini onions; cover.
3. Bake at 350° for 4 hours or until brisket is tender. Remove from oven,

cover, and let stand 30 minutes. Transfer brisket to a cutting board and onions to a large bowl, reserving liquid in Dutch oven. Cover brisket and onions loosely with aluminum foil.

4. Bring reserved liquid to a boil over high heat, stirring often; boil, stirring often, 10 minutes or until liquid is reduced by half. Stir in onions and remaining ½ tsp. rosemary. Cut brisket across the grain into thick slices. Serve with onion mixture.
NOTE: We tested with Rex-Goliath Merlot.

Sweet Potato Latkes

MAKES: 27 latkes
HANDS-ON TIME: 45 min.
TOTAL TIME: 1 hr., 5 min., including applesauce

Vegetable oil
2 large baking potatoes, peeled and coarsely grated (about 2 lb.)
1 large sweet potato, peeled and coarsely grated (about 1 lb.)
3 green onions, thinly sliced
6 Tbsp. panko (Japanese bread-crumbs)
3 Tbsp. all-purpose flour
1 tsp. kosher salt
3 large eggs, lightly beaten
Thyme-Scented Applesauce

1. Pour oil to depth of ¼ inch into a large skillet, and heat over medium-high heat to 350°. Combine potatoes and green onions in a large bowl. Sprinkle with panko, flour, and salt; gently toss. Stir in eggs.
2. Drop potato mixture, in batches, by ¼ cupfuls into hot oil in skillet; slightly flatten each mound with a spatula or fork. Cook 2 to 3 minutes on each side or until lightly browned. Drain latkes on a wire rack over paper towels. Place latkes on a wire rack in a jelly-roll pan, and keep warm in a 200° oven. Serve immediately with Thyme-Scented Applesauce.

Thyme-Scented Applesauce

MAKES: 1½ cups
HANDS-ON TIME: 20 min.
TOTAL TIME: 20 min.

1. Sauté 1 McIntosh apple, unpeeled and chopped, in 2 Tbsp. melted butter over medium-high heat 3 to 4 minutes or until tender. Remove from heat, and stir in 1 cup sweetened applesauce, 2 tsp. fresh lemon juice, ½ tsp. each chopped fresh thyme and salt, and ¼ tsp. pepper. Serve at room temperature.

SUNDAY, DECEMBER 16

Chicken for a Crowd

SERVES 8

Roast Chicken with
Sweet Potatoes
and Apples

Roast Chicken with Sweet Potatoes and Apples

MAKES: 8 servings
HANDS-ON TIME: 40 min.
TOTAL TIME: 2 hr., 20 min.

1 lemon
½ cup butter, softened
2 garlic cloves, minced
1 tsp. kosher salt, divided
1 tsp. freshly ground pepper, divided
1 (5- to 6-lb.) whole chicken
3 fresh thyme sprigs
Kitchen string
1 large sweet potato (about 1 lb.)
2 large Granny Smith apples (about 1 lb.)
¼ cup firmly packed dark brown sugar
¼ cup butter, melted

1. Preheat oven to 425°. Grate zest from lemon to equal 2 tsp; reserve lemon. Combine zest, softened butter, garlic, and ½ tsp. each salt and pepper. If applicable, remove neck and giblets from chicken, and reserve for another use. Rinse chicken, and pat dry. Loosen and lift skin from chicken breast with fingers (do not totally detach skin); spread half of butter mixture underneath skin, and place thyme sprigs under skin. Carefully replace skin.
2. Cut reserved lemon in half. Squeeze lemon juice into cavity of chicken, and place lemon halves in cavity. Tie ends of legs together with string; tuck wingtips under. Rub remaining butter mixture over chicken, and sprinkle with remaining ½ tsp. each salt and pepper. Place chicken, breast side up, on a lightly greased rack in a lightly greased large, shallow roasting pan.
3. Bake chicken at 425° for 30 minutes.
4. Meanwhile, peel sweet potato and apples. Cut potato in half lengthwise, and cut into ¼-inch-thick half-moon slices. Cut apples in half vertically through stem and bottom ends, and cut into ¼-inch-thick wedges. Arrange half of sweet potatoes in bottom of a 9-inch oval gratin dish. Sprinkle with 1 Tbsp. brown sugar. Arrange apple wedges in a single layer over sweet potatoes; sprinke with 1 Tbsp. brown sugar. Top with remaining sweet potatoes, and sprinkle with remaining 2 Tbsp. brown sugar; drizzle with ¼ cup melted butter. Season with desired amount of salt and pepper. Cover with aluminum foil.
5. Reduce oven temperature to 350°. Bake chicken 15 minutes. Add potato mixture to oven, and bake chicken and potato mixture at the same time for 35 minutes. Uncover potato mixture, and bake 40 more minutes or until a meat thermometer inserted into thickest portion of chicken thigh registers 180° and potatoes and apples are tender and lightly browned.

Panini

Spread outsides of sandwiches with butter. Cook in a preheated panini press 2 to 3 minutes or until golden.

PICK A STURDY BREAD

- Raisin-nut bread
- French bread slices
- Slider buns or dinner rolls
- Challah or brioche bread
- Pumpernickel, rye, or hearty white bread

CHOOSE A CHEESE

- Brie
- Sharp white Cheddar
- Blue cheese
- Gruyère or Swiss
- Creamy goat cheese
- Cream cheese

SPREAD SOME FLAVOR

- Apple butter
- Coarse-grained, Dijon, or honey mustard
- Herbed butter (great for spreading on the outside of sandwiches before grilling!)
- Fruit preserves
- Pepper jelly

ADD A FAVORITE TOPPING (OR TWO)

- Caramelized onions
- Sautéed apples or pears
- Sliced fresh fruit or vegetables
- Dried apricots
- Fresh herbs
- Thinly sliced deli meat
- Cooked bacon slices
- Smoked salmon
- Chopped toasted nuts

SUNDAY, DECEMBER 23

Wine & (Grilled) Cheese Bar

S E R V E S   A   C R O W D

Let guests build their own panini with a selection of different breads, cheeses, and toppings.

Five Combos We Love

Wine Director Richard Robinson of The Wine Shop at Western Supermarket in Mountain Brook, Alabama, shares some delicious (and affordable!) pairings for these melt-in-your-mouth ideas.

{1}

Brie with apple butter and bacon, on raisin-walnut bread: For white, try Chenin Blanc such as Champalou Vouvray from the Loire Valley ($17), or a California version like Ballentine Vineyards ($17). A richer-style Riesling from the Pfalz or Rhiengau areas would also work well. And if you just have to have red, then try Beaujolais or California Pinot Noir.

{2}

Creamy goat cheese with smoked salmon on hearty white bread brushed with dill butter: The obvious choice here is Sauvignon Blanc—specifically Sancerre or a South African version like Neil Ellis ($14) or Southern Right ($13). The smoked salmon element opens the door to a topflight Pinot Grigio, such as Jermann ($22).

{3}

Blue cheese with caramelized onions and sautéed pears on brioche or challah bread: The intense complexity of ingredients calls for a wine of equal complexity but one that will complement, not compete. Leitz Dragonstone Riesling ($16) would be a great choice, but any good-quality Spatlese or even Auslese-level Riesling will be wonderful. A village level red Burgundy or an Oregon Pinot Noir such as Stoller ($21) would be fine choices for red.

{4}

Gruyère with coarse-grained mustard, thinly sliced ham, apricot halves, and toasted pistachios on French bread slices: Chardonnay comes first to mind, and white Burgundy in particular. But my heart leads to rosé, a vibrant, exhilarating Bandol ($29-$34) or slightly softer version from Cassis ($29). Less expensive Rosé kike by Cune from Spain ($10) or Domainede Fonsainte "Gris du Gris" from Corbieres ($13) would also work beautifully.

{5}

Sharp white Cheddar with honey mustard, thinly sliced Golden Delicious apples, and toasted pecans on slider buns or dinner rolls: A good, crisp, cool-climate Chardonnay will be great with this one, but I would encourage giving white Rhône a try. Rich and exotic, these wines possess wonderful food affinity and crowd-pleasing versatility. La Vieille Ferme from the Luberon ($8) will fill the bill without overfilling it! Côtes du Rhône Blanc from Famille Perrin ($11) or E. Guigal ($14) would be even better.

New Year's Eve Eve

S E R V E S 8

Peach-Mustard Glazed
Pork Tenderloin

Red Bliss Potato Salad
with Chives

COCKTAIL OF THE
MONTH

Black Currant Champagne

Fill a Champagne flute with equal
parts chilled Champagne or
sparkling wine and black currant
nectar. Other nectars—such as
peach, mango, tropical, or pear—
may be substituted.

Peach-Mustard Glazed Pork Tenderloin

MAKES: 8 servings
HANDS-ON TIME: 25 min.
TOTAL TIME: 1 hr.

- 2 (1¼-lb.) pork tenderloins
- ½ tsp. salt
- ½ tsp. freshly ground pepper
- 2 Tbsp. olive oil
- 2 Tbsp. butter
- 1 large shallot, minced
- ½ cup peach preserves
- ⅓ cup bourbon
- ¼ tsp. dried crushed red pepper
- 2 Tbsp. country-style Dijon mustard
- ½ cup low-sodium fat-free chicken broth

1. Preheat oven to 400°. Sprinkle tenderloins with salt and pepper. Cook in hot
oil in a large ovenproof skillet over high
heat 3 to 4 minutes on each side or until
lightly browned.
2. Melt butter in a small skillet over
medium-high heat; add shallot, and sauté
2 to 3 minutes or until tender. Remove
from heat, and stir in peach preserves
and next 3 ingredients. Cook over
medium heat, stirring often, 1 minute or
until preserves are melted. Pour mixture
over tenderloins.
3. Bake at 400° for 20 minutes or until
a meat thermometer inserted in thickest
portion registers 150°. Transfer tenderloins to a cutting board, reserving pan
drippings in skillet. Cover loosely with
aluminum foil, and let stand 10 minutes
before slicing.
4. Meanwhile, stir broth into reserved
drippings, and cook over medium-high
heat, stirring constantly, 5 minutes
or until drippings are reduced by half.
Serve with sliced tenderloins.

Red Bliss Potato Salad with Chives

MAKES: 8 servings
HANDS-ON TIME: 20 min.
TOTAL TIME: 50 min.

- 2 lb. small red bliss potatoes, quartered
- 5 Tbsp. olive oil, divided
- 2 Tbsp. Champagne vinegar
- 1 tsp. lemon juice
- 1 tsp. Dijon mustard
- ¼ tsp. kosher salt
- ¼ tsp. freshly ground pepper
- 1 small shallot, minced
- 2 Tbsp. crème fraîche
- 2 Tbsp. chopped fresh chives
  Kosher salt and pepper to taste

1. Preheat oven to 400°. Toss together
potatoes with 2 Tbsp. olive oil, and place
in a jelly-roll pan. Bake 30 to 35 minutes
or until golden.
2. Meanwhile, whisk together vinegar
and next 4 ingredients in a large bowl.
Add shallot, and gradually whisk in
vegetable oil crème fraîche, and remaining
3 Tbsp. olive oil, whisking until well
blended. Remove potatoes from oven,
and gently toss with vinegar mixture
and chives. Season with kosher salt and
pepper to taste.

Sophisticated Cocktail Supper

Holiday Get-Together

SERVES 8

Sparkling Rum Punch

Crispy Goat Cheese-Topped Arugula Salad with Pomegranate Vinaigrette

Fingerling Potatoes with Dilled Avocado and Smoked Salmon

Salt-Roasted Beef Tenderloin Sliders with Chimichurri Pesto

Mini Crab Cakes with Pineapple-Cucumber Salsa

Coconut Crème Brûlée

Sparkling Rum Punch

MAKES: about 9 cups
HANDS-ON TIME: 10 min.
TOTAL TIME: 1 hr., 10 min.

- 2 cups fresh orange juice
- ½ cup orange liqueur
- ½ cup dark rum
- 2 (750-milliliter) bottles sparkling wine, chilled

1. Stir together first 3 ingredients in a medium bowl; cover and chill 1 hour. Pour mixture into a large pitcher or punch bowl, and top with sparkling wine. Serve immediately.

NOTE: We tested with Cointreau orange liqueur and Asti Spumante sparkling wine.

Crispy Goat Cheese-Topped Arugula Salad with Pomegranate Vinaigrette

MAKES: 8 servings
HANDS-ON TIME: 25 min.
TOTAL TIME: 1 hr., 50 min., including vinaigrette

Dip a knife in hot water to get clean slices of cheese.

- 4 (4-oz.) goat cheese logs
- ½ cup all-purpose flour
- ½ tsp. pepper
- 2 egg whites
- 1 cup panko (Japanese bread-crumbs)
- 4 Tbsp. olive oil
- 2 (5-oz.) containers baby arugula
- 4 large navel oranges, peeled and sectioned
  Pomegranate Vinaigrette

1. Cut each goat cheese log into 6 (½-inch) slices. Combine flour and pepper in a shallow dish. Whisk together egg whites and 2 Tbsp. water in another shallow dish. Place panko in a third shallow dish. Dredge goat cheese rounds in flour mixture, dip in egg mixture, and dredge in panko. Arrange goat cheese slices in a single layer in an aluminum foil-lined jelly-roll pan; cover and chill 30 minutes to 4 hours.

2. Cook half of goat cheese rounds in 2 Tbsp. hot olive oil in a large nonstick skillet over medium heat 2 to 3 minutes on each side or until lightly browned. Drain on paper towels. Repeat with remaining olive oil and goat cheese rounds.

3. Divide arugula and orange sections among 8 plates; drizzle with Pomegranate Vinaigrette. Top each salad with 3 goat cheese rounds.

Pomegranate Vinaigrette

MAKES: about ⅔ cup
HANDS-ON TIME: 20 min.
TOTAL TIME: 55 min.

1. Bring 1½ cups pomegranate juice to a boil in a medium saucepan over medium-high heat; reduce heat to medium, and cook, stirring occasionally, 15 minutes or until reduced to ¼ cup. Transfer to a small bowl; cool completely (about 30 minutes). Whisk in ⅓ cup olive oil, 5 tsp. honey, 1 Tbsp. white wine vinegar, 1 tsp. Dijon mustard, ¼ tsp. pepper, and ⅛ tsp. salt.

Fingerling Potatoes with Dilled Avocado and Smoked Salmon

MAKES: 8 servings
HANDS-ON TIME: 15 min.
TOTAL TIME: 55 min.

- 1 lb. fingerling potatoes, halved lengthwise
- 1 Tbsp. olive oil
- ½ tsp. salt
- ¼ tsp. pepper
- 1 ripe avocado, halved
- 1 Tbsp. minced fresh dill
- 1 tsp. lemon zest
- 2 tsp. fresh lemon juice
- ⅛ tsp. salt
- 1 (4-oz.) package thinly sliced smoked salmon
  Garnish: fresh dill sprigs

1. Preheat oven to 400°. Toss together first 4 ingredients in a large bowl. Place potatoes, cut sides down, in a lightly greased jelly-roll pan. Bake 20 to 22 minutes or until tender and cut sides are browned. Cool completely (about 20 minutes).

2. Meanwhile, scoop avocado pulp into a medium bowl; mash with a fork. Stir in dill and next 3 ingredients. Spoon avocado mixture onto cut sides of potatoes, and top each with 1 salmon slice.

Salt-Roasted Beef Tenderloin Sliders with Chimichurri Pesto

MAKES: 8 servings
HANDS-ON TIME: 20 min.
TOTAL TIME: 1 hr., 25 min., including pesto

The tenderloin can be cooked a day ahead, covered, and stored in the refrigerator. Bring to room temperature before serving.

- 1 (1½-lb.) beef tenderloin, trimmed
- 1 tsp. cracked pepper
- 1 Tbsp. olive oil
- 6 cups kosher salt
- 1 cup cold water
- 24 small rolls or buns, split and toasted
  Chimichurri Pesto

1. Preheat oven to 400°. Sprinkle beef with pepper. Cook beef in hot oil in a large skillet over medium-high heat, turning occasionally, 5 minutes or until browned on all sides. Transfer to a plate.
2. Stir together salt and 1 cup cold water. Spread half of salt mixture in a rectangle (slightly larger than beef) in a large roasting pan; top with beef. Pat remaining salt mixture over beef, covering completely.
3. Bake at 400° for 45 to 50 minutes or until a meat thermometer inserted into center of beef registers 145°. Immediately tap salt crust with a wooden spoon to loosen, and remove crust. (Beef will continue to cook if crust remains on.) Transfer beef to cutting board; cover loosely with aluminum foil, and let stand 10 minutes before slicing. Brush off excess salt; cut beef into 24 thin slices. Serve on rolls with Chimichurri Pesto.

Chimichurri Pesto

MAKES: about 1 cup
HANDS-ON TIME: 10 min.
TOTAL TIME: 10 min.

1. Process 1 cup firmly packed fresh flat-leaf parsley leaves; 1 cup firmly packed fresh cilantro leaves; ½ cup chopped toasted walnuts; ½ cup freshly grated Parmesan cheese; 1 tsp. fresh lemon juice; 1 small garlic clove, chopped; ¼ tsp. dried crushed red pepper; and ¼ tsp. salt in a food processor until finely chopped. With processor running, pour ¼ cup extra virgin olive oil through food chute in a slow, steady stream, processing until smooth.

Mini Crab Cakes with Pineapple-Cucumber Salsa

MAKES: 8 servings
HANDS-ON TIME: 30 min.
TOTAL TIME: 1 hr., 30 min., including salsa

Pineapple-Cucumber Salsa
- 1½ lb. fresh crabmeat, drained
- ¼ cup mayonnaise
- 1 large egg
- 1 Tbsp. Dijon mustard
- 1 tsp. lemon zest
- ¼ cup panko (Japanese breadcrumbs)
- 3 Tbsp. minced green onions
- 3 Tbsp. diced red bell pepper
- 4 Tbsp. butter
  Lime wedges

1. Prepare salsa.
2. Pick crabmeat, removing any bits of shell.
3. Whisk together mayonnaise and next 3 ingredients in a large bowl. Gently stir in crabmeat, panko, and next 2 ingredients. Shape mixture into 16 (2-inch) cakes (about ¼ cup each). Cover and chill 1 to 4 hours.
4. Melt 2 Tbsp. butter in a large nonstick skillet over medium heat. Add 8 crab cakes, and cook 2 to 3 minutes on each side or until browned. Repeat with remaining butter and crab cakes. Serve with Pineapple-Cucumber Salsa and lime wedges.

Pineapple-Cucumber Salsa

MAKES: 3¾ cups
HANDS-ON TIME: 20 min.
TOTAL TIME: 1 hr., 20 min.

1. Stir together 2 cups diced fresh pineapple; 1 English cucumber, peeled and diced (about 1½ cups); 2 green onions, thinly sliced (about ¼ cup); 1 jalapeño pepper, seeded and minced; ¼ cup chopped fresh basil; 1 Tbsp. fresh lime juice; and ⅛ tsp. salt. Cover and chill 1 to 24 hours.

Coconut Crème Brûlée

MAKES: 6 servings
HANDS-ON TIME: 20 min.
TOTAL TIME: 9 hr., 40 min.

- 1 (13½-oz.) can unsweetened coconut milk
- 1¼ cups heavy cream
- 8 egg yolks
- ⅔ cup sugar
- ¼ tsp. coconut extract
- 6 tsp. sugar
  Garnish: toasted sweetened flaked coconut

1. Preheat oven to 325°. Whisk together first 5 ingredients until smooth. Divide mixture among 6 (6-oz.) shallow crème brûlée dishes. Place dishes in a large roasting pan; add hot water to pan to come halfway up sides of dishes. Carefully place in oven.
2. Bake at 325° for 45 to 50 minutes or just until centers are set. Cool in pan on a wire rack 25 minutes. Remove from water; cover and chill 8 to 24 hours.
3. Preheat broiler with oven rack 5 inches from heat. Sprinkle 1 tsp. sugar over each custard. Fill a large roasting pan or 15- x 10-inch jelly-roll pan with ice; arrange dishes in pan. Broil 3 minutes or until sugar melts and lightly caramelizes, rotating pan as needed to allow sugar to brown evenly. Let stand 5 minutes for sugar to harden.
NOTE: We tested with A Taste of Thai Coconut Milk.

Sit Down for a Wintry Feast

This simple, no-stress dinner menu invites you to relax and enjoy your holiday company.

Simple Winter Supper

SERVES 8

Sweet Potato Soup

Arugula-Pear-Blue Cheese Salad

Cranberry Roasted Winter Vegetables

Pork Roast with Sweet Onion-Pumpkin Seed Relish

Wild Rice with Bacon and Fennel

Gingerbread Soufflé

Sweet Potato Soup

MAKES: 8 cups
HANDS-ON TIME: 35 min.
TOTAL TIME: 1 hr.

Make the soup through Step 2 the day before. Reheat, and stir in the sour cream and lime juice before serving.

- 2 Tbsp. butter
- 1 medium onion, chopped
- 2 garlic cloves, minced
- 5½ cups low-sodium fat-free chicken broth
- 2 lb. sweet potatoes, peeled and chopped (3 large)
- 1 cup apple cider
- 1 tsp. minced canned chipotle pepper in adobo sauce
- 1 tsp. salt
- 2 Tbsp. fresh lime juice
- ½ cup sour cream
- 2 tsp. fresh lime juice

1. Melt butter in a large saucepan over medium-high heat; add onion, and sauté 5 to 7 minutes or until tender. Add garlic; sauté 1 minute. Stir in broth and next 4 ingredients. Bring to a boil; reduce heat to medium-low, and simmer 20 minutes or until potatoes are tender.
2. Process mixture with a handheld blender until smooth. (If you don't have a handheld blender, cool mixture 10 minutes, and process, in batches, in a regular blender until smooth. Return mixture to saucepan, and proceed as directed in Step 3.)
3. Cook over low heat, stirring occasionally, 5 minutes or until thoroughly heated. Stir in 2 Tbsp. lime juice. Whisk together sour cream and 2 tsp. lime juice. Ladle soup into bowls, and drizzle with sour cream mixture.

Arugula-Pear-Blue Cheese Salad

MAKES: 8 servings
HANDS-ON TIME: 15 min.
TOTAL TIME: 15 min.

- ¼ cup plus 2 Tbsp. pear preserves
- ½ cup Champagne vinegar
- 1 shallot, sliced
- 2 tsp. Dijon mustard
- ½ tsp. salt
- ¼ tsp. freshly ground pepper
- ½ cup olive oil
- 8 cups loosely packed arugula
- 2 Bartlett pears, cut into 6 wedges each
- 4 oz. blue cheese, crumbled
- ¼ cup chopped toasted walnuts

1. Process ¼ cup pear preserves and next 5 ingredients in a food processor 30 seconds to 1 minute or until smooth. With processor running, pour oil through food chute in a slow, steady stream, processing until smooth. Transfer to a 2-cup measuring cup or small bowl, and stir in remaining 2 Tbsp. pear preserves.
2. Place arugula in a large serving bowl, and top with pears, blue cheese, and walnuts. Drizzle with vinaigrette.

Cranberry Roasted Winter Vegetables

MAKES: 8 servings
HANDS-ON TIME: 30 min.
TOTAL TIME: I hr., 5 min.

Roast the vegetables before the Pork Roast (recipe at right). Then, toss them back in the oven to reheat while the pork rests.

- 4 large carrots (about I½ lb.), halved lengthwise and cut into I-inch pieces
- 3 large turnips (about 2 lb.), peeled and cut into I-inch pieces*
- I lb. Brussels sprouts, halved (quartered, if large)
- I Tbsp. minced fresh rosemary
- 2 Tbsp. olive oil
- ¾ tsp. salt
- ¼ tsp. pepper
- I cup fresh or thawed frozen cranberries
- 4 tsp. molasses

1. Preheat oven to 400°. Lightly grease 2 large jelly-roll pans; place carrots and turnips in one pan and Brussels sprouts in second pan. Divide rosemary and next 3 ingredients among carrot mixture and Brussels sprouts; toss each to coat.
2. Bake both pans at 400° at the same time. Bake carrot mixture 30 minutes, stirring once; add cranberries, and bake 5 minutes or until carrots and turnips are tender and browned and cranberries begin to soften. Bake Brussels sprouts I5 to 20 minutes or until tender and browned, stirring once.
3. Combine vegetables in a large serving bowl. Drizzle with molasses, and toss to coat.

*2 lb. parsnips may be substituted.

Pork Roast with Sweet Onion-Pumpkin Seed Relish

MAKES: 8 servings
HANDS-ON TIME: 20 min.
TOTAL TIME: I hr., 40 min.

Be sure to ask the butcher to cut the chine bone and French the rib rack for easy carving and elegant presentation.

- I¼ tsp. salt, divided
- ½ tsp. freshly ground pepper
- I (5-lb.) 8-rib bone-in pork loin roast, chine bone removed
- I Tbsp. minced fresh rosemary
- 4 tsp. minced fresh thyme, divided
- 3 large sweet onions (about 2 lb.), cut into ½-inch-thick rings
- 2 Tbsp. olive oil
- ⅛ tsp. freshly ground pepper
- I tsp. white wine vinegar
- I tsp. light brown sugar
- ¼ cup toasted pumpkin seeds

1. Preheat oven to 450°. Sprinkle I tsp. salt and ½ tsp. pepper over pork; rub rosemary and I Tbsp. thyme over pork. Place pork in a lightly greased roasting pan.
2. Toss together onions, olive oil, ⅛ tsp. pepper, and remaining ¼ tsp. salt until coated. Arrange onions around pork.
3. Bake at 450° for 30 minutes; reduce heat to 375°, and cook 50 more minutes or until a meat thermometer inserted into thickest portion registers I45°, stirring onions once. Transfer pork to a cutting board; cover loosely with aluminum foil, and let stand I0 minutes before slicing.
4. Meanwhile, coarsely chop onions; transfer to a medium bowl. Stir in vinegar, brown sugar, and remaining I tsp. thyme. Stir in pumpkin seeds just before serving.

Wild Rice with Bacon and Fennel

MAKES: 8 servings
HANDS-ON TIME: 40 min.
TOTAL TIME: I hr., 5 min.

- I⅓ cups uncooked wild rice
- 4 bacon slices
- I large fennel bulb, thinly sliced
- I large onion, cut into thin wedges
- 2 garlic cloves, minced
- ½ cup low sodium fat-free chicken broth
- ⅓ cup golden raisins
- ¼ tsp. salt
- ⅛ tsp. pepper
- ¼ cup chopped fresh fennel fronds or flat-leaf parsley
- I Tbsp. white wine vinegar
- ½ cup chopped toasted walnuts

1. Cook wild rice according to package directions; drain.
2. Meanwhile, cook bacon in a large nonstick skillet over medium-high heat 7 to 8 minutes or until crisp; remove bacon, and drain on paper towels, reserving I Tbsp. drippings in skillet. Chop bacon.
3. Sauté fennel bulb and onion in hot drippings over medium-high heat 5 minutes or until softened. Add garlic; sauté I minute. Add broth and next 3 ingredients, and bring to a boil. Reduce heat to medium-low; cover and simmer 8 minutes or until vegetables are tender.
4. Stir in rice and bacon; cook, stirring often, 3 minutes. Transfer to a large serving bowl. Stir in fennel fronds and vinegar. Stir in walnuts just before serving.

Gingerbread Soufflé

MAKES: 8 servings
HANDS-ON TIME: 20 min.
TOTAL TIME: 1 hr., 30 min.

After the vegetables and pork are finished, reduce the oven temp to 350°, and pop the soufflés in the oven before sitting down to dinner.

- 1 cup milk
- ½ cup sugar
- ¼ cup all-purpose flour
- ¼ tsp. salt
- ⅓ cup molasses
- 2 Tbsp. butter, softened
- 2 tsp. pumpkin pie spice
- 1 tsp. ground ginger
- 2 tsp. vanilla extract
- 6 large eggs, separated
- ⅛ tsp. cream of tartar
  Sweetened whipped cream or vanilla ice cream

1. Preheat oven to 350°. Whisk together first 4 ingredients in a medium saucepan until smooth. Bring to a boil over medium heat, whisking constantly. Transfer to a large bowl, and whisk in molasses and next 4 ingredients. Cool 15 minutes. Whisk in egg yolks.

2. Butter a 2½-qt. dish; sprinkle with sugar to coat, and shake out excess.

3. Beat egg whites and cream of tartar at high speed with an electric mixer until stiff peaks form. Fold one-third of egg white mixture into milk mixture just until well blended. Repeat twice with remaining egg white mixture. Spoon batter into prepared dish.

4. Bake at 350° for 55 to 60 minutes or until puffy and set. Serve immediately with whipped cream or ice cream.

Southern-Style Appetizers

GRITS

Brisket Shooters

MAKES: 12 servings
HANDS-ON TIME: 30 min.
TOTAL TIME: 40 min., including coleslaw

Pick up smoked brisket and sauce from your favorite barbecue joint.

- 2 cups milk
- 1 cup uncooked regular grits
- ½ tsp. salt
- 1 cup (4 oz.) shredded smoked Gouda cheese
- ½ cup (2 oz.) shredded Parmesan cheese
- 1½ lb. shredded smoked beef brisket
  Coleslaw
  Barbecue sauce

1. Bring milk and 2 cups water to a boil in a medium saucepan over medium heat, stirring occasionally. Gradually whisk in grits and salt; return to a boil. Cover, reduce heat to low, and simmer, stirring occasionally, 10 to 15 minutes or until thickened. Remove from heat, and stir in cheeses until blended.

2. Layer brisket, grits, and Coleslaw in 12 (8-oz.) glasses; drizzle with barbecue sauce. Serve immediately.

Coleslaw

1. Whisk together ⅓ cup mayonnaise, 2 Tbsp. minced green onions, 1 Tbsp. sugar, 2 Tbsp. fresh lemon juice, and ¼ tsp. each salt and freshly ground pepper in a large bowl. Add 1 (10-oz.) package shredded coleslaw mix, and toss to coat. Makes: about 3 cups. Hands-on time: 10 min., Total time: 10 min.

Grits Spanakopita

MAKES: about 4 dozen
HANDS-ON TIME: 30 min.
TOTAL TIME: 8 hr., 50 min.

- 1 cup uncooked regular grits
- 1 (10-oz.) package frozen chopped spinach, thawed
- 2 (4-oz.) packages feta cheese, crumbled
- ½ cup finely chopped green onions
- ¼ cup chopped fresh basil
- 2 garlic cloves, pressed
- 1 Tbsp. fresh lemon juice
- ¾ tsp. salt
  Freshly ground pepper to taste
- 2 cups panko (Japanese breadcrumbs)
- ½ cup grated Parmesan cheese
- ¼ cup finely chopped fresh parsley
  Canola oil or vegetable cooking spray

1. Prepare grits according to package directions. Drain spinach well, pressing between paper towels. Stir spinach, feta cheese, and next 5 ingredients into hot cooked grits until blended. Season with freshly ground pepper to taste.

2. Stir together panko and next 2 ingredients; sprinkle half of breadcrumb mixture over bottom of a well-greased 13- x 9-inch baking dish. Pour hot grits mixture into prepared pan. Sprinkle remaining breadcrumb mixture over grits. Cover and chill 8 hours.

3. Invert chilled grits onto a cutting board, and cut into 24 squares. Cut each square diagonally into 2 triangles. Brush 1 side of triangles with canola oil, using a pastry brush, or coat well with cooking spray.

4. Place grits cakes, non-oiled sides down, on a hot greased griddle or in nonstick skillet, and cook, in batches, over medium heat 2 to 3 minutes on each side or until golden brown. Place spanakopita in a single layer on a wire rack on a baking sheet, and keep warm in a 200° oven up to 30 minutes.

Grits-and-Gumbo Tarts

MAKES: 3 dozen
HANDS-ON TIME: 35 min.
TOTAL TIME: 1 hr., 40 min.

- 36 unpeeled, medium-size raw shrimp
- 2 cups chicken broth
- 1 cup milk
- 1 cup uncooked regular grits
- 4 Tbsp. butter, divided
- ½ cup finely chopped andouille sausage
- ½ cup finely diced green bell pepper
- ⅓ cup finely diced red onion
- 2 garlic cloves, minced
- 36 (½-inch-thick) fresh okra slices (8 to 10 pods)
- 2 tsp. Creole seasoning
- 36 (4-inch) wooden skewers

1. Preheat oven to 350°. Peel and devein shrimp.
2. Bring broth and milk to a boil in a large saucepan over medium-high heat. Gradually whisk in grits; return to a boil. Reduce heat to low, and simmer, stirring occasionally, 10 to 15 minutes or until thickened.
3. Melt 3 Tbsp. butter in a medium skillet over medium-high heat; add sausage and next 3 ingredients, and sauté 5 minutes. Stir sausage mixture into cooked grits. Spoon 1 rounded tablespoonful grits mixture into each of 3 lightly greased 12-cup miniature muffin pans, pressing lightly.
4. Bake at 350° for 20 to 25 minutes or until lightly browned. Remove from oven, and make an indentation in center of each tart, using back of a spoon. Cool completely in pans on wire racks (about 30 minutes). Remove tarts from muffin pans, and place in a 15- x 10-inch jelly-roll pan.
5. Sprinkle shrimp and okra with Creole seasoning. Melt remaining 1 Tbsp. butter in a large skillet over medium-high heat; add shrimp and okra, and sauté 3 to 5 minutes or just until shrimp turn pink. Thread 1 shrimp and 1 okra slice onto each skewer, and place 1 on each grits tart. Bake at 350° for 8 to 10 minutes or just until warm. Serve immediately.

Grits Crostini

MAKES: about 5 dozen
HANDS-ON TIME: 30 min.
TOTAL TIME: 1 hr., 25 min., including topping

- 1 cup all-purpose flour
- 4 tsp. baking powder
- ¼ tsp. salt
- 1 Tbsp. sugar
- ¼ cup butter, melted
- 2 large eggs, beaten
- 1 cup milk
- 1½ cups cooked grits
  Caramelized Apple-and-Onion Topping
- 1 cup (4 oz.) shredded fontina cheese
- 1 Tbsp. minced fresh thyme leaves

1. Preheat oven to 425°. Sift together first 4 ingredients into a large bowl. Whisk together melted butter and next 2 ingredients in a separate bowl; add to flour mixture, stirring just until dry ingredients are moistened. Whisk in grits. Spoon batter into 2 greased 12-cup muffin pans (about 1 Tbsp. per cup).
2. Bake, in batches, at 425° for 12 to 15 minutes or until golden. Immediately remove from pans to wire racks; cool completely (about 30 minutes). Reduce oven temperature to 375°.
3. Meanwhile, prepare Caramelized Apple-and-Onion Topping.
4. Place cooled crostini in a single layer on a baking sheet. Top each crostini with 1 tsp. Caramelized Apple-and-Onion Topping; sprinkle with shredded cheese. Bake at 375° for 8 to 10 minutes or until cheese is melted and golden. Remove from oven, and sprinkle with fresh thyme. Serve immediately.
NOTE: Prepare and bake crostini as directed through Step 2. Cool completely, and freeze in zip-top plastic freezer bags up to 1 month, if desired.

Caramelized Apple-and-Onion Topping

MAKES: 2¾ cups
HANDS-ON TIME: 30 min.
TOTAL TIME: 30 min.

1. Melt 3 Tbsp. butter in a large skillet over medium-high heat; add 4 cups diced sweet onions, and sauté 10 minutes or until golden. Stir in 2 cups diced Granny Smith apple, and sauté 10 minutes or until mixture is caramel colored. Remove from heat, and stir in ¼ tsp. each salt and freshly ground pepper.

Pepper Jack Grits Poppers

MAKES: about 10 appetizer servings
HANDS-ON TIME: 35 min.
TOTAL TIME: 8 hr., 40 min.

You'll need about ½ cup uncooked grits to make this recipe. Pepper Jack cheese adds a nice little zip to these tasty holiday appetizers.

- 1 cup hot cooked grits
- 1 cup (4 oz.) freshly shredded pepper Jack cheese
- ½ cup (2 oz.) shredded Parmesan cheese
- 2 Tbsp. chopped fresh cilantro
- 1 garlic clove, pressed
  Salt and pepper to taste
- 18 to 20 sweet mini bell peppers (about 2 inches long)

1. Stir together first 5 ingredients in a small bowl until cheeses are melted; season with salt and pepper to taste. Cover and chill 8 hours.
2. Preheat broiler with oven rack 6 inches from heat. Cut bell peppers in half lengthwise, leaving stems intact; remove seeds. Spoon grits mixture into bell pepper halves. Place stuffed peppers on a broiling pan. Broil 4 to 5 minutes or until golden brown.

Chicken Salad Pitas

MAKES: 4 dozen
HANDS-ON TIME: 30 min.
TOTAL TIME: 4 hr., 30 min.

- ½ cup mayonnaise
- ⅓ cup red pepper jelly
- ¼ cup minced green onions
- 2 Tbsp. chopped fresh cilantro
- 1 tsp. lime zest
- ¼ tsp. ground red pepper
- 2 cups finely chopped cooked chicken
- ½ cup finely chopped celery
- ½ cup finely chopped toasted pecans
  Salt and freshly ground black
  pepper to taste
- 24 mini pita pockets, halved
- 1 bunch fresh watercress

1. Whisk together first 6 ingredients in a large bowl; stir in chicken and next 2 ingredients until blended. Season with salt and freshly ground pepper to taste. Cover and chill 4 hours. Fill each pita half with a watercress sprig and chicken salad mixture. Serve immediately.

Pork Tenderloin Crostini

MAKES: about 4 dozen
HANDS-ON TIME: 30 min.
TOTAL TIME: 2 hr., 50 min., including jelly

- 24 frozen tea biscuits
- 2 (¾- to 1-lb.) pork tenderloins
- 1 tsp. salt
- 2 tsp. freshly ground pepper
- 2 Tbsp. olive oil
- 5 Tbsp. butter, melted
  Cranberry-Pepper Jelly
- 1 bunch fresh watercress

1. Preheat oven to 350°. Bake frozen tea biscuits according to package directions. Cool completely on a wire rack (about 20 minutes).
2. Preheat grill to 350° to 400° (medium-high) heat. Remove silver skin from each tenderloin, leaving a thin layer of fat. Sprinkle salt and pepper over pork; rub olive oil over pork. Grill pork, covered with grill lid, 10 to 12 minutes on each side or until a meat thermometer inserted into thickest portion registers 145°. Remove from grill; cover with aluminum foil, and let stand 15 minutes.
3. Meanwhile, cut biscuits in half, and brush cut sides with melted butter. Arrange biscuits, cut sides up, on a baking sheet. Bake at 350° for 8 to 10 minutes or until edges are golden.
4. Cut pork into ¼-inch-thick slices (about 24 slices each). Place pork on toasted biscuit halves; top with desired amount of Cranberry-Pepper Jelly and a watercress sprig. Serve immediately.

Cranberry-Pepper Jelly

MAKES: 3 cups
HANDS-ON TIME: 25 min.
TOTAL TIME: 1 hr., 10 min.

1. Bring 1 (12-oz.) package fresh cranberries, 1 (10-oz.) jar red pepper jelly, 1½ cups peeled and diced Granny Smith apple, ¾ cup sugar, ½ cup water, and ¼ tsp. dried crushed red pepper to a boil in a large saucepan over medium-high heat, stirring often. Reduce heat to medium-low, and simmer, stirring often, 10 to 15 minutes or until cranberries begin to pop and mixture starts to thicken. Remove from heat, and stir in ½ cup sweetened dried cranberries. Cool completely (about 45 minutes). Serve at room temperature, or cover and chill 8 hours before serving. Store in an airtight container in refrigerator up to 2 weeks.

Pepper Jelly Margaritas

MAKES: 3 cups
HANDS-ON TIME: 10 min.
TOTAL TIME: 10 min.

- 1 cup tequila
- 1 cup fresh lime juice
- ½ cup orange liqueur
- ⅓ cup powdered sugar
- ¼ cup green pepper jelly

1. Stir together all ingredients in a large pitcher until sugar and pepper jelly are dissolved. Fill cocktail shaker with ice cubes; pour desired amount of mixture into cocktail shaker. Cover with lid, and shake vigorously until thoroughly chilled (about 30 seconds). Strain into chilled cocktail glasses. Repeat with remaining mixture. Serve immediately.
NOTE: We tested with Grand Marnier orange liqueur.

Pepper Jelly-Pecan Rugelach

MAKES: about 5 dozen
HANDS-ON TIME: 30 min.
TOTAL TIME: 3 hr., 15 min.

2¼ cups all-purpose flour
1 cup cold butter, cut into pieces
1 (8-oz.) package cream cheese, cut into pieces
½ tsp. salt
1 (10-oz.) jar red pepper jelly
1 cup finely chopped toasted pecans
Parchment paper

1. Pulse first 4 ingredients in a food processor 3 or 4 times or until dough forms a small ball and leaves sides of bowl. Divide dough into 8 portions, shaping each portion into a ball. Wrap each ball separately in plastic wrap, and chill 1 to 24 hours.
2. Preheat oven to 375°. Cook pepper jelly in a small saucepan over medium heat, stirring often, 2 to 3 minutes or just until melted. Roll 1 dough ball into an 8-inch circle on a lightly floured surface. Brush dough with 1 to 2 Tbsp. melted jelly; sprinkle with 2 Tbsp. pecans. Cut circle into 8 wedges, and roll up wedges, starting at wide end, to form a crescent shape. Place, point sides down, on a lightly greased parchment paper-lined baking sheet. Repeat procedure with remaining dough balls, pepper jelly, and pecans.
3. Bake at 375° for 15 to 20 minutes or until golden brown. Remove from baking sheets to wire racks. Cool completely (about 30 minutes).

Pepper Jelly-Goat Cheese Cakes

MAKES: 2 dozen
HANDS-ON TIME: 20 min.
TOTAL TIME: 2 hr., 50 min.

To melt the pepper jellies, place in a microwave-safe bowl, and microwave at HIGH 20 to 25 seconds or until melted.

24 aluminum foil miniature baking cups
Vegetable cooking spray
¼ cup fine, dry Italian-seasoned breadcrumbs
¼ cup ground toasted pecans
2 Tbsp. grated Parmesan cheese
2 Tbsp. butter, melted
1 (8-oz.) package cream cheese, softened
1 (4-oz.) goat cheese log, softened
1 large egg
2 Tbsp. heavy cream
1 Tbsp. Asian Sriracha hot chili sauce
¼ cup green pepper jelly, melted
¼ cup red pepper jelly, melted

1. Preheat oven to 350°. Place baking cups in 2 (12-cup) miniature muffin pans; coat baking cups with cooking spray.
2. Stir together breadcrumbs and next 3 ingredients. Firmly press about 1 tsp. breadcrumb mixture into bottom of each baking cup.
3. Beat cream cheese and goat cheese at medium speed with an electric mixer until light and fluffy; add egg and next 2 ingredients, beating just until blended. Spoon batter into baking cups, filling three-fourths full.
4. Bake at 350° for 10 minutes or until set. Cool completely in pans on a wire rack (about 20 minutes). Spoon 1 tsp. melted green pepper jelly over each of 12 cheesecakes. Spoon 1 tsp. melted red pepper jelly over remaining 12 cheesecakes. Cover and chill 2 to 12 hours before serving.

BACON

Bacon-Wrapped Bourbon Figs

MAKES: 2 dozen
HANDS-ON TIME: 20 min.
TOTAL TIME: 55 min.

The size of your figs will determine how much cheese you need.

12 dried Calimyrna figs
¼ cup bourbon
1 (2- to 4-oz.) wedge Gorgonzola cheese, cut into 24 pieces
24 pecan halves, toasted
12 fully cooked ready-to-serve bacon slices, cut in half crosswise
24 wooden picks

1. Combine first 2 ingredients and 1½ cups water in a medium saucepan. Cook, covered, over low heat 15 to 20 minutes or until figs are plump and softened. Remove from heat, and cool slightly (about 15 minutes). Drain figs, and gently pat dry with paper towels.
2. Preheat oven to 350°. Cut figs in half lengthwise. Place 1 cheese piece and 1 toasted pecan half on cut side of each fig half. Wrap 1 bacon piece around each fig half, and secure with a wooden pick. Place figs on a wire rack in a 15- x 10-inch jelly-roll pan.
3. Bake at 350° for 6 to 8 minutes or until bacon is crisp and browned.
NOTE: We tested with Oscar Mayer Fully Cooked Bacon.

Bacon-Wrapped Shrimp

MAKES: 2 dozen
HANDS-ON TIME: 20 min.
TOTAL TIME: 1 hr., 8 min.

- 24 unpeeled, large raw shrimp
- ¼ cup canola oil
- ¼ cup balsamic vinegar
- 3 Tbsp. chopped fresh basil
- 2 shallots, minced
- 1 garlic clove, minced
- 1 Tbsp. light brown sugar
- ¼ tsp. ground red pepper
- ⅛ tsp. salt
- 12 bacon slices, cut in half crosswise
- 24 wooden picks

1. Preheat oven to 450°. Peel and devein shrimp, leaving tails on. Combine canola oil and next 7 ingredients in a zip-top plastic freezer bag. Add shrimp; seal and chill 30 minutes, turning once.

2. Meanwhile, arrange bacon pieces in a single layer in a 15- x 10-inch jelly-roll pan. Bake at 450° for 6 to 8 minutes or just until bacon slices begin to brown. (Bacon will be partially cooked, not crisp.) Remove bacon from pan, and drain on paper towels. Reduce oven temperature to 400°.

3. Place a lightly greased wire rack in an aluminum foil-lined 15- x 10-inch jelly-roll pan. Remove shrimp from marinade, discarding marinade. Wrap 1 bacon piece around each shrimp, and secure with a wooden pick threaded through both ends of shrimp. Arrange shrimp in a single layer on wire rack, and bake at 400° for 8 to 10 minutes or until bacon is crisp and shrimp turn pink. Serve immediately.

Bacon-Wrapped Potatoes with Queso Blanco Dip

MAKES: 16 servings
HANDS-ON TIME: 30 min.
TOTAL TIME: 1 hr., 10 min.

Look for white American cheese in the deli section of the supermarket.

- 2 medium-size red potatoes, cut into 8 wedges each
- ½ tsp. salt
- 16 center-cut bacon slices
- ½ tsp. pepper
- ½ cup diced red onion
- 1 Tbsp. canola oil
- 1 garlic clove
- 12 oz. queso blanco pasteurized prepared cheese product, cubed
- 1 (8-oz.) block pepper Jack cheese, shredded
- ½ cup half-and-half
- 1 (4-oz.) can chopped green chiles
- 1 plum tomato, seeded and diced
- ¼ cup chopped fresh cilantro

1. Place a lightly greased wire rack in an aluminum foil-lined 15- x 10-inch jelly-roll pan.

2. Preheat oven to 425°. Sprinkle potato with salt. Wrap each with 1 bacon slice, wrapping bacon around potato wedge in a single layer. Arrange potatoes in a single layer in prepared pan. Sprinkle with pepper.

3. Bake at 425° for 40 to 45 minutes or until bacon is crisp and browned.

4. Meanwhile, sauté onion in hot oil in a skillet over medium-high heat 5 minutes or until tender. Add garlic, and sauté 1 minute. Remove from heat.

5. Combine queso blanco, next 3 ingredients, and onion mixture in a large microwave-safe glass bowl. Microwave at HIGH 2½ minutes; stir and microwave 2½ more minutes or until cheese is melted and mixture is smooth, stirring at 1-minute intervals. Stir in diced tomato and cilantro. Serve with potatoes.

NOTE: We tested with Velveeta Queso Blanco for prepared cheese product.

Chicken-and-Bacon Satay

MAKES: 16 to 20 servings
HANDS-ON TIME: 40 min.
TOTAL TIME: 1 hr., 35 min., including sauce

- 4 skinned and boned chicken thighs (about 1 lb.)
- ½ cup lite soy sauce
- ⅓ cup sake
- 2 Tbsp. light brown sugar
- 1 Tbsp. grated fresh ginger
- ½ tsp. dried crushed red pepper
- 16 to 20 (4-inch) wooden skewers
- 8 to 10 fully cooked bacon slices, cut in half crosswise
  Garnish: thinly sliced green onions
  Peanut Sauce

1. Place chicken between 2 sheets of plastic wrap, and flatten to ¼-inch thickness using a rolling pin or flat side of a meat mallet. Cut chicken into 16 to 20 (1-inch) strips.

2. Combine soy sauce and next 4 ingredients in a large zip-top plastic freezer bag; add chicken, turning to coat. Seal and chill 45 minutes, turning once.

3. Meanwhile, soak skewers in water 30 minutes; drain.

4. Preheat grill to 350° to 400° (medium-high) heat. Remove chicken from marinade, discarding marinade. Thread 1 bacon piece and 1 chicken strip onto each skewer.

5. Grill, covered with grill lid, 4 to 5 minutes on each side or until chicken is done. Serve with Peanut Sauce.

Peanut Sauce

MAKES: about 1⅓ cups
HANDS-ON TIME: 10 min.
TOTAL TIME: 10 min.

1. Process ½ cup creamy peanut butter; ⅓ cup lite soy sauce; ¼ cup loosely packed fresh cilantro leaves; and 3 Tbsp. each fresh lime juice, honey, and dark sesame oil in a blender or food processor until smooth. Add 1 to 2 Tbsp. water, 1 tsp. at a time, to blender for desired consistency.

Bacon-Wrapped Cheese Sticks with Collard Green Pesto

MAKES: about 2 dozen
HANDS-ON TIME: 20 min.
TOTAL TIME: 45 min., plus 24 hr. for chilling

Before you chop the collard greens, be sure to trim out the thick stalk.

- 3 cups firmly packed chopped fresh collard greens
- ⅓ cup chopped toasted pecans
- 2 garlic cloves, sliced
- ½ cup olive oil
- ½ cup freshly grated Asiago cheese
- ½ tsp. salt
- ¼ tsp. dried crushed red pepper
- 26 to 28 fully cooked bacon slices
- 1 (26-oz.) package frozen breaded mozzarella sticks

1. Cook collard greens in boiling water to cover 3 minutes; drain. Plunge into ice water to stop the cooking process; drain well.
2. Process pecans and garlic in a food processor until finely ground. Add greens, oil, next 3 ingredients, and ¼ cup water; process 2 to 3 seconds or until smooth, stopping to scrape down sides as needed. Cover and chill 24 hours.
3. Preheat oven to 425°. Place a lightly greased wire rack in an aluminum foil-lined 15- x 10-inch jelly-roll pan. Wrap 1 fully cooked bacon piece around each frozen cheese stick. (Do not thaw cheese sticks.) Arrange cheese sticks in a single layer on rack.
4. Bake at 425° for 10 to 12 minutes or until bacon is crisp and browned. Serve with collard green mixture.
NOTE: We tested with Farm Rich breaded mozzarella sticks.

Layer Cake Pancakes

Indulge in a Christmas morning meal that will remind you of your favorite holiday dessert.

Three Steps to Perfect Pancakes

{1}

To cook pancakes, pour about ¼ cup batter for each pancake onto a hot buttered griddle or large nonstick skillet. Cook pancakes 3 to 4 minutes or until tops are covered with bubbles and edges look dry and cooked. Turn and cook 3 to 4 minutes or until done. Place pancakes in a single layer on a baking sheet, and keep warm in a 200° oven up to 30 minutes.

{2}

Use a light hand when stirring the batter; overmixing will cause a rubbery texture. Batter should be lumpy.

{3}

When using a griddle to cook pancakes, set the temperature dial to 350°.

The Loveless Café's Red Velvet Pancakes

MAKES: 24 pancakes
HANDS-ON TIME: 35 min.
TOTAL TIME: 50 min., including butter

- 2 cups all-purpose flour
- 1 cup powdered sugar
- ½ cup unsweetened cocoa
- 1½ tsp. baking powder
- ½ tsp. baking soda
- ½ tsp. salt
- 1½ cups buttermilk
- 2 large eggs
- ½ cup granulated sugar
- 2 Tbsp. red liquid food coloring
  Sweet Cream-Cheese Butter
  Garnish: powdered sugar

1. Sift together first 6 ingredients into a large bowl. Whisk together buttermilk and next 3 ingredients in another bowl. Gradually stir buttermilk mixture into flour mixture just until dry ingredients are moistened. Cook as directed at left. Serve with Sweet Cream-Cheese Butter.

Sweet Cream-Cheese Butter

MAKES: 4 cups
HANDS-ON TIME: 15 min.
TOTAL TIME: 15 min.

1. Beat 1 (8-oz.) package cream cheese, softened, and 1 cup butter, softened, at medium speed with an electric mixer until creamy. Gradually add 3 cups powdered sugar, beating at low speed until blended after each addition. Add 1 tsp. vanilla extract, beating until blended.

Italian Cream Pancakes

MAKES: about 18 pancakes
HANDS-ON TIME: 35 min.
TOTAL TIME: 50 min., including syrup

- ⅔ cup finely chopped pecans
- ½ cup sweetened flaked coconut
- 2 cups all-purpose flour
- ⅓ cup sugar
- 1 tsp. baking powder
- ½ tsp. baking soda
- ½ tsp. salt
- 1 cup buttermilk
- ¾ cup heavy cream
- 2 Tbsp. butter, melted
- 2 tsp. vanilla extract
- 2 large eggs, separated
  Cream Cheese Syrup
  Garnish: chopped toasted pecans

1. Preheat oven to 350°. Bake pecans and coconut in a single layer in a shallow pan. Bake 5 to 7 minutes or until lightly toasted and fragrant, stirring halfway through.
2. Stir together flour and next 4 ingredients in a large bowl. Whisk together buttermilk, next 3 ingredients, and 2 egg yolks in another bowl. Gradually stir buttermilk mixture into flour mixture just until dry ingredients are moistened. Stir in pecans and coconut. Beat egg whites at high speed with an electric mixer until stiff peaks form, and fold into batter. Cook as directed on page 301. Serve with Cream Cheese Syrup.

Cream Cheese Syrup

MAKES: about 1¼ cups
HANDS-ON TIME: 10 min.
TOTAL TIME: 10 min.

1. Beat ½ (8-oz.) package cream cheese, softened; ¼ cup butter, softened; ¼ cup maple syrup; and 1 tsp. vanilla extract at medium speed with an electric mixer until creamy. Gradually add 1 cup powdered sugar, beating until smooth. Gradually add ¼ cup milk, beating until smooth. If desired, microwave syrup in a microwave-safe bowl at HIGH 10 to 15 seconds or just until warm; stir until smooth.

German Chocolate Pancakes

MAKES: about 20 pancakes
HANDS-ON TIME: 35 min.
TOTAL TIME: 55 min., including syrup

- 2 cups all-purpose flour
- ½ cup sugar
- ½ cup unsweetened cocoa
- 1½ Tbsp. baking powder
- 1 tsp. salt
- 2 cups milk
- 2 large eggs, lightly beaten
- ½ (4-oz.) sweet chocolate baking bar, finely chopped
- 3 Tbsp. butter, melted
- 1 tsp. vanilla extract
  German Chocolate Syrup
  Garnish: white and sweet chocolate curls

1. Whisk together first 5 ingredients in a large bowl. Whisk together milk and next 4 ingredients in another bowl. Gradually stir milk mixture into flour mixture just until dry ingredients are moistened. Cook as directed on page 301. Serve with German Chocolate Syrup.
NOTE: We tested with Baker's German's Sweet Chocolate Bar.

German Chocolate Syrup

MAKES: about 1½ cups
HANDS-ON TIME: 15 min.
TOTAL TIME: 20 min.

- ⅔ cup chopped pecans
- ⅔ cup sweetened flaked coconut
- 1 (5-oz.) can evaporated milk
- ½ cup firmly packed light brown sugar
- ¼ cup butter, melted
- 2 egg yolks, lightly beaten
- ½ tsp. vanilla extract

1. Preheat oven to 350°. Bake pecans and coconut in a single layer in a shallow pan 5 to 7 minutes or until lightly toasted and fragrant, stirring halfway through.
2. Cook evaporated milk and next 3 ingredients in a 2-qt. heavy saucepan over medium heat, stirring constantly, 8 to 10 minutes or until mixture bubbles and begins to thicken. Remove from heat, and stir in vanilla, pecans, and coconut. Serve immediately, or store in an airtight container in refrigerator up to 1 week.
TO REHEAT: Microwave syrup in a microwave-safe bowl at HIGH 10 to 15 seconds or just until warm; stir until smooth.

Hummingbird Pancakes

MAKES: about 18 pancakes
HANDS-ON TIME: 30 min.
TOTAL TIME: 45 min., including anglaise

- 1½ cups all-purpose flour
- 2 tsp. baking powder
- ¾ tsp. salt
- ½ tsp. ground cinnamon
- 1½ cups buttermilk
- 1 cup mashed very ripe bananas
- ½ cup drained canned crushed pineapple in juice
- ⅓ cup sugar
- 1 large egg, lightly beaten
- 3 Tbsp. canola oil
- ½ cup chopped toasted pecans
  Cream Cheese Anglaise
  Garnishes: sliced bananas, pineapple chunks

1. Stir together first 4 ingredients in a large bowl. Whisk together buttermilk and next 5 ingredients in another bowl. Gradually stir buttermilk mixture into flour mixture just until dry ingredients are moistened. Fold in pecans. Cook as directed on page 301. Serve with Cream Cheese Anglaise.

Cream Cheese Anglaise

MAKES: about 1¾ cups
HANDS-ON TIME: 15 min.
TOTAL TIME: 15 min.

- 1½ cups half-and-half
- ½ (8-oz.) package cream cheese, softened
- ⅓ cup sugar
- 3 egg yolks
- 1 Tbsp. cornstarch
- ⅛ tsp. salt
- 2 Tbsp. butter
- 1 tsp. vanilla extract

1. Process first 6 ingredients in a blender until smooth. Bring mixture to a boil in a medium saucepan over medium heat, whisking constantly. Boil, whisking constantly, 1 minute. Remove from heat, and whisk in butter and vanilla. Serve immediately.

Carrot Cake Pancakes

MAKES: about 24 pancakes
HANDS-ON TIME: 40 min.
TOTAL TIME: 50 min., including cream

Use small holes of a box grater to finely grate the carrots by hand; if you use a food processor, the carrots will be too wet, making the pancakes dense and less tender.

- 1¾ cups all-purpose flour
- 1½ tsp. baking powder
- 1 tsp. baking soda
- 1 tsp. ground cinnamon
- 1 tsp. salt
- 2 cups buttermilk
- ⅓ cup firmly packed light brown sugar
- ¼ cup butter, melted
- 2 large eggs, lightly beaten
- 2 tsp. vanilla extract
- 2 cups finely grated carrots (about 1 lb.)
- ½ cup chopped toasted pecans
- ⅓ cup chopped golden raisins
  Mascarpone Cream
  Garnish: carrot curls

1. Stir together first 5 ingredients in a large bowl. Whisk together buttermilk and next 4 ingredients in another bowl. Gradually stir buttermilk mixture into flour mixture just until dry ingredients are moistened. Fold in carrots and next 2 ingredients. Cook as directed on page 301. Serve with Mascarpone Cream.

Mascarpone Cream

MAKES: about 2½ cups
HANDS-ON TIME: 10 min.
TOTAL TIME: 10 min.

1. Whisk together 1 (8-oz.) container mascarpone cheese, ¼ cup powdered sugar, and 2 tsp. vanilla extract in a large bowl just until blended. Beat 1 cup whipping cream at medium speed with an electric mixer until stiff peaks form. Fold whipped cream into mascarpone mixture.

Caramel Cake Pancakes

MAKES: about 15 pancakes
HANDS-ON TIME: 30 min.
TOTAL TIME: 40 min., including syrup

- 2 cups self-rising flour
- ½ cup sugar
- 1 cup milk
- 2 large eggs
- 3 Tbsp. butter, melted
- 2 tsp. vanilla extract
  Caramel Syrup

1. Whisk together first 2 ingredients in a large bowl. Whisk together milk and next 3 ingredients in another bowl. Gradually stir milk mixture into flour mixture just until dry ingredients are moistened. Cook as directed on page 301. Serve with Caramel Syrup.

Caramel Syrup

MAKES: 1¾ cups
HANDS-ON TIME: 10 min.
TOTAL TIME: 10 min.

1. Melt ½ cup butter in a heavy saucepan over medium heat; add 1 cup sugar and 1 tsp. fresh lemon juice, and cook, stirring constantly, 5 to 6 minutes or until mixture turns a caramel color. Gradually add ¾ cup whipping cream, and cook, stirring constantly, 1 to 2 minutes or until smooth. Serve immediately, or store in an airtight container in refrigerator up to 1 week. To reheat, microwave syrup in a microwave-safe bowl at HIGH 10 to 15 seconds or just until warm; stir until smooth.

Dreaming of a White Christmas Cake

Meet the finalists in our second annual white cake contest. Plus, try the scrumptious white cake our Test Kitchen created for the cover of this year's *Southern Living Annual Recipes*.

Layer Cake Secrets

- Allow butter and eggs to stand at room temperature 30 to 45 minutes.

- Add extracts to butter-and-sugar mixture instead of at the end to fully incorporate into the batter.

- Cooking spray with flour works like a charm to keep cakes from sticking to pans.

- Bake cakes on the same oven rack, but be sure to leave 2 inches of space between pans so heat can circulate freely.

Mrs. Billett's White Cake

MAKES: 10 to 12 servings
HANDS ON TIME: 40 min.
TOTAL TIME: 2 hr., including frosting

Don't let the cake bosses and bakers extraordinaire fool you. Smooth, pliable, decorative fondant is easy to use, particularly one straight from the box. Follow our directions (see White Cake Decorating 101 at right), applying a little edible glitter and pearl sparkling dust (such as Wilton Shimmer Dust). Don't forget the pearls!

Parchment paper
1   cup milk
1½ tsp. vanilla extract
1   cup butter, softened
2   cups sugar
3   cups cake flour
1   Tbsp. baking powder
5   egg whites
    Vanilla Buttercream Frosting
    Garnish: Fondant Snowflakes
    (directions on opposite page)

1. Preheat oven to 350°. Grease 3 (8-inch) round cake pans; line bottoms with parchment paper, and grease and flour paper.
2. Stir together milk and vanilla.
3. Beat butter at medium speed with a heavy-duty electric stand mixer until creamy; gradually add sugar, beating until light and fluffy. Sift together flour and baking powder; add to butter mixture alternately with milk mixture, beginning and ending with flour mixture. Beat at low speed just until blended after each addition.

4. Beat egg whites at medium speed with an electric mixer until stiff peaks form; gently fold into batter. Pour batter into prepared pans.
5. Bake at 350° for 20 to 23 minutes or until a wooden pick inserted in center comes out clean. Cool in pans on wire racks 10 minutes. Remove from pans to wire racks; discard parchment paper. Cool completely on wire racks (about 40 minutes).
6. Spread Vanilla Buttercream Frosting between layers (about 1 cup per layer) and on top and sides of cake.

Vanilla Buttercream Frosting

MAKES: 4½ cups
HANDS-ON TIME: 10 min.
TOTAL TIME: 10 min.

1   cup butter, softened
¼   tsp. salt
1   (2-lb.) package powdered sugar
6   to 7 Tbsp. milk
1   Tbsp. vanilla extract

1. Beat butter and salt at medium speed with an electric mixer 1 to 2 minutes or until creamy; gradually add powdered sugar alternately with 6 Tbsp. milk, beating at low speed until blended and smooth after each addition. Stir in vanilla. If desired, beat in remaining 1 Tbsp. milk, 1 tsp. at a time, until frosting reaches desired consistency.

SUE WINTER
GILLETTE, WYOMING

White Cake Decorating 101

HOLLY FONDANT: Frost cake as directed. Roll one-fourth of 1 (24-oz.) package white rolled fondant to ¼-inch thickness on a flat surface lightly dusted with powdered sugar. Cut fondant with a 1¾-inch holly leaf cutter. Use a small knife to add decorative veins. Crumple 2 (14-inch-long) pieces aluminum foil into 1-inch-wide ropes; place on a parchment paper-lined baking sheet. Gently drape each fondant leaf over foil to give it a natural-looking shape. Let stand at room temperature 12 hours. Lightly brush leaves with vodka, and sprinkle with white edible glitter and pearl sparkling dust (such as Wilton Shimmer Dust). Arrange leaves and fresh cranberries on cake as desired, pressing gently to adhere.

ALMOND BARK AND RASPBERRIES: Frost cake as desired. Melt 1 (24-oz.) package almond bark candy coating in a large saucepan according to package directions. Spread about ¾ cup melted candy coating into a thin 4- x 12-inch rectangle on parchment paper, using an offset spatula. Transfer parchment paper to top of a 12-cup muffin pan (this will give the candy coating gentle curves); freeze 20 minutes or until set. Remove frozen candy coating on parchment paper from muffin pan, and place in freezer until ready to assemble cake. Repeat process with remaining candy coating. When ready to assemble cake, let frozen candy coating stand at room temperature 10 minutes; break into pieces. Attach pieces to sides of cake with frosting. Top cake with about 2 (4-oz.) containers fresh raspberries; dust berries with powdered sugar.

DOT-PUSH PATTERN: Frost cake as desired. Insert a round ¼-inch tip into a large decorating bag; fill with Vanilla Buttercream Frosting (see page 304). Pipe 1 column of dots on side of cake, from top edge of cake to bottom, making sure dots touch each other. Using a small offset spatula, gently smear each dot horizontally, 1 at a time. Repeat to decorate entire sides; add 1 row of dots around top outer edge of cake, smearing dots as directed.

MERINGUE: Frost cake as desired. Stack store-bought mini meringues on top of cake, and dust generously with powdered sugar.

FONDANT SNOWFLAKES: Frost cake as desired. Roll half of 1 (24-oz.) package white rolled fondant to ¼-inch thickness on a flat surface lightly dusted with powdered sugar. Cut fondant with small and large snowflake cutters. Transfer to baking sheets; let stand at room temperature 12 hours. Lightly brush dry snowflakes with vodka, and sprinkle with white edible glitter and pearl sparkling dust (such as Wilton Shimmer Dust). Arrange on cake as desired, using frosting to adhere. Press white no. 5 dragees around bottom edge of cake, if desired.

Dreamy White Cake with Chocolate-Mint Cheesecake Layers and Mint Buttercream Frosting

MAKES: 12 servings
HANDS-ON TIME: 50 min.
TOTAL TIME: 11 hr., 50 min., including cheesecake layers and frosting

Chocolate-Mint Cheesecake Layers have to chill before the cake is assembled, so make them the day before you plan to serve the cake. This one was created by our Test Kitchen—a candy curl garnish adds a festive touch. (Pictured on cover)

2¾   **cups cake flour**
1⅔   **cups sugar**
1   **Tbsp. baking powder**
½   **tsp. salt**
¾   **cup butter, softened**
4   **egg whites**
1   **large egg**
1   **cup milk**
2   **tsp. vanilla extract**
    Mint Buttercream Frosting
    Chocolate-Mint Cheesecake Layers
    Garnish: Candy Curls (recipe on opposite page)

1. Preheat oven to 350°. Combine first 4 ingredients in a bowl of a heavy-duty electric stand mixer; beat at low speed until blended. Add butter, beating until crumbly. Gradually add egg whites, beating until blended after each addition, and stopping to scrape bowl as needed. Add egg, beating just until blended.
2. Stir together milk and vanilla; add to flour mixture, ⅓ cup at a time, beating just until blended after each addition, and stopping to scrape bowl as needed. Pour batter into 3 greased and floured 8-inch round cake pans.
3. Bake at 350° for 20 to 22 minutes or until a wooden pick inserted in center comes out clean. Cool in pans on wire racks 10 minutes. Remove from pans to wire racks, and cool completely (about 1 hour).

4. Place 1 white cake layer on a serving plate or cake stand; spread with ⅓ cup Mint Buttercream Frosting. Top with 1 Chocolate-Mint Cheesecake Layer; spread with ⅓ cup Mint Buttercream Frosting. Repeat procedure once. Top with remaining white cake layer.
5. Spread a thin layer of Mint Buttercream Frosting on top and sides of cake. Chill 30 minutes. Spread remaining Mint Buttercream Frosting over top and sides of cake. Cover and chill 1 to 24 hours before serving. Store cake in refrigerator. Garnish, if desired.

Chocolate-Mint Cheesecake Layers

MAKES: 2 layers
HANDS-ON TIME: 10 min.
TOTAL TIME: 7 hr., 50 min.

    Parchment paper
8   **(1-oz.) semisweet chocolate baking squares**
3   **(8-oz.) packages cream cheese, softened**
1   **cup sugar**
1   **(8-oz.) package mascarpone cheese**
2   **tsp. vanilla extract**
½   **tsp. peppermint extract**
3   **large eggs**

1. Preheat oven to 325°. Line bottoms of 2 lightly greased 8-inch round cake pans with parchment paper; lightly grease parchment paper.
2. Melt chocolate in a microwave-safe bowl at HIGH 1 to 1½ minutes or until melted and smooth, stirring at 30-second intervals.
3. Beat cream cheese and sugar at low speed with an electric mixer until smooth. Add melted chocolate, beating just until blended. Add mascarpone cheese and extracts, beating just until blended. Add eggs, 1 at a time, beating just until blended after each addition. Pour batter into prepared pans.

4. Bake at 325° for 30 minutes or until set. Cool completely in pans on wire racks (about 1 hour). Cover and chill 6 to 24 hours. Gently run a knife around edge of cheesecakes to loosen. Invert each onto a separate sheet of parchment paper.

Mint Buttercream Frosting

MAKES: 5½ cups
HANDS-ON TIME: 10 min.
TOTAL TIME: 10 min.

1   **cup butter, softened**
2   **(16-oz.) packages powdered sugar**
½   **cup whipping cream**
1   **Tbsp. vanilla extract**
1   **tsp. peppermint extract**

1. Beat butter at medium speed with an electric mixer until creamy; gradually add half of powdered sugar, beating at low speed until blended after each addition. Add remaining powdered sugar alternately with cream, beating at low speed until blended after each addition. Add extracts; beat at medium speed 2 minutes or until fluffy.

Peppermint-Hot Chocolate Cake

MAKES: 10 to 12 servings
HANDS-ON TIME: 40 min.
TOTAL TIME: 2 hr., 25 min., including filling and frosting

- ½ cup boiling water
- 1 (4-oz.) milk chocolate baking bar, chopped
- 1 cup butter, softened
- 2 cups sugar
- 4 large eggs, separated
- 1 tsp. vanilla extract
- 2 cups all-purpose flour
- ¼ cup unsweetened cocoa
- 1 tsp. baking soda
- 1 tsp. salt
- 1 cup buttermilk
  Fudge Filling
  Peppermint-Cream Frosting
  Garnish: French vanilla cream-filled rolled wafer cookies dusted with powdered sugar, hard peppermint candies, fresh mint sprig

1. Preheat oven to 350°. Grease and flour 3 (8-inch) round cake pans.

2. Pour boiling water over milk chocolate in a small heatproof bowl. Stir until chocolate is melted and smooth. Cool to room temperature (about 30 minutes).

3. Beat butter at medium speed with a heavy-duty electric stand mixer until creamy; gradually add sugar, beating until light and fluffy. Add egg yolks, 1 at a time, beating until blended after each addition. Add vanilla and melted chocolate, beating until blended.

4. Combine flour and next 3 ingredients; add to butter mixture alternately with buttermilk, beginning and ending with flour mixture. Beat at low speed just until blended after each addition.

5. Beat egg whites at medium speed until soft peaks form; gently fold into batter. Pour batter into prepared pans.

6. Bake at 350° for 20 to 30 minutes or until a wooden pick inserted in center comes out clean. Cool in pans on wire racks 10 minutes; remove from pans to wire racks, and cool completely (about 40 minutes).

7. Meanwhile, prepare Fudge Filling.

8. Spread filling between layers. Spread Peppermint-Cream Frosting on top and sides of cake.

Fudge Filling

MAKES: 2 cups
HANDS-ON TIME: 10 min.
TOTAL TIME: 30 min.

1. Cook 1 (14-oz.) can sweetened condensed milk and 1 (12-oz.) package semisweet chocolate morsels in a saucepan over medium-low heat, stirring constantly, 4 to 6 minutes or until chocolate is melted and smooth. Remove from heat; stir in ¼ tsp. peppermint extract. Cool to room temperature (about 20 minutes).

Candy Curls

Line 4 (5- x 3-inch) loaf pans with aluminum foil, allowing 1 to 2 inches to extend over all sides. Melt 2 cups white candy coating wafers according to package directions. Spoon about 4 Tbsp. melted white candy in bottom of each pan, spreading to cover completely. Let stand approximately 10 minutes or until set. Melt 1 cup red candy coating wafers according to package directions. Spoon about 2 Tbsp. over each white candy layer, spreading to cover completely. Let stand approximately 10 minutes or until set. Spoon about 4 Tbsp. melted white candy over each red layer, spreading to cover completely. Let stand 10 minutes or until completely set. Remelt candy, if necessary for 30-second intervals. Lift layered candy from pans, using foil sides as handles. Microwave each 10 seconds or until warm. Pull a vegetable peeler along narrow edge of layered candy, making curls.

Peppermint-Cream Frosting

MAKES: 3 cups
HANDS-ON TIME: 5 min.
TOTAL TIME: 5 min.

1. Beat 1 (7-oz.) jar marshmallow crème; 1 (8-oz.) container frozen whipped topping, thawed; and ⅛ tsp. peppermint extract at high speed with an electric mixer 1 to 2 minutes or until glossy and stiff peaks form.

NOTE: We tested with Nielsen-Massey Pure Peppermint Extract.

BRITAINY SHAW
BURLESON, TEXAS

Marbled Pumpkin-Praline Cake

MAKES: 10 to 12 servings
HANDS-ON TIME: 50 min.
TOTAL TIME: 2 hr., 15 min.

PUMPKIN BATTER

- Parchment paper
- 2 cups all-purpose flour
- 2 tsp. baking soda
- 2 tsp. ground cinnamon
- ½ tsp. salt
- ¼ tsp. ground nutmeg
- ¼ tsp. ground ginger
- ¼ tsp. ground cloves
- 1½ cup granulated sugar
- ¾ cup firmly packed light brown sugar
- ¾ cup vegetable oil
- 3 large eggs
- 1½ cups canned pumpkin
- ¾ cup buttermilk

CREAM CHEESE BATTER

- 2 (3-oz.) packages cream cheese, softened
- ½ cup granulated sugar
- 6 Tbsp. butter, softened
- 2 Tbsp. all-purpose flour
- 1 tsp. vanilla extract
- 2 large eggs, lightly beaten

PECAN-PRALINE FILLING

- ½ cup firmly packed light brown sugar
- ¼ cup butter
- ¼ cup corn syrup
- ½ cup half-and-half
- 2 Tbsp. cornstarch
- 1 cup chopped toasted pecans
- 1 tsp. vanilla extract

SPICED WHIPPED CREAM

- 2 cups heavy cream
- 6 Tbsp. powdered sugar
- ¾ tsp. vanilla extract
- ⅛ tsp. ground cinnamon

GARNISH

- Fresh bay leaves sprayed with silver food color spray, sugared pecan halves, and halved and whole kumquats

1. Prepare Pumpkin Batter: Preheat oven to 350°. Grease 3 (9-inch) round cake pans. Line bottoms with parchment paper, and grease and flour paper.

2. Combine flour and next 6 ingredients in a small bowl. Beat 1½ cups granulated sugar and next 3 ingredients at medium speed with a heavy-duty electric stand mixer until blended. Add pumpkin, beating until blended. Add buttermilk, beating until blended. Gradually add flour mixture, beating at low speed just until blended after each addition. Pour batter into prepared pans.

3. Prepare Cream Cheese Batter: Beat cream cheese and next 4 ingredients at medium speed until creamy. Add eggs, beating until blended. Drop by heaping tablespoonfuls onto batter in pans, and gently swirl with a knife.

4. Bake at 350° for 25 minutes or until a wooden pick inserted in center comes out clean. Cool in pans on wire racks 10 minutes; remove from pans to wire racks, and cool completely (about 40 minutes).

5. Meanwhile, prepare Pecan-Praline Filling: Bring ½ cup brown sugar and next 2 ingredients to a boil in a saucepan over medium heat, whisking constantly. Boil, whisking constantly, 1 minute or until sugar is dissolved. Whisk together half-and-half and cornstarch in a small bowl until smooth; gradually add to brown sugar mixture, whisking constantly. Return to a boil, and boil, whisking constantly, 1 minute or until thickened. Stir in toasted pecans and 1 tsp. vanilla. Cool 20 minutes.

6. Spread filling between cake layers.

7. Prepare Spiced Whipped Cream: Beat cream at medium speed 1 minute. Add powdered sugar and next 2 ingredients, beating until soft peaks form. Spread frosting on top and sides of cake.

MARILYN BOONE
BARTLESVILLE, OKLAHOMA

Red Velvet Revelry

This season enjoy a few twists on this Southern Christmas classic dessert.

Red Velvet Cake with Coconut-Cream Cheese Frosting

MAKES: 10 to 12 servings
HANDS-ON TIME: 30 min.
TOTAL TIME: 2 hr., 35 min., including frosting

Though it may appear that this batter fits in two pans, we recommend dividing the batter among four pans. If you need additional cake pans, 8-inch aluminum foil disposable pans work fine. Just be sure to place them on a baking sheet for easy in and out of the oven.

- ¾ **cup butter, softened**
- 2 **cups sugar**
- 3 **large eggs**
- 3 **Tbsp. red liquid food coloring**
- 1 **Tbsp. vanilla extract**
- 2¾ **cups all-purpose flour**
- ½ **cup unsweetened cocoa**
- 1 **Tbsp. baking powder**
- ¾ **tsp. baking soda**
- ¼ **tsp. salt**
- 1½ **cups buttermilk**
  Coconut-Cream Cheese Frosting

1. Preheat oven to 350°. Beat butter at medium speed with a heavy-duty electric stand mixer until light and fluffy. Gradually add sugar, beating until blended. Add eggs, 1 at a time, beating until blended after each addition. Add food coloring and vanilla, beating until blended.

2. Whisk together flour and next 4 ingredients; add to butter mixture alternately with buttermilk, beginning and ending with flour mixture. Beat at low speed just until blended after each addition. Spoon batter into 4 greased and floured 8-inch round cake pans.

3. Bake all pans at the same time, with 2 pans on the top rack and 2 pans on the bottom rack, at 350° for 10 minutes; rotate pans, and bake 10 to 12 minutes or until a wooden pick inserted in center comes out clean. Cool in pans on wire racks 10 minutes. Remove from pans to wire racks, and cool completely (about 1 hour).

4. Spread about 1 cup Coconut-Cream Cheese Frosting between layers; spread remaining frosting on top and sides of cake.

Coconut-Cream Cheese Frosting

MAKES: about 8 cups
HANDS-ON TIME: 15 min.
TOTAL TIME: 15 min.

1. Beat 2 (8-oz.) packages cream cheese, softened, and 1 cup butter, softened, at medium speed with a heavy-duty electric stand mixer until smooth. Add ½ tsp. coconut extract, beating until blended. Gradually add 8 cups powdered sugar, beating until smooth. Stir in 4 cups sweetened shredded coconut.

Red Velvet-Raspberry Tiramisù Trifle

MAKES: 10 servings
HANDS-ON TIME: 20 min.
TOTAL TIME: 5 hr., 5 min., including madeleines

- 1 **cup seedless raspberry jam**
- ¼ **cup black raspberry liqueur**
- ¼ **cup fresh orange juice**
- 2 **(8-oz.) containers mascarpone cheese**
- 2 **cups heavy cream**
- ⅓ **cup sugar**
- 1 **tsp. vanilla extract**
  Red Velvet Madeleines (without powdered sugar) (see recipe, page 310)
- 3 **(6-oz.) containers fresh raspberries**

1. Whisk together first 3 ingredients in a small bowl.

2. Stir together mascarpone cheese in a large bowl just until blended.

3. Beat heavy cream at high speed with an electric mixer until foamy; gradually add sugar and vanilla, beating until soft peaks form. Stir one-fourth of whipped cream into mascarpone using a rubber spatula; fold in remaining whipped cream.

4. Arrange one-third of Red Velvet Madeleines in a 3-qt. trifle dish; drizzle with one-third of jam mixture, top with 1 container of raspberries, and dollop raspberries with one-third of mascarpone mixture. Repeat layers twice. Cover and chill 4 to 24 hours before serving.

Red Velvet Madeleines

MAKES: 2 dozen
HANDS-ON TIME: 15 min.
TOTAL TIME: 45 min.

- ¾ cup granulated sugar
- 3 large eggs
- 2 egg yolks
- 1 tsp. vanilla extract
- ¾ cup butter, melted
- 2 Tbsp. red liquid food coloring
- 1⅓ cups cake flour
- 2 Tbsp. unsweetened cocoa
- ½ tsp. baking powder
- ¼ tsp. salt
  Powdered sugar (optional)

1. Preheat oven to 400°. Beat first 4 ingredients at medium-high speed with an electric mixer 5 minutes or until thick and pale. Add butter and food coloring, beating until blended.
2. Sift together cake flour and next 3 ingredients; fold flour mixture into egg mixture. Spoon batter into 2 lightly greased shiny madeleine pans, filling three-fourths full (about 1 Tbsp. per madeleine).
3. Bake at 400° for 8 to 10 minutes or until centers of madeleines spring back when lightly touched. Immediately remove from pans to wire racks, and cool completely (about 20 minutes). Dust with powdered sugar just before serving, if desired.

Red Velvet Madeleine Tree

Make a madeleine tree by pinning about 5 dozen Red Velvet Madeleines to an 18-inch-tall white foam cone, available at Michaels and other crafts stores. (You can use any height of cone for these and cut them to size, if you wish. Number of madeleines will vary.) Start with a row at the top, and work your way down the cone, securing the bottom of each madeleine with wooden picks and overlapping the consecutive rows to hide the picks (similar to staggering shingles on a roof). Dust with powdered sugar for a snowy finish.

Red Velvet-Peppermint Swirl Brownies

MAKES: about 2 dozen
HANDS-ON TIME: 20 min.
TOTAL TIME: 1 hr., 50 min.

- 1 (4-oz.) bittersweet chocolate baking bar, chopped
- ¾ cup butter
- 2¼ cups sugar, divided
- 4 large eggs
- 1 (1-oz.) bottle red liquid food coloring
- ¼ tsp. peppermint extract
- 2 tsp. vanilla extract, divided
- 1½ cups all-purpose flour
- ⅛ tsp. salt
- ½ (8-oz.) package cream cheese, softened
- 2 egg whites
- 2 Tbsp. all-purpose flour

1. Preheat oven to 350°. Line bottom and sides of a 13- x 9-inch pan with aluminum foil, allowing 2 to 3 inches to extend over sides; lightly grease foil.
2. Microwave chocolate and butter in a large microwave-safe bowl at HIGH 1½ to 2 minutes or until melted and smooth, stirring at 30-second intervals. Whisk in 2 cups sugar. Add eggs, 1 at a time, whisking just until blended after each addition. Add food coloring, peppermint extract, and 1 tsp. vanilla. Gently stir in 1½ cups flour and ⅛ tsp. salt. Pour batter into prepared pan.
3. Beat cream cheese and remaining ¼ cup sugar at medium speed with an electric mixer until fluffy. Add egg whites and remaining 1 tsp. vanilla, and beat until blended. Stir in flour until smooth. Drop cream cheese mixture, by heaping tablespoonfuls over batter in pan, and gently swirl with a knife.
4. Bake at 350° for 30 to 32 minutes or until a wooden pick inserted in center comes out with a few moist crumbs. Cool completely in pan on a wire rack (about 1 hour). Lift brownies from pan, using foil sides as handles. Gently remove foil; cut brownies into squares.

Red Velvet Cake Roll

MAKES: 8 to 10 servings
HANDS-ON TIME: 25 min.
TOTAL TIME: 2 hr., 10 min.

Parchment paper
1 cup semisweet chocolate chunks
5 large eggs, separated
1 cup granulated sugar, divided
2 Tbsp. red liquid food coloring
¼ cup powdered sugar
1 cup whipping cream
2 Tbsp. amaretto liqueur

1. Preheat oven to 325°. Lightly grease a 15- x 10-inch jelly-roll pan; line bottom with parchment paper, and lightly grease paper. Microwave chocolate chunks and ¼ cup water in a large microwave-safe glass bowl at HIGH 1 minute or until chocolate is melted and smooth, stirring at 30-second intervals.

2. Beat egg yolks and ¾ cup granulated sugar at high speed with an electric mixer 3 minutes or until mixture is thick and pale. Whisk into chocolate mixture; stir in food coloring.

3. Beat egg whites at high speed until stiff peaks form; fold into chocolate mixture. Pour batter into prepared pan.

4. Bake at 325° for 15 minutes or until cake springs back when lightly touched. Remove from oven, and cover with a clean, damp towel. Cool completely in pan on a wire rack (about 30 minutes).

5. Remove towel. Sift powdered sugar onto a clean, dry cloth towel in a 15- x 10-inch rectangle. Run a knife around edges of pan to loosen cake, and turn cake out onto prepared towel. Carefully peel parchment paper from cake, and discard.

6. Beat whipping cream, amaretto, and remaining ¼ cup granulated sugar at high speed until stiff peaks form. Spread cream mixture over top of cake, leaving a 1-inch border on all sides. Lift and tilt towel, and carefully roll up cake, jelly-roll fashion, starting at 1 short side and using towel as a guide. Place cake, seam side down, on a serving platter. Cover and chill 1 to 8 hours before serving.

Chocolate Latte

MAKES: about 5¼ cups
HAND-ON TIME: 10 min.
TOTAL TIME: 10 min.

1. Cook 4 cups strong brewed, hot coffee, 1 cup half-and-half, ¼ cup chocolate syrup, 2 Tbsp. sugar, and ½ tsp. vanilla extract in a medium saucepan over medium-low heat, stirring often, 5 minutes or until thoroughly heated. Serve immediately.

Test Kitchen Intervention

Let There Be Peace on Earth (or at least serenity in your kitchen).

Like you, we often find ourselves caught in the holiday vortex of entertaining, shopping, cleaning, and cooking, all while trying to keep up with everyday chores and family meals. Here's how we regroup and bring joy to the hours spent in the kitchen.

ANGELA SELLERS

"I listen to the soundtrack from *A Charlie Brown Christmas* all month long." (Find our holiday playlist at *southernliving.com*)

PAT YORK

"After everyone has gone and the kitchen is clean, I like to take a walk in the woods—it's physically and mentally rejuvenating."

DONNA FLORIO

"I sit down with Truman Capote's *A Christmas Memory*, about an Alabama Christmas in a simpler time. It almost—but not quite—makes me want to make fruitcake. And the end always makes me cry."

MARY ALLEN PERRY

"I plant a window garden of snowy paperwhites."

PAM LOLLEY

"I make myself a latte and warm up a leftover sweet roll." (Get the recipe for Pam's famous Orange Rolls at *myrecipes.com*)

SHANNON SATTERWHITE

"My mother would always play Elvis to take the edge off while making tins of fudge. For me, a little Widespread Panic or Karl Denson kicks things up a notch, but the King always seems to find a spot on my playlist."

Frostings and Fillings

Chocolate Filling

MAKES: 2⅓ cups
HANDS-ON TIME: 15 min.
TOTAL TIME: 7 hr., 15 min.

- 2 cups heavy cream
- ⅓ cup sugar
- ¼ cup all-purpose flour
- ¼ cup Dutch process cocoa
- 2 large eggs
- 1 Tbsp. vanilla extract

1. Whisk together first 5 ingredients in a heavy saucepan. Cook over medium-low heat, whisking constantly, 8 to 10 minutes or until mixture reaches a chilled pudding-like thickness. Remove from heat; stir in vanilla. Cool to room temperature (about 1 hour). Place plastic wrap directly onto mixture (to prevent a film from forming), and chill 6 to 24 hours before using.

Gingerbread Latte Filling

MAKES: 2 cups
HANDS-ON TIME: 15 min.
TOTAL TIME: 7 hr., 15 min.

- 1⅔ cups heavy cream
- ⅓ cup molasses
- ¼ cup all-purpose flour
- 2 large eggs
- 2 tsp. espresso powder
- ½ tsp. ground ginger
- ¼ tsp. ground cinnamon
- 1 tsp. vanilla extract

1. Whisk together first 7 ingredients in a heavy saucepan. Cook over medium-low heat, whisking constantly, 10 to 12 minutes or until mixture reaches a chilled pudding-like thickness. Remove from heat; stir in vanilla. Cool to room temperature (about 1 hour). Place plastic wrap directly onto mixture (to prevent a film from forming), and chill 6 to 24 hours before using.

Eggnog Filling

MAKES: 2 cups
HANDS-ON TIME: 15 min.
TOTAL TIME: 7 hr., 15 min.

- 1¾ cups heavy cream
- ⅓ cup sugar
- ¼ cup all-purpose flour
- 2 large eggs
- ¼ tsp. ground nutmeg
- ¼ cup bourbon
- 1 Tbsp. vanilla extract

1. Whisk together first 5 ingredients in a heavy saucepan. Cook over medium-low heat, whisking constantly, 10 to 12 minutes or until mixture reaches a chilled pudding-like thickness. Remove from heat; stir in bourbon and vanilla. Cool to room temperature (about 1 hour). Place plastic wrap directly onto mixture (to prevent a film from forming), and chill 6 to 24 hours before using.

Lemon-Thyme Curd Filling

MAKES: 2 cups
HANDS-ON TIME: 20 min.
TOTAL TIME: 8 hr., 25 min.

- 4 large eggs
- 3 egg yolks
- ½ cup sugar
- 2 Tbsp. lemon zest
- ½ cup fresh lemon juice
- ½ tsp. chopped fresh thyme
- 1 vanilla bean, split
- 6 Tbsp. cold butter, cut into small pieces
  Pinch of salt

1. Pour water to depth of 1 inch into bottom of a double boiler over medium-high heat; bring to a boil. Reduce heat to medium-low, and simmer. Whisk eggs and egg yolks in top of double boiler off heat; whisk in sugar and next 3 ingredients. Scrape vanilla bean seeds into egg mixture, and whisk until blended. Place top of double boiler over simmering water. Cook, whisking constantly, 10 minutes or until mixture thickens.

2. Remove top of double boiler from simmering water, and add butter and salt, whisking until butter is melted. Place plastic wrap directly onto warm curd (to prevent a film from forming), and chill 8 hours before using.

Merry Berry Filling

MAKES: 2 cups
HANDS-ON TIME: 15 min.
TOTAL TIME: 6 hr., 45 min.

- 1 cup fresh cranberries
- 1 cup fresh raspberries
- ½ cup sugar
- 2 Tbsp. cornstarch
- 1 Tbsp. cold water
- 1 cup chopped fresh strawberries
- 1 Tbsp. butter

1. Cook first 3 ingredients and 3 Tbsp. water in a medium saucepan over medium-low heat, stirring often, 3 to 4 minutes or until cranberries begin to pop. Whisk together cornstarch and 1 Tbsp. cold water in a small bowl until smooth; add to cranberry mixture, and cook, stirring constantly, 1 minute. Stir in strawberries and butter. Cool to room temperature (about 30 minutes). Cover and chill 6 hours before using.

White Chocolate Buttercream

MAKES: about 6 cups
HANDS-ON TIME: 15 min.
TOTAL TIME: 45 min.

- 1 (4-oz.) white chocolate baking bar, broken into small pieces
- ⅓ cup heavy cream
- 1 cup butter, softened
- 1 (2-lb.) package powdered sugar
- ¼ cup heavy cream
- ⅛ tsp. kosher salt
- 2 tsp. vanilla extract

1. Microwave white chocolate and ⅓ cup heavy cream in a microwave-safe bowl at MEDIUM (50% power) 1 to 1½ minutes or until melted and smooth, stirring at 30-second intervals. (Do not overheat.) Let cool to room temperature (about 30 minutes).

2. Beat butter at medium speed with an electric mixer until creamy; gradually add powdered sugar and ¼ cup heavy cream, 1 Tbsp. at a time, beating at low speed until blended after each addition. Beat in salt and white chocolate mixture until light and fluffy. Stir in vanilla.

Crème de Menthe Frosting

MAKES: 6 cups
HANDS-ON TIME: 15 min.
TOTAL TIME: 15 min.

- 1 cup butter, softened
- 1 (2-lb.) package powdered sugar
- 4 Tbsp. green crème de menthe
- ½ cup plus 2 Tbsp. milk
- 2 tsp. vanilla extract
- ⅛ tsp. salt

1. Beat butter at medium speed with an electric mixer until creamy; gradually add powdered sugar alternately with crème de menthe and milk, beating at low speed just until blended after each addition. Stir in vanilla and salt.

Bourbon-Vanilla Bean Frosting

MAKES: 6 cups
HANDS-ON TIME: 15 min.
TOTAL TIME: 15 min.

- 1 cup butter, softened
- 1 (2-lb.) package powdered sugar
- 5 Tbsp. bourbon
- ½ cup milk
- 2 Tbsp. vanilla bean paste
- ⅛ tsp. salt

1. Beat butter at medium speed with an electric mixer until creamy; gradually add powdered sugar alternately with bourbon and milk, beating at low speed just until blended after each addition. Stir in vanilla bean paste and salt.

White Russian Frosting

MAKES: 6 cups
HANDS-ON TIME: 15 min.
TOTAL TIME: 15 min.

- 1 cup butter, softened
- 1 (2-lb.) package powdered sugar
- ½ cup plus 2 Tbsp. coffee liqueur
- 2 tsp. vanilla extract
- ⅛ tsp. salt

1. Beat butter at medium speed with an electric mixer until creamy; gradually add powdered sugar alternately with coffee liqueur, beating at low speed just until blended after each addition. Stir in vanilla and salt.

Salted Caramel Frosting

MAKES: 5 cups
HANDS-ON TIME: 20 min.
TOTAL TIME: 20 min.

- 1 cup butter
- 1 cup firmly packed dark brown sugar
- ⅓ cup heavy cream
- 4 cups powdered sugar, sifted
- 1 tsp. vanilla extract
- ½ tsp. sea salt

1. Bring first 2 ingredients to a rolling boil in a 3½-qt. saucepan over medium heat, whisking constantly.
2. Stir in cream, and return to a boil; remove from heat. Pour into bowl of a heavy-duty electric stand mixer. Gradually beat in powdered sugar and vanilla at medium speed, using whisk attachment; beat 7 to 10 minutes or until thickened. Use immediately. Sprinkle with sea salt.

Casseroles for Every Occasion

Whether you need a dish to host the in-laws or take to the neighbor's potluck, try one of these perfectly portable chicken bakes.

Swiss Chicken Crêpes

MAKES: about 4 to 6 servings
HANDS-ON TIME: 20 min.
TOTAL TIME: 1 hr., 5 min.

1 (12-oz.) jar roasted red bell peppers, drained
Swiss Cheese Sauce
3 cups finely chopped cooked chicken
1 (5-oz.) package fresh baby spinach, chopped
1 cup (4 oz.) shredded Swiss cheese
¼ cup chopped fresh basil
1 garlic clove, pressed
1 tsp. seasoned pepper
8 egg roll wrappers

1. Preheat oven to 350°. Process peppers in a blender until smooth, stopping to scrape down sides as needed. Pour into 4 lightly greased 7- x 4½-inch baking dishes.
2. Prepare Swiss Cheese Sauce. Stir together next 6 ingredients, and 1 cup Swiss Cheese Sauce.
3. Divide chicken mixture evenly among wrappers, spooning down centers; gently roll up. Place, seam side down, over red peppers in baking dish. Top with remaining Swiss Cheese Sauce. Cover with aluminum foil.
4. Bake, covered, at 350° for 15 minutes or until thoroughly heated.

Swiss Cheese Sauce

MAKES: about 4 cups
HANDS-ON TIME: 20 min.
TOTAL TIME: 20 min.

⅓ cup dry vermouth
1 garlic clove, pressed
3 cups half-and-half
3 Tbsp. cornstarch
1 tsp. salt
½ tsp. pepper
2 cups (8 oz.) shredded Swiss cheese

1. Bring vermouth and garlic to a boil in a large skillet over medium-high heat; reduce heat to medium-low, and simmer 7 to 10 minutes or until vermouth is reduced to 1 Tbsp. Whisk together half-and-half and cornstarch in a small bowl. Whisk salt, pepper, and half-and-half mixture into vermouth mixture; bring to a boil over medium-high heat, whisking constantly. Boil, whisking constantly, 1 minute or until mixture is thickened. Add Swiss cheese; reduce heat to low, and simmer, whisking constantly, 1 minute or until cheese is melted and sauce is smooth. Remove from heat, and use immediately.

Tortellini-Chicken-Broccoli Bake

MAKES: 6 to 8 servings
HANDS-ON TIME: 30 min.
TOTAL TIME: 1 hr., 15 min.

½ cup butter
½ cup chopped sweet onion
½ cup chopped red bell pepper
2 garlic cloves, minced
¼ cup all-purpose flour
3 cups chicken broth
1½ cups half-and-half
½ cup dry white wine
1 cup (4 oz.) freshly shredded Parmesan cheese
¼ tsp. salt
¼ tsp. ground red pepper
1 (20-oz.) package refrigerated cheese-filled tortellini
4 cups chopped fresh broccoli
4 cups chopped cooked chicken
½ cup grated Parmesan cheese
15 round buttery crackers, crushed
½ cup chopped pecans
3 Tbsp. butter, melted

1. Preheat oven to 350°. Melt ½ cup butter in a Dutch oven over medium-high heat; add onion and next 2 ingredients, and sauté 5 to 6 minutes or until tender.
2. Add flour, stirring until smooth. Cook, stirring constantly, 1 minute. Whisk in broth, half-and-half, and white wine. Reduce heat to medium, and cook, stirring constantly, 6 to 8 minutes or until mixture is thickened and bubbly.
3. Remove from heat; add 1 cup Parmesan cheese and next 2 ingredients, stirring until cheese melts. Stir in tortellini and next 2 ingredients. Spoon into a lightly greased 13- x 9-inch baking dish. Stir together ½ cup grated Parmesan cheese and next 3 ingredients. Sprinkle over casserole.
4. Bake at 350° for 40 to 45 minutes or until bubbly.

Chicken-Mushroom-Sage Casserole

MAKES: 6 servings
HANDS-ON TIME: I hr.
TOTAL TIME: I hr., 40 min.

This is a saucier casserole, but when it stands, the liquid absorbs into the rice to make a creamy texture.

½ cup butter, divided
6 skinned and boned chicken breasts
3 shallots, chopped
2 garlic cloves, minced
I lb. assorted fresh mushrooms, coarsely chopped
¼ cup sherry
3 Tbsp. all-purpose flour
2 (14-oz.) cans chicken broth
I (6-oz.) box long-grain and wild rice mix
½ cup grated Parmesan cheese
2 Tbsp. chopped fresh flat-leaf parsley
I Tbsp. chopped fresh sage
½ tsp. salt
½ tsp. pepper
½ cup sliced toasted almonds

1. Preheat oven to 375°. Melt I Tbsp. butter in a large skillet over medium-high heat; add half of chicken, and cook 3 minutes or until browned; turn and cook I minute. (Chicken will not be cooked completely.) Transfer to a plate. Repeat procedure with I Tbsp. butter and remaining chicken. Wipe skillet clean.
2. Melt 2 Tbsp. butter in skillet over medium-high heat. Add shallots, and sauté 3 minutes or until translucent. Add garlic, and sauté 30 seconds. Add mushrooms, and cook, stirring often, 4 to 5 minutes or until tender. Stir in sherry, and cook, stirring often, I minute.
3. Melt remaining ¼ cup butter in a 3-qt. saucepan over medium-high heat. Whisk in flour; cook, whisking constantly, I minute. Gradually whisk in broth. Bring to a boil, whisking constantly, and cook, whisking constantly, I to 2 minutes or until slightly thickened. Remove from heat,

and add rice mix (reserve flavor packet for another use), next 5 ingredients, and shallot mixture. Spoon into a lightly greased 13- x 9-inch baking dish. Top with chicken.
4. Bake at 375° for 30 to 35 minutes or until a meat thermometer inserted in thickest portion of chicken registers 165°. Remove from oven, and let stand 10 minutes. Sprinkle with almonds.

Cajun Chicken Cassoulet

MAKES: 6 servings
HANDS-ON TIME: 35 min.
TOTAL TIME: I hr., 15 min., not including topping

I (16-oz.) package Cajun smoked sausage, cut into ½-inch slices
6 skinned and boned chicken thighs (about 2¼ lb.)
I tsp. salt
I large onion, chopped
I medium-size green bell pepper, chopped
2 celery ribs, chopped
4 garlic cloves, chopped
2 (16-oz.) cans cannellini beans, drained and rinsed
I (14½-oz.) can diced tomatoes
1½ cups chicken broth
½ (16-oz.) package frozen sliced okra, thawed
1½ tsp. Cajun seasoning
Toasted Herbed Breadcrumb Topping (optional)

1. Preheat oven to 400°. Cook sausage in a large cast-iron Dutch oven over medium heat, stirring occasionally, 4 to 5 minutes or until browned. Remove sausage with a slotted spoon, and drain on paper towels, reserving drippings in Dutch oven.
2. Sprinkle chicken with salt. Cook chicken in hot drippings over medium-high heat 2 to 3 minutes on each side or until browned. Remove from Dutch oven. Add onion and next 3 ingredients to Dutch oven, and cook, stirring often, 5 minutes or until onion is tender. Add beans, next 4 ingredients, chicken, and sausage.

3. Bake, covered, at 400° for 40 minutes or until bubbly. Uncover and, if desired, sprinkle with Toasted Herbed Breadcrumb Topping.
TOASTED HERBED BREADCRUMB TOPPING: Sauté 2½ cups soft, fresh French-bread breadcrumbs (about 3 slices) and I garlic clove, pressed, in 2 Tbsp. hot olive oil in a large nonstick skillet over medium-high heat 5 minutes or until golden brown and crisp. Remove from heat, and transfer to a small bowl. Stir in 2 Tbsp. chopped fresh flat-leaf parsley.

Bow-Tie Cheese Casserole

MAKES: 8 to 10 servings
HANDS-ON TIME: 15 min.
TOTAL TIME: I hr., 5 min.

I (16-oz.) package farfalle (bow-tie) pasta
4 cups chopped cooked chicken
6 Tbsp. butter
4 Tbsp. all-purpose flour
4 cups milk
2½ cups (10 oz.) freshly shredded sharp Cheddar cheese
I tsp. salt
½ tsp. pepper
I (24-oz.) jar tomato-and-basil pasta spaghetti sauce
I cup (4 oz.) shredded Italian six-cheese blend

1. Preheat oven to 350°. Prepare pasta according to package directions. Place pasta and chicken in a large bowl.
2. Melt butter in a medium saucepan over medium-high heat. Whisk in flour; cook, whisking constantly, I minute or until smooth. Gradually whisk in milk until smooth. Bring mixture to a boil, reduce heat to medium-low, and gradually stir in Cheddar cheese until smooth. Stir in salt and pepper. Stir cheese sauce into pasta mixture.
3. Spoon pasta mixture into a lightly greased 13- x 9-inch baking dish. Top with pasta sauce, and sprinkle with Italian cheese blend.
4. Bake at 350° for 35 to 40 minutes or until bubbly.

Community Cookbook

A taste of what received the highest raves in the *Southern Living* Test Kitchen.

FROM THE KITCHEN OF
ROBIN WARREN
CLARKESVILLE, GEORGIA

"The cornmeal adds a crunchy texture to the cookies—a change of pace from ordinary sugar cookies."

Cornmeal Sugar Cookies

1. Preheat oven to 300°. Beat I cup granulated sugar and I cup butter, softened, at medium speed with a heavy-duty electric stand mixer until creamy. Add 2 egg yolks, I at a time, beating until blended after each addition. Whisk together I½ cups all-purpose flour and I cup plain white cornmeal; gradually add to sugar mixture, beating just until blended. Roll dough to ¼-inch thickness on a well-floured surface. Cut with a 3¼-inch round (or desired shape) cutter, and decorate with sparkling sugar. Place cookies 2 inches apart on lightly greased baking sheets. Bake 14 to 16 minutes or until lightly browned. Transfer to wire racks, and cool completely (about 20 minutes). Makes: about 3 dozen.

JOIN OUR RECIPE SWAP!

Share your favorite—if it wows the Test Kitchen, we'll feature it here and send you a SL cookbook: *southernliving.com/recipeswap*.

NOTE: All submitted recipes become the property of *Southern Living* and may be used for any purpose.

FROM THE KITCHEN OF
ELLIE LEESE
MURFREESBORO, TENNESSEE

Honey-Orange-Ginger Cookies

1. Preheat oven to 350°. Beat ⅔ cup sugar and ½ cup butter, softened, at medium speed with a heavy-duty electric stand mixer until creamy. Add ½ cup honey, I tsp. orange extract, and I large egg, beating until blended. Stir together 2¼ cups all-purpose flour, I Tbsp. orange zest, I tsp. ground ginger, ½ tsp. baking soda, and ½ tsp. baking powder; gradually add to sugar mixture, beating until blended. Cover and chill 30 minutes to I hour. Shape dough into I-inch balls, and roll in sugar. Place 2 inches apart on ungreased baking sheets, and slightly flatten each with bottom of a glass. Bake 8 to 10 minutes or until lightly browned. Transfer to wire racks, and cool completely (about 20 minutes). Makes: about 4 dozen.

FROM THE KITCHEN OF
JENNIFER HEICHEL
ANDALUSIA, ALABAMA

"Even if you don't care for the traditional cake version that you re-gift every year, you'll love these cookie bites."

Fruitcake Cookies

1. Preheat oven to 300°. Beat I½ cups sugar and I cup butter, softened, at medium speed with a heavy-duty electric stand mixer until creamy. Add 3 large eggs, I at a time, beating until blended after each addition. Stir in I tsp. vanilla extract. Sift together 3 cups all-purpose flour, I tsp. baking soda, and a pinch of salt; gradually add to sugar mixture, beating until blended. Stir in I lb. mixed candied fruit and peel; 4 cups chopped toasted pecans; I cup raisins; and I cup maraschino cherries, chopped. Drop dough by tablespoonfuls I inch apart onto lightly greased baking sheets. Bake 18 to 20 minutes or until lightly browned. Transfer to wire racks, and cool completely (about 20 minutes). Makes: about 9 dozen.

Don't Forget the Milk Punch

It's not the holidays without this spiked Southern classic.

Here are six delicious ways to enjoy it, hot or cold. (Beware, they go down very easy!) For the perfect make-ahead punch, cover and cool to room temperature (about 30 minutes) after simmering, and pour into a pitcher. Then, cover and chill about 8 hours before serving to let the flavors mingle. Top with soft whipped cream for extra frothiness.

Peanut Brittle Milk Punch

MAKES: 6 cups
HANDS-ON TIME: 20 min.
TOTAL TIME: 1 hr., 40 min.

1. Preheat oven to 350°. Bake 2 cups unsalted, blanched peanuts in a single layer in a shallow pan, 15 minutes or until toasted and fragrant, stirring halfway through. Bring 7 cups milk, 3 cups heavy cream, ½ cup firmly packed light brown sugar, 2 Tbsp. honey, ⅛ tsp. salt, 2 (3-inch-long) lemon zest strips, and roasted peanuts to a boil in a large heavy saucepan over medium-high heat; reduce heat to low, and simmer, stirring occasionally, 45 minutes. Remove from heat, and stir in 4 tsp. vanilla bean paste. Let stand 15 minutes. Discard lemon zest strips. Process mixture with a handheld blender until smooth. Pour through a wire-mesh strainer into a pitcher; discard solids. Serve hot or cold. If desired, stir in 2 to 3 Tbsp. bourbon per 1 cup punch just before serving. Garnish with crushed peanut brittle, if desired.

Mint-and-White-Chocolate Milk Punch

MAKES: about 7 cups
HANDS-ON TIME: 20 min.
TOTAL TIME: 30 min.

1. Bring 2 cups heavy cream; 1 qt. 2% reduced-fat milk; ½ cup sugar; and 1 vanilla bean, split, to a simmer in a large saucepan over medium heat, stirring often. Remove from heat; add 3 fresh mint sprigs. Cover and let stand 8 minutes. Discard mint and vanilla bean. Add 1 (4-oz.) white chocolate baking bar, chopped, and cook over low heat, stirring constantly, 2 minutes or until chocolate is melted. Serve hot or cold. If desired, stir in 2 Tbsp. vodka per 1 cup punch just before serving.

Caramel-and-Chicory Milk Punch

MAKES: 6 cups
HANDS-ON TIME: 20 min.
TOTAL TIME: 20 min.

You will need 2 cups strong brewed chicory coffee for this recipe.

1. Cook ½ cup granulated sugar, ¼ cup firmly packed light brown sugar, and ¼ cup strong brewed chicory coffee in a large saucepan over medium heat, stirring constantly with a long-handled wooden spoon, 4 to 5 minutes or until mixture reaches syrup-like consistency. Stir 1¾ cups strong brewed chicory coffee, 1 qt. half-and-half, and 1 tsp. vanilla extract into sugar mixture, and bring to a simmer over medium heat, stirring occasionally. Serve hot or cold. If desired, stir in 2 Tbsp. chocolate liqueur per 1 cup punch just before serving.

Chocolate-Raspberry Milk Punch

MAKES: 7 cups
HANDS-ON TIME: 15 min.
TOTAL TIME: 15 min.

1. Bring 1 qt. 2% reduced-fat milk, 2 cups heavy cream, and 2 (2-inch-long) orange zest strips to a simmer in a large saucepan over medium heat, stirring often. Remove from heat; whisk in ¾ cup chocolate syrup and ½ cup seedless raspberry jam until smooth. Discard orange zest. Serve hot or cold. If desired, stir in 2 Tbsp. brandy per 1 cup punch just before serving.

Ginger-Vanilla Milk Punch

MAKES: 6½ cups
HANDS-ON TIME: 15 min.
TOTAL TIME: 35 min.

1. Bring 1 qt. 2% reduced-fat milk; 2 cups heavy cream; ¾ cup sugar; 2 (¼-inch-thick) fresh ginger slices; 2 (2-inch-long) lemon zest strips; 1 (2-inch-long) orange zest strip; and 1 vanilla bean, split, to a simmer in a large saucepan over medium heat, stirring often. Cover and let stand 20 minutes. Pour mixture through a wire-mesh strainer into a pitcher; discard solids. Serve hot or cold. If desired, stir in 2 Tbsp. dark rum per 1 cup punch just before serving.

Indian Spice Milk Punch

MAKES: 6¾ cups
HANDS-ON TIME: 20 min.
TOTAL TIME: 20 min.

1. Bring 1 qt. 2% reduced-fat milk, 1 (13.5-oz.) can coconut milk, 1 (8.75-oz.) can cream of coconut, 1 (2-inch-long) lemon zest strip, 1 star anise pod, 1 tsp. whole cloves, ¼ tsp. ground ginger, and ⅛ tsp. ground cardamom to a simmer in a large saucepan over medium heat, stirring often. Pour through a wire-mesh strainer into a heatproof pitcher; discard solids. Serve hot or cold. If desired, stir in 2 Tbsp. amaretto liqueur per 1 cup punch just before serving.

Cheese Straw Sampler

One basic recipe yields a delicious variety of holiday treats.

Basic Cheese Straw Dough

1. Beat 2½ cups (10 oz.) freshly shredded sharp Cheddar cheese; ½ cup butter, softened; 1 Tbsp. half-and-half; and 1 tsp. kosher salt at medium speed with a heavy-duty electric stand mixer until blended. Gradually add 1½ cups all-purpose flour, beating just until combined. Form dough into a ball. Hands-on time: 10 min., Total time: 10 min.

Test Kitchen Tip

Reroll dough scraps only once. Dough may be wrapped in plastic wrap, sealed in a zip-top plastic freezer bag, and chilled up to 3 days. Let stand 15 minutes before rolling out.

PECAN-ROSEMARY-CHEDDAR BUTTONS: Preheat oven to 350°. Prepare dough as directed, increasing half-and-half to 2 Tbsp. and adding 2 cups chopped toasted pecans and 1 Tbsp. finely chopped fresh rosemary with flour. Turn dough out onto a well-floured surface. Divide dough into 4 equal portions, and flatten each into a disk; roll each disk to ⅛-inch thickness. Cut with a 2-inch round cutter. Place 1 inch apart on parchment paper-lined baking sheets. Bake 15 to 18 minutes or until golden; cool on baking sheets on wire racks 30 minutes. Makes: about 6 dozen. Hands-on time: 30 min.; Total time: 2 hr., including dough.

OLIVE-BLUE MOONS: Preheat oven to 350°. Prepare dough as directed, adding 1 (6-oz.) can Spanish olives, drained and finely chopped, and 2 oz. blue cheese, crumbled, before adding flour. Turn dough out onto a well-floured surface. Divide dough into 2 equal portions, and flatten each into a disk; roll each disk to ⅛-inch thickness. Cut with a 2½-inch moon-shaped cutter. Place 1 inch apart on parchment paper-lined baking sheets. Bake 15 to 20 minutes or until golden; cool on baking sheets on wire racks 30 minutes. Makes: about 8 dozen. Hands-on time: 30 min.; Total time: 2 hr., 10 min., including dough.

BACON-SMOKED PAPRIKA CHEDDAR BARS: Preheat oven to 350°. Prepare dough as directed, adding 4 cooked and crumbled applewood-smoked bacon slices, 1 tsp. smoked paprika, and ½ tsp. ground red pepper with flour. Turn dough out onto a well-floured surface. Divide dough into 2 equal portions; flatten each into a square. Roll out each square to ⅛-inch thickness. Cut each square into 2½- x ¾-inch strips, using a fluted pastry wheel. Place 1 inch apart on parchment paper-lined baking sheets. Bake 15 to 20 minutes or until golden; cool on baking sheets on wire racks 30 minutes. Makes: about 6 dozen. Hands-on time: 30 min.; Total time: 2 hr., 30 min., including dough.

PIMIENTO CHEESE SQUARES: Preheat oven to 350°. Drain 1 (4-oz.) jar diced pimiento; pat dry with paper towels, and finely chop. Stir 1 tsp. ground mustard and ¼ tsp. ground red pepper into 1½ cups flour in dough recipe. Gradually add chopped pimiento to flour mixture, tossing to coat. Prepare dough as directed, omitting half-and-half. Turn dough out onto a well-floured surface. Divide dough into 2 equal portions; flatten each into a square. Roll each square to ⅛-inch thickness. Cut with a 1½-inch square cutter. Place 1 inch apart on parchment paper-lined baking sheets. Bake 15 to 20 minutes; cool on baking sheets on wire racks 30 minutes. Makes: about 5 dozen. Hands-on time: 30 min.; Total time: 1 hr., 50 min., including dough.

PARMESAN-BASIL-CHEDDAR STARS: Preheat oven to 350°. Prepare dough as directed, increasing half-and-half to 3 Tbsp. and adding 1½ cups grated Parmigiano-Reggiano cheese and 3 Tbsp. finely chopped fresh basil with flour. Turn dough out onto a well-floured surface. Divide dough into 4 equal portions, and flatten each into a disk; roll each disk to ⅛-inch thickness. Cut with a 1½-inch star-shaped cutter. Place 1 inch apart on parchment paper-lined baking sheets. Bake 11 to 14 minutes or until golden; cool on baking sheets on wire racks 30 minutes. Makes: about 15 dozen. Hands-on time: 30 min.; Total time: 2 hr., 40 min., including dough.

Shortbread Sampler

Basic Shortbread Cookies

MAKES: 4 dozen
HANDS-ON TIME: 30 min.
TOTAL TIME: 2 hr., 40 min.

- 1 cup butter, softened
- ¾ cup powdered sugar
- 2 tsp. vanilla extract
- ½ tsp. almond extract
- 2 cups all-purpose flour
- ¼ tsp. baking powder
- ⅛ tsp. salt
- Wax paper
- Parchment paper

1. Beat butter at medium speed with an electric mixer until creamy. Gradually add powdered sugar, beating until smooth. Stir in vanilla and almond extracts until blended.
2. Stir together flour and next 2 ingredients. Gradually add flour mixture to butter mixture, beating at low speed until blended.
3. Divide dough in half; flatten each half into a disk. Roll each disk to ¼-inch thickness between 2 sheets of wax paper. Transfer rolled dough in wax paper to a baking sheet; chill 1 hour.
4. Preheat oven to 350°. Working with 1 portion of dough at a time, remove top sheet of wax paper, and cut into 2½- x ¾-inch rectangles, rerolling dough scraps once. Place 1 inch apart on parchment paper-lined baking sheets.
5. Bake at 350° for 12 to 14 minutes or until edges are golden. Cool on baking sheets 1 minute; transfer to wire racks, and cool completely (about 20 minutes). Store in airtight containers.

CHOCOLATE-PEPPERMINT BARS: Prepare recipe as directed. Microwave ¾ cup dark chocolate morsels in a microwave-safe bowl at HIGH 1½ minutes or until melted and smooth, stirring at 30-second intervals. Drizzle over cookies. Sprinkle 12 crushed hard peppermint candies over cookies. Let stand until firm (about 30 minutes). Makes: 4 dozen. Hands-on time: 20 min.; Total time: 3 hr., 30 min.

BOURBON-PECAN SNOWFLAKES: Prepare recipe as directed through Step 2, omitting almond extract, adding 1 cup chopped toasted pecans and 4 Tbsp. bourbon with vanilla in Step 1, and increasing flour to 2½ cups. Proceed as directed, cutting with a 3-inch snowflake-shaped cutter and increasing bake time to 14 to 16 minutes. Makes: 2½ dozen. Hands-on time: 30 min.; Total time: 2 hr., 50 min.

CHERRY-CHOCOLATE THUMBPRINTS: Soak 1 cup chopped dried cherries in 4 Tbsp. cherry liqueur for 1 hour. Prepare recipe as directed through Step 2, omitting almond extract and stirring in soaked cherries and ¾ cup Dutch process cocoa with vanilla in Step 1. Shape dough into 1-inch balls (about 1 Tbsp. per ball), and place 2 inches apart on parchment paper-lined baking sheets. Press thumb or end of a wooden spoon into each ball, forming an indentation. Bake and cool as directed. Microwave ½ cup white chocolate morsels and 2 Tbsp. heavy cream in a microwave-safe bowl at HIGH 1 minute or until melted and smooth, stirring at 30-second intervals. Spoon ½ tsp. white chocolate mixture into each indentation. Let stand until white chocolate mixture is firm (about 1 hour). Makes: 4 dozen. Hands-on time: 30 min.; Total time: 3 hr., 20 min.

CINNAMON-ORANGE SQUARES: Prepare recipe as directed through Step 2, omitting vanilla and almond extracts, increasing flour to 2¼ cups, and adding 2 Tbsp. orange zest, ¾ tsp. ground cinnamon, and ¼ tsp. ground nutmeg to flour mixture in Step 2. Proceed with recipe as directed through Step 4, cutting with a 2-inch square cutter. Stir together 1 Tbsp. sugar and ¼ tsp. ground cinnamon, and sprinkle over cookies. Bake and cool as directed. Makes: 3 dozen. Hands-on time: 30 min.; Total time: 3 hr., 5 min.

KEY LIME STARS: Prepare recipe as directed through Step 2, omitting vanilla and almond extracts and adding 1 Tbsp. Key lime zest and 2 Tbsp. Key lime juice after sugar in Step 1 and increasing flour to 2¼ cups. Stir together 2 Tbsp. white sanding sugar and 1 Tbsp. lime zest. Proceed with recipe as directed through Step 4, cutting with a 2-inch star-shaped cutter. Sprinkle cookies with sugar mixture, pressing gently to adhere. Bake and cool as directed, increasing baking time to 14 to 16 minutes or until tips of stars just begin to brown. Makes: about 4 dozen. Hands-on time: 30 min.; Total time: 2 hr., 50 min.

SWEET POTATO-MARSHMALLOW COOKIE SANDWICHES: Prepare recipe as directed through Step 2, omitting almond extract and adding ¾ cup canned sweet potato puree with vanilla in Step 1, increasing flour to 2½ cups, and adding 1 tsp. freshly grated nutmeg, ¾ tsp. ground cardamom, ½ tsp. ground ginger, and ½ tsp. ground cinnamon to flour mixture in Step 2. Proceed as directed, cutting with a 2-inch round cutter and sprinkling with 1 Tbsp. Demerara sugar before baking. Beat ½ cup marshmallow crème and ½ cup butter, softened, with a heavy-duty electric stand mixer at medium speed 2 minutes or until smooth; gradually add 2 cups powdered sugar. Add 1¼ tsp. meringue powder, and beat at high speed 2 minutes or until fluffy. Stir in 1 tsp. vanilla extract. Spread about 2 tsp. marshmallow mixture on 1 side of half of cooled shortbread rounds; top with remaining shortbread rounds, and press gently. Makes: 2½ dozen sandwich cookies. Hands-on time: 1 hr.; Total time: 3 hr., 20 min.

Pound Cake Truffle Sampler

Million Dollar Pound Cake

MAKES: 1 (9-inch) layer
HANDS-ON TIME: 15 min.
TOTAL TIME: 2 hr., 30 min.

You'll need only half of this cake for each truffle recipe—save the other half for other truffles or just nibbling. Use your favorite frosting or Vanilla Buttercream Frosting on page 304.

- 1   **cup butter, softened**
- 1½ **cups sugar**
- 3   **large eggs**
- 2   **cups all-purpose soft-wheat flour**
- ½   **cup milk**
- ½   **tsp. almond extract**
- ½   **tsp. vanilla extract**

1. Preheat oven to 300°. Beat butter at medium speed with a heavy-duty electric stand mixer until creamy. Gradually add sugar, beating 3 to 5 minutes or until light and fluffy. Add eggs, 1 at a time, beating just until yellow disappears.

2. Add flour to butter mixture alternately with milk, beginning and ending with flour. Beat at low speed just until blended after each addition. Stir in extracts. Pour batter into a lightly greased and floured 9-inch round cake pan.

3. Bake at 300° for 50 to 60 minutes or until a wooden pick inserted in center comes out clean. Cool in pan on a wire rack 10 minutes. Remove from pan to wire rack, and cool completely (about 1 hour).

NOTE: We tested with White Lily All-Purpose Flour.

BOURBON-PECAN POUND CAKE TRUFFLES: Crumble half of Million Dollar Pound Cake into a large bowl; stir in ½ cup Vanilla Buttercream Frosting, ⅓ cup chopped toasted pecans, and 2 Tbsp. bourbon until mixture holds its shape. Shape into 1-inch balls, and place on wax paper. Roll truffles in ¾ cup finely chopped toasted pecans, and dust with powdered sugar. Makes: about 3 dozen.

CANDIED GINGER POUND CAKE TRUFFLES: Crumble half of Million Dollar Pound Cake into a large bowl; stir in ½ cup Vanilla Buttercream Frosting, ⅓ cup finely chopped crystallized ginger, and ¼ cup amaretto liqueur until mixture holds its shape. Shape into 1-inch balls, and place on wax paper. Pour water to depth of 1 inch into bottom of a double boiler over medium heat. Bring to a boil; reduce heat, and simmer. Place 2 (4-oz.) 60% cacao bittersweet chocolate baking bars, chopped, and 1 (4-oz.) semisweet chocolate baking bar, chopped, in top of double boiler over simmering water. Cook, stirring occasionally, 15 minutes or until melted. Remove from heat. Dip truffles in melted chocolate, and place on a wax paper-lined baking sheet. Immediately sprinkle tops with finely chopped crystallized ginger. Makes: about 3 dozen.

CHOCOLATE-ESPRESSO POUND CAKE TRUFFLES: Crumble half of Million Dollar Pound Cake into a large bowl. Microwave 1 (4-oz.) semisweet chocolate baking bar and 3 Tbsp. heavy cream in a medium-size microwave-safe bowl at HIGH 1 to 1½ minutes or until melted and smooth, stirring at 30-second intervals. Stir in 1 single-serve packet from a 0.93-oz. package of ready-brew Colombian medium-roast instant coffee (such as Starbucks VIA). Stir ⅓ cup Vanilla Buttercream Frosting and chocolate mixture into crumbled cake until mixture holds its shape. Shape into 1-inch balls. Roll each truffle in Dutch process cocoa 2 times (This helps to get a good coating.) Makes: 3 dozen.

NOTE: We tested with Scharffen Berger Semisweet Fine Artisan Dark Chocolate bar.

RASPBERRY POUND CAKE TRUFFLES: Crumble half of Million Dollar Pound Cake into a large bowl; stir in ½ cup Vanilla Buttercream Frosting, ¼ cup seedless raspberry fruit spread, and ¼ tsp. vanilla extract until mixture holds its shape. Shape into 1-inch balls, and place on wax paper. Roll truffles in ½ cup finely chopped toasted almonds, and top each with 2 toasted sliced almonds. Makes: about 2½ dozen.

Holiday Favorites

Family Celebration

Host a crowd of loved ones with this bounteous meal that begins with a tasty bisque and ends with a luscious tart. And the dinner plate will win raves in between.

Family Get-Together

SERVES 12

Roasted Root Vegetable Bisque

Ham with Bourbon, Cola, and Cherry Glaze

Holiday Potato Bake

Roasted Brussels Sprouts and Cauliflower with Bacon Dressing

Chocolate-Orange Velvet Tart

Roasted Root Vegetable Bisque

MAKES: 17 cups
HANDS-ON TIME: 1 hr., 14 min.
TOTAL TIME: 2 hr., 14 min.

This appetizer soup will get your family gathering off to a delicious start. It's a thick puree of winter's best ingredients, blended with cream and Cajun seasoning.

- 6 **parsnips, peeled and chopped (1 lb.)**
- 4 **small turnips, peeled and chopped (1 lb.)**
- 2 **medium celeriac, peeled and chopped (1 lb.)**
- 1 **large butternut squash, peeled and chopped (2 lb.)**
- ¼ **cup olive oil**
- 10 **cups chicken broth, divided**
- ¼ **cup butter**
- 1 **large onion, chopped (about 2 cups)**
- 4 **garlic cloves, minced**
- 3 **Tbsp. all-purpose flour**
- 3 **Tbsp. tomato paste**
- 2 **tsp. Cajun seasoning**
- 1 **cup heavy whipping cream**
- ½ **tsp. salt**

1. Preheat oven to 450°. Combine parsnips and next 4 ingredients in a large bowl; toss to coat. Transfer vegetables to a large roasting pan, spreading into a single layer.

2. Roast at 450° for 1 hour to 1 hour and 10 minutes or until very tender and browned. Process half of roasted vegetables and 3 cups chicken broth in a blender until smooth. Pour vegetable puree into a large stockpot. Repeat with remaining roasted vegetables and 3 cups chicken broth; set aside.

3. Melt butter in a large skillet over medium-high heat; add onion and garlic, and sauté 7 minutes. Reduce heat to medium. Add flour; cook, stirring constantly, 3 minutes or until browned. Stir in tomato paste and Cajun seasoning; cook, stirring often, 3 minutes. Process onion mixture and remaining 4 cups broth in blender until smooth. Transfer to stockpot with vegetable mixture. Stir in cream and salt. Bring to a boil over medium heat; reduce heat to medium-low, and simmer, stirring often, 15 minutes.

NOTE: To make ahead, prepare this soup up to the point of sautéing the onion in Step 3. Freeze the pureed vegetable mixture in zip-top plastic freezer bags up to 1 month.

⭐ Holiday Favorites

Ham with Bourbon, Cola, and Cherry Glaze

MAKES: 12 to 14 servings
HANDS-ON TIME: 4 hr.
TOTAL TIME: 5 hr.

This holiday ham sizzles with Southern comfort. Pick a ham with an intact fat layer that will crisp when baked and show off its pepper-and-clove crust.

- 1 (12- to 14-lb.) fully cooked, bone-in ham shank
- 1 Tbsp. black peppercorns
- 30 whole cloves
- 1 (12-oz.) can cola soft drink, divided
- ¼ cup bourbon, divided
- 6 Tbsp. firmly packed brown sugar, divided
- 1 (13-oz.) jar cherry preserves, divided
  Garnishes: kumquats, cherries

1. Preheat oven to 350°. Remove skin from ham; trim fat to ¼-inch thickness. Make shallow cuts in fat 1 inch apart in a diamond pattern. Place peppercorns in a small zip-top plastic freezer bag. Tap peppercorns with a meat mallet or small heavy skillet until coarsely crushed. Rub peppercorns over surface of ham; insert cloves in centers of diamonds. Insert a meat thermometer into ham, making sure it does not touch fat or bone. Place ham in a lightly greased 13- x 9-inch pan; set aside.
2. Combine ¼ cup cola, 2 Tbsp. bourbon, and 2 Tbsp. brown sugar; set aside. Combine remaining cola, bourbon, and brown sugar; pour over ham.

3. Bake at 350° for 2 hours, basting with cola mixture every 15 minutes. Remove ham from oven; leave oven on.
4. Meanwhile, combine reserved cola mixture and ⅔ cup cherry preserves in a medium saucepan. Cook over medium heat 3 minutes or until glaze is hot and sugar dissolves; brush ham with glaze. Return ham to oven; bake at 350° for 1 hour and 45 more minutes or until thermometer registers 140°. (Cover ham with aluminum foil during the last hour, if necessary, to prevent excessive browning.) Let ham stand 1 hour before carving.
5. Transfer baked ham to a serving platter; cover with foil. Remove fat from drippings in pan. Whisk remaining ½ cup cherry preserves into drippings in pan. Transfer mixture to a saucepan, if desired, or continue cooking in roasting pan placed over 2 burners on the stovetop. Bring to a boil; reduce heat, and simmer until slightly thickened (8 to 10 minutes). Serve glaze with ham. Garnish, if desired.

Holiday Potato Bake

MAKES: 10 to 12 servings
HANDS-ON TIME: 29 min.
TOTAL TIME: 1 hr., 14 min.

Simple mashed potatoes get dressed up in this comfort food dish inspired by twice-baked potatoes.

- 6 large baking potatoes, peeled and cut into chunks
- ¼ cup butter
- 1 cup chopped green onions
- 4 garlic cloves, minced
- 2 cups milk
- 2 cups (8 oz.) shredded extra-sharp Cheddar cheese, divided
- 2 tsp. salt
- 1 (12-oz.) jar roasted red bell peppers, drained and finely chopped
- 4 oz. cream cheese, softened
- 2 large eggs, lightly beaten

1. Preheat oven to 375°. Cook potatoes in boiling water to cover 15 to 20 minutes or until tender; drain well.
2. Meanwhile, melt butter in a large skillet over medium-high heat; add green onions and garlic. Sauté 5 minutes or until tender.
3. Combine potatoes and green onion mixture in a large bowl; mash using a potato masher. Add milk, 1 cup cheese, and next 4 ingredients; mash. Spoon into a lightly greased 13- x 9-inch baking dish. Top with remaining 1 cup cheese.
4. Bake at 375° for 45 to 50 minutes or until browned and bubbly.

Roasted Brussels Sprouts and Cauliflower with Bacon Dressing

MAKES: 12 servings
HANDS-ON TIME: 29 min.
TOTAL TIME: 1 hr., 15 min.

This is one of the best side dish offerings of the holiday season. Brussels sprouts and cauliflower develop a nutty flavor once roasted, and the bacon vinaigrette adds a smoky hit.

- 1½ **lb. fresh Brussels sprouts**
- 2 **medium heads cauliflower (about 2 lb. each), cut into florets**
- ¼ **cup olive oil**
- 2 **Tbsp. sugar**
- 10 **bacon slices**
- 2 **Tbsp. white wine vinegar**
- 1 **Tbsp. olive oil**
- 2 **garlic cloves, minced**
- 1 **tsp. salt**
- ½ **tsp. pepper**
- ¾ **cup pitted kalamata olives, coarsely chopped**
- 1 **Tbsp. chopped fresh parsley**
- 1 **tsp. chopped fresh thyme**

1. Preheat oven to 450°. Rinse Brussels sprouts thoroughly; remove any discolored leaves. Trim stem ends; cut in half lengthwise. Combine sprouts and next 3 ingredients in a large roasting pan; toss to coat. Spread into a single layer. Roast at 450° for 45 to 48 minutes or until vegetables are tender and browned, stirring after 30 minutes.
2. Meanwhile, cook bacon in a large skillet over medium-high heat 15 minutes or until crisp; remove bacon, and drain on paper towels, reserving 2 Tbsp. drippings. Crumble bacon. Whisk together drippings, vinegar, and next 4 ingredients.
3. Drizzle vinaigrette over roasted vegetables. Add crumbled bacon, olives, parsley, and thyme; toss to coat.

Chocolate-Orange Velvet Tart

MAKES: 8 to 12 servings
HANDS-ON TIME: 20 min.
TOTAL TIME: 4 hr., 31 min.

This luxurious tart is more like a truffle than a pie. Serve slivers or slices; coffee's a must.

- 1¼ **cups cinnamon-flavored graham cracker crumbs (about 8 sheets)**
- 3 **Tbsp. brown sugar**
- ¼ **cup butter, melted**
- ¾ **cup heavy whipping cream**
- ½ **cup milk**
- ¼ **cup turbinado sugar**
- 1 **Tbsp. orange zest**
- 1 **tsp. ground cinnamon**
- 3 **(4-oz.) semisweet chocolate baking bars, coarsely chopped**
  Garnishes: sweetened whipped cream, orange zest

1. Preheat oven to 375°. Combine first 3 ingredients; press firmly into a lightly greased 9-inch pie plate.
2. Bake at 375° for 11 minutes or until lightly browned. Remove from oven; let cool.
3. Combine cream and next 4 ingredients in a saucepan. Bring to a simmer over medium-low heat. Remove from heat; add chocolate, and stir until chocolate is melted and mixture is smooth. Pour filling into baked crust. Refrigerate 4 hours or until firm. Garnish, if desired.
NOTE: We tested with Ghirardelli semi-sweet chocolate baking bars.

Bite-Size Desserts

Good things come in small packages, and it's especially true with these festive desserts.

Chocolate-Praline Sundae Shots

MAKES: 12 servings
HANDS-ON TIME: 11 min.
TOTAL TIME: 23 min.

Use vintage shot glasses for serving these mini indulgences. Bake the candied pecans ahead, and assemble desserts in a snap.

- 1 **Tbsp. brown sugar**
- 1 **tsp. butter, melted**
- 12 **pecan halves**
- 2½ **cups butter pecan ice cream**
- ½ **cup hot fudge sauce**

1. Preheat oven to 350°. Combine brown sugar and butter in a small bowl, stirring well. Add pecans; toss to coat. Spread pecans on an ungreased baking sheet in a single layer. Bake at 350° for 12 minutes, stirring halfway through. Cool completely.
2. Using a 1 Tbsp. cookie scoop, place 2 scoops of ice cream into each of 12 chilled shot glasses or other tiny dessert glasses. Top each dessert with 2 tsp. room-temperature hot fudge sauce and either a praline pecan half or chopped praline pecan. Serve immediately.

Fruitcake-Bourbon Custard Dessert Shots

MAKES: 12 servings
HANDS-ON TIME: 46 min.
TOTAL TIME: 3 hr., 26 min., including custard

- ½ **cup chopped dates**
- ½ **cup raisins**
- ½ **cup chopped candied pineapple**
- ⅓ **cup orange juice**
- ¼ **cup dried apricots**
- ½ **cup butter, softened**
- ½ **cup firmly packed light brown sugar**
- 3 **large eggs**
- 1¼ **cups all-purpose flour**
- ½ **tsp. baking soda**
- ¼ **tsp. salt**
- ½ **cup chopped pecans**
- 2 **tsp. orange zest**
- ½ **cup bourbon**
  Vanilla Bean-Bourbon Custard
  Sweetened whipped cream

1. Combine first 5 ingredients in a medium bowl; cover and let stand 30 minutes.
2. Preheat oven to 325°. Beat butter at medium speed with an electric mixer until creamy; gradually add sugar, beating until blended. Add eggs, 1 at a time, beating until blended after each addition.
3. Combine flour, baking soda, and salt; gradually add flour mixture to butter mixture, beating until blended. Stir in pecans and orange zest.
4. Drain fruit mixture; discard orange juice. Fold fruit mixture into batter. Spoon batter into a lightly greased 8-inch square pan.
5. Bake at 325° for 40 minutes or until a wooden pick inserted in center comes out clean. Poke holes in warm cake with a wooden skewer; pour bourbon over cake, allowing it to seep into holes. Cool completely on a wire rack (about 1 hour).
6. Coarsely crumble half of fruitcake. (Reserve remaining fruitcake for another use.) Layer fruitcake and Vanilla Bean-Bourbon Custard in 4-oz. cordial glasses or shot glasses. Top with whipped cream.

Vanilla Bean-Bourbon Custard

MAKES: 3 cups
HANDS-ON TIME: 17 min.
TOTAL TIME: 2 hr., 17 min.

- ½ **cup sugar**
- 3 **Tbsp. cornstarch**
- ¼ **tsp. salt**
- 2¼ **cups milk**
- 3 **egg yolks**
- 3 **Tbsp. bourbon**
- 1 **Tbsp. butter**
- 1 **tsp. vanilla bean paste or vanilla extract**

1. Combine sugar, cornstarch, and salt in a large saucepan; whisk in milk. Cook, whisking constantly, over medium heat 7 minutes or until mixture comes to a boil; boil 1 minute.
2. Whisk egg yolks until thick and pale. Gradually stir about one-fourth of hot milk mixture into yolks; add yolk mixture to remaining hot milk mixture, stirring constantly. Bring mixture to a boil, and cook 3 minutes, whisking constantly. Remove from heat; stir in bourbon, butter, and vanilla. Cover and chill 2 to 24 hours. Whisk custard until smooth before assembling desserts.

Baby Bananas Foster Cheesecakes

MAKES: 3 dozen
HANDS-ON TIME: 24 min.
TOTAL TIME: 5 hr., 12 min.

- ¾ **cup cinnamon graham cracker crumbs (about 4 sheets)**
- ¼ **cup finely chopped pecans**
- ¼ **cup butter, melted**
- 1 **(8-oz.) package cream cheese, softened**
- ⅓ **cup firmly packed light brown sugar**
- 2 **large eggs**
- 2 **Tbsp. sour cream**
- 2 **Tbsp. dark rum, divided**
- ½ **tsp. ground cinnamon**
- 3 **medium bananas**
- ½ **cup caramel topping**

1. Preheat oven to 325°. Stir together graham cracker crumbs, pecans, and butter in a bowl. Press crumb mixture into bottom of 3 (12-cup) miniature muffin pans. Bake at 325° for 8 minutes; let cool.
2. Beat cream cheese at medium speed with an electric mixer until creamy. Gradually add brown sugar, beating just until blended. Add eggs, 1 at a time, beating just until yellow disappears after each addition. Stir in sour cream, 1 Tbsp. rum, and cinnamon.
3. Mash 1 banana; add mashed banana to cream cheese mixture, beating at low speed just until blended. Spoon cream cheese batter into prepared crust in pans, filling full.
4. Bake at 325° for 18 minutes or until set. Remove cheesecakes from oven; cool completely in pans on a wire rack (about 15 minutes). Cover and chill 4 hours.
5. Heat caramel topping in a saucepan over low heat 2 to 3 minutes. Remove from heat; add remaining 1 Tbsp. rum. Slice remaining 2 bananas into 36 slices (about ¼ inch thick); add to caramel sauce, stirring to coat.
6. Remove cheesecakes from pans. Place 1 caramel-coated banana slice on each cheesecake. Arrange cheesecakes on a serving platter.

Test Kitchen Notebook

Perfect for a holiday pickup dessert, these one-bite cheesecakes deliver all the goodness of traditional Bananas Foster.

German Chocolate Cake Truffles

MAKES: 8½ dozen
HANDS-ON TIME: 58 min.
TOTAL TIME: 2 hr., 58 min.

Whether you call these truffles or cake balls, they're easy to make and fun to dip. Drizzle with white icing, or sprinkle with sanding sugar for alternate garnishes.

- 1 (18.25-oz.) package German chocolate cake mix
- 1 (16-oz.) container ready-to-spread milk chocolate frosting
- 2 cups toasted coconut, divided
- 1¾ cups toasted finely chopped pecans, divided
- 4 (7-oz.) containers milk chocolate dipping chocolate
  Candy dipping fork

1. Prepare cake mix according to package directions in a lightly greased 13- x 9-inch pan. Let cool completely in pan (about 30 minutes).
2. Crumble cake into a large bowl. Scoop frosting by spoonfuls over cake crumbs. Sprinkle with 1 cup each coconut and pecans; stir gently just until thoroughly blended. Using a cookie scoop, scoop cake mixture into 1¼-inch balls; roll in hands, and place balls on wax paper-lined baking sheets. Cover and chill 1 hour.
3. Meanwhile, combine remaining 1 cup coconut and ¾ cup pecans; stir well. Melt dipping chocolate, 1 container at a time, according to package directions; dip chilled balls into melted chocolate, using candy dipping fork and allowing excess chocolate to drip off. Place coated truffles on wax paper-lined baking sheets. Sprinkle tops with coconut-pecan mixture; chill 30 minutes or until set. Place truffles in paper or aluminum-foil baking cups.

Maple-Walnut Blondie Stacks

MAKES: 3 dozen
HANDS-ON TIME: 32 min.
TOTAL TIME: 2 hr., 44 min., including frosting

A popular national restaurant chain serves a blonde brownie à la mode with a maple-walnut butter sauce. Our recipe has all the same appeal stacked up in one brownie bite.

- ⅓ cup butter, softened
- ¾ cup firmly packed light brown sugar
- 2 large eggs
- 1 tsp. vanilla extract
- ¾ cup all-purpose flour
- ¾ tsp. baking powder
- ⅛ tsp. salt
- ⅓ cup finely chopped, toasted walnuts
- ⅓ cup coarsely crushed hard butter-toffee candies
  Maple-Brown Sugar Frosting
  Garnishes: coarsely crushed hard butter-toffee candies; chopped, toasted walnuts

1. Preheat oven to 350°. Line bottom and sides of an 8-inch square pan with aluminum foil, allowing 2 to 3 inches to extend over sides; lightly grease foil. Set aside.
2. Beat butter and sugar in a large bowl at medium speed with an electric mixer until creamy. Add eggs, 1 at a time, beating after each addition and scraping down sides of bowl. Stir in vanilla.
3. Combine flour, baking powder, and salt in a small bowl, stirring well. Gradually add flour mixture to butter mixture, beating just until blended. Stir in ⅓ cup each walnuts and crushed toffee candies. Spread batter into prepared pan.
4. Bake at 350° for 22 to 25 minutes or until a wooden pick inserted in center comes out with a few moist crumbs. Cool in pan on a wire rack 15 minutes.

5. Lift warm uncut brownies from pan, using foil sides as handles; place on a cutting board. Remove foil; cool uncut brownies completely (about 1 hour). Cut brownies into 4 equal portions. Cut each portion in half horizontally.
6. Spread ¼ cup Maple-Brown Sugar Frosting onto each of 4 brownie portions; top with remaining 4 brownie portions. Cut each stack into 9 pieces. (We recommend using an electric knife.)
7. Spoon remaining frosting into a zip-top plastic freezer bag. Snip 1 corner of bag to make a small hole. Pipe about 1 tsp. frosting onto each brownie stack. Garnish, if desired.

Maple-Brown Sugar Frosting

MAKES: 2 cups
HANDS-ON TIME: 20 min.
TOTAL TIME: 35 min.

- 1 cup firmly packed light brown sugar
- ½ cup evaporated milk
- ⅓ cup butter
- 2 Tbsp. light corn syrup
- 3 cups powdered sugar
- 2 Tbsp. maple syrup
- 1 tsp. vanilla extract

1. Combine first 4 ingredients in a medium saucepan; cook over medium-low heat, stirring constantly, 7 minutes. Bring to a boil over medium-low heat; cook 5 minutes over medium-low heat, stirring constantly. Remove from heat; stir in powdered sugar, syrup, and vanilla. Cool in pan 15 minutes.
2. Transfer warm frosting mixture to a mixing bowl. Beat at medium-high speed with an electric mixer until smooth and spreading consistency (about 8 to 10 minutes).

Cozy Christmas Eve Dinner

Set an intimate table for two and toast the season—fireside with this Mediterranean-inspired meal.

Dinner for Two

SERVES 2

Creamy Turnip Soup with Bacon, Caramelized Pears, and Onions

Roast Pork with Provençal Breadcrumb Crust

Greens with Goat Cheese, Pecans, and Sherry Vinaigrette

Broccoli with Roasted Garlic and Tomatoes

Mini Chocolate-Cherry Layer Cakes

Creamy Turnip Soup with Bacon, Caramelized Pears, and Onions

MAKES: about 2 cups
HANDS-ON TIME: 35 min.
TOTAL TIME: 55 min.

Right before serving, prepare the bacon, pear, and onion topping.

- 2 **Tbsp. butter, divided**
- 1 **cup thinly sliced leek (about 1 small)**
- ½ **lb. turnips, peeled and diced into ½-inch pieces (1½ cups)**
- 1 **cup low-sodium fat-free chicken broth**
- 3 **Tbsp. whipping cream**
- ¼ **tsp. salt**
- ¼ **tsp. ground white pepper**
- 1 **bacon slice**
- ½ **firm pear, peeled and thinly sliced**
- ½ **small onion, halved and thinly sliced**
- 2 **tsp. sugar**

1. Melt 1 Tbsp. butter in a medium-size heavy saucepan over medium heat. Add leeks; sauté 5 minutes or until tender. Add turnips, broth, and ½ cup water; bring to a boil. Cover, reduce heat, and simmer 20 minutes or until turnips are very tender.

2. Process soup, in batches, in a blender or food processor until smooth, stopping to scrape down sides as needed. Return to saucepan; stir in cream, salt, and pepper. Set aside, and keep warm.

3. Cook bacon in a large skillet over medium heat 5 minutes or until crisp; remove bacon, and drain on paper towels. Crumble bacon; set aside. Wipe skillet clean with a paper towel. Melt remaining 1 Tbsp. butter in skillet over medium-high heat. Add pear and onion; sprinkle with sugar. Sauté 9 to 11 minutes or until golden brown.

4. To serve, ladle soup into bowls, and top with crumbled bacon and pear mixture.

Roast Pork with Provençal Breadcrumb Crust

MAKES: 2 to 3 servings
HANDS-ON TIME: 6 min.
TOTAL TIME: 1 hr., 16 min.

A French-inspired crusting gives this roast an incredible aroma as it cooks. Ask your butcher to french the roast for you. If you do it yourself, be sure to cut all the fat from the rib bones and scrape them clean to make a beautiful presentation.

⅓ cup fresh breadcrumbs
¼ cup freshly grated Parmesan cheese
3 Tbsp. finely chopped pitted kalamata olives
1½ Tbsp. finely chopped fresh thyme
2 garlic cloves, pressed
3 Tbsp. olive oil, divided
1 (3-rib) (1¼- to 1½-lb.) pork loin roast, frenched
Salt and freshly ground pepper
3 Tbsp. Sherry Glaze

1. Preheat oven to 350°. Combine first 5 ingredients in a small bowl; stir in 2 Tbsp. oil.
2. Place pork roast, bone side down, in a small greased roasting pan. Rub remaining 1 Tbsp. oil over meaty top side of roast; sprinkle with desired amount of salt and pepper, and pat breadcrumb mixture over oil to adhere.
3. Bake at 350° for 45 to 55 minutes or until a meat thermometer inserted into thickest portion registers 155°. Let stand 15 minutes or until thermometer registers 160°. Carve roast between bones into 3 chops. Drizzle each serving with Sherry Glaze.

Sherry Glaze

MAKES: ¼ cup
HANDS-ON TIME: 19 min.
TOTAL TIME: 19 min.

Reserve 1 tablespoon of this glaze for the next recipe.

2 cups cream sherry

1. Bring sherry to a boil in a medium saucepan over medium-high heat; boil until syrupy and reduced to ¼ cup. Remove from heat; let cool.
NOTE: To make a nonalcoholic reduction, substitute 1 cup apple cider for cream sherry. Bring cider to a boil over medium-high heat in a small saucepan; boil 15 minutes or until reduced to ¼ cup.

Greens with Goat Cheese, Pecans, and Sherry Vinaigrette

MAKES: 2 servings
HANDS-ON TIME: 5 min.
TOTAL TIME: 5 min.

1 Tbsp. Sherry Glaze (see recipe, above)
1½ tsp. sherry vinegar
¼ tsp. salt
¼ tsp. freshly ground pepper
1½ Tbsp. extra virgin olive oil
3 cups mixed baby greens
1 oz. goat cheese, crumbled
¼ cup sugared pecans

1. Combine first 4 ingredients in a small bowl, stirring with a wire whisk; gradually whisk in oil.
2. Place greens on 2 salad plates. Sprinkle salads with goat cheese and pecans; drizzle with vinaigrette.

Broccoli with Roasted Garlic and Tomatoes

MAKES: 2 servings
HANDS-ON TIME: 5 min.
TOTAL TIME: 47 min.

Roasted broccoli and tomatoes make a festive pairing for pork.

4 large garlic cloves
3 cups broccoli florets (about ½ lb.)
1 Tbsp. olive oil
1 cup grape tomatoes
2 Tbsp. unsalted butter, softened
¼ tsp. salt
¼ tsp. freshly ground pepper
3 Tbsp. freshly grated Parmesan cheese (optional)

1. Preheat oven to 425°. Fold a sheet of aluminum foil in half, creasing it to form a double sheet. Place garlic in center; drizzle with 1 tsp. water. Fold foil to seal. Bake at 425° for 20 minutes or until lightly browned and tender. Transfer to a small bowl; mash garlic with a fork. Increase oven temperature to 450°.
2. Combine garlic, broccoli, and oil in a lightly greased cast-iron skillet. Spread vegetables in a single layer.
3. Roast at 450° for 10 minutes or until broccoli begins to brown. Add tomatoes and next 3 ingredients to skillet, tossing to combine. Roast 12 more minutes or until tomato skins begin to split. Sprinkle with cheese, if desired.

Mini Chocolate-Cherry Layer Cakes

MAKES: 4 servings
HANDS-ON TIME: 13 min.
TOTAL TIME: 3 hr., 57 min., including syrup, mousse, and glaze

Share one of these tender-rich chocolate mousse cakes with your sweetie, and freeze the other up to 2 weeks.

> Parchment paper
> ¼ cup all-purpose flour
> ¼ cup unsweetened cocoa
> ¼ tsp. salt
> 3 large eggs, at room temperature
> ½ cup sugar
> 2 tsp. hot water
> 2 Tbsp. unsalted butter, melted
> Cherry Syrup
> Chocolate Mousse
> Chocolate Glaze

1. Preheat oven to 400°. Grease an 8-inch square cake pan. Line bottom of pan with parchment paper; flour edges of pan. Set aside.

2. Sift ¼ cup flour, cocoa, and salt into a small bowl. Combine eggs, sugar, and hot water in a small, deep bowl; beat at medium-high speed with an electric mixer 5 minutes or until thick and pale. Sift half of flour mixture over egg mixture; gently fold into egg mixture. Repeat procedure with remaining flour mixture. Drizzle butter over batter; fold butter into batter. (Do not overmix.) Pour batter into prepared pan.

3. Bake at 400° for 17 to 20 minutes or until a wooden pick inserted in center comes out clean. Cool in pan on a wire rack 10 minutes; remove from pan to a wire rack to cool completely.

4. Brush Cherry Syrup over cake. Cut cake into 4 squares. Spoon Chocolate Mousse onto 2 cake squares, spreading to edges. Place remaining 2 squares on top of mousse, and press gently to adhere. Chill 30 minutes.

5. Pour Chocolate Glaze over cakes, spreading to cover tops and sides. Chill 2 to 24 hours before serving.

Cherry Syrup

MAKES: 3 Tbsp.
HANDS-ON TIME: 5 min.
TOTAL TIME: 5 min.

> 3 Tbsp. cherry preserves
> 2 tsp. cherry brandy or ¼ tsp. almond extract

1. Press preserves through a fine wire-mesh strainer into a bowl using the back of a spoon to yield 2 Tbsp. sieved preserves; stir in liqueur.

Chocolate Mousse

MAKES: ¾ cup
HANDS-ON TIME: 5 min.
TOTAL TIME: 5 min.

> 1½ oz. bittersweet chocolate, finely chopped (about ⅓ cup)
> ⅓ cup whipping cream

1. Microwave chocolate in a small microwave-safe bowl at HIGH 30 seconds or until chocolate melts; stir until smooth. While chocolate is warm, beat whipping cream with an electric mixer until stiff peaks form; beat in chocolate.

Chocolate Glaze

MAKES: ½ cup
HANDS-ON TIME: 5 min.
TOTAL TIME: 20 min.

> ⅓ cup whipping cream
> 1 Tbsp. light corn syrup
> 2 oz. bittersweet chocolate, finely chopped (about ½ cup)
> 2 tsp. cherry brandy or ¼ tsp. almond extract

1. Bring whipping cream and corn syrup to a boil in a small saucepan. Remove from heat; stir in chocolate and liqueur. Stir until smooth. Cool 15 minutes or until mixture is thickened but still pourable.

IT'S NOT THANKSGIVING WITHOUT…

The Year's Best Nap

We interrupt our scheduled food programming for some shut-eye.

The turkey carcass is down to bones. The mashed potatoes are nothing more than a sad, hopeful, metallic scraping—some people just can't accept that gone is gone. The pinto beans and ham are in Tupperware, divided 14 ways. The last biscuit is a memory. (Or so it seems. My mama always hides one or two away for my boy, Jake.) Over the last crumbs of dressing, old women say, "Don't know what happened…it just wasn't fit to eat."

It is time for my people to gather in the living room and unburden themselves of all the fine gossip they have been holding onto since September, like money. I will be there, with them, sometimes with a half-eaten piece of chocolate cake balanced dangerously on one knee, but I will hear almost none of it.

I would rather be awake, to find out whose garden did well and whose didn't, and whose foreign car isn't running good—because you know they should have known better—and whose children have misbehaved. I would like to know what is happening to our kin across the state line—my Aunt Juanita calls them "the Georgia people," like they are a new species—and who last killed a snake. They will say that the snakes seem to have stayed out longer this year, and no one will say it any more but we're pretty sure it's because those men walked on the moon. I want to hear it all, swirling around me, assuring me that no matter what happens in this uncertain world the things that truly matter, things here, are all right.

But the same peace of mind that settles on me as that talk drifts around the room is the same peace and comfort that tugs me into the calm darkness. My mama will look at me from across the wood floor and say, quickly, "Let him sleep." I know this because sometimes I am not quite out, and it is the last thing I hear.

It would be all right with me if it was the last thing I ever hear.

I will blame the chair. I bought it out of a catalog a quarter-century ago, what the catalog called a British club chair, but it just looks like a leather chair to me. It is firm and soft at the same time, and there is some kind of drug in it, I swear, that makes my chin droop, and makes me begin to snore softly. The talk continues around me, and I would like to tell you what it is all about but of course I do not know. I just know I love the idea of it, of the stories being told with me and yet without me, at the same time. The old white dog sleeps, too, across the room. In human years she is…well, a miracle.

I am not a napper, and do not even sleep well at night. But here, in this chair on Thanksgiving Day, it is automatic, certain. Maybe I should steal the chair from my mama's and take it to live with me all the time. Then, at least, I could hear all the news at home.

But I do not believe I will. They tell me sometimes I am out for only a few minutes, but that cannot be. I wake feeling restored, feeling alive and happy to be. It is almost enough to make a person believe in magic, because I know there are hours and hours worth of good things happening as I shut my eyes.

BY RICK BRAGG

Make-Ahead Favorites

Appealing Appetizers

Mushroom Turnovers

MAKES: 3½ dozen
HANDS-ON TIME: 30 min.
TOTAL TIME: 1 hr., 45 min.

1½ (8-oz.) packages cream cheese,
   softened
2¼ cups all-purpose flour
¾ cup butter, softened
3 Tbsp. butter
1 cup chopped onion
1 lb. mushrooms, chopped
¼ tsp. dried thyme
¼ tsp. salt
½ tsp. pepper
2 Tbsp. all-purpose flour
¼ cup sour cream
3 Tbsp. sherry
1 Tbsp. butter, melted

1. Combine first 3 ingredients. Shape dough into a ball; cover and chill 1 hour.
2. Meanwhile, melt 3 Tbsp. butter in a large skillet over medium heat; add onion, and sauté 12 minutes or until onion is golden. Stir in chopped mushrooms, and sauté 3 minutes. Stir in thyme, salt, and pepper. Sprinkle 2 Tbsp. flour evenly over mushroom mixture. Stir in sour cream and sherry. Remove from heat, and set aside.
3. Preheat oven to 400°. Pat or roll chilled dough to ⅛-inch thickness on a lightly floured surface; cut out circles with a 3-inch round cutter. Spoon 1 tsp. mushroom mixture on half of each dough circle; fold dough over filling. Press edges together with a fork to seal. Place turnovers on an ungreased baking sheet.

4. Bake at 400° for 15 to 20 minutes or until edges are lightly browned; brush tops with melted butter.
NOTE: To make ahead, place uncooked turnovers in a single layer on baking sheets, and freeze. Transfer frozen turnovers to large zip-top plastic freezer bags, seal, and freeze up to 1 month. Place frozen turnovers on ungreased baking sheets. Bake as directed.

Bacon-and-Greens Salsa

MAKES: 4 cups
HANDS-ON TIME: 15 min.
TOTAL TIME: 22 min.

8 bacon slices
1 (16-oz.) package frozen mixed
   greens, thawed and drained
½ medium-size sweet onion,
   chopped
1 tsp. jarred minced garlic
1½ cups frozen corn, thawed
1 serrano chile pepper, minced
¼ tsp. salt
¼ tsp. pepper
2 Tbsp. cider vinegar

1. Cook bacon in a large skillet over medium-high heat 7 to 9 minutes or until crisp; remove bacon, and drain on paper towels, reserving 2 Tbsp. drippings in skillet. Crumble bacon.
2. Sauté greens, onion, and garlic in hot drippings 7 to 10 minutes or until tender. Stir in corn and next 3 ingredients, and cook 3 minutes or until thoroughly heated. Remove from heat, and stir in vinegar. Sprinkle with bacon.
NOTE: We also loved this salsa over cream cheese (a great idea for leftovers). You can prepare the recipe up to a day ahead—just reheat the salsa before serving.

Fresh Herb-Tomato Crostini

MAKES: about 20 appetizer servings
HANDS-ON TIME: 30 min.
TOTAL TIME: 40 min.

¼ cup olive oil
2 garlic cloves, pressed
1 (8.5-oz.) French bread baguette,
   cut into ¼-inch-thick slices
3 Tbsp. fresh lemon juice
2 Tbsp. olive oil
¼ tsp. salt
⅛ tsp. pepper
1 large tomato, finely chopped
¾ cup finely chopped green onions
½ cup chopped fresh parsley
1 Tbsp. chopped fresh mint
⅓ cup crumbled feta cheese

1. Preheat oven to 350°. Stir together olive oil and garlic; brush on 1 side of each bread slice. Place bread slices, garlic sides up, on a baking sheet. Bake 10 to 12 minutes or until lightly toasted.
2. Whisk together lemon juice and next 3 ingredients in a large bowl. Add tomato and next 3 ingredients; gently toss to coat.
3. Top each bread slice with tomato mixture (about 2 rounded teaspoonfuls each). Sprinkle with cheese.

TRY THIS TWIST!
Green Tomato-Fresh Herb Crostini: Substitute 1 finely chopped large green tomato for red tomato. Proceed with recipe as directed.
NOTE: Prepare tomato topping up to 2 days ahead; cover and store in the refrigerator. Toast bread slices 1 day ahead; store at room temperature in an airtight container.

Easy Soups

Spiced Butternut-Pumpkin Soup

MAKES: 15 cups
HANDS-ON TIME: 30 min.
TOTAL TIME: 1 hr., 35 min.

- 2 Tbsp. butter
- 1 large sweet onion, diced
- 1 large red bell pepper, chopped
- 3 garlic cloves, minced
- 2 Tbsp. finely grated fresh ginger
- 1 medium butternut squash, peeled and cubed (about 1¾ lb.)
- 1 small pumpkin, peeled and cubed (about 1¾ lb.)
- 1 large sweet potato, peeled and cubed
- 1 large Granny Smith apple, peeled and cubed
- 1 (32-oz.) container low-sodium chicken broth
- 2 bay leaves
- 1½ tsp. red curry paste*
- ½ tsp. pepper
- ¾ cup whipping cream
- 1 Tbsp. fresh lime juice
  Salt and pepper to taste

1. Melt butter in a large Dutch oven over medium-high heat; add onion and bell pepper, and sauté 8 minutes or until onion is golden. Stir in garlic and ginger, and cook 1 minute. Add squash, next 7 ingredients, and 4 cups water. Bring to a boil, reduce heat to medium-low, and simmer 20 minutes or until vegetables are tender. Remove from heat, and let stand 30 minutes, stirring occasionally. Remove and discard bay leaves.

2. Process soup, in batches, in a blender until smooth. Return to Dutch oven, and stir in cream. Bring to a simmer over medium heat; stir in lime juice, and season with salt and pepper to taste.

*1 tsp. curry powder may be substituted.
NOTE: 3 lb. butternut squash may be substituted for 1¾ lb. butternut squash and 1¾ lb. pumpkin.

Corn-and-Zucchini Queso Chowder

MAKES: 11 cups
HANDS-ON TIME: 40 min.
TOTAL TIME: 1 hr.

- ¼ cup butter
- 1 cup finely chopped red bell pepper
- 1 cup finely chopped onion
- 3 poblano peppers, seeded and finely chopped
- 2 garlic cloves, minced
- 2 cups frozen whole kernel corn, thawed
- 2 cups chopped zucchini
- ¼ tsp. ground cumin
- 2 (14-oz.) cans low-sodium fat-free chicken broth
- ⅓ cup all-purpose flour
- 1½ cups milk
- 1 cup half-and-half
- 1 cup (4 oz.) freshly shredded asadero cheese*
- 1 cup (4 oz.) freshly shredded sharp Cheddar cheese
- ½ tsp. kosher salt
  Toppings: chopped cooked bacon, shredded Cheddar cheese, diced red onion

1. Melt butter in a Dutch oven over medium-high heat; add bell pepper and next 3 ingredients, and sauté 4 to 5 minutes or until tender. Add corn, zucchini, and cumin, and sauté 5 minutes or until tender. Gradually stir in broth, stirring to loosen particles from bottom of Dutch oven. Bring to a boil; cover, reduce heat to low, and simmer 15 minutes.

2. Whisk together flour and next 2 ingredients. Stir into zucchini mixture, and cook over medium heat, stirring constantly, 5 minutes or until thickened. Reduce heat to low.

3. Add asadero cheese, 1 cup shredded Cheddar cheese, and salt, and cook, stirring constantly, until cheeses melt and mixture is thoroughly heated. Serve with desired toppings.

*Monterey Jack cheese may be substituted.

Freeze Ahead

{1}

COOL. Refrigerators and freezers cannot cool soups quickly enough to be food safe. Speed up the cooling process by placing the pot of soup in a bath of ice water in the sink. Stir soup often to help release the heat.

{2}

PACKAGE. Label and date gallon- or quart-size zip-top plastic freezer bags, place in a bowl, and cuff the bag over the edge. Ladle soup into each bag; let out any excess air, and seal.

{3}

FREEZE. Lay bags flat in a single layer in the freezer; when frozen. stack bags to save space.

Turkey Chili

MAKES: 6 servings
HANDS-ON TIME: 15 min.
TOTAL TIME: 1 hr., 5 min.

- 1 onion, chopped
- 1 green bell pepper, chopped
- 1 lb. ground turkey
- 1 lb. ground turkey sausage
- 1 tsp. vegetable oil
- 1 (16-oz.) can chili beans
- 2 cups tomato sauce
- 2 cups tomato juice
- 1 garlic clove, minced
- 1 (1.75-oz.) envelope chili seasoning mix
- 1 (10-oz.) can diced tomatoes and green chiles
- 1 tsp. sugar
  Garnishes: sour cream, shredded Cheddar cheese

1. Cook onion, bell pepper, ground turkey, and sausage in hot oil in a Dutch oven over medium heat, stirring until meat crumbles and is no longer pink. Drain well.
2. Add chili beans and next 6 ingredients to Dutch oven; bring to a boil, stirring frequently. Reduce heat, and simmer 30 minutes, stirring occasionally. Garnish each serving, if desired.
NOTE: This chili freezes well, so package any leftovers in single-serving containers for quick meals another day.

Cozy Casseroles

Classic Chicken Tetrazzini

MAKES: 8 to 10 servings
HANDS-ON TIME: 20 min.
TOTAL TIME: 55 min.

- 1½ (8-oz.) packages vermicelli
- ½ cup butter
- ½ cup all-purpose flour
- 4 cups milk
- ½ cup dry white wine
- 2 Tbsp. chicken bouillon granules
- 1 tsp. seasoned pepper
- 2 cups freshly grated Parmesan cheese, divided
- 4 cups diced cooked chicken
- 1 (6-oz.) jar sliced mushrooms, drained
- ¾ cup slivered almonds

1. Preheat oven to 350°. Prepare pasta according to package directions.
2. Meanwhile, melt butter in a Dutch oven over low heat; whisk in flour until smooth. Cook 1 minute, whisking constantly. Gradually whisk in milk and wine; cook over medium heat, whisking constantly, 8 to 10 minutes or until mixture is thickened and bubbly. Whisk in bouillon granules, seasoned pepper, and 1 cup Parmesan cheese.
3. Remove from heat; stir in diced cooked chicken, sliced mushrooms, and hot cooked pasta.
4. Spoon mixture into a lightly greased 13- x 9-inch baking dish; sprinkle with slivered almonds and remaining 1 cup Parmesan cheese.
5. Bake at 350° for 35 minutes or until bubbly.

King Ranch Chicken Casserole

MAKES: 6 servings
HANDS-ON TIME: 13 min.
TOTAL TIME: 45 min.

- 1 (10-oz.) package frozen seasoning blend
- 2 cups chopped cooked chicken
- 1 (10¾-oz.) can cream of chicken soup
- 1 (10¾-oz.) can cream of mushroom soup
- 1 (10-oz.) can diced tomatoes and green chiles
- 1 tsp. chili powder
- ½ tsp. garlic salt
- 12 (6-inch) corn tortillas
- 2 cups (8 oz.) shredded Cheddar cheese, divided

1. Preheat oven to 350°. Stir together first 7 ingredients.
2. Tear tortillas into 1-inch pieces; layer one-third of tortilla pieces in a lightly greased 13- x 9-inch baking dish. Top with one-third of chicken mixture and ⅔ cup cheese. Repeat layers twice.
3. Bake at 350° for 32 minutes or until casserole is thoroughly heated and bubbly.
NOTE: Freeze casserole up to 1 month, if desired. Thaw in refrigerator overnight, and bake as directed.

Make-Ahead Favorites

Pizza Spaghetti Casserole

MAKES: 6 servings
HANDS-ON TIME: 15 min.
TOTAL TIME: 55 min.

We prefer turkey pepperoni in this recipe. Freeze the unbaked casserole up to I month. Thaw overnight in the refrigerator; let stand 30 minutes at room temperature, and bake as directed.

- 12 oz. uncooked spaghetti
- ½ tsp. salt
- 1 (I-lb.) package mild ground pork sausage
- 2 oz. turkey pepperoni slices (about 30), cut in half
- 1 (26-oz.) jar tomato-and-basil pasta sauce
- ¼ cup grated Parmesan cheese
- 1 (8-oz.) package shredded Italian three-cheese blend

1. Preheat oven to 350°. Prepare spaghetti with ½ tsp. salt according to package directions. Drain well, and place in a lightly greased 13- x 9-inch baking dish.
2. Brown sausage in a large skillet over medium-high heat, stirring occasionally, 5 minutes or until sausage crumbles and is no longer pink. Drain and set aside. Wipe skillet clean. Add pepperoni, and cook over medium-high heat, stirring occasionally, 4 minutes or until slightly crisp.
3. Top spaghetti with sausage; pour pasta sauce over sausage. Arrange half of pepperoni slices evenly over pasta sauce. Sprinkle with cheeses. Arrange remaining half of pepperoni slices evenly over cheese. Cover with nonstick or lightly greased aluminum foil.
4. Bake at 350° for 30 minutes; remove foil, and bake 10 more minutes or until cheese melts and just begins to brown.

Cajun Shrimp Casserole

MAKES: 6 servings
HANDS-ON TIME: 30 min.
TOTAL TIME: I hr., 6 min.

This long ingredient list is worth the effort for a special-occasion meal. If you're not a fan of okra, you can leave it out of this dish.

- 2 lb. unpeeled, large raw shrimp
- ¼ cup butter
- 1 small red onion, chopped*
- ½ cup chopped red bell pepper*
- ½ cup chopped yellow bell pepper*
- ½ cup chopped green bell pepper*
- 4 garlic cloves, minced
- 2 cups fresh or frozen sliced okra
- 1 Tbsp. lemon juice
- 1½ tsp. salt
- 3 cups cooked long-grain rice
- 1 (10¾-oz.) can cream of shrimp soup**
- ½ cup dry white wine
- 1 Tbsp. soy sauce
- ½ tsp. ground red pepper
- ¼ cup grated Parmesan cheese
  Garnishes: quartered lemon slices, chopped parsley leaves

1. Preheat oven to 350°. Peel shrimp; devein, if desired.
2. Melt ¼ cup butter in a large skillet over medium-high heat. Add onion and next 3 ingredients; sauté 7 minutes or until tender. Add garlic, and sauté I minute. Stir in okra, lemon juice, and salt; sauté 5 minutes. Add shrimp, and cook 3 minutes or until shrimp turn pink. Stir in rice and next 4 ingredients until blended. Pour into a lightly greased II- x 7-inch baking dish. Sprinkle evenly with Parmesan cheese.
3. Bake at 350° for 15 to 20 minutes or until casserole is bubbly and cheese is lightly browned. Garnish, if desired.

*I (10-oz.) package frozen onions and peppers may be substituted for fresh onion and bell peppers.

**I (10¾-oz.) can cream of mushroom soup may be substituted for cream of shrimp soup.

NOTE: An unbaked casserole may be made I day in advance. Cover and refrigerate. Let stand at room temperature 30 minutes before baking as directed. To freeze an unbaked casserole, prepare as directed, omitting Parmesan cheese. Cover tightly, and freeze. Let stand at room temperature 30 minutes before baking. Bake, covered, at 350° for 50 minutes. Uncover; sprinkle evenly with Parmesan cheese, and bake 10 more minutes or until cheese is lightly browned.

Sweet Endings

Brownie Buttons

MAKES: 20 brownies
HANDS-ON TIME: 15 min.
TOTAL TIME: 1 hr.

- 1 (18.9-oz.) package triple chunk brownie mix
- 1 bag of assorted miniature peanut butter cup candies and chocolate-coated caramels

1. Preheat oven to 350°. Prepare brownie mix according to package directions. Spray miniature (1¾-inch) muffin pans with cooking spray, or line pans with paper liners, and spray liners with cooking spray.
2. Spoon brownie batter into each cup, filling almost full. Bake at 350° for 19 to 20 minutes. Cool in pans 3 to 4 minutes, and then gently press a miniature candy into each baked brownie until the top of candy is level with top of brownie. Cool 10 minutes in pans. Gently twist each brownie to remove from pan. Cool on a wire rack.

Chocolate-Coffee Cheesecake Tartlets

MAKES: 15 tartlets
HANDS-ON TIME: 30 min.
TOTAL TIME: 2 hr., 38 min.

Treat yourself to this bite-size dessert featuring coffee-flavored chocolate cheesecake in a mini phyllo shell. Easy pick-up desserts like this one are perfect for entertaining, so you may want to double the recipe. You can make them ahead and chill them overnight.

- 2 Tbsp. slivered almonds
- 1 (2.1-oz.) package frozen mini-phyllo pastry shells, thawed
- 2 Tbsp. heavy cream, divided
- ½ tsp. instant espresso powder
- 1 (3-oz.) package cream cheese, softened
- 3 Tbsp. powdered sugar
- 2 Tbsp. light brown sugar
- 1 oz. bittersweet chocolate

1. Preheat oven to 350°. Place almonds in a single layer in a shallow pan. Bake at 350°, stirring occasionally, 5 to 7 minutes or until lightly toasted and fragrant, stirring halfway through.
2. Place thawed pastry shells on a baking sheet, and bake at 350° for 3 to 5 minutes or until crisp.
3. Stir together 1 Tbsp. cream and ½ tsp. espresso powder in a small microwave-safe ramekin or cup. Microwave at HIGH 10 seconds; stir until espresso is dissolved.
4. Beat cream cheese and sugars at medium-high speed with an electric mixer until smooth. Gradually add espresso mixture, and beat 30 seconds or until creamy and light. Spoon 1 rounded teaspoonful into each phyllo shell.
5. Microwave chocolate and remaining 1 Tbsp. cream in a small microwave-safe ramekin or cup at HIGH 20 seconds, stirring after 10 seconds and at end until smooth. Spoon ¼ tsp. chocolate mixture over each tart. Top immediately with almonds. Cover and chill 2 hours or up to 24 hours.

Chocolate-Ginger Pound Cake

MAKES: 12 servings
HANDS-ON TIME: 12 min.
TOTAL TIME: 2 hr., 32 min.

- 1 (12-oz.) package semisweet chocolate morsels
- 1¼ cups butter, softened
- 2 cups sugar
- 5 large eggs
- 3 cups all-purpose flour
- 1 tsp. baking powder
- 1 tsp. ground ginger
- ⅛ tsp. salt
- 1 cup buttermilk
- ½ cup crystallized ginger, finely chopped
- 1 tsp. vanilla extract

Make-Ahead Favorites

1. Preheat oven to 325°. Place chocolate morsels in a small microwave-safe glass bowl. Microwave at HIGH 1½ to 2 minutes or until melted and smooth, stirring at 30-second intervals.

2. Beat butter at medium speed with a heavy-duty electric stand mixer until creamy. Gradually add sugar, beating at medium speed until light and fluffy. Add eggs, 1 at a time, beating just until yellow disappears. Add melted chocolate, beating just until blended.

3. Sift together flour and next 3 ingredients. Stir together buttermilk and crystallized ginger. Add flour mixture to butter mixture alternately with buttermilk mixture, beginning and ending with flour mixture. Beat at low speed just until blended after each addition. Stir in vanilla. Pour into a greased and floured 10-inch tube pan.

4. Bake at 325° for 1 hour and 10 minutes or until a long wooden pick inserted in center comes out clean. Cool in pan on a wire rack 10 minutes. Remove cake from pan to wire rack, and cool 1 hour or until completely cool.

TO FREEZE: Wrap cooled cake tightly with plastic wrap. Wrap loosely with aluminum foil. Freeze up to 1 month.

Luscious Lemon Bars

MAKES: about 2 dozen
HANDS-ON TIME: 20 min.
TOTAL TIME: 2 hr., 5 min.

Classic lemon squares are always a popular dessert at teas, luncheons, and showers. As an added bonus, you can make them ahead and freeze for up to 1 month.

- 2¼ cups all-purpose flour, divided
- ½ cup powdered sugar
- 1 cup cold butter, cut into pieces
- 4 large eggs
- 2 cups granulated sugar
- 1 tsp. lemon zest
- ⅓ cup fresh lemon juice
- ½ tsp. baking powder
  Powdered sugar

1. Preheat oven to 350°. Line bottom and sides of a 13- x 9-inch pan with heavy-duty aluminum foil or parchment paper, allowing 2 to 3 inches to extend over sides; lightly grease foil.

2. Stir together 2 cups flour and ½ cup powdered sugar. Cut in butter using a pastry blender or fork until crumbly. Press mixture onto bottom of prepared pan.

3. Bake at 350° for 20 to 25 minutes or until lightly browned.

4. Meanwhile, whisk eggs in a large bowl; whisk in granulated sugar, lemon zest, and lemon juice. Stir together baking powder and remaining ¼ cup flour; whisk into egg mixture. Pour mixture over hot baked crust.

5. Bake at 350° for 25 minutes or until filling is set. Let cool in pan on a wire rack 30 minutes. Lift from pan, using foil sides as handles. Cool completely on a wire rack (about 30 minutes). Remove foil, and cut into bars; sprinkle with powdered sugar.

Strawberry Semifreddo Shortcake

MAKES: 16 servings
HANDS-ON TIME: 30 min.
TOTAL TIME: 5 hr., 45 min.

- 2 (3-oz.) packages soft ladyfingers
- 2 pt. strawberry ice cream, softened
- 1 pt. strawberry sorbet, softened
- 1 pt. fresh strawberries, hulled
- 2 Tbsp. powdered sugar
- ½ (7-oz.) jar marshmallow crème
- 1 cup heavy cream

1. Arrange ladyfingers around sides and on bottom of a 9-inch springform pan, cut sides in. (Reserve any remaining ladyfingers for another use.) Spread strawberry ice cream over ladyfingers, and freeze 30 minutes.

2. Spread softened strawberry sorbet over ice cream. Freeze 30 minutes.

3. Process strawberries and powdered sugar in a food processor 1 minute or until pureed. Reserve ¼ cup strawberry mixture. Whisk remaining strawberry mixture into marshmallow crème until well blended.

4. Beat cream at high speed with an electric mixer until stiff peaks form. Fold into marshmallow mixture. Pour over sorbet in pan. Drizzle reserved strawberry mixture over top, and gently swirl with a paring knife. Freeze 4 hours or until firm. Let ice-cream cake stand at room temperature 15 minutes before serving.

NOTE: We tested with Blue Bell Strawberry Ice Cream and Häagen-Dazs Strawberry Sorbet.

METRIC EQUIVALENTS

The recipes that appear in this cookbook use the standard United States method for measuring liquid and dry or solid ingredients (teaspoons, tablespoons, and cups). The information on this chart is provided to help cooks outside the U.S. successfully use these recipes. All equivalents are approximate.

METRIC EQUIVALENTS FOR DIFFERENT TYPES OF INGREDIENTS

A standard cup measure of a dry or solid ingredient will vary in weight depending on the type of ingredient. A standard cup of liquid is the same volume for any type of liquid. Use the following chart when converting standard cup measures to grams (weight) or milliliters (volume).

Standard Cup	Fine Powder (ex. flour)	Grain (ex. rice)	Granular (ex. sugar)	Liquid Solids (ex. butter)	Liquid (ex. milk)
1	140 g	150 g	190 g	200 g	240 ml
¾	105 g	113 g	143 g	150 g	180 ml
⅔	93 g	100 g	125 g	133 g	160 ml
½	70 g	75 g	95 g	100 g	120 ml
⅓	47 g	50 g	63 g	67 g	80 ml
¼	35 g	38 g	48 g	50 g	60 ml
⅛	18 g	19 g	24 g	25 g	30 ml

USEFUL EQUIVALENTS FOR DRY INGREDIENTS BY WEIGHT
(To convert ounces to grams, multiply the number of ounces by 30.)

1 oz	=	¹⁄₁₆ lb	=	30 g
4 oz	=	¼ lb	=	120 g
8 oz	=	½ lb	=	240 g
12 oz	=	¾ lb	=	360 g
16 oz	=	1 lb	=	480 g

USEFUL EQUIVALENTS FOR LENGTH
(To convert inches to centimeters, multiply the number of inches by 2.5.)

1 in					=	2.5 cm		
6 in	=	½ ft			=	15 cm		
12 in	=	1 ft			=	30 cm		
36 in	=	3 ft	=	1 yd	=	90 cm		
40 in					=	100 cm	=	1 m

USEFUL EQUIVALENTS FOR LIQUID INGREDIENTS BY VOLUME

¼ tsp					=	1 ml	
½ tsp					=	2 ml	
1 tsp					=	5 ml	
3 tsp	=	1 Tbsp		=	½ fl oz	=	15 ml
		2 Tbsp	=	⅛ cup	=	1 fl oz	=	30 ml
		4 Tbsp	=	¼ cup	=	2 fl oz	=	60 ml
		5⅓ Tbsp	=	⅓ cup	=	3 fl oz	=	80 ml
		8 Tbsp	=	½ cup	=	4 fl oz	=	120 ml
		10⅔ Tbsp	=	⅔ cup	=	5 fl oz	=	160 ml
		12 Tbsp	=	¾ cup	=	6 fl oz	=	180 ml
		16 Tbsp	=	1 cup	=	8 fl oz	=	240 ml
		1 pt	=	2 cups	=	16 fl oz	=	480 ml
		1 qt	=	4 cups	=	32 fl oz	=	960 ml
					33 fl oz	=	1000 ml	= 1 l

USEFUL EQUIVALENTS FOR COOKING/OVEN TEMPERATURES

	Fahrenheit	Celsius	Gas Mark
Freeze Water	32° F	0° C	
Room Temperature	68° F	20° C	
Boil Water	212° F	100° C	
Bake	325° F	160° C	3
	350° F	180° C	4
	375° F	190° C	5
	400° F	200° C	6
	425° F	220° C	7
	450° F	230° C	8
Broil			Grill

Menu Index

This index lists every menu by suggested occasion. Recipes in bold type are provided with the menu and accompaniments are in regular type.

Menus for Family

Build a Better Hot Dog

SERVES 4 TO 8

(page 193)

Thai-Style Hot Dogs
Greek-Style Dogs
Muffuletta Dogs
Dixie Caviar Dogs
Assorted baked potato chips and pita chips

Super-Easy Soup & Salad

SERVES 8

(page 288)

Southern Italian Chicken Soup
Shredded Kale Salad with Bacon and Chopped Dates

Family Get-together

SERVES 12

(page 322)

Roasted Root Vegetable Bisque
Ham with Bourbon, Cola, and Cherry Glaze
Holiday Potato Bake
Roasted Brussels Sprouts and Cauliflower with Bacon Dressing
Chocolate-Orange Velvet Tart

Sunday Supper

SERVES 4 TO 6

Roast Chicken *(page 39)*
Mashed potatoes
Waldorf Spinach Salad *(page 60)*
Winter Blackberry Cobbler *(page 41)*
Iced Tea

Pasta Night

SERVES 2 TO 3

Shrimp Destin Linguine *(page 80)*
Mixed salad greens
Strawberry-Basil Frozen Yogurt *(page 83)*

Saturday Morning Breakfast

SERVES 8

Fried Chicken Thighs & Biscuits *(page 90)*
Fresh fruit

Sandwich & Salad Supper

SERVES 4

Country Ham-and-Peach Panini *(page 128)*
Spring Garden Strawberry Salad *(page 86)*
Icebox Butter Cookies *(page 220)*

Relaxing Summer Evening

SERVES 4

Salad in a Soup *(page 129)*
Old-fashioned Tomato Pie *(page 154)*
TennTucky Blackberry Cobbler *(page 160)*

Barbecue Night

SERVES 10

The *Southern Living* Pulled Pork Sandwich *(page 144)*
Grandma Gwen's Beans *(page 145)*
Chipotle-Bacon Mac and Cheese *(page 146)*
Spinach-Artichoke Dip Potato Salad *(page 147)*
Sweet, Salty, and Spicy Watermelon Refresher *(page 147)*

Menus for Company

Spring Brunch

SERVES 8
(page 62)

Peach-Basil Iced Tea
Sunshine Citrus Platter
Herbed Dip with Baby Vegetables
Spring Greens with Strawberries
Chutney Chicken Salad
Creamy Egg Strata
Brown Sugar Bacon
Chilled Carrot Soup
Lemon-Rosemary Coffee Cake

The Dainty & Delicious Menu

SERVES 6
(page 68)

Neiman Marcus Cheddar Cheese
   Biscuits
Tomato-Basil Bisque
Tarragon Chicken Salad
Cranberry-Strawberry Salad
Mixed greens
Caramelized Onion Quiche
Crowd-Pleasing Tea Sandwiches
Assorted desserts

Easter Egg Hunt

SERVES 6
(page 92)

GROWN-UPS
Beef-and-Arugula Ciabatta
   Sandwiches
Ham-and-Fontina Sourdough
   Sandwiches
Roasted Vegetable Salad

YOUNG ONES
Hazelnut-Strawberry Sandwiches
"Rabbit Food" Cups
Two-Ingredient Chicken Strips

EVERYONE
Pineapple-Coconut or Pineapple-
Carrot Cake Cupcakes with
   Buttermilk-Cream Cheese
   Frosting

Toast to the Derby

SERVES 12
(page 106)

Roasted Brown-Butter Pecans with
   Rosemary
Spring-on-a-Plate Salads
Assorted vegetables with **Whipped
   Lemon Aïoli**
Fluffy Cream Cheese Biscuits filled
   with **Ginger Ale-Brown Sugar
   Smoked Ham** served with **Figgy
   Port Chutney** and **Blue Cheese
   Butter**
Ginger Ale-Brown Sugar Smoked
   Ham
Watercress Canapés
Derby Truffles
Mint julep bar

The Backyard Menu Planner

SERVES 6
(page 130)

PICK A MEAT
Buttermilk-Brined Grilled Chicken
Grilled Molasses Flank Steak with
   Watermelon Salsa

CHOOSE TWO SIDES
Fresh Herb Potato Salad
Heirloom Tomato Salad with
   Lady Pea Salsa
Broccoli Slaw with Candied Pecans
Shrimp Rémoulade Deviled Eggs

SIP WITH
Sweet Tea Spritzer

CAP IT OFF WITH
Icebox pie

Our Summer Fish Fry Menu

SERVES 8
(page 194)

FISH FRY
Beer-Battered Fried Fish
Malt Vinegar Mignonette
Buttermilk-Ranch-Herb Sauce
Peach-Ginger Slaw
Grilled Corn-and-Butter Bean Salad
Hush Puppies

SIP WITH
Sparkling Cherry Limeade

SAVE ROOM FOR
Peanut-Cola Cake

Scavenger Hunt Menu

SERVES 6
(page 203)

Honeysuckle-Watermelon Cocktails
Stuffed Jalapeño Poppers
Smoked Chicken Summer Salad
Cobbler sundaes

Make-Ahead Tex-Mex Menu

SERVES 8
(page 216)

DRINKS
Pink Cadillac Margaritas
Iced Hibiscus Sweet Tea

STARTERS
Spicy Roasted Chile Peanuts and
    Pepitas
Chipotle Shrimp Cocktail

THE MAIN DISH & SIDES
Chicken Enchiladas
Three Sisters Salad
Mango Tango

DESSERT
Mexican Chocolate Ice-cream Pie

Rustic Feast

SERVES 8
(page 230)

COCKTAIL
Umatilla Smash

STARTERS
Farmer Salad
Butternut Squash Soup

MAIN COURSE
Grilled Ribeye Steaks with Béarnaise
    Butter and Onion Relish
Grilled Fingerling Potato Salad
Marinated Kale Salad with Gouda
    and Shaved Apples

DESSERT
Pineapple Upside-Down Cake

Backyard Bash

SERVES 8
(page 246)

APPETIZER
Plum-Glazed Sausage Board

MAIN COURSE
Dry-Brined Beer-Can Chicken
Tart Apple-and-Cabbage Toss
Warm Lentil-and-Potato Salad

DESSERT
Black Forest Pound Cake

Chicken for a Crowd

SERVES 8
(page 289)

Roast Chicken with Sweet Potatoes
    and Apples

Wine & (Grilled) Cheese Bar

SERVES A CROWD
(page 290)

Let guests build their own panini with a
    selection of different breads, cheeses,
    and toppings.

Simple Winter Supper

SERVES 8
(page 294)

Sweet Potato Soup
Arugula-Pear-Blue Cheese Salad
Cranberry Roasted Winter
    Vegetables
Pork Roast with Sweet Onion-
    Pumpkin Seed Relish
Wild Rice with Bacon and Fennel
Gingerbread Soufflé

Menus for Special Occasions

Deep South Meat 'n' Three

SERVES 8
(page 262)

THE MEAT
Herb-Roasted Turkey with Easy
    Turkey Gravy

THE THREE
Cornbread Dressing with Smoked
    Bacon and Pecans
Mashed Sweet Potatoes with
    Autumn Spices
Fried Collards and Apples

THE TEA
Clementine Tea

Texas Meat 'n' Three

SERVES 8
(page 265)

THE MEAT
Grilled Turkey Breast with Parsley-
    Mint Salsa Verde

THE THREE
Roasted Carrot and Avocado Salad
Cauliflower Galettes with Chipotle
    Crème Fraîche
Poblanos Stuffed with Goat Cheese
    Mashed Potatoes

THE TEA
Hibiscus-Mint Margaritas

Lowcountry Meat 'n' Three

SERVES 8
(page 267)

THE MEAT
Turkey Tenderloins with Madeira
    Gravy

THE THREE
Brussels Sprouts with Applewood
    Bacon
Orange-Glazed Sweet Potatoes
Cornbread, Chestnut, and Country
    Ham Dressing

THE TEA
Pineapple-Basil Tea

Hanukkah Celebration

SERVES 8
(page 288)

Red Wine-Braised Brisket with
    Caramelized Onions
Sweet Potato Latkes
Thyme-Scented Applesauce

New Year's Eve Eve

SERVES 8
(page 291)

Peach-Mustard Glazed Pork
    Tenderloin
Red Bliss Potato Salad with Chives

Holiday Get-Together

SERVES 8
(page 292)

Sparkling Rum Punch
Crispy Goat Cheese-Topped
    Arugula Salad with Pomegranate
    Vinaigrette
Fingerling Potatoes with Dilled
    Avocado and Smoked Salmon
Salt-Roasted Beef Tenderloin Sliders
    with Chimichurri Pesto
Mini Crab Cakes with Pineapple-
    Cucumber Salsa
Coconut Crème Brûlée

Dinner for Two

SERVES 2
(page 327)

Creamy Turnip Soup with Bacon,
    Caramelized Pears, and Onions
Roast Pork with Provençal
    Breadcrumb Crust and Sherry
    Glaze
Greens with Goat Cheese, Pecans,
    and Sherry Vinaigrette
Broccoli with Roasted Garlic and
    Tomatoes
Mini Chocolate-Cherry Layer Cakes

Recipe Title Index

This index alphabetically lists every recipe by exact title.

Month-by-Month Index

This index alphabetically lists every food article and accompanying recipes by month.

General Recipe Index

This index lists every recipe by food category and/or major ingredient.

Favorite Recipes Journal

Jot down your family's and your favorite recipes for quick and handy reference. And don't forget to include the dishes that drew rave reviews when company came for dinner.

Recipe	Source/Page	Remarks